# Advancing Cybersecurity at the Intersection of Parallel Computing and Blockchain

Valentina E. Balas
https://orcid.org/0000-0003-0885-1283
*Aurel Vlaicu University of Arad, Romania*

Qin Xin
https://orcid.org/0000-0002-6178-8538
*University of the Faroe Islands, Denmark*

Ambeth Kumar V. D.
https://orcid.org/0000-0001-7722-2398
*Mizoram University, India*

IGI Global
Scientific Publishing
Publishing Tomorrow's Research Today

Vice President of Editorial Melissa Wagner
Director of Acquisitions Mikaela Felty
Director of Book Development Jocelynn Hessler
Production Manager Mike Brehm
Cover Design Jose Rosado

Published in the United States of America by
IGI Global Scientific Publishing
701 East Chocolate Avenue
Hershey, PA, 17033, USA
Tel: 717-533-8845 | Fax: 717-533-7115
Website: https://www.igi-global.com E-mail: cust@igi-global.com



Library of Congress Cataloging-in-Publication Data

Names: Balas, Valentina Emilia editor | Xin, Qin, 1977- editor | V. D., Ambeth Kumar, 1983- editor
Title: Advancing cybersecurity at the intersection of parallel computing and blockchain / edited by Valentina E. Balas, Qin Xin, and Ambeth Kumar V. D.
Description: Hershey, PA : IGI Global Scientific Publishing, [2027] | Includes bibliographical references and index. | Summary: "This book provides a comprehensive and authoritative reference on emerging cybersecurity solutions built upon parallel computing and blockchain technologies. It advances secure, efficient, and trustworthy computing ecosystems"-- Provided by publisher.
Identifiers: LCCN 2026011285 (print) | LCCN 2026011286 (ebook) | ISBN 9798337390536 h/c | ISBN 9798337390543 s/c | ISBN 9798337390550 ebook
Subjects: LCSH: Computer security | Blockchains (Databases)--Security measures | Parallel processing (Electronic computers)--Security measures | Artificial intelligence--Security measures | Computer networks--Security measures
Classification: LCC QA76.9.A25 A3794 2026 (print) | LCC QA76.9.A25 (ebook)
LC record available at https://lccn.loc.gov/2026011285
LC ebook record available at https://lccn.loc.gov/2026011286

British Cataloguing in Publication Data
A Cataloguing in Publication record for this book is available from the British Library.

# Table of Contents

**Preface** ........ xvi

**Chapter 1**
AI and Blockchain-Enabled Architectures for Secure and Resilient Digital Systems ........ 1
*Ashutosh Bhardwaj, Poornima University, Jaipur, India*

**Chapter 2**
Parallel Computing and Blockchain for AI-Driven Cybersecurity: A Secure and Scalable Framework for Distributed Digital Infrastructures ........ 27
*Rocky Kumar, Poornima University, Jaipur, India*

**Chapter 3**
A Distributed Framework for Adaptive Cybersecurity via Convergence of Parallel AI and Blockchain Architectures: AICyber-Chain ........ 59
*B. Shaji, Mahaguru Institute of Technology, Kayamkulam, India*
*Ram Mohan N. R., Panimalar Engineering College, Chennai, India*
*Nisha K. L., Amrita Vishwa Vidyapeetham, Amritapuri, India*

**Chapter 4**
Decentralized Application (DApps): Secure Blockchain Ecosystems ........ 99
*Kanupriya Gupta, School of Engineering and Technology, Vivekananda Institute of Professional Studies - Technical Campus, India*
*Divay Pahuja, School of Engineering and Technology, Vivekananda Institute of Professional Studies - Technical Campus, India*
*Om Mishra, School of Engineering and Technology, Vivekananda Institute of Professional Studies - Technical Campus, India*
*Monika Bansal, School of Engineering and Technology, Vivekananda Institute of Professional Studies - Technical Campus, India*
*Nishi Jain, School of Engineering and Technology, Vivekananda Institute of Professional Studies - Technical Campus, India*

**Chapter 5**
Blockchain-Based Forest Plant Record Storage System Using Hyperledger Fabric ........ 141
*Abhisake Sinha, Tripura University, India*
*Sukanta Chakraborty, Tripura University, India*
*Abhishek Majumder, Tripura University, India*

**Chapter 6**
High-Performance Computing for Advanced Cybersecurity: GPU and TPU-Based Security Optimisation Techniques ........ 165
*Jyoti Kumari, GD Goenka University, India*
*Pradeep Yadav, Institute of Technology and Management, Gwalior, India*
*Chandra Prakash Bhargava, Institute of Technology and Management, Gwalior, India*

**Chapter 7**
AI-Based Approaches to Intrusion Detection and Privacy Preservation in Autonomous Systems ........ 191
*Vikas Sharma, Department of Computer Applications, SRM Institute of Science and Technology, Delhi NCR, India*
*Tarun Kumar Vashishth, Department of Computer Applications, Vidya University, Meerut, India*
*Shashiraj Teotia, Department of Computer Applications, Swami Vivekanand Subharti University, Meerut, India*
*Devendra Singh, Department of Mechanical Engineering, Ajay Kumar Garg Engineering College, Ghaziabad, India*
*Sonal Shah, Department of IT, Auro University, Surat, India*
*Sachin Chaudhary, School of Computer Science and Applications, IIMT University, Meerut, India*
*Pushpendra Kumar Verma, School of Computer Science and Applications, IIMT University, Meerut, India*

**Chapter 8**
AI-Driven Cloud-Enabled Cybersecurity Framework for Intelligent IoT Intrusion Detection ........ 219
*Rudhrananth Baladhandapani, Intel, USA*
*Bhanutheja Nagabhushana Reddy Kasinayakanahally, Apple Inc., USA*
*Sri Harsha Grandhi, Intel, USA*
*T Kalaikumaran, Department of Artificial Intelligence and Data Science, VSB College of Engineering Technical Campus, Coimbatore, India*
*Elegbeleye Femi Abiodun, Walter Sisulu University, South Africa*
*Biplov Paneru, Department of Electronics Engineering, Pokhara University, Nepal*

**Chapter 9**
Advanced Threat Modeling via KM Generator-Driven Mutation Engines and Fork-Based Attack Simulation ........ 255
*Keshav Sinha, University of Petroleum and Energy Studies, Dehradun, India*
*Roopa Vuppula, Woxsen University, India*

**Chapter 10**
Advanced GhostNet Architecture for Cyber Attack Classification ........ 283
*G. Geetha, Department of Computing Technologies, SRM Institute of Science and Technology, Kattankulathur, India*
*Manjula Rajagopal, Department of Computing Technologies, SRM Institute of Science and Technology, Kattankulathur, India*

**Chapter 11**
A Hybrid VGG16–CNN Framework for Deepfake Image Detection in Cloud-Enabled Environments ........ 301
*Ali Zaheer Agha, United College of Engineering and Research, Prayagraj, India*
*Ratnesh Mishra, BIT Mesra, Patna, India*

**Chapter 12**
AI Applications in Body Area Networks ........................................................ 329
*Priyadarshini Radhakrishnan, IBM Corporation, USA*
*Vijai Anand Ramar, Delta Dental Insurance Company, USA*
*Karthi Kushala, Taylor Corporation, USA*
*Venkataramesh Induru, Piorion Solutions Inc., USA*
*Yashwant Kumar Kolli, Cognizant Technology Solutions US Corp., USA*
*R. Pushpakumar, Department of Information Technology, Vel Tech Rangarajan Dr. Sagunthala R&D Institute of Science and Technology, Chennai, India*

**Chapter 13**
An Advanced Hybrid Holmes-Tinker-Tent Map (HTTM) Chaotic Encryption Framework for Secure Distribution and Retention of Medical Images ............ 365
*Sujarani Rajendran, SASTRA (Deemed to be) University, India*
*Supriya Sridharan, SASTRA (Deemed to be) University, India*
*M. Vanitha, SASTRA (Deemed to be) University, India*
*P. Umamaheswari, SASTRA (Deemed to be) University, India*
*D. Rubidha Devi, SASTRA (Deemed to be) University, India*

**Chapter 14**
Integration of Classical and Quantum Cryptography in IoT ............................ 391
*Jayavardhanarao Sahukaru, Aditya Institute of Technology and Management, India*
*Balajee Maram, SR University, India*
*Padala Ashok, Vignana Bharathi Institute of Technology, India*
*Kuppala Swapna, Siddhartha Institute of Technology and Sciences, India*

**Chapter 15**
Quantum-Safe Email Client Using Simulated Quantum Key Distribution ...... 425
*J. Gayathri, Panimalar Engineering College, India*
*B. Alice Franny, Panimalar Engineering College, India*
*Kavitha Subramani, Panimalar Engineering College, India*

**Compilation of References** ........................................................................ 457

**About the Contributors** ............................................................................. 499

**Index** ........................................................................................................ 509

# Detailed Table of Contents

**Preface** ............ xvi

**Chapter 1**
AI and Blockchain-Enabled Architectures for Secure and Resilient Digital Systems ............ 1
*Ashutosh Bhardwaj, Poornima University, Jaipur, India*

The mushrooming digitalization of industries has heightened the need to have secure and resilient system design as well as smart system design that is prone to address intricate cyber threats and data breaches. Artificial Intelligence (AI) and Blockchain have become the new influential technological innovations that could contribute greatly to the security, visibility, and reassurances of any digital ecosystem. AI can be used to provide smart threat detection and predictive analytics, intelligent decision-making, and blockchain can be employed to provide decentralization trust, immutability, and secure data sharing. The chapter discusses the prospects of AI and blockchain in the design of secure digital architectures and how the two can be used concurrently to enhance cybersecurity, keep data intact, and ensure operational resilience. It talks about architectural structures, practical implementation in industries, and ethical or regulatory implications as well as the future opportunities to create a solid and reliable digital systems in a more globalized world.

**Chapter 2**
Parallel Computing and Blockchain for AI-Driven Cybersecurity: A Secure and Scalable Framework for Distributed Digital Infrastructures ............ 27
*Rocky Kumar, Poornima University, Jaipur, India*

The multiplication of digital infrastructures and cloud services and of cyber-physical systems connected with each other has resulted in the significant growth of cybersecurity challenges. Traditional security mechanisms are usually not qualified to process large quantities of security data and identify complex cyber threats in real-time. The combination of artificial intelligence (AI), parallel computing, and blockchain technologies show a promising way forward on creating secure, scalable and resilient cybersecurity frameworks for distributed digital infrastructures. This Chapter puts forth a conceptual framework that incorporates parallel computing architectures and block-chain enabled security mechanisms in order to increase the efficiency and trustworthiness of AI-enabled Cybersecurity systems. Parallel computing helps high-performance processing of big amounts of network traffic and security logs, so that AI models can perform better analysis of picker threat patterns and find out anomalies more efficiently.

**Chapter 3**
A Distributed Framework for Adaptive Cybersecurity via Convergence of Parallel AI and Blockchain Architectures: AICyber-Chain ................................ 59
*B. Shaji, Mahaguru Institute of Technology, Kayamkulam, India*
*Ram Mohan N. R., Panimalar Engineering College, Chennai, India*
*Nisha K. L., Amrita Vishwa Vidyapeetham, Amritapuri, India*

As the digital landscape expands, centralised cybersecurity frameworks grow increasingly vulnerable to sophisticated threats, creating single points of failure and targets for adversarial data manipulation. While AI enables real-time threat detection and big data analytics, its centralised deployment limits efficacy and exposes training data to poisoning and evasion attacks. To address this, the AICyber-Chain model proposes a distributed framework combining parallel AI and blockchain architectures. It leverages a hybrid Proof-of-Stake (PoS) and Byzantine Fault Tolerance (BFT) mechanism with IPFS and Private Data Centres (PDCs) for secure decentralised storage and processing. Generative Adversarial Networks (GANs) refine security rules, while Ethereum-based smart contracts enable automated responses and trustless data sharing. Results on the Rinkeby test network show 1.8× faster authentication, 25% lower gas consumption, F1 score of 0.92, and 1.2 s response time, with a medical data sharing use case ensuring data provenance and tamper-proof control.

**Chapter 4**
Decentralized Application (DApps): Secure Blockchain Ecosystems................. 99
*Kanupriya Gupta, School of Engineering and Technology, Vivekananda Institute of Professional Studies - Technical Campus, India*
*Divay Pahuja, School of Engineering and Technology, Vivekananda Institute of Professional Studies - Technical Campus, India*
*Om Mishra, School of Engineering and Technology, Vivekananda Institute of Professional Studies - Technical Campus, India*
*Monika Bansal, School of Engineering and Technology, Vivekananda Institute of Professional Studies - Technical Campus, India*
*Nishi Jain, School of Engineering and Technology, Vivekananda Institute of Professional Studies - Technical Campus, India*

A Decentralized Application (DApp) is a distributed, open-source software application that runs on a peer-to-peer (P2P) blockchain network. DApps are emerging as a transformative force across various sectors, leveraging blockchain technology to create applications that operate autonomously, offer enhanced security and transparency, and function without a central authority. Common security issues with DApps include smart contract and blockchain vulnerabilities, phishing and social engineering attacks, and key management challenges. Mitigation strategies involve thorough code audits, formal verification, multi-signature wallets, and robust security frameworks. This chapter provides a detailed analysis of DApp security, focusing on theoretical aspects, architectural components, and specific vulnerabilities in smart contracts, oracles, blockchain protocols, front-end interfaces, and cross-chain interoperability mechanisms.

**Chapter 5**
Blockchain-Based Forest Plant Record Storage System Using Hyperledger Fabric ........ 141
*Abhisake Sinha, Tripura University, India*
*Sukanta Chakraborty, Tripura University, India*
*Abhishek Majumder, Tripura University, India*

In today's era, securing data related to environmental and forest department has become a crucial aspect. Integrating blockchain based technologies with the forest data management is an effective solution. Blockchain technology such as Hyperledger Fabric is a permissioned blockchain. It can be helpful in storing the forest data in a more accurate, secure and tamper-proof manner. In this work a Hyperledger Fabric based framework has been developed to store the forest data in a secure and cost effective manner. The developed system can be used in the forest department to improve security and to monitor forest activities like illegal logging. In the developed system all the records are stored in an immutable manner. Its decentralized and permissioned nature helps to prevent any unauthorized participants, which means it only allows the participants that are authorized or permitted to perform within the network. The proposed technique has been implemented on Fabric 2.5 Test-Network. Performance analysis revels that the proposed system can be implemented in real time.

**Chapter 6**
High-Performance Computing for Advanced Cybersecurity: GPU and TPU-Based Security Optimisation Techniques ........ 165
*Jyoti Kumari, GD Goenka University, India*
*Pradeep Yadav, Institute of Technology and Management, Gwalior, India*
*Chandra Prakash Bhargava, Institute of Technology and Management, Gwalior, India*

Cybersecurity operations at enterprise and carrier scale are increasingly constrained by computational throughput rather than analytical capability. Modern threat actors exploit distributed systems to launch attacks beyond traditional CPU-based defenses. This chapter examines how GPU and TPU computing redefine security operations, covering parallel architectures, GPU-accelerated cryptography, and post-quantum schemes. It further explores machine learning-based analytics for intrusion detection and malware classification, real-time high-throughput threat detection, deployment challenges, HPC security risks, and emerging areas such as federated learning, homomorphic encryption, neuromorphic processors, and quantum-classical systems.

**Chapter 7**
AI-Based Approaches to Intrusion Detection and Privacy Preservation in Autonomous Systems ........................................................................ 191

*Vikas Sharma, Department of Computer Applications, SRM Institute of Science and Technology, Delhi NCR, India*
*Tarun Kumar Vashishth, Department of Computer Applications, Vidya University, Meerut, India*
*Shashiraj Teotia, Department of Computer Applications, Swami Vivekanand Subharti University, Meerut, India*
*Devendra Singh, Department of Mechanical Engineering, Ajay Kumar Garg Engineering College, Ghaziabad, India*
*Sonal Shah, Department of IT, Auro University, Surat, India*
*Sachin Chaudhary, School of Computer Science and Applications, IIMT University, Meerut, India*
*Pushpendra Kumar Verma, School of Computer Science and Applications, IIMT University, Meerut, India*

Cybersecurity is one of the most pressing concerns with regard to autonomous systems' ever-increasing adoption across multiple sectors, including transportation, health care, and smart city developments. The aim of this chapter is to focus on the various methods of securing autonomous systems through artificial intelligence (AI)-powered intrusion detection systems (IDS) and privacy-preserving mechanisms. For example, this chapter will explore the use of machine learning for anomaly detection as well as secure federated learning and blockchain technology to enhance the integrity of data in autonomous systems. Furthermore, it will provide an overview of the use of adversarially attacking AI models and provide recommendations for reducing cyber risk. Utilizing AI-based security frameworks, autonomous systems can identify threats and respond to them almost instantly, while ensuring user privacy. Finally, this chapter addresses the regulatory hurdles surrounding autonomous technology, as well as potential areas for future research related to security in autonomous systems.

**Chapter 8**

AI-Driven Cloud-Enabled Cybersecurity Framework for Intelligent IoT Intrusion Detection .................... 219

*Rudhrananth Baladhandapani, Intel, USA*
*Bhanutheja Nagabhushana Reddy Kasinayakanahally, Apple Inc., USA*
*Sri Harsha Grandhi, Intel, USA*
*T Kalaikumaran, Department of Artificial Intelligence and Data Science, VSB College of Engineering Technical Campus, Coimbatore, India*
*Elegbeleye Femi Abiodun, Walter Sisulu University, South Africa*
*Biplov Paneru, Department of Electronics Engineering, Pokhara University, Nepal*

As the number of IoT devices has expanded rapidly, the risk of exposure to rapidly evolving threats has also increased, resulting in a broader attack surface (i.e., the networked devices that an attacker may have access to). Thus, with the large-scale IoT installations come high-dimensional signal data that pose a challenge to accurately detect intrusions. This paper develops a cyber-physical system composed of multiple cloud-based cybersecurity frameworks that leverage AI technology as well as signal data from IoT devices in order to detect intrusions. The proposed framework uses Sugeon-type fuzzy feature extraction (after preprocessing) to extract a set of features necessary for classification by a table prior-based IoT intrusion detection system that uses a transformer. Results of the cloud-based model demonstrate an accuracy rate of 98.46% and precision of 98.59% with inference latency of 69.67 ms.

**Chapter 9**

Advanced Threat Modeling via KM Generator-Driven Mutation Engines and Fork-Based Attack Simulation .................... 255

*Keshav Sinha, University of Petroleum and Energy Studies, Dehradun, India*
*Roopa Vuppula, Woxsen University, India*

The fast development of cyber threats has revealed significant weaknesses in traditional threat modeling systems, which majorly rely on fixed attack patterns and deterministic or weakly random mutation algorithms that do not reflect the adaptive and unpredictable behavior of real-world adversaries. This paper presents a new threat modeling paradigm that uses the KM Generator as the source of randomness in a mutation engine in a fork-based attack simulation model. The KM Generator, determined by the recurrence, generates high-entropy statistics that drive non-deterministic mutation selection and allow independent branching of parallel simulation forks. Every fork is a distinct and repeatable attack trajectory and enables thorough exploration of complicated threat spaces. The suggested framework defines a mathematically rigorous, reproducible, and scalable basis of next-generation adaptive threat modeling in the areas of smart city, IoT, healthcare, and critical infrastructure.

**Chapter 10**
Advanced GhostNet Architecture for Cyber Attack Classification .................. 283
*G. Geetha, Department of Computing Technologies, SRM Institute of Science and Technology, Kattankulathur, India*
*Manjula Rajagopal, Department of Computing Technologies, SRM Institute of Science and Technology, Kattankulathur, India*

Cyberattacks have become one of the most serious threats in today's digital world, affecting individuals, organizations, and even governments. As technology continues to grow, so does the complexity and frequency of malicious activities carried out over networks and computer systems. To better understand, detect and prevent these threats, these cyberattacks are commonly grouped into different categories based on their methods, targets, and objectives, and the process known as cyberattack classification. This classification helps security professionals analyze attack patterns, design defensive strategies, and respond more effectively to incidents. From malware and phishing to denial-of-service and insider attacks, each type has distinct characteristics and impacts. By organizing cyber threats into structured classes, cybersecurity efforts become more systematic, proactive, and efficient, ultimately strengthening digital protection and risk management.

**Chapter 11**
A Hybrid VGG16–CNN Framework for Deepfake Image Detection in Cloud-Enabled Environments ........................................................................... 301
*Ali Zaheer Agha, United College of Engineering and Research, Prayagraj, India*
*Ratnesh Mishra, BIT Mesra, Patna, India*

Deepfakes technologies are capable of an authentic and significant manipulation of images, audio, and video with threats of identity theft, false information, blackmail, and financial fraud. Their increasing abuse is the primary challenge of both digital forensics and cybersecurity. In this paper, a hybrid deep learning architecture, Deepfake Predictor (DFP), will be suggested as a way of image recognition of manipulated faces. The model uses a pre-trained VGG16 network that is used with other convolutional layers to enhance classification. It was trained and tested using a dataset of 2041 images (1081 real, 960 fake). The metrics that were used to compare performance to Xception, NASNet, and MobileNet included accuracy, precision, F1-score, specificity, geometric mean, and loss. The model proposed had 94% accuracy and 95% precision that is better than the baseline methods. Its performance and scalability can be used to detect in real time and can be used in the cloud-based and active cybersecurity systems.

**Chapter 12**
AI Applications in Body Area Networks ........................................................ 329
*Priyadarshini Radhakrishnan, IBM Corporation, USA*
*Vijai Anand Ramar, Delta Dental Insurance Company, USA*
*Karthi Kushala, Taylor Corporation, USA*
*Venkataramesh Induru, Piorion Solutions Inc., USA*
*Yashwant Kumar Kolli, Cognizant Technology Solutions US Corp., USA*
*R. Pushpakumar, Department of Information Technology, Vel Tech Rangarajan Dr. Sagunthala R&D Institute of Science and Technology, Chennai, India*

Energy-efficient communication paradigms, anomaly detection techniques and machine learning algorithms are being researched due to the increased demand for secure and efficient communication protocols. the Deep Neural Network performs best with 92.8 percent accuracy, 93.4 percent precision, 91.9 percent recall and an AUC-ROC of 95.7 percent, demonstrating its dominance over Random Forest and Support Vector Machine. Beacon mode enjoys the maximum latency of 20 ms but minimum energy usage of 15 mW for the communication protocols. In contrast, emergency mode which was designed for applications in real time of aminimum latency of 10 ms but maximum energy use of 25 mW. In a study in energy efficiency, more efficient MAC protocols provided the highest energy savings 40 percent. The results highlight how, within different operating circumstances, efficiency, energy consumption and computing cost are traded off.

**Chapter 13**
An Advanced Hybrid Holmes-Tinker-Tent Map (HTTM) Chaotic Encryption Framework for Secure Distribution and Retention of Medical Images ............ 365
*Sujarani Rajendran, SASTRA (Deemed to be) University, India*
*Supriya Sridharan, SASTRA (Deemed to be) University, India*
*M. Vanitha, SASTRA (Deemed to be) University, India*
*P. Umamaheswari, SASTRA (Deemed to be) University, India*
*D. Rubidha Devi, SASTRA (Deemed to be) University, India*

The increasing digitization of healthcare and the expansion of telemedicine have made the secure transmission of medical imagery, such as ultrasound and MRI scans, a critical challenge, as these images are highly susceptible to cyberattacks due to their significant data volume and inherent pixel redundancy. To address these vulnerabilities, this research proposes a Robust Secure Communication Framework for Medical Imagery based on a novel Hybrid Non-Linear Chaotic Oscillator system. Unlike traditional linear encryption methods, the proposed framework leverages the complex, multi-dimensional, and unpredictable dynamics of hybrid chaotic maps to achieve superior confusion and diffusion properties, scrambling pixel positions and modifying pixel values with high efficiency.The system utilizes these oscillators to generate high-entropy keystreams that exhibit extreme sensitivity to initial conditions, thereby providing a vast key space that is mathematically resistant to brute-force and differential attack.

**Chapter 14**
Integration of Classical and Quantum Cryptography in IoT ............................ 391
*Jayavardhanarao Sahukaru, Aditya Institute of Technology and Management, India*
*Balajee Maram, SR University, India*
*Padala Ashok, Vignana Bharathi Institute of Technology, India*
*Kuppala Swapna, Siddhartha Institute of Technology and Sciences, India*

The chapter will act as an appositive and definitive boundary review on the integration of the classical and quantum cryptographic means into the Internet of Things (IoT) system through the position of the recent scholarly, industrial, and standards-related sources. The literature being evaluated is concerned with the increased awareness that the old cryptographic solutions will not be adequate with respect to the new security threats of the large, heterogeneous and highly distributed deployments of IoT. In such a scenario, quantum cryptography or simply quantum key distribution has been given a lot of attention since quantum key distribution is theoretically proved to be secure against both classical and quantum adversary. The literature however also speaks of the fact that there are significant limitations in the application of quantum cryptographic in the IoT world which can be broadly termed as a limitation being constrained by the consumption of energy.

**Chapter 15**
Quantum-Safe Email Client Using Simulated Quantum Key Distribution ...... 425
*J. Gayathri, Panimalar Engineering College, India*
*B. Alice Franny, Panimalar Engineering College, India*
*Kavitha Subramani, Panimalar Engineering College, India*

Email has long been a vital tool for personal and professional communication, but its security relies on traditional cryptographic algorithms that are expected to become vulnerable due to developments in quantum computing. The paper presents a secure application-layer email model compatible with existing frameworks, enhancing confidentiality using quantum-resistant methods. The system supports OAuth 2.0 and OpenID Connect, eliminating password-based authentication and improving access security while enabling integration with services like Gmail and Outlook. It uses symmetric encryption and a hybrid one-time pad–based key mechanism to simulate post-quantum secure keys. All encryption and decryption occur at the application layer, ensuring end-to-end security without modifying SMTP or IMAP, while maintaining compatibility with existing email systems.

**Compilation of References** ........ 457

**About the Contributors** ........ 499

**Index** ........ 509

# Preface

## INTRODUCTION

The accelerating pace of digital transformation has fundamentally reshaped the way information is generated, processed, shared, and protected. As organizations, governments, and societies increasingly depend on interconnected digital infrastructures, the demand for secure, scalable, and resilient computing environments has never been greater. While advances in high-performance computing, distributed architectures, cloud platforms, and intelligent systems have unlocked remarkable opportunities for innovation, they have also expanded the sophistication, scale, and frequency of cyber threats. Addressing these challenges requires the convergence of complementary technologies capable of delivering both computational efficiency and trusted security mechanisms.

Among the most influential developments in this evolving landscape are parallel computing and blockchain technologies. Parallel computing enables the efficient processing of massive datasets and complex computational workloads through concurrent execution, providing the performance required by modern artificial intelligence, big data analytics, cloud computing, and Internet of Things (IoT) applications. Blockchain, on the other hand, introduces decentralized trust, immutable recordkeeping, and transparent transaction validation, offering robust mechanisms for preserving integrity, accountability, and resilience across distributed environments. Together, these technologies present exciting opportunities for building secure, intelligent, and highly scalable digital ecosystems while simultaneously introducing new cybersecurity considerations that demand innovative approaches.

*Advancing Cybersecurity at the Intersection of Parallel Computing and Blockchain* has been developed to explore this rapidly emerging convergence. Bringing together distinguished researchers and practitioners from around the world, including selected and substantially extended contributions presented at iCONNECT 2026 alongside invited chapters from leading experts, this volume presents current advances in cybersecurity frameworks that leverage parallel computing, blockchain, and complementary intelligent technologies. The collection reflects the growing recognition that future cybersecurity solutions must combine computational scalability, decentralized trust, adaptive intelligence, and real-time responsiveness to effectively defend increasingly complex digital infrastructures.

The chapters presented throughout this volume examine a broad spectrum of contemporary topics that collectively define the next generation of secure computing systems. Readers will encounter research on blockchain-enabled security architectures, distributed cybersecurity frameworks, artificial intelligence-driven threat detection, privacy-preserving computation, secure cloud and edge environments, intelligent intrusion detection systems, secure Internet of Things infrastructures, federated learning, trust management, decentralized identity, cryptographic innovations, and scalable cyber defense mechanisms. Together, these contributions illustrate how interdisciplinary approaches can strengthen cybersecurity while supporting the growing computational demands of modern digital ecosystems.

A defining strength of this volume is its balance between theoretical advancement and practical implementation. The contributing authors present novel algorithms, architectural frameworks, experimental evaluations, and application-driven case studies that demonstrate how emerging technologies can be translated into real-world cybersecurity solutions. The chapters not only investigate current technological capabilities but also identify existing limitations, unresolved research questions, and future opportunities for innovation. In doing so, the book provides valuable guidance for researchers seeking to advance the state of the art while offering practical insights for professionals responsible for designing and securing contemporary computing infrastructures.

As editors, our objective has been to assemble a comprehensive reference that reflects the multidisciplinary nature of cybersecurity research at the intersection of parallel computing and blockchain. We hope this volume serves as an authoritative resource for researchers, faculty members, doctoral scholars, postgraduate students, cybersecurity professionals, software architects, industry practitioners, and policymakers who are working to build secure, intelligent, and trustworthy digital systems. By presenting peer-reviewed, conference-validated, and internationally contributed research within a single collection, this book seeks to foster collaboration across academic, industrial, and governmental communities while encouraging continued innovation in advanced cybersecurity technologies.

We extend our sincere appreciation to all chapter authors for their outstanding scholarly contributions and their commitment to advancing research in this dynamic field. We are equally grateful to the anonymous reviewers whose thoughtful evaluations strengthened the quality and rigor of each chapter. Finally, we acknowledge the editorial and production teams whose dedication and professionalism have been instrumental in bringing this volume to completion.

It is our hope that *Advancing Cybersecurity at the Intersection of Parallel Computing and Blockchain* will inspire new research directions, encourage interdisciplinary collaboration, and contribute meaningfully to the development of secure, scalable, and resilient computing environments capable of addressing both today's cybersecurity challenges and those that will emerge in the years ahead.

## ORGANIZATION OF THE BOOK

The volume opens by establishing the technological foundations that underpin secure, resilient, and intelligent digital ecosystems. Chapter 1 explores the convergence of artificial intelligence and blockchain technologies as complementary enablers of trustworthy digital architectures. The chapter examines how AI-driven analytics, predictive threat detection, and intelligent decision-making can be integrated with blockchain's decentralized trust and immutability to strengthen cybersecurity while maintaining data integrity and operational resilience. Beyond architectural models and implementation strategies, the discussion also considers ethical, regulatory, and future research implications associated with deploying these technologies across increasingly interconnected digital environments.

Building upon this foundation, Chapter 2 presents a conceptual framework that integrates artificial intelligence, parallel computing, and blockchain into a unified cybersecurity architecture for distributed digital infrastructures. The chapter demonstrates how parallel processing enables high-performance analysis of massive security datasets, allowing AI models to identify sophisticated cyber threats more efficiently, while blockchain enhances trust, transparency, and resilience throughout the security ecosystem. This contribution illustrates the importance of combining computational scalability with decentralized security mechanisms to meet the demands of modern cloud and cyber-physical systems.

Continuing the exploration of distributed cybersecurity, Chapter 3 introduces the AICyber-Chain framework, an innovative architecture that combines parallel AI, blockchain technologies, decentralized storage, and automated smart contracts to overcome the limitations of centralized cybersecurity models. By integrating hybrid consensus mechanisms, secure distributed storage, generative adversarial networks, and blockchain-enabled automation, the chapter demonstrates how adaptive cybersecurity frameworks can improve authentication efficiency, reduce operational costs, and enhance secure data sharing within practical application domains such as healthcare.

Chapter 4 shifts attention to decentralized applications (DApps), examining both their transformative potential and their evolving security landscape. The chapter provides a comprehensive overview of DApp architectures while analyzing vulnerabilities associated with smart contracts, blockchain protocols, oracle services, front-end interfaces, and cross-chain interoperability. Equally important, it presents practical mitigation strategies, including formal verification, code auditing, multi-signature authentication, and secure development practices that collectively contribute to more robust blockchain ecosystems.

Expanding blockchain applications into environmental information systems, Chapter 5 presents a permissioned blockchain framework based on Hyperledger Fabric for the secure storage and management of forest plant records. The chapter demonstrates how decentralized, immutable recordkeeping can improve data integrity, prevent unauthorized access, and support monitoring activities such as illegal logging. Through real-world implementation and performance evaluation, this contribution illustrates how blockchain technologies can extend beyond conventional cybersecurity applications to safeguard critical environmental information infrastructures.

The focus then turns toward computational performance in Chapter 6, which examines how high-performance computing technologies, including GPU and TPU architectures, are transforming cybersecurity operations. The chapter discusses GPU-accelerated cryptography, post-quantum security techniques, large-scale intrusion detection, malware classification, and emerging technologies such as homomorphic encryption, federated learning, neuromorphic processors, and hybrid quantum-classical systems. Collectively, these discussions demonstrate the increasingly important role of advanced computational platforms in supporting scalable and intelligent cyber defense.

Chapter 7 addresses the growing security requirements of autonomous systems by examining AI-based intrusion detection and privacy-preserving mechanisms across domains such as transportation, healthcare, and smart cities. The chapter explores machine learning techniques for anomaly detection alongside federated learning and blockchain-based data protection strategies while also considering adversarial machine learning, regulatory challenges, and future research opportunities. This contribution highlights the need to balance intelligent threat detection with strong privacy guarantees as autonomous technologies continue to evolve.

Extending AI-enabled cybersecurity into the Internet of Things, Chapter 8 presents a cloud-enabled intrusion detection framework that combines artificial intelligence with advanced feature extraction and transformer-based classification techniques. Designed to address the expanding attack surface created by large-scale IoT deployments, the proposed framework demonstrates high detection accuracy with low inference latency, illustrating how cloud computing and AI can be effectively combined to provide scalable, real-time protection for cyber-physical systems.

The importance of proactive cyber defense is emphasized in Chapter 9, which introduces a novel threat modeling methodology driven by high-entropy mutation engines and parallel fork-based attack simulation. By employing mathematically rigorous mutation generation and independent simulation pathways, the framework enables comprehensive exploration of adaptive attack scenarios across critical domains including healthcare, IoT, smart cities, and critical infrastructure. The chapter offers an innovative perspective on predictive cybersecurity through scalable and reproducible threat modeling techniques.

Complementing these detection strategies, Chapter 10 focuses on cyberattack classification as a critical component of modern cybersecurity operations. The chapter reviews the taxonomy of contemporary cyber threats, ranging from malware and phishing attacks to denial-of-service incidents and insider threats, while highlighting the importance of structured classification for improving threat analysis, defensive planning, incident response, and organizational risk management.

Addressing one of today's most pressing cybersecurity concerns, Chapter 11 presents a hybrid deep learning framework for detecting manipulated facial images generated through deepfake technologies. Combining a pretrained VGG16 model with additional convolutional neural network layers, the proposed architecture demonstrates strong detection performance while supporting real-time deployment in cloud-enabled cybersecurity environments. The chapter underscores the growing significance of AI-powered digital forensics in combating misinformation, identity fraud, and synthetic media attacks.

Healthcare cybersecurity is further explored in Chapter 12, which investigates the application of artificial intelligence within Body Area Networks (BANs). The chapter evaluates machine learning techniques for anomaly detection alongside communication protocols designed to balance energy efficiency, latency, and computational performance. Through comparative analysis of deep learning models and communication strategies, the chapter illustrates the trade-offs involved in designing secure, intelligent, and resource-efficient healthcare monitoring systems.

Continuing the healthcare theme, Chapter 13 introduces an advanced chaotic encryption framework for securing medical image transmission and storage. Utilizing a novel hybrid nonlinear chaotic oscillator to generate high-entropy encryption keys, the proposed system enhances resistance to brute-force and differential attacks while providing efficient protection for sensitive diagnostic imagery used in telemedicine and digital healthcare applications. This contribution highlights the growing importance of specialized cryptographic techniques for protecting high-value medical data.

Looking toward the future of secure communications, Chapter 14 examines the integration of classical and quantum cryptographic techniques within Internet of Things environments. The chapter reviews recent developments in quantum key distribution alongside traditional cryptographic methods, discussing both the promise of quantum-safe communication and the practical limitations associated with deploying quantum technologies within resource-constrained IoT ecosystems. The discussion provides valuable insight into emerging directions for post-quantum cybersecurity.

The volume concludes with Chapter 15, which presents a quantum-safe email client that incorporates simulated quantum key distribution alongside modern authentication protocols to strengthen secure digital communication. By combining OAuth 2.0, OpenID Connect, application-layer encryption, and hybrid post-quantum key generation techniques while maintaining compatibility with existing email infrastructure, the chapter demonstrates a practical pathway toward future-ready communication systems capable of withstanding emerging quantum computing threats.

## CONCLUSION

As editors, we believe that the contributions assembled in *Advancing Cybersecurity at the Intersection of Parallel Computing and Blockchain* demonstrate both the remarkable progress that has been achieved and the significant challenges that remain in securing an increasingly interconnected digital world. The convergence of parallel computing, blockchain, artificial intelligence, cloud technologies, and emerging quantum-safe approaches is fundamentally redefining the way cybersecurity solutions are conceived, implemented, and evaluated. Collectively, the chapters in this volume illustrate that effective cyber defense can no longer rely on isolated technologies but must instead embrace integrated, intelligent, and decentralized frameworks capable of adapting to rapidly evolving threat landscapes.

The diverse perspectives presented throughout this book highlight the interdisciplinary nature of modern cybersecurity research. From distributed architectures and high-performance computing to intrusion detection, digital forensics, secure healthcare systems, Internet of Things security, blockchain-enabled applications, and post-quantum cryptography, each contribution offers valuable theoretical insights alongside practical innovations that address pressing security challenges across a wide range of application domains. Together, these chapters not only advance current knowledge but also identify promising avenues for future investigation, emphasizing the importance of collaboration among researchers, industry practitioners, and policymakers.

It is our sincere hope that this volume will serve as a trusted reference for scholars, educators, graduate students, cybersecurity professionals, software architects, and technology leaders seeking to understand and advance the integration of parallel computing and blockchain within secure digital ecosystems. By bringing together peer-reviewed research presented at iCONNECT 2026 alongside invited international contributions, this collection reflects the global effort to develop scalable, resilient, and trustworthy cybersecurity solutions for the next generation of digital infrastructures.

We extend our deepest appreciation to all contributing authors for sharing their expertise and innovative research, and to the reviewers whose thoughtful evaluations have strengthened the quality and scholarly rigor of every chapter. We also express our gratitude to the editorial and production teams whose dedication and professionalism made the publication of this volume possible.

We trust that the ideas presented throughout this book will stimulate continued research, foster interdisciplinary collaboration, and inspire new technological innovations that strengthen cybersecurity in an era increasingly defined by distributed intelligence, decentralized trust, and high-performance computing. As digital systems continue to evolve, we hope this volume will contribute meaningfully to the development of secure, resilient, and intelligent computing environments capable of meeting both current and future cybersecurity challenges.

# Chapter 1
# AI and Blockchain-Enabled Architectures for Secure and Resilient Digital Systems

**Ashutosh Bhardwaj**
http://orcid.org/0009-0008-3311-8335
*Poornima University, Jaipur, India*

## ABSTRACT

*The mushrooming digitalization of industries has heightened the need to have secure and resilient system design as well as smart system design that is prone to address intricate cyber threats and data breaches. Artificial Intelligence (AI) and Blockchain have become the new influential technological innovations that could contribute greatly to the security, visibility, and reassurances of any digital ecosystem. AI can be used to provide smart threat detection and predictive analytics, intelligent decision-making, and blockchain can be employed to provide decentralization trust, immutability, and secure data sharing. The chapter discusses the prospects of AI and blockchain in the design of secure digital architectures and how the two can be used concurrently to enhance cybersecurity, keep data intact, and ensure operational resilience. It talks about architectural structures, practical implementation in industries, and ethical or regulatory implications as well as the future opportunities to create a solid and reliable digital systems in a more globalized world.*

DOI: 10.4018/979-8-3373-9053-6.ch001

# 1. INTRODUCTION

## 1.1 Background of Digital Transformation

Online revolution has become one of the determining factors of contemporary societies, economies, and industries. The enormous use of digital technologies including cloud computing, big data analytics, mobile locations, and the Internet of Things (IoT) have changed the way organizations conduct their activities and provide the services. Companies have found themselves depending on the digital infrastructures as tools to deal with information, automation processes and also increase customer participation. This revolution has facilitated live linkage, synergies globally, and scaled innovativeness, and has fundamentally transformed the conventional ways of operation in industries.

The adhesion of digital technologies has contributed to the enlargement of the area covered by data creation and utilization. Organizations have gone to deal with huge amounts of structured and non-structured data being produced by various sources, such as social media, sensors, enterprise systems, and digital platforms. This capability of processing and analysis of this data has enhanced decision-making, efficiency and strategies in its operations. Digital tools have also contributed to increased transparency, responsiveness and service delivery, enabling organizations to also keep pace with the ever-growing technology driven environment (Cohen, 1960).

Digital ecosystems have, however, presented new vulnerabilities and complexities owing to its rising dependence on them. The more connected the systems, the more vulnerable it is to cyber threats, system failures and unauthorized access. Digital infrastructures are no longer restricted to single network systems, but are integrated into international systems that expose them to risks. The importance of protecting these systems has been pressing due to the increasing impact of digital platforms on the financial transaction, healthcare services, governance and industrial processes.

Digital change is not just a change in technology only but a socio-economical wave that changes the interaction between technology and society. It determines the way people socialize, the way organizations operate and the way governments deliver services. With the further development of digital systems, their security, reliability, and resilience are now the key to sustainable development and confidence in technological progress.

## 1.2 Need for Secure and Resilient Digital Architectures

The growing reliance on digital technologies has created the timely necessity to secure robust and resilient digital architecture. The conventional security models that were centralized due to the control and response based processes are not adequate in dealing with the contemporary cyber attacks. Such advanced attacks as ransomware, phishing, insider threats, and distributed denial-of-service (DDoS) attacks are used to attack an organization, taking advantage of vulnerabilities in the system. These threats require active and dynamic security strategies that are able to detect threats before they have inflicted massive losses.

One important requirement has become resilience when it comes to designing a digital system. In addition to ready automatic defenses against attacks, the systems should also have the ability to sustain themselves quickly upon being hit by disruptions. The secure architectures must use redundancy, fault tolerance and adaptive response systems to ensure that the systems can keep on functioning even in unfavorable situations. This is especially critical to such crucial sectors as healthcare, finance and energy, where failure of a system may cause dire outcomes (Navimipour & Charband, 2016).

The second important factor is the necessity to have trust and transparency in digital interactions. As digital transactions and exchange of data is increasingly becoming part and parcel of life, various stakeholders demand that systems are reliable and secure. There is need of the trust in digital payments, controls on identities and sharing of information. The secure architectures need to provide provisions on data integrity, authenticity, and confidentiality and transparency and accountability in operations (Kumari et al., 2026).

A multidisciplinary strategy based on technology, governance, and human factors is also needed in the change toward resilient architectures. To address changing risks, organizations need to invest in safe system design, regulatory compliance as well as training workforce. The development of resilient digital infrastructures cannot effectively be regarded as a technological challenge only, but also a strategic requirement that can guarantee resilience, reliability, and trust in digital ecosystems.

## 1.3 Role of Artificial Intelligence and Blockchain in Modern Security

The development of Artificial Intelligence (AI) and Blockchain have become revolutionary technologies that minimize the shortcomings of digital security systems in the past. Intelligent capabilities of AI allow systems to identify anomalies, predict potential threats and also respond automatically. With help of machine learning algorithms, which process Big Data and other extensive data volumes to extract regularities and anomalies, organizations can predict the risks before that happen and reinforce preventive actions. This is a proactive method that allows making the cybersecurity more effective and shortens the response period in case of an incident.

The blockchain technology brings in a decentralized trust and transparency to the digital systems. Blockchain makes the transactions of data secure, immutable and verifiable by adopting distributed ledger mechanisms. Every transaction is registered in several nodes and distorting or manipulating data is virtually impossible. This has the benefit of strengthening the integrity of data and decreasing the dependence on centralized authorities and as such, this will decrease the associated risks of single points of failure (Charband & Jafari Navimipour, 2016).

*Figure 1. Integrated AI–blockchain architecture for secure and resilient digital systems*

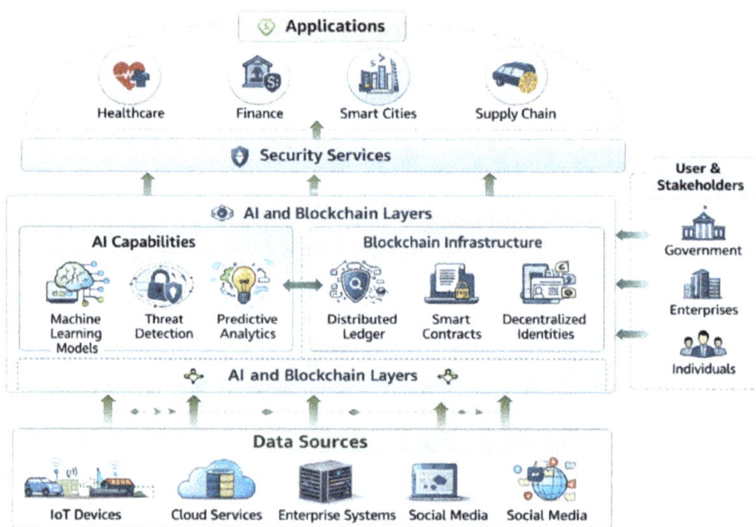


AI and blockchain integration make a strong platform of secure digital architectures. The AI complements blockchain systems by allowing intelligent information on the patterns of transactions and identification of fraud. In the meantime, blockchain assists AI through secure and transparent data space which enhances integrity of machine learning models. The synergy promotes the creation of intelligent, trustworthy and robust digital systems.

The utilization of AI and the use of blockchain technologies jointly will probably transform the security paradigms as digital frameworks get improved. Through these technologies, bases of automated, transparent and decentralized solutions that can respond to emerging threats are being offered. Their use in industries is a testimony that they can make digital ecosystems stronger and more sustainable in the future in the world that is becoming more interconnected (Kaur et al., 2018).

# 2. EVOLUTION OF DIGITAL SYSTEMS AND SECURITY CHALLENGES

## 2.1 From Centralized Systems to Distributed Digital Ecosystems

The digital systems have experienced a massive change in the its separated computational systems into integrated worldwide infrastructure. The initial digital systems were centralized and were based on either low levels of network connectivity hence they were simpler to control and protect. Companies kept their data and process hidden in private space and limited the scope of vulnerability to toxic or malicious activities. Nevertheless, these systems were not very scalable and flexible and thus could not support large scale operations.

As the internet began to spread and also with the new-fangled cloud computing, the digital systems were made more distributed and accessible. In order to increase productivity and cooperation, organizations embraced the use of online services, remote services, and digital communication communication tools. The shift has facilitated real-time exchange of data and connectivity globally, relying on it has transformed the models of business activity and service delivery. Nevertheless, the rise in connectivity also put systems at a risk of novel security weaknesses and cyber threats (Kumari & Goyal, 2026).

The attachment of IoT devices and smart technologies had an additional enlarging effect on the digital environment. The linked devices produce endless data feeds and communicate with other systems in real time to form complex online eco systems. Although this connectivity is improving to make the process more automated and efficient, it also expands the attack perimeter of the cyber threats. The security of interconnected networks and devices has turned out to be a significant issue to organizations and policy makers.

The shift towards distributed systems out of centralized systems has offered both prospects and threats. Digital ecosystems can facilitate the development of innovation and scale-ability, although this must be accompanied by sophisticated mechanisms of security that would respond to dynamic threats. Adaptable and robust digital architectures have gained acuity in the operation of this compound technological environment more than ever (Niranjanamurthy et al., 2019).

## 2.2 Emerging Cybersecurity Threats in the Digital Era

The cybersecurity threat has significantly increased in the digital age by attacking organizations, governments, and individuals. The cyberattacks have taken a rogue turn in that they use complex methods to attack the systems. Types of threats like ransomware, phishing, identity theft, and malware attacks interfere with the operations, steal confidential information, and cost money. These threats underscore the shortcomings of conventional security practices that are mainly based on the reactive practice.

The increasing use of the cloud services and home-based working setups has also increased the complexity of cybersecurity. Information is currently saved on and can now be accessed in a number of different platforms, posing risks of unauthorized access and breach. Networks are penetrated by attackers, which use weak authentication systems and misconfigurations of system. Due to increased interactions via the digital platform, organizations need to implement proactive security models in order to protect their digital resources (Bhutta et al., 2021).

The other issue is the problem of insider threats where employees or authorized users inadvertently or intentionally breach system security. Lack of awareness, human error and inadequate training are causes of weakness within organizations. To deal with these problems the technological solutions are not the only way to follow, but the awareness programs and organizational policies that encourage responsible online actions should be involved.

Cyber security threats have been dynamic with the technological change, and therefore conventional forms of defense have found it hard to adapt. Digital ecosystems are getting ever more complex, which requires smart solutions to security issues that will be able to identify and act on the threats in real time. The development of new advanced technologies like AI and blockchain is becoming one of the main instruments in solving these issues and reinforcing digital resilience.

## 2.3 Data Privacy, Trust, and System Vulnerabilities

The privacy of data has taken a critical concern in the digital era as companies gather and handle a lot of personal and sensitive data. Users would like their information to be treated safely and in a morally acceptable way, but the violations and unauthorized access are destroying the trust. In addition to personal lives being compromised due to invasion of their privacy, privacy also harms the reputation of organizations as well as their credibility. Preservation of data privacy has thus been mandated as a key requirement in designing of digital systems (Sharma et al., 2026).

The other necessary component of digital ecosystems is trust. Electronic communications, payment processing, exchange of information are relying on the dependability of systems and platforms. In case users have the perception that there is less security and reliability of the systems to use, the adoption levels drop and the efficiency in operations is distorted. This can only be achieved through transparent mechanisms that can instill trust and secure authentication process and a sound data protection framework.

The vulnerabilities of the system are usually in old infrastructure, poor encryption system, and wrong security system. With the changes in technologies, old systems found it difficult to meet the current security demands. The organizations need to keep on upgrading their systems, use secure security measures and create the use of sophisticated technologies to address the weaknesses. The consequences of not responding to these weaknesses may be extreme operational and monetary.

Data privacy, trust, and vulnerabilities are a holistic effort that needs intelligence and advancement in technology together with policy frameworks and awareness of the user. The technologies of the AIs and blockchains present such path-indeed solutions as improving the level of transparency, automatizing the process of threat detection, and ensuring the safety of theoretical data processing. Incorporating them into digital architectures is a major move to developing secure and resilient digital systems that can withhold the future technological developments (Rawat et al., 2020).

## 3. FUNDAMENTALS OF ARTIFICIAL INTELLIGENCE IN SECURE ARCHITECTURES

### 3.1 Role of Artificial Intelligence in Cybersecurity

The use of Artificial Intelligence (AI) has become one of the most essential aspects of creating safe digital architectures because it has the capability to handle a lot of information and draw trends that can lead to the emergence of a threat. The conventional cybersecurity solutions can be restricted by predefined rules and reactive mechanisms that are not enough in dealing with the dealings that are dynamic and flexible in response to cyber risks. Machine learning and deep learning, which are part and parcel of AI, allow the systems to identify abnormality, anticipate threats and act proactively to security attacks. The ability increases the efficiency and effectiveness of the digital security frameworks.

AI-controlled cybersecurity infrastructures support real-time behavior, user, and data analysis on networks. AI models are capable of detecting abnormal patterns by analyzing historical data and warn organizations about possible breaches before it starts to happen. This predictiveught enables the organizations to move beyond the reactive security models to the proactive defence measures. AI-based intrusion detection systems, say, may do the detection of suspicious activity and attach preventive actions automatically and ensure the minimum damage and response time (Xu et al., 2016).

Automation can be also identified as another important benefit of AI in cybersecurity. The activities performed by security operations seem to be repetitive (checking network activity, feeding threat databases, investigating security alerts, etc.). The AI automates these operations and minimizes the efforts of people and shortens the time to react to any threats. Accuracy is also enhanced by the use of automated security systems since human errors are usually a significant source of vulnerability (Farooqi et al., 2026).

The negative aspects of AI implementation in cybersecurity are challenges, too, even in spite of the benefits it offers. AI systems need data of high quality in order to be trained, and are vulnerable to adversarial attacks and biases. The attackers will be able to control AI models by providing them with incorrect information, which will result in the false observation of a threat. Companies are hence advised to have stringent training and monitoring and validation systems to uphold the trustworthiness of the AI-fueled security systems.

## 3.2 Machine Learning and Predictive Threat Intelligence

Machine learning (ML), which is a part of AI, is critical to the development of predictive threat intelligence and risk management. ML algorithms examine the patterns of cyber attacks, system logs, and behavior patterns of the past to predict patterns and forecast a potential security threat. Such forecasting ability helps companies to do preventive measures, which minimizes the risk of attacks and enhances the overall system robustness.

Machine learning-based predictive threat intelligence assists organizations in foreseeing vulnerabilities: machine learning anticipates and prevents vulnerables before being exploited. As one example, ML models are able to discuss the profiles of previous cyberattacks and single out the vulnerable areas of systems. Training results can be applied to make organizations strengthen their assets, refresh security policies, and reserve resources more efficiently. Risk assessment is another field that is supported by predictive analytics that analyzes possible threats and the effects they will have on digital infrastructures (Alam et al., 2022).

Machine learning improves self-defense capabilities, which keep up with new threats. In contrast to the traditional systems which are based on the fixed set of rules, the ML-based security frameworks change and learn with a new information. This flexibility will make the digital systems resistant to emerging cyber threats and advanced methods of attacks. It also allows the organizations to be dynamically responsive to shifting threat environments.

Nevertheless, to introduce machine learning into security architectures, there is a need to solve the data privacy challenges, transparency of the algorithms, and computation requirements. Huge datasets are important in the initiation of ML models and can include sensitive data. Trust is a vital requirement of ensuring that data are used ethically and privacy is ensured. Moreover, it is a possibility that the complexity of ML algorithms might reduce their interpretability, and as a result, organizations are unable to comprehend decision-making processes.

### 3.3 AI-Driven Automation and Decision Support Systems

AI based automation and decision support solutions can be used to reinforce secure digital architectures. These systems help organizations with the task of making good security decisions based on a high volume of data, the possible dangers, and suggestions regarding the relevant course of action. Artificial intelligence based decision support tools will be used to enhance situational awareness and improve the organizations response to security incidents.

Electronic security has automation in threat detection, optimization of vulnerability, response to the incident and monitoring of the systems. When used to oversee digital infrastructures, AI-based tools are able to continually monitor them and take corrective actions automatically upon identifying anomalies. This will lower the response time and will ensure that smaller problems do not grow into bigger security breach cases. The automation systems additionally enhance uniformity to security operations since they provide a common approach to responses (Sharma et al., 2021).

The AI-based decision support systems can help security experts assess complicated situations. These systems allow organizations to focus on the risks and allocate resources by giving real-time insights and predictive analytics. They are also used to uphold a strategic planning, as they check the new threats that may emerge and provide preventive remedies. This automation and intelligence combination will increase the organizational resilience and business preparedness.

No matter how many advantages can be associated with AI-controlled automation, the issue of excessive dependence on technology is also present. Over-sourcing to computerized systems can lead to the lack of human control and critical thinking in the decision-making process. Companies need to balance the automation and human capabilities to achieve successful and ethical security practices (Goyal et al., 2026).

## 4. BLOCKCHAIN TECHNOLOGY AND DECENTRALIZED SECURITY MODELS

### 4.1 Fundamentals of Blockchain Technology

The application of the blockchain technology has adopted a striking solution in improving the security, transparency, and trust of digital systems. It is a decentralized registry that stores operations between various nodes such that information is unmodifiable and unverifiable. A chain of transactions is cryptographically secured and chained with other blocks turning each block in the chain into a durable structure. This is a decentralized system that minimizes the use of centralized authorities and improves the integrity of data.

The major characteristics of blockchain are decentralization, transparency, immutability, and consensus. Decentralization implies that there is no central authority over the whole system, and the possibility of being manipulated or affected is lower. Transparency enables participants to authenticate transactions whereas immutability attests that information accepted cannot be modified after it is accepted. The consensus mechanisms provide a way in which the various parties to a network are able to agree with each other on the validity of the transaction in the system and keeping the system reliable (Emmanuel et al., 2023).

The applications of blockchain technology in financial operations, supply chain management, medical information exchange, and identification systems are very common. It enjoys a promising future of establishing reputable digital ecosystems because of its capacity to deliver secure and transparent records. Weeding out the middlemen and making the process of data transfer secure, blockchain improves efficiency and responsibility of online operations.

Blockchain also has issues of scalability, energy usage, and regulatory issues despite the benefits of blockchain. Massive adoption would demand effective consensus mechanism and upgrading of infrastructure. To incorporate the blockchain in secure digital architecture, it is necessary to address these limitations (Islam et al., 2023).

## 4.2 Decentralized Security and Trust Mechanisms

The blockchain-based decentralized security models offer a solid model to safeguard digital systems against aggression in the cyber domain. In contrast to centralized networks which depend on one authority, decentralized ones spread data and control over two or more nodes. This can minimize the susceptibility of single points of failure, and improves resiliency in the system. In case one of the nodes is compromised, the entire network is not in danger.

Blockchain has mechanisms of trust that rely on cryptographic algorithms and consensus. The transactions get authenticated by encryption and are validated by the network members, which makes them authentic and reliable. Such processes make intermediaries unnecessary and promote greater transparency between the digital interactions. The blockchain-based systems are applicable in the applications which need high level of trust as it ensures secure peer-to-peer communication.

Another important use of blockchain technology is identity management that is decentralized. People are able to manage their online identities and disseminate data safely without the need to use centralized authorities. This improves privacy and minimizes chances of identity theft. Identity systems that are based on blockchain also enhance access control and authentication procedures (Goyal et al., 2026).

Nevertheless, decentralized security models must be established properly and governed. Interoperability, network complexity control, and legal and regulatory issues are some of the main challenges. Companies should establish a preconceived policy and standard that will guarantee the success of adopting blockchain-based security systems.

## 4.3 Smart Contracts and Secure Digital Transactions

Smart contracts are computer-generated contracts which are kept on blockchain networks and which have predetermined rules and conditions that are automatically enforced. Such contracts do not involve the use of arm-length intermediaries and provide transparency in transactions. Smart contracts decrease the involvement of humans in the operations of digital systems and increase the efficiency of their work by automating every process.

Smart contracts of safe digital designs support automated procedures, access description, and certification measures. They make sure that the agreements are fulfilled with a set of said conditions but also reduce risks related to manual operations. This proves useful especially in industries like finance, supply chains and digital governance whereby, secure and transparent transactions are critical (Hu et al., 2021).

Digital interactions are also made more accountable and traceable with the use of smart contracts. Every transaction is conducted in the blockchain, which offers an audible trail. This enhances predisposition among the parties concerned and diminishes the possibilities of fraud or corruption. Smart contracts help organizations to make operations easier and guarantee their conformity with regulatory provisions.

Smart contracts are not without some challenges as they are vulnerable to coding errors, lack legal recognition and are limited in scale. Mistakes in the construction of the contract may have unplanned outcomes and regulatory frameworks of smart contracts are under development. These issues are crucial in order to secure the trustworthiness and popularization of digital systems built using blockchain (Li et al., 2020).

## 5. INTEGRATION OF AI AND BLOCKCHAIN FOR SECURE DIGITAL ECOSYSTEMS

### 5.1 Convergence of AI and Blockchain Technologies

The combination of Artificial Intelligence (AI) and a blockchain is a major breakthrough in the creation of safe digital ecosystems. AI offers intelligent analytics, predictive capabilities and automation whereas blockchain offers decentralization, transparency and data integrity. These technologies are used together and fill in on the shortcomings of the old centralized digital systems. The intersection of them allows building intelligent, secure, and resilient infrastructures that will be able to deal with complex cyber threat conditions and handle operations of a massive scale in digital activities (Dandotiya et al., 2026).

AI also improves the effectiveness of blockchain networks by allowing intelligent transactions tracking and detecting abnormalities in transaction real-time. Machine learning algorithms have the capability to examine blockchain information and present irregularities, fraudulence, and potential weaknesses. This enhances consistency of the blockchain systems and proactive risk management. Concurrently, blockchain reinforces AI systems by offering tamper-proof and secure data environments, which assures AI training data authenticity and integrity of the knowledge used to develop AI models.

AI in combination with blockchain enhances cross-organizational data sharing as well as collaboration. Blockchain facilitates blocking of data between the stakeholders and AI converts this data into insights to aid decision-making. This integration supports trusted data ecosystems in terms of which organizations are able to work together without loss of security and privacy. As the industry is going toward the data-driven workflow, the combination of AI and blockchain becomes critical towards the construction of credible digital infrastructures.

Although there could be positive outcomes, the adjustment of AI and blockchain involves addressing technical issues like scalability, interoperability, and complexity of the system. Organizations should need to take care that these technologies are put in position that conforms with the operational needs and security standards. The full potential of AI-blockchain integration should be realised through strategic planning, development of infrastructure, and regulatory assistance (Krichen et al., 2022).

### 5.2 AI-Enabled Blockchain Security Mechanisms

AI is instrumental in enhancing the security of a blockchain with its ability to monitor this very aspect intelligently and detect any threats beforehand and take the appropriate response. Although blockchain networks are secure, the networks remain vulnerable to threats like network attacks and malicious nodes as well as exploiting smart contracts. AI systems are capable of determining the trends of transactions, detecting any suspicious activity, and blocking illegal actions before they affect the network.

Machine learning models result in better blockchain consensus mechanism by improving network operation and identifying abnormalities in checking transactions. Based on the AI algorithm, the behavior of nodes can be assessed, malicious activities recognized, and the trustworthiness of the network provided. This leads to the formulation adaptive blockchain systems that can react to changing threats as well as providing stability to operations (Chanson et al., 2023).

Another use of AI in blockchain-based financial systems is the fraud detection. AI systems are able to detect and notify the stakeholders of possible fraud patterns by examining the transaction data and user behaviour patterns. It is especially useful in fields where secure transactions are especially important like cryptocurrency, executing digital payments, and financial services. AI-based analytics enhance the level of transparency and minimize the chances of financial fraud.

Nevertheless, the implementation of AI into blockchain security systems must pay close attention to such aspects as data privacy, system bias, and complexity. To sustain trust, it is necessary to ensure the transparency of AI decision-making and prevent sensitive information. The use of AI-based blockchain security methods by organizations needs to take ethical and responsible approaches.

## 5.3 Decentralized Intelligence and Autonomous Systems

The intersection of AI and blockchain has created a concept of decentralized intelligence whereby decision-making processes are shared between participants in the network as opposed to having central authority. This strategy improves resilience of the system as well as minimizing single points of failure. Revolutionary AI-powered autonomous systems and blockchain may act on their own, track activity, and react to threats without the need of human human resources.

The decentralized intelligence encourages growth of autoregulating digital ecosystems. AI is applied to data and makes decisions, whereas blockchain gets control over transparency and responsibility in the process. This is especially useful in areas of life like smart cities, supply chains, and autonomous financial systems where extensive tracking is needed and fast reaction is necessary (Kumari et al., 2026).

Autonomous systems are also effective in enhancing the efficiency of operations through process automation and availability of real-time decision-making. As an illustration, AI-based blockchain may be used to automatically handle transactions, oversee network usage, and implement security measures. This decreases the need to have human intervention and improves the functionality of the system.

Regardless of its benefits, decentralized intelligence presents some issues concerning governance, accountability and ethical issues. To achieve responsible use of autonomous technologies, organizations need to put clear policies and structures in place to provide a guideline. The automation and the presence of human control are the key to ensuring trust and reliability in AI-supported blockchain-based systems (Habib et al., 2022).

## 6. ARCHITECTURE DESIGN FOR RESILIENT DIGITAL SYSTEMS

### 6.1 Principles of Resilient Digital Architecture

Resilient digital architecture works upon designing a system with the ability to withstand disruptions, be able to adapt to changes, and remain functional in a bad state. Resilience is now a paramount need during the digital system design in the time when the number of cyber attacks and technological challenges grows. To achieve operational continuity, secure architectures should have redundancy, flexibility and continuous checkups.

The concepts encompassed by resilient architecture are decentralization, modulatory design, fault tolerance, and real-time responsiveness. Decentralization ensures the lack of dependence on individual systems, and its components can work independently and restart fast with the help of modular design. Fault tolerance is to guarantee that systems are capable of carrying on even when some of its components fail. Instantaneous responsiveness will also allow organizations to notice a threat and act on it in real-time (Singh et al., 2021).

The use of AI and blockchain as part of the resilient architectures can increase the capacity of the resilience to address the risks and achieve stability. Artificial intelligence can assist with predictive analytics and responsiveness whereas blockchain also provides a secure and transparent handling of data. The combination enhances digital structures and increases their ability to manage disruptions.

Holistic approach that takes into consideration the technology factors, organizational factors and human factors are also needed because they are all required in resilient architectures. To create the systems that would be able to adjust to the new threats and operational challenges, organizations have to invest in the development of infrastructure, strategies to ensure the safety of the cyber-space and training of the workforce (Sheikh et al., 2026).

## 6.2 Layered Architecture for Secure Digital Systems

A popular method of security system design that is widely applied in digital systems is layered architecture. It separates the components of the system into various layers, which perform certain functions like data management, network security, processing of the application and interaction with the user. This framework increases the organization, scalability and security of the system.

*Figure 2. Layered AI–blockchain security architecture for resilient digital systems*

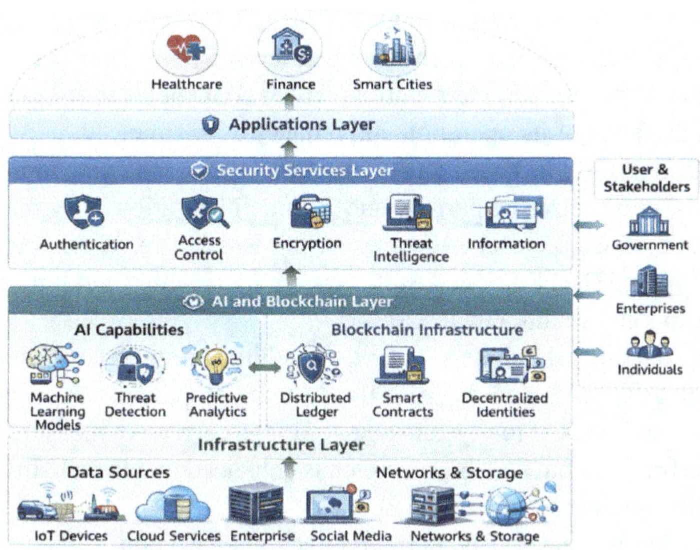


Layered architecture in the AI-blockchain-enabled systems has data layers, blockchain layers, AI analytics layers, application layers, and user interface layers. The information storage and access is controlled by the data layer and the blockchain layer provides the secure and transparent transactions. The data processing layer, known as the AI analytics layer, is used to support the decision making process, and the application layer is the system functionality (Saad et al., 2020).

This multifaceted implementation contributes to the increase of security by isolating possible weaknesses and facilitating specific security implementing mechanisms. When it is breached on one layer, the others are safe giving the system fewer chances of risk. It also enhances the flexibility of the system giving the organizations the ability to update or make certain changes without interfering with the whole infrastructure.

Layered architecture implementation is a process that needs proper planning and coordination between the stakeholders. Organizations have to make sure that there is compatibility between layers and data integrity, and that the security protocols are clear and well-defined. Strong digital resilience and efficient operations are connected with effective implementation of AI and blockchain into more layers to integrate and analyze data.

## 6.3 Adaptive and Self-Healing System Architectures

The next step of resilient design of digital systems can be adaptive and self-healing architectures. These systems apply AI to use tracking of performance, resolving anomalies, and automatic corrective measures. Systems can self-heal to recuperate failures without human intervention, which contributes to the sustainability of the system in terms of its operation and reduces downtime.

Adaptive systems based on AI can analyze real-time data to modify the configurations to optimize the performance. As an illustration, they may put traffic on a new path, revise security measures, or put isolated forsaken components to avoid further harm. The ability makes the system more stable and it minimizes the effect of disruptions (Bathula et al., 2024).

Blockchain will enable an adaptive architecture where the communication and data integrity are secured across the system components. It allows one to clearly track the activities of the system and verify the corrective measures. Artificial intelligence brings about flexibility, which is enhanced by blockchain-powered security that will enhance system resistance.

As adaptive and self-healing architectures have considerable advantages, they demand highly sophisticated infrastructure, computing and highly proficient staff. Companies have to respond to these needs and the responsible execution of the requirements. There must be a balance between automation and the human factor to ensure reliability, accountability, and ethical system running (Sharma et al., 2026).

# 7. APPLICATIONS IN CRITICAL SECTORS

## 7.1 Healthcare Systems

The internet of Artificial Intelligence (AI) and blockchain technology has greatly revolutionized the healthcare systems because it improves the security of data, interoperability, and efficiency in operations. Health facility institutions produce and handle large volumes of sensitive patient data, such as medical history, review of diagnostics, and history of treatments. AI aids in the fields of healthcare, helping to predict the end result with the help of analytics and detecting diseases, as well as recommend the patient individual treatment options; meanwhile, blockchain assures the safety of patient data storage and sharing across more than just one stakeholder (Bhumichai et al., 2024).

AI-driven systems can help healthcare workers with early-stage diagnosis and clinical decision-making by collecting patient-related data and outlining trends of certain diseases. Such technologies enhance precision and minimize time used on diagnosis and eventually better patient outcomes. Meanwhile, blockchain provides an opportunity to have the health records secure and transparently managed so that the information about a patient could be accessible only to authorized individuals and could not be modified without verification.

Telemedicine and remote healthcare services are also improved by the understanding of AI and integration with blockchain. Involving patient information and coordinating work across national boundaries is enabled by secure digital platforms where healthcare providers can share the information they have. Consent management through blockchain guarantees privacy of the patients and control over the medical data. AI assists with remote monitoring systems and evaluates health indicators and offers real-time notification to medical workers (Kaur et al., 2022).

Nevertheless, there are regulatory compliance, costs of infrastructure, and data standardization challenges in the AI-blockchain system implementation into healthcare in spite of its advantages. According to successful implementation, it is essential to ensure that patient data are used ethically and the systems are interoperable. However, these technologies promise much in enhancing the delivery of healthcare, security, and trust in patients.

## 7.2 Financial Services and FinTech

One of the first sectors to embrace AI and blockchain technologies is financial services and FinTech industries because of the necessity to maintain secure, transparent and efficient transaction systems. Blockchain also provides a secure digital operation based on decentralized records, whereas AI improves the fraudulent detection, risk control, and customer analysis. These technologies help to enhance the financial eco-systems and enhance trust among the stakeholders.

Financial analytics enabled by AI are used to track the trends of transactions and identify anomalies that can suggest fraud. With machine learning models, data is analyzed in bulk in the financial industry to detect unusual betting and stop fraud. Blockchain also contributes to security by making the records of the transactions to be immutable and verifiable to reduce the chances of manipulation and unauthorized access (Ressi et al., 2024).

FinTech involves the automation of financial procedures with the utilization of smart contracts, i.e., payment, insurance claims, and compliance validation. Such contracts are automated to operate automatically when certain pre-established conditions are satisfied, and the cost of operation is lowered in addition to enhancing efficiency. The AI assists these systems with trends in the market, customer preferences, and strategies to invest.

Nonetheless, regulatory and technological issues also arise in the area of AI implementation and blockchain use in financial services. Financial institutions need to make sure that they follow the legal frameworks, deal with scalability and system integration. Regardless of these issues, AI-blockchain is transforming financial services between increased transparency, efficiency, resilience.

## 7.3 Smart Cities and Internet of Things (IoT)

Smart cities have inter-related digital infrastructure to control infrastructure, transport, energy, and social services. The AI and blockchain technologies are vital in ensuring safe and efficient smart city ecosystems. AI is used to helps in real-time data analysis and decision-making whereas blockchain will be used to guarantee secure communication and data transfer between connected devices (Martinez et al., 2024).

Smart cities are AI-based systems that can be used to optimize traffic, energy usage and safety according to sensor and IoT evaluations of the city. Predictive analytics also assist authorities in predicting the need of the infrastructure and responding to an emergency in a better manner. Blockchain can also be used to improve security since it offers decentralized networks that prevent the IoT devices against cyber attacks and unauthorized intrusion.

The existence of AI and blockchain integration helps to enhance citizen services as well to create clear governance and effective resource management. These technologies generate online platforms to provide services to citizens, enable them to give feedback and contributions to operations of decision making. In the field of a public administration, blockchain provides the transparency and accountability of data (Minh et al., 2022).

The introduction of the AI-blockchain systems into the context of smart cities will be associated with overcoming certain limitations including infrastructure building, interoperability, and privacy of data. The system to establish long-term sustainable and inclusive smart city ecosystems is a guarantee of equitable access to technology and ethical use of technology.

### 7.4 Supply Chain and Logistics

The combination of AI and blockchain has helped supply chain and logistics systems enhance their level of transparency, efficiency, and security. Contemporary supply chains have a great number of stakeholders, such as manufacturers, distributors, and retailers, and this information demands consistent data transfer and alignment. Demand forecasting, route optimization, and inventory are supported with the use of AI, whereas traceability and secure data exchange are guaranteed by blockchain.

Supply chain systems based on blockchain also ensure clear record keeping on product movement and transactions that decrease fraud and counterfeiting. The transactions are stored in a decentralized registry, and the stakeholders have access to the authenticity of products and shipment of products in real-time. The AI adds value to these systems by interpreting the data to improve the operations in the logistics and predict disruption (Chamola et al., 2023).

AI and blockchain also enhance the sustainability of supply chains through the optimization of resource use, as well as minimization of waste. Predictive analytics assist in assisting organizations to spot inefficiencies and take corrective actions. The technologies facilitate sourcing ethically and in accordance with regulatory standards.

Nonetheless, to implement AI-blockchain systems in supply chains, it is necessary to address the issues of infrastructure, standardization, and collaboration between stakeholders. To maximize their investment in these innovations, organizations have to ensure that they invest in technology integration and workforce training. Nevertheless, AI and blockchain are changing supply chains to secure and robust digital ecosystems and overcoming these challenges.

## 8. DATA PRIVACY, TRUST, AND ETHICAL CONSIDERATIONS

### 8.1 Privacy Protection in AI–Blockchain Systems

Having information privacy is a core issue with digital systems that incorporate AI and blockchain technologies. These systems store and handle huge volume of a sensitive information such as identities, financial records, health care records among others. To ensure privacy, it is necessary to have sound security measures, encryption, and strict access control policies that ensure that data is not used by the unauthorised (Thakur et al., 2021).

AI systems use big data to train and analyze information, and this increases the issue of data ownership and consent. Privacy-safe AI methods and the anonymization, as well as anonymization, are the privacy-preservation methods adopted by organizations that need to be ready to protect individual identities. Blockchain also improves the privacy of data since it allows safety in sharing data and sharing the information transparently without revealing sensitive data.

AI together with blockchain facilitates decentralized identity management whereby individuals can manage their personal data. Users are able to give themselves or withdraw their access to their information and this gives users more privacy and control. This will build confidence and minimize dependence on the central authority.

Even though there are these benefits, privacy restraint under the AI blockchain needs sustained observation and control by regulatory authorities. Companies cannot afford to compromise data protection laws and ethical principles because of lack of confidence by the people and reliability of the systems used to conduct business over the internet.

## 8.2 Building Trust in Digital Ecosystems

Adoption of digital systems using AI and blockchain will require trust to be successful. Users ought to be convinced that their information is safe, transactions are clear and systems are dependable. The blockchain also leads to trust as it offers immutable records and decentralized verification systems whereas the AI increases trust as it is intelligent in monitoring and making decisions.

Efficient accountability and open systems of governance plays a central role in developing confidence in digital ecosystems. Companies should make sure that AI algorithms are human-readable and blockchain systems can be just and transparent. This fosters trust in the users and the wider use of digital technologies (Merhej et al., 2024).

Ethical use of technology and collaboration with the stakeholders is also vital in building trust. To come up with structures that would implement technology responsibly, organizations need to consult with the policymakers, regulators, and users. For building confidence in new digital systems, there must be public awareness and education.

Nonetheless, there are technological abuses, artificial intelligence partiality amid anti-trust, and transparency as erosion of trust. To solve such issues, it will be necessary to assess these problems and maintain ethical standards and high-quality governance systems with a focus on equity and responsibility.

## 8.3 Ethical Challenges and Responsible Technology Use

The use of AI and blockchain combines multiple ethical issues in data applications, algorithmic bias, and the question of technological responsibility. Due to the risk of biased results, AI systems can be trained using unrepresentative or incomplete data, which will result in unjust decisions. To avoid inequality and discrimination, organizations need to be fair and inclusive during the development of AI (Venkatesan & Rahayu, 2024).

Another ethical concern that blockchain systems attract is concerning energy, governance, and accessibility. As much as the blockchain increases the level of transparency, the application should take into account the ecological sustainability and equal access to technology. Responsible innovation involves striking a balance between the social and environmental effects as well as technology benefits.

The aspect of ethics is stretched into the application of autonomous systems and decision-making processes. With the increasing numbers of AI-driven systems, it is necessary that a system has human control and accountability. Companies also need to set up moral standards that will be used to regulate the creation and implementation of such technologies.

The efforts to promote the responsible use of technology ought to be done by a network of stakeholders who can include governments, industry leaders as well as academic institutions. Ethical codes, legal frameworks and constant oversight are required to make sure that AI and blockchain technologies can benefit society, and reduce possible risks and unwanted outcomes (Ressi et al., 2024).

## CONCLUSION

Artificial Intelligence and blockchain technologies are being converged to transform the design of secure and robust digital systems in all industries. With the ever-growing and increasing level of interconnectivity of digital infrastructures, conventional security is no longer adequate to handle any further cyber threat, data vulnerability, and operational risks. Intelligent automation, predictive analytics and adaptive threat detection come with AI and transparency, decentralized trust, and data integrity come with blockchain. Combined these technologies constitute a strong base of creating digital ecosystems that are safe, dependable, and able to carry out complicated and massive operations.

Whether it is healthcare, finance, smart cities, and supply chains, the integration of too AI and blockchain has shown good potential in vital areas. These technologies not only increase the efficiency of operations, improve the security of information, but also facilitate safe cooperation between the stakeholders. Nevertheless, their implementation is too is associated with scalability, regulatory compliance, data privacy, ethical issues, and governance problems. It would take a middle-ground strategy that includes the technological innovation, policy frameworks, building infrastructure and preparing the workforce to handle these challenges. Responsible implementation and persistent improvement are required in organizations in the quest to deliver sustainable digital transformation.

## REFERENCES


Alam, S., Shuaib, M., Ahmad, S., Jayakody, D. N. K., Muthanna, A., Bharany, S., & Elgendy, I. A. (2022). Blockchain-based solutions supporting reliable healthcare for fog computing and internet of medical things (IoMT) integration. *Sustainability (Basel)*, *14*(22), 15312. DOI: 10.3390/su142215312

Bathula, A., Gupta, S. K., Merugu, S., Saba, L., Khanna, N. N., Laird, J. R., Sanagala, S. S., Singh, R., Garg, D., Fouda, M. M., & Suri, J. S. (2024). Blockchain, artificial intelligence, and healthcare: The tripod of future—a narrative review. *Artificial Intelligence Review*, *57*(9), 238. DOI: 10.1007/s10462-024-10873-5

Bhumichai, D., Smiliotopoulos, C., Benton, R., Kambourakis, G., & Damopoulos, D. (2024). The convergence of artificial intelligence and blockchain: The state of play and the road ahead. *Information (Basel)*, *15*(5), 268. DOI: 10.3390/info15050268

Bhutta, M. N. M., Khwaja, A. A., Nadeem, A., Ahmad, H. F., Khan, M. K., Hanif, M. A., Song, H., Alshamari, M., & Cao, Y. (2021). A survey on blockchain technology: Evolution, architecture and security. *IEEE Access : Practical Innovations, Open Solutions*, *9*, 61048–61073. DOI: 10.1109/ACCESS.2021.3072849

Chamola, V., Hassija, V., Sulthana, A. R., Ghosh, D., Dhingra, D., & Sikdar, B. (2023). A review of trustworthy and explainable artificial intelligence (XAI). *IEEE Access : Practical Innovations, Open Solutions*, *11*, 78994–79015. DOI: 10.1109/ACCESS.2023.3294569

Chanson, M., Bogner, A., Bilgeri, D., Fleisch, E., & Wortmann, F. (2023). Blockchain for the IoT: privacy-preserving protection of sensor data. *Journal of the Association for Information Systems, 20*(Article 10), 1271-1307.

Charband, Y., & Jafari Navimipour, N. (2016). Online knowledge sharing mechanisms: A systematic review of the state of the art literature and recommendations for future research. *Information Systems Frontiers*, *18*(6), 1131–1151. DOI: 10.1007/s10796-016-9628-z

Cohen, J. (1960). A coefficient of agreement for nominal scales. *Educational and Psychological Measurement*, *20*(1), 37–46. DOI: 10.1177/001316446002000104

Dandotiya, M., Goyal, N. K., Yadav, P., Sankhla, K., & Kumari, M. (2026). GENALYTICS: A Deep Dive Into Real-Time Insights via Generative AI. In Elbaghazaoui, B. (Eds.), *Generative AI-Powered Data Architectures* (pp. 105–134). IGI Global Scientific Publishing., DOI: 10.4018/979-8-3373-5616-7.ch005

Emmanuel, A. A., Awokola, J. A., Alam, S., Bharany, S., Agboola, P., Shuaib, M., & Ahmed, R. (2023). A hybrid framework of blockchain and IoT technology in the pharmaceutical industry: A comprehensive study. *Mobile Information Systems*, *2023*(1), 3265310. DOI: 10.1155/2023/3265310

Farooqi, A., Das, D., Tripathi, M., Dutta, R., Goyal, N. K., & Sheikh, M. F. (2026). Navigating Ethical Frontiers in AI-Driven Geriatric Care. In Stolakis, K., & Efthymiou, I. (Eds.), *AI for Geriatric Care in an Aging Society* (pp. 243–266). IGI Global Scientific Publishing., DOI: 10.4018/979-8-3373-5462-0.ch009

Goyal, N. K., Goyal, N. K., Kumar, S., Dutta, R., Kothari, V., & Sinha, S. K. (2026). Empowering Elderly Care Through Artificial Intelligence. In Stolakis, K., & Efthymiou, I. (Eds.), *AI for Geriatric Care in an Aging Society* (pp. 1–28). IGI Global Scientific Publishing., DOI: 10.4018/979-8-3373-5462-0.ch001

Habib, G., Sharma, S., Ibrahim, S., Ahmad, I., Qureshi, S., & Ishfaq, M. (2022). Blockchain technology: Benefits, challenges, applications, and integration of blockchain technology with cloud computing. *Future Internet*, *14*(11), 341. DOI: 10.3390/fi14110341

Hu, B., Zhang, Z., Liu, J., Liu, Y., Yin, J., Lu, R., & Lin, X. (2021). A comprehensive survey on smart contract construction and execution: Paradigms, tools, and systems. *Patterns (New York, N.Y.)*, *2*(2), 100179. DOI: 10.1016/j.patter.2020.100179 PMID: 33659907

Islam, S., Islam, M. J., Hossain, M., Noor, S., Kwak, K. S., & Islam, S. R. (2023). A survey on consensus algorithms in blockchain-based applications: Architecture, taxonomy, and operational issues. *IEEE Access : Practical Innovations, Open Solutions*, *11*, 39066–39082. DOI: 10.1109/ACCESS.2023.3267047

Kaur, D., Uslu, S., Rittichier, K. J., & Durresi, A. (2022). Trustworthy artificial intelligence: A review. *ACM Computing Surveys*, *55*(2), 1–38. DOI: 10.1145/3491209

Kaur, H., Alam, M. A., Jameel, R., Mourya, A. K., & Chang, V. (2018). A proposed solution and future direction for blockchain-based heterogeneous medicare data in cloud environment. *Journal of Medical Systems*, *42*(8), 156. DOI: 10.1007/s10916-018-1007-5 PMID: 29987560

Krichen, M., Ammi, M., Mihoub, A., & Almutiq, M. (2022). Blockchain for modern applications: A survey. *Sensors (Basel)*, *22*(14), 5274. DOI: 10.3390/s22145274 PMID: 35890953

Kumari, M., & Goyal, N. K. (2026). Artificial Intelligence in the Cryptocurrency Ecosystem: Crime Mechanisms, Detection Strategies, and Legal Perspectives. In *Innovations in Cryptocrime and Financial Fraud* (pp. 245-282). IGI Global Scientific Publishing.

Kumari, M., Khan, S. T., Gulati, K., Sharma, P., Goyal, N. K., & Sheikh, M. F. (2026). *Innovative Procedural Content Generation (PCG) Using Generative AI*. IGI Global Scientific Publishing., DOI: 10.4018/979-8-3373-4637-3.ch007

Li, X., Jiang, P., Chen, T., Luo, X., & Wen, Q. (2020). A survey on the security of blockchain systems. *Future Generation Computer Systems*, *107*, 841–853. DOI: 10.1016/j.future.2017.08.020

Martinez, D., Magdalena, L., & Savitri, A. N. (2024). Ai and blockchain integration: Enhancing security and transparency in financial transactions. *International Transactions on Artificial Intelligence*, *3*(1), 11–20. DOI: 10.33050/italic.v3i1.651

Merhej, J., Harb, H., Abouaissa, A., & Idoumghar, L. (2024). Toward a new era of smart and secure healthcare information exchange systems: Combining blockchain and artificial intelligence. *Applied Sciences (Basel, Switzerland)*, *14*(19), 8808. DOI: 10.3390/app14198808

Minh, D., Wang, H. X., Li, Y. F., & Nguyen, T. N. (2022). Explainable artificial intelligence: A comprehensive review. *Artificial Intelligence Review*, *55*(5), 3503–3568. DOI: 10.1007/s10462-021-10088-y

Navimipour, N. J., & Charband, Y. (2016). Knowledge sharing mechanisms and techniques in project teams: Literature review, classification, and current trends. *Computers in Human Behavior*, *62*, 730–742. DOI: 10.1016/j.chb.2016.05.003

Niranjanamurthy, M., Nithya, B. N., & Jagannatha, S. J. C. C. (2019). Analysis of Blockchain technology: Pros, cons and SWOT. *Cluster Computing*, *22*(S6, Suppl 6), 14743–14757. DOI: 10.1007/s10586-018-2387-5

Rawat, D. B., Chaudhary, V., & Doku, R. (2020). Blockchain technology: Emerging applications and use cases for secure and trustworthy smart systems. *J Cybersecur Priv*, *1*, 4–18. DOI: 10.3390/jcp1010002

Ressi, D., Romanello, R., Piazza, C., & Rossi, S. (2024). AI-enhanced blockchain technology: A review of advancements and opportunities. *Journal of Network and Computer Applications*, *225*, 103858. DOI: 10.1016/j.jnca.2024.103858

Saad, M., Spaulding, J., Njilla, L., Kamhoua, C., Shetty, S., Nyang, D., & Mohaisen, D. (2020). Exploring the attack surface of blockchain: A comprehensive survey. *IEEE Communications Surveys and Tutorials*, *22*(3), 1977–2008. DOI: 10.1109/COMST.2020.2975999

Sharma, A., Kaur, S., & Singh, M. (2021). A comprehensive review on blockchain and Internet of Things in healthcare. *Transactions on Emerging Telecommunications Technologies*, *32*(10), e4333. DOI: 10.1002/ett.4333

Sharma, P., Kumawat, R., Jain, G., Keswani, G., Goyal, N. K., & Sheikh, M. F. (2026). Machine Learning-Based Intrusion Detection Systems for Healthcare IoT. https://doi.org/DOI: 10.4018/979-8-3373-7610-3.ch007

Sheikh, M.F.A., Kapoor, S.K., Goyal, N.K., Tuba, E., Rao, A. (2026). Enhancing Healthcare Security with Fog Computing and Blockchain Technology. https://doi.org/DOI: 10.1007/978-981-96-7760-3_38

Singh, S., Hosen, A. S., & Yoon, B. (2021). Blockchain security attacks, challenges, and solutions for the future distributed iot network. *IEEE Access : Practical Innovations, Open Solutions*, *9*, 13938–13959. DOI: 10.1109/ACCESS.2021.3051602

Thakur, T., Mehra, A., Hassija, V., Chamola, V., Srinivas, R., Gupta, K. K., & Singh, A. P. (2021). Smart water conservation through a machine learning and blockchain-enabled decentralized edge computing network. *Applied Soft Computing*, *106*, 107274. DOI: 10.1016/j.asoc.2021.107274

Venkatesan, K., & Rahayu, S. B. (2024). Blockchain security enhancement: An approach towards hybrid consensus algorithms and machine learning techniques. *Scientific Reports*, *14*(1), 1149. DOI: 10.1038/s41598-024-51578-7 PMID: 38212390

Xu, X., Pautasso, C., Zhu, L., Gramoli, V., Ponomarev, A., Tran, A. B., & Chen, S. (2016, April). The blockchain as a software connector. In *2016 13th Working IEEE/IFIP Conference on Software Architecture (WICSA)* (pp. 182-191). Ieee. DOI: 10.1109/WICSA.2016.21

# Chapter 2
# Parallel Computing and Blockchain for AI-Driven Cybersecurity:
## A Secure and Scalable Framework for Distributed Digital Infrastructures

**Rocky Kumar**
http://orcid.org/0009-0002-6995-2037
*Poornima University, Jaipur, India*

## ABSTRACT

*The multiplication of digital infrastructures and cloud services and of cyber-physical systems connected with each other has resulted in the significant growth of cybersecurity challenges. Traditional security mechanisms are usually not qualified to process large quantities of security data and identify complex cyber threats in real-time. The combination of artificial intelligence (AI), parallel computing, and blockchain technologies show a promising way forward on creating secure, scalable and resilient cybersecurity frameworks for distributed digital infrastructures. This Chapter puts forth a conceptual framework that incorporates parallel computing architectures and block-chain enabled security mechanisms in order to increase the efficiency and trustworthiness of AI-enabled Cybersecurity systems. Parallel computing helps high-performance processing of big amounts of network traffic and security logs, so that AI models can perform better analysis of picker threat patterns and find out anomalies more efficiently.*

DOI: 10.4018/979-8-3373-9053-6.ch002

# 1. INTRODUCTION: AI-DRIVEN CYBERSECURITY IN DISTRIBUTED DIGITAL INFRASTRUCTURES

The booming growth of digital technologies, cloud computing, IoT devices and distributed systems have revolutionized modern information infrastructures. While these technologies address and enhance the scalability and efficiency of operations, they also introduce major cybersecurity challenges because of the complex architectures and increased attack surfaces. Cyber attackers exploit vulnerabilities in distributed networks through different types of cyber-attacks such as ransomware, DDoS attacks, and data breaches. Artificial intelligence has become one of the effective solutions for detecting cyber threats by analysing massive amounts of network data. However, AI systems have strong need of computational support. Integrating parallel computing with blockchain technology is what allows for scalable data processing, secure information sharing and threat detection for protecting modern distributed digital ecosystems (Ali et al., 2025).

## 1.1 Evolution of Cybersecurity in Distributed Systems

Cybersecurity approaches have drastically changed with the development of distributed computing environments. Early information systems were mainly running on standalone computers or small-scale networks where security measures centered around basic access control mechanisms and firewalls for protection. As organizations started spinning to client-server architectures and to internet-based communication systems, cybersecurity solutions started to expand with intrusion detection systems, encryption protocols, and network monitoring systems.

With the advent of cloud computing, edge computing and IoT-based digital infrastructures, digital environments have become decentralized, interconnected and over networked. These are distributed systems that provide organizations to process vast amounts of data at multiple locations and in multiple devices. However, the distributed nature of these systems also brings forward security concerns such as unauthorized access, data leakage from them and network vulnerabilities. Cyber attackers often exploit weak links in the distributed networks and use the Internet to access sensitive information or block critical services.

In light of these changing threats, the response has shifted in the cybersecurity solutions to be ones that embrace intelligent and adaptive approaches that leverage artificial intelligence and advanced analytics. With AI as its backbone, secure network architectures can constantly monitor network traffic, analyse behaviour patterns and detect suspicious activities and in real time. The integration of AI technologies with distributed computing infrastructures helps organizations implement proactive defense mechanism which could respond to complex cyber threats (Aljawarneh et al., 2018).

## 1.2 Challenges of Securing Modern Digital Infrastructures

Modern digital infrastructures are defined by their large scale, heterogeneity and dynamics. These infrastructures are the set of cloud communication's interlinked services, the IoT devices, edge computing's nodes and enterprise networks that are together, basically supporting various digital applications and services. While these types of technologies offer a lot of benefits, particularly in terms of scalability and efficiency, they also open up many security vulnerabilities that can be exploited by attackers.

One of the greatest problems in securing distributed infrastructures is the huge amount of data produced from network devices and digital applications. Security systems have to analyse huge network traffic, system logs, and user activities to identify potential threats. The more tremendous scale of such huge data set is quite difficult for traditional security tools in order to process data in real time, which leads to delayed detection of threats and easy cyber incidents. Another challenge is the complexity of the hot modern cyberattacks. Attackers are also graduating to bigger and better techniques such as polymorphic malware, encrypted communication channels and multi-stage attack methods to bypass normal security mechanisms. These sophisticated attacks mandate intelligent systems for detecting information that can identify delicate behavioural patterns throughout distributed networks (Apruzzese et al., 2018).

## 1.3 Role of Artificial Intelligence in Cyber Defense

Artificial intelligence has been a game-changing technology in the field of cybersecurity; it has become possible to analyse complex datasets and identify patterns linked to cyber threats. AI-powered cybersecurity systems can use machine learning, deep learning, and data analytics techniques to identify data and respond to security incidents faster and more effectively than traditional rule-based systems. Machine learning algorithms: Machine learning algorithms are popularly used for many things such as detecting attacks, malwares, phishing, and detecting anomalies.

These algorithms are trained to learn patterns from the historical data of the network and identify the anomalous behaviour that differentiates normal system behaviour from malicious activities. Once they have been trained, AI models can be used to analyse real-time network traffic and automatically identify any suspicious activities for further investigation. Deep learning models purify cybersecurity all further, because it allows automated feature extraction and complex pattern recognition. Neural network architectures (Convolutional Neural Networks), Convolution Neural Networks (CNNs), Recurrent Neural Networks (RNNs) etc. are particularly effective for analysing the network traffic patterns and identifying advanced cyber-attacks. AI-based cybersecurity systems can integrate data on threat intelligence from a variety of sources as well to enhance detection capabilities and anticipate new attack patterns (Berman et al., 2019).

## 1.4 Importance of Parallel Computing and Blockchain Integration

Parallel computing is important in shaping AI-based cybersecurity systems that can process massive amounts of data without slowing the process. In parallel computing architectures, the execution of complex computational tasks is being divided into subsets of elementary computations which are executed concurrently at several processors or computing nodes. This approach major impact on processing speed paving the way to perform real-time analysis on massive datasets generated from distributed networks. In cybersecurity applications, parallel computing is used to use artificial intelligence (AI) models to analyse the network traffic stream, system logs and behavioural data in parallel.

This capability deploys the detection latency and optimizing the detection capabilities of the security systems to detect cyber threats as it's happening. High performance computing associations that are close to the graphics processing unit (GPU), distributed to assist the cluster to help with the parallel processing in cyber security programs to are typical. Blockchain technology is complementary to parallel computing terms of how blockchain technology offers decentralized security mechanism that can help bring trust and data integrity in a distributed environment (Buczak & Guven, 2015).

## 1.5 Objectives and Organization of the Chapter

The main goal of this chapter is to discuss the potential of the marriage of artificial intelligence, parallel computing and blockchain technologies to increase cybersecurity for distributed digital infrastructures. Specifically, the chapter has set out to deal with the role of AI in identifying cyber threats, analyse the value of parallel computing used to process large amounts of security data, and assess the role of blockchain technology in strengthening trust and transparency within distributed cybersecurity environments.

The following is the organization of the chapter. Section 2 is devoted to discourse on conceptual bases of distributed cybersecurity systems and role played by emerging technologies for superior digital security. Section 3 discusses the principles of parallel, and blockchain technologies, and how they can be used for cybersecurity applications. Section 4 talks about the framework proposed for integration of AI based threat detection, parallel computing and trust management based on blockchain. Section 5 is the real application and case study on actual usage of above technologies in Cyber security systems.

*Figure 1. Convergence of AI, parallel computing, and blockchain in cybersecurity*

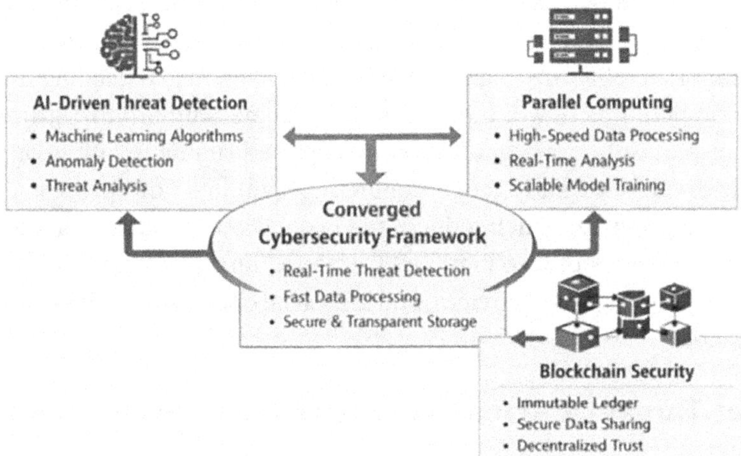


The figure illustrates the combination of artificial intelligence, parallel computing and blockchain technologies to create a secure and scalable cybersecurity framework that will be capable of real-time threat detection and trusted data management.

## 2. FOUNDATIONS OF DISTRIBUTED CYBERSECURITY SYSTEMS

Distributed cybersecurity systems is the building blocks for securing modern digital infrastructures which is spread across cloud-based systems, IoT networks and connected computing environments. These systems are focused at securing data, applications and communication processes which is distributed among multiple nodes in the network. Unlike centralized security approaches, distributed cybersecurity approaches are the solutions to the problems related to large-scale network traffic, heterogeneous devices and complex threat landscapes. Advanced technologies such as artificial intelligence, machine learning and blockchain are also being used to enhance such systems (Casino et al., 2019).

## 2.1 Overview of Distributed Digital Infrastructures

Distributed digital infrastructures can be called the computing environments where data processing, storage and application services are spread across multiple interconnected nodes, as opposed to being centralized within one system. These infrastructures often combine cloud computing platforms, data centers, edge computing point, IoT devices and enterprise networks and all work in tandem for seamless offerings of digital services. Distributed architectures allow organizations to process large amount of data processing tasks, to support global connectivity and offer better system reliability thanks to redundancy and load balancing mechanism.

Cloud computing is now a large part of distributed digital infrastructures, and consumes resources for an organization to store and run data with geographically distributed servers. Similarly, edge computing facilitates the processing of data closer to the data source, which reduces the latency and enhances the performance of the system. IoT devices also increase distributed infrastructures and connections of vital billion sensors, smart devices, and industrial operations to the world network (Das et al., 2025).

## 2.2 Cyber Threat Landscape in Distributed Environments

The security challenge posed by cyber threats in distributed digital world environments separated from the growing penetration of interconnected technologies. Cyber attackers are constantly creating new methods to exploit vulnerabilities in distributed systems; they attack both network infrastructure and application-level services.

One of the most common distributed environment threats is the distributed denial-of-service (DDoS) attack. In a DDoS attack, elements of the network attack, compromised machines or networks are used to overwhelm the target systems with a huge amount of traffic, disrupting the normal services. Distributed infrastructures can be especially vulnerable to these kinds of attacks, due to their inter-connections and dependence on network communication.

Another major threat is with the data breaches and unauthorized access to sensitive data that is stored across distributed cloud platforms. Attackers can harvest weak authentication mechanisms, insecure APIs or misconfiguration through the use of cloud services for unauthorized access of critical information. Insider threats are also a major threat in distributed systems, as employees or authorized users of the system may cause or accidentally expose sensitive information (Diro & Chilamkurti, 2018).

## 2.3 Limitations of Traditional Cybersecurity Approaches

Traditional cybersecurity methods mostly depend on centralized security structures that come with firewalls, antivirus tools, and signature-based intrusion detection systems. While these tools have been effective in securing conventional networks, they have typically been found inadequate for securing modern distributed digital infrastructures. One of the main shortcomings of traditional security systems is that they are based on predetermined attack signatures. Signature-based detection methods are methods in which threats are identified by comparing the network activities with the known patterns of malicious behaviour.

However, these methods are not very good when it comes to zero-day attacks detection, or newly appearing cyber threats that do not follow existing signatures. There are other limitations too such as issue with scalability. Possible Meaning Traditional security tools may be built to function inside the borders of a single network, and may not handle large amounts of data generated by distributed infrastructures easily. As network traffic increases, centralised security systems could also prove to be a bottleneck and cause a delay in threat detection and lower system efficiency (Ferrag et al., 2017).

## 2.4 Need for Scalable and Intelligent Security Frameworks

The complexity of distributed digital infrastructures is increasing, which makes the need for scalable and intelligent cybersecurity frameworks that are able to solve modern security challenges very urgent. Advanced cybersecurity solutions should be capable of analysing large amounts of network data, and identifying emerging threats in real-time, as well as reacting to potential cyber incidents as quickly as possible. Artificial intelligence plays an important role in enabling intelligent cybersecurity systems with its superior data analytics and pattern recognition capabilities.

Machine learning algorithms can analyse the historical data collected from the network and identify the abnormal behaviours and detect the cyber threats that might be recognizable through traditional security methods. AI-fuelled cybersecurity systems are also found using it to support predictive analysis of its threats and help organisations "anticipate" the possible cyberattacks in the future, before they take place. Parallel computing also helps to increase the cybersecurity structures because the computing nodes can make high-speed data processing. By breaking up computational tasks, however, and assigning them to different parallel processors, security systems can then be employed to analyse very large data sets in the moment they occur and increase the efficiency of threat detection (Ferrag et al., 2020).

*Table 1. Cybersecurity challenges in distributed digital systems*

| Challenge | Description | Impact on Security Systems | Possible Solutions |
|---|---|---|---|
| Large-Scale Network Traffic | Massive volumes of data generated by distributed devices and cloud systems | Difficult real-time monitoring | AI-based traffic analysis |
| Distributed Attack Surface | Multiple nodes and devices increase vulnerability points | Higher risk of cyber intrusions | Zero-trust security models |
| Data Integrity Risks | Shared data across distributed systems may be manipulated | Loss of trust and reliability | Blockchain-based verification |
| Complex Threat Patterns | Multi-stage cyberattacks across networks | Hard to detect using traditional systems | Machine learning–based anomaly detection |
| Scalability Challenges | Traditional security tools cannot process large datasets efficiently | Delayed threat detection | Parallel computing architectures |

The table summarizes some of the key security issues in distributed infrastructures and some of the possible technological solutions for improving cybersecurity resiliency.

## 3. ARTIFICIAL INTELLIGENCE IN CYBERSECURITY

Artificial intelligence (AI) has been the game-changing technology in cybersecurity systems today. With the rapid growth of the digital infrastructures and the increase in the complex of cyber threats, the traditional security mechanisms are often not enough to detect the advanced cyber security attacks. AI-driven cybersecurity solutions: Organizations can use AI-powered cybersecurity solutions to analyse vast amounts of network data and detect out-of-the-ordinary activity and detect malicious activities in real-time.

By taking advantage of machine learning as well as deep finding styles, these systems have the ability to identify designs in network behaviour as well as make security alerts automatically. AI also promotes automated incident response so it can be faster when it comes to mitigating any threat. As cyber threats keep adapting, incorporating AI into cybersecurity architectures is significant to create intelligent and adaptive cybersecurity (Gilbert & Gilbert, 2024).

### 3.1 Machine Learning for Threat Detection

Machine learning algorithms examine past information and learn about the patterns of what constitutes normal behaviour by the system and what constitutes a cyber threat. Then, once trained, these models are able to handle real-time network traffic and route activities as legitimate or suspicious.

Common techniques of machine learning applied to cybersecurity analysis are decision trees, support vector machines, random forests, and logistic regression. Such algorithms study different network features like packet size, connection time, the source and destination address, and the frequency of the communication between devices. By looking for these types of characteristics, machine learning models have the potential to detect suspicious activities potentially indicative of cyberattacks such as unauthorized access attempts or the spread of malware. Machine learning-based threat detections offer a number of benefits over traditional security approaches. They are able to automatically adapt to new types of attacks, helps to reduce the need for the manually defined rules for an attack, and is able to improve the success of detecting a threat. Additionally, the machine learning models can also constantly learn from updated datasets, enabling cybersecurity systems to adapt with the evolving cyber threats (Gupta et al., 2018).

## 3.2 Deep Learning for Intrusion and Anomaly Detection

Deep learning is a higher level of artificial intelligence featuring multi-layer neural networks for the application of deep analysis to large amounts of data. In applications such as cybersecurity, deep learning techniques are generally used in intrusion detection, anomaly detection, and classification of malware. These models are able to automatically extract meaningful features from raw data with no need for extensive features engineering. Convolution to Google Neural Networks CNN, Recurrent Neural Networks RNN, Convolution al Neural Networks, Convolution Neural Network referrer to one of the most used deep learning architectures in cybersecurity systems.

CNN models are especially helpful in pattern detection of network traffic information and malware communication or abnormal packet flows. RNN models such as long short-term memory (LSTM) networks are helpful for analysing information over time and recognizing patterns in the data points of the network activities. Intrusion detection systems that are based on deep learning algorithms can identify subtle anomalies that may not be detected by traditional machine learning algorithms. These systems examine patterns in the network traffic and system logs, as well as user patterns to identify possible security threats. However, deep learning models can be resource-intensive to train, with large amounts of data needed to get teaching algorithms to learn and with large amounts of computational power to train them, which can be an issue for organizations with limited infrastructure (Hamad et al., 2025).

## 3.3 AI-Based Threat Intelligence and Predictive Security

AI-powered cybersecurity systems are starting to be applied more to enable threat intelligence systems as well as predictive security measures. Threat intelligence refers to gathering and researching the information related to possible cyber threats, attack patterns, and vulnerabilities in digital systems. By integrating artificial intelligence into threat intelligence platforms, organizations can analyse large quantities of security-related information from different sources, and better identify the present and future menace. Predictive security systems are based on machine learning models that are used to predict potential cyberattacks based on historical data and behavioural patterns.

These systems are used to analyse the trends in the network activities and identify the suspicious indicators and predict the possible scenarios before the attackers do. For instance, predictive analytics can be used to detect phishing campaigns patterns, malware dissemination or coordinated cyberattacks against certain organizations. AI-based threat intelligence platforms can also combine information from globally used cybersecurity databases and security incident reports, including network monitoring systems. This integration gives the organizations to share the threat intelligence information securely and work together to identify the emerging cyber threats. By tapping the power of predictive analytics technologies with real-time monitoring capabilities, artificial intelligence-enabled cybersecurity frameworks have made it possible to become proactive in terms of detecting threats as well as increasing overall cyber defense capabilities (Hamid et al., 2016).

## 3.4 Challenges of AI-Driven Security Systems

Despite the myriad benefits of artificial intelligence in cybersecurity, artificial intelligence security systems have a number of challenges and limitations. One of the main areas of complications relates to the availability and quality of the data in which the model will be trained. Machine learning models require huge amounts of labelled data to correctly identify the patterns that are associated with cyber threats. However, the quality of the data gathered on cyberattacks can be a challenge to gather due to privacy issues and the fact that cyberattacks are dynamic in nature. The other challenge has to do with the adversarial attacks against AI models themselves.

Cyber attackers might attempt to take control of machine learning systems by feeding them malicious data and data to try to take control of, by exploiting the flaws in the algorithms. This lack of transparency may lead to trust concerns as well as hinder adoption of solutions that use AI for cybersecurity in critical infrastructures (Hodo et al., 2017).

*Table 2. AI techniques and their applications in cybersecurity*

| AI Technique | Method Type | Cybersecurity Application | Key Advantages |
|---|---|---|---|
| Decision Trees | Machine Learning | Intrusion detection and network classification | Easy interpretation and fast decision-making |
| Support Vector Machines (SVM) | Machine Learning | Malware detection and network anomaly detection | High accuracy in high-dimensional data |
| Random Forest | Machine Learning | Network traffic classification and threat detection | Reduces overfitting and improves prediction accuracy |
| Convolutional Neural Networks (CNN) | Deep Learning | Malware detection and network traffic analysis | Automatic feature extraction |
| Recurrent Neural Networks (RNN/LSTM) | Deep Learning | Detection of sequential cyberattack patterns | Effective for time-series network data |
| Reinforcement Learning | AI Learning Model | Automated cyber defense and response systems | Adaptive learning and dynamic decision-making |

The table concentrates on some of the key Artificial Intelligence techniques used in Cybersecurity systems as well as its use in Threat detection, Anomaly analysis and Cyber defense Automated cyber defense.

## 4. PARALLEL COMPUTING FOR HIGH-PERFORMANCE CYBERSECURITY

Parallel computing plays an integral role in boosting the performance of the cybersecurity systems in modern times by facilitating the processing of huge security data sets at a faster pace. As digital infrastructures generate inputs of immense amounts of network traffic, system logs, and security events, the process of efficiently analysing data, done with old fashioned sequential approaches of computing, often face a tough time. Parallel computing trends to solve this issue by distributing the computational operations on a group of processors to enable the simultaneous processing of data. This capability contributes to network monitoring on a real-time basis, threat detection at a faster rate, and better security analytics capabilities. When concentrated with man-made intellect and cloud-based organizations, parallel computing exponentially enhances adaptability, productivity, and reactors of cybersecurity frameworks made for ensuring distributed computerized settings (Javaid et al., 2016).

## 4.1 Overview of Parallel and Distributed Computing

Parallel computing is a computing paradigm in which a computing task is divided into multiple processing units which work in parallel to solve complex problems more efficiently. Instead of running computations one after the other on a single processor, parallel computing incorporates dividing a big computation task into smaller sub-computations that can run in parallel on multiple processors or computing nodes. This approach reduces the amount of processing time considerably and enhances the overall performance value of the computational systems. Distributed computing which goes hand in hand with parallel computing in which a network of interconnected computers works together to perform computational tasks. In the case of distributed systems, processing resources are distributed among many different machines that communicate over a network to accomplish some common goal (Lv et al., 2024).

These systems allow organizations to be able to process large-scale datasets and support high-performance applications across geographically distributed infrastructures. In the application of cybersecurity, we refer to parallel and distributed computing architectures that will help to control network data, security logs, and threat intelligence information in a short period. By having data processing distributed among several computing nodes, security schemes can process large levels of network activities without racking the computing performance. This ability is especially useful in the context of large enterprise networks, and in cloud computing environments in which the security systems need to process streams of data continuously in real time (Moustafa & Slay, 2015).

## 4.2 Parallel Data Processing for Network Traffic Analysis

Network traffic analysis is a major part in identifying illicit activities and identifying potential cyber threats in digital infrastructure. Modern networks generate huge amounts of network traffic containing data on characterizing the packet transmissions, the type of communication protocol and the connection patterns between devices. Analysing this data in methods that satisfy the various of the work with conventional sequential processing techniques, can be slow and inefficient, specially in large-scale distributed settings. Parallel computing offers an effective solution for dealing with this network traffic data processing by spreading the task of analysis around multiple processors. Security analytics platforms can split incoming network traffic into multiple data streams, and as such processes them in parallel by using parallel algorithms. This approach helps organizations to use cybersecurity systems to continuously monitor their network activities and identify any suspicious patterns that might be indicative of cyberattacks.

For instance, intrusion detection systems can utilize parallel coding methods to assess information together with the stated the items in the network or on the packets level at various nodes in parallel. These systems can also reuse traffic data in parallelized fashion to have strategies that easily identify anomalies such as unusual communication patterns, unauthorized access attempts or unusual traffic spikes in immediate fashion. Parallel processing also aids in the training of machine learning models that are used in cybersecurity analytics by speeding up the computation of large datasets required for the training and evaluation of machine learning models (Nguyen & Reddi, 2021).

## 4.3 GPU and Cloud-Based Parallel Cybersecurity Systems

Graphics Processing Units (GPUs) have become an integral part of parallel computing architectures of the modern age because of their capability to perform large number of computations at a time. Unlike conventional central processing units (CPUs), which are optimized for sequential processing tasks, GPUs have hundreds or thousands of smaller processing cores that can perform parallel processing tasks with high efficiency. This capability makes GPU's especially suitable for applications that require the processing of complex data in a short amount of time such as machine learning and cybersecurity analytics.

In the real of cybersecurity systems, GPUs are widely employed for accelerator applications like malware detection, intrusion detection, large data network traffic reveal, etc. Deep learning models applied to cybersecurity applications often demand a lot of computational resources for the training and inference processes. GPU-based computing platforms allow these models to process large amounts of data in a short period of time and optimize the performance of AI-driven security systems.

Cloud computing platforms further support parallel cybersecurity capabilities by offering scalable computing resources to be used as required. Cloud-based security infrastructures provide organizations with the ability to deploy distributed cybersecurity infrastructures that can dynamically scale computing resources according to the workload requirement. Security analytics tasks like threat detection, log analysis and training machine learning models can be distributed across several cloud servers which allows organizations to process massive volumes of security data efficiently. Combination of GPU implementation with cloud based parallel computing is therefore a powerful infrastructure for high-performance cybersecurity systems (Nithyavani & Raja, 2025).

*Figure 2. Parallel computing architecture for cybersecurity analytics*

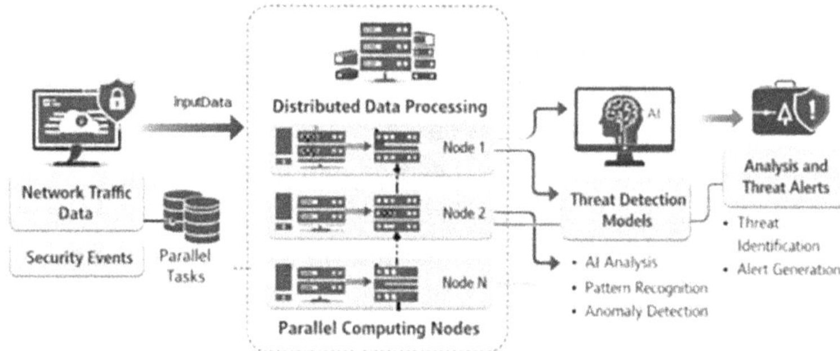


In this distributed architecture of parallel computing, network traffic data is processed across various computing nodes for AI-based threat detection, real-time cybersecurity analytics, etc.

## 5. BLOCKCHAIN TECHNOLOGY FOR SECURE CYBER INFRASTRUCTURES

Blockchain technology has become a successful, and effective solution to the problems of improving security, transparency, and trust in modern digital infrastructures. As distributed systems grow with the rise of cloud computing, IoT networks and decentralized platforms, it is becoming more difficult to preserve data integrity and authenticity. Traditional centralized security systems are reliant upon the use of singular databases, which are at risk for cyberattack and data manipulation. Blockchain helps overcome these problems by offering a decentralized and undatable register for safe data sharing. Through the cryptographic verification and consensus mechanisms, blockchain ensures safe transaction records. When combined with Artificial Intelligence and Parallel Computing, Blockchain enables scalable Cybersecurity mechanisms that have the ability to safeguard distributed digital spaces from advanced cyber threats (Owezarski, 2023).

### 5.1 Fundamentals of Blockchain Security

Blockchain security is constructed on some of the most important features like decentralization, security of internet users and consensus validation. Unlike traditional centralized data storage methods in the form of centralized databases, in blockchain network storage of data over multiple nodes in a peer-to-peer network. Each node has a copy of the blockchain ledger so that no single person has control over the system. The decentralised nature of such architecture reduces the risk of data modification or system breaching to a huge extend.

Cryptographic techniques play an important role in the blockchain transaction security. Public-key cryptography is this technology to verify whether transactions are authentic or not and for making sure that there are only authorized participants of the network to have access to or modify data that includes in the network. Hash functions are also used to link a series of blocks together to create a chain of records which is secure in that any alteration of a previous block would necessitate changing all subsequent blocks as well. This is the mechanism that takes care of immutability of the data stored on the Blockchain. Consensus mechanisms of various types such as Proof of Work (PoW), Proof of Stake (PoS) and other distributed agreement protocols are implemented for validating transactions and for keeping the network operational. These mechanisms are to ensure that all the involved participating nodes are in agreement on the state of the blockchain before adding new transactions to the ledger. As a result, blockchain networks have created a secure and transparent space to manage cybersecurity-related data and transactions (Padhiar & Patel, 2023).

## 5.2 Decentralized Identity and Authentication

Identity management and authentication are essential parts of cybersecurity systems. Traditional authentication mechanisms usually make use of centralized identity management systems that store passwords in centralized databases. While these systems remain convenient access control solutions, they do open up some potential opportunities for compromised computer systems since attackers may target centralized identity servers to achieve unauthorized access to sensitive computer systems. Blockchain technology offers decentralized identity management solutions that allow users to have access to and verification of their digital identities without having to rely on references to centralized authorities.

In decentralized identity systems, identity credentials are securely stored within a blockchain network by means of a cryptographic method. Using cryptographic keys instead of traditional username and password combinations, the users are able to authenticate themselves. This approach makes it much more secure in the sense that it decreases the risk of stolen credentials and hampered identity. In addition to this, decentralized identity systems are critical to ensure authentication in distributed digital infrastructures for things like cloud platforms, IoT networks and enterprise systems (Rajendran et al., 2024).

## 5.3 Smart Contracts for Cybersecurity Automation

Smart Contracts are self-executing programs, which are individually stored at the blockchain networks, to automatically impose predefined rules and contracts among the network's participants. These contracts operate under principles of conditional logic which implies that you automatically cause certain actions to occur whenever certain conditions are meeting. Smart contracts can offer a great deal to cybersecurity operations as they allow the automation of security operations and reduce the need for manual intervention. In the application of cybersecurity, smart contracts can be used in the automation processes of some business operations, such as the control of access, incident response procedures, the monitoring of compliance.

For example, using a smart contract, it is possible to automatically revoke access to the system, if the system detects suspicious activity, or enforce security policies, if certain conditions exist on the network. This automation is helpful to reduce the amount of time it takes to respond to cyber incidents, as well as help to increase the efficiency of cybersecurity operations. Smart contracts can also be used to facilitate secure data sharing between organizations that are cooperating in the field of cybersecurity. For example, organizations that are engaged in threat intelligence sharing networks can use smart contracts to authenticate data and enforce data access policies. On the one hand, by making cybersecurity operations automated by using blockchain-based smart contracts, organizations will be able to manage security operations more effectively, with reduced operational complexity (Sarker et al., 2020).

*Table 3. Blockchain applications in cybersecurity*

| Blockchain Application | Description | Cybersecurity Benefit |
|---|---|---|
| Decentralized Identity Management | Blockchain-based digital identity verification | Reduces identity theft and credential attacks |
| Smart Contract Security Automation | Automated enforcement of security policies | Faster incident response and compliance |
| Secure Data Integrity | Immutable storage of security logs and records | Prevents data tampering |
| Threat Intelligence Sharing | Secure sharing of cyber threat data between organizations | Improves collaborative defense |
| Distributed Access Control | Blockchain-based authentication mechanisms | Eliminates single points of failure |

The table brings attention to some of the major applications of blockchain in cybersecurity that provide trust, data integrity, and automated security management in distributed digital infrastructures.

# 6. INTEGRATED FRAMEWORK: PARALLEL COMPUTING AND BLOCKCHAIN FOR AI-DRIVEN CYBERSECURITY

This increased complexity of cyber threats combined with the expansion of digital distributed infrastructures maps a need for advanced cybersecurity frameworks that are able to process large scales of security data while maintaining trust and integrity of data. Traditional security systems can find it difficult to analyse a large volume of traffic in the network and to coordinate responses throughout distributed environments. Integrating Artificial Intelligence, parallel computing, and the Blockchain to provide an innovative approach to combating cyber security challenges for scalability in the modern day. AI helps smart threat detection by studying network behaviour and the parallel computing helps in processing in huge set of data in real-time. Blockchain technology is used for secure purposes of data-sharing and logging security events which cannot be altered. Together, these technologies form a secure and expandable infrastructure for cybersecurity for the protection of distributed digital infrastructures (Shone et al., 2018).

## 6.1 Framework Architecture and System Design

The architecture of the integrated cybersecurity framework is aimed at supporting distributed data processing, intelligent threat detection, and secure communication between network participants. The framework is composed of multiple layers which are interconnected to each other, to ensure that all-around cybersecurity is maintained. These layers include data collection layer, processing layer, AI analytics layer, blockchain security layer and finally response management layer.

The data collection layer takes security-related information from various sources including network traffic monitors, system logs, IoT devices, and cloud platforms. This data offers valuable information about the activities within the system and possible cyber threats. The gathered data is then delivered to the processing layer, with the help of parallel computing techniques, which are used to process large scale data sets efficiently. The AI analytics layer makes use of the machine learning algorithms and deep learning algorithms to analyse the processed data and look for the patterns related to the malicious activities.

These models keep a constant check on the network behaviour and flag the anomalies that can be a result of cyberattacks. Once the potential threats are identified then the relevant security events are recorded on the blockchain layer, which guarantees the integrity and transparency of security records. The security layer of the blockchain is used to manage decentralized trust by keeping unchangeable records of cybersecurity incidents and enabling the secure communication between nodes on the blockchain network. Finally, the response management layer ensures the coordination of automated security responses, such as blocking suspicious connections or triggering incident response procedures. This layered architecture guarantees efficient co-ordination between AI-based threat detection, high performance data processing and also secure blockchain chunk-wise data management (Szymoniak et al., 2025).

## 6.2 Data Flow and Security Protocols

Efficient data flow management plays an important part in ensuring effectiveness of cybersecurity frameworks for distributed digital environments. In the proposed framework, security data passes through several stages of processing, starting with data collection and finishing with the detection and responding to a threat. The system gathers the network traffic data, user activity logs and the system performance data from distributed nodes across the digital infrastructure. Once the data is collected it is transmitted to parallel processing units where it is analysed simultaneously over multiple computing nodes. This parallel approach to data processing allows the system to process large amounts of security data much faster in real time to speed up threat detection mechanisms and make them faster and more accurate.

The data that has been processed is then fed to the artificial intelligence (AI) based analytics modules, where machine learning algorithms analyse data and detect anomaly and suspicious pattern. In order to ensure data integrity and confidentiality, the framework utilizes protected communication protocols, such as encryption and digital signatures. Blockchain technology is useful to enhancing security, where authenticated security events are written in the distributed ledger. Each security event is then validated through blockchain consensus techniques before its permanent recording on the blockchain network. This process ensures that no unauthorized data modification happens and to create transparency between participating nodes. By combining the secure communication protocols and the blockchain validation mechanisms, reliable and trustworthy Cybersecurity data management are provided by the framework (Vinayakumar et al., 2019).

## 6.3 AI-Based Threat Detection within Blockchain Networks

Artificial intelligence is an integral part of the process of identifying cyber threats as part of the integrated cybersecurity framework. AI algorithms can analyse network behaviour and detect patterns that may be evidence of malicious activities, such as unauthorized access attempts, malicious communications between malware or an abnormal network traffic pattern. Machine learning models are trained with historical datasets of cybersecurity information so as to identify both known and emerging cybersecurity threats. Within blockchain networks, applications created with AI capabilities detect network security issues by analysing data stored across the decentralized nodes and be able to identify a potential security incident in real time. For example, AI models can be used to analyze patterns of transactions on the blockchain and detect suspicious activities that may indicate fraudulent transactions or unauthorized access to the system. Used together, AI analytics and blockchain data verification mechanisms make the threat detection processes more reliable (Wang et al., 2017).

## 6.4 Parallel Processing for Real-Time Security Monitoring

Real-time cybersecurity monitoring allows for the need to process and analyze huge amounts of network traffic and system logs on a continuous basis. Parallel computing is an important part of enabling such real-time analytics by distributing such computational tasks to multiple processing units. In the integrated cybersecurity framework, multiple, parallel processing architectures analyse incoming streams of network traffic in real time, and the cybersecurity system is able to detect the threat as it is occurring. Parallel processing is also used to support the training and execution of machine learning models that are used for cybersecurity analytics. Training the deep learning models may take huge computation resources especially when we use a big cybersecurity data set. By leveraging parallel computing infrastructure like GPCs and made distributed computing clusters, cybersecurity systems will be able to improve model training processes and improve detection accuracy. In addition to making the process of detecting faster, parallel computing also helps to build cybersecurity infrastructures that can be scaled up to accommodate larger and larger networks. As digital infrastructures are expanding and generating more and more data, parallel processing systems can be available as a dynamic learning system that can be used to assign computing resources according to the performance of detecting threats. This capability ensures that cybersecurity frameworks are kept effectively operating within a very dynamic environment and large-scale distributed environments (Yin et al., 2017).

*Figure 3. Integrated AI–blockchain–parallel computing cybersecurity framework*

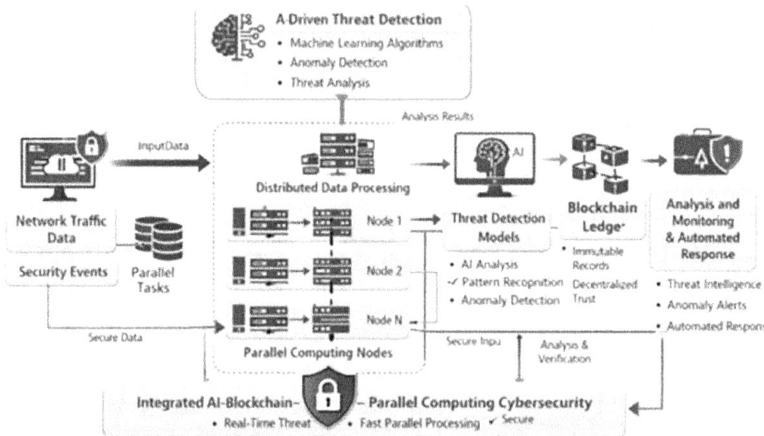


The figure shows a complete cybersecurity with an artificial intelligence of threat detection, parallel computing of high-speed data processing and a blockchain of secure and transparent security event management.

## 7. CASE STUDY: DISTRIBUTED CYBER THREAT DETECTION USING AI AND BLOCKCHAIN

The explosive growth of distributed digital infrastructures have confronted the cybersecurity systems with huge challenges in detection and control of threats in massive networks. Traditional centralized security frameworks can have a difficult time handling heavy loads of Network Traffic generated by cloud platforms, IoT devices and enterprise systems. And to overcome these limitations, advanced technologies like artificial intelligence, parallel computing, and blockchain can be integrated to provide better cyber threat detection. In this case study, network traffic is constantly monitored through AI based threat detection models. Parallel computing helps in speeding up data processing and training models, which results in analysing big data faster. Meanwhile, blockchain technology provides for a secure and unalterable storage of security events. The merging of these technologies results in an increase of threat detection success, data integrity, and the ability of teams to work together in a collaborative cybersecurity environment in a distributed digital environment (Nithyavani & Raja, 2025).

## 7.1 Problem Context and Threat Scenario

Modern distributed digital infrastructures include interconnected cloud servers, IoT and enterprise network systems operating alongside one another and generating huge volumes of network traffic and system activity logs. These infrastructures are often a target for cyber attackers, who use their vulnerabilities in distributed networks to gain unauthorized access, steal sensitive information and disrupt services.

In this case study the threat situation has to do with detection of distributed cyberattacks in a large enterprise network environment. Some types of potential attacks include distributed denial-of-service (DDoS) attacks, attempts to gain unauthorized access, propagation of malware, and insider threats. These attacks are frequently occurring at multiple network nodes at the same time and harder to detect by traditional centralized security systems. The goal of the case study is to build a distributed cybersecurity framework that could detect these cyber threats in real-time while ensuring security record integrity. Artificial intelligence models are employed to analyse the network traffic data and determine suspicious patterns, and blockchain technology is used to keep a validated security event in a decentralized ledger. Parallel computing infrastructure is used for high-speed data processing and helps the system analyse large scale data efficiently (Owezarski, 2023).

## 7.2 Dataset and Experimental Setup

To applaud the effectiveness of the proposed cybersecurity framework, the cybersecurity data available in the public domain such as CICIDS2017 and UNSW-NB15 were used for experimental analysis. These datasets contain realistic network traffic records which include both normal system activities and different types of cyberattacks. The datasets present the detailed information about network packets, communication protocols, connection durations, and attack categories, which could be used for training and evaluating the intrusion detection models.

The experimental setup is to first preprocess the network traffic data in order to extract relevant features that could be used to perform machine learning analysis. Data preprocessing steps, such as removing redundant attributes, fixing missing values and normalizing feature values to bring consistency in representing the data, were followed. The dataset was further split into subsets of training and testing in an 80:20 ratio. In addition, a blockchain network was implemented for recording the verified cybersecurity events and security logs to guarantee the integrity of security (Das et al., 2025).

## 7.3 AI Model Development and Parallel Training

Machine learning algorithms have been used to create the AI-based detection models of threat used in this case study. Several classification algorithms were implemented in order to analyse network traffic data and identify possible cyber threats. These algorithms were decision trees, random forest classifiers, support vector machines, and deep neural networks. The training process entailed feeding the machine learning models labelled network traffic data to enable the models to learn the patterns of normal and malicious activities.

Parallel computing techniques were applied to speed up the training process by distributing the computation process to multiple processing units. GPU-based parallel processing helped to speed up the model training time, as well as increase the overall system efficiency. Deep learning models were also implemented including convolutional neural networks to analyse complex patterns in the network traffic data. For each of those, these models automatically found features in raw data and found subtle anomalies that might signal cyberattacks. As the AI models were enabled to process massive datasets efficiently by using parallel computing infrastructure, a better accuracy of threat detection was achieved (Aljawarneh et al., 2018).

## 7.4 Blockchain-Based Security Validation

Blockchain technology was incorporated into the cybersecurity applying for secure and transparent validation of security events. When the AI-based threat detection system detected any suspicious activities, the appropriate security events were collected in a blockchain ledger. Each event was cryptographically verified and stored in a distributed blockchain network which meant that the security records could not be changed or tampered with. The blockchain network also was the platform for securely sharing threat intelligence information among participating network nodes. For instance, if a cyber threat was observed in one area of the distributed infrastructure, the corresponding threat information could be shared via the blockchain network in a secure manner with other nodes.

This is a collaborative approach and resulted in an improvement in the ability of the cybersecurity system to fraudulently respond to emerging threats. Smart contracts were used to automate security verification processes on the blockchain network. These contracts automatically validated security events and enforced security predefined policies. Then, the smart contracts offered an automatized reaction to security activities that could be taken (e.g. block malicious network connections or activate incident response procedures) depending on the nature of the work, if suspicious activities were detected (Gilbert & Gilbert, 2024).

*Table 4. Performance metrics of AI-based cybersecurity models*

| Model | Accuracy | Precision | Recall | F1-Score | Key Strength |
|---|---|---|---|---|---|
| Decision Tree | 90% | 88% | 87% | 87% | Simple and interpretable |
| Random Forest | 96% | 94% | 93% | 94% | High detection accuracy |
| Support Vector Machine | 94% | 92% | 91% | 91% | Effective for high-dimensional data |
| Neural Network | 95% | 93% | 92% | 92% | Detects complex attack patterns |
| CNN Deep Learning | 97% | 95% | 94% | 95% | Advanced pattern recognition |

The table compares the performance of various machine learning and deep learning models that were used for distributed cyber threat detection against the parameters of accuracy, precision, recall, and F1-score.

## 8. FUTURE RESEARCH DIRECTIONS

As the digital infrastructures continue to evolve as they transition to cloud computing, edge computing, and large-scale distributed systems, the structure of cybersecurity needs to evolve to meet current and future cybersecurity challenges and threats. The combination of artificial intelligence, blockchain technology and parallel computing has made a big difference in the ability of cybersecurity systems to detect and respond to cyber threats more rapidly. However, there are new challenges that need to be researched and technologically innovated, such as the need for more transparency and trust in the AI systems we use, the need for more data, and the need for more adaptable attack strategies.

Future research on cybersecurity can be expected to focus on improving the transparency of security systems that are based on AI, collaborative learning capabilities implemented between a distributed infrastructure, and evolution technologies in cryptography that can withstand incipient cyber threats like quantum computing attacks, etc. Additionally, the development of autonomous systems that can identify and react to cyber security threats without the need for a human to intervene will be a primary component of securing complicated cyber security systems. This section sheds light on the path ahead on a few promising research directions and how they might evolve as a development platform for the next generation of intelligent frameworks focused on cybersecurity. (Lv et al., 2024).

## 8.1 Explainable AI for Cybersecurity Systems

Explainable artificial intelligence (XAI) has become an important research area in cybersecurity with the rise of complex machine learning and deep learning models for the detection of threats. Many AI-based cybersecurity systems are "black box", so it is hard for security analysts to understand how these models derive their predictions or identify cyber threats. This lack of transparency may lead to a lack of trust in automated cybersecurity systems and create challenges in investigating security incidents. Explainable AI techniques are focused on dispelling this problem by giving interpretable insights on how AI models analyse the data and identify potential threats.

For example, explainable AI techniques can be used to identify specific features in the network or patterns in the behaviour that helped identify suspicious activities. This enables the use of this transparency to validate the model predictions and identify potential biases in the predictions, as well as enhance the reliability of the threat detection system. Future research in explainable AI for cybersecurity will focus on creating interpretable machine learning models that will be able to maintain high detection accuracy with clear explanations of the model's predictions. The combination of explainable AI and intrusion detection systems or security analytics platforms will help in boosting the transparency and trust of AI-powered cybersecurity solutions (Nguyen & Reddi, 2021).

## 8.2 Federated Learning for Distributed Security

Federated learning is a new paradigm in machine learning which can work for collaborative machine learning in a distributed environment without the need to share data in a centralized way. In traditional machine learning systems, data from multiple sources is gathered in a central place for training the machine learning model. However, this code may raise privacy and security issues, especially if sensitive cybersecurity data is called into play.

Federated learning overcomes this issue by allowing organizations to train machine learning models in distributed settings by training the models with their own data and exchanging the model parameters rather than the raw data. This decentralized approach to learning helps to keep data private and enables organizations to collaborate to create better and healthier cybersecurity models. In distributed cybersecurity systems, federated learning can help to facilitate collaborative threat detection across different organizations, cloud platforms and IoT networks. And by exchanging updates to their models but not the sensitive data itself, organizations can all improve on their set of intrusion detection systems, without revealing their data. Future research will involve the improvement of federated learning algorithms, optimization of communication efficiency of the statements between the distributed nodes and security consideration for the model aggregation processes (Padhiar & Patel, 2023).

## 8.3 Quantum-Resistant Blockchain Security

The development of quantum computing technologies is advancing rapidly and may threaten the existing cryptographic security mechanisms that are in use in the modern digital infrastructure. Many of the current encryption algorithms are dependent on mathematical problems that could possibly be solved more efficiently by quantum computers and this could threaten security of digital communication systems and blockchain networks. To meet such a challenge, researchers are trying to find quantum-resistant cryptographic algorithms that can resist attacks by quantum computing systems. These algorithms, commonly called post-quantum cryptography, are based to keep to be very safe against powerful quantum processors. In a cybersecurity system based on the blockchain, it will be necessary to employ cryptographic protocols capable of resisting quantum computing attacks, so as to guarantee the security and trust of this system over time. Future research will be done with the integration of post-quantum cryptographic methods into blockchain architectures and will test its performance under distributed cybersecurity conditions (Sarker et al., 2020).

*Table 5. Emerging technologies for next-generation cybersecurity*

| Emerging Technology | Description | Cybersecurity Application | Key Benefit |
|---|---|---|---|
| Explainable AI (XAI) | Interpretable machine learning models | Transparent threat detection | Improves trust in AI security systems |
| Federated Learning | Decentralized collaborative model training | Distributed intrusion detection | Preserves data privacy |
| Post-Quantum Cryptography | Quantum-resistant encryption algorithms | Secure blockchain networks | Protects against quantum attacks |
| Autonomous Cyber Defense | AI-driven automated security response | Real-time cyber threat mitigation | Faster incident response |
| Edge AI Security | AI processing at network edge devices | IoT security monitoring | Low-latency threat detection |

The table brings out the emerging technology which is supposed to play an important role in the development of advanced and smart cybersecurity systems for the future digital infrastructures.

*Figure 4. Future intelligent cybersecurity ecosystem*

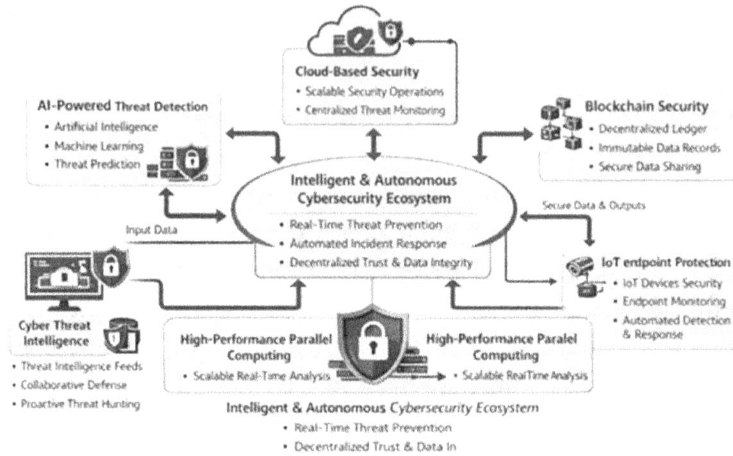


The figure depicts the implementation of an advanced cyber security ecosystem that includes AI, Block Chain, Cloud security, and Parallel computing to provide autonomous detection of the threat, decentralized trust and real-time threat detection for cyber security.

## CONCLUSION

The rate at which the distributed digital infrastructures, cloud platforms, and connected systems are developing has introduced a multitude of layers of complexity to our contemporary-day cybersecurity issues. Traditional cybersecurity mechanisms are often not adequate to detect advanced cyber threats that are aimed at attacking large-scale distributed networks. As cyberattacks become more advanced and dynamic, the integration of emerging technologies into cybersecurity legislation has become essential as ways of creating secure and scalable cybersecurity frameworks like artificial intelligence, parallel computing, and blockchain integration. These technologies together increase the capacity of organizations to oversee the activities in networks, analyse huge amounts of data and detect cyber threats in real-time. Artificial intelligence provides the option for intelligent threat detection which can detect patterns and anomalies in the network traffic and system behaviour. Parallel computing provides data processing capabilities that have capability for high performance and may enable Cybersecurity systems to process a huge data in an efficient way and make real-time security monitoring feasible. Blockchain technology adds extra levels to the cybersecurity infrastructures because it adds data integrity and can also help share secure data as well as store immutable data security across a spread network. The integrated framework presented in this chapter brings to light the potential of converging different disciplines of AI, parallel computing and blockchain to help build a cybersecurity ecosystem that is both secure and scalable and has the potential to protect the modern digital infrastructure. Future research needs to be focused on improving transparency of AI-driven security systems, improving collaborative learning via federated models, and coming up with quantum resistant cryptographic solutions. These advancements will play an important role while building resilient cybersecurity architectures for the next generation of distributed digital environments.

## REFERENCES


Ali, M., Raza, A., Akram, M. A., Arif, H., & Ali, A. (2025). Enhancing IOT Security: A review of Machine Learning-Driven Approaches to Cyber Threat Detection: Enhancing IOT Security: A review of Machine Learning-Driven Approaches to Cyber Threat Detection. *Journal of Informatics and Interactive Technology*, *2*(1), 316–324. DOI: 10.63547/jiite.v2i1.64

Aljawarneh, S., Aldwairi, M., & Yassein, M. B. (2018). Anomaly-based intrusion detection system through feature selection analysis and building hybrid efficient model. *Journal of Computational Science*, *25*, 152–160. DOI: 10.1016/j.jocs.2017.03.006

Apruzzese, G., Colajanni, M., Ferretti, L., Guido, A., & Marchetti, M. (2018, May). On the effectiveness of machine and deep learning for cyber security. In *2018 10th international conference on cyber Conflict (CyCon)* (pp. 371-390). IEEE. DOI: 10.23919/CYCON.2018.8405026

Berman, D. S., Buczak, A. L., Chavis, J. S., & Corbett, C. L. (2019). A survey of deep learning methods for cyber security. *Information (Basel)*, *10*(4), 122. DOI: 10.3390/info10040122

Buczak, A. L., & Guven, E. (2015). A survey of data mining and machine learning methods for cyber security intrusion detection. *IEEE Communications Surveys and Tutorials*, *18*(2), 1153–1176. DOI: 10.1109/COMST.2015.2494502

Casino, F., Dasaklis, T. K., & Patsakis, C. (2019). A systematic literature review of blockchain-based applications: Current status, classification and open issues. *Telematics and Informatics*, *36*, 55–81. DOI: 10.1016/j.tele.2018.11.006

Das, R., Zhou, L., Bi, S., Wang, T., & Hou, T. (2025). Towards the Safety of Intelligent Transportation: A Survey on the Security Challenges and Mitigations in Internet of Vehicles (IoV). *ACM Transactions on Sensor Networks*.

Diro, A. A., & Chilamkurti, N. (2018). Distributed attack detection scheme using deep learning approach for Internet of Things. *Future Generation Computer Systems*, *82*, 761–768. DOI: 10.1016/j.future.2017.08.043

Ferrag, M. A., Maglaras, L., Moschoyiannis, S., & Janicke, H. (2020). Deep learning for cyber security intrusion detection: Approaches, datasets, and comparative study. *Journal of Information Security and Applications*, *50*, 102419. DOI: 10.1016/j.jisa.2019.102419

Ferrag, M. A., Maglaras, L. A., Janicke, H., Jiang, J., & Shu, L. (2017). Authentication protocols for internet of things: A comprehensive survey. *Security and Communication Networks*, *2017*(1), 6562953. DOI: 10.1155/2017/6562953

Gilbert, C., & Gilbert, M. A. (2024). Advancing privacy standards through education: The role of academic initiatives in enhancing privacy within Cardano's blockchain ecosystem. *International Research Journal of Advanced Engineering and Science*, *9*(4), 238–251.

Gupta, B. B., Arachchilage, N. A., & Psannis, K. E. (2018). Defending against phishing attacks: Taxonomy of methods, current issues and future directions. *Telecommunication Systems*, *67*(2), 247–267. DOI: 10.1007/s11235-017-0334-z

Hamad, N. A., Bakar, K. A., Qamar, F., Jubair, A. M., Mohamed, R. R., & Mohamed, M. A. (2025). Systematic analysis of federated learning approaches for intrusion detection in the Internet of Things environment. *IEEE Access : Practical Innovations, Open Solutions*, *13*, 95410–95444. DOI: 10.1109/ACCESS.2025.3574672

Hamid, Y., Sugumaran, M., & Journaux, L. (2016, August). Machine learning techniques for intrusion detection: a comparative analysis. In *Proceedings of the International Conference on Informatics and Analytics* (pp. 1-6). DOI: 10.1145/2980258.2980378

Hodo, E., Bellekens, X., Hamilton, A., Tachtatzis, C., & Atkinson, R. (2017). Shallow and deep networks intrusion detection system: A taxonomy and survey. *arXiv preprint arXiv:1701.02145.*

Javaid, A., Niyaz, Q., Sun, W., & Alam, M. (2016). A deep learning approach for network intrusion detection system. *Eai Endorsed Transactions on Security and Safety*, *3*(9), 21. DOI: 10.4108/eai.3-12-2015.2262516

Lv, L., Xu, D., Hu, R. Q., Ye, Y., Yang, L., Lei, X., & Nallanathan, A. (2024). Safeguarding next-generation multiple access using physical layer security techniques: A tutorial. *Proceedings of the IEEE*, *112*(9), 1421–1466. DOI: 10.1109/JPROC.2024.3420127

Moustafa, N., & Slay, J. (2015, November). UNSW-NB15: a comprehensive data set for network intrusion detection systems (UNSW-NB15 network data set). In *2015 military communications and information systems conference (MilCIS)* (pp. 1-6). Ieee.

Nguyen, T. T., & Reddi, V. J. (2021). Deep reinforcement learning for cyber security. *IEEE Transactions on Neural Networks and Learning Systems*, *34*(8), 3779–3795. DOI: 10.1109/TNNLS.2021.3121870 PMID: 34723814

Nithyavani, G., & Raja, G. N. (2025). A comprehensive survey on security and privacy challenges in internet of medical things applications: Deep learning and machine learning solutions, obstacles, and future directions. *IEEE Access : Practical Innovations, Open Solutions*, *13*, 188955–188989. DOI: 10.1109/ACCESS.2025.3588489

Owezarski, P. (2023, May). Investigating adversarial attacks against Random Forest-based network attack detection systems. In *NOMS 2023-2023 IEEE/IFIP Network Operations and Management Symposium* (pp. 1-6). IEEE. DOI: 10.1109/NOMS56928.2023.10154328

Padhiar, S., & Patel, R. (2023, April). Outside the Closed World: On Using Machine Learning for Network Intrusion Detection. In *International Conference on Information and Communication Technology for Intelligent Systems* (pp. 265-270). Singapore: Springer Nature Singapore. DOI: 10.1007/978-981-99-3982-4_23

Rajendran, T., Imtiaz, N. M., Jagadeesh, K., & Sampathkumar, B. (2024, April). Cybersecurity threat detection using deep learning and anomaly detection techniques. In *2024 International Conference on Knowledge Engineering and Communication Systems (ICKECS)* (Vol. 1, pp. 1-7). IEEE. DOI: 10.1109/ICKECS61492.2024.10617347

Sarker, I. H., Kayes, A. S. M., Badsha, S., Alqahtani, H., Watters, P., & Ng, A. (2020). Cybersecurity data science: An overview from machine learning perspective. *Journal of Big Data*, *7*(1), 41. DOI: 10.1186/s40537-020-00318-5

Shone, N., Ngoc, T. N., Phai, V. D., & Shi, Q. (2018). A deep learning approach to network intrusion detection. *IEEE Transactions on Emerging Topics in Computational Intelligence*, *2*(1), 41–50. DOI: 10.1109/TETCI.2017.2772792

Szymoniak, S., Piątkowski, J., & Kurkowski, M. (2025). Defense and security mechanisms in the internet of things: A review. *Applied Sciences (Basel, Switzerland)*, *15*(2), 499. DOI: 10.3390/app15020499

. Vinayakumar, R., Soman, K. P., Poornachandran, P., Mohan, V. S., & Kumar, A. D. (2019). ScaleNet: scalable and hybrid framework for cyber threat situational awareness based on DNS, URL, and email data analysis. *Journal of Cyber Security and Mobility*, 189-240.

Wang, W., Sheng, Y., Wang, J., Zeng, X., Ye, X., Huang, Y., & Zhu, M. (2017). HAST-IDS: Learning hierarchical spatial-temporal features using deep neural networks to improve intrusion detection. *IEEE Access : Practical Innovations, Open Solutions*, *6*, 1792–1806. DOI: 10.1109/ACCESS.2017.2780250

Yin, C., Zhu, Y., Fei, J., & He, X. (2017). A deep learning approach for intrusion detection using recurrent neural networks. *IEEE Access : Practical Innovations, Open Solutions*, *5*, 21954–21961. DOI: 10.1109/ACCESS.2017.2762418

# Chapter 3
# A Distributed Framework for Adaptive Cybersecurity via Convergence of Parallel AI and Blockchain Architectures:
## AICyber-Chain

**B. Shaji**
http://orcid.org/0000-0001-9688-6333
*Mahaguru Institute of Technology, Kayamkulam, India*

**Ram Mohan N. R.**
http://orcid.org/0000-0002-0624-145X
*Panimalar Engineering College, Chennai, India*

**Nisha K. L.**
http://orcid.org/0000-0002-3495-4668
*Amrita Vishwa Vidyapeetham, Amritapuri, India*

## ABSTRACT

*As the digital landscape expands, centralised cybersecurity frameworks grow increasingly vulnerable to sophisticated threats, creating single points of failure and targets for adversarial data manipulation. While AI enables real-time threat detection and big data analytics, its centralised deployment limits efficacy and exposes training data to poisoning and evasion attacks. To address this, the AICyber-Chain model*

DOI: 10.4018/979-8-3373-9053-6.ch003

*proposes a distributed framework combining parallel AI and blockchain architectures. It leverages a hybrid Proof-of-Stake (PoS) and Byzantine Fault Tolerance (BFT) mechanism with IPFS and Private Data Centres (PDCs) for secure decentralised storage and processing. Generative Adversarial Networks (GANs) refine security rules, while Ethereum-based smart contracts enable automated responses and trustless data sharing. Results on the Rinkeby test network show 1.8× faster authentication, 25% lower gas consumption, F1 score of 0.92, and 1.2 s response time, with a medical data sharing use case ensuring data provenance and tamper-proof control.*

## 1. INTRODUCTION

### 1.1 The Evolution of Cyber Threats in Big Data Environments

The rapid evolution of the digital landscape, characterised by the proliferation of the Internet of Things (IoT), enterprise cloud computing, and integrated cyber-physical systems, has led to an unprecedented explosion in data generation. The volume, velocity, and variety characteristics of big data also apply to cybersecurity information, which continuously flows across global networks. Until now, cybersecurity paradigms were based on relatively static perimeter-based network defence models with firewalls and intrusion detection signatures at strategic points within an infrastructure (Samuel & Jessica, 2019). However, as we increasingly move toward a "perimeterless" network environment through interconnecting these infrastructures—the internet-of-everything—hampers perimeter-based security solutions. Therefore, cyberthreats have become dynamic and highly distributed. Attackers use automated scripts for launching attacks against vulnerabilities in web services or hosts, which form weak links in a new type of fragmented infrastructure that was physically exposed through a DDoS attack on Dyn (Batchu et al., 2024). Data generated in today's Internet world is uncontrolled by individuals whom it represents but is scattered across institutions, and its sharing control lacks consensus or regulation anywhere in the current infrastructure. Conventional security measures are inadequate to detect zero-day exploits or subtle behavioural anomalies across vast datasets, requiring considerable engineering effort across multiple conflicting issues between privacy protection requirements, regulatory compliance requirements, identity theft, etc., until this data can be used for research according to acceptable standards, leaving critical infrastructure operation vulnerable.

To confront these challenges, new national H2020 R&I efforts (Steeman et al., 2025) are needed, proportional to those made after 9/11 for Terrorism related R&D. To address these challenges, we need orchestration & regulation measures geared toward incentivising Dev(web-designers) + Net-Op(operators) communities to co-develop secure SDN (info)-infrastructures within regulatory bounds, simultaneously improving throughput while reducing time/cost/complexity of end-to-end provisioning.

## 1.2 The Role of Artificial Intelligence in Modern Cybersecurity

To counter the growing sophistication of cyber threats, Artificial Intelligence (AI) and Machine Learning (ML) have emerged as the key building blocks of next-generation cybersecurity. AI forms an essential ingredient in big data analytics, where it provides computational power to analyse large volumes of unstructured data in real-time. In complicated cyberspaces, intelligent algorithms probe network traffic, system logs, and user activities to extract relevant insights leading to evidential traces (Ndibe, 2025).

Herein, employing supervised learning for known threat detection and unsupervised learning for zero-day anomaly detection, AI models can recognise even subtle deviations from normal operational patterns with high accuracy. Additionally, AI enables the automation of security event triaging and incident response by assigning priorities to security alerts, thus resulting in lower cognitive overload on human analysts (Tariq et al., 2025). Since adversaries are increasingly using AI-driven models to automate their attacks too, adopting self-sufficient AI-enabled defensive strategies is not a choice but becoming more evident need.

In addition, predictive analytics, along with reinforcement (Majumder, 2025), allows such protective systems to evolve with varying contours of adversarial landscape over time, turning security from a reactive human-involved discipline into a proactive intelligent immune system that can eliminate threats before their actualisation.

## 1.3 Limitations of Centralised Defence Mechanisms

Despite the promise of AI in threat detection, its deployment within state-of-the-art centralised computing architectures introduces new and increasing risks. The accuracy and performance of any machine learning solution strongly depend on the quality, integrity, and sheer quantity of training data. Within centralised systems, massive amounts of sensitive data are consolidated into single locations, creating high-value targets for sophisticated adversaries. Such a consolidation also implies a drastic single point of failure: if the central repository or server gets compromised, all confidentiality is lost.

Moreover, centralised AI models (Kryś et al., 2025) prove to be extremely brittle against adversarial attacks: poisoning attackers can inject corrupted training data to degrade their effectiveness; evasion attackers can craft adversarial samples that evade static AI-based detection mechanisms; or inversion attackers can exploit access to black-box machine learning APIs to recover information about their training dataset. Theft is also an issue with central storage since it poses easier access for theft attempts, compromising security professionals employed by third-party platforms that apply machine learning at scale.

In addition to adversarial threats, the very aggregation of sensitive data under a proprietary service raises fundamental privacy and trust concerns. Enterprises and organisations are often reluctant to share knowledge about increasingly stealthy cyber threats as well as operationally valuable telemetry with monolithic third-party services out of fear for accidental disclosure (e.g., through misconfigurations), man-in-the-middle leakage, or subpoenas. Consequently, the very monolithic architectural approach needed by AI semantically constrains how threat intelligence could be shared among different peers, both within corporate silos and across them.

## 1.4 Chapter Mission and Objectives

Recognising the critical limitation of current centralised AI defences, and the exponentially growing complexity of increasingly large-scale big data cyber threats, this chapter advocates for a required architectural transition to ever more distributed and parallelised security ecosystems becoming necessary. The prime goal of this chapter is to introduce the AICyber-Chain model (Chaudhary & Lee, 2024), an encompassing enterprise-scale framework fusing, on one hand, the adaptive intelligence of parallelled AI with, on the other hand, decentralised immutable trust provided by blockchain.

In particular, to bring forth the realisation that only at the meeting point of these two disruptive technologies can robust protection against dependence on single points of control and failure, as well as firm guarantees of privacy, ownership privacy (within the GDPR context), regulations compliance, and even guarantees about soundness around the integrity of AI training data. In particular, we will sketch such a system architecture based on our presented AICyber-Chain model. Using hybrid interlinked blockchains consensus combined with IPFS (Inter Planetary File System) (Uysal et al., 2026) for secure parallelled storage + retrieval, leveraging RES components linked between whilst keeping their responsibility in privatised PDC (Private Data Centre). As well as by integrating GANs into dynamic learning, generating hardened RULES via compositional cellular automata-based HACS component deployed as DApps.

## 2. THEORETICAL BACKGROUND AND RELATED WORK

The proposed AICyber-Chain architecture is built on the integration of several different but cooperative computer science fields. This section reviews the theoretical foundations of Artificial Intelligence (AI) applied to threat detection, unveils blockchain technology operations and features, and presents network security parallel computing schemes, followed by a discussion on research gaps.

### 2.1 AI and Machine Learning in Threat Detection (Deep Learning, Neural Networks)

Artificial Intelligence and Machine Learning (ML) have revolutionised cybersecurity into an era where defence mechanisms are not as static signature-based as before, but defence strategy has become dynamic, behavioural-analysis-oriented, thanks to AI/ML. This has attracted worldwide concerns that the figure reached more than equal to or greater than US$96 billion in global spending on AI and ML for cybersecurity applications. Also, in highly complicated cyberspace environments, AI algorithms collect valuable features from large-scale unstructured data-set mining in order to detect novel malware patterns.

Recent literature illustrates the wide employment of different ML models for specific security tasks (Nandish et al., 2025). Deep learning has received substantial attention and has been extensively used with RNN, LSTM network, and CNN architectures to classify malware traffic and detect anomalous intrusion attacks. These deep neural network models achieve high accuracy in zero-day attack detection by learning complex hierarchical data representations. Yet, these deep learning models are often computationally expensive; hence, their adoption is limited in resource-constrained environments. Researchers have consequently deployed Decision Tree and Naive Bayes models as alternatives to develop systems able to detect malicious behaviour as well as anomalies at lower computational expenses. However, these models lack precise classification or labelling of the security-relevant dataset, which presents some difficulties when using this data for training and evaluating purposes. SVM combined with rule-based systems, as well as Hidden Markov models paired with reinforcement learning, have also been considered in the literature for semantic-based phishing detection and DDoS attacks detection, achieving promising results. Nevertheless, the described AI methods encounter one common problem: they operate within a centralised architecture that makes them prone to poisoning when adversarial input is injected into legitimate training datasets (Pernice, 2025) and evasion with which an adversary attempts either to make his malicious activity change its benign label prediction by modifying its activity features or target another user by manipulating variables accessible to them.

## 2.2 Blockchain Technology: Distributed Ledgers and Smart Contracts

To overcome these weaknesses of centralised data processing, a decentralised blockchain can be a suitable solution. Technically, a blockchain is an open-source, decentralised, and immutable ledger that is distributed across multiple nodes in the network (Preethi et al., 2025). It forms a chain of blocks, in which each block records transaction information and is cryptographically linked with the previous one via its hash.

The adoption of blockchain for secure data sharing and transmission has gained huge popularity. For instance, a blockchain-based framework was proposed to ensure secure and transparent data sharing in healthcare while maintaining data integrity and traceability. Also focusing on the medical field, MeDShare employs blockchain technology to achieve provenance, auditing, aggregation, and sharing of medical data over cloud storage solutions. In the supply chain management arena, OriginChain was presented to enable tamper-proof product tracking with transparency among involved parties, since they can query consistent data from it.

A key feature of contemporary blockchain networks like Ethereum is the execution of smart contracts, which are basically self-executing scripts with a set of predefined terms and conditions, where policies can be automatically enforced without reliance on a third party. This showcased how smart contracts could be utilised to automate and enforce security policies during data transmission in IoT networks, achieving a substantial reduction in the possibility of data breaches. The elimination of the need for central authorities by means of blockchain-enabled technology delivers a transparent, decentralised, traceable, and tamper-evident ledger, which results in a trustless environment for executing security policies with algorithmic certainty.

## 2.3 Parallel Computing Principles in Network Security

The integration of parallel computing paradigms is critical to scaling the blockchain and AI approaches to the enterprise level. Centralised cloud storage, however, poses a single point of failure vulnerability and a high-payoff opportunity for cyber attackers. Hence, decentralised designs employ peer-to-peer distribution to parallelise the storage and retrieval of data. The Inter Planetary Filesystem (IPFS), for instance, is a distributed file system that addresses content rather than location, similar to traditional (HTTP) approaches (Dhingra et al., 2025). By disassembling data into cryptographic shards and distributing them among nodes on a network, IPFS obviates the need for central authorities when requesting files. Data can thereby be retrieved independently from grand simultaneous sources in parallel. The introduction of such a distributed ledger system as the IPFS considerably reduces single points of failure.

Within this context exists the abstraction of Private Data Centres (PDCs) acting as both physical and logical secure storage repositories, which are not feasible within centralised public clouds due to the lack of fine-grained uniform data access controls being possible exclusively at a site level. A user's digital identity is thereby partitioned across several trusted PDCs while using IPFS as an abstraction, so that even if one node or gateway is compromised by an attacker then they cannot retrieve/extract a complete digital file containing personal information from it without direct modification or analysis (seed key inference attacks) action against every other related party nodes they are connected with on the network graph. This exploitation model, coupled with parallel AI processing—AI-based Secure Computing (ASC)—allows multiple disjointed and sequestered nodes to operate/process security policies simultaneously yet share learned behaviour/knowledge confidentially without direct exposure risk and avoid sharing actual sensitive private information unnecessarily.

## 2.4 Gaps in Existing Literature: The Need for Convergence

While the individual merits of AI, blockchain, and parallel storage systems are known in literature and practice, a systematic literature review reveals that no work has provided a comprehensive architectural integration. Most current solutions address data security through isolated mechanisms and do not consider security in a holistic manner. An example here is AI-oriented studies, which do not explore the architecture deficiencies of centralised data lakes (ADLs) and the weaknesses they may introduce in such environments. On the other hand, although SecNet provides an assured architecture based on blockchain, it is operationally suboptimal because users' data would be spread all over the network instead of being managed by controlled PDCs, making overall AI training unenriched. Similarly, approaches that rely on OpenPDS allow for virtual management but are based on scarce trust foundations, meaning that this does not provide an enriched volume or variety for better ML/AI results due to overall scarcity concerns. Furthermore, stand-alone intrusion detection systems often suffer from imbalanced datasets and a high false positive rate, as well as using unsupervised learning, inadvertently compromising raw dataset privacy.

A careful comparison of existing models reveals that most do not synergise Secure Storage, Smart Contracts, Forwarding Efficiency, and Network Performance at the same time. For instance, works of (Bhavana et al., 2025). do not utilise blockchain and forwarding efficiency, while works (Xie et al., 2025) do not adopt smart contract functionalities at all.

Although existing studies have investigated blockchain-based security architectures, most focus primarily on secure data storage, access control, or transaction integrity. Comparatively fewer studies integrate adaptive AI-driven threat intelligence with decentralized security enforcement. The proposed AI Cyber-Chain framework combines GAN-based adaptive threat detection, blockchain-enabled trust management, and distributed data storage through IPFS, thereby providing a unified architecture for intelligent and decentralized cybersecurity management.

So we observe a noticeable need for an architecture with enterprise-scale combining storage security, dynamic threat detection using parallel AI, along with policy control based on distributed ledgers in automating fashion. The proposed AICyber-Chain model aims to fill this particular need by blending hybrid blockchain consensus, adaptive machine learning, and IPFS-based distributed storage within a meshed secure cyberspace structure.

## 3. THE VULNERABILITIES OF CENTRALISATION

### 3.1 The Architecture of Centralised AI Systems

The increasing use of Artificial Intelligence (AI) in cybersecurity has been facilitated by centralised architectures. In such architectures, huge amounts of data are collected from edge devices, network nodes, and user endpoints and sent to a single centralised server or cloud system, where it is combined and analysed. AI algorithms analyse the data to extract features used for anomaly detection and threat identification in increasingly complex cyberspaces.

The centralisation inherent in most AI systems poses several fundamental security challenges (Hui & Tucker, 2025). The central repository hosts comprehensive private data as well as the intelligence of the defence, making it an attractive target for adversaries. Any compromised node would allow attackers access to all clients and their respective endpoints, sharing information with this server; excessive reliance on the performance of a single processing point induces a serious bottleneck.

### 3.2 Adversarial Attacks on Machine Learning Models

Beyond the issues of centralisation, we also find that the AI models themselves are vulnerable to a form of subtle attack known as adversarial attacks, which play on the underlying mathematical and statistical mechanics of machine learning algorithms, rather than attempting to brute-force network perimeters. However, because centralised systems share a single model in common, such attacks grow exponentially more potent as an adversary striking mechanism—once a model is compromised, for example, it effectively blinds an entire network security ecosystem.

Table 1 provides an overview of the main adversarial attacks against artificial intelligence and machine models within real-world environments (in both pre-deployment preparation and operational phases), highlighting how attackers can leverage vulnerabilities found in AI systems to undermine services or gain sensitive information.

*Table 1. AI attack techniques that can be applied to real-world situations*

| Attack Method | Description of Attack |
|---|---|
| **Poisoning Attack** | This attack disrupts machine learning models by injecting new corrupted data into training datasets. |
| **Evasion attacks** | Attacks that generate some hostile samples to evade detection by significantly reducing the overall security of the target system. |
| **Impersonation attack** | To misclassify the original sample, specific hostile samples are generated to mislead existing machine-learning-based systems. |
| **Inversion attacks** | Attacks that use the API (Application Programming Interface) of the machine learning system to collect some basic information about the target system model and reverse engineer it to steal sensitive data. |

### 3.2.1 Data Poisoning Attacks

One of the most dangerous long-term threats to centralised AI is the data poisoning attack. This involves an attacker injecting malicious and carefully crafted samples into training datasets, which a centralised system must constantly consume to assimilate billions of factors external to it, which are endlessly updating and re-optimising as they learn from context (Alber et al., 2025). Provided unauthorised access can be gained to one part of the system's streaming pipeline and substitute-passivity utility, generative synthesis then goes to work on designing new-level-zero-input patterns (i.e., maintaining adversarial control without resorting to evolutionary games based on PDE fronting) and surreptitiously introducing them at scale during semiotic parsing and synthesising stages of the greatest probabilistic models associated with belief propagation representing value extraction.

### 3.2.2 Evasion and Impersonation Attacks

While poisoning occurs in the training phase, evasion and impersonation attacks aim at the AI model during its active operational (inference) phase. Evasion attacks generate a set of specific hostile samples to evade detection by reducing the overall security of the target system significantly. Attackers perturb slightly malicious payloads, often with perturbations imperceptible to human analysts, to be misclassified as benign network traffic by the AI (Claudel et al., 2026). Similar to this approach are impersonation attacks where specific hostile samples are generated to misclassify an original sample on which existing machine-learning-based systems have been trained. Adversaries can leverage this idea, mimicking legitimate user behaviour or authorised network protocols, such that they can pass a firewall based on AI without security alerts.

### 3.2.3 Inversion Attacks and API Vulnerabilities

Centralised AI systems generally use APIs for the interaction of edge devices/external software components with the centralised analytical model. However, these APIs introduce a high security threat in terms of data confidentiality (Tanveer et al., 2025). An inversion attack is performed by using the API of a machine learning system to fetch some primary information about the target system model, and then it is reconstructed to fetch the proprietary/sensitive data. By continuous query and investigating the output probability space of the API, the adversary is able to reconstruct the model by which proprietary/sensitive data on which the ML model was trained can be extracted easily. This issue becomes more critical in the case of centralised architecture, as most sensitive information resides within the weights/parameters of the centralised model.

## 3.3 Data Fragmentation and Privacy Challenges in Cyberspace

Although powerful AI depends on access to large amounts of high-quality training data, the present information age is inherently a fractured landscape. Internet data is both fragmented and controlled by multiple entities, making it difficult to authorise and legitimate its use. In the case of modern medicine, medical data are located in many kinds of environments (fractured silos) that are controlled by different authorities that may have competing (e.g., business) interests; these authorities are not part of any standard trust infrastructure either. Consequently, we cannot legitimately and securely share useful data based on today's complications due to auditability and prior consent (Widjaja, 2025).

These privacy concerns become even more apparent when one considers the fact that AI architectures tend toward centralisation. To build highly effective models, developers must centralise physically scattered (this "big") fractured data into single proprietary servers or third-party mediated repositories. Truly put: When it comes to big-data analytics—because of security issues with excessive sharing—no sane individual or organisation would be willing to help train anyone else's servers operating beyond their legal or direct control with their property, regulatory deliverables, or trade secrets/data since the risk for exposure is too great. As a result, they do not contribute sufficient quantities and diversity of potentially sensitive data needed for training cybersecurity models.

The levels of fragmentation and reluctance outlined above suggest an inherent limitation in being able to leverage available resources properly in this information era because technologically enforced rules formulated around decentralisation can be unconditionally followed only if all contributors autonomously operate from behind perfectly secure firewalls while maintaining ownership control over their digital property indefinitely.

# 4. THE AICYBER-CHAIN ARCHITECTURE: A CONVERGENCE OF TECHNOLOGIES

## 4.1 Overview of the Distributed Framework

The AICyber-Chain model represents a new dawn in the Era of cybersecurity, where traditional vulnerable centralised repositories are replaced with a highly powerful, resilient distributed structure. The three-layer AICyber-Chain architecture not only seamlessly integrated the blockchain and AI-based cybersecurity applications but also provided a strong, secure platform for conducting data operations in an enterprise-scale environment using the scaleless approach. The philosophy of this architecture is to combine the power of decentralised ledger and immutability forms of blockchain technology, along with real-time threat detection and self-updating learning abilities of modern Artificial Intelligence systems.

Distributing data as well as security processing across a networked parallel node (Xu et al., 2025) together with strong integration among its components has not only prevented any point attack but also provided quality, originality, and immunity from compromised data setup. To achieve a reception-complete, elegant defence structure, this architectural model is structured into three major interacting components: Blockchain component, AI component, and finally Smart Contracts component; together they perform all features necessary for securely storing data forms without high performance degradation at runtime environments present in all IoT networks without vulnerabilities, loopholes, or possible attacks at each layer.

Figure 1 illustrates the dual-layered architecture (Neto et al., 2025) of our proposed AICyber-Chain model. The macroscopic view (left) depicts that numerous PDCs are interconnected through a distributed Blockchain-Based System to provide the capabilities of state synchronisation, consensus algorithms, and smart contract execution for trustless value and data exchange. Whereas the microscopic view (right) presents the internal structure of a single PDC in detail. It encompasses the deployment of a local Blockchain Ledger, Access Control Scheme, and Data Storage Module together with an intelligent Operation Support System (OSS), comprising GAN, AI-based Secure Computing (ASC), and Knowledge Computing Modules (KCM).

*Figure 1. The overall aicyber-chain architecture*

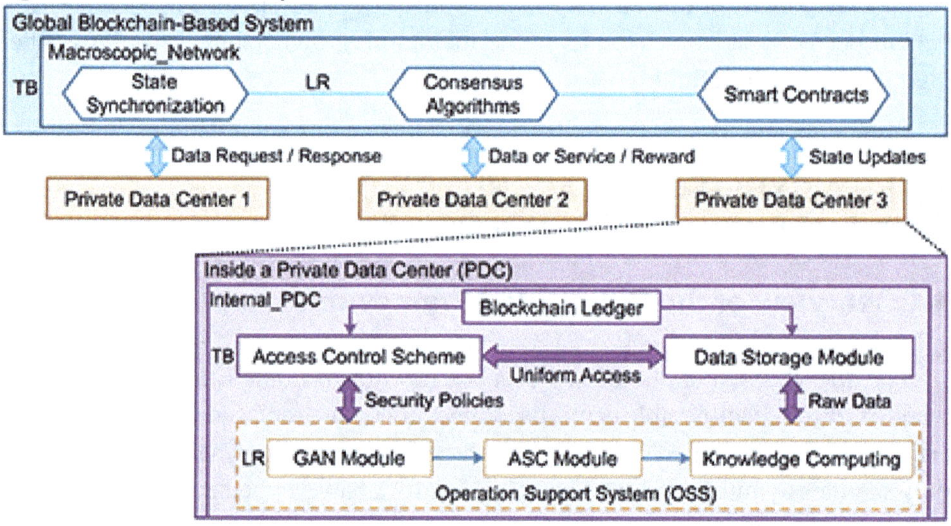


## 4.2 The Blockchain Layer: Ensuring Immutable Data Integrity

The first component of the AICyber-Chain model is the Blockchain Layer, which provides an immutable foundation for the overall security ecosystem. In conventional systems, centralised databases are susceptible to silent tampering; if an attacker penetrates beyond the outer defences, then they can modify access logs and security event records to hide their activity. In contrast, within our approach, a decentralised ledger or blockchain is used to durably store all transactions and system logs between participants. Once a log record or data transaction has been added to this blockchain layer, it is hashed with a cryptographic hash function (Yang et al., 2025) to produce a unique identifier (hash), timestamped with metadata from consensus timestamps of all peer nodes within the network, and persisted across globally distributed copies of that ledger on participating peer nodes within that network. It becomes almost impossible computationally for any peer node participant to alter blocks in such a ledger without a consensus majority because every other copy in other redundant globally synchronised ledgers also differs.

### 4.2.1 Hybrid Consensus Mechanism: Proof-of-Stake (PoS) and Byzantine Fault Tolerance (BFT)

To keep the tamper-proof and tamper-evident properties of blockchain, a consensus algorithm is fundamentally required in a blockchain network. However, typical consensus mechanisms such as Proof-of-Work (PoW) are very energy-consuming and suffer from serious scalability problems. It is not suitable for enterprise cybersecurity scenarios that need real-time data processing. To alleviate the energy consumption and improve the scalability of the common blockchain to meet the requirements of cyber-range use cases, a sophisticated hybrid consensus mechanism is adopted by AICyber-Chain, named Proof-of-Stake (PoS) (John et al., 2025) with Byzantine Fault Tolerance (BFT).

In this hybrid model, PoS largely reduces the computational overhead by selecting validators based on their stake in the cryptocurrency by being part of it or other methods; In addition to that, PoS ensures validators do not stall each other's proposals during the block generation phase to finish the blockchain process faster due to low voting stakes. And BFT guarantees that those validators can achieve an agreement when reaching consensus, since they may likely be conflicting with each other. Such a mathematical guarantee works well against attacks at the network layer, where attackers send wrong messages between nodes or at the transaction validation function, a secret development process through which they will launch more concurrency between servers (the fractions due to the missing wrong-doing message amount in response).

### 4.2.2 High Throughput and Low Latency Adjustments

The most important reason we utilise a hybrid PoS-BFT consensus mechanism is that the legacy blockchain itself has limitations and could be a performance bottleneck in such a complex parallel computing environment to analyse network transactions simultaneously through multiple nodes. In particular, its underlying ledger should have capabilities of high volume and low latency as well. High volume means that it can record thousands of logs and access information every second without a bottleneck in the big data era. Low latency requires that the time interval between an accident or security attack occurring when a data packet arrives at the corresponding node, and when it is permanently recorded into the blockchain by all nodes, should be as short as possible. It is especially important for performing real-time monitoring & response on security services so that the Blockchain Layer will not become a performance bottleneck for the AI Layer and Smart Contract Layer.

## 4.3 The AI Layer: Real-Time Threat Detection

While the Blockchain Layer establishes the foundation for security, the AI Layer acts as the passive intelligent defence mechanism of the architecture. Operating in real-time on trusted information provided by blockchain, several machine learning algorithms are applied, which have been trained to detect cyber-attacks (Sekhar et al., 2025). Raw data, such as network traffic logs, user activity, and system performance gathered from various sources, is pre-processed and then presented to the AI engine for analysis. The integrity of data upon which training takes place is ensured through security guarantees offered by blockchain, thus making it resilient against typical adversarial evasion, abuse, and high detection rate attacks.

### 4.3.1 Supervised and Unsupervised Learning Integrations

To achieve complete threat visibility, the AI Layer leverages a two-pronged approach. It employs a combination of supervised and unsupervised learning to perform real-time analysis of network behaviour. Supervised learning models are trained on large, labelled datasets containing exhaustive sets of known malware signatures, phishing attacks, and specific patterns for various types of intrusions, providing a fine-grained method for quickly determining whether an incoming traffic stream is malicious (using well-understood attack vectors).

However, because the adversary's tactics constantly change over time and some APTs lack historical perspectives (i.e., zero-day attacks) (SakthiMurugan et al., 2024), supervised models frequently fail to detect such threats. Thus, the AI Layer also employs unsupervised models that focus primarily on anomaly detection and clustering. By modelling granular behaviours across multiple dimensions—from per-machine/application TCP/UDP entropy to per-destination-country or per-user DNS request bursts or anomalies—it is possible to extract signs that an ongoing traffic trace contains previously never-seen-before threats.

### 4.3.2 Continuous Adaptation via Reinforcement Learning

The most important innovation in the AI Layer is that it is living. The machine learning models used in the AICyber-Chain are not static; they are based on reinforcement learning, so they can learn over time as new threats emerge. In a conventional system, an AI model will become less and less accurate as the environment within which it operates changes (a phenomenon called concept drift). This usually means that one has to send data scientists to retrain and or reconfigure the AI model manually.

In contrast, through reinforcement learning, the models implemented in AICyber-Chain realise that cyberspace is a dynamic environment. By closing feedback loops with downstream effectors, the models can automatically learn from history and effectively self-configure their internal parameters to detect new kinds of threats more effectively. When an adversary attempts novel operations and breaches are detected by human controllers applying security patches or operators taking countermeasures manually, these risks multiply — also spreading thanks to vulnerability-sharing marketplaces available on the invisible web darknet discussed when referring to crypto-locking products above — this malfunctioning fixation tends to reinforce mechanisms triggered during previous successful episodes for mitigating novel risks/attacks.

## 4.4 The Smart Contract Layer: Automated Security Execution

The final part of the AI Cyber-Chain's defensive workflow is the Smart Contract Layer. The AI Layer identifies threats, but it needs a method for effectively and securely implementing security policies. This implementation is performed by smart contracts. These are self-executing pieces of code with predefined rules and agreements, which activate automatically once certain conditions are met. Using AICyber-Chain terminology, smart contracts manage and effectuate the enforcement of security policies solely based on provided threat assessments generated by the AI Layer.

### 4.4.1 Solidity Implementations on Ethereum

To ensure reliability and security, these contracts are written in Solidity, which is a specialised object-oriented programming language, and are deployed on the Ethereum blockchain. By adopting Ethereum as our platform solution, we take advantage of a well-known Turing-complete virtual machine (the EVM), being able to deal with complex programmatic logic.

More specifically, inside the framework, since we focus on the interaction of the AI detection with the blockchain, several procedures step in that contain specific algorithmic logic. Examples are Register Data, which is used by an application owner to register data-providing CI-technologies so they can offer their services within contract negotiation processes; Request Data also acts between an application owner and a subscribed CI-technology, but for retrieving requested data instead of registering it; finally, Subscribe Data that works between any subscriber and data-providing CI-technology, meaning that firstly a subscriber gets registered or deletes its subscription. The same holds for managing access permissions, e.g., available via Register App, interested subscribers register at the Subscription Platform App (SPA) towards having access from decentralised apps under trust SP's umbrella, go through RegisterAccess_p2(). Since all these contracts are deployed onto the distributed ledger, every action performed through them is determined with full transparency and non-reputability. Neither can there be any hidden information nor any entity circumventing security mechanisms, as those counterforces are hardcoded in our contracts accessible by SPA's APIs! Every adaptation happening automatically or/and/or executed security measure leaves its footprint recorded on the blockchain.

### 4.4.2 Zero-Latency Human Intervention Removal

One of the most glaring time lags in conventional cybersecurity operations is the time required for human intervention. Any flag raised by standard security software generally goes into a queue for examination by a human analyst. In the hours or days, it takes to cover all steps required for an investigation, bad actors have used that time to move laterally within the network, escalate privileges, and exfiltrate data.

This problem is unequivocally solved by the Smart Contract Layer through immediate response activities if a flagged incident is deemed of high enough confidence. The AI Layer counterpart flags decent-likelihood threats e.g., compromising of a node identified through behavioural analytics; or detection that, on balance, data leakage occurred. This causes an instant activation of the smart contract instance in which interpretation occurs – i.e., automatically enforce response activities, e.g., isolation node from general access; termination token access permission; initiate multi-factor authentication process, etc. In sum, by automatically activating these response activities, AICyber-Chain provides near-zero-latency response mitigation, thus suppressing cyber threats at machine speed before significant damage has been done to enterprise infrastructure.

## 5. PARALLEL COMPUTING AND DECENTRALISED DATA STORAGE

The performance and security of any advanced cybersecurity framework depend on how safely and rapidly it can store, transmit, and process a huge amount of data. In this age of big data and hyper-connected enterprise networks, the traditional centralised storage mechanism is not suitable because it serves as a performance bottleneck and has an attractive point for cyber criminals (Dai et al., 2025). AICyber-Chain should be based on a decentralised approach, so we have to use a high-performance parallel computer using a distributed storage device in our proposed AICyber-Chain model too. Legacy cloud-based architecture will not achieve this objective. Therefore, we propose that some new concepts, such as the integration of Private Data Centres (PDCs), Inter Planetary File System (IPFS), together with blockchains for data recordation (Data Recording Blockchains or DRBs), will be used to build our fully functional AI Cyber-Chain's resilient parallel cyberspace ecosystem.

## 5.1 Private Data Centres (PDCs) vs. Centralised Cloud Storage

Contemporary organisations rely extensively on centralised cloud computing for the storage and processing of data. Many people tend to misinterpret cloud computing as nothing more than a secure way of storing and processing data digitally, but in practice, more than fifty per cent of breaches publicly reported in the last few years are because cloud instances have been misconfigured. As organisations migrate more workloads containing sensitive information to the cloud, we will see increasingly hostile efforts put into compromising these central repositories by adversaries. Centralised clouds inevitably introduce a single point of failure – one compromised administrator account or one vulnerable API can expose petabytes worth of intellectual property.

To address this centralised vulnerability, the AICyber-Chain model introduces Private Data Centres (PDC) that help implement uniform data access control and storage amongst users with which they transact, i.e., interact/communicate/process. They present new opportunities to improve privacy not possible with past systems based on silos, Personal Data Stores (PDS), like openPDS, that are completely implemented within software algorithms within virtualised environments. PDC is essentially a physical container centrally secured where each user/entity-specific data is physically maintained therein by its partner members/entities, etc. Compared with PDS, it is indeed smarter because it utilizes human-in-the-loop validation to augment automated intelligence.

The PDC acts as the central repository, or like an information sink, for all information on an entity in cyberspace. This calls for the implementation of two important characteristics within the PDC architecture: Uniform Data Representation (UDR) and Uniform Access Control (UAC). UDR involves defining a format representation that enables data that is associated with an entity to be easily parsed by applications that adhere to this representation and to avoid any derivation of format conflicts while sharing it among different entities. UAC provides direct control over what can be done with a user's data by a service; specifically, whether or not a request to perform specific operations (e.g., CRUD operations) on the user's data made by a service is valid or not. The advantage of UDR and UAC over systems like traditional cloud storage systems is taking localised yet standardised control such that neither can the users' service provider manipulate their data nor access to their confidential data be granted/misused.

Figure 2 gives an overview of how, with IPFS, we will transition from centralised silos of monolithic files representing a complete set of related datasets associated with a Physical-Identity-based Data Storage Module of Private Data Centre (PDC). A PDC acts as a virtual clone, more rightly 'a digital twin', of an individual/organisation represented in cyberspace. A consolidated form or part(s) for easier-to-manage view/access generation from these large source files for entities in cyberspace belonging only/to multiple physical identities should not be mistaken as a similar/preferred approach.

*Figure 2. IPFS-based decentralised data storage and sharding*

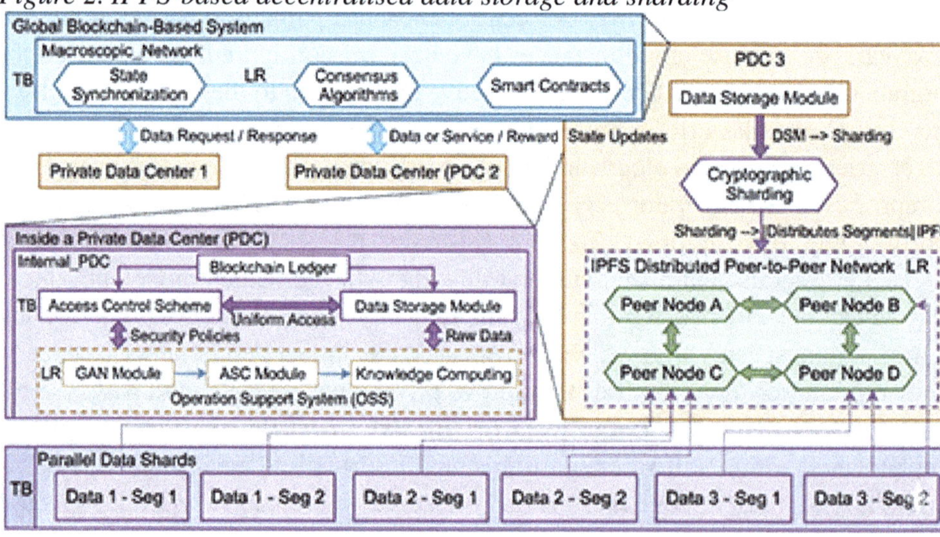


## 5.2 Operation Support Systems (OSS) and AI-Based Secure Computing (ASC)

A PDC is not a passive vault, but needs an intelligent management engine to protect the data it contains as well as to enable secure and privacy-conscious communications with the external network. Thus, each PDC in the AICyber-Chain framework possesses an OSS utilising AI-based Secure Computing (ASC), which serves as the autonomic nervous system for PDC, automatically constructing security policies and knowledge bases based on internal storage data to discern abnormal behaviour against data resources.

The ASC component augments the AICyber-Chain OSS with enhanced computing capabilities and protects the owned storage data accordingly. Since raw data (e.g., medical records or enterprise proprietary intelligence) is too sensitive to be transmitted through the open Internet. Instead of uploading raw data into some centralised servers for AI calculations, by throwing AI algorithms into storage directly, different entities can perform these operations locally and safely share only results via blockchain after such parallel computing, so that raw data always resides inside a user's trusted PDC; this measure essentially minimises energy consumption and communication bandwidth while maximising privacy sensitivity.

Furthermore, the ASC module uses GANs to produce strong dynamic security rules. As a result, the entire OSS infrastructure can become an adaptive autonomous system that constantly adapts and reacts to new threats in its environment. With this powerful localised processing mechanism, PDCs can be seen as part of a globally parallelised supercomputer dedicated to the proactive detection of threats.

## 5.3 Integration of the Inter Planetary File System (IPFS)

While PDCs secure data locally, the exclusive dependency on isolated physical centres can introduce localised vulnerabilities (e.g., physical destruction or targeted network isolation). In order to achieve real decentralisation, data redundancy and parallel processing capabilities, the AICyber-Chain framework employs Inter Planetary File System (IPFS), which is a peer-to-peer, distributed, and decentralised file system, changing completely how we store and retrieve data from the internet.

By using IPFS as the underlying data exchange layer for PDCs, the system transforms from a client-server model to a highly resilient distributed network. This decentralised way prevents privacy leaks by storing isolated data into multiple different network nodes so that the failure of one node won't lead to the leaking of all information.

### 5.3.1 Content-Based Addressing vs. Location-Based Addressing

The most fundamental architectural difference between traditional web protocols, such as HTTP, and IPFS is the way they locate data. In HTTP (and all other systems using location-based addressing), a user must know which server exactly (i.e., its IP address or domain name) hosts the file they want to access. If that server goes down, is under a DDoS attack, or if the file simply moves elsewhere on the web directory structure, then that data can't be accessed anymore due to the system's server outage being unable to return anything but an error code instead of the actual data.

In the Inter Planetary File System (IPFS), content-based addressing replaces traditional location-based retrieval by assigning each file a unique identifier derived from a cryptographic hash function. This hash acts as a digital fingerprint, ensuring that any modification to the file results in a completely different address. Consequently, data is requested and verified based on its content rather than its storage location. This mechanism inherently prevents spoofing and tampering, as any attempt to substitute or alter data would produce a mismatch between the requested and retrieved content. For instance, when requesting a specific public key, only the exact corresponding key can satisfy the query, as it must match the predefined hash. This paradigm not only guarantees data integrity and immutability but also secures data during transmission. Techniques such as content-aware byte caching further leverage these properties to optimise data retrieval while preserving trust and consistency within the network.

### 5.3.2 Data Sharding and Parallel Retrieval

IPFS achieves this goal of optimising network performance and security by exploiting data sharding and parallel retrieval. When integrating large-scale datasets into the network, they are not imported as a single huge monolithic file. The PDC acts as a manager of the distributed data storage cloud within the enterprise-class private cloud environment, which uniformly disperses all the data fragments into the entire infrastructure underlying the abstraction layer in an object-oriented manner. All these fragments, hereafter also called blocks in a content-addressable fashion, are linked with each other via content-addressable hyperlinks.

Therefore, true parallelism in computing can be exploited. Without needing to find where exactly a specific piece of data is located, IPFS will download multiple different blocks referencing similar content from multiple different nodes on the P2P network (Heimbach et al., 2025) concurrently as well.

Such a mechanism of parallel downloading contributes not only to an improved forwarding efficiency but also to better system resilience. Moreover, such explicit partitioning designs can benefit security because even if an attacker gains one particular block or manages to tamper with certain nodes (private clouds), it cannot acquire or construct any complete file/dataset since all those low-level infrastructure-based objects will lead it only to isolated, encrypted, and undecipherable garbage.

To summarise the architectural shift required for enterprise-scale cybersecurity, Table 2 compares and reviews the structural and economic benefits of migrating from legacy cloud infrastructures to the proposed IPFS-integrated one.

*Table 2. Comparison between cloud-based and blockchain-based storage systems*

| Characteristics | Traditional Cloud Storage | Blockchain / IPFS Storage (AICyber-Chain) |
|---|---|---|
| Architecture | Centralised (Client-Server model) | Decentralized (Peer-to-Peer network) |
| Open-Source | Typically, proprietary and closed-source (controlled by major tech providers) | Entirely open-source protocols, promoting transparency and community auditing |
| Privacy & Security | Moderate. Relies on trusting a third-party provider; vulnerable to internal misconfigurations. | High. Data is cryptographically sharded; ownership is guaranteed via smart contracts and Data Recording Blockchains (DRBs). |

continued on following page

*Table 2. Continued*

| Characteristics | Traditional Cloud Storage | Blockchain / IPFS Storage (AICyber-Chain) |
|---|---|---|
| Data Addressing | Location-based addressing (HTTP/IP). | Content-based addressing (Cryptographic Hashes). |
| Scalability | High, but requires massive vertical and horizontal infrastructure investments by the central provider. | Highly scalable. Network capacity inherently increases as more peer nodes join the ecosystem. |
| Cost Efficiency | High ongoing costs (monthly subscription fees and bandwidth surcharges). | Lower overall storage costs; IPFS reduces bandwidth overhead, and hybrid PoS/BFT reduces gas consumption. |
| Single Point of Failure | **Yes.** A targeted attack on the central server can compromise the entire dataset. | **No.** Data is distributed across numerous nodes; destroying one node does not compromise the complete file. |

## 5.4 Data Recording 2Blockchains (DRBs) and Ownership Rights

In a decentralised ecosystem where data is sharded, distributed and processed in parallel, it is technically challenging to define ownership and access clearly. There is no central authority that grants permission based on policies. In the AI Cyber- Chain business scenario, we need a trustless mechanism that guarantees data owners have full control over their digital asset (data) even when they are distributed over the IPFS network. To tackle this challenge, it was necessary to design Data Recording Blockchains (DRBs) (Alotaibi et al., 2025).

A DRB refers to a specific instance of blockchain infrastructure that organises the proliferation and provides management functions of a set of local ledgers that make up a DRB implementation. The collection addressed all data elements uniquely.

The primary goal associated with the use case implementation of a DRB defines work items for creating implemented or reusable artifacts relevant to achieving that goal. For instance, an important work item directly assigned under a defined primary goal would improve support for multi-party workflow execution scenarios.

Through DRBs, real-time, trustless data sharing is enabled. Each time a third party (i.e., not the Data Owner) requests access to specific data, the transaction is processed and recorded on the chain. This ensures that all inbound data is validated and that only the DRB can deliver valid and true data to the entity making a request. In addition, by recording ownership and interactions immutably, conflicts of interest are greatly reduced by DRBs, thus opening up opportunities for value-exchange ecosystems. Data owners may securely monetise their data or AI-generated security rules through smart contracts, being assured by the cryptographic unforgeable proof delivered by a DRB of their provenance and rights.

Having established the decentralized storage and ownership mechanisms through IPFS and DRBs, the next stage of the framework focuses on intelligent threat detection and adaptive defence through artificial intelligence.

## 6. INTELLIGENT DEFENCE: GANS AND DYNAMIC RULE GENERATION

The journey from a reactive cybersecurity posture to a proactive, intelligent defence ecosystem requires the infusion of advanced machine learning paradigms that possess the ability of self-evolution. The static firewalls and rule-based intrusion detection systems (IDS) the invention of the last century are not at all powerful to deal with polymorphic malware and sophisticated adversarial attacks. To overcome this literature gap, we utilised Generative Adversarial Networks (GANs) (Ali et al., 2025) in the design of the AICyber-Chain framework, where GAN is a part of the core network architecture. This section presents the theoretical aspect as well as practical usage/application of GAN within the network; the mechanism for adversarial training and algorithmic workflows responsible for governing interaction between artificial intelligence and blockchain-based smart contracts.

### 6.1 Generative Adversarial Networks (GANs) in Cybersecurity

Generative Adversarial Networks (GANs) are a novel deep learning breakthrough, operating on a zero-sum game model with two neural networks competing against each other: a Generator network and a Discriminator network. GANs are conventionally used to generate synthetic data that is statistically indistinguishable from the real data. We reuse this adversarial feature to strengthen the network defence of the AICyber-Chain model.

Minimax Objective Function: The adversarial training process can be formally defined by the value function V(D,G):

$$\min_{G} \max_{D} V(D, G) = E_{x \sim p_{data}}[\log D(x)] + E_{z \sim p_z}[\log(1 - D(G(z)))] \quad (1)$$

$$L_D = -\left(E_{x \sim p_{data}}[\log D(x)] + E_{z \sim p_z}[\log(1 - D(G(z)))]\right) \quad (2)$$

$$L_G = -E_{z \sim p_z}[\log D(G(z))] \quad (3)$$

Equation (1) represents the adversarial objective function of the GAN. Equation (2) defines the Discriminator loss, which measures the ability to distinguish legitimate requests from generated attacks. Equation (3) defines the Generator loss, which evaluates the capability of generated attacks to evade detection. The iterative optimization of these functions enables adaptive threat detection and autonomous security rule generation.

The AI-based Secure Computing (ASC) component is injected into the OSS of each Private Data Centre (PDC) for data protection support. Within its evolutionary-developmental security-enhanced computing-injection initial stage, with added adversarial GAN module updates, more powerful and active dynamically evolving security policies are created by incorporating the power deployment of GANs. Systemically injecting these high-level ASC functions into PDC's runtime architecture establishes, in essence, an operational Ossicle - i.e., localised parallel learning ecosystem. A suitable, secure, advanced and intelligent OSS is developed herein, which can self-patch through autonomous processes, thus precluding the risks associated with controllable human operative error or unavailability being involved in efficacy recalibrations, or central software patches uploads; hence aiming towards living-immune system-like 'living' computer systems.

## 6.2 Adversarial Training: Forging Access Requests to Strengthen Defences

The realisation of GANs in the AICyber-Chain is an outcome of opportunistic adversarial training. In such a training environment, the Generator network models the operation of an advanced and stealthy cyber adversary while the Discriminator network represents a main-component defence mechanism of the PDC's OSS.

When equipped with the GAN module, a PDC begins by actively learning this inherited security policy. Once it has achieved sufficient confidence about normal operations and legitimate security rules, this knowledge is utilised by its Generator counterpart to generate access requests that look deceptively identical to some real requester-specific information. Here, these synthetic requests are intentionally meant to mislead and confuse the PDC's OSS/Discriminator network, aiming to sample points for which they might fail in correctly classifying that access request.

This adversarial interaction forms a closed-loop, high-speed training mechanism. Whenever the Generator gain passes through the Discriminator grip, the defence use case system feeds back the experience of failure into updating its internal weights and anomaly detection parameters. Meanwhile, if a synthetic attack gets blocked by the grip, then this also gets fed back for updating the AEIF and fine-tuning of an even more lethal attack against it. The OSS of such a PDC can strengthen itself after each round of generation and classification by the GAN algorithm. Eventually forged access credentials and zero-day exploits can hardly pose viable threats competing with such a reliable and comprehensive OSS.

## 6.3 Algorithmic Logic and Operational Workflow

To understand how they work, we need to technically expose the algorithmic logic that manages the interaction between AI detection and blockchain execution. In particular, two algorithms are developed whose functioning actually implements the theoretical soundness of AICyber-Chain obtained through GAN-trained OSS into practice. Therefore, they act as linkers between off-chain AI analysis and on-chain security enforcement.

### 6.3.1 Algorithm 1: AI-Driven Threat Detection and Response

The first algorithm is responsible for the continuous monitoring and identification phase that represents the vanguard of AI Cyber-Chain, indeed. It starts by initialising AI models for threat detection. They receive as input a continuous stream of network traffic data, system logs and users' behaviour data.

So, as the real-time data is flowing to the system, it enters into a pre-processing phase (pre_processing_I) where normalisation and feature extraction are employed in order to clean and get the suitable format of the data for Neural Network (NN) analysis. Once this is done, potential adversaries' breach attempts are analysed by the Threat Detection Module (DM). It utilises the trained machine learning models. Notice now that these models are hardened through GAN's adversarial training apprentice generation. Hence, their precision to capture subtle, multi-vector attacks, among others, is significantly increased.

Adversarial Potentialities within breach detection if DM results turn out positive in the previous step, reaching here alerts all AI models (i.e., A4, A5, A6 and A7) since every single one of them has its own very distinctive particularities.

If any one of them detects an attack (positive results), then Defensive-In-Depth's algorithm logic moves on immediately to II) Adversarial Detection Mode Response, the threat response module being responsible only due to the triggered event for:

### 6.3.2 Algorithm 2: Adaptive Smart Contract Execution

While Algorithm 1 copes with immediate mitigation, Algorithm 2 is responsible for the long-term resilience of the network. To achieve this, it periodically updates the overall security posture. The inputs are the threat alerts produced by the AI module and the policies that are pre-defined at installation and adaptation times.

When a new threat alert arrives, it is parsed by extracting its associated threat information, such as type and severity. This information then feeds into the Policy Adjustment Module that compares current security policies evolutionarily with historical attack data to decide if an existing policy does not dominate another one and if there is a need for its adaptation due to the newly arrived attack that is being exploited within the next-believed slots (corresponding to simulating multiple generations of those using evolutionary games).

Crucially, this adaptation requires the re-compilation of smart contract logic (if required). Thereafter, in order to enforce the updated security mechanisms on the decentralised network, execution of the smart contract by the system is done. This adaptive execution makes sure that the occurrence of a new attack vector upon identification by a single PDC leads to updated immunity across the network, with aggregated awareness of the entire ecosystem.

## 6.4 Smart Contract Operations (Register Data, Request Data, Subscribe Data)

The operational workflow of the AICyber-Chain heavily depends on the execution of specific smart contract operations for managing information and value exchanges in a secure manner among participants. In particular, these operations ensure that data provenance, auditing, and access control are guaranteed in a tamper-proof way.

Register Data: This operation is used by a DO to start the life cycle of its secure data. With this operation (Register Data), the DO registers its data on the blockchain. For privacy protection, rather than directly uploading its raw dataset into the ledger, it posts only the cryptographic hash of its dataset (usually derived from an underlying representative part of it). Besides this hash, it also provides details about both: i) the network address where users can consume to this data, and ii) an imposed fee for accessing it.

Subscribe Data: This is used when another entity needs access to registered data. By using the Subscribe Data function, a Data User (DU) can read descriptions of registered data from the blockchain and subscribe to specific data. The DU invokes this smart contract with a payment of a subscription fee specified by the DO in order to get access to the subscribed data.

Request Data: For very sensitive use cases, it might not be appropriate for a DU to automatically subscribe to registered data. In such a case, Request Data allows users to request explicit authorisation for accessing specific registered data. This function generates an access permission request that will be logged on the BC. If this request is valid and authorised (typically verified by an ASC module checking that the requesting transaction has no known malicious content), a reference will be returned pointing to the now authorised and authenticated DU on how they can download/access.

By performing these operations on the Ethereum blockchain, the AICyber-Chain ensures the integrity of the structure. Users cannot tamper with the execution of smart contracts with Ethereum and the process of value exchange as well. Every transaction, policy change, access request, etc., can be viewed immutably in log files with non-repudiation and transparency at an unprecedented level across the enterprise network.

The preceding sections described the architectural components of AI Cyber-Chain. To demonstrate its practical applicability, the following section presents a healthcare-oriented use case.

## 7. USE CASE SCENARIO: SECURE MEDICAL DATA SHARING

To concretely apply the theoretical framework of the AICyber-Chain to a real-life scenario, this section presents an in-depth use case: secure sharing of Electronic Health Records (EHR) in a trustless medical care system. The healthcare industry is one of the most hostile sectors in terms of cybersecurity and data handling, hence it makes a suitable example to demonstrate that double AI parallelism with blockchains can be a solution.

### 7.1 The Complexities of Healthcare Data Management

The lack of integral handling for health records has been an obstacle to building an integral, global, effective healthcare system. Nowadays, patients' health records are spread across different types of healthcare environments such as primary care clinics, specialised hospitals or independent diagnostic laboratories. These different silos are governed by legally separated entities that might even have commercial competing interests among them; thus, they store their assets using proprietary (often incompatible) database technologies.

Because they do not belong to one entity that everyone inherently trusts, data coming from such different sources is difficult to audit and control. Therefore, valuable medical data cannot be shared in a safe and ethically sound manner. Patients need to collect their records, either physically or digitally, at each new organisation they visit (although the previous organisation already has them). Lack of standardisation and lack of economic incentives prevent this process from being smooth. Moreover, these medical records are full of highly sensitive personal information. Privacy concerns result in regulations that often also forbid patients themselves from accessing their own data easily. But this is not what we need when accurate/comprehensive medication analysis becomes critically needed! There is thus a need for secure decentralised solutions that take sensor analytics to the next level.

## 7.2 Workflow for Trustless Medical Data Transfer (Hospital A to Hospital B)

To address these complexities, AICyber-Chain adopts a decentralised workflow that enables secure and trustless sharing of Electronic Health Records (EHR), as illustrated in Figure 3. Consider a scenario where Hospital A (requesting institution) requires access to the medical record of a patient, Alice, for an emergency intervention, while the corresponding data $MD_{Alice}$ is stored at Hospital B (data provider). The process begins when Hospital A generates a data request $R_{MD}$ through its Private Data Centre A and forwards it to Private Data Centre B (Step 1). Simultaneously, the request is logged on the blockchain layer (Step 2), ensuring an immutable record of the transaction.

Upon receiving the request, Hospital B employs its ASC Module / AI Verification to validate the behaviour and authenticity of the request (Step 3). Based on this verification, the system authorises or rejects access to the requested data (Step 4), thereby preventing impersonation or malicious activity. Once authorisation is granted, the process triggers the smart contract layer (Step 5), where Smart Contract 1 (Hospital Payment) manages the financial transaction between the institutions (Step 6a/6b), and Smart Contract 2 (Patient Reward) ensures that the patient, Alice, receives compensation for her data consent (Step 7).

Following the successful execution of the smart contracts, the encrypted medical data $MD_{Alice}$ is securely transferred from Hospital B to Hospital A (Step 8). Finally, Hospital A integrates the received data into its Knowledge Computation Module for further analysis and clinical decision-making (Step 9). This workflow ensures data integrity, transparency, and accountability through immutable logging, while simultaneously enabling secure and privacy-preserving data exchange across institutions.

*Figure 3. Trustless medical data sharing workflow via aicyber-chain*

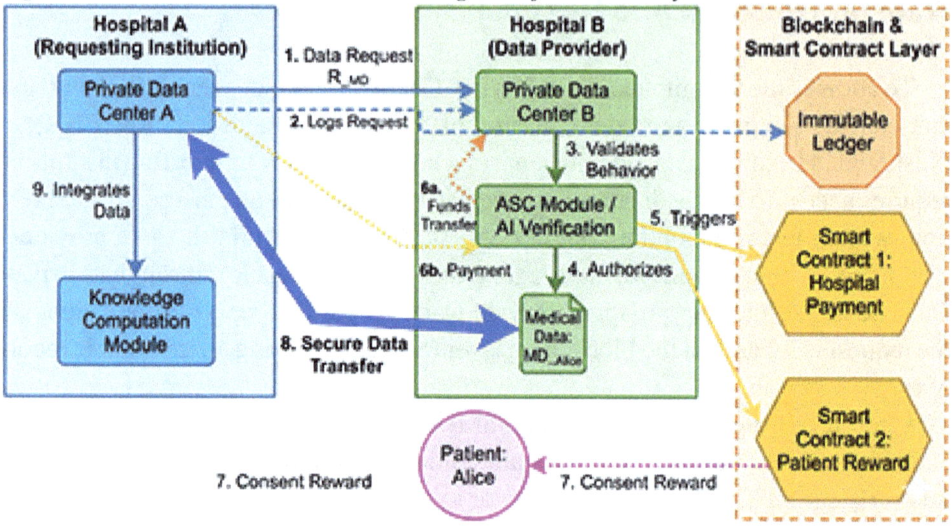


## 7.3 ASC Module Verification and Malicious Intent Filtration

Recording the request in blockchain is not enough; it must also be ensured that the hospital HB cryptographically verifies that the request from HA is legitimate and not a sophisticated impersonation attack aiming to exfiltrate EHRs. When the blockchain ledger updates the request, secure data reconciliation relies on an AI-based Secure Computing (ASC) module, which is a part of the Operation Support System (OSS) of PB.

The ASC module does not rely on static digital certificates, which can easily be forged. Instead, it has a sub-module, namely Generative Adversarial Network (GAN), using an AI-based approach to actively detect behavioural features of an incoming Request RMD. Ranging from network routing, frequency analysis, and comparison of PA's cryptographic signature with its dynamically-built security rules by artificial intelligence incorporated into ASC acts as a gatekeeper to prevent denial of service or penetration attempts through spoofing behaviour or malicious access. After validating requester entity integrity by the AI layer, injecting validated Request-RMD securely between the ASC module and Data Storage Module, with PB authorising MDAlice preparation for encrypted transfer

## 7.4 Value-Exchange Mechanisms and Incentive-Driven Data Sharing

A major historical barrier in this domain is the lack of financial motivation for institutions to share their proprietary datasets. This is directly addressed by the AICyber-Chain, as an automated incentive-based value-exchange mechanism governed by on-chain smart contracts is introduced.

Upon the AI validation of $R_{MD,}$ $MD_{Alice}$, a proposed SC1 automatically executes between HB and HA. It calculates and securely transfers via the AICyber-Chain a certain amount (e.g., cryptocurrency or network tokens), which HA has to pay to HB for the provided service of data transfer. Concurrently, another smart contract, proposed SC2, is triggered between hospital HB and patient Alice itself.

As soon as hospital HA successfully gets the desired medical data, $MD_{Alice}$, both on-chain smart contracts SC1 and SC2 automatically execute their final clauses and immediately swap the corresponding assets through the network. Now, a more competent and incentive-based ecosystem is created in which HB makes money by hosting and sharing the data, and Alice also gets rewarded for her consent. Last but not least, to achieve maximal benefits of this privacy-respected data swap and use it in future AI-oriented medical research, the Knowledge Computation Module (KCM) of the receiver institution can aids to encode received-data that includes several important parts of patients' records, such as patient history, disease diagnostics, and medication, which can be used.

The proposed framework supports privacy-preserving data management by storing sensitive information within Private Data Centres and exchanging only authorized data references through blockchain transactions. Such an approach can assist organizations in meeting privacy and data governance requirements while maintaining transparency and auditability.

# 8. EMPIRICAL VALIDATION AND PERFORMANCE METRICS

To validate the theoretical claims and structural benefits of the proposed AI Cyber -Chain framework, a stringent practical validation was performed. Theoretical architectural models need to be evaluated under real-world network scenarios to justify their suitability for deployment at an enterprise scale. This section presents a description of the simulation environment, comparative performance evaluation with the traditional centralised model, effectiveness of the AI-driven threat detection layer and overall resilience of the system against massive distributed attacks.

## 8.1 Simulation Environment Setup (Ethereum Rinkeby Testnet, Remix, Geth)

Performance evaluation for the AI-driven threat detection and adaptive smart contract execution model has been purposely conducted in an environment designed on a high-performance computing (HPC) platform. The base hardware configuration consisted of an Intel Core i7 processor with a clock speed of 3.6 GHz, supported by 16GB of memory using 64-bit Ubuntu 20.04 LTS OS.

The blockchain simulation was implemented based on the Ethereum network, more precisely the official Ethereum test network Rinkeby (and Goerli for broader smart contract deployment testing), to simulate a real-world decentralised ledger without real monetary costs. The blockchain node environment was set up with Ethereum's Geth client. For the development, compilation, and deployment of the smart contracts, we used the Remix Integrated Development Environment (IDE). We scripted the smart contracts responsible for implementing our automated security policies as well as our data sharing protocols in Solidity, which is also considered Ethereum's main object-oriented programming language. Metamask served as intermediary software in charge of generating cryptographic accounts and signing transactions.

On the artificial intelligence part of our prototype, we built our analytical models using Python 3.8 and the TensorFlow 2.4 framework to abstract the complex machine learning process from us. Our test environment included multiple nodes that continuously generated benign operating traffic with simulated attack vectors like malware programs, phishing emails, or Distributed Denial of Service (DDoS) attacks to achieve the realism of an enterprise-like network.

To evaluate the proposed framework, a simulated enterprise network environment was constructed containing a mixture of normal network traffic, system logs, and representative cyberattack scenarios. The GAN model was trained using adversarial learning, where the generator produced synthetic attack patterns and the discriminator learned to distinguish legitimate behaviour from malicious activity. Model performance was evaluated using standard classification metrics, including precision, recall, and F1-score. Simulated attack scenarios included malware activity, phishing attempts, and distributed denial-of-service (DDoS) attacks.

## 8.2 Comparative Performance Analysis against Centralised Models

The existing centralised system performance should not be compromised while migrating to the proposed decentralised, parallel approach. The simulation considered throughput, latency and economic efficiency in the case of the AI Cyber-Chain model.

### 8.2.1 Authentication Speed and Latency

Traditional centralised models usually have severe bottlenecks in peak traffic because a single server has to process and authenticate every incoming request. The AI Cyber -Chain model alleviated this bottleneck by distributing the workload in parallel nodes and using content-based addressing via IPFS, as explained before. Empirical results showed that the proposed model sped up the authentication process 1.8 times compared to equivalent centralised models.

Furthermore, the system realised an average response time, namely, the duration from the initial threat detection by the AI module to the successful execution of the corresponding smart contract, as low as 1.2 seconds. The underlying blockchain has been operated with a robust transaction throughput equal to 50 Transactions Per Second (TPS), and a minimum transaction latency of 200 milliseconds. Notably, upon detecting new threats for protection networks' real-time learning, it took around 3.5 seconds for our system to achieve policy adjustment in practice that further verified its ability to dynamically rewrite and enforce updated security rules over the network in near-real-time.

### 8.2.2 Economic Efficiency: Gas Consumption Reduction

Operating over the Ethereum network requires computational effort, which is denoted as gas. In enterprise settings, high gas fees can make blockchain-based security mechanisms impractical economically. To overcome this issue, AI Cyber -Chain outsources heavy data storage to IPFS and intensive AI computations to the localised Private Data Centres (PDCs), and processes only lightweight metadata, security logs, and value-exchange triggers on-chain. This structural optimisation reduces 20%–25% of total gas consumption as compared with a generic blockchain integration approach. These savings guarantee that large-scale enterprise deployment is able to afford continuous automated execution of security smart contracts.

### 8.2.3 Real-World Considerations for Smart Contract Execution Costs

The practical deployment of blockchain-based cybersecurity frameworks requires consideration of smart contract execution costs. In Ethereum-compatible networks, transaction costs are determined by gas consumption, which depends on the complexity of the executed operation.The transaction cost can be estimated as:

$$\text{Cost} = \text{Gas Used} \times \text{Gas Price} \times \text{ETH Price}$$

For example, assuming a gas price of 20 Gwei and an Ether value of USD 3,000, a transaction consuming 80,000 gas units would cost approximately USD 4.80. Actual costs vary according to network conditions and transaction complexity.

In the proposed AI Cyber-Chain architecture, only metadata and security logs are stored on-chain, while large datasets remain within IPFS and Private Data Centres (PDCs). This design helps minimise blockchain storage requirements and reduces operational costs, making the framework more suitable for enterprise-scale deployment.

## 8.3 AI Model Efficacy: Detection Accuracy and F1-Scores

The effectiveness of the smart contract layer depends entirely on the accuracy of the underlying AI threat detection models. The AI models were evaluated against a realistically labelled dataset that contains different types of network traffic, system logs and malicious samples. In this work, we used conventional statistical standard metrics such as precision, recall and their harmonic mean, F1-score, to measure the effectiveness.

The simulation results indicated that the AI models achieved an F1-score of 0.92, demonstrating effective discrimination between benign and malicious activities. The empirical results yielded from the simulation of the AI Cyber -Chain framework on the Ethereum Rinkeby test network are encapsulated in Table 3. The metrics represent the performance analysis of the system's efficiency, accuracy in detecting AI threats, and elapsed time for smart contract automated enforcement of security policy.

*Table 3. Performance evaluation metrics of the aicyber-chain model*

| Performance Metric | Recorded Result | Description |
|---|---|---|
| Detection Accuracy (F1-Score) | 0.92 | High precision and recall in distinguishing malicious anomalies from benign network traffic. |
| Average Response Time | 1.2 seconds | The time taken from initial threat detection to the execution of automated mitigation. |
| Transaction Throughput | 50 TPS | The number of security logs and transactions the hybrid blockchain processes per second. |
| Transaction Latency | 200 ms | The delay before a security event is permanently and immutably recorded on the ledger. |
| Policy Adjustment Time | 3.5 seconds | The time required to dynamically rewrite and enforce updated smart contract security rules across the network. |

## 8.4 Network Resilience: Mitigating Distributed Denial of Service (DDoS) Attacks

Enterprise infrastructures and their critical web applications remain a preferred target for attackers, such as those launching Distributed Denial of Service (DDoS) attacks. These attacks drain network bandwidth and computing resources. In a centralised network, if the primary server fails due to a DDoS attack, the whole network will fail, resulting in operational risks and economic impact.

### 8.4.1 Analysing System Vulnerability vs. Shared Security Rules

The AI Cyber -Chain framework inherently prevents DDoS attacks by allocating security costs to the peer-to-peer network. In this simulation, four independent and equal DDoS attacks ($\lambda$=0.2, $\lambda$=0.4, $\lambda$=0.6, and $\lambda$=0.8) were simulated with a Poisson distribution in order to consider whether this also holds for the Blockchain as a Service automation use case.

The experiment results are then described, and we simulate the impact of the overall AICyber-Chain system vulnerability as a function of the amount of security rules being dynamically exchanged among the network's nodes. With respect to this relationship, we concluded that an inequality of inverse exponential dependence is taking place since one can intuitively assume that the more security rules are distributed over in-network nodes (at a reasonable level), there lesser damage risk occurs on specific AI Cyber -Chain's cyber component or constituents.

Figure 4 shows the network resilience against DDoS attacks. As we see, we have an inverse exponential dependency: while more dynamically generated security rules are shared between decentralised nodes, i.e., if their concentration in some part related to the cyber-component/constituents-system increases, generally it tends to lower overall network vulnerability in a significant manner. It also perfectly visualises the notion that the crowning provided by P2P architecture collective intelligence certainly grants safe protections against massively destructive attacking methods.

*Figure 4. System vulnerability vs. shared security rules under DDoS attacks*

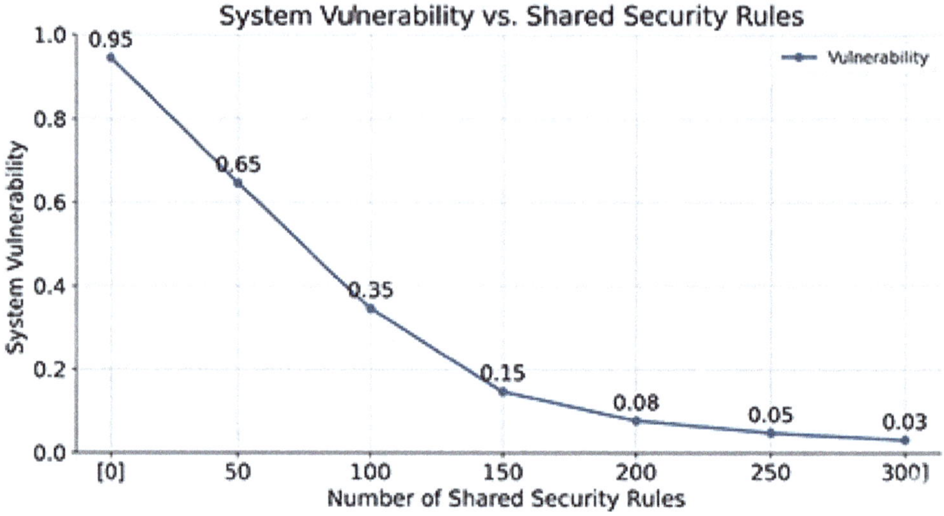


By leveraging blockchain to share threat intelligence and defensive strategies in real-time, the entire ecosystem gradually forms an active immunity over time. The richer information repository surfaces the attack probability much better. Sustained attacking a distributed system is considered more and more difficult in terms of the attacker's investment, with high operational costs meaning higher failure risks. It indicates collective parallel protective effects can be modelled on cyberspace, which increases the difficulty of big and brute- force networks being damaged.

While the proposed architecture demonstrates promising performance, large-scale enterprise deployment may introduce additional challenges related to network management, blockchain synchronization, and computational resource allocation. Future work will investigate scalability optimization, resource-efficient consensus mechanisms, and deployment strategies for large distributed environments.

## 9. CONCLUSION AND FUTURE DIRECTIONS

### 9.1 Summary of the AICyber-Chain Contributions

The AICyber-Chain framework proposed in this chapter, as a holistic solution to the exposed vulnerabilities of the centralised cybersecurity paradigm, which converges parallel Artificial Intelligence with blockchain, has resolved the single point of failure concern for enhancing data integrity. Through experimental evaluation, our results indicated that integrating IPFS and hybrid consensus can boost authentication performance by 1.8 times for both types of consensus under up to 25%, and the AI layer presented robust threat classification with an F1-score at 0.92; the average response for automated smart contracts was even less than 1.2 seconds.

## 9.2 Advancing Cybersecurity Infrastructures

The proposed model significantly advances current cybersecurity infrastructures by shifting from static, reactive defence perimeters to dynamic, self-evolving ecosystems. Through the combination of Generative Adversarial Networks (GANs) and localised Private Data Centres (PDCs), the framework in parallel learns and generates dynamic security rules. Additionally, the decentralised dissemination of security rules over blockchain can reduce networks' susceptibility to enormous Distributed Denial of Service (DDoS) attacks by harnessing peer-to-peer networks' collective intelligence. Ultimately, the AI Cyber - Chain architecture provides an all-encompassing, tested and structurally solid design for building resilient, transparent and intelligent enterprise networks.

## 9.3 Future Work: Unreliable Network Environments and Advanced Smart Contracts.

Notwithstanding that AI Cyber - Chain has provided a sturdy foundation for decentralisation of security, research must overcome emergence issues when deploying these complex systems under highly volatile or constrained conditions. Further efforts will be devoted towards more elaboration with particularly highly trusted smart contracts for imposing nuanced data-sharing agreements as well as managing distributed AI-based computing tasks. Meanwhile, examining the trustworthiness performances of such decentralised architectures under unreliable network environments represents the next grand challenge.

## REFERENCES


Alber, D. A., Yang, Z., Alyakin, A., Yang, E., Rai, S., Valliani, A. A., Zhang, J., Rosenbaum, G. R., Amend-Thomas, A. K., Kurland, D. B., Kremer, C. M., Eremiev, A., Negash, B., Wiggan, D. D., Nakatsuka, M. A., Sangwon, K. L., Neifert, S. N., Khan, H. A., Save, A. V., & Oermann, E. K. (2025). Medical large language models are vulnerable to data-poisoning attacks. *Nature Medicine*, *31*(2), 618–626. DOI: 10.1038/s41591-024-03445-1 PMID: 39779928

Ali, M., Ali, M., Hussain, M., & Koundal, D. (2025). Generative adversarial networks (GANs) for medical image processing: Recent advancements. *Archives of Computational Methods in Engineering*, *32*(2), 1185–1198. DOI: 10.1007/s11831-024-10174-8

Alotaibi, E. M., Issa, H., & Codesso, M. (2025). Blockchain-based conceptual model for enhanced transparency in government records: A design science research approach. *International Journal of Information Management Data Insights*, *5*(1), 100304. DOI: 10.1016/j.jjimei.2024.100304

Batchu, R. K., Bikku, T., Thota, S., Seetha, H., & Ayoade, A. A. (2024). A novel optimization-driven deep learning framework for the detection of DDoS attacks. *Scientific Reports*, *14*(1), 28024. DOI: 10.1038/s41598-024-77554-9 PMID: 39543174

Bhavana, G. B., Anand, R., Ramprabhakar, J., Guerrero, J. M., Thakkar, N., & Ambikapathy, A. (2025). Comparative evaluation and simulation of blockchain consensus mechanisms for secure and scalable peer-to-peer energy trading in microgrids. *Scientific Reports*, *15*(1), 43546. DOI: 10.1038/s41598-025-27431-w PMID: 41372270

Chaudhary, D., & Lee, C.-C. (2024). *Anonymous quantum-safe secure and authorized communication protocol under dynamic identities for Internet of Drones. Computers and Electrical Engineering*. Elsevier., DOI: 10.1016/j.compeleceng.2024.109774

Claudel, N., Guo, W., & Xing, Y. (2026). AI Evasion and Impersonation Attacks on Facial Re-Identification with Activation Map Explanations. arXiv preprint arXiv:2603.15396.

Dai, F., Hossain, M. A., & Wang, Y. (2025). State of the art in parallel and distributed systems: Emerging trends and challenges. *Electronics (Basel)*, *14*(4), 677. DOI: 10.3390/electronics14040677

Dhingra, L., Meetei, L. S., Ojha, V., Lodi, M. K., Sheela, A. S., & Agarwal, A. (2025, March). The Role of Blockchain Technology in Enhancing Network Security. In *2025 International Conference on Automation and Computation (AUTOCOM)* (pp. 559-564). IEEE. DOI: 10.1109/AUTOCOM64127.2025.10956764

Heimbach, L., Vonlanthen, Y., Villacis, J., Kiffer, L., & Wattenhofer, R. (2025). Deanonymizing Ethereum Validators: The {P2P} Network Has a Privacy Issue. In 34th USENIX Security Symposium (USENIX Security 25) (pp. 1319-1338).

Hui, X., & Tucker, C. (2025). Decentralization, blockchain, artificial intelligence (AI): Challenges and opportunities. *Journal of Product Innovation Management*, *42*(5), 947–957. DOI: 10.1111/jpim.12800

John, K., Rivera, T. J., & Saleh, F. (2025). Proof-of-work versus proof-of-stake: A comparative economic analysis. *Review of Financial Studies*, *38*(7), 1955–2004. DOI: 10.1093/rfs/hhaf013

Kryś, J., Sharma, Y., & Egan, J. (2025). Distributed and Decentralised Training: Technical Governance Challenges in a Shifting AI Landscape. arXiv preprint arXiv:2507.07765.

Majumder, R. Q. (2025). Machine Learning for Predictive Analytics: Trends and Future Directions. Available at *SSRN* 5267273.

Nandish, H. D., Rahul, R., Dasari, H. C., Kumaran, U., & Umah, B. (2025). Machine learning-powered intrusion detection for network security. In Proceedings of International Conference on Recent Trends in Computing (ICRTC 2024), Lecture Notes in Networks and Systems, vol. 885. Springer. https://doi.org/DOI: 10.1007/978-981-97-8836-1_9

. Ndibe, O. S. (2025). AI-driven forensic systems for real-time anomaly detection and threat mitigation in cybersecurity infrastructures. International journal of research publication and reviews, 6(5), 389-411.

Neto, G. F., Macêdo, B. D. S., Boratto, T. H., Gontijo, T. S., Bodini, M., Saporetti, C., & Goliatt, L. (2025). Stratified metamodeling to predict concrete compressive strength using an optimized dual-layered architectural framework. *Mathematical & Computational Applications*, *30*(1), 16. DOI: 10.3390/mca30010016

Pernice, E. (2025). AI Model Training: Consent or Legitimate Interest? Guidance on Choosing the Most Appropriate Legal Basis. JL, Mkt. &. *Innovation*, •••, 584.

Preethi, M., Kale, A., Satheesh, P., Harshitha, R., & Vaidya, R. (2025, March). Decentralised Cloud Architecture: Blockchain Driven Integrity and Raptor Codes for Enhanced Data Transmission. In 2025 IEEE 14th International Conference on Communication Systems and Network Technologies (CSNT) (pp. 358-365). IEEE.

. SakthiMurugan, S., Sanjay Kumaar, A., Vishnu Vignesh, & Santhi, P. (2024). Assessment of zero-day vulnerability using machine learning approach. EAI Endorsed Transactions on Internet of Things, 10(1). https://doi.org/DOI: 10.4108/eetiot.4978

Samuel, T., & Jessica, L. (2019). From Perimeter to Cloud: Innovative Approaches to Firewall and Cybersecurity Integration. *International Journal of Trend in Scientific Research and Development*, *3*(5), 2751–2759.

Sekhar, J. C., Priyanka, R., Nanda, A. K., Josephson, P. J., Ebinezer, M. J. D., & Devi, T. K. (2025). Stochastic gradient boosted distributed decision trees security approach for detecting cyber anomalies and classifying multiclass cyber-attacks. *Computers & Security*, *151*, 104320. DOI: 10.1016/j.cose.2025.104320

Steeman, J. T., Peiffer-Smadja, O., & Ravet, J. (2025). A comparative analysis of public R&I funding in the EU, US, and China (No. KI-01-25-090-EN-N). Directorate General for Research and Innovation (DG RTD) of the European Commission.

Tanveer, F., Iradat, F., Iqbal, W., & Ahmad, A. (2025). Towards Secure APIs: A Survey on RESTful API Vulnerability Detection. *Computers, Materials & Continua*, *84*(3), 4223–4257. DOI: 10.32604/cmc.2025.067536

Tariq, S., Baruwal Chhetri, M., Nepal, S., & Paris, C. (2025). Alert fatigue in security operations centres: Research challenges and opportunities. *ACM Computing Surveys*, *57*(9), 1–38. DOI: 10.1145/3723158

Uysal, F., Demirkesen, S., Tezel, A., Elghaish, F., & Hoxha, J. (2026). A blockchain and Interplanetary File System (IPFS) based project risk register for construction organizations. *International Journal of Construction Management*, •••, 1–27. DOI: 10.1080/15623599.2026.2636732

Widjaja, G. (2025). PRIVACY AND SECURITY IN DIGITAL COMMUNICATIONS: CHALLENGES AND SOLUTIONS IN CYBERSPACE. In Prosiding Seminar Nasional Indonesia (Vol. 2, No. 2, pp. 26-33).

Xie, Z., Zhang, X., & Liu, X. (2025). Enhanced efficiency and security in cross-chain transmission of blockchain internet of ports through multi-feature-based joint learning. *Scientific Reports*, *15*(1), 6199. DOI: 10.1038/s41598-025-85330-6 PMID: 39979319

Xu, Q., Ren, S., Wang, J., Li, Z., & Gao, W. (2025, May). A Research of Compute First Networking Based on Information-Centric Networking Cache Mechanism. In 2025 5th International Conference on Electronics, Circuits and Information Engineering (ECIE) (pp. 783-791). IEEE. DOI: 10.1109/ECIE65947.2025.11087005

Yang, Y., Wan, H., Yan, X., Zhao, M., Zeng, J., & Li, B. (2025). Parallel cryptographic hash function based on cellular automata and random diffusion model. *Applied Soft Computing*, *169*, 112546. DOI: 10.1016/j.asoc.2024.112546

# Chapter 4 Decentralized Application (DApps): Secure Blockchain Ecosystems

**Kanupriya Gupta**
*School of Engineering and Technology, Vivekananda Institute of Professional Studies - Technical Campus, India*

**Divay Pahuja**
*School of Engineering and Technology, Vivekananda Institute of Professional Studies - Technical Campus, India*

**Om Mishra**
*School of Engineering and Technology, Vivekananda Institute of Professional Studies - Technical Campus, India*

**Monika Bansal**
http://orcid.org/0000-0003-0178-4727
*School of Engineering and Technology, Vivekananda Institute of Professional Studies - Technical Campus, India*

**Nishi Jain**
http://orcid.org/0000-0002-0311-3866
*School of Engineering and Technology, Vivekananda Institute of Professional Studies - Technical Campus, India*

## ABSTRACT

*A Decentralized Application (DApp) is a distributed, open-source software application that runs on a peer-to-peer (P2P) blockchain network. DApps are emerging as a transformative force across various sectors, leveraging blockchain technology to create applications that operate autonomously, offer enhanced security and*

DOI: 10.4018/979-8-3373-9053-6.ch004

*transparency, and function without a central authority. Common security issues with DApps include smart contract and blockchain vulnerabilities, phishing and social engineering attacks, and key management challenges. Mitigation strategies involve thorough code audits, formal verification, multi-signature wallets, and robust security frameworks. This chapter provides a detailed analysis of DApp security, focusing on theoretical aspects, architectural components, and specific vulnerabilities in smart contracts, oracles, blockchain protocols, front-end interfaces, and cross-chain interoperability mechanisms.*

## 1. INTRODUCTION

### 1.1 Definition and Significance of Decentralized Applications (DApps)

The concept of decentralization can be used in numerous areas, situations, and spaces. The examination of decentralization of different fields begins with the definition of technical decentralization and the discussion of its networking reasons. We shift the focus of our inquiry of technical network incentives to the wider social, political and economic, advantages of decentralization as shown in Figure 1. This research tries to demonstrate how the social outcomes of the studies on technical decentralization are realized and political as well as economic kinds of decentralization rather than making comparisons across contexts.

*Figure 1. Decentralization*

The blockchain network enables the operation of software applications called DApps and usually called Decentralized Applications (Dhananjay et al., 2019). They are important because they provide a number of advantages over traditional applications:

- *Decentralization:* No single entity controls DApps, they are more resistant to censorship and cooking attacks.
- *Transparency:* A DApp offers transparency since all transactions made are recorded on the blockchain.
- *Security:* DApps built on blockchain technology are more secure and immune to hacking and fraud.
- *Efficiency:* The automation of processes by DApps would decrease the need for intermediaries, resulting in lower costs and increased efficiency.
- *User autonomy:* Users are often given more autonomy over their data and digital assets in a DApp.

## 1.2 Evaluation of DApps: From Bitcoin Scripting to Ethereum and Web3 Ecosystem

Over the past several months now, the Total Value Locked (TVL) in the DeFi platform and crypto protocols is reached 44 billion USD (Binance USD), with over 82 million wallets and users around the world. Since Bitcoin was created, the underlying technology used by this type of platform has advanced, opening up room for many other tools besides currency. The terms of agreements between buyers and sellers go into self-executing code structured within smart contracts which stores and replicates its programming across blockchain networks to execute automatically without any third-parties. Smart contracts acknowledge the hack-proof and transparent nature of the Blockchain, allowing them to provide users with a method to enforce agreements and streamline processes. These systems work independently and the deployment process prevents any alterations from happening afterward (Open Knowledge Repository, n.d.). The deployment of a blockchain-based smart contract makes it available to all users who have blockchain network access for use and interaction.

## 1.3 Importance of Security in Decentralized System

In this digital age, blockchain technology is an innovative mechanism used to essentially record and secure data. Blockchain has come a long way since its inception along with Bitcoin in 2008 and has evolved beyond its primary use case in cryptocurrencies. It offers specific opportunities and challenges, especially to the case of its decentralized architecture - identity management and contract security as shown in Figure 2. Give me a chance to explain: On the most fundamental level, blockchain is an secure, transparent and immutable record keeping system that is independent from a central authority is called a type of distributed ledger system. This is a critical aspect, and its implications on security and trust of digital infrastructures are significant. Further, the peculiar feature of decentralized structure of at least some blockchain networks is a radical, paradigm-shifting change in the manner of how data storage systems, data access and validation procedures should be done (Fan, n.d.). A change with potential, so far as ways to address old issues on cyber security and digital ID management.

*Figure 2. Decentralized security*

## 2. THEORETICAL FOUNDATION OF DAPPS

### 2.1 Distribution Ledger Technologies (DLT) and Blockchain

The term consists of distributed digital systems which enable nodes to add data into verified storage databases that distributed across complete or partial system nodes (distributed ledger). A software protocol determines the functionality of every DLT system in operation. The protocols follow a structure with three fundamental elements that maintain their connection. The first pillar of every DLT system determines both data structure and the possible information storage format in the distributed ledger. Nodes operate according to specified criteria which are defined in the second pillar of the DLT system.

- Permissionless (Open) Distributed Ledgers

The two types of distributed ledger systems differ through open or permissionless and permissioned operations. Both Bitcoin and Ethereum represent the decisive examples of fully permissionless blockchain platforms which enable participants to join or leave the network without any pre-approval processes from organizational entities. A computer with proper software constitutes the sole prerequisite for joining an open network and adding transactions to the ledger.

- Permissioned Distributed Ledgers

The owner or administrator of permissioned distributed ledgers (DLs) selects all participants and controls network entry as well as determines operational rules for the ledger (Alchemy, n.d.). By allowing cherry-picked participants to join permissioned distributed ledgers this approach establishes solutions for the issues governments and regulators have with permissionless distributed ledgers regarding network participant identification processes and licensing requirements and ledger ownership definition. Such arrangements diminish a fundamental advantage of permissionless blockchains since they rely on the ability to operate without relying on any single entity responsible for coordination functions.

## 2.2 Smart Contact as the Backbone of DApps

Smart contracts are structured as computer protocols enabling users to negotiate agreements digitally in a secure and user-friendly manner. Within the blockchain framework, smart contracts represent intricate applications wherein digital assets are managed directly through code. These smart contracts function as self-operating agents operating on the blockchain, each recognized by a distinct address and holding a balance of ether. Each time the contract's account detects incoming messages from other contracts or transactions from external users a specific programmed segment activates to manage its balance and key/value storage system for tracking persistent variables. Users must transmit transactions that contain specific gas value along with ABI-formatted data payload to trigger engagement with a contract.

EVM bytecode emanates from programming in Solidity and Vyper languages but developers write initial smart contract code using higher-level languages such as Solidity and Vyper that share similarities with Python and JavaScript. The EVM bytecode operates under a virtual machine present in the Ethereum execution environment. Code execution works through an endless loop that executes operations at the bytecode beginning from the current program counter before progressing to the next instruction with each repetition. The code execution process stops at three points: the bytecode reaches its natural termination or it encounters an error and it detects either a STOP or RETURN instruction (Alchemy, n.d; Apillon, 2023).

Every resource users need for computations demands payment from them including computing power and bandwidth and data storage capabilities. Each operation in a smart contract incurs computing expenses defined using base units of "gas." The operations start with gas calculation before their execution begins.

*Figure 3. Smart contract*

## 2.2.1 EVM/ WASM/ eWASM Bytecode

This section contrasts the design choices as well as execution mechanics between EVM and WASM and eWASM bytecode (Apillon, 2023).

EVM Bytecode: EVM refers to Ethereum Virtual Machine. After transformation Ethereum smart contracts achieve a low-level form known as EVM bytecode which has stack-oriented structure. The code follows a specific order of programming commands. The three different storage types within the system are stack storage, memory storage, and long-term storage. Data on both the stack and memory get erased following the calculation but long-term storage preserves all saved data until further updates. The EVM offers various high-level functions that include SSTORE for saving 256-bit integers to storage alongside CREATE to start new child contracts and CALL to run methods between contracts as well as SHA3 implementation for Keccak-256 hashing. The base data component in EVM consists of 256-bit integers but also supports decreasing data sizes through 8-bit integer operations. The EVM requires all calculations under 256-bits to convert into 256-bit format for its execution. Maintaining determinism requires the EVM to refrain from complete float-point support.

WASM: The internet has become the largest implementation platform for running multiple application types. The native support of JavaScript on the internet cannot meet the rising performance needs of complex web applications that include games and interactive 3D graphics. Browsers developers in the year 2017 developed Web Assembly as a secure low-level compilation target which provides rapid performance together with portability. Web Assembly or WASM functions as a binary instruction format meant for stack-based virtual machine execution that delivers nearly native performance levels..

eWASM: The term eWASM describes WebAssembly that Ethereum has specifically designed for its platform. WASM contains small set of instructions designed specifically for Ethereum smart contracts ones. The Ethereum Environment Interface (EEI) serves as a connection framework that WASM execution entities utilize to interface with the Ethereum environment because WASM itself lacks fundamental operation codes. Since blockchain nodes must run operations precisely eWASM restricts float operations which are non-deterministic. The eWASM project includes a backward compatibility system using an EVM transpiler while the calculation of computational costs operates similarly to EVM.

## 2.3 Decentralised Storage and Data Availability

Nodes operate in distributed computer networks to form decentralized cloud storage services which contrast permissioned cloud providers since they reduce excessive control. The P2P network of nodes maintains connections between storage systems which are operated by entities and individuals who provide paid disk space. The Blockchain takes responsibility for tracking all transactions that occur on these storage platforms which work as a ledger. The blockchain maintains records with unalterable security. The advantages of decentralized cloud storage .

Decentralized cloud storage addresses vulnerability problems through its distributed peer-to-peer network system of servers called nodes which functions without central control (Posey, 2025).

This distributed data storage system offers three main advantages to its users:

1) No central point of failure

Information maintained in decentralized networks exists in continuous availability because it spreads across multiple locations. The information remains accessible throughout all nodes even when one of them experiences failure.

2) Enhanced security

The combination of encryption and hashing algorithms allows data to break into numerous nodes which protect information from unauthorized modification or access by centralized entities.

3) Greater data privacy and control

People holding ownership of their data have complete authority to establish criteria about data storage and access permissions and sharing limitations.

4) Cost effectiveness

Cloud storage provided by decentralized networks usually proves to be less expensive than standard data storage systems yet providers maintain different pricing structures. Users obtain rewards or tokens because they share their extra storage capacity to reduce their storage expenses.

## 2.4 Interoperability and Oracles in DApps

### 2.4.1 Decentralized ORACLES Networks - Chainlink, Band Protocol

Smart contracts on blockchain or main chains get expanded and improved capabilities through Decentralized Oracle Networks illustrate in Figure 4 which extend protocol functions that blockchain lacks natively. These resources reach computing systems through the supply of networking capabilities alongside computation processing and data storage functions. The main goal of a Distributed Oracle Network is to provide its resources with strong confidentiality along with integrity and availability features while ensuring accountability measures.

Reliable services from DONs are achieved through permanent partnerships between oracle nodes which establish cooperative working groups to serve clients. The development process of DONs operates independently from any blockchain system. On any suitable main chain developers can establish off-chain smart contract support through the powerful flexible resource provided by DONs (Sharma et al., 2021)

*Figure 4. Decentralized oracle network*

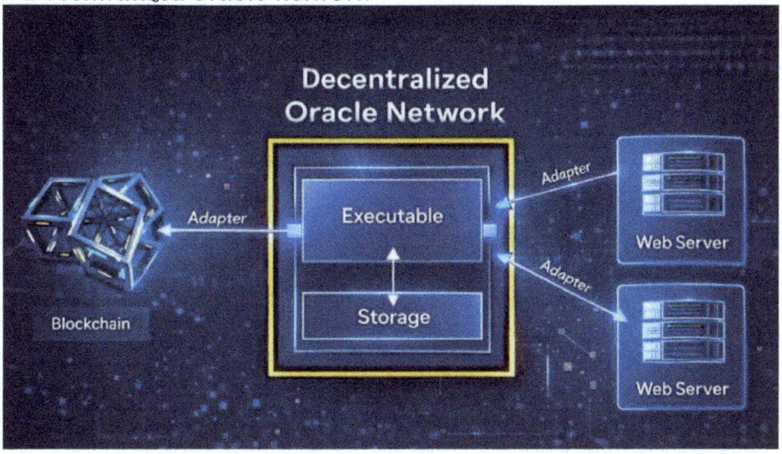


## 2.4.2 ChainLink Network (LINK)

Figure 5 illustrates Chainlink exists as the top-decentralized oracle solution that powers data feeds for almost every major DeFi project. The off-chain oracle works through autonomous node operators whose responsibility is data collection for transmission to its middleware application. The middleware application takes this data through its programming to present a single organized input prior to blockchain transmission where smart contracts can later access it.

*Figure 5. Chainlink software aggregates inputs from all operators*

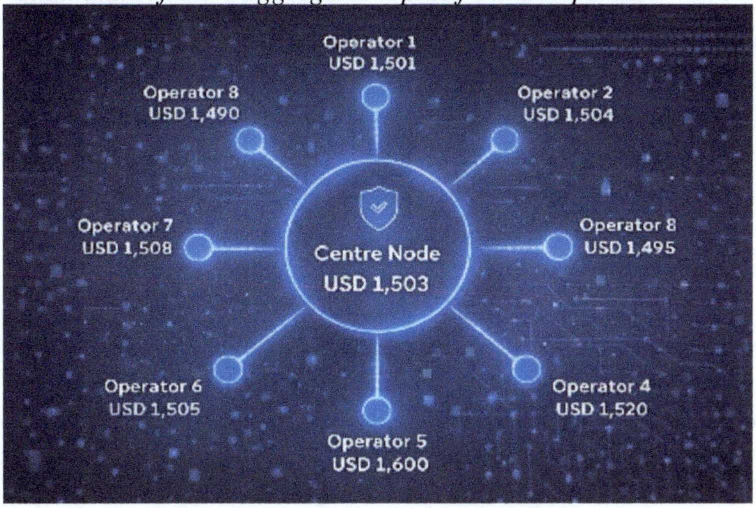

Any blockchain interface becomes accessible to developers through Chainlink network because it functions outside particular blockchain structures. LINK functions as both payment currency for Ethereum users and operator security measure on the Ethereum network for dapps. The LINK token will gain access to additional smart-contract based blockchain platforms to provide oracle services that facilitate cross-platform integration (Bitcoin Wiki, n.d.).

The assessment of the Chainlink initiative along with its LINK token economic system is available within the February Digital Investor – Chainlink Investment Thesis.

### 2.4.3 Band Protocol

The Band Protocol service works as an on-chain oracle through the standalone Band Chain blockchain based on Cosmos technology while serving different smart platform blockchains. Through its capability developers can generate unique oracle scripts which extract needed data for dapps functionality. The Band Chain under its Delegated Proof of Stake consensus bases its operation on a network of over 100 validators who collect requested data and distribute it first to Band Chain then to its associated platform chain. The BAND token serves as validator payment for data delivery while validators must stake BAND tokens to ensure data integrity through penalty systems. A data query takes about 6 seconds to fulfill through Band Chain because its block period reaches only 2 seconds. Band Chain functions autonomously so network difficulties on requesting chains do not impact its operations such as delays in block times and fee rate increases.

## 3. SECURITY RISKS IN DAPPS

### 3.1 Smart Contract- Level Weaknesses

There are many weaknesses in smart contacts and one can visit a large amount of money or even compromise the security within these dynamics. Common vulnerabilities are amonst themas shown in Figure 6:

1. Reentrancy Attacks

.It happens when a function makes an external call to another untrusted contract during its actual execution operations. If indeed the contract you thought is untrusted, actually triggers a call again back to original function, well then you will possibly invoke unknown. responses. The infamous reentrancy attack of the DAO exploit in

2016, which then wiped around $50 million worth of Ether, was a good example of a reentrancy attack (Chainlink, 2022).

2. Integer Overflow/Underflow

Several programming languages (Solidity being one of the main language for smart contracts in Ethereum, integer values have hard minimum and maximum). Going over the limits makes values wrap, often resulting in spooky behavior. Earlier, an integer overflow vulnerability let a 2018 BEC token theft automize the generation of a large amount of tokens (*International Journal of Engineering and Technology Research,* 2024).

3.Timestamp Dependence

Block timestamps are used by many smart contracts for several functions. Nevertheless, miners can adjust these timestamps to some degree which may affect the timing-sensitive contracts results.

4.Front-Running

MEMEPOOL, where all transactions are viewable before they are mined in blockchain networks. When this happens people can see it and thus potentially act on this data before hand than the original transaction (Wan et al., 2021). Decentralized exchanges an alternative to front-running, which is when an attacker submits buy and sell order right before/just after a big order in hopes that they can make profit from quickly changing price.

5. Access Control Issues

An access control too lax gets the job done, but poorly. The Parity multi-sig wallet bug, which locked 280 M$ or so of Ether under control insufficient access control in 2017.

*Figure 6. Severity and financial risk of smart contract security issues*

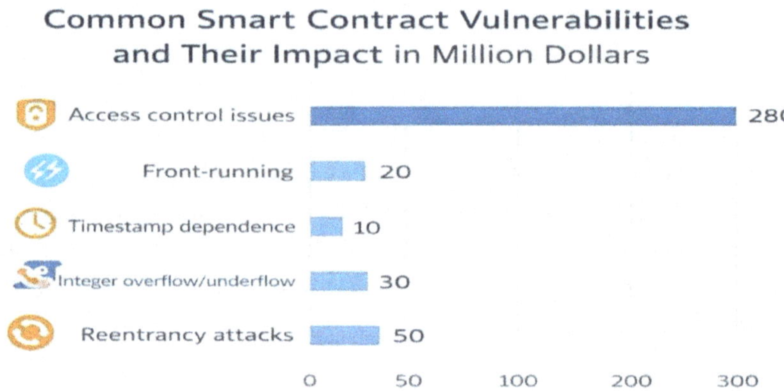


## 3.2 Blockchain-Level Security Risks

### 3.2.1 Blockchain Security Attacks and Challenges

The double-spending threat poses an essential danger to blockchain security because a warning occurs when miners acquire mining power above 51%. A solution to this issue combines Proof of Work and Proof of Stake algorithms (2-hop Blockchain). This technique establishes barriers which minimize the risk for a miner who possesses greater than 51% mining power to carry out duplicitous behavior (Szabo, 1996).

### 3.2.2 Blockchain Security Issues

1)Transaction Malleability: The agreement process for arranged transactions includes detailed hash computation but certain modified network transactions occasionally succeed in avoidance of verification process. According to Christian Decker and Roger Wattenhofer transaction malleability describes the process of transaction interception followed by alteration and subsequent rebroadcast that makes the entity participant believe the initial transaction was not confirmed.

2) Network Security: Under an eclipse attack an adversary controls network communication parts to segment the network in a logical manner which results in synchronization delay extension as a base denial of service attack serves to boost double-spending capabilities. In an eclipse attack the adversary chooses information

that hides from one or more network participants although blocking potential block transfers to nodes.

3) Privacy: The fundamental problem of blockchain transactions involves privacy since nodes have full visibility into all transactions and accessible data. Researchers introduced multiple solutions to overcome privacy challenges but these solutions work within limited application domains and lack solutions for all present problems.

## 3.3 Frontend Security Threats In DApps

### 3.3.1 Phishing Attacks

Phishing is the attempt to gain sensitive information under false pretenses by disguising oneself as an trustworthy entity (i.e., in electronic communications). The most common social engineering attack method is messages pretending to come from widespread social media platforms, auction sites, online payment services or IT administrators, tricking stupid people. Phishing: Malware infected websites that are linked in the form of phishing emails (Zheng et al., 2018).

*Figure 7. Phishing attack*

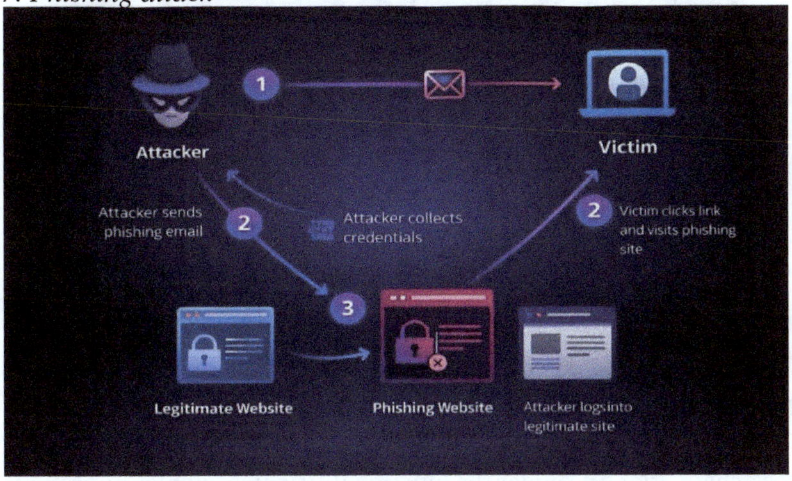


Phishing is a perfect example for Social Engineering. It is commonly used in email breaches (i.e. the hacker emails a victim a link with bank details or some personal data). Then, the user clicks that and gives all info asked by the hacker who will get all of user details. An illustration of a phishing is shown in Figure 7.

### 3.3.2 Unveiling Vulnerabilities of Web Attacks

With heavy web use, web based applications are also common. Websites form a conduit for communication with servers and the client, These applications are absolutely fundamental to everyday operations in many businesses, education systems, banking sectors for sale of goods retail and more making them incredible for work quality. Web is nothing but a centralized place where all of the data are stored of user like personal and sensitive information. Websites get hit more often because the sheer volume of internet users. Exist a software code-processing weakness, or system setting weakness in conjunction with defects discovered throughout website or web applications of OOTB. These flaws are distinct from the kind of flaws that affect either networks or resources (Jiang et al., 2019; Cong et al., 2024).

*Figure 8. Types of web-based attack*

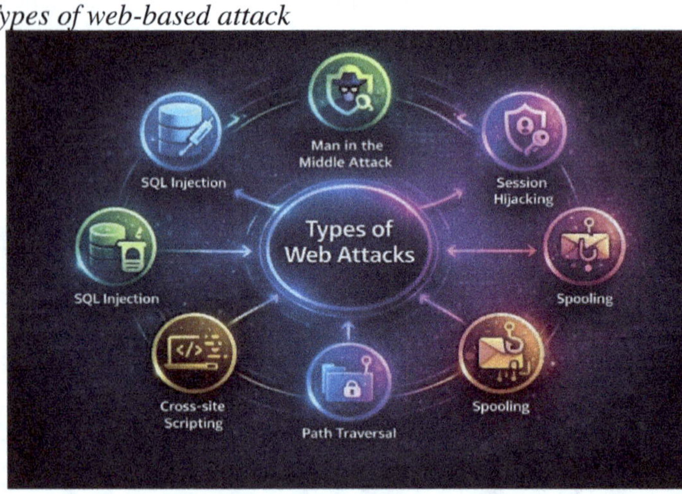


## 3.4 Cross-Chain Bridge Vulnerabilities

A cross-chain bridge provides the functionality which enables migration of assets and data between different blockchain networks and finally to bridge them together. Right now, assets in one blockchain are isolated from other blockchain networks ("USDT" on Solana is not able to be used in Ethereum as a different "USDT"). It allows users get the most of the pros and cons of different blockchains instead of limited the user to operate within a single one. Consider an Ethereum-based assets transfer to Solana network, this means the person can derive the massive speed of transactions and lesser cost that comes inearch Solana (GeeksforGeeks, 2025).

Cross-chain bridges are able to do this by locking the original assets on the source chain and creating corresponding tokens on the target chain, so that total supply stays the same.

### 3.4.1 Cross-Chain Vulnerability

The smart contracts of cross-chain bridges contain special types of defects known as Cross-chain vulnerability (CCV) (Contrast Security, n.d.; Nicholls, 2024). A fundamental problem with these contracts stems from their unintended lack of adequate access control alongside inconsistency with bridge semantics during two-blockchain asset transfers. Figure 9 illustrate following two examples CCV. The attack-inflicted contracts originated from two real circumstances involving Chain Swap and ThOR Chain (Sebastian Sinclair 2021). Our team has structured the original contract code for better readability purposes.

*Figure 9. Two motivating examples of CCV.*

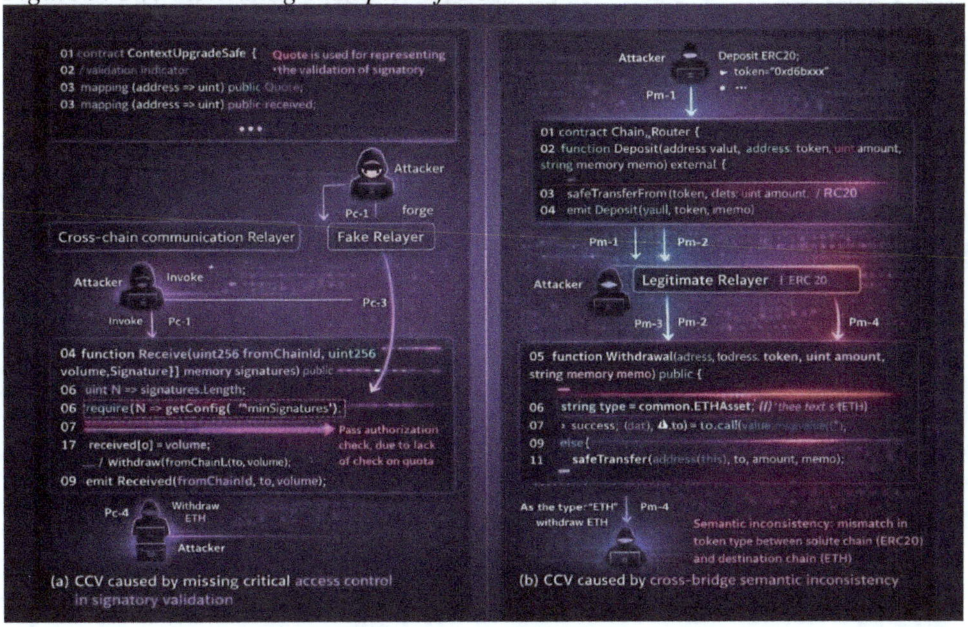

# 4. SECURITY BEST PRACTICE IN DAPPS DEVELOPMENT

In general, security is an inherent part of the development process, rather than a hindsight. This initiative will save you a great amount of frustration and time. Another point worth remembering is that the deployment of applications in a decentralized network exposes them to the possibility of being hacked, and therefore proactive is undoubtedly a crucial factor (Class Central, 2026).

## 4.1 Formal Verification and Smart Contract Security

Smart contracts have a code structure that allows developers to create applications that integrate decentralization with resilience and reliability in new applications that enhance user value. Such deals are security measures to secure handling of large volumes. Formal verification is one of the most appropriate approaches to strengthening the security of smart contracts (Fortinet, n.d.).

### 4.1.1 Techniques for Formal Verification of Smart Contracts

#### *Model Checking*

Formal verification Model checking is a complement to smart contracts in the form of complete verification of their formal models against registered operational requirements. These kinds of contracts are state-transition systems where the particular features are brought out in the temporal logic notation. The model checking entails the definition of mathematical abstractions of systems and propositional logic properties. It is due to this that the model-checking algorithm succeeds in the process of assessing system compliance with presented logical standards.

#### *Theorem Proving*

Theorem proving stands as a technical evaluation method which analyzes computational systems through mathematical logic to test their precision. The method transforms system and requirements information from contracts into mathematical equations for logical representation. The main objective of theorem proving is to create logical consistency among statements that follow a 'logical equivalence' also called 'logical bi-implication' relationship. The logical relationship between models of contracts and their characteristics becomes verifiable through theorem statements that formal inference systems confirm.

*Symbolic Execution*

Smart contracts get verified through symbolic execution because this method performs operations with symbolic data instead of real-world values. The organized structure enables users to get particular features from within the codebase of smart contracts.

An SMT solver enables users to check path predicate satisfiability through mathematical expressions made from symbolic execution traces using input values to find satisfying values. A particular value emerges from the SMT solver in case a weak point exists which demands further analysis of that specific region.

## 4.2 Static and Dynamic Analysis

*Static Analysis*- Static code analysis testing encompasses two primary methods: pattern-based and flow-based methodologies.Static code analysis through pattern detection verifies that code adheres to predetermined coding guidelines by scanning for faulty coding patterns that break these rules.

*Dynamic Analysis*- The testing approach of dynamic analysis detects program-based issues directly during runtime execution of those programs using an uncertain number of testing techniques. The internal analysis of application functions makes up dynamic analysis when testing embedded systems despite disregarding external behavior assessment. When the white box testing is applied by the testing professionals, the improvement of the code execution is determined (El-Hajj & Roelink, 2024).

### 4.2.1 Fuzzing

The ancillary quality assurance method, called Fuzz testing, assists programmers in finding bugs and security vulnerabilities within operating systems and network settings and code. This computational approach subjects software architectures to an extensive number of randomly produced inputs with the goal of triggering system errors or crashes. When a vulnerability becomes evident the fuzz testing platform enables marking the source of the matter.

### 4.2.2 RunTime Monitoring

Runtime Security serves as a complete protective system for software throughout its entire development cycle that extends from creation through testing to production and additional stages. The approach extends its security monitoring from a single application to include the entire application stack that contains frameworks alongside applications and APIs and libraries and custom code. The combination of real-time monitoring services with protective measures enables Runtime Security to identify security threats by studying application conduct and data movement and operational settings.

### 4.2.3 Automated Penetration Testing

The automated pen testing framework is an entire process of identifying weaknesses that are present in the security platform of a system. This was developed as a result of machine learning advances in technology that provided better outcomes than the antique vulnerability scanning processes. In the case of organizations, the use of sophisticated software tools is done, automated penetration test to identify familiar security vulnerabilities that manifest in un-patched servers and machines with poor internet security.

## 4.3 Secure Smart Contract Design Patterns

Blockchain transactions involving digital contracts are self-directed computer-generated programs (Kanga University, 2025; Freeman Law, 2023). Smart contract design patterns provide developers with reusable coding methods through established patterns which enhances code efficiency as well as lowers redundancy. The can serve a wide range of purposes, but can be seen as offering four main functions:

- Security patterns – To protect your contract against breaches.
- Efficiency patterns – To reduce the cost of executing your contract.
- Access control patterns – To manage who can execute the functions of your contract.
- Contract management patterns – To organize your contracts and how they interact,

### 4.3.1 CEI Pattern

Conducting business through the Check-Effects-Interactions (CEI) as shown in Figure 10 paradigm constitutes a standard procedure for Solidity language contracts that helps limit reentrancy security breaches (Isabella, 2023). A structured procedure for contract logic exists in the Check-Effects-Interactions (CEI) paradigm which begins by confirming essentials and proceeds with operations that modify state followed by mutual contacts with external agreements. The ordered sequence exists for the purpose of minimizing disturbances from unanticipated contacts with external agreements.

*Figure 10. CEI pattern*

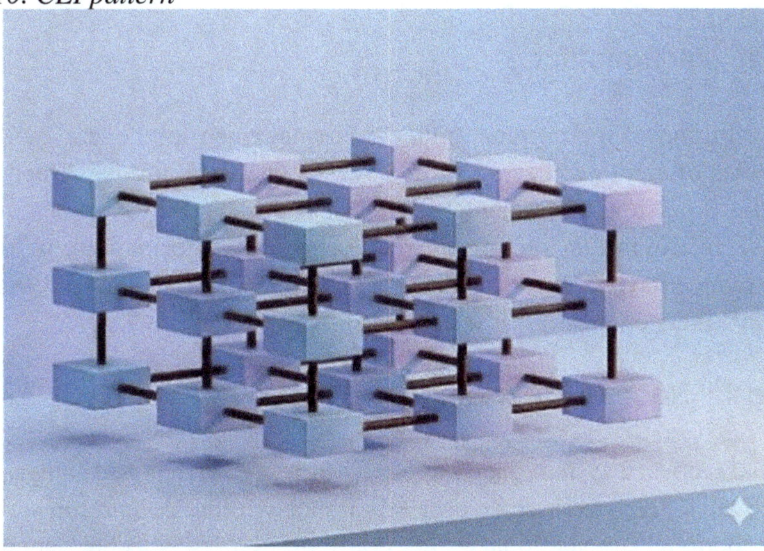

## 4.3.2 Fail-Safe Mechanism, Emergency Stop Function

The protective system known as a fail-safe mechanism as shown in Figure 11 provides protection against severe failures simultaneously assisting in fast system recovery. The protection of both users and the network through different protocol features exists within the cryptocurrency framework (Balawejder et al., 2019; Fortinet, n.d.). The redundant design of blockchain technology spreads replicated data across multiple nodes to keep the system functional after one failure occurs. Furthermore, security measures shield against hacks and fraud.

*Figure 11. Fail safe design*

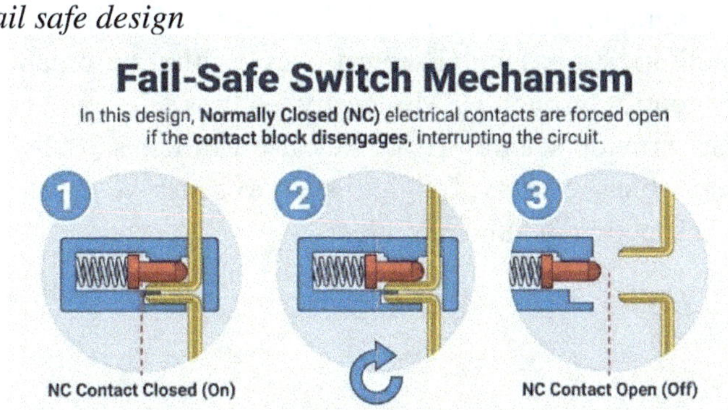

## 4.4 User Security Considerations

### 4.4.1 Key Management

The definition of the cryptographic key management procedures will involve the processes of creating cryptographic keys which are then safeguarded with secure storage provisions and safeguarded distribution and control management. The practice is effective in data integrity as well as encrypted information confidentiality based on reduced cyber threats to digital assets to achieve guaranteed availability (Planet Compliance, n.d.).

### 4.4.2 Social Recovery Wallet

A social recovery system added to cryptocurrency wallets adds a new security approach which helps to improve user experience without compromising the self-custody functions. Conventional wallet configuration leads to permanent money loss when functioning users lose their private keys or forget their passwords but social key recovery wallets ensure security for the user with the assistance of trusted network pals.

Social Recovery Wallets Work:- Social recovery wallets use the decentralized key reconstruction solutions that fall under the category of cryptographic recovery protocols. The recovery procedure involves the designated trusted entities having separate portions of both keys and key recovery essentials. When a recovery starts the designated persons work together to reconstruct necessary keys which restores ownership of digital assets and wallet to the account holder.

### 4.4.3 Hardware Security Modules

Security specialists build hardware security modules (HSM) as specific devices that defend cryptographic keys against illicit access while allowing management of authorized authorization. Digital security keys within an organization receive enforced access control through HSM security features.

Organizations provide secure private key use to their staff by implementing HSM encryption which restricts straight access to sensitive cryptographic assets and decreases their potential vulnerabilities.

# 5. CASE STUDIES OF HIGH-PROFILE DAPP SECURITY INCIDENTS

## 5.1 The DAO Hack (2016): Reentrancy Attack and Ethereum Governance Implications

### 5.1.1 What is a Distributed Autonomous Organization (DAO)?

The Ethereum community needed a hard fork to deal with a security breach that let a large amount of investor funds get stolen. The network partition into two separate chains led to the creation of Ethereum Classic and Ethereum following this operational choice. Ethereum split into separate chains known as Ethereum and Ethereum Classic because its members held distinct viewpoints on what the network should operate after the breach occurred (Anglen, 2024).

A distinctive aspect of blockchain elements comprises the Distributed Autonomous Organization (DAO) that showcases decentralized management through blockchain-operated organizational patterns. They differ from standard organizations as DAOs use code and smart contracts to run instead of traditional central command systems. Ethereum along with other blockchain networks let stakeholders and investors execute their governance role in essential business decisions.

### 5.1.2 A Brief History of The DAO Hack

The DAO appeared in 2015 as the collaborative outcome of Ethereum community development to enable collective human activities by applying smart contracts together with decentralized decision processes and verifiable code modules.

The DAO implementation began its operation on the Ethereum Mainnet3 in April 2016 after developers spent one year working on the proposal design as shown in Figure 12. The project developed an investment fund with distributed management that enabled community members to operate it for Ethereum's general advancement.

The DAO project obtained funding from its members through Ether contributions that served as initial investment capital after achieving operational status. The DAO finalized its aggregated funds from token holder investments to initiate investments based on their account. At the time of its launch The DAO drew substantial interest from Ethereum users because of its new architecture of autonomous decentralized platforms (DAOs) which yielded about 11,000 investors and accumulated approximately $150 million in Ether.

*Figure 12. How DAO hack works*

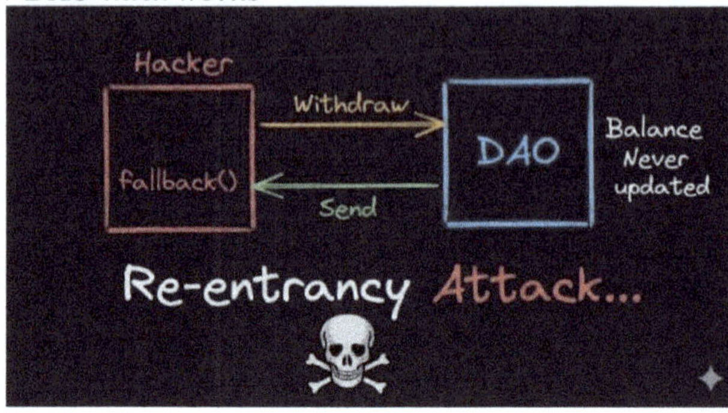


## 5.1.3 Response to The DAO Hack

Investors in The DAO experienced extreme distress when hackers concealed their funds transfer from the platform's system. The stakeholders of The DAO experienced significant trust crisis after this major security breach which produced significant levels of anxiety that prompted them to initiate extensive talks about a suitable response strategy.

Whitehats assembled as a group of hacktivists constructed a countermeasure to resolve the situation. The hacktivists implemented the reentrancy exploits for rapid fund extraction as their countermeasure against the attacker during The DAO incident. A quick escape pod function allowed investors to withdraw funds before their capital became exposed to loss.

The Ethereum founder Vitalik Buterin introduced a soft-fork proposal to cure DAO vulnerability retroactively when he appeared before the public on June 17, 2016. The proposal introduced Ethereum framework code that functioned to blacklist the attacker preventing unauthorized transfers of funds from The DAO together with its related organizations. The plan aimed to safeguard permanently all assets acquired by the original attacker.

## 5.1.4 The Hard-Fork Proposal

After the soft fork failure the Ethereum development team proposed a hard fork which targeted modifications of Ethereum blockchain historical records. Although its developers had technical capabilities to run the hard fork alone the team could not push the modification through without everyone agrees. The execution of the hard fork required cooperation among project stakeholders, such as exchanges, miners, and node operators, through a consensus-driven method. The successful hard fork took effect at block 192,000 on July 20, 2016 to revamp Ethereum network records and redirect the DAO funds in another smart contract for investor fund retrieval (Cyberscope, n.d.).

### 5.1.5 Responses to the Hard Fork

The DAO attack demonstrated smart contract vulnerabilities as shown in Figure 13 which serve as critical lessons for blockchain platform security instead of exposing Ethereum blockchain weaknesses. Ethereum introduced substantial security improvements after the attack occurred.

The blockchain transformed itself as a direct result of the hard fork that happened after the attack. Key stakeholders made difficult choices that transformed Ethereum and protected it during its most vulnerable period.

*Figure 13. Figures of DAO hack*

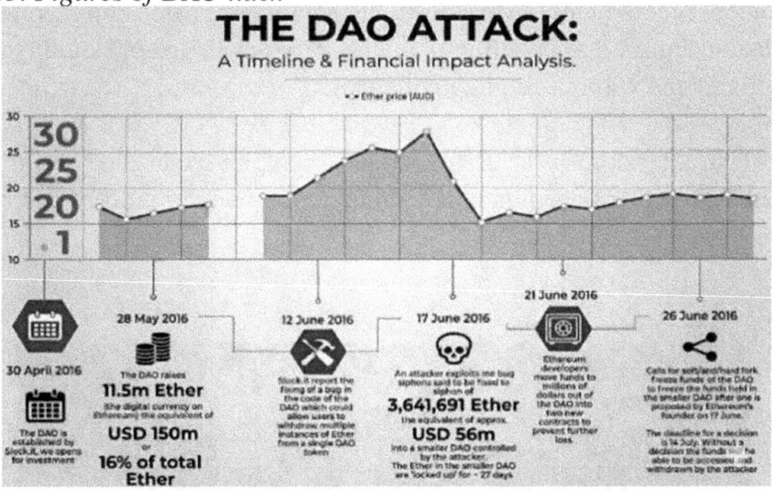


## 5.2 DeFi Flash Loan Attacks (2020-2023): Arbitrage-Based Exploitation, Governance Takeovers

### 5.2.1 Flash Loan

A flash loan system permits borrowers to borrow any amount of money from blockchainSupply without requiring any collateral during a single blockchain transaction. The DeFi-specific financial instrument serves TradFi replacement purposes through code-based protocols and distributed ledger technology but eliminates the need for trust in traditional financial organizations and intermediaries (Jain, n.d.).

### 5.2.2 Flash Loan Attacks Work

Flash loan attacks exploit protocol-provided temporary liquidation opportunities to execute price manipulation schemes as well as to exploit smart contract vulnerabilities and steal funds.

Flash loan attacks work through three sequential phases which form the whole operation.

1) The perpetrator takes out a loan by removing a considerable quantity of cryptocurrency from a DeFi platform without offering any form of security.
2) The funds obtained through borrowing must be used either for price manipulation of targeted cryptocurrencies or to detect weaknesses in DeFi smart contracts.
3) The attacker completes the loan repayment within the same mining block where the loan originated thus letting the temporary advantage of liquidity flow unmonitored and without needing collateral.

Flash loan attacks are successful because exploiters can repay their debts in the same block without needing collateral therefore making it difficult for lending platforms to prevent these attacks.

*Figure 14. Flash loan example*

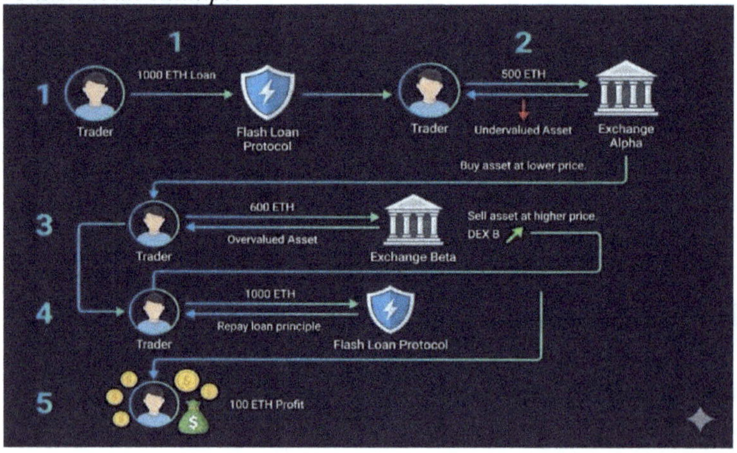

## 5.2.3 Real-World Cases of Flash Loan Attacks

### *1) Euler Finance: $197m (March 2023)*

The Euler Finance platform experienced a critical cyber assault because hackers took advantage of the interest rate calculation weakness. Fund transfer vulnerabilities in the eToken function of the platform enabled an attacker to exploit the system design. Borrowed assets could be erroneously converted into collateralized assets through this platform vulnerability to execute a complicated assault.

The attacker obtained funds through Tornado Cash and did so with on-chain entities along with a front-running bot and their private wallet. The attackers borrowed $30 million in DAI through Aave protocol flash loans to change how the platform functioned with its borrowing characteristics.

### *2) Cream Finance: $130m (October 2021)*

A $130 million loss resulted from the October 2021 decentralised finance (DeFi) attack on CREAM Finance. The USDV ault system of CREAM Finance experienced an exploitable weakness that caused this security vulnerability.

Two utilizers of Maker DAO and AAVE flash loans conducted a string of transactions through which they manipulated the underlying value of USDVault tokens. Through a meticulously planned manipulation the entity received a major increase of USDVault tokens and YUSD.

The entity reached a total sum of $1.5 billion USD and $500 million USDVault through repeated execution of the procedure. A portion of the USDVault tokens were exchanged for USD through redemption by the entity thus reducing the overall supply of USDVault. After this action the entity surged a matching value into the vault so its overall value from CREAM's valuation process doubled because it considers token supply as a value factor.

The entity controlled by the attacker was recorded to have USD valued at $3 billion on the vault system after converting $1.5 billion USD through the vault system values. After the flash loans were paid back the attacker stole $130 million from CREAM's vulnerable storage network.

### *3) BZx: $1m (November 2021)*

A sophisticated hacking was comprised of 2 separate attacks in which each process successfully exploited a different vulnerability in the BZx protocol. The attack vector was based on the reliance on a single oracle to determine the price of an asset, exposing the collateral pool to a flash loan manipulation as shown in Figure 15. After exploiting this vulnerability at the beginning, the hacker performed a second attack using another method. The second attack took advantage of the vulnerability of

BZx's use of the Uniswap spot price as an oracle, which was manipulated in order to make the value of the collateral seem higher than it was.

In the first attack, he borrowed a large amount of ETH using a flash loan and placed a 5x short position on the ETH-wBTC trading pair, which caused significant slippage. As such, a second transaction actually exploited the vulnerability by causing the Uniswap Synthetix USD price to change, thus enabling a double-dipping borrowing of more ETH via BZx as collateral.

These incidents showed the need to implement strong security measures and improve the price determination process using multiple trusted oracles to relieve the critical vulnerabilities that exist in the BZx protocol. These malicious attacks had unfortunate results, with losses of over $985K.

*Figure 15. Flash loan*

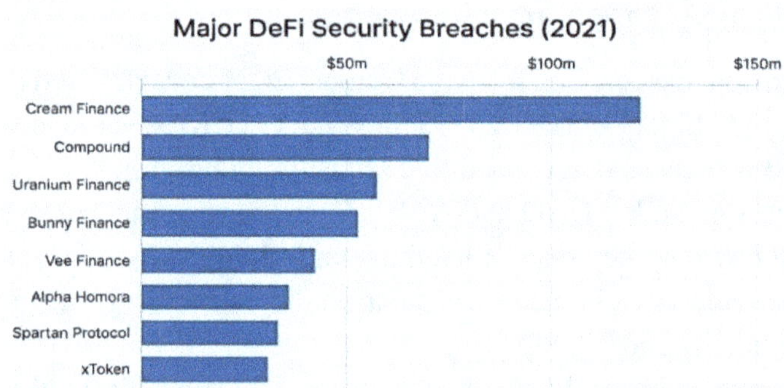


## 6. EMERGING SECURITY TECHNOLOGIES FOR DAPPS

### 6.1 Zero-Knowledge Proofs (ZKPs) and Privacy Enhancements

Zero-knowledge proofs are a complex and profound cryptographic technique that allows a "prover" to prove knowledge of a special piece of data relevant to a claim using advanced algorithms. This validation can take place as part of an interactive or non-interactive manner.

This is exemplified by a cavernous cave with a circular path, an entrance that isn't marked, and a door that's hidden. Somewhat similarly, Alice, the advocate, has the key to open the hidden door, and Bob, the validator, wishes to verify Alice's knowledge without learning more than whether Alice's claim is valid. Alice is just going to show that she knows the key because she can walk the circular path forever.

Each instance of her doing this increases her chances of picking the right exit. Thus, Bob can conclude that Alice holds the key because she has a high probability of picking the right exit, and he is not privy to any of the secret information.

### 6.1.1 ZK-SNARKs

This is made possible by the ZK-SNARKs proof, where a statement's correctness can be checked without repeating calculations and some inputs can be kept secret.

The succinctness of this protocol guarantees that the verification is not much longer than the computation itself, so that a verifier does not need to independently compute the output. This is done using empirical sampling methods. But using random sampling means it stops being deterministic about finding purposefully introduced falsehoods. This is done thanks to polynomial commitments which has three main implementations: the Fast Reed-Solomon Verification Algorithm (FRI), bulletproofs and Kate.

One of the key characteristics of a ZK-SNARK is that they are Non-Interactive, meaning that the prover does not need to interact multiple rounds with the verifier. On the other hand, interactive proving would need back-and-forth communication, potentially making it less effective.

### 6.1.2 ZK-STARKs

When used with large witnesses, ZK-STARKs (zero-knowledge succinct non-interactive argument of knowledge, a variant of zk-SNARKs) are more scalable ZKSnark family.

The STARK protocols are cheaper than other more scalable, characterized with high overhead on verification, and as such they are preferred when scaling is key to this level.

One of the key advantages of STARK protocol uniquely lacked a trusted setup, instead using publicly verifiable randomness to derive public parameters, reducing transparency for a common reference string (CRS) generation process that is not trusted, especially in some cases the credibility of how public parameters derived.

### 6.1.3 Bulletproofs

Bulletproofs are more of a weird zero-knowledge argument of knowledge that asserts the existence of a secret in a small interval. In combination of being so succinct, non-interactive and not necessarily based on trusted setup they are a great way to establish commitments in Confidential Transactions.

Bulletproofs differ from other proving systems of a similar ilk due to a combination of multiple range proofs in one super succinct proof vs. lengthier proofs when compared with zk-SNARKs and despite a longer verification times compared to the usual.

## 6.2 Multi-Party Computation (MPC) and Threshold Cryptography

MPC (Multi-Party Computation) and Threshold Cryptography are two cryptographic methods for maintaining the security and privacy in decentralized systems which are very important. MPC enables multiple parties to jointly compute a function with their private inputs using MPC in the clear, while not revealing any information about those inputs to other parties. This ensures that no party learns another's input and is therefore appropriate in a setting like secure computation where keeping the privacy of data is desireable (secure auctions, joint data analysis).

In contrast, Threshold Cryptography means you take a secret (think private key) and split it into various shares to need a predetermined quantity of shares to use it for tasks like decryption or signing. It reduces this to a requirement of one party not having the whole secret, which increases stabilization. In reality one may split a private key among five people with three of them to regroup and work with the key. In this way, a system will still secure even if some participants are compromised or non available.

### 6.2.1 Threshold Signatures

Advanced digital asset management and the need for more robust security protocols speaks to the need to be encrypting private keys from prying eyes. Threshold Signatures Scheme (TSS) is an entirely new class of cryptographic signature which builds upon security further. New comer to the industry and has been taken hold by service providers as it serves to shield a secure information flow allowing for limiting external influence at the moment, especially when it comes to so called enemy sharks — the hackers and phishers

Threshold Signatures Scheme work(TSS): It would be a great misconception to think of threshold signatures without heading to the basic idea of cryptocurrencies from root. The most important part here is the public key cryptography—which is based on a cryptographically bound pair of keys (the public one you have to encrypt the message and the corresponding private one for decryption).

### 6.2.2 Decentralized Custody Models

Decentralized Custody Model Describes the architecture for managing digital assets (such as cryptocurrencies) with multiple participants and no reliance on one central organization.

These assets, that require split control of private keys (access and handling for assets) by techniques such in multi-signature wallets or secret sharing.

*Decentralized custody models work:* The model works on splitting the private keys into pieces, custodians store one fragment each. A multi-signature wallet for instance might make a transaction require more than one to consent so it is not all or nothing decision-making. It prevents unauthorised access and limits the risks on events such as hacking or fraud which are found when using centralized storage. However, this framework comes with the requirement of coordinating and a trusted custodian key management. Difficulties are still here, such as complexity and scalability but it offers exceptional security and user oversight. As decentralized finance (DeFi) proliferates, this is a bright outlook of secure and independent asset management in the ever-evolving digital space.

## 7. REGULATORY AND COMPLIANCE CONSIDERATIONS FOR DAPPS SECURITY

### 7.1 Legal Challenges in Smart Contract Enforcement

The blockchain-based software program known as smart contracts enables automated agreement authentication and execution. The software program known as Smart Contracts carries out self-executing functions because the entire contract code gets translated into programming code yet execution happens only after all stated conditions are met. The technology operates under the name Distributed Ledger Technology.

Smart contracts operate on the principle of "code as law," where predefined conditions execute automatically eliminating the need for intermediaries. However, they face legal jurisdictional constraints that challenge their enforcement as shown in Figure 16.

### 7.1.1 Code as Law

1. Based on blockchain protocols, smart contracts self-execute which eliminates the need of intermediaries.

2. Advocates argue that before the deployment of the code, the execution of code should be a final while improving operational efficiency and minimising legal disputes.

*Technological Challenges*

1. Scalability and Transaction Speed of the contracts.
2. Interoperability and Integration of the smart contracts.
3. Smart contracts need evaluation of their cyber safety to determine their security status.
4. Key Management (Consensus Protocol).
5. Lack of Maturity and Mass Adoption in the smart contracts.
6. Data privacy features should be implemented in contracts to protect information confidentiality.

*Legal Challenges*

1. Cross border issues - The decentralized structure of blockchains creates problems when trying to identify which jurisdiction applies to settlement disputes between parties.
2. Contract law compliance - Smart contracts often fail to meet traditional contract standards since they lack Legal requirements like mutual consent, consideration, and individual capacity to enter agreements.
3. Immutability issues - Code errors alongside unforeseen circumstances as well as issues and errors in the code become extremely challenging to fix properly in a proper manner when legal intervention is unavailable.
4. Consumer protection and regulatory concerns - Government protection measures and regulatory standards exist to safeguard users from unsatisfactory and faulty smart contract operations.
5. Lack of legal recognition - Various jurisdictions fail to acknowledge smart contracts as binding legal agreements. Smart contracts face legal obstacles because various jurisdictions refuse to provide them with legally binding agreement status.
6. Smart contract operations remain unclear because jurisdictions fail to define ownership boundaries while contract laws cannot enforce the agreements and the industry lacks standardized regulations.

### 7.1.2 Navigating Compliance in Decentralized Finance (DeFi)

*Figure 16. Illustrating the challenges in decentralized finance*

Decentralized Finance (DeFi) works as a revolutionary force that transforms financial operations into new directions. DeFi improves transparency while eliminating reliance on intermediaries, and reducing the transaction fees of the platforms which are providing peer-to-peer lending, decentralized exchanges, and automated market makers. DeFi networks present major difficulties for compliance operations although they deliver several financial advantages.

## 7.2 KYC and AML Challenges

Implementing KYC and AML measures in the decentralized finance is a big challenge. Traditional finances mandate the identification of the customers by the institutions to ensure that they are not involved in illegal activities. However, Transactions occur directly between users through blockchain technology because DeFi platforms often do not have a central body to perform this verification makes it difficult to track identities. Analyzing how KYC and AML procedures decrease criminal activity leads to a need for innovative methods to perform these standards within decentralized systems.

### 7.2.1 Regulatory Frameworks and Guidelines

*Financial Action Task Force (FATF)*

With the rise of cryptocurrencies and decentralized platforms, the FATF introduced guidelines that apply to Virtual Asset Service Providers (VASPs). These guidelines serve to fight both anti-money laundering (AML) and Combating the financing of Terrorism(CFT). The FATF's "Travel Rule" is a regulation that requires

Virtual Asset Service Providers (VASPs) to gather and share information about the people involved in cryptocurrency transactions. This rule is particularly affecting decentralized finance (DeFi) platforms as they work to implement Know Your Customer (KYC) and Anti-Money Laundering (AML) processes

### *U.S. Securities and Exchange Commission (SEC)*

The commission has displayed a keen interest in DeFi, in particular, when the platforms are providing their services comparable to traditional financial services like lending, borrowing, and trading of securities. Under U.S. law, there is a test known as the Howey Test for determining if an asset is a security or not. Assuming the DeFi token or platform satisfies these criteria it becomes subject to SEC regulation and therefore requires registration and reporting.

### *European Union's Markets in Crypto-Assets (MiCA)*

The European Union has introduced MiCA regulation that assists in creating a general regulatory framework about digital assets. MiCA aims to control the services of DeFi, such as stablecoins, exchanges and token offerings, to ensure that investors are not left vulnerable to financial risk. This probably demands DeFi platforms, which issues tokens or delivers some types of services to satisfy disclosure, KYC, and operational requirements.

### *Bank Secrecy Act (BSA) in the U.S.*

BSA also requires financial institutions to assist the U.S. government agencies in identifying and intercepting money laundering. When a DeFi platform is viewed as a financial institution, it might have to submit to AML regulations, which necessitates the provision of suspicions reports, as well as maintaining customer records.

### *Decentralized Compliance Models*

Decentralized compliance models spread the responsibility and decision-making throughout an organization so that localized knowledge and flexibility are combined with alignment and compliance with strategic organization. This approach is different from the centralized models since there is a centralized authority who makes all the decisions.

### *Key Characteristics of the Decentralized Compliance Model*

- Distributed Decision-Making:

Instead of having all decisions made by one central authority, the power to make decisions is shared among different departments or business units.

- Local Expertise:

Each unit can customize its compliance strategies to fit its unique needs and risks.

- Increased Agility:

Decentralized models allow for quicker responses to changing regulations and emerging threats.

- Enhanced Empowerment:

Different levels within the organization can take responsibility for compliance, fostering a culture of security awareness.

- Resilience:

Decentralization lowers the risk of failures because different units can operate independently.

## 7.4 Ethical and Governance Considerations

DAOs are organizations built on blockchain technology that are managed by their community. DAOs follow a set of self-executing governance rules written in their blockchain operation that runs autonomously from the outside influence of a central authority. Risks of DAO goverance are shown in Table 1.

*Table 1. Risks of DAOs governance*

| **Lack of Participation** | **Voting is optional in DAOs which can affect the number of community members and results in lack of participation.** |
|---|---|
| Rigidity | Voting systems are time-consuming, which can hamper the project to change and adapt quickly. |
| Voting Manipulation | Power concentration together with corruption and bribery and inappropriate and rigorous behaviours can damage the DAO governance structure. |
| Lack of legal clarity | The system experiences destructive activities because it lacks established legal frameworks. |

# 8. FUTURE DIRECTIONS AND OPEN RESEARCH CHALLENGES

## 8.1 Post-Quantum Cryptography for Blockchain and Dapps

Businesses remain concerned about data security because quantum computing vulnerabilities inherent in the future and this is why urgent adoption of post-quantum cryptographic systems is necessary. Blockchain security experts actively work to prevent potential future attacks known as "harvest now, decrypt later" since such intrusions can result in the decryption of stolen data.

### 8.1.1 Quantum Resistant Cryptographic Algorithms

The post quantum techniques used within this blockchain system protect against quantum computers' computational power. Through its implemented techniques Quantum-resistant blockchains delivers protection of transactions data and overall system integrity. Quantum-resistant blockchains have been designed to protect from dangers which quantum computing poses to conventional cryptographic algorithms because they become exposed to vulnerabilities.

*Key Algorithms*

Quantum systems operate based on key algorithms which determines the efficiency and capability of the quantum systems. These algorithms are employed to overcome the problems that are unsolvable from classical computers. Algorithms such as the Quantum Approximate Optimization Algorithm (QAOA) and the Variational Quantum Eigensolver (VQE) are designed to tackle optimization problems and simulate molecular structures, respectively. These algorithms allow researchers to model quantum systems with incredible accuracy, unlocking new discoveries in physics, biology, and engineering.

Shor's algorithm stands out as the most celebrated quantum algorithm because it factors large integers at an exponential speed outperforming classical algorithms for the best-known results. Security of RSA and other encryption schemes depends on factoring large numbers being difficult to solve since their security relies on this computational intractability. The discovery of Shor's algorithm creates an immediate requirement for quantum-resistant cryptographic methods because it breaches standard encryption standards.

Another quantum algorithm known as Grover's algorithm gives exponential speedup to search through unstructured problems. While not as dramatic as Shor's exponential advantage, it still provides a substantial improvement for certain applications. The search process through databases and solution of NP-complete problems becomes faster with Grover's algorithm compared to traditional computing methods.

The technique offers good opportunities for implementation across multiple domains including optimization, machine learning and cryptography.

## 8.2 Security in Multi-Chain and Layer-2 Scaling Solutions

Layer 2 scaling solutions bring enhanced transaction speed and scalability to Ethereum blockchain while preserving all the security characteristics provided by its system. Some popular solutions include:

### 1. State Channels

Users can perform off-chain transactions through state channels with final states recorded on-chain.

How it works:

Two parties create an open connection between each other. The parties exchange a number of transactions off-chain. After completion the final on-chain state becomes recorded.

- Examples: Bitcoin Lightning Network, Raiden Network (Ethereum).

### 2. Plasma

Plasma serves as an application development platform which shifts transactions to child chains called Plasma chains that are linked to Ethereum's main blockchain

How it works:

Plasma chains are operating independently while remaining linked to Ethereum. Plasma chains submit a summary(or checkpoint) to Ethereum for Transactions to occur. Users can use the main chain for resolving disputes when they submit proofs.

- Examples:OMG Network (OmiseGo).

### 3. Optimistic Rollups

The optimistic rollup system combines various transactions into dense packages and submit it to Ethereum as a compressed transaction. Optimistic rollups operate under the principle that all transactions submitted should be considered valid unless strong evidence proves otherwise.

How it works:

Ethereum receives one condensed batch form of multiple off-chain transactions and submitted as a compressed version of this batch to Ethereum. Validators have the ability to create fraud proof reports during transaction detection of fraudulent activity which can be submitted to challenge freely.

- Examples: Optimism, Arbitrum.

### 4. ZK-Rollups (Zero-Knowledge Rollups)

ZK-Rollups aggregates transactions into one batch like other rollups yet relies on zero-knowledge proofs (zk-SNARKs) to validate the batch instantly before Ethereum processing.

How it works:

Off-chain processing of multiple transactions produces a zero knowledge proof as a validity verification which gets submitted to Ethereum for validation.

- Examples:ZKSync, StarkWare.

### 5. Hybrid Rollups (Optimistic + ZK-Rollups)

HYBRID ROLLUPS features all essential components from the group of optimistic and zk-rollup protocols. The solution seeks to integrate both positive attributes and negative aspects of these technologies. Optimistic rollups helps in general-purpose contracts and ZK-rollups in specific high-throughput use cases.

## 8.3 Automated Security Verification Tools for Smart Contracts

### 1. Cyberscan

The investors benefit from Cyberscan as one of the Cyberscope products designed for informed investment decisions. The tool provides security evaluations of smart contracts with its particular focus. The single source of truth offered by Cyberscan contains all necessary metrics. Users benefit from this system because it combines different source checks to discover risks that may exist in blockchain ventures.

### 2. Safescan

Safescan serves as a necessary tool for Web3 security since it fights against criminal activities in the field. Background checks run automatically by this program examine the transactions from the specified address. This product generates reports containing associated findings that present users with wallet history insights and warning alerts which link to particular transactions.

### 3. Similarityscan

Similarityscan detects how similar any smart contract is to available popular smart contracts that exist within databases. The Similarity Scan technology evaluates two source codes based on character matching and phrase analysis between the contracts. The security analysis process includes token comparison and commonality detection where it matches code units called tokens before identifying shared elements.

### 4. MythX

As a cloud-based tool MythX enables programmers to access different security analysis applications including static and dynamic analysis applications to find vulnerabilities in Ethereum smart contracts. Smart contract developers choose to deploy MythX and identify and fix all code vulnerabilities before launching their Ethereum network. Through its automatic 6 features MythX generates exploits which demonstrate potential damages from found vulnerabilities.

### 5. Echidna

The intuitive smart contract security tool Echidna works in the Remix and Truffle development tools. It supports Multiple contract languages, Solidity, Vyper, and Bamboo, to make it a flexible solution for blockchain developers.Echidna has robust reporting of security vulnerabilities and of property violations running alongside 2y advanced testing features – it's easy for developers to find and fix any potential issues

## 9. CONCLUSION

In short, despite the benefits that dApps have, like enhanced privacy, a higher level of transparency, and more control over the user, they also have severe security implications. The safety of smart contracts depends on the manner in which they were written; whether they had vulnerabilities, or whether a human error occurred during the development process, or because of malicious dApps and data breaches. The only way to be able to fully address these risks and prevent this situation is to have a rigorous process for smart contract auditing, secure development practices, and ongoing monitoring of the deployment process. As always, educating users on security best practices and developing strict privacy mechanisms will be important to create trust and assure the future of dApps in the blockchain ecosystem.This chapter provide us with the knowledge of how there are legal challenges in the enforcement of the Smart Contract.These challenges includes both technological and legal challenges, because the smart contract operate on the principle of code as law. This chapter also includes Decentralized finance, it's regulatory frame work and Decentralized conelience models.This chapter creates a foundation of dapps by introducing the readers with distribution ledger technologies, decentralized storage. For readers understanding this includes some case studies, real world cases on some dapps security incidents. Security in multi-chain and layer to scaling solutions are some ways to overcome these challenges. This chapter also provide the readers some automated security verification tools for smart contracts to ensure security, transparency of their data.

## REFERENCES


Alchemy. (n.d.). *List of 26 decentralized storage tools (2025).* https://www.alchemy.com/dapps/best/decentralized-storage-tools

Anglen, J. (2024, December 6). *Future-proofing blockchain: Embracing quantum-resistant cybersecurity in 2024.* Rapid Innovation. https://www.rapidinnovation.io/post/quantum-resistant-blockchain-preparing-for-the-future-of-cybersecurity-in-2024

Apillon. (2023, November 22). *The top 7 decentralized cloud storage platforms in 2023.* Medium. https://blog.apillon.io/the-top-7-decentralized-cloud-storage-platforms-in-2023-d9bdfc0e1f2d

Balawejder, B., Dankiewicz, R., & Ostrowska-Dankiewicz, A. (2019). The role of insurance in cyber risk management in enterprises. *Humanities and Social Sciences Quarterly*, *26*. Advance online publication. DOI: 10.7862/rz.2019.hss.33

Bitcoin Wiki. (n.d.). *Hash time locked contracts.* https://en.bitcoin.it/wiki/Hash_Time_Locked_Contracts

Chainlink. (2022, November 3). *Introducing the Chainlink on-chain data directory: Data.eth.* Chainlink Blog. https://blog.chain.link/introducing-the-chainlink-on-chain-data-directory

Class Central. (2026, January 15). *Solidity advanced: Secure smart contracts & DApp development.* https://www.classcentral.com/course/coursera-packt-solidity-advanced-secure-smart-contracts-dapp-development-fqajl-352879

Cong, N., Toan, L., & Thanh, T. (2024). An overview of static and dynamic analysis in application security testing. *Journal of Military Science and Technology*, *99*, 1–11. DOI: 10.54939/1859-1043.j.mst.99.2024.1-11

Contrast Security. (n.d.). *What is runtime security?* https://www.contrastsecurity.com/glossary/runtime-security

Cyberscope. (n.d.). *The top 10 smart contract security tools.* https://www.cyberscope.io/blog/the-top-10-smart-contract-security-tools

Dhananjay, S., Kumar, V., Agrawal, H., Patankar, P., & Jain, S. A. (2019). Distributed ledger technology based data minimization of digital identities. *International Journal of Advance Research, Ideas and Innovations in Technology, 5*(3). https://www.ijariit.com

El-Hajj, M., & Roelink, B. O. (2024). Evaluating the efficiency of ZK-SNARK, ZK-STARK, and Bulletproof in real-world scenarios: A benchmark study. *Information (Basel), 15*(8), 463. Advance online publication. DOI: 10.3390/info15080463

Fan, T. (n.d.). *Ethereum 2.0 for dummies—Part 1: Why upgrade?* Medium. https://medium.com/coinmonks/ethereum-2-0-for-dummies-part-1-why-upgrade-112d8f5b6d88

Fortinet. (n.d.). *What is cyber insurance? Why is it important? Risk coverages.* https://www.fortinet.com/resources/cyberglossary/cyber-insurance

Fortinet. (n.d.). *What is hardware security module (HSM)?* https://www.fortinet.com/resources/cyberglossary/hardware-security-module

Freeman Law. (2023, October 12). *Decentralized governance mechanisms: Blockchain technology.* https://freemanlaw.com/decentralized-governance-mechanisms/

GeeksforGeeks. (2025, July 23). *Static testing vs dynamic testing.* https://www.geeksforgeeks.org/software-engineering/difference-between-static-and-dynamic-testing/

*International Journal of Engineering and Technology Research.* (2024). IAEME Publication. https://iaeme.com/Home/issue/IJETR?Volume=9&Issue=2

Isabella, M. (2023, March 23). *Bounties within the DAO ecosystem.* Lifespan.io. https://www.lifespan.io/topic/bounties-within-the-dao-ecosystem

Jain, J. (n.d.). Smart contracts & blockchain—Evolving jurisprudence in India. *Journal of Applicable Law & Jurisprudence, 1*(1). https://calr.in/wp-content/uploads/2021/01/Smart-Contracts-Blockchain-%E2%80%93-Evolving-Jurisprudence-in-India.pdf

Jiang, X., Liu, M., Yang, C., Liu, Y., & Wang, R. (2019). A blockchain-based authentication protocol for WLAN mesh security access. *Computers, Materials & Continua, 58*(1), 45–59. DOI: 10.32604/cmc.2019.03863

Kanga University. (2025, June 3). *What are threshold signatures?* https://kanga.exchange/university/en/courses/4-primus-course/lessons/43-what-are-threshold-signatures/

Nicholls, M. (2024, March 25). *A brief guide to automated penetration testing.* Redscan. https://www.redscan.com/news/a-brief-guide-to-automated-penetration-testing

Open Knowledge Repository. (n.d.). *Open Knowledge Repository.* https://openknowledge.worldbank.org/entities/publication/c3df3394-494f-5941-8a49-93c6e2fe236f

Planet Compliance. (n.d.). *Navigating compliance in decentralized finance (DeFi).* https://www.planetcompliance.com/financial-compliance/navigating-compliance-defi/

Posey, B. (2025, April 24). *Compare 7 decentralized data storage networks.* SearchStorage. https://www.techtarget.com/searchstorage/tip/Comparing-4-decentralized-data-storage-offerings

Sharma, P., Jindal, R., & Borah, M. D. (2021). Blockchain-based decentralized architecture for cloud storage system. *Journal of Information Security and Applications*, *62*, 102970. Advance online publication. DOI: 10.1016/j.jisa.2021.102970

Szabo, N. (1996). *Smart contracts: Building blocks for digital markets.* https://www.scribd.com/document/786841851/Nick-Szabo-Smart-Contracts-Building-Blocks-for-Digital-Markets-1996

Wan, Z., Xia, X., Lo, D., Chen, J., Luo, X., & Yang, X. (2021, May). Smart contract security: A practitioners' perspective. *In 2021 IEEE/ACM 43rd international conference on software engineering (ICSE) (pp. 1410-1422). IEEE.*\

Zheng, Z., Xie, S., Dai, H.-N., Chen, X., & Wang, H. (2018). Blockchain challenges and opportunities: A survey. *International Journal of Web and Grid Services*, *14*(4), 352–375. DOI: 10.1504/IJWGS.2018.095647

Chapter 5

# Blockchain-Based Forest Plant Record Storage System Using Hyperledger Fabric

**Abhisake Sinha**
http://orcid.org/0009-0001-8779-0003
*Tripura University, India*

**Sukanta Chakraborty**
http://orcid.org/0000-0003-0205-8532
*Tripura University, India*

**Abhishek Majumder**
http://orcid.org/0000-0001-8451-0451
*Tripura University, India*

## ABSTRACT

*In today's era, securing data related to environmental and forest department has become a crucial aspect. Integrating blockchain based technologies with the forest data management is an effective solution. Blockchain technology such as Hyperledger Fabric is a permissioned blockchain. It can be helpful in storing the forest data in a more accurate, secure and tamper-proof manner. In this work a Hyperledger Fabric based framework has been developed to store the forest data in a secure and cost effective manner. The developed system can be used in the forest department to improve security and to monitor forest activities like illegal logging. In the developed system all the records are stored in an immutable manner. Its decentralized and permissioned nature helps to prevent any unauthorized participants, which*

DOI: 10.4018/979-8-3373-9053-6.ch005

*means it only allows the participants that are authorized or permitted to perform within the network. The proposed technique has been implemented on Fabric 2.5 Test-Network. Performance analysis revels that the proposed system can be implemented in real time.*

## INTRODUCTION

In this digital era data security has become a crucial aspect, for ensuring data confidentiality, integrity and transparency. To address these challenges Hyperledger Fabric is used in the field of forest management. Earth has a vast variety of flora and fauna that almost covers half of the land. They are the reason for life on earth and are home for many living organisms. So preserving the forest becomes a very important factor (Paulino et al., 2024). The forest department acts as a protector of these vast forest ecosystems. They play an important role in protecting animals and plants, conserving the environment and also ensuring the potential use of forest resources (Bhatt et al., 2024). The work carried out by the forest department for protecting the forest includes afforestation, monitoring all kinds of plant species, preventing illegal logging and organizing activities and programs regarding forest conservation (Bhatt et al., 2024). The records, data or the information that are collected by the forest department are stored in traditional data storage systems and are mostly centralized. The data stored in the centralized traditional data storage system are very likely to have security issues as they lack in providing security. Some of such security issues are unauthorized access, interpreting the data or missing data. Integrating blockchain in forest department data management systems can prevent most of the security issues faced by the traditional data storage system (Ucbas et al., 2023). Blockchain technology such as Hyperledger fabric is a permissioned blockchain. It is well fitted in industrial and enterprise applications used in the forest department. It can resolve the security issues because of its decentralization, temper-proofing and immutability nature.

Emerging technology such as Blockchain helps organizations in resolving the security issues by providing immutability, transparency and various data management processes. Blockchain platforms specifically Hyperledger Fabric works efficiently in the forest department and can ensure proper sustainable management.

### Hyperledger Fabric

Public blockchains are open for everyone like Ethereum and Bitcoin. Unlike public blockchain, hyperledger fabric is known to operate in a closed environment. It is a permissioned blockchain platform that is often used at the enterprise level.

Hyperledger fabric stands out to be very flexible, efficient and secure with the development process due to its various features that the public blockchain lacks. It is used and well known for its compatible nature of decentralization, transparency and immutability. Some of the key features of Hyperledger fabric are:

- Permissioned platform: Hyperledger fabric is a permissioned blockchain platform that is basically designed for industrial and enterprise applications. To be a part of the network, users must be verified and authorized. Hyperledger fabric is most suitable for the organizations that rely on trust and confidentiality. The users must have proper identification and credentials for joining the network, which helps in resolving the issues related to security and accountability.
- Modular architecture: One of the important features of Hyperledger fabric is its modular architecture that helps in maintaining and building blockchain driven solutions to carry out specific tasks. It helps in structuring the blockchain network in such a manner that a high degree of scalability, security, resiliency and confidentiality is ensured.
- Channels: It is a feature of hyperledger fabric which allows participants within the network to communicate securely and privately. The network can have a single channel for communication or it can have multiple channels based on the organization's needs. It works within the network in such a way that the participants can share information or data through a dedicated channel which cannot be accessed by other entities providing fully secure and private communication.
- Chaincode: It is like a smart contract that automates business logic which helps in ensuring accuracy and efficiency for the ongoing processes. It includes several rules and policies that help in maintaining the flow of transactions and the operations that are to be executed. Basically chaincodes are responsible for the interaction with the network's ledger enforcing the rules and policies that are defined.
- Scalability and high performance: The scalability and high performance issues are often faced in various blockchain platforms which can be controlled with the help of Hyperledger fabric. This feature allows for large scale deployment resulting in efficient and faster transactions (Melo et al., 2022).

The hyperledger fabric platform is well suited for organizations that rely on security, confidentiality and trust. The various features of the fabric help an organization to form a network with many participants who interact with each other in an organized and secure manner with proper identifications. It provides privilege to every participant in the network. Each network participant has its role to play and performs according to that which helps in keeping the network cleanly functional and reduces the chances of mistakes. It also helps in reducing the workload because of its chaincode feature which automates the operations that are to be carried out. The chaincode automatically activates in the network when certain criteria and arguments are triggered and stops when the operations are completed. Each and every transaction in the network is stored in the ledger and shared to every participant in the network.

## Why Hyperledger Fabric in the Forest Department?

Hyperledger fabric is a permissioned blockchain platform that is mostly used at the enterprise level. It can be utilized by the forest department to counter most of the key challenges faced by traditional forest management systems (Melo et al., 2022). It can overcome the challenges and make the forest management system more reliable due to its ability such as data transparency, authorized access, tamper-proof data storage, and immutability. The forest department's traditional system stores crucial forest data such as forest conservation plans, logging records, data related to wildlife tracking into various databases and handwritten registry that eventually leads to inefficiencies, high risk of corruption, very limited data transparency, and data tempering. By including blockchain technology such as hyperledger fabric into the forest department, it is possible to develop a permissioned, tamper-proof, decentralized and immutable ledger where information, transactions and every slice of data are securely maintained, stored and shared in the blockchain network and can be easily accessed in real-time.

The proposed Hyperledger fabric based system developed for the forest department mainly focuses on conservation of plants to keep the forest areas alive and evergreen. The technology helps to track tree details such as species, location, tress use, logging etc. in an efficient, secure, tamperproof and immutable manner that is transparent. It can be accessed by everyone who is part of the network. The main goal is to keep track of tree details such that if a tree gets missing or had been cut down illegally within the reach of forest department area it would immediately get recorded on the network which will ultimately help the forest officers to gather information about the missing tree. In such cases the features of the hyperledger fabric stands out to be a crucial factor and makes the system efficient and reliable.

## Motivation

Hyperledger Fabric is a permissioned blockchain platform that allows only authenticated and authorized participants for accessing and interacting with the network system, making it ideal for the environment that runs on confidentiality and trust. It provides components that are customizable like membership services and different consensus mechanisms, to overcome the problems and to provide efficient solutions for the specific needs of an organization. By keeping transaction records in a decentralized, tamper-proof and immutable manner, Hyperledger Fabric ensures accountability and reduces high chances of corruption and data tempering. The fabric network is known for its high scalability and performance, which is capable of processing huge transactions and large-scale data. The channels in Hyperledger fabric allows for private and secure transactions between the network participants, resulting in data confidentiality. Smart contracts (or chaincode) within Hyperledger Fabric automate business logic, maintaining functionalities and performing operations efficiently which results in better accuracy. All these features of Hyperledger Fabric make it a better option to use it in forest management where security, confidentiality and trust are required.

## Background and Problem Definition

Integration of Hyperledger fabric into the systems of the forest department for managing and recording plant details entails a balanced approach that ensures decentralization, transparency, security, immutability, well organized management and safety of forest resources. The modular architecture of the Hyperledger fabric enables accountability, security, and communication between the stakeholders, addressing several systematic problems faced by the forest department (Balaji et al., 2022). Hyperledger Fabric is a permissioned blockchain platform where all the network participants need to be authorized to be a part of the network. This network feature ensures the protection of sensitive plant details such as details of rare plant species, or logging details from unknown access (Girma et al., 2023). Public blockchains such as Bitcoin and Ethereum are mostly permission-less platforms where the network can be accessed and joined by any user, making the network vulnerable. So Hyperledger Fabric stands out as the most reliable and efficient blockchain platform to be used in the forest department due to its modular architecture, security services, and permissioned nature. The main goal of integrating Hyperledger fabric into the forest department is to bring transparency in managing the forest data, to securely store the plant records as well as monitor forestry activities.

## Objective

The blockchain technology such as Hyperledger fabric which is a permissioned blockchain platform, provides enhanced security and trust ensuring that only authenticated participants can join and interact within the network. It aims to create an immutable and decentralized ledger where all transactions and data are securely recorded, enabling accountability and real-time access. The main objective of using Hyperledger fabric in forest management is to maintain a secure, transparent, and tamper-proof record of trees, including species, location, plant status, and logging activities. By integrating Hyperledger fabric in the forest management system, its operations can be streamlined. The system aims at sustainable management of resources, and protection of forest ecosystems with higher precision and accountability.

The chapter is organized as; the second section discusses existing related works. The methodology is presented in the third section. The fourth section discusses the proposed system. Results have been analyzed in the fifth section. Conclusion and future work are presented in the sixth section.

## LITERATURE SURVEY

A sizable section of India is covered by forest ecosystems, which are rich in diversity and variety. Millions of people rely on these woods for their livelihoods. It is very important for the nation's biodiversity, water conservation, and climate management. The forests vary from the dry thorn forests of Rajasthan to the thick tropical rainforests of the Andaman and Nicobar Islands and the northeastern states (Balaji et al., 2022). Various plant and animal species rely on the forest ecosystem and are supported by these ecosystems. Additionally, the forest plays an important role in reducing global warming by retaining water, conserving soil, and in taking carbon dioxide. India is known for its vast plant biodiversity, which includes a variety of medicine plants, wood plants and timber species. It maintains the forest ecosystem and livelihood of millions of animals and human beings. The forest department plays a crucial role for plant conservation in India, mainly prioritizing the management of forest resources and preserving diverse flora and fauna. The forest department keeps records of all the plant species which are then stored in databases or written down in paper sheets, ensuring the conservation of rare plant species or the plants that are important for economic development. It is done through various management plans and security acts (Girma et al., 2023). For taking initiative to ensure security aspects, various modern technologies are being used. One such technology is blockchain technology.

The introduction of blockchain technology in public domains has dominated in recent years. The emerging blockchain technology provides a framework for permissioned and permissionless blockchain networks such as Ethereum, Bitcoin, Hyperledger fabric etc. This work focuses on Hyperledger fabric as it is a permissioned blockchain network and useful in the field of forest department. Hyperledger fabric has several features that offer modular architecture, allowing for consensus protocols to be customized, secured, private, and highly scalable (Dias et al., 2024). In the context of forest conservation by the forest department, blockchain's immutability, transparency and decentralized nature provides outstanding advantages compared with the traditional forest management systems. Use of blockchain technology such as the Hyperledger fabric into the forest department stands out to be reliable and very efficient. Permissioned blockchain platforms such as Hyperledger Fabric can be helpful in forest conservation and in forest department operations in many ways. Managing forest resources is an important aspect in forest conservation. Use of blockchain technology enables to carry out transparent, secure, accurate and data driven resource planning.

The traditional forest management system used by the forest department faces the problem with transparency, as a result of which several details such as wildlife sightings, logging information, or member details may become prone to unauthorized access, data manipulation, or data hiding. Traditionally, the data related to forest management are often circulated across several systems, making it challenging to prevent tempering and ensuring accuracy. Many solutions have been carried out using blockchain technology that helps in the conservation of forest as well as wildlife. For instance, Stopfer´ et al. (2024) proposed a blockchain technology in the wood supply chains that fulfills the requirements for timber industry and forestry. Mario et al. (2021) proposed a blockchain solution for tracking and certifying wood volumes. Similarly, Mechik, E., & Von Hauff, M. (2022). analysed blockchain-based forest conservation methods along with various forest communities' economic activities in India, Brazil, and Thailand. The study proposes a concept that aims to reduce unauthorized illegal logging and also mitigate climate change with the help of a blockchain-based contract management system. Their work is designed for tropical forest preservation and mainly focuses on economic incentives and contract management, whereas the proposed Hyperledger Fabric system concentrates on forest data collection, real-time tracking of individual plant records, and multi-level role-based validation. There are blockchain technologies that are aligned along several enterprise settings that ensure accountability and better security (Aliyu et al., 2022). Several blockchain technologies are being used for the conservation of the forest yet the possibilities of using blockchain technology such as Hyperledger fabric in the forest department can be advantageous and supportive in many ways.

Various blockchain technologies have been used in different sectors according to the need. Some of the sectors are healthcare, agriculture and supply chain management. Extending blockchain in the agricultural sector, Wang, Xiaoding, et al (2025) designed a blockchain-Empowered H-CPS Architecture for smart agriculture. The proposed framework integrates Hyperledger Fabric with AI-driven analytics, IOT devices, and various sensing technologies to enable data-driven decision-making, transparent transactions in the supply chain, and real-time crop management. The proposed H-CPS architecture has some significant similarities, such as role-based data collection and the use of Hyperledger Fabric with our proposed plant record storage system. However, this architecture fails to address the requirement of plant record tracking by different domains for multi-level validations by the forest guards, foresters, and the forest range officers. With a similar technological implementation, 470 TPS of read throughput with an average latency of 5 seconds are reported for the H-CPS system by using Hyperledger Caliper. Table 1 summarizes a comparison among various blockchain technologies used in different sectors. Sizan et al. (2025) proposed the ethereum blockchain platform along with IoT to enhance data recommendation using sensor devices. The system has been implemented on public blockchain that is not suitable for enterprise settings. The system proposed by Kaushal et al. (2025) uses Hyperledger Fabric with IoT in healthcare, which helps in monitoring patients and collects real-time patient's data, but the system is developed to be used in specific domains with complex technicality, and real-world scalability issues. An approach similar to the use case discussed can be carried out using Hyperledger Fabric in the forest department for storing plant records that eventually enhances the storage management system without depending on complex data models and IoT based systems. Similarly, Wickremasinghe et al. (2024) demonstrated use of Hyperledger Fabric in the supply chain focusing mainly on filtering and data privacy. The system proposed by Al-Sumaidaee et al. (2023) is used in healthcare, which is also domain specific and only stores key-value pairs of patients. It lacks both real time on-field validation and role based actions. The system developed by Hu et al. (2024) focuses on security of agricultural data and provides a user-friendly interface because the system architecture is very complex and needs to be cost effective. Similarly, Ferr´andez-Pastor et al. (2022) proposed a traceability model with IoT embedded systems but the model heavily relies on IoT based devices. Sheng and Wicha (2024) in the context of teak forestry proposed a decentralized application for implementing a traceable teak identity that is based on Ethereum blockchain. The system includes stakeholders such as farmers, manufacturers and forestry officers who does the verification and registration of the details related to teak on to the blockchain.

The comparison and relevance study of blockchain technology shows the flexibility of blockchain in various domains by delivering data-integrity, transparency and tamper-proofing for storage management. Blockchain used in the various sectors gives a clear vision when compared with the use cases and encourages using the technology for forest management. For instance, the ethereum blockchain platform with IoT is used as a public blockchain. It is not suitable for enterprise settings. Hyperledger Fabric has been used with IoT in healthcare and supply chain management which requires data privacy. An approach similar to the Hyperledger Fabric use cases discussed can be used in the forest department for storing plant records that eventually enhances the storage management system. By putting the storage management system alongside the use cases, table 1 not only indicates the usefulness of Hyperledger fabric in forest data management but also highlights the various applications of blockchain in different other domains.

*Table 1. Comparison of blockchains used in various sectors*

| Sl. No. | Work | Methodology | Features |
|---|---|---|---|
| 1 | Muhanned et al. (2025) | Etherium blockchain | Public blockchain is used here. It is not suitable for enterprise settings |
| 2 | Sizan et al. (2025) | Etherium blockchain, IOT | It uses public blockchain and is cost effective |
| 3 | Rahaman et al. (2024) | Hyperledger Fabric | It is designed for supply chain management using private blockchain. |
| 4 | Kaushal et al. (2025) | Hyperledger Fabric, IOT | It is designed for remote patient monitoring using private blockchain. |
| 5 | Wickremasinghe et al. (2024) | Hyperledger Fabric | Supply chain framework was designed in this work using private blockhain. |
| 6 | Al-Sumaidaee et al. (2023) | Hyperledger Fabric | Healthcare system has been developed using private blockchain. |
| 7 | Hu et al. (2024) | Hyperledger Fabric | Agricultural data security has been developed using private blockchain. |
| 8 | Ferr´andez-Pastor et al. (2022) | Hyperledger Fabric, IOT | An agricultural traceability model has been developed using private blockchain. |

## METHODOLOGY

The traditional forest department system often relies highly on processing the data manually, and pen paper work is easily prone to mistakes, interference and corruptions. To overcome all these obstacles, the chapter uses blockchain technology, mainly the Hyperledger Fabric, to create a tamper-proof ledger that records plant details and each and every transaction performed within the range of forest department. The Hyperledger fabric is designed to be a private blockchain. In this work Hyperledger fabric used in the forest department will be implemented by the forest guards, foresters and the forest range officers of the forest department. The chaincode (smart contract) used in the network allows for the automation of the workflows. The chaincode is developed for managing plant details on a Fabric blockchain. It is mainly focused on the forest department for conservation of plants to keep the plant data temper-proof. It is also designed to make the system verifiable for tracking and recording data related to forestry. It ensures that only the authorized and officials can register details of plants such as species, plant-Id, location and health status. This process of digitally registering plant details makes it verifiable and helps to remove duplications or data manipulation that are being faced by the system used in traditional data management. It also supports modification and retrieval of plant data and allows authorized officials to access the plant details that are being registered, ensuring decision making and proper monitoring. In certain cases where plants are being cut or affected by natural calamity, its position can be updated accordingly, maintaining current plant details at ground level. Synchronization between the real time forestry data and the digitally stored data provides monitoring of the illegal logging activities and unauthorized access in the zones that are covered by the forest departments. As all the operations such as data collection, process updation and ownership transfer are all stored in a distributed ledger; the blockchain system ensures accountability and traceability at each and every level (Nedaković et al, 2023). Use of the chaincode for the conservation of forest workflows converts the way how the plant data are being stored, updated, monitored and verified. This type of system turns out to be very important for addressing challenges such as inefficient reporting, deforestation and other factors that affect the sustainability of forest management. The main objective of applying blockchain technology such as Hyperledger Fabric in forest department is to track the plant records and other activities within the range of forest department so that there would be no scope of any illegal exercise.

The methodological choices of the proposed system have been taken by countering the four specific requirements of the traditional data storage management.

- Tamper resistance: Records stored in the traditional storage system can be manipulated or altered by any authorized user without a proper audit trail. The used methodology overcomes this issue by storing the plant records in the Hyperledger Fabric. In the proposed system, once a record is committed no one can alter it.
- Accountability: The plant record stored in the system should be traceable to every official responsible. To keep track of each record, a workflow of three-stage validation has been implemented where each and every transaction is digitally signed.
- Query efficiency: During field inspection the forest officers require immediate access to the records. The methodology helps the system to prioritize the read operation over the write operation.

## PROPOSED SYSTEM

Use of permissioned blockchain platforms such as Hyperledger Fabric in the forest department database helps ensure that only authenticated participants, such as forest guards, foresters, and the forest range officers, can access the system. This feature of access control keeps the system safe from unauthorized access. The proposed system is used to store the plant records in a secure, transparent, and immutable manner preventing it from data manipulation, data hiding and also bringing in trust and confidentiality. The system helps to keep track of each and every plant along with its attributes such as species, location, and plant status so that if any plant gets missing or is being cut illegally without anyone noticing, it can get tracked easily. With the help of the chaincode attributes of the plant such as its location, health status and species are recorded immutably which ensures that each and every plant is verifiable and identifiable. In case a plant has been cut down or goes missing, the information can be gathered by querying the record stored using the chaincode function. The ability of the system to access the records in real-time ensures that no unauthorized access gets unnoticed. The system thus, helps the officials of the forest department to trace each and every plant and monitor changes improving accountability and transparency in forest data management.

### Entities in the System

Following are entities in the proposed system,

- **Forest Guard (FG):** Forest Guard plays an important role within the forest department's management system. In forest department, the FG constantly patrols and monitors the plant species, wildlife activities, and logging activities over a particular area. They are mainly responsible for collecting the details of each and every plant such as species, location, and health status within the area they are assigned. In the blockchain network, work of the FG is to collect plant data and digitally submit them in the network which is then sent to the Forester.
- **Forester:** In forest department the Forester looks after the work of the FG, making sure that the work done by the FG is carried out properly without any mistake. Foresters are engaged in several activities, but in the blockchain network the work of the forester is to validate the plant data that have been collected by the FG. After validating the forester marks the transaction as validated and sends the transaction for further process to the Forest Range Officer.

- **Forest Range Officer (FRO):** FROs look after the work of both Forester and FG, making sure that everything lines up with forest management plans and activities. FRO is responsible for planning and managing programs related to forest management, including logging activities, projects related to reforestation, wildlife activities and so on. In the blockchain network, FROs are responsible for the last validation of the transaction sent from the forester. They make sure that the transaction is validated and endorsed by the forester. They perform the final validation function before storing it to the network ledger.

## System Architecture

The system architecture has been designed using Hyperledger Fabric and it describes how the data (in this case the plant records) is transferred through each nodes present in the blockchain network. The network consists of three organizations namely, Org1 (Forest Guard), Org2 (Forester) and Org3 (Forest Range Officer). It will also contain one Ordering service.

## Blockchain architecture

The system architecture has been presented in fig. 1. The proposed Hyperledger fabric network consists of entities such as forest guard, foresters and forest range officers who will act as peer nodes and also certificate authority (CA) and membership service provider (MSP). The components of has been discussed below,

- **Fabric SDK:** Hyperledger Fabric provides the Fabric Software Development Kit (SDK) that is used to interact with the network. It empowers several applications that are written in java, go, python etc. to communicate with the network in a programmatic way. All the operations such as network connection, transaction submission, ledger query and identity management are carried out by the Fabric SDK in a simple and easy way.
- **Certificate Authority (CA):** In Hypeledger Fabric the CA provides digital certificates for the network participants that consists of keys (public key /private key), and digital identities which helps in managing access control. The admin, peer or order registers with the Fabric CA. With the help of the Fabric CA client, new users are registered by the admin which is stored in the CA database. On the time of enrollment the CA server receives a request from the Fabric CA client for the key generation.
- **Membership Service Provider (MSP):** The CA provides digital certificates for the network components and with the help of these certificates the MSP

specifies the identities, permissions, roles and policies for the network participants. The roles define the actions such as plant data collection, plant data submission, endorsement and validation which are carried out by the network participants.

- **Chaincode:** The chaincode used in the system has been written in Go language, which automates the operation for managing plant details within the network. The chaincode manages the interaction between FG, Forester and FRO. A data structure named PlantData is defined in the chaincode that includes the required fields for identifying plant details. The transaction functions consist of CollectPlantData, Forester Validation, Officer Validation and a query function ReadPlantData.

## Working of the proposed System

The proposed system brings efficiency and reliability into the forest department data management system. With the integration of smart contract (chaincode), each operation such as collection of plant data, validation and updation are all automatically stored into the ledger ensures data traceability throughout its life cycle. The proposed system is built upon the existing features and capabilities of the Hyperledger Fabric. Unlike other implementations of the blockchain technology or Fabric application used in various sectors, the originality of the proposed work focuses mainly on its domain-specific system of forest plant record management embodied into a three-tier validation workflow that consists of Forest Guard, Forester, and Forest Range officer. The operations within the networks performed by different entities are described in this section. Notations used in this work is listed in Table 2.

*Table 2. Symbols used*

| Symbols | Description |
|---|---|
| *P* | Plant data |
| *TX* | Transaction Output |
| *cert_FG* | Forest Guard Certificate |
| *cert_F* | Forester Certificate |
| *cert_FRO* | Forest Range Officer Certificate |
| *P_FG* | Forest Guard PublicKey |
| *P_F* | Forester PublicKey |
| *P_FRO* | Forest Range Officer PublicKey |
| *i* | Loop variable |
| *Org_ID* | MSPID |
| *ctx.GetClientIdentity()* | Retrieves client details |
| *ctx.GetStub()* | Read/Write TX info |

In the fabric network the CA is responsible for providing certificates and keys to the network participants. At first the entities have to go through the registration process where they are provided with the user ID by the CA. Then the enrollment process is carried out in which the entities are provided with the keys. The credentials provided by the CA identify each network participant uniquely and allow verifications and secure communications between the participants. Once the network participants get the necessary credentials, the MSP verifies the authenticity during validation and transaction proposal by using these credentials. In the system the FG is responsible for collecting the plant data which is then sent to the next step for validation. The plant data which are collected by the FG are signed with his/her private key provided by the CA. The data is then sent to the forester for the validation process. Algorithm 1 shows the steps performed by the FG for collecting the plant data.

Forester in the network is responsible for the validation process. The forester validates the transaction record that is the plant data sent by the FG. To verify the transaction proposal the forester verifies the signature of the FG on the transaction proposal. If the transaction is valid, the forester endorses the transaction proposal with his/her remark and a timestamp and sends the updated proposal to the Forest Range Officer for further processing. Algorithm 2 shows the steps that are carried out by the forester for validation.

After getting the updated transaction proposal (TX) along with the remarks and validation of the forester, the FRO is responsible for the final validation of the transaction proposal. The FRO checks if the validation process performed by the forester complies with the validation dependencies. If the validation process succeeds, the FRO then updates the transaction proposal with its remarks and a timestamp and writes it into the ledger. Algorithm 3 shows the final validation process carried out by the FRO.

The algorithm discussed in this section show the sequential flow of operation carried out by the different entities of the forest department from the time a plant data has been collected till the time it gets stored in the blockchain ledger. Every entity is assigned with specific tasks which are to be performed by that particular entity itself ensuring accountability and efficiency.

```
Algorithm 1: Plant Data collection process
Input: P = (ID, species, Height, diameter, location, Health-Status)
Output: Tx = [ID, validated, remarks]

1: Retrieving cert_FG from MSP
2: For each plant P
3:  cert_FG = MSP.getcert(FG_ID)
```

```
Extract P_FG from CA
P_FG = CA.extractP_FG(cert_FG)
Authentication using MSP_ID
Org_ID ← ctx.GetClientIdentity( ).GetMSP_ID( )
if Org ID ≠ "Org1MSP" then
        log: "Only forest guard can collect plant data"
                End process
        end if
        Verify unique plant record
        exists ← s.PlantDataExists(ctx,ID)
        if exists = true then
                Log: "Plant ID already exists"
                End process
        end if
        Prepare plant data structure
        collector ← ctx.GetClientIdentity( ).GetID( )
        timestamp = ctx.GetStub( ).GetTxTimestamp( )
        Initialize 'P' object with ID, species, height, diameter, location, healthStatus
        CollectedBy = collector
CollectionDate = timestamp
        ForesterValidated = false
        OfficerValidated = false
        Write to ledger
        plantDataJSON ← json.Marshal(plantData)
        ctx.GetStub( ).PutState(ID, plantDataJSON)
end for
```

Algorithm 2: Forester Validation

Input: TX = (ID, validated, remarks)

Output: Updated TX = (validated and remarks)

```
Retrieving cert_F from MSP
For each plant P
 cert_F = MSP.getcert(F_ID)
 Extract P_F from CA
 P_F = CA.extractP_F(cert_F)
 Authentication using MSP_ID
 Org_ID ← ctx.GetClientIdentity( ).GetMSP_ID( )
 if Org ID ≠ "Org2MSP" then
        log: "Only forester can validate"
```

```
                End process
        end if
        Retrieve plant data from ledger
        plantDataJSON ← ctx.GetStub( ).GetState(ID)
        if plantDataJSON = nil then
                Log: "Plant_ID does not exist"
                End process
        else
                Unmarshal JSON to 'P' object
        end if
        Update validation fields
        timestamp ← ctx.GetStub( ).GetTxTimestamp( )
        F_Validated = validated
F_Remarks = remarks
        F_Date = timestamp
        Write updated data to ledger
        updatedJSON = json.Marshal(plantData)
        ctx.GetStub().PutState(ID, updatedJSON)
end for
```

Algorithm 3: Forest Range Officer Validation

Input: TX = (ID, validated, remarks)

Output: Updated TX with OfficerValidated = (validated and remarks)

```
Retrieving cert_FRO from MSP
For each plant P
 cert_FRO = MSP.getcert(FRO_ID)
 Extract P_FRO from CA
 P_FRO = CA.extractP_FRO(cert_FRO)
 Authentication using MSP_ID
 Org_ID ← ctx.GetClientIdentity().GetMSP_ID()
 if Org ID ≠ "Org3MSP" then
        log: "Only forest range officer can validate"
                End process
        end if
        Retrieve plant data from ledger
        plantDataJSON ← ctx.GetStub().GetState(ID)
        if plantDataJSON = nil then
                Log: "Plant ID does not exist"
                End process
```

```
        else
              Unmarshal JSON to 'P' object
        end if
        Validation dependency check
        if plantData.ForesterValidated = false then
              Log: "Forester must validate before officer validation"
        End process
        else
              Proceed to update fields
        end if
        Update officer validation fields
        timestamp = ctx.GetStub().GetTxTimestamp()
  FRO_Validated = validated
  FRO_remarks = remarks
  FRO_Date = timestamp
  Writing Updated Data to Ledger
  updatedJSON = json.Marshal(plantData)
  ctx.GetStub().PutState(ID, updatedJSON)
  end for
```

## RESULTS AND ANALYSIS

The performance of the Hyperledger Fabric used in the forest department for the record storage system is evaluated with the help of Hyperledger Caliper which is very simple and a compatible benchmarking tool. Conducting tests using the caliper benchmarking tool provides thorough information about the chaincode that is being deployed into the system. The tests that were performed outline the real world usage and communications with the blockchain network, specifically giving attention towards the plant data collection and data retrieving activities. The system was built on a Fabric 2.5 Test-Network which is very compatible with the benchmarking process. The network consists of one ordering service and three organizations namely, Org1 (Forest guard), Org2 (Forester), Org3 (Forest Range Officer). The chaincode used in the system includes several operations but the main objective for the test being done is to understand how the fabric network and the chaincode respond with the CollectPlantData (createAsset) operation and the ReadPlantData (readAsset) operation. Before the benchmarking test is carried out it is crucial to set up certain files and a workload module. Caliper starts the benchmarking process by running the chaincode functions starting with the creatAsset (CollectPlantData) operation, the work that is carried out by the Org1 (Forest Guard). For testing, 1000 plant data transactions were used by the caliper and were successfully processed. The test resulted in successfully transacting 1000 plant data and zero failure with a send rate (TPS) of 67.2. The test gave a maximum latency of 79.70 seconds, minimum latency of 0.71 seconds and an average latency of 37.43 seconds. The throughput achieved is 10.7 TPS. Table 3 presents the test results of the createAsset operation.

*Table 3. Test results of createAsset operation*

| Name | Success | Fail | Send Rate (TPS) | Max Latency (S) | Min Latency (S) | Avg Latency (S) | Throughput (TPS) |
|---|---|---|---|---|---|---|---|
| createAsset | 1000 | 0 | 67.2 | 79.70 | 0.71 | 37.43 | 10.7 |

While performing the readAsset (ReadPlantData) operation, the results were comparatively better. The caliper easily processed 25366 successful read operations and zero failure with a send rate (TPS) of 429.9. The test gave a maximum latency of 0.07 seconds, minimum latency of 0.01 seconds and an average latency of 0.01 seconds with a throughput of 429.9 TPS. Table 4 presents the test results of the readAsset operation.

*Table 4. Test results of readAsset operation*

| Name | Success | Fail | Send Rate (TPS) | Max Latency (S) | Min Latency (S) | Avg Latency (S) | Throughput (TPS) |
|---|---|---|---|---|---|---|---|
| readAsset | 25366 | 0 | 429.9 | 0.07 | 0.01 | 0.01 | 429.9 |

By taking notes of the caliper test result shown in table 3 and table 4, it can be seen that the system works well for the forest data management. During the create-Asset (CollectPlantData) operation, it took more time to complete as compared to readAsset (ReadPlantData) operation as the createAsset operation has to go through several endorsement requirements.

During the createAsset (CollectPlantData) operation, it took more time to complete as compared to the readAsset (ReadPlantData) operation. It gave 37.43 seconds of average latency with a throughput of 10.7 TPS, resulting in relatively higher latency as write operation in Hyperledger Fabric requires endorsement carried out by the forest guards peer node, specific required validation by the forester, forest range officers' final validation and approval, as well as ordering and committing the validated transaction into the ledger. At the time of initial transactions, when the chaincode is deployed, a maximum latency of 79.70 has been captured. As for the readAsset operation, the average latency and the captured throughput result in a fast response time for any queries of the plant records in the field, for instance, finding the location of a specific plant species or gathering information on illegal logging of plants in the field.

## Security Analysis

The proposed system provides several layers of security that a traditional forest management system lacks. Each transaction carried out comes across proper authentication and access control, its data immutability and tamper-proofing feature ensure the information recorded stays in its original state. The system prevents various common attacks that are encountered in traditional systems, such as the

Sybil attack, which can be prevented by proper identity verification with the help of MSP, the Man-in-the-middle attack, prevents by encrypting communications between peers, and lastly, from the insider threat that is resolved by its role-based validation feature.

## Scalability Considerations

As for the current benchmarking 1000 of plant records has been used, there might be millions of records that can come up in terms of some real-world cases. To counter large number of records various scalability measures has to be considered:

- Ledger Size: For each plant data approximately 500 bytes are used. For 1 million plant records, the size of the ledger would go up to ~500 MB, which is reasonable for modern storage devices. However, if the number grows to 10 million, the size of the ledger would go up to ~5 GB, requiring sufficient storage on each node.
- Transaction Throughput: During the testing, it has been found that the throughput of 10.7 TPS gives out ~38,500 records per hour. A vast forest area can add up like 12,000 new plants per day, which would approximately be completed in ~13 minutes, which remains under the operational time limit.
- Query Performance: For any queries of the plant records, even if it is a large volume of data, the system performance would remain the same and would consume a very small amount of time compared to writing the records.
- Network Scalability: peers can be added depending on the forest areas that are covered within the network. The Fabric supports features where multiple channels can be made, where different regional operators can communicate through the channel without congesting the network.

## CONCLUSION AND FUTUREWORK

The use of blockchain technology such as Hyperledger Fabric into the forest department brings transparency and security and helps in various forest management plans. By taking the advantage of Fabrics data is stored in an immutable manner. The system helps in keeping the records of all the plant species and the activities performed in a secure and tamper-proof manner. Each organization of the system has separate smart contract functions and are all kept together under a single smart contract, making the system less complex. The system performance has been tested out with the help of Hyperledger Caliper. The performance analysis shows that the proposed system can be implemented in real life. Overall, the plan of introducing Hyperledger Fabric into the forest department minimizes the technological gaps in the traditional forest management systems. In the future, Hyperledger Fabric in forest management can be combined with other technologies which may include, artificial intelligence, internet of things (IoT) devices to develop a better forest data management system. IOT integration such as, drone-based imaging, camera traps, and soil moisture sensors can provide real-time data monitoring and activity into the blockchain network directly. By installing GPS-enabled tags or attaching QR codes on certain trees could help in recording the location and status updates of the trees automatically, reducing the workload of Forest Guards. Deploying AI-driven monitoring systems which may include deep learning models could help in analyzing satellite or drone imagery that will help in monitoring forest health, identifying infected trees or detecting unwanted or illegal logging activities. This is because with the help of IoT devices and AI many of the works that are carried out physically can be automated resulting in better accuracy and efficiency.

## REFERENCES


Al-Sumaidaee, G., Alkhudary, R., Zilic, Z., & Swidan, A. (2023). Performance analysis of a private blockchain network built on Hyperledger Fabric for healthcare. *Information Processing & Management*, *60*(2), 103160. DOI: 10.1016/j.ipm.2022.103160

Aliyu, I., Van Engelenburg, S., Mu'Azu, M. B., Kim, J., & Lim, C. G. (2022). Statistical detection of adversarial examples in blockchain-based federated forest in-vehicle network intrusion detection systems. *IEEE Access : Practical Innovations, Open Solutions*, *10*, 109366–109384. DOI: 10.1109/ACCESS.2022.3212412

Balaji, G., Sharma, G., & Jayanth, R. S. S. (2022). Forest cover in India: A victim of technicalities. *Ecological Economics*, *193*, 107306. DOI: 10.1016/j.ecolecon.2021.107306

Bhatt, H., Jugran, H. P., & Pandey, R. (2024). Cultural ecosystem services nexus with Socio-Cultural attributes and traditional ecological knowledge for managing community forests of indian western Himalaya. *Ecological Indicators*, *166*, 112379. DOI: 10.1016/j.ecolind.2024.112379

Dias, P., Gonçalves, H., Silva, F., Duque, J., Martins, J., & Godinho, A. (2024). Blockchain technologies: A scrutiny into Hyperledger Fabric for higher educational institutions. *Procedia Computer Science*, *237*, 213–220. DOI: 10.1016/j.procs.2024.05.098

Ferrández-Pastor, F. J., Mora-Pascual, J., & Díaz-Lajara, D. (2022). Agricultural traceability model based on IoT and Blockchain: Application in industrial hemp production. *Journal of Industrial Information Integration*, *29*, 100381. DOI: 10.1016/j.jii.2022.100381

Girma, G., Melka, Y., Haileslassie, A., & Mekuria, W. (2023). Participatory forest management for improving livelihood assets and mitigating forest degradation: Lesson drawn from the Central Rift Valley, Ethiopia. *Current Research in Environmental Sustainability*, *5*, 100205. DOI: 10.1016/j.crsust.2022.100205

Hu, Z., Kim, B., & Jeong, J. (2024). A Study on mechanization, data, and insurance challenges for agriculture based on hyperledger fabric. *IEEE Access : Practical Innovations, Open Solutions*, *12*, 144855–144869. DOI: 10.1109/ACCESS.2024.3468430

Kaushal, R. K., Kumar, N., Kukreja, V., & Boonchieng, E. (2025). Hyperledger fabric based remote patient monitoring solution and performance evaluation. *Peer-to-Peer Networking and Applications*, *18*(3), 105. DOI: 10.1007/s12083-025-01921-0

Mechik, E., & Von Hauff, M. (2022). The fight against deforestation of tropical forests—the contribution of the blockchain-based contract management method to minimize illegal logging. In Climate and development (pp. 439-463)

Melo, C., Oliveira, F., Dantas, J., Araujo, J., Pereira, P., Maciel, R., & Maciel, P. (2022). Performance and availability evaluation of the blockchain platform hyperledger fabric. *The Journal of Supercomputing*, *78*(10), 12505–12527. DOI: 10.1007/s11227-022-04361-2

Nedaković, A., Hasselgren, A., Kralevska, K., & Gligoroski, D. (2023). Hyperledger fabric platform for healthcare trust relations—Proof-of-Concept. Blockchain. *Research and Applications*, *4*(4), 100156.

Paulino, E. R., Schlerf, M., Röder, A., Stoffels, J., & Udelhoven, T. (2024). Forest disturbance characterization in the era of earth observation big data: A mapping review. *International Journal of Applied Earth Observation and Geoinformation*, *128*, 103755. DOI: 10.1016/j.jag.2024.103755

Sheng, S. W., & Wicha, S. (2024). Blockchain-based traceability for teak identity: A transformational approach. Journal of Mobile Multimedia, 20(2), 267-306. Sheng, S. W., & Wicha, S. (2024). Blockchain-based traceability for teak identity: A transformational approach. *Journal of Mobile Multimedia*, *20*(2), 267–306. DOI: 10.13052/jmm1550-4646.2022

Sizan, N. S., Dey, D., Layek, M. A., Uddin, M. A., & Huh, E. N. (2025). Evaluating blockchain platforms for iot applications in industry 5.0: A comprehensive review. Blockchain: Research and Applications, 100276. Rahaman, M., Tabassum, F., Arya, V., & Bansal, R. (2024). Secure and sustainable food processing supply chain framework based on Hyperledger Fabric technology. *Cyber Security and Applications*, *2*, 100045.

Stopfer, L., Kaulen, A., & Purfürst, T. (2024). Potential of blockchain technology in wood supply chains. *Computers and Electronics in Agriculture*, *216*, 108496. DOI: 10.1016/j.compag.2023.108496

Ucbas, Y., Eleyan, A., Hammoudeh, M., & Alohaly, M. (2023). Performance and scalability analysis of ethereum and hyperledger fabric. *IEEE Access : Practical Innovations, Open Solutions*, *11*, 67156–67167. DOI: 10.1109/ACCESS.2023.3291618

Wang, Xiaoding, et al. "Blockchain-Empowered H-CPS Architecture for Smart Agriculture." Advanced science 12.27 (2025): 2503102.

Wickremasinghe, G., Frost, S., Rafferty, K., & Sharma, V. (2024). Demonstrating a Hyperledger Fabric-based Blockchain with Knowledge Graphs for a Supply Chain Ecosystem. In *IEEE International Conference on Blockchain and Cryptocurrency (ICBC)* (pp. 15-16). DOI: 10.1109/ICBC59979.2024.10634370

## KEY TERMS AND DEFINITIONS

**Blockchain:** Blockchain is a decentralized ledger technology. It is used to store transactions and track the records. It facilitates sharing of data electronically ensuring immutability and transparency. There are four types of block chains namely, public block chain, private block chain, consortium block chain and hybrid block chain. In the case of a public block chain, it is permission-less and non-restrictive. Every participant can do all the activities in the block chain like, mining, verification of records and data access. Examples of public block chains are Bitcoin, Ethereum, and Litecoin etc. A private block chain is suitable for closed network like enterprise or organization which has a limited number of participants. It is also known as permissioned block chain. The level of accessibility, permission, authorization security will be decided by the organization. Corda and Hyperledger are examples of private blockchain. Consortium block chain can be managed by one or more organizations. Many organizations can also participate in the block chain, exchange information and perform mining. An example of Consortium block chain is Quorum. A combined form of public and private blockchain is hybrid blockchain. The users can specify which data are available in public and which will remain private. The access rights and the user capacities can also be specified.

**Chaincode:** Java, node.js and Go languages are used to write chain code. Docker container is used to run chain codes. From endorsing peer process it is isolated. Initialization and management of ledger state is done by the chaincode using transactions which are submitted by the applications. Business logic on which the members of network reach an agreement is handled by chaincode. Therefore, it can be said that it is a smart contract. If a chaincode creates a state, no other chaincode can access it directly except that chaincode. For accessing the state other chaincodes need appropriate permission.

**Hyperledger Fabric:** Developers who aim to design an application with security and permissioned blockchain, for them Hyperledger fabric is very good option. For large applications requiring protection of data, its adaptive architecture is well suited. It has been designed with modules. So, the customization of the blockchain network can be done according to the requirements of the users. In comparison with other blockchains, Hyperledger fabric is very unique. Peers or endorsers/committers will distribute the computation burden of the transaction processing among them. Orderers are responsible for building the consensus, ordering transactions and putting transactions into blocks.

**Latency:** Total time required from transaction initialization to inclusion or confirmation of the transaction in the block is known as latency. For performance analysis it is one of the important factors. After initialization of transaction, it is transmitted to the blockchain network nodes. For achieving consensus the transactions will be verified by the nodes. When the block gets confirmed, transaction is added in the blockchain. The time required for the entire process is known as latency. It is a key performance indicator.

**Throughput:** It is used to measure number of actions completed within a time unit. In the context of blockchain, throughput calculates the number of transactions performed per time unit. The time unit is usually seconds. But it can be minutes or hours. Therefore the units of throughput can be transactions per second (TPS), transactions per minute (TPM) and transactions per hour (TPH). The throughput of a blockchain depends on the underlying blockchain, consensus mechanism and scenario. It is a key performance papramete.

Chapter 6

# High-Performance Computing for Advanced Cybersecurity: GPU and TPU-Based Security Optimisation Techniques

**Jyoti Kumari**
http://orcid.org/0000-0001-9648-2494
*GD Goenka University, India*

**Pradeep Yadav**
http://orcid.org/0000-0003-1073-7076
*Institute of Technology and Management, Gwalior, India*

**Chandra Prakash Bhargava**
http://orcid.org/0009-0004-4751-9149
*Institute of Technology and Management, Gwalior, India*

## ABSTRACT

*Cybersecurity operations at enterprise and carrier scale are increasingly constrained by computational throughput rather than analytical capability. Modern threat actors exploit distributed systems to launch attacks beyond traditional CPU-based defenses. This chapter examines how GPU and TPU computing redefine security operations, covering parallel architectures, GPU-accelerated cryptography, and post-quantum schemes. It further explores machine learning-based analytics for intrusion detection and malware classification, real-time high-throughput threat*

DOI: 10.4018/979-8-3373-9053-6.ch006

*detection, deployment challenges, HPC security risks, and emerging areas such as federated learning, homomorphic encryption, neuromorphic processors, and quantum-classical systems.*

## 1. INTRODUCTION

Something changed in the world of threats around the time that commodity cloud infrastructure made petaflop-scale computing available for the price of a credit card. Threat actors found access to the sort of raw computing power that previously only national programs could afford to maintain.

Password databases could be audited against a billion guesses per second, machine learning models could be trained to produce realistic phishing attacks at industrial scales and distributed denial of service attacks could mobilize hundreds of gigabits of synthetic traffic with a few lines of code rented from botnet-as-a-service providers. The defenders armed with multi-core CPUs optimized for sequential logic and moderate thread counts found themselves in a race that they were structurally ill-equipped to win.

That imbalance started to close with the recognition of the GPU previously a peripheral in a pixel-pushing role as a general-purpose parallel processing device available for application against security problems. A flagship data centre GPU from 2024 boasts over 80 billion transistors thousands of arithmetic execution pipelines and memory bandwidth of over three terabytes per second.

These figures are not mere marketing boasts; they directly equate to verification of over hundreds of billions of SHA-256 hashes per second, inspection of tens of millions of network packets per second against a full ruleset and execution of deep learning (Chen et al., 2018) inference on incoming telemetry fast enough to make a blocking decision before the arrival of the next packet.

TPUs are an extension of this line of thinking but in a different computational form, optimized around matrix operations and therefore suited to inference-oriented tasks typical of a production-level security operations centre.

The technical literature however has not kept up with the practitioner's requirements. There is a lack of clear correspondence between performance sheets for the hardware and security workload profiles. There are few research papers on security applications of GPU acceleration for hashing or intrusion detection systems that discuss the engineering pipeline around the accelerator.

There are few deployment guides that discuss the new surface that the drivers and shared memory provide to attackers. In the following chapters we hope to provide a useful resource for the researcher seeking a theoretical framework as well as the practitioner seeking a practical guide, from the hardware foundations through to the latest research frontiers that will define the field in the next ten years.

The chapter outline continues like this. In Section 2 we discuss the architectural foundation of parallelism in GPUs and TPUs and we discuss the reasons why security workloads fit this parallelism model so nicely. In Section 3 we discuss cryptography in GPUs in detail. In Section 4 we discuss machine learning-based security analytics. In Section 5 we discuss the analysis of real-time scalable threat detection architectures. In Section 6 we discuss deployment engineering. In Section 7 we discuss research trends. In Section 8 we discuss strategic conclusions.

## 2. ARCHITECTURAL FOUNDATIONS: PARALLEL COMPUTING FOR CYBERSECURITY WORKLOADS

### 2.1 Why Security Workloads Parallelise Well

Computational tasks fall broadly into two categories. Some are inherently serial: the next step depends on the last there are few opportunities for instruction-level parallelism and the key performance characteristics are clock speed and out-of-order execution depth. The CPU is very good at these. The other type are data-parallel: many operations need to be performed in parallel on a very large number of data elements and there are few or no data dependencies between operations. The GPU was designed for these.

But a surprising number of fundamental security operations belong to the second category. Hashing a password dictionary where each hash is independent of the others. Encrypting a packet stream in counter mode, where each counter is independent of the others. Scanning one million packets against a signature ruleset where each packet is independent of the others. Running inference on a batch of network flow feature vectors where each vector is independent of the others and makes no reference to its neighbours in the batch.

This label embarrassingly parallel is an old term from high-performance computing, referring to a set of subproblems that share no state and it is why a system with several thousand weak cores in a GPU can outperform a system with sixty strong cores in a CPU by one or two orders of magnitude on these operations.

Even seemingly sequential workloads may have hidden parallelism. The Aho-Corasick multi-pattern string search algorithm which underpins network signature scanning may be parallelized to the extent that separate threads process the automaton for a given packet or a given portion of a given packet.

The parallelism in Bloom filters for IP reputation may be exploited to process groups of incoming IP addresses in parallel. The key scheduling step in the AES encryption process while sequentially executed in most implementations may be parallelized when many sessions are processed concurrently. The recognition and exploitation of such hidden parallelism is the key mental challenge in porting security software to GPU architectures.

## 2.2 GPU Architecture: The Mechanics Behind the Performance

The execution model for NVIDIA GPUs has a three-level hierarchy for computation. The lowest-level computation is the threads where one private set of registers is dedicated to arithmetic computation. A set of 32 threads is called a warp and all the threads in a warp execute the same instruction simultaneously according to the SIMT model. Divergent control flow is handled at the warp level where predication is used to disable threads that should not execute a particular branch. A set of thread blocks is dispatched to the SMs, and many SMs are used to make up the device.

The memory hierarchy plays a part in the performance just as the arithmetic units do. The registers (fast, private, and very small) the shared memory (fast and block-shared with configuration options) the L1 and L2 cache (automatic and low-latency) and the main high-bandwidth memory (large and high-throughput but higher latency) need to be well managed.

Security kernels that store their working set in shared memory and registers achieve the best throughput; those that "thrash the HBM bandwidth boundary" have their performance dominated by the memory system rather than the arithmetic units. Knowing which class a security workload falls into and restructuring it to keep it in the fast tier is a big part of the expertise that experienced security engineers on the GPU bring to the table.

The Tensor Cores which were added with Volta are a further specialisation of this type of unit able to perform a 4x4 matrix FMADD in a single clock period achieving a throughput of over a thousand teraflops per second with BF16 or FP8 operations on an H100 device. It should be noted that while deep learning inference is the direct beneficiary of this technology there is a matrix multiply operation in certain polynomial multiplication schemes that are of use in lattice cryptography so Tensor Cores are becoming more useful in this field. Table no.1 shows the comparative overview of GPU and TPU architecture specifications.

*Table 1. Comparative overview of GPU and TPU architecture specifications and security relevance*

| Processor | Peak TFLOPS / TOPS | Memory BW (GB/s) | Primary HPC Role | Key Security Use |
|---|---|---|---|---|
| NVIDIA H100 SXM5 | 67 TF (FP32) | 3,350 | Large-model training | Threat detection, hash audit |
| NVIDIA RTX 4090 | 82.6 TF (FP32) | 1,008 | Consumer AI / forensics | Password analysis, fuzzing |
| AMD Instinct MI300X | 163 TF (FP32) | 5,300 | LLM inference / HPC | Anomaly detection, SIEM |
| Google TPU v4 | 275 TOPS (BF16) | 1,200 | ML training at cloud scale | Real-time intrusion detection |
| Google TPU v5e | 197 TOPS (INT8) | 1,600 | Inference-optimised edge | Edge inference, TLS offload |

*Figure 1. Relative throughput — CPU vs. GPU vs. TPU across core security workloads (log scale)*

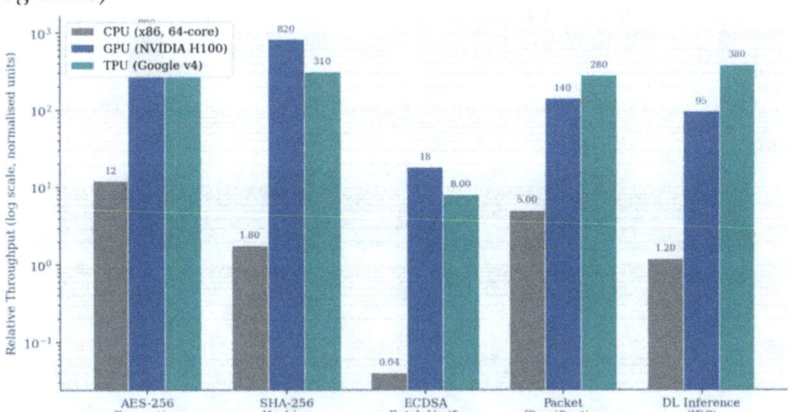


## 2.3 TPU Architecture: Systolic Arrays and Security Inference

While the GPU generalizes from its original focus on graphics processing to a very broad range of computations the TPU as shown in figure no.1, specializes from a general matrix-multiply-oriented design to a very specialized form with data flowing through a regular grid of "multiply-accumulate" operations with data flowing in one direction and weights flowing in a perpendicular direction with each cell performing a multiply-add operation on data as it flows by.

This design achieves very high utilization of the MAC units for large dense matrix multiplications with very little energy spent on memory access or control logic which might be required in a more general design. For a tensor-contraction operation whose dimensions are a good match for the width of a systolic array it's hard to compete with a TPU in operations per joule.

The implication for security is that TPUs are the correct technology to deploy for large-scale deployment of standardized ML models such as transformer-based intrusion classification models, LSTM-based behavioral sequence analysis models, BERT models fine-tuned for security text classification and so on.

They are the wrong technology to deploy if you need to deploy models that require custom low-level kernels novel cryptographic primitives or unusual memory access patterns that cannot be efficiently supported by the systolic array architecture. Security practitioners who deploy TPUs for inference, CPUs or FPGAs for cryptographic offload and GPUs for the hybrid tasks in between are likely to deploy the most cost-efficient architectures. Figure 2 shows the GPU accelerated cybersecurity architecture with data flow diagram.

*Figure 2. GPU-accelerated cybersecurity architecture — data-flow from ingestion to response*

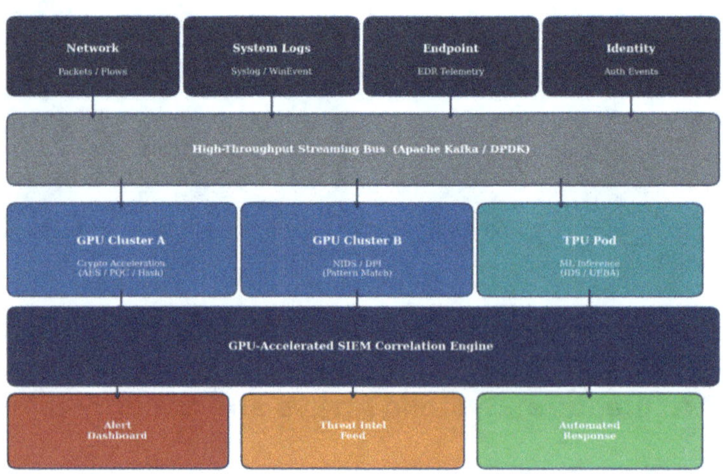

# 3. GPU-ACCELERATED CRYPTOGRAPHIC OPERATIONS

## 3.1 Symmetric Cipher Acceleration

AES in counter mode is an archetypal "embarrassingly parallel" cipher with no dependencies between blocks, just a current counter and round keys required for each 16-byte block of counter mode encryption. A thousand threads are dispatched by a GPU and a terabyte per second is achievable for AES-128 encryption on an H100 notwithstanding data transfer times over PCIe. This is in stark contrast to what a CPU-based cluster of comparable cost might achieve if the payload is larger than a few megabytes, a figure above which the crossover point is exceeded and AES-NI is no longer an efficient solution on a CPU.

In GCM an authentication tag is computed and this multiplication is sequential in Galois fields but carry-less multiplication extensions provide a means to parallelise this operation over blocks. AES-GCM is already in use in high-throughput storage encryption devices, TLS accelerators and VPN concentrators where the encryption rate saturates available CPU core resources. ChaCha20-Poly1305, the other TLS 1.3 workhorse achieves a similar level of acceleration by a different mechanism where each 64-byte chunk of keystream is independent providing a level of flexibility to implement whichever cipher is required by regulatory frameworks without sacrificing acceleration benefits.

## 3.2 Cryptographic Hash Functions: Throughput and Password Auditing

The security of all enterprises that store hashed credentials is only as strong as the resistance of the hash to brute force recovery by an attacker with today's GPU technology. According to Costan, V., & Devadas, S. (2016), the SHA-256 rate on a single NVIDIA H100 board exceeds 50 billion operations per second; for an attacker with eight such boards this becomes 400 billion possibilities per second .

Against a simple SHA-256 hash with no salt and no stretching an eight-character lowercase alphanumeric password is trivially recovered in seconds. This is not a theoretical problem; this is the reality that all incident response professionals know when they get a leaked hash dump and see what GPU-enabled attackers can recover from it overnight.

The defensive corollary is just as important. Security teams should and can proactively audit their own user database with the same GPU-enabled toolset that attackers will bring to bear before their user database is ever exfiltrated. Detecting accounts that are protected by weak credentials such as short passwords, dictionary words and known-compromised patterns from previous breaches and forcing their reset is far more cost-effective than fighting the credential stuffing attack that will follow the breach.

Table 2 shows the GPU/TPU cryptographic acceleration performance vs. CPU baseline. Bcrypt, scrypt, and Argon2 were specifically developed to counter the trend towards GPU parallelism and the strength of existing authentication infrastructure should be reassessed as GPU memory capacities increase.

*Table 2. GPU/TPU cryptographic acceleration performance vs. CPU baseline*

| Algorithm | Platform | Throughput vs. CPU Baseline | Operational Security Context |
|---|---|---|---|
| SHA-256 parallel hashing | CUDA (H100) | ~800× | Log integrity, blockchain audit |
| AES-GCM bulk encryption | GPU + CPU AES-NI | ~120× | VPN, encrypted storage |
| ECDSA batch verification | cuBLAS (A100) | ~300× | TLS handshake, PKI |
| ML-KEM / Kyber-768 NTT | GPU (Hopper) | ~50–70× (early) | Post-quantum TLS, KEM |
| FHE bootstrapping | CUDA-HE / cuFHE | ~20–40× | Privacy-preserving analytics |

### 3.3 Public-Key Operations: Batch Verification and ECC Acceleration

This is because elliptic curve arithmetic is fundamentally different from the arithmetic performed in symmetric ciphers; a single ECDSA signature verification operation requires a series of modular multiplications on the curve and the data dependencies in this chain mean that the speedup of a single operation on the GPU is not realized for a single signature verification operation.

The speedup of the GPU is realized for batch operations. This is because a transparency log auditor may need to verify a million signatures in a single operation or a certificate authority may need to validate thousands of certificate signing requests per second.

Studies on the implementation of GPU acceleration for ECDSA batch verification on the NIST P-256 elliptic curve show that throughputs reach tens of millions of operations per second or roughly three hundred times the throughput of a single-threaded CPU.

In the case of RSA modular exponentiation, parallelisation is not as clean-cut as the long carry chains in multi-precision arithmetic are hard to map to the GPU's

SIMD model. Batch RSA decryption for large key sizes does show speedups in the range of twenty to fifty times for appropriately sized payloads to justify the dispatch overhead. The move in industry towards ECC for new deployments replacing RSA makes the ECC acceleration curve even more important for future planning.

## 3.4 Post-Quantum Cryptography: GPU Acceleration as a Necessity

The NIST post-quantum standardisation process was completed in 2024 resulting in the publication of FIPS 203 (Bos et al., 2018), FIPS 204 (Ducas et al., 2018) and FIPS 205 (SLH-DSA, based on SPHINCS+). These algorithms have significantly higher computational costs than the traditional algorithms they are based on.

According to Bernstein (2025), a key encapsulation in Kyber-768 is about six times more computationally expensive than an ECDH key exchange operation at a similar security level. A signature generation in Dilithium-3 is about twelve times more computationally expensive than an ECDSA P-256 signature generation. This arithmetic expense cannot be easily absorbed at the CPU headroom required by today's internet infrastructure which needs millions of TLS handshakes per second.

The most compute-intensive operation in both Kyber and Dilithium is the Number Theoretic Transform the polynomial multiplication algorithm operating over a prime modulus field. NTT is a butterfly network equivalent to the FFT in structure and contains the same level of hierarchical parallelism: all operations within a given stage are independent in the O(n log n) stages of the NTT.

Figure No. 3 show the classical vs. Post-Quantum cryptographic key operation throughput the CPU, GPU, and TPU.

In the GPU implementation, independent butterfly operations are executed in separate threads, achieving NTT throughputs on the H100 that exceed fifty million Kyber-768 key generation operations per second. The NIST transition recommendations also advise running post-quantum and classical algorithms in parallel during the transition period effectively doubling the available compute budget for cryptographic operations and increasing the strength of the case for offload to the GPU.

*Figure 3. Classical vs. post-quantum cryptographic key-operation throughput — CPU, GPU, and TPU (ops/sec, log scale)*

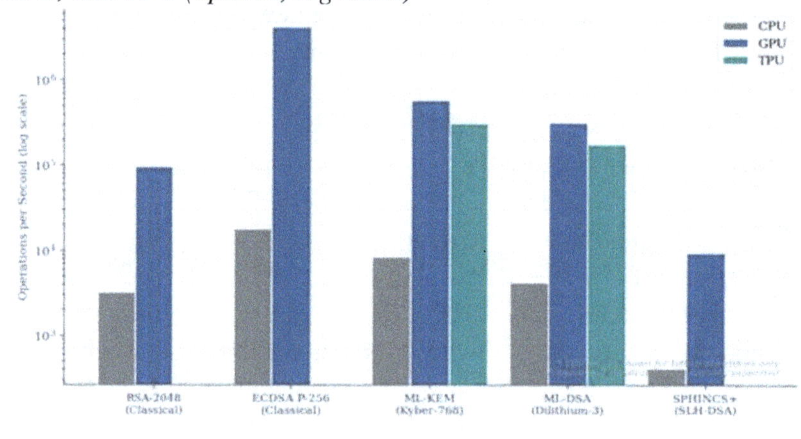


# 4. MACHINE LEARNING-BASED SECURITY ANALYTICS ON GPU AND TPU PLATFORMS

## 4.1 Intrusion Detection: From Signatures to Learned Representations

Signature-based intrusion detection is fast, deterministic and limited in its capabilities. It detects what it is configured to detect and nothing else and the person crafting signatures is always one step behind an attacker crafting new signatures to evade detection. A machine learning-based approach fundamentally changes the paradigm from signature generation to representation learning.

Given enough labeled normal and malicious data a rich enough model learns to identify the fundamental features that differentiate normal and malicious data and generalizes to detect unknown attacks that share those features regardless of their actual byte-level differences.

CNN models when trained on raw representations of network packets as a grid of byte-level information analyze a network flow as a two-dimensional grid of information, akin to an image. The CNN filters learn local patterns within a byte stream such as header field combinations, protocol state patterns, payload signatures which are indicative of malicious behavior.

LSTM/GRU recurrent network architectures analyze the temporal nature of network flows consisting of multiple packets, modeling the state machine nature of attack protocols. Transformer architectures use self-attention to analyze network flows consisting of multiple packets recognizing long-range relationships between packets occurring at different points within a network flow particularly relevant when considering multi-stage attacks where reconnaissance packets are related to exploitation attempts.

Not only is GPU acceleration important for training these models but it's also necessary in the sense of "condition of possibility." An enterprise network generating two terabytes of flow records per day with realistic sampling might produce 500 million labeled feature vectors for a training epoch.

Performing this epoch of training might take hours on a well-parallelised GPU cluster but would take weeks on a CPU cluster of similar cost. Weeks versus hours means the difference between a model that can be re-trained in response to fresh threat intelligence in a reasonable timeframe and one that effectively becomes fossilised in its initial deployment.

## 4.2 Behavioural Anomaly Detection and UEBA

User and entity behaviour analytics is a different position in the detection pipeline from traffic classification. Instead of asking if a given flow of data is consistent with a known bad pattern, UEBA asks if the aggregate of an entity's recent behaviour is different from its normal behaviour (Demmler et al., 2015). This means that you must build and maintain a probabilistic model of thousands of users and entities simultaneously and score new events against this model in near real time while events are arriving in rates of millions per minute in an enterprise environment.

GPU-based autoencoder architectures for UEBA are now the dominant form of implementation. The autoencoder learns a compressed representation of normal user activity; the error in reconstructing incoming events is used as an anomaly score. Large error in reconstructing an event indicates that the event cannot be compactly represented under a model of normality; in other words the event is structurally anomalous. This approach naturally extends to open-set insider threat detection: the analyst doesn't need to know what the attack patterns look like in advance, he only needs to know what normal looks like.

The application of graph neural networks (McMahan et al., 2017) to enterprise network topology represents a spatial extension of UEBA systems. Any form of lateral movement requires that attackers cross edges of the graph that are statistically rare, a workstation communicating with a domain controller it has never before contacted a service account authenticating to a production database from a novel source and so on.

According to Goodfellow et al. 2018, the use of a graphics processing unit to perform inference on graphs with billions of edges represents a form of topological anomaly detection, where attackers are revealed through patterns that are not anomalous on a per-entity basis but where no entity is behaving anomalously even as the collective pattern is highly anomalous.

### 4.3 Malware Analysis at Scale

Antivirus companies and threat intelligence services combine receive tens of millions of new binaries per day. Manually analyzing a small fraction of that number is impractical without automation. The GPU classification pipeline acts as the first stage of triage assigning a known malware family to the sample or marking it as a high-priority unknown for further analysis, usually in a matter of milliseconds from the time it was received.

The visualisation malware classification method where the raw binary data is converted to a grayscale image and then passed through a CNN exploits the inherent textural patterns that are characteristic of the code infrastructure and packers/configurations shared across malware families.

Classification accuracy for existing benchmarks is consistently above 97% for within-family classification and inference latency is below one millisecond per sample allowing for real-time classification at submission rates exceeding hundreds of thousands per second per node.

LLM-based malware analysis appears to be an emerging technology which warrants keeping an eye on. Capabilities such as explaining code attributing actor groups to code and generating YARA rules based on training or fine-tuning on decomposed code, assembly code and natural language-based threat intelligence reports have been successfully demonstrated.

Due to the inference costs associated with large language models acceleration via a GPU or TPU is a necessity for any practical deployment. National Institute of Standards and Technology, 2024 shows the techniques such as FP8 quantization and speculative decoding as implemented in TensorRT-LLM have reduced costs to a level which enterprise SOCs can afford.

## 5. REAL-TIME THREAT DETECTION AT NETWORK SCALE

### 5.1 GPU-Accelerated Network Intrusion Detection

The network link speed of 100 Gbps provides an ability to process approximately 149 million minimum-size Ethernet frames per second. A signature-based NIDS that checks all frames needs to finish all pattern-matching operations within 6.7 nanoseconds per packet and this needs to be done before even a single CPU cache miss. Table no.3 shows the network intrusion detection performance with CPU, GPU and TPU Architectures.

The GPU-based NIDS architectures achieve this by restructuring the pattern-matching process as a batch process. The packets are grouped in batches in a ring buffer and then copied to the GPU memory by the DMA controller. Thousands of threads then process the packets in parallel.

The Aho Corasick algorithm underlying Snort/Suricata rule engines has been implemented as a data structure resident on a GPU. Each thread processes an individual packet through a state transition graph representing an Aho Corasick algorithm (Jouppi et al., 2017). Collective throughput of thousands of threads results in 50 to 200 million packets per second pattern matching throughput on mid-range to high-end GPUs, a 20 to 100 times increase over CPU-based implementations.

Engineering challenges: While not trivial, the state transition graph representing a full set of production rules may exceed the size of a GPU's L2 cache. A PCIe bus-based data path from a network interface card to a GPU needs to be bypassed via kernel-space network capture frameworks like DPDK.

*Table 3. Network intrusion detection performance — CPU, GPU, and TPU architectures*

| NIDS Configuration | Accelerator | Throughput (Mpps) | Detection Latency |
|---|---|---|---|
| Suricata / Snort (CPU only) | Multi-core CPU | 1–5 Mpps | High (several ms) |
| GPU-accelerated Suricata | NVIDIA A100 | 50–200 Mpps | Moderate (<1 ms) |
| TPU + ML classifier | Google TPU v4 | ~100–300 Mpps* | Low (10–100 μs) |
| FPGA + GPU hybrid | Xilinx VU9P + H100 | >300 Mpps | Very low (<10 μs) |

## 5.2 DDoS Detection and Mitigation

Distributed denial of service attacks sit in a particularly awkward position in the realm of network defence: the attack is the problem and the act of analyzing the attack utilizes the same resources that the attack is attempting to deny.

A successful DDoS detection system needs not only to be fast but asymmetrically fast, that is it needs to have a high rate of detection with a low cost per packet, lest the detection engine become a bottleneck that the attack can exploit.

GPU-resident traffic statistics provide a way to achieve this asymmetry. Keeping source IP statistics for the entire ipv4 address space requires an allocation of approximately 16 GB memory for 32-bit counter width easily within the memory allocation for a data centre GPU.

Updating these statistics for incoming packets requires an atomic increment operation on the GPU taking a few nanoseconds. Calculation of aggregate entropy for the source address distribution or the ratio of SYN to SYN-ACK packets for the entire flow table can be performed in a single GPU reduction kernel running in microseconds over billions of flow table entries. These statistics are then used by a classifier to identify volumetric attacks, protocol reflection attacks and application-layer attacks in real time triggering mitigation responses such as route announcements, ACL pushes and scrubbing centre diversion before attack traffic even saturates uplink capacity.

## 5.3 SIEM Acceleration and Event Correlation

In modern enterprise environments, a SIEM system collects data from firewalls, endpoint systems, identity providers, cloud-native systems and many other sources and aggregates all these data streams into a normalized stream that can be processed by correlation rules. This stream contains many billions of events per day in an enterprise environment and the correlation rules that security engineers create to detect complex attacks involving multiple steps such as a reconnaissance scan followed by an authentication failure followed by a successful login from the same source must be executed against all possible combinations of matching events within specified time windows.

This combinatorial evaluation process is where CPU-based SIEM systems often reach their throughput limit, and the only options for the practitioner are to simplify the rule complexity or extend the aggregation window both of which increase the FN rate.

The GPU correlation engine maintains the state for the evaluation of millions of concurrent rule evaluations within the time window and executes the evaluation logic for thousands of in-flight windows in parallel for each tick of the clock cycle. Preliminary benchmarks for the research implementation show that the correlation throughput can reach hundreds of millions of event-rule evaluations per second well in excess of the event rate for even the largest of enterprises with sub-second detection latency for a threat that a CPU-based engine would take minutes to present as shown in table no.4.

*Table 4. GPU/TPU-accelerated cybersecurity threat detection — summary of performance and accuracy metrics*

| Threat Category | HPC Technique | Approx. Detection Accuracy | Response Latency |
|---|---|---|---|
| Volumetric DDoS | GPU traffic stats | >99% | Real-time (<1 ms) |
| Zero-day exploits | TPU anomaly model | ~92–96% | Near-real-time |
| APT lateral movement | GPU graph analytics | ~88–94% | Batch + streaming |
| Insider threat (UEBA) | GPU autoencoder | ~85–91% | Near-real-time |
| Ransomware activity | GPU I/O behaviour model | ~95–98% | Real-time (<5 ms) |

# 6. DEPLOYMENT FRAMEWORKS AND OPERATIONAL ENGINEERING

## 6.1 Programming Models and Toolchain Selection

CUDA remains the most capable and best-supported programming model for security applications that need custom computation. The CUDA toolchain which includes the nvcc compiler, Nsight profiler, compute-sanitizer memory checker, cuDNN, cuBLAS, cuSPARSE,

Thrust and RAPIDS has been developed over the last seventeen years and now includes all the numerical primitives a security programmer might need. For fixed hardware deployments, CUDA is the correct choice unless a constraint forces a different choice.

OpenCL offers a cross-vendor implementation for Intel, AMD and NVIDIA cards as well as certain FPGA types. The performance differential between a hand-optimized CUDA code and a corresponding OpenCL code on NVIDIA cards is typically between 10% and 30%. This is not a major issue for security analytics but could be significant for crypto code where every clock cycle is important.

The HIP framework provided by AMD allows code written in CUDA to be compiled for AMD cards with moderate porting effort giving MI300X-class cards access to the CUDA environment with adaptation rather than rewrite overhead.

PyTorch, TensorFlow, and JAX eliminate the need for programming GPUs and TPUs for ML tasks which account for the majority of the security analytics workload. These libraries abstract the underlying hardware for memory allocation, data transfer, kernel launch and distributed computation freeing the security data scientist from worrying about the hardware and focusing on the model architecture and training flow (Wei et al., 2023).

TensorRT and ONNX Runtime offer accelerated inference services with quantization, kernel fusion and dynamic batching for minimizing inference latency and cost in a SOC environment.

## 6.2 Security Risks in GPU-Accelerated Environments

The GPU is not a neutral accelerator that is dropped in an existing infrastructure and it comes with its own set of risks which must be understood by those responsible for the security of a system that utilizes a GPU accelerator.

GPU memory does not reset to zero when deallocated. In a multi-tenant cloud environment where GPU memory may be dynamically allocated between workloads or between customers, data from a previous workload may be readable by a subsequent tenant. This represents a serious risk if a workload handles plaintext credentials, private keys, or personal data which are exactly the workloads that many security-oriented workloads fall into. NVIDIA's Hopper architecture provides a memory scrubbing feature but this requires operational effort to take full advantage of the feature not simply purchasing a newer generation of NVIDIA hardware.

GPU driver vulnerabilities are another concern that needs to be addressed. The GPU driver code runs in the kernel privilege level is one of the most complex closed-source codebases in use today and has historically been subject to less rigorous security analysis than OS kernel code.

A privilege escalation vulnerability in a GPU driver allows an attacker to gain kernel-level access to a host system completely disregarding all application-level security measures in place. GPU driver versions need to be included in the patch management process in the same way that OS kernel and hypervisor patches are treated.

Side-channel attacks against computations performed on GPUs have been shown to be possible in a research context. Time side-channel attacks against GPUs where the time it takes to execute a kernel is data-dependent can leak information about data being computed. Resource contention on shared resources such as memory bandwidth, caches and execution resources in a multi-tenant scenario can leak side-channel information across security domains.

Side-channel attacks against GPUs are more difficult to exploit than those against CPUs but in a cryptographic context where such computations are likely to be performed in a cloud-based scenario the easiest solution is to run such computations on dedicated non-shared instances of GPUs.

## 6.3 Infrastructure Integration and Capacity Planning

The construction of the data pipeline to the GPU accelerator is equally important to the choice of the accelerator itself. The throughput capacity of a GPU is only realized when it is supplied with data at a rate and in a form that can be efficiently processed by the GPU. A common failure mode of first-generation GPU security systems is a CPU-bound pre-processing step that starves the GPU or a PCIe data transfer bottleneck that causes the GPU to wait for data.

Measuring the entire system pipeline under realistic conditions, not just the performance of the GPU kernel itself is the key diagnostic to determine whether acceleration is being provided or the accelerator is simply sitting idle.

Apache Kafka has become the de facto streaming backbone for GPU-accelerated security pipelines offering a long-term partitioned log of events that can be consumed independently of the ingestion and processing rates without any back-pressure propagating upstream to the log sources.

The NVIDIA DOCA framework and DPDK library's userspace networking stack bypass the OS kernel for packet capture operations and deliver them directly to GPU memory via RDMA operations, avoiding the need for a copy that would otherwise limit the rate of incoming packets to a fraction of the GPU's potential throughput as shown in figure no.4 the ML based IDS.

*Figure 4. ML-Based IDS model training time vs. dataset size — CPU, GPU, and TPU comparison (log-log scale)*

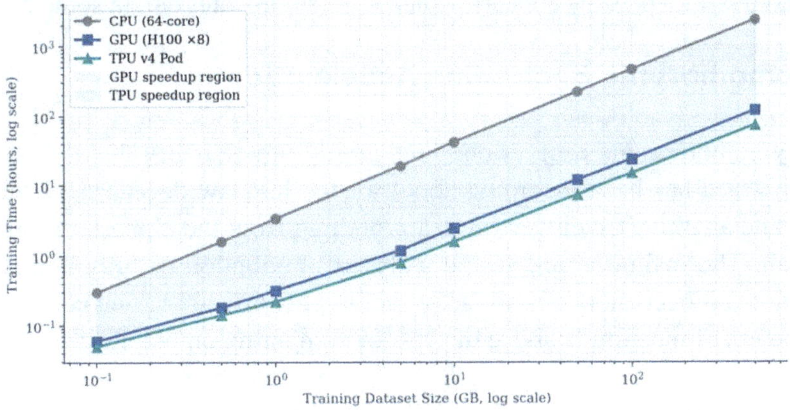

# 7. EMERGING RESEARCH DIRECTIONS

## 7.1 Federated Learning for Cross-Organisational Threat Intelligence

The most accurate intrusion detection models are learned from the most diverse datasets but the most diverse datasets are those for which organisations would be forced to share raw security event data with one another, a situation that regulations, competition and organizational conservatism make impossible.

Federated learning provides a way out of this apparent no-win situation. Each organisation learns a model on their data adds up gradients over a fixed training round and sends those gradients to a central aggregator that combines them to improve the global model. The raw data never crosses the organizational border; only derived information in the form of gradients does (Dwork, C., & Roth, A. (2014)).

The acceleration of computations on a participant's GPU is what enables the local training step to occur at a rate which keeps the federation cycle running at a rate which is operationally relevant. Without such acceleration a federation round might take days to run but with modern GPU technology, a federation round consisting of a day's worth of telemetry data takes just a few hours which enables a daily refresh cycle which adapts to a changing threat landscape. The addition of differential privacy noise to gradients before transmission, a calculation which can be parallelised across a GPU gives a formal mathematical guarantee about what an adversary controlling the aggregation server can learn about a participant's data which addresses a privacy concern which gradient updates can in some cases leak.

## 7.2 Homomorphic Encryption Acceleration

Fully homomorphic encryption is the crypto functionality that the crypto and security world has been dreaming about for the last few decades. It's the ability to compute anything on ciphertext, learn nothing from the ciphertext and decrypt the result. The main obstacle to the widespread adoption of fully homomorphic encryption has been an overhead factor that has historically varied between five to seven orders of magnitude above the cost of computing on plaintext.

The acceleration of FHE by GPU technology has been gradually closing the gap. Libraries such as CUDA-HE, cuFHE and the recently announced TensorFHE provide an implementation of NTT-based polynomial operations which dominate FHE computations and are now available on GPU hardware achieving speedups between 20 to 40 times compared to an optimized CPU implementation for the BFV and CKKS schemes.

The use case that appears most relevant to practical deployment is privacy-preserving collaborative threat intelligence: two organisations, each possessing partial indicators of compromise wish to compute the union or intersection of their indicator sets without either revealing to the other which of their indicators did not match.

Private set intersection protocols based on GPU acceleration of homomorphic encryption or oblivious PRF can perform such a computation on sets of millions of indicators in seconds which appears to be a practical speed for operational threat intelligence sharing without the legal and competitive risk of disclosure.

## 7.3 Neuromorphic Computing and Spiking Neural Networks

The "always on" nature of network security monitoring poses a power budget problem and traditional GPU architectures are not well-suited to solve it. A GPU running at full utilization for constant monitoring consumes hundreds of watts; in most enterprise network segments the attack traffic that the system is monitoring for arrives sporadically amidst a flood of benign traffic (Vaswani et al., 2025).

The GPU is wasting power monitoring benign traffic with only occasional bursts of interesting traffic. Neuromorphic processors such as Intel's Loihi 2 only operate when events occur and their power consumption is proportional to the rate of events, not their frequency and that is potentially transformative for ambient monitoring workloads.

The accuracy of spiking neural network anomaly detectors implemented on neuromorphic hardware has been shown to be within a few percent of their conventional deep learning equivalent implemented in simulation but with energy consumption reduced by a factor of ten or more.

The tool chain for converting a trained model into an equivalent form suitable for implementation on the target platform is in a very early stage of development but the research path is promising. The training infrastructure for surrogate gradient training of SNNs on GPUs is an active research path providing the training path for neuromorphic security even before the deployment platform is mature.

## 7.4 Quantum-Classical Hybrid Security Architectures

The impact of quantum computing on cybersecurity has two parts, one as a potential threat and the other as a potential opportunity. The threat of Shor's algorithm breaking RSA and ECC on a fault-tolerant quantum computer has already begun to be addressed in the transition to post-quantum cryptography.

The opportunity for quantum algorithms to improve security analytics has several parts including Grover's algorithm offering a quadratic speedup in unstructured search problems applicable to key space search, quantum machine learning offering polynomial speedups for specific classification problems and quantum simulation offering improved modeling of adversaries in complex network systems.

Realistic assessment of the prospects for quantum security analytics in the near term is necessarily measured. Realistic estimates suggest that practical fault-tolerant quantum processors with the qubit count and gate quality levels required to support these algorithms will not be forthcoming for at least ten years.

The relevant near-term research direction is not quantum security analytics but rather quantum-safe security infrastructure to guarantee that existing systems are not vulnerable to the quantum computers that will be available in fifteen to twenty years. The relevant near-term action item is actually GPU-accelerated post-quantum cryptography.

## 8. DISCUSSION: STRATEGIC CONSIDERATIONS FOR PRACTITIONERS AND RESEARCHERS

Three strategic observations may be drawn from the technical discussion above that are worth making explicit. First, the performance gap between GPU-accelerated and CPU-only security infrastructure has grown to the point where it no longer feels like a marginal improvement in performance but rather a matter of capability.

Organizations that do not have GPU-accelerated cryptographic processing will not be able to complete their TLS migration to post-quantum TLS without CPU hardware investments that are more expensive than what's necessary for GPU offload.

Organizations that do not have GPU-accelerated security analytics will not be able to run the ML-based detection models that their security vendor has increasingly made their default offering. This is not a future problem that's going to become relevant in several years. It's a decision that needs to be made in the next twelve to thirty-six months for organizations that are currently planning their budgets.

The second observation relates to the skills gap. The ability to do secure GPU engineering requires parallel computing and security domain expertise. This is a very rare combination. CUDA programming, memory hierarchy optimisation, kernel profiling and distributed execution are not skills that security engineers normally develop.

The parallel computing world also has not traditionally been very interested in security profiles. Organisations that are doing this effectively are doing one of three things: building hybrid engineers, building a thin abstraction layer over the GPU to allow security engineers to leverage the acceleration without having to write CUDA code or leveraging a managed cloud service that provides GPU-as-a-service for training or TPUs for inference and hides the hardware completely.

The third observation is adversarial resilience. While the introduction of the new class of ML-based detection systems with GPU acceleration is significant, it is not the last step in the detection arms race but rather an escalation thereof. Adversarial players given the same access to the same hardware can develop adversarial perturbation generators to evade detection develop traffic patterns that by design will always be placed in the low-confidence region of the decision boundary or even exploit the training cycle to temporarily stop detection during the training gap between epochs.

The key defenses are the use of adversarial training, i.e., training with adversarial perturbations and ensemble detection architectures, i.e., the combination of many classes of models. Diversity rather than relying on a single model class and single vendor is the key to the strategic defense.

## 9. CONCLUSION

In this chapter the journey from hardware basics to deployment of acceleration in advanced cybersecurity with GPUs and TPUs has been explored. The argument for HPC in cybersecurity is not based on a future hardware roadmap but rather on a current throughput improvement that is measured in hundreds for the most important workloads in cybersecurity: cryptographic hashing, packet classification, ML inference and SIEM correlation. At this level of improvement the discussion is no longer about whether to deploy a GPU-based solution but rather about how to prioritize such a deployment based on other pressing needs and budget constraints.

There are a few conclusions that should be highlighted in particular. Firstly, post-quantum cryptography acceleration is an investment with the greatest time constraints as the cryptographic change is a mandatory requirement, algorithms are standardised and compute costs are high enough to warrant offloading to a GPU.

ML-based intrusion detection is an analytics investment with the greatest leverage as the gap between classical signature-based and ML-based solutions is high and widening. Federated learning and homomorphic encryption acceleration are research investments with the greatest strategic impact for data-processing organisations with cross-organisational boundaries.

The underlying theme common to all these particular observations is the computational aspect of security in general. The threats that were previously constrained by the attackers' computing resources – brute-force cryptanalysis, ML-assisted spear phishing, real-time adaptive evasion of detection systems now enjoy the same unconstrained computing as the defenders do thanks to commodity GPU systems. The security position of any organisation that has not taken account of the computational aspect of its security is actually in a weaker position than it might appear to be. High-performance computing is no longer a luxury that a security program might enjoy; it is increasingly becoming the fundamental infrastructure upon which a security program relies.

## REFERENCES


Bernstein, D. J. (2025). Post-quantum cryptography. In *Encyclopedia of Cryptography, Security and Privacy* (pp. 1846-1847). Cham: Springer Nature Switzerland. http://dx.doi.org/DOI: 10.1007/978-3-030-71522-9_386

Bos, J., Ducas, L., Kiltz, E., Lepoint, T., Lyubashevsky, V., Schanck, J. M., Schwabe, P., Seiler, G., & Stehlé, D. (2018). CRYSTALS-Kyber: A CCA-secure module-lattice-based KEM. 2018 IEEE European Symposium on Security and Privacy (EuroS&P), 353–367. https://doi.org/DOI: 10.1109/EuroSP.2018.00032

Chen, T., Moreau, T., Jiang, Z., Zheng, L., Yan, E., Shen, H., & Krishnamurthy, A. (2018). {TVM}: An automated {End-to-End} optimizing compiler for deep learning. In *13th USENIX symposium on operating systems design and implementation (OSDI 18)* (pp. 578-594). https://doi.org/DOI: 10.48550/arXiv.1802.04799

Costan, V., & Devadas, S. (2016). Intel SGX explained. IACR Cryptology ePrint Archive, 2016(086). https://eprint.iacr.org/2016/086

Demmler, D., Schneider, T., & Zohner, M. (2015). ABY: A framework for efficient mixed-protocol secure two-party computation. *Proceedings of the 22nd Annual NDSS Symposium*, 1–15. https://doi.org/DOI: 10.14722/ndss.2015.23113

Ducas, L., Kiltz, E., Lepoint, T., Lyubashevsky, V., Schwabe, P., Seiler, G., & Stehlé, D. (2018). CRYSTALS-Dilithium: A lattice-based digital signature scheme. IACR Transactions on Cryptographic Hardware and Embedded Systems, 2018(1), 238–268. https://doi.org/DOI: 10.13154/tches.v2018.i1.238-268

Dwork, C., & Roth, A. (2014). The algorithmic foundations of differential privacy. *Foundations and Trends in Theoretical Computer Science*, *9*(3–4), 211–487. DOI: 10.1561/0400000042

Goodfellow, I., McDaniel, P., & Papernot, N. (2018). Making machine learning robust against adversarial inputs. *Communications of the ACM*, *61*(7), 56–66. DOI: 10.1145/3134599

Jouppi, N. P., Young, C., Patil, N., & Patterson, D. (2017). In-datacenter performance analysis of a tensor processing unit. *Proceedings of the 44th ISCA*, 1–12. https://doi.org/DOI: 10.1145/3079856.3080246

Lecuyer, M., Atlidakis, V., Geambasu, R., Hsu, D., & Jana, S. (2019). Certified robustness to adversarial examples with differential privacy. Proceedings of the 2019 IEEE S&P, 656–672. https://doi.org/DOI: 10.1109/SP.2019.00044

McMahan, H. B., Moore, E., Ramage, D., Hampson, S., & Agüera y Arcas, B. (2017). Communication-efficient learning of deep networks from decentralised data. *Proceedings of the 20th AISTATS*, 1273–1282. https://doi.org/DOI: 10.48550/arXiv.1602.05629

National Institute of Standards and Technology, S. (2024). FIPS 204, module-lattice-based digital signature standard. https://doi.org/DOI: 10.6028/NIST.FIPS.204

NIST. (2024). *Module-lattice-based key-encapsulation mechanism standard (FIPS 203)*. National Institute of Standards and Technology., DOI: 10.6028/NIST.FIPS.203

Vaswani, A., Shazeer, N., Parmar, N., Uszkoreit, J., Jones, L., Gomez, A. N., Kaiser, Ł., & Polosukhin, I. (2025). Attention is all you need. *Advances in Neural Information Processing Systems*, *30*, 5998–6008. DOI: 10.48550/arXiv.1706.03762

Wei, Y., Wang, S., Nait-Abdesselam, F., & Benlarbi-Delai, A. (2023, December). Study of spiking neural network-based regressor on applications in digital predistortion for power amplifiers. In 2023 6th International Conference on Advanced Communication Technologies and Networking (CommNet) (pp. 1-7). IEEE. http://dx.doi.org/DOI: 10.1109/CommNet60167.2023.10365305

## KEY TERMS AND DEFINITIONS

**CUDA (Compute Unified Device Architecture):** NVIDIA's parallel computing platform and API that exposes GPU hardware to general-purpose programming via a C/C++ extension, giving direct control over thread hierarchy and the memory subsystem.

**Federated Learning:** A distributed training paradigm in which each participating node trains a local model on its own data and shares only gradient updates with a central aggregator, preserving data locality and supporting privacy regulations.

**GPU (Graphics Processing Unit):** A massively-parallel processor built around thousands of lightweight arithmetic cores. Originally designed for real-time 3D rendering, it is now the dominant accelerator for scientific computing, machine-learning training, and cryptographic workloads.

**Homomorphic Encryption (HE):** A family of cryptographic constructions allowing arithmetic on ciphertexts; the decrypted result matches what would be obtained by operating on plaintexts directly, enabling privacy-preserving delegated computation (Lecuyer et al., 2019).

**Intrusion Detection System (IDS):** A monitoring component — host-based or network-based — that analyses activity streams against known-bad signatures or learnt behavioural baselines, raising alerts or triggering automated countermeasures when anomalies are identified.

**Post-Quantum Cryptography (PQC):** The cryptographic algorithms conjectured to remain hard even for fault-tolerant quantum computers, including the lattice-based schemes standardised by NIST as FIPS 203 and FIPS 204 and the hash-based scheme FIPS 205.

**SIMT (Single Instruction Multiple Thread):** NVIDIA's execution model in which a warp of 32 threads simultaneously executes the same instruction on distinct data elements, amortising instruction-decode cost across the warp while permitting per-thread predication.

**Tensor Core:** Purpose-built execution units within NVIDIA GPUs that perform mixed-precision matrix fused-multiply-add operations in a single clock cycle, yielding throughput far exceeding the standard FP32 CUDA cores for deep-learning arithmetic.

**TPU (Tensor Processing Unit):** A domain-specific ASIC developed by Google whose systolic-array design maximises the efficiency of matrix-multiply-accumulate operations central to neural-network training and inference, trading programmability for throughput and energy efficiency.

**UEBA (User and Entity Behaviour Analytics):** A security-analytics discipline that constructs probabilistic models of normal operational patterns for users, hosts, and services, then raises risk scores for deviations indicative of account compromise, insider threats, or undetected lateral movement.

# Chapter 7
# AI-Based Approaches to Intrusion Detection and Privacy Preservation in Autonomous Systems

**Vikas Sharma**
http://orcid.org/0000-0001-8173-4548
*Department of Computer Applications, SRM Institute of Science and Technology, Delhi NCR, India*

**Tarun Kumar Vashishth**
http://orcid.org/0000-0001-9916-9575
*Department of Computer Applications, Vidya University, Meerut, India*

**Shashiraj Teotia**
http://orcid.org/0000-0002-0849-3642
*Department of Computer Applications, Swami Vivekanand Subharti University, Meerut, India*

**Devendra Singh**
*Department of Mechanical Engineering, Ajay Kumar Garg Engineering College, Ghaziabad, India*

**Sonal Shah**
*Department of IT, Auro University, Surat, India*

**Sachin Chaudhary**
http://orcid.org/0000-0002-8415-0043
*School of Computer Science and Applications, IIMT University, Meerut, India*

**Pushpendra Kumar Verma**
http://orcid.org/0000-0003-2777-5626
*School of Computer Science and Applications, IIMT University, Meerut, India*

## ABSTRACT

*Cybersecurity is one of the most pressing concerns with regard to autonomous systems' ever-increasing adoption across multiple sectors, including transportation, health*

DOI: 10.4018/979-8-3373-9053-6.ch007

*care, and smart city developments. The aim of this chapter is to focus on the various methods of securing autonomous systems through artificial intelligence (AI)-powered intrusion detection systems (IDS) and privacy-preserving mechanisms. For example, this chapter will explore the use of machine learning for anomaly detection as well as secure federated learning and blockchain technology to enhance the integrity of data in autonomous systems. Furthermore, it will provide an overview of the use of adversarially attacking AI models and provide recommendations for reducing cyber risk. Utilizing AI-based security frameworks, autonomous systems can identify threats and respond to them almost instantly, while ensuring user privacy. Finally, this chapter addresses the regulatory hurdles surrounding autonomous technology, as well as potential areas for future research related to security in autonomous systems.*

## 1. INTRODUCTION

The fast-paced growth of automation and artificial intelligence is changing how we think about Autonomous Systems (i.e., systems that perform tasks without human intervention) in various industries, such as Transportation, Healthcare, Smart Cities, and Industrial Automation. Most Autonomous Systems use a large number of connected devices and a central computer system that uses AI for decision-making to allow them to run independently from humans. Therefore, Autonomous Technologies are becoming increasingly prevalent in the world, resulting in numerous cybersecurity issues, such as Data Breaches, Adversarial Attacks, and other Cybersecurity Threats. Because of their decentralized nature and ability to operate in real time, traditional security methods may not be sufficiently secure against Cybersecurity Threats. To increase Security in Autonomous Systems, AI-based Intrusion Detection Systems (IDSs) and privacy-preserving capabilities will be critical. AI-based IDSs leverage Deep Learning to detect anomalous behaviour in real-time by processing large volumes of data and analysing the patterns in that data as well as the identification of unknown threats. On the other hand, Privacy-Preserving Mechanisms will support the development of Federated Learning by allowing the training of AI Models on Autonomous Systems to be completed without any disclosure of confidential information. The first two points highlight how decentralised models like Federated Learning enhance the security of data while still allowing for efficient and effective threat detection through the use of AI. Furthermore, blockchain technology offers a decentralized and tamper-proof method to ensure data integrity. It provides secure communication and validates transactions within autonomous networks. Autonomous systems still face a high level of challenge when it comes to cyber adversaries targeting AI systems using adversarial attacks, meaning adversaries attack the input into A.I. decision-making systems (Mollashaik, 2025) to cause misclassification or erroneous behaviour of the autonomous system. Cybersecurity practitioners will need strong defence mechanisms against such attacks, which will include adversarial training, differential privacy and anomaly detection algorithms. The regulatory challenges posed by cybersecurity policy and compliance frameworks will also complicate the secure operation of autonomous systems because current regulations must evolve to meet the new risks of A.I. autonomous technology. Machine learning anomaly detection, secure federated learning and blockchain technology offer a path toward providing greater security for autonomous systems. The impact of adversarial attacks on the performance of A.I. models will also be presented, along with a discussion of how various cyber security solutions may be available to mitigate these attacks and improve the overall security posture of artificial intelligence. A.I. security frameworks have the potential to deliver tremendous value to autonomous systems through the ability to conduct continuous automatic identification and response to emerging cyber threats while safeguarding the privacy of users. This chapter discusses various challenges associated with developing a regulatory structure for autonomous technology, as well as the complementary trajectories for future research that are necessary to enhance safety and trust in autonomous technology within our increasingly connected and digital environment (Cheng et al., 2025).

## 1.1 Overview of Autonomous Systems in Various Domains

The development of autonomous systems leveraging AI (Artificial Intelligence), ML (Machine Learning) and advanced sensor systems is leading the way in many sectors and creating next-generation solutions to many existing problems e.g., autonomous vehicles can provide a safer form of transportation, mitigate congestion, and maximize fuel efficiency through intelligent navigation and real-time decision making. Please note that we refer to autonomous vehicles or driverless cars throughout; however, the use of AI perception, planning, and control provides drivers and riders with a plethora of choices of various types of transportation modes, including the following, automated delivery drones, ride serving companies and automated public transit. In healthcare, for example, autonomous systems are increasingly used to assist in the performance of surgery, provide automated diagnostic systems, and enable remote patient monitoring (Vashishth et al., 2024). For example, medical robots are capable of performing surgery with precision, while AI capable of diagnosing conditions using images from x-rays, MRIs, and CTs with high accuracy is providing improved outcomes for patients by detecting disease at an earlier stage. Similarly, smart cities are leveraging autonomous systems to enhance urban infrastructure and improve the management of urban resources. AI-based tracking, intelligence based tracking, and automatic trash management solutions help with safety in society, decrease energy usage while developing urban layout. Drones and

Robots are supporting with disaster relief activities as well as the management of our environment by providing us real-time streaming info to make better decisions. Autonomous systems such as autonomous robots and AI-based predictive maintenance in producing industries streamline the manufacturing process to produce more products at a lower cost. The agriculture sector is improving how we monitor, water, and harvest crops with the use of drones and AI controlled machines. These developments promote sustainable farming for a better environment. The rapid expansion of autonomous systems is causing incomparable cybersecurity and privacy issues. Most all autonomous systems are connected via network infrastructure, therefore they transmit large amounts of information on a real-time basis, to be processed by AI and make real-time decisions. This increases the opportunity for cyber-attacks, adversary penetration, and unauthorised access to information. In order to maintain the trust and reliability of autonomous technology, it is necessary to create strong security standards, develop AI-based intrusion detection systems and work toward designing privacy-preserving technology solutions for all autonomous systems (Dhinakaran et al., 2024).

## 1.2 Growing Cybersecurity Threats in Autonomous Technologies

As industries such as transportation, healthcare, smart cities, and industrial automation continue to automate processes, there will be increased sophistication and frequency of cyber threats to autonomous technologies as well. Because of the interconnected nature of autonomous systems, the need for real-time data processing, and reliance on AI for decision making, autonomous technologies will have an increased vulnerability to cyber attackers. The connectedness of autonomous systems and the reliance on real-time data processing provide cybercriminals with numerous opportunities to exploit weaknesses within those systems and conduct a variety of cyber-attacks (e.g., data breaches, Denial of Service attacks, adversarial AI manipulation). Such attacks may prevent operations of autonomous systems, interfere with operations, threaten safety and privacy, and create substantial risks for public safety. A prime example is how cybercriminals can manipulate the sensors/ GPS of an autonomous vehicle, which may put the passenger and pedestrian safety at risk because of incorrect navigation decisions. Adversarial AI attacks may also be one of the most concerning types of cyber-attacks in the autonomous technology industry. Cybercriminals can feed purposely crafted inputs into AI models to deceive the AI model, resulting in the AI model misclassifying, bypassing security measures, or malfunctioning under certain conditions. Furthermore, autonomous technologies create and process enormous amounts of sensitive data, which provides another avenue for cybercriminals to gain access to that data through data breaches and identity theft. Unauthorized access to medical robots, smart surveillance systems, or industrial automation systems creates a variety of ethical and regulatory issues and exposes confidential patient information. One of the biggest challenges in protecting Autonomous Systems from Distributed Denial of Service (DDoS) attacks and ransomware is how to secure them because they rely heavily on cloud and edge computing technologies. Cybercriminals exploit vulnerabilities within the networks that support these systems to interrupt or take control of operations as ransom. Due to the distributed architectures of Autonomous Systems and the way they need to be able to operate in near real-time, securing Autonomous Systems is unique and considerably different than most other types of systems, so traditional cyber protection techniques may not be sufficient for every Autonomous System. New approaches to Cybersecurity are emerging to help alleviate some of the complexity of securing Autonomous Systems (Andreoni et al., 2024).

## 2. CYBERSECURITY CHALLENGES IN AUTONOMOUS SYSTEMS

Across multiple industries, there is growing reliance on autonomous systems that have introduced cybersecurity challenges of complex nature that can compromise or jeopardize the reliability, safety, and integrity of the systems. Autonomous Systems interface with the physical world in dynamic, complex, and interconnected environments. Because of that there is a vast array of cyber threats these systems face, including but not limited to unauthorized access, adversarial attacks on AI (Artificial Intelligence), compromises to data, and network vulnerabilities. Of the greatest challenges of Autonomous Systems, is to secure the way these systems make real-time decisions. Real-time decision making is based on overwhelming amounts of data created from sensor information, images, and Communication Networks. Should the integrity of any data source be compromised, this could result in erroneous decisions and could, in turn, result in catastrophic failure, such as accidents in Autonomous Vehicle, Diagnostic Errors, in AI Medical Diagnostics, or Cyber Security Breaches, within Smart City Infrastructure. A second, and perhaps equally important challenge of Autonomous Systems, is weaknesses of AI Models used within Autonomous Systems, which may be exploited through adversarial attacks, whereby cybercriminals exploit weaknesses with input data and trick AI algorithms into misclassifying objects, misinterpreting threats, or behaving erratically. This is an especially critical issue for Safety Critical Systems, such as those used in Self-Driving Cars and Autonomous Drones, where split-second decisions are required to protect human safety. As companies deal with the difficulties associated with complying with regulatory requirements regarding AI, they are also finding themselves under a great deal of additional regulatory compliance issues that are complicating their ability to manage their cyber security risks. Companies should take a proactive approach toward cyber security by utilising a number of different types of security technologies, including intrusion detection systems that use AI; secure data storage and management systems that use blockchain technology; encryption methods; and strong authentication systems. When proactive systems are deployed, autonomous systems will be able to defend themselves from cyber threats better than ever, allowing for both safe and ethical use of these systems in the market place (Vyas et al., 2024).

## 2.1 Threat Landscape in Autonomous Systems

Emerging and adopting autonomous systems have introduced a greater risk of cyber threats to these systems as the result of how they operate in critical sectors i.e. transportation, healthcare, smart cities, industrial automation. The reliance of autonomous systems on artificial intelligence (AI), machine learning (ML), sensor networks, and cloud computing makes them subject to a rapidly expanding and increasingly complex set of cyber threats from criminals targeting autonomous system networks and the AI-based decision-making capabilities and exploiting vulnerabilities in those networks. Threats to autonomous technology will continue to evolve because criminal actors will be inventing new ways of acquiring and using the information that is created by autonomous systems. Understanding the types of threats posed to autonomous systems is important in creating effective cybersecurity strategies that protect these systems from being exploited. Adversarial AI attacks by malicious actors is one of the most serious threats to the security of autonomous technologies. Adversarial AI is when a criminal uses adversarial artificial intelligences to manipulate the input information of the AI model used by an autonomous system in order to mislead or deceive the AI model. Autonomous vehicles are vulnerable to attacks that may potentially harm their operators. A common method used by some of these attackers is the alteration of traffic signs so that an autonomous vehicle's AI model is unable to determine what how a stop sign and speed limit should be interpreted. Loss of control in the event of an altercation caused by an attacker would lead to serious consequences, including the potential for an accident. Attacks against medical AI systems are similar. In both cases of altered input data, an adversary creates a situation that puts a patient and consumer in harm's way. In both examples described above, the risk associated with improper input data to an AI model is significant and poses a risk of harm to society at large. Another major concern that attackers have caused through the act of cyber threats around data breach and the presumed illegal access of confidential information are that, as AI systems create large amounts of data (i.e., personally identifiable information, financial information, operational data, etc.), any data that could potentially be targeted as a result of the attack could result in identity theft, financial fraud, and/or corporate espionage.

*Figure 1. Autonomous system architecture with AI models*

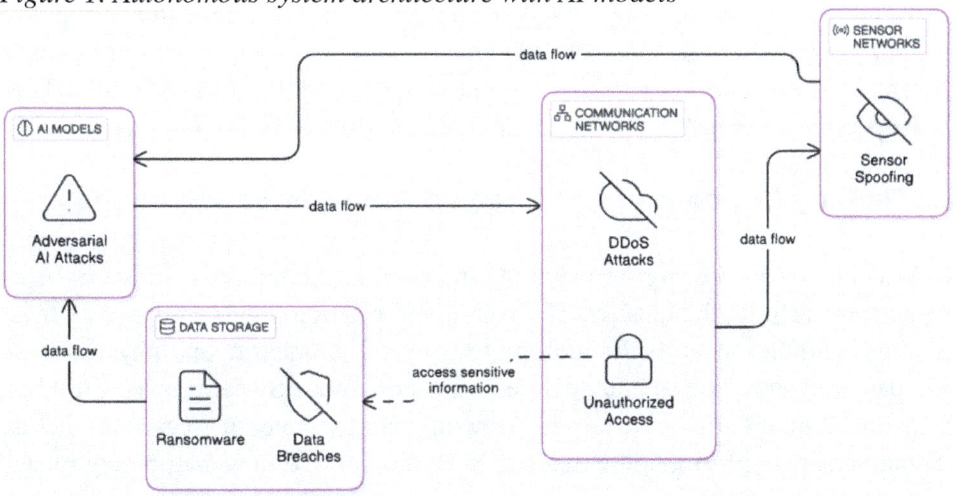


The attacks of DDoS and ransomware pose increasing layers of complexity and challenges to the cybersecurity of autonomous systems. They disrupt the operation of autonomous networks by filling them with surplus traffic and preventing access to critical systems, e.g., if there were a DDoS attack on the smart cities system, this would interfere with the operation of traffic management systems leading to excessive congestion and accidents. Ransomware attacks against autonomous healthcare systems could render healthcare professionals unable to access medical equipment and patient records until the ransom was paid. These types of attacks can have devastating financial and operational consequences. There currently exist frameworks and protocols for protecting against such attacks and the potential for cyber-physical attacks from sensor spoofing, which also represents an extreme risk to the safety and integrity of Autonomous Systems, (Nasir et al.,2024) which rely on a number of sensor technologies including LiDAR, radar, and GPS to navigate and make decisions. Spoofing sensor inputs using false signals, jamming GPS coordinates, or injecting harmful data onto a sensor network represents an immense risk to the safe operation of these systems and to the lives of the individuals who depend on them. The use of encryption, authentication, and forms of anomaly detection can prevent the potential for these types of cyber threats. Due to the interconnected and ever-changing nature of autonomous systems, they are extremely attractive to cybercriminals, nation-state actors, and malicious insiders. The present methods of securing these types of intelligent and automated systems by relying on strict rules and static methods of defence are insufficient to protect these types of systems. (Moustafa et al. 2023). Adapting to the evolving threat environment necessitates the use of AI-based Security Solutions (Cybersecurity Applications) along with Blockchain-based Data Integrity solutions (Blockchain based Solutions), to Secure Federated Learning (Privacy Preserving for AI) and Threat Monitoring capabilities depicted in figure 1. Autonomous Systems implementing Proactive Security Solutions can, therefore, continue to mitigate and respond to Cybersecurity threats in Real Time (to help maintain their S/RC in a growingly Digital World) (Alqubaysi et al. 2025).

## 2.2 Privacy Concerns in AI-Enabled Autonomous Systems

With an ever-increasing number of AI empowered (Autonomous) Systems being created and utilised, the quantity of sensitive information (data) produced by these systems continues to grow. In addition to personal, biometric, and physical location data collected, stored and analysed by Autonomous Systems in Health Care, Transport, Smart Cities etc.; rapidly growing Privacy concerns regarding the use of such sensitive information will also need addressing. Below are privacy-related issues surrounding the use of AI powered autonomous systems.

**1. Data Collection and Surveillance Risks:** Data collection, continual improvement of functionality, improving user experience and personalisation are all crucial components of AI enabled autonomous systems. In order to further these goals, a substantial amount of data must be collected by and from Autonomous Systems and as such, this collection can be construed to be surveillance. Smart cities deploy AI-enabled (Camera and IoT) systems, which constantly monitor the behaviour of individuals using both the public space and the road systems, but excessive monitoring can impede or infringe on an individual's right to privacy. The greatest challenge for society is to strike a proper balance between leveraging the advantages of the data collection from AI enabled autonomous systems and protecting users' privacy and rights to control their own personal information (Sharma and Bairwa 2025).

**2. Unauthorized Access and Data Breaches:** The most damaging form of data breach involves an AI healthcare system being breached and exposing sensitive personal patient information, enabling identity thieves to steal their identities and commit financial fraud. The potential for breaches in autonomous financial services could affect the banking transactions of the consumers involved, as well as expose their personal and private financial information. Furthermore, adversarial attacks against AI models and dataset via unauthorized access provides an opportunity for cybercriminals to manipulate AI predictions for fraudulent purposes. Therefore, encryption, effective access control systems, and use of blockchain technology to protect data storage should all be required to help mitigate the risk of data breaches and/or unauthorized access in AI-enabled autonomous systems.

**3. Lack of User Consent and Data Ownership:** Due to the nature of autonomous technologies, the collection and processing of their data is done in real-time. Given how difficult it is, in most cases, to obtain explicit consent for processing real time data in AI-enabled Autonomous Technologies, ethical and legal issues arise. In addition, it is unclear what parties hold ownership of processed data in AI-enabled Autonomous Technologies (i.e., the user, service provider, or developer of the AI Model) and what, if any, limits exist as to how service providers can levy processed data. Ultimately, establishing clear data protection policies and allowing users to control access to their own data will help provide compliance to privacy legislation (e.g., GDPR and CCPA).

**4. Privacy Risks in Federated Learning and AI Training:** Federated learning provides organizations with a means of enhancing the capabilities of AI models without requiring the organization to centralize their datasets into a single location. As the use of federated learning becomes more common for developing autonomous systems, organizations will need to weigh the benefits of this privacy-preserving method of training against the potential threats posed by malicious actors who may participate in their federated learning networks. Once a malicious user can access a Federated Learning system, they may try to recover any information contained in the individual's model updates from the federated learning system. In addition to attempting to recover an individual user's information, these malicious users may also try to manipulate the organization's model through the introduction of contaminated (biased or invalid) data.

The protection of user privacy must be considered by organizations in order to build and maintain trust in the use of AI-enabled autonomous systems. Organizations will also have to take proactive measures to protect against any potential malicious attacks that may occur as the use of AI-enabled autonomous systems continues to grow.

## 3. AI-BASED INTRUSION DETECTION FOR AUTONOMOUS SYSTEMS

Due to their static methods of detecting threats, traditional methods of detecting intrusion threats (IDS) cannot keep pace with the rapid changes in autonomous systems threats. As a result, AI-based intrusion detection systems (AI-IDS) have been proposed to address this shortcoming. By leveraging machine learning (ML) and deep learning (DL), AI-IDS can quickly identify, analyse, and mitigate cyber threats in real-time (Vikas et al., 2023). AI-IDS utilise both supervised and unsupervised learning approaches, allowing them to detect all types of attacks, including those already identified and those still unknown (Laghari et al., 2025).

## 3.1 Fundamentals of Intrusion Detection Systems (IDS) in Autonomous Systems

Autonomous systems rely on an Intrusion Detection System (IDS) to protect them from cyber threats and are therefore important components in the protection of autonomous systems. Due to the complex nature of these systems (involving many interconnected sensors, networks, and AI systems), they are prone to attack by sophisticated cyber threats. Some examples of cyber threats are malware, denial of service (DoS) attacks, data breaches, and unauthorized access attempts, all of which can greatly affect the operation, reliability, and safety of autonomous systems. To mitigate the potential risks of cybersecurity violations against the organizations utilizing autonomous technology, IDS continually monitors network traffic (system traffic) and application activities by users while seeking to ensure compliance with security policies. In addition to improving the operational resilience of autonomous systems through the timely identification and response to cybersecurity violations, NABM helps position organizations mitigating cyber threats that may impact autonomous technologies by providing organizations with the ability to quickly isolate, contain, and remediate potential security breaches. Cybersecurity threats in the autonomous space are dynamic and present unique challenges within the context of a self-driving car, as cyber attackers can take advantage of flaws in the vehicle's V2V communication protocols to create false sensor readings resulting in erroneous navigation decisions. Smart healthcare technology is also susceptible to cyber threats. Cybercriminals will also attempt to gain unauthorized access to patient medical information or disrupt the normal operation of IoT-enabled medical devices. To help combat these types of threats, IDS employs sophisticated techniques to detect and neutralize cyber threats prior to their infliction of harm on the system, including signature-based detection, anomaly detection, and behavioural analysis. When correctly installed, an IDS will help differentiate between standard system operations and unusual activity so that reduce the number of false positives. In addition, modern IDS use AI and machine learning to improve the accuracy of detection, allow for adjustments to changing cyber threats and decrease the time taken to respond (Muneer & al., 2024). By analyzing extensive amounts of data, intelligent security systems can find patterns and irregularities that indicate cyber-attacks, which are then utilized to proactively defend against them.

*Figure 2. Intrusion Detection Systems (IDS) in autonomous systems*

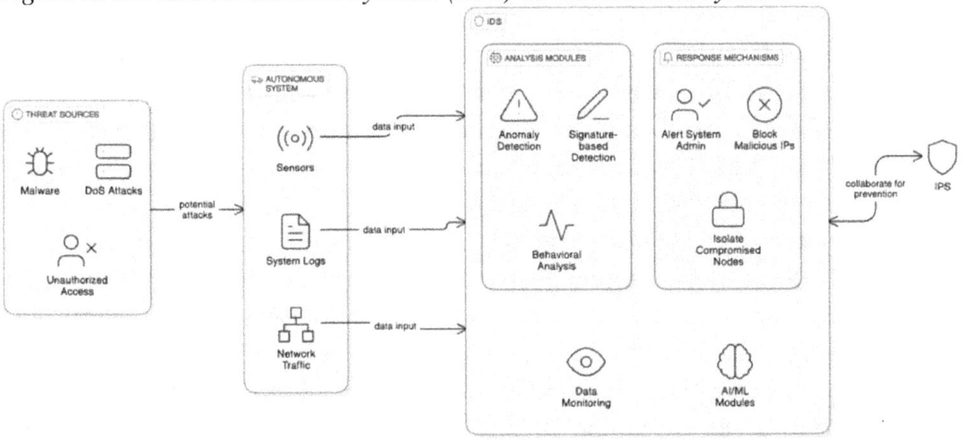


## 3.1.1 Types of Intrusion Detection Systems (IDS) in Autonomous Systems

An IDS's primary purpose is to collect key information on autonomous systems and the way that autonomous systems operate within an increasingly vulnerable world. The significant characteristics of traditional IDSs are NIDSS (network intrusion detection systems) and HIDS (host intrusion detection systems). NIDSS provides monitoring capabilities across an entire network and alerts administrators to potential unauthorised activity on the network.

**1. Network-Based Intrusion Detection Systems (NIDS):** A Network Intrusion Detection System (NIDS) monitors a network by detecting evidence of malicious software (malware), unauthorized use of computer systems, and other such events through examining packets that pass over the network for signs of unauthorized interference with the network and the data contained therein by would-be hackers or other nefarious entities. NIDS installations can be placed at various locations throughout a network, including gateways, routers, or specific segments within the network itself. All traffic flowing between every device associated with the network will also be monitored by a NIDS without requiring users to intervene. NIDS can identify unusual traffic patterns that may represent potential threats to a network, such as denial-of-service (DoS) attacks, man-in-the-middle (MITM) attacks, and malware infections. In addition to monitoring user-computer interaction, NIDS can secure Autonomous Systems (AS) from outside interference along the communication route between autonomous agents, as in the case of a self-driving auto. NIDS will be able to monitor traffic between all autonomous vehicles to identify any cyberattacks aimed at disrupting the navigation system or their ability to transfer sensor data to other autonomous vehicles or the infrastructure in which they operate. In a Smart City environment, NIDS can provide similar protection to Internet of Things (IoT) devices used for traffic management, power generation and distribution, and security.

**2. Host-Based Intrusion Detection Systems (HIDS):** HIDS are fixed to standalone machines (hosts) that are set up to monitor the activities of every endpoint connected to the network. HIDS monitor activities by observing application and operating system logs, application activities, and behaviour exhibited by endpoints. Because HIDS monitoring activities focus on the host operating system and application(s), HIDS provide a much clearer picture of activity that occurs at this level than do network-based IDSs. As such, HIDS are able to identify many more types of activity that may take place on a host operating system such as unauthorised logins, changes to files, excessive numbers of system calls. Therefore, HIDS can effectively serve as a means of protecting autonomous systems from internal & external threats. An additional benefit that comes with utilising HIDS is their ability to detect both internal and external threats and zero-day attacks that may not be detectable by network-based IDSs. Since HIDS continuously monitor the host and associated logs, they consume a large amount of processing power (Vashishth et al., 2026).

## 3.2 Machine Learning and Deep Learning for Anomaly Detection

In particular, IDSs trained via supervised learning techniques, such as decision trees, support vector machines (SVMs), and random forests, use labelled datasets of benign and malicious activity to train the IDS. These IDSs learn from previous attacks and have the ability to identify the same types of threats in real-time. The major drawback of using supervised learning to train IDS is that it requires large, well-annotated datasets and, therefore, it does not perform well against new cyber-attack types. An alternative to supervised learning is to use unsupervised learning and deep learning. Examples of unsupervised learning methods include clustering (e.g., k-means clustering and DBSCAN) and autoencoders; both types of unsupervised learning use system behaviour to build a profile of normal behaviour. If an anomaly occurs in system behaviour, it is flagged as a potential threat, regardless of whether or not it has previously been identified. With respect to anomaly detection, CNNs and RNNs increase anomaly detection ability through their capability to automatically extract features from traffic and logs. CNNs and RNNs excel at detecting advanced, complex attack patterns, including stealthy and polymorphic malware. The combined learning of LSTM and GAN-based IDS will eventually provide more reliable and useful models for the detection and mitigation of future adversarial threats, thus improving the adaptability of IDS systems to real-world environments. When additional capabilities are combined with Federated Learning (FL), both LSTM and GAN-based IDS will benefit from the enhanced notification of abnormal behaviour and reduce the amount of time required for analysis. FL will allow for the creation of shared IDS training models amongst multiple autonomous systems without exchanging raw data, thereby preserving individual data privacy while also enhancing the overall threat intelligence for the IDS as a whole. This will be particularly beneficial for smart cities and autonomous vehicles whose networks require high levels of data privacy to secure their networks from both internal and external threats (Zhang et al., 2025).

## 3.3 Real-Time Threat Detection and Response Mechanisms

To protect autonomous systems from fast-moving cyber threats, organizations must use real-time threat detection and response processes. Autonomous technologies must function in rapidly changing environments and, as such, timely detection of security threats along with the ability to rapidly respond can help reduce the risk of extensive impact (e.g., disruption to services, compromise of sensitive information, and injury to people). Unlike traditional security methods, which are based on fixed rules, new autonomous technologies can use artificial intelligence (AI) based adaptive security frameworks to detect, investigate, and counteract cyber threats in real-time. Through continuous network traffic monitoring, sensor data gathering, and system log analysis, organizations can quickly recognize malicious behaviour and conduct investigations to eliminate it. Machine Learning (ML) and Deep Learning (DL) based Advanced Intrusion Detection Systems (IDS) monitor system activity to identify both known cyber threats (e.g., malware) and unknown cyber threats (e.g., new attack techniques) (Moulahi et al., 2023). Signature-based IDS can identify previously known threats, but they may not be equipped to identify new threats. To address this limitation, organisations are turning to anomaly detection-based detection methods utilizing unsupervised machine learning techniques (clustering, autoencoders, and GANs) to identify anomalous system behaviour. For example, in the field of autonomous vehicles, many of the current mechanism that monitor the vehicle-to-vehicle (V2V) and vehicle-to-infrastructure (V2I) communications for the identification and blocking of potential cyber threats (e.g., GPS spoofing and denial of service (DoS) attacks) also include the ability to detect and stop unauthorized control commands.

## 4. PRIVACY-PRESERVING MECHANISMS IN AUTONOMOUS SYSTEMS

As autonomous systems grow in use across multiple industries, such as in transportation, healthcare, smart cities, and industrial automation, it is important to secure the data associated with them, both for the sake of the user and for the integrity of the systems themselves. Autonomous systems rely heavily on large amounts of data collected from sensors, IoT devices, and AI-powered decision-making processes; therefore, they face many risks associated with privacy breaches, unauthorized data access, and abuse of data.

### 4.1 Secure Federated Learning for Data Privacy

Federated Learning (FL) is a method of developing machine learning models, that takes advantage of decentralization of computing power when training an Artificial Intelligence (AI) model. The idea for federated learning originated from many different user domains where there was a concern for the confidentiality of user data, especially in regard to healthcare and transportation applications. Traditionally, in order to create and train an AI model, there must be a central location where the training data is stored. With federated learning, instead of having all the data sent to a single location, users can locally train their own data and then send updates to a single group or organization that will use those updates. FL has significantly decreased the risk of both data breaches and unauthorized access to users' private information because of this. The application of federated learning in health care is when medical devices are employed to collect patient health information, which is then compiled with other medical devices across all medical devices at one centralized location. By aggregating and training multiple datasets, the health care sector can improve upon AI-based models to diagnose diseases and remain compliant with privacy rules and regulations like GDPR and HIPAA. Federated learning also enables autonomous vehicles to learn from the way that the vehicle operates in different types of driving situations, while still preserving sensitive private driving information or the location of the vehicle and its occupants. While federated learning has many advantages, it is susceptible to various privacy attacks, including model inversion (where an adversary reconstructs the original training data set from updates received from users as part of the training process), data poisoning, and adversarial learning. Secure Federated Learning (SFL) is an enhancement of FL and works to address these security concerns by using advanced privacy-preserving algorithms such as homomorphic encryption, differential privacy, and secure multi-party computation (SMPC). Smart cities use FL in many ways, including in traffic systems, cameras that recognize faces for surveillance purposes, and monitoring of IoT-enabled infrastructure. FL also helps city administrators provide better urban services by allowing them to train their model on data without having to reveal the identity of their citizens. As autonomous systems continue to grow, secure FL will allow for AI development while still providing very high levels of privacy (Narayan, 2025).

## 4.2 Homomorphic Encryption and Differential Privacy

The protection of sensitive data from being lost as a result of the processing and generation of enormous amounts of sensitive data in AI-based autonomous systems presents challenges associated with both data privacy and computation efficiency. The privacy-securing techniques of homomorphic encryption (HE) and differential privacy (DP) are two examples of techniques that can be used to securely process data while also protecting the confidentiality of users' data in an AI-controlled autonomous environment illustrated in Figure 3. There are many examples of how these two advanced techniques will help try to eliminate a host of privacy risks within many sectors (e.g., autonomous healthcare, smart transportation, intelligent surveillance systems) in the event of a breach of data or any other kind of violation of electronic private Web communications (Hendaoui et al., 2024). An example of the capability of HE is that computations can be conducted upon the encrypted data without the requirement of encryption being removed from the data in order to perform computations upon the data. So, for example, an individual's sensitive data (i.e., medical records, vehicle telemetry, and even identifying personal data) can remain encrypted during the entire processing of that data, thus reducing the exposure of the individual's sensitive data. Similarly, for smart cities, HE allows for encrypted data collected via surveillance cameras and traffic sensors to be analysed without a person necessarily being able to identify a specific individual (Hendaoui et al., 2024). Even though homomorphic encryption offers a high degree of privacy-security, HE is not optimally efficient in terms of computing; therefore, it will need to continue to be optimized so it can effectively serve in a scalable manner in many of today's rapidly-evolving autonomous vehicle applications. DP is an alternative privacy-boosting technique that prevents unauthorized entities from deriving sensitive personal data from a dataset. Through differential privacy, noise is added to datasets or results so that the individual pieces of information can't be pinpointed, allowing the data to provide many useful insights. This is critical for training models in artificial intelligence because there are attackers who will conduct model inversion attacks to recover the original data.

*Figure 3. Homomorphic Encryption (HE) and Differential Privacy (DP) in autonomous system*

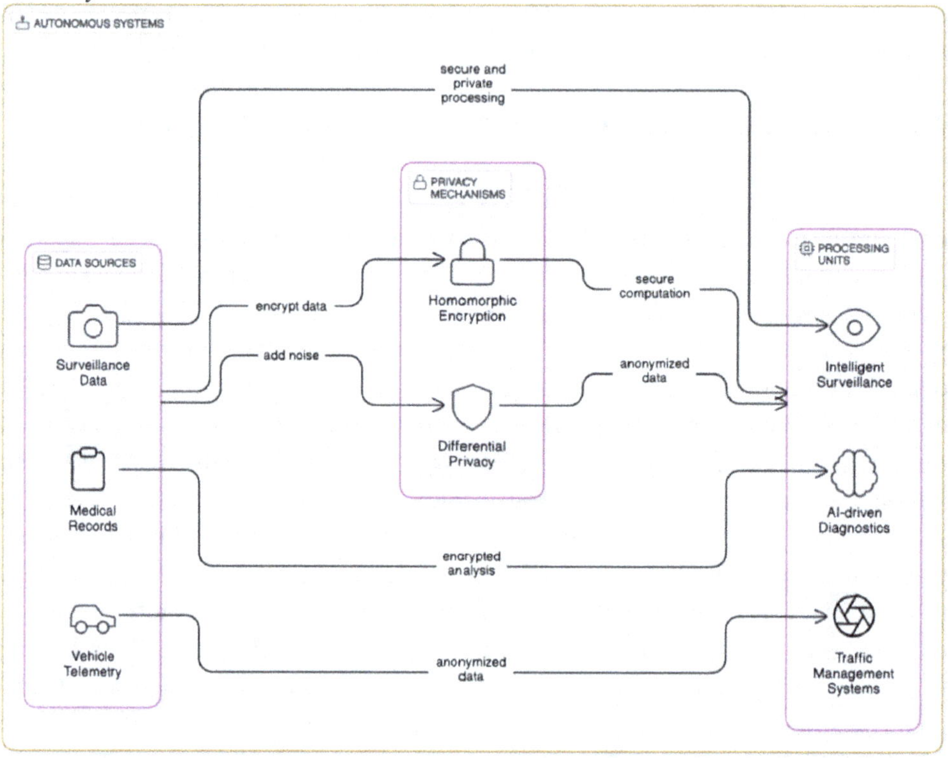


Homomorphic encryption and differential privacy both present viable solutions to the privacy problems faced in autonomous systems. Homomorphic encryption protects the confidentiality of the data through the course of computation, whereas differential privacy provides the assurance of statistical privacy by making it impossible to extract sensitive information. As such, both methods have their limitations; therefore, research continues to focus on the potential for both methods to have a computational cost, the ease of use with real-time AI, and the need for an appropriate level of privacy and accuracy.

## 4.3 Blockchain for Data Integrity and Secure Communications

The use of blockchain technology will play a growing role in ensuring the integrity and security of the information flow within autonomous systems. Autonomous systems depend upon real-time data being exchanged; they require multiple sensors connected to one another and are fully automated via artificial intelligence for decision making. A blockchain offers an alternative method of data security through its decentralized, distributed, immutable ledger. Everything that is written in a blockchain is unalterable so that it cannot be changed or deleted. Furthermore, all data within a blockchain is made available to everyone using the blockchain, making it easy for them to verify the accuracy of the information contained within the blockchain. In the case of autonomous vehicles, blockchain technology will store the sensor readings from the vehicle as well as the location information provided by the GPS receiver. Also, blockchain technology will record all vehicle-to-vehicle (V2V) communications, which is vital for the operation of autonomous vehicles, making it nearly impossible for anyone to forge or otherwise manipulate the critical driving data used in making driving decisions. Therefore, blockchain allows for the reliability of data input into autonomous systems, thus decreasing the risk of cyber-attacks against autonomous vehicles. For smart cities, which have vast IoT networks that control and monitor services and devices for things such as traffic control and traffic management, surveillance, and environmental monitoring, blockchain will also offer data security by encrypting all communication between IoT devices and validating all transactions using a consensus process (Castro et al., 2023). In addition to providing data integrity, Blockchain provides enhanced security in communications between autonomous entities via cryptographic encryption, identity verification, and access control. In the Autonomous Healthcare system, for example, patient data may be Shared securely by Hospitals, Physicians, and AI Based Diagnostics without the potential for privacy violation. Additionally, the Blockchain records all access requests and Transactions in a visibility manner. By Having a Secure Blockchain ledger, only authorized personnel will have access to sensitive medical information, reducing risk for data breaches and Identity Theft. The Use of Smart Contracts allows Trust to Be Automated between Autonomous Systems. Automated Trust-Based Interactions are achieved by Smart Contracts, a type of Self-Executing Agreement Stored in the Blockchain. Smart Contracts are Geared to Enforce Security Protocols, Verify Identity, Facilitate Secure Transactions, and Eliminate the Need for Middleman for Automated Transactions. In the case of Industrial Automation Smart Contracts will be utilized to Control Communication between Machines to reduce Cyber-attack (Padmavathi and Saminathan, 2025)

## 5. ADVERSARIAL ATTACKS ON AI MODELS AND DEFENSE STRATEGIES

The implementation of adversarial attacks against AI models that are operating within autonomous systems is of escalating concern. Adversaries will find and exploit the vulnerabilities inherent with machine learning algorithms to adversely affect the manner in which an AI Model takes action on its input by way of the way it was created. Typically, an adversarial attack consists of a "crafted input" that is designed for a human to be unable to detect but has a XY-low probability of causing the AI Model output to produce an incorrect reaction by causing the AI to misclassify or misinterpret data.

## 5.1 Understanding Adversarial Attacks on AI-Based IDS

In cybersecurity, adversarial attacks against AI-based Intrusion Detection Systems (IDS) pose one of the largest threats to our current security architecture. Adversaries will use many different methods to modify the output results of the machine learning algorithms used by an IDS to ensure that they can pass through the IDS undetected or in some cases as a false positive. Furthermore, by exploiting the vulnerabilities in AI-based algorithms, adversarial attackers can circumvent the ability to detect cyber threats, as well as a validation of these threats as being authenticated or valid to the IDS. For instance, evasion attacks against AI-based IDS can be seen where an adversary alters traffic transmitted over the Internet or changes his/her user behavior within the system prior to their submitting their threat to the IDS. As a result, the IDS would view the traffic as being normal, rather than looking for signs of a threat. Another type of adversarial attack is a poisoning attack. This occurs during the initial training of an AI-based IDS wherein the data being used for training is tainted or corrupted, increasing the likelihood of misclassification and limiting the model's ability to recognize true threats. Through model extraction, attackers can exploit the AI detection mechanisms and use this information to build targeted attacks and identify vulnerabilities within the system. Attackers utilize model probing techniques that have been developed to extract an adversarial model from an AI-DIS. As a result, the detection systems ultimately fail to achieve their intended goal. It is essential to develop resilient defenses that can protect the function, integrity, and performance of AI-based intrusion detection systems that operate in autonomous modes. These defenses could include, but are not limited to: using adversarial training techniques to develop models capable of learning from the adversarial examples and adapting to the patterns of the attack, implementing feature-space hardening techniques that reduce the susceptibility of IDS feature-extraction methods to minor changes in input data, and creating ensemble methods that utilize multiple models with various architectures to decrease the chances that one adversarial methodology could cause a total failure of any one deployed model. Additionally, the use of blockchain technology for logging and verifying activities/evidence contained in IDS creates a permanent history of each recorded event, making it impossible to alter or corrupt this data after the fact. The continuous evolution and increasing interconnection of autonomous systems has created a need to protect AI-based IDS from adversarial threats through ongoing research and development. Organizations must have adaptive AI security frameworks, share threat intelligence in real-time, update their IDS models continually, allowing for resiliency and maintaining the ability to detect intrusions within a dynamic environment (Sharma et al., 2025).

## 5.2 AI-Driven Defense Mechanisms Against Adversarial Attacks

AI-based defense strategies provide essential protection for autonomous systems from adversarial threats. The utilization of these defense strategies will ultimately allow for the effectiveness and integrity of AI-based Intrusion Detection Systems (IDS) and other security measures. By taking advantage of weaknesses in machine learning models, adversaries can create altered inputs to fool AI algorithms.

**1. Adversarial Training:** Adversarial training is designed to serve as one type of defense against adversarial attacks on AI-based IDS models. This training procedure creates the potential adversarial examples by adding adversarial modifications to the training data set. This training allows the AI model to identify and respond to similar adversarial challenges in operational use. The primary benefit is that adversarially trained AI models are able to differentiate between authentic and adversarial input and thus, are better able to protect against adversarial attacks.

**2. Defensive Distillation:** Defence Distillation (DD) refers to a training method where one (the distilled or defence model) of two AI models(s) trained together, recognises the output probability distributions of another primary (defender) model. Distilled output probability distributions allow for smooth recognition boundaries that allow for making predictions based on inputs.

**3. Feature-Space Hardening:** Feature-Space Hardening (FSH) allows AI to be more effective in differentiating between legitimate users and adversarial (malicious) users by providing the AI system with a wide variety of helpful and important features. The goal of the FSH process is to maximise the amount, quality, and relevance of relevant features that are extracted and represented by the AI, and ultimately reduce the ability of malicious inputs to corrupt the model.

**4. AI-Powered Anomaly Detection:** The Anomaly Detection (AD) function of AI is critical in detecting adversarial attacks on an ongoing basis. In AD, continuous monitoring of the entire system and all of the systems network traffic, sensor data, and any external devices connected to the system, will allow the algorithms of the machine learning and deep learning techniques to classify the various activity patterns being recognised and subsequently to analyse those patterns of activity to detect any abnormal patterns of activity this could indicate that an adversary is trying to compromise the security of the system and/or an attack is forthcoming.

As AI continues to grow and develop, many advances in AI security will focus on developing self-adaptive learning models that are capable of automatically detecting and mitigating the adversarial threats to AI without requiring human input.

## 6. REGULATORY AND ETHICAL CHALLENGES IN SECURING AUTONOMOUS SYSTEMS

The ubiquity of the use of autonomous systems in a variety of sectors (such as transportation, healthcare, and smart cities) brings with it a wide array of cybersecurity & regulatory; and ethical; hurdles. Because these technologies are reliant on the use of artificial intelligence (AI), machine learning (ML), as well as a web of interconnected networks, they also present challenges with regard to susceptibility to cyber threats, data privacy, and algorithmic bias.

**1. Lack of Standardized Cybersecurity Regulations:** The lack of standardised Cybersecurity Regulations is one of the major regulatory issues associated with the development and use of autonomous systems. There are many different regulations regarding Cybersecurity for AI, Data Protection for Autonomous Systems and AI Accountability within different jurisdictions and industries; therefore, each organisation and country must attempt to comply with many different regulations (and often cannot do so due to those regulations being inconsistent). For Example: This inconsistency of regulation makes it extremely difficult for Companies operating in multiple jurisdictions to comply with all regulatory standards, while simultaneously putting the company at risk. In order to address this challenge, governments and international organisations must develop a comprehensive Global Cybersecurity Framework which allows for effective Interoperability of Cybersecurity among Autonomous Technologies (Ighofiomoni et al 2025).

**2. Data Privacy and Compliance with Legal Frameworks:** Collecting and processing copious amounts of personal and sensitive information not only impacts people's ability to maintain their right to privacy but also increases the need for data protection from a legal compliance perspective. The European Union's General Data Protection Regulation (GDPR) and California's Consumer Privacy Protection Act (CCPA), for example, have detailed regulations regarding how data can be obtained, maintained, and disposed of. However, real-time data collection and processing found within autonomous vehicles (AVs), healthcare monitoring devices, or smart cities is fundamentally at odds with both of these laws' current legal frameworks. Therefore, there are a number of technical solutions that can help mitigate the privacy risks associated with the rapid development of these technologies (i.e., differential encryption, federated learning, and other cryptographic methods) while preserving the person's right to privacy. These solutions will not only protect the rights of the individual, but they will also enable AI models to learn from and gain insights into non-centralized sources of information (Holubenko et al., 2025).

**3. Ethical Concerns in AI Decision-Making:** As mentioned previously, an individual's privacy will be compromised; however, in addition to the challenges associated with protecting the individual's privacy, ethical concerns exist as a result of the reliance upon machine learning (ML) models to assist in making decisions. Because of that reliance, the outcome of a decision made based upon a ML model may contain inherent bias or produce unintended consequences. For instance, there will be instances where self-driving cars (AVs) must make ethical decisions regarding the relative priority of both avoiding an accident or mitigating the damage in the event of an unavoidable collision. Likewise, AI applications utilized in healthcare must be committed to treating patients equally regardless of their respective social class and providing equitable medical diagnoses and recommendations for treatment.

**4. Security Risks in Autonomous Critical Infrastructure:** Many autonomous systems are integrated into critical infrastructure, such as power grids, traffic management systems, and smart healthcare facilities. A cyberattack on these infrastructures could lead to catastrophic consequences, including public safety hazards and service disruptions. Regulatory bodies must enforce strict security standards to protect critical autonomous infrastructure from cyber threats. Measures such as intrusion detection systems (IDS), blockchain-based data integrity mechanisms, and AI-driven threat mitigation strategies should be mandated to ensure robust security. Governments and organizations must also conduct regular security audits and risk assessments to proactively address emerging threats (Dhanushkodi and Thejas, 2024).

**5. Accountability and Liability in Autonomous System Failures:** Cyberattacks on the power grid and other types of autonomous critical infrastructures will have widespread impacts due to potential consequences that threaten public safety and disrupt services. As regulators enforce stringent security standards upon autonomous critical infrastructures, they should also mandate the use of IDS, blockchain, AI-based intrusion detection systems (IDS), among other measures. Governments and organisations should perform ongoing security audits and risk assessments as needed to continuously reinforce their defence against emerging threats.

When it comes to dealing with the legislative and ethical issues associated with Autonomous Technologies; in establishing secure approaches to safeguarding the implementation of Autonomous Technologies in the modern Industry while maintaining Privacy, Security and Fairness.

## 7. FUTURE RESEARCH DIRECTIONS AND CHALLENGES

As the technology for Autonomous Systems continues to grow and develop, the focus of future research will also need to be directed to improving security, privacy and resilience against ever-changing cyber threats. Important areas for further review to support the development of robust and reliable autonomous systems have been identified below:

## 7.1. Future Research Directions in Securing Autonomous Systems

To be successful in our continuing efforts to develop Autonomous Systems in a responsible and safe manner, we should collectively focus on the following near-term and long-term avenues of Future Research:

**1. Advancing AI-Driven Security Frameworks:** Security associated with autonomous systems is implementing enhanced A.I.-based security frameworks which can provide real-time threat detection and response for autonomous systems. The current machine learning (ML) and deep learning (DL) capabilities must advance beyond the current capabilities of the current ML and DL models to allow the models to be more flexible, capable of detecting 'unknown' or previously 'unseen' attack patterns (i.e. Zero-Day Vulnerabilities). Also essential in A.I. based security applications is the utilization of Explainable A.I. (XAI). In autonomous systems environment, XAI is helpful to the making of operational decisions by A.I. models to reduce the potential of being exploited by cyber attackers.

**2. Privacy-Preserving AI Techniques:** in addition to this ongoing concern of the AI technologies, privacy-preserving AI technologies will support the continued development and implementation of advanced AI technologies. AI models can be trained securely and without the use of their raw data by utilizing secure federated learning, homomorphic encryption, and differential privacy techniques. Each of these techniques has potential issues with computing overhead and trade-offs in performance. Future research efforts should be directed toward developing and optimizing privacy preserving ai techniques and technologies to make them scalable and more efficient for use in the real world with large scale autonomous networks.

**3. Blockchain for Secure Data Integrity and Communication:** The decentralised and immutable nature provided by blockchain technology provides enhanced data integrity and communication control to autonomous systems. Future research will focus on the creation of lightweight and scalable blockchain technologies that can be incorporated into autonomous network infrastructures for the efficient validation of transactions and execution of smart contracts without having a negative impact on the overall system performance. The combination of AI-based IDS and blockchain technology provides a clear audit trail of the cyber threat level and provides an enhanced level of accountability in autonomous decision-making (Soomro et al., 2024).

**4. Proactive Threat Intelligence and Automated Security Response:** Autonomous systems will use proactive cyber security measures to help identify and mitigate potential threats before any damage occurs to an organization. Further research should lead to the development of AI-based Threat Intelligence Platforms that collect information on threats from around the world; using the information that has been collected, Analysts will be able to use the threats' aggregated information to predict where future vulnerabilities will occur based on previous successful attacks, and to make proactive countermeasure recommendations. Automated cybersecurity response mechanisms can be deployed to enable autonomous systems to autonomously identify and mitigate cyber threats without any effort from human operators.

## 7.2 Challenges in Securing Autonomous Systems

Innovation must continue in the creation of AI-based Cybersecurity Frameworks, as well as through cooperation and collaboration between Researchers and Policymakers to develop scalable, resilient, and privacy-preserving solutions to protect the growing threat of Cyber Attacks on Autonomous Systems.

**1. Complexity and Diversity of Autonomous Systems:** Autonomous systems provide solutions across multiple industries and each of these sectors operates with its own unique Cybersecurity criteria; therefore, applying a "one size fits all" Cyber Security Solution to all these sectors is not realistic. Further complicating the security of autonomous systems are the numerous opportunities for a cyber-attack, as a result of the vast number of components that comprise autonomous systems. The use of Artificial Intelligence (AI), Internet of Things (IOT), Cloud Computing, and Edge Computing creates an extremely large Attack Surface for attackers to exploit, while simultaneously creating barriers to effectively managing vulnerabilities within an autonomous system (Ndibe, 2025).

**2. Vulnerabilities in AI Models and Machine Learning Algorithms:** These ML models are vulnerable to a wide variety of different attacks including: adversarial attacks, model poisoning, and data manipulation, meaning that attackers can leverage weaknesses in AI algorithms to trick autonomous systems to make faulty decisions such as: tricking self-driving cars to read wrong road signs and tricking intelligent healthcare systems into misdiagnosing patients. Therefore, having a robust defence against adversarial attacks, as well as establishing security protocols around the entire ML pipeline is an engineering challenge that must be tackled.

**3. Real-Time Threat Detection and Response:** Autonomous systems need real-time threat detection and response capabilities when faced with cyber threats. Existing standard intrusion detection systems (IDS) and cybersecurity solutions usually cannot handle fast, complex autonomous systems since cyber threats are detected and mitigated much sooner than the industry can provide. This has led to catastrophic failures such as vehicle crashes in autonomous transport and incorrect medical intervention in healthcare systems.

**4. Data Privacy and Secure Communication:** Autonomous Vehicles generate and use vast amounts of sensitive information. There are challenges associated with balancing an individual's right to privacy with security measures taken to secure communications between Autonomous Vehicles that are connected to each other.

Recent AI technologies have been developed to help protect an individual's right to privacy (e.g., Federated Learning, Differential Privacy), but they also increase Computational Load and Decrease Performance across the Autonomous Vehicle System. The industry should continue pursuing ways of providing privacy-preserving functionality without impairment to overall performance.

## 8. CONCLUSION

The introduction of autonomous systems in various fields has brought along with-it new forms of potential attacks and compromised IT by exposing the vulnerabilities inherent in these autonomous systems to numerous forms of cyber-attacks (including ransomware and phishing), the adoption of IoT, Advanced Computing, AI and all forms of autonomous systems also create new risk factors. This chapter discusses available intrusion detection (IDS) models developed of AI-based methodologies in correlation with characteristics of machine learning/deep learning detection for anomaly detection and real-time detection and response to cases of imminent threats. The illustration of various privacy-preserving methodologies addressed in this chapter such as (but not limited to): Secure Federated Learning, encrypt-based models using homomorphic encryption, and SECURE Blockchain are designed to effectively protect user privacy and to allow for secure sharing of communication. The need to protect against adversarial attacks on AI-based models that are utilized within autonomous systems indicates the necessity for developing better methods of protecting from those adversarial attacks. The methods which can improve the security architecture resilience of AI-based autonomous systems are implementing adversarial training and explanation-based AI. Future applied research will focus on developing lightweight cybersecurity protection products and improving identification of imminent threats through real-time threat detection, while also incorporating Blockchain Technology and Quantum Cryptography into the existing framework of our AI Security Solutions

## REFERENCES


Alqubaysi, T., Asmari, A. F. A., Alanazi, F., Almutairi, A., & Armghan, A. (2025). Federated learning-based predictive traffic management using a contained privacy-preserving scheme for autonomous vehicles. *Sensors (Basel)*, *25*(4), 1116. DOI: 10.3390/s25041116 PMID: 40006346

Andreoni, M., Lunardi, W. T., Lawton, G., & Thakkar, S. (2024). Enhancing autonomous system security and resilience with generative AI: A comprehensive survey. *IEEE Access : Practical Innovations, Open Solutions*, *12*, 109470–109493. DOI: 10.1109/ACCESS.2024.3439363

Castro, O. E. L., Deng, X., & Park, J. H. (2023). Comprehensive survey on AI-based technologies for enhancing IoT privacy and security: Trends, challenges, and solutions. Human-centric Computing and Information Sciences, 13(39).

Cheng, X., Oun, A., & Wince, K. (2025). *The Role of Artificial Intelligence in Boosting Cybersecurity and Trusted Embedded Systems Performance: A Systematic Review on Current and Future Trends*. IEEE.

Dhanushkodi, K., & Thejas, S. (2024). AI enabled threat detection: Leveraging artificial intelligence for advanced security and cyber threat mitigation. *IEEE Access : Practical Innovations, Open Solutions*, *12*, 173127–173136. DOI: 10.1109/ACCESS.2024.3493957

Dhinakaran, D., Sankar, S. M., Selvaraj, D., & Raja, S. E. (2024). Privacy-preserving data in IoT-based cloud systems: A comprehensive survey with AI integration. arXiv preprint arXiv:2401.00794.

Hendaoui, F., Ferchichi, A., Trabelsi, L., Meddeb, R., Ahmed, R., & Khelifi, M. K. (2024). Advances in deep learning intrusion detection over encrypted data with privacy preservation: A systematic review. *Cluster Computing*, *27*(7), 8683–8724. DOI: 10.1007/s10586-024-04424-4

Holubenko, V., Gaspar, D., Leal, R., & Silva, P. (2025). Autonomous intrusion detection for IoT: A decentralized and privacy preserving approach. *International Journal of Information Security*, *24*(1), 7. DOI: 10.1007/s10207-024-00926-9

Ighofiomoni, M. O., Ojerinde, J. S., Olaniyan, I., Issah, P. P., Adepitan, O. S., Oyenuga, O., & Chinonyerem, C. A. (2025). Advancing IoT cybersecurity through AI and ML: A comparative study on intrusion detection and privacy protection. *Asian Journal of Advanced Research and Reports*, *19*(8), 159–174. DOI: 10.9734/ajarr/2025/v19i81122

Laghari, A. A., Khan, A. A., Ksibi, A., Hajjej, F., Kryvinska, N., Almadhor, A., Mohamed, M. A., & Alsubai, S. (2025). A novel and secure artificial intelligence enabled zero trust intrusion detection in industrial internet of things architecture. *Scientific Reports*, *15*(1), 26843. DOI: 10.1038/s41598-025-11738-9 PMID: 40702039

Mollashaik, A. S. (2025). Advancing data security through AI-driven classification: A framework for intelligent threat detection and privacy preservation. [IJCET]. *International Journal of Computer Engineering and Technology*, *15*(6), 467–481. DOI: 10.34218/IJCET_16_01_040

Moulahi, T., Jabbar, R., Alabdulatif, A., Abbas, S., El Khediri, S., Zidi, S., & Rizwan, M. (2023). Privacy-preserving federated learning cyber-threat detection for intelligent transport systems with blockchain-based security. *Expert Systems: International Journal of Knowledge Engineering and Neural Networks*, *40*(5), e13103. DOI: 10.1111/exsy.13103

Moustafa, N., Koroniotis, N., Keshk, M., Zomaya, A. Y., & Tari, Z. (2023). Explainable intrusion detection for cyber defences in the internet of things: Opportunities and solutions. *IEEE Communications Surveys and Tutorials*, *25*(3), 1775–1807. DOI: 10.1109/COMST.2023.3280465

Muneer, S., Farooq, U., Athar, A., Ahsan Raza, M., Ghazal, T. M., & Sakib, S. (2024). A critical review of artificial intelligence-based approaches in intrusion detection: A comprehensive analysis. *Journal of Engineering*, *2024*(1), 3909173. DOI: 10.1155/2024/3909173

Narayan, S. B. (2025). Safeguarding Intelligence: A Comprehensive Analysis of AI Security and Privacy in the Era of Autonomous Systems. Available at *SSRN* 5718122. DOI: 10.2139/ssrn.5718122

Nasir, Z. U. I., Iqbal, A., & Qureshi, H. K. (2024). Securing cyber-physical systems: A decentralized framework for collaborative intrusion detection with privacy preservation. *IEEE Transactions on Industrial Cyber-Physical Systems*, *2*, 303–311. DOI: 10.1109/TICPS.2024.3425794

Ndibe, O. S. (2025). Ai-driven forensic systems for real-time anomaly detection and threat mitigation in cybersecurity infrastructures. *International Journal of Research Publication and Reviews*, *6*(5), 389–411. DOI: 10.55248/gengpi.6.0525.1991

Padmavathi, V., & Saminathan, R. (2025). A federated edge intelligence framework with trust-based access control for secure and privacy preserving IoT systems. *Scientific Reports*, *15*(1), 35832. DOI: 10.1038/s41598-025-19712-1 PMID: 41087484

Sharma, D. P., Habibi Lashkari, A., Firoozjaei, M. D., Mahdavifar, S., & Xiong, P. (2025). Defense Methods for Adversarial Attacks and Privacy Issues in Secure AI. In *Understanding AI in Cybersecurity and Secure AI: Challenges, Strategies and Trends* (pp. 159–195). Springer Nature Switzerland. DOI: 10.1007/978-3-031-91524-6_9

Sharma, S. B., & Bairwa, A. K. (2025). Leveraging AI for Intrusion Detection in IoT Ecosystems: A Comprehensive Study. *IEEE Access : Practical Innovations, Open Solutions*, *13*, 66290–66317. DOI: 10.1109/ACCESS.2025.3550392

Soomro, I. A., Hussain, S. J., Ashraf, Z., Alnfiai, M. M., & Alotaibi, N. N. (2024). Lightweight privacy-preserving federated deep intrusion detection for industrial cyber-physical system. *Journal of Communications and Networks (Seoul)*, *26*(6), 632–649. DOI: 10.23919/JCN.2024.000054

Vashishth, T. K., Sharma, V., Chaudhary, S., Sharma, R., Chauhan, P., & Sharma, B. K. (2026). Adoption of Artificial Intelligence Techniques for Enhancing Host-Based Intrusion Detection Systems. In *AI Solutions for Detecting Cyber-Attacks in Information Systems* (pp. 133–164). IGI Global Scientific Publishing.

Vashishth, T. K., Sharma, V., Sharma, K. K., Kumar, B., Chaudhary, S., & Panwar, R. (2024). Intrusion Detection and Prevention Techniques in FL Cloud-Based Healthcare 5.0: A Comprehensive Review. Pioneering Smart Healthcare 5.0 with IoT, Federated Learning, and Cloud Security, 152-174.

Vikas, D. R. P., Kumar, D., Charan, P., Ingilela, R. S. K., & Rastogi, R. (2023). Intrusion detection in wireless sensor networks using hybrid Deep Belief Networks and Harris Hawks optimizer. 2023 4th International Conference on Electronics and Sustainable Communication Systems (ICESC), 1631–1636. DOI: 10.1109/ICESC57686.2023.10193270

Vikas, & Teotia, S. (2025). Optimization of Graph Neural Networks for real-time intrusion detection in dynamic mobile ad-hoc networks. International Journal of Environmental Sciences, 11(11s), 740–748.

Vyas, A., Lin, P. C., Hwang, R. H., & Tripathi, M. (2024). Privacy-preserving federated learning for intrusion detection in IoT environments: A survey. *IEEE Access : Practical Innovations, Open Solutions*, *12*, 127018–127050. DOI: 10.1109/ACCESS.2024.3454211

Zhang, C., Wang, N., Hou, Y. T., & Lou, W. (2025). Machine Learning-Based Intrusion Detection Systems: Capabilities, Methodologies, and Open Research Challenges. *Authorea Preprints*. DOI: 10.1002/9781394293773.ch03

Chapter 8

# AI-Driven Cloud-Enabled Cybersecurity Framework for Intelligent IoT Intrusion Detection


**Rudhrananth Baladhandapani**
http://orcid.org/0009-0003-2497-1979
*Intel, USA*

**Bhanutheja Nagabhushana Reddy Kasinayakanahally**
*Apple Inc., USA*

**Sri Harsha Grandhi**
http://orcid.org/0009-0000-8425-4144
*Intel, USA*

**T Kalaikumaran**
*Department of Artificial Intelligence and Data Science, VSB College of Engineering Technical Campus, Coimbatore, India*

**Elegbeleye Femi Abiodun**
*Walter Sisulu University, South Africa*

**Biplov Paneru**
*Department of Electronics Engineering, Pokhara University, Nepal*



## ABSTRACT

*As the number of IoT devices has expanded rapidly, the risk of exposure to rapidly evolving threats has also increased, resulting in a broader attack surface (i.e., the networked devices that an attacker may have access to). Thus, with the large-scale IoT installations come high-dimensional signal data that pose a challenge to accurately detect intrusions. This paper develops a cyber-physical system composed of multiple cloud-based cybersecurity frameworks that leverage AI technology as well as signal data from IoT devices in order to detect intrusions. The proposed framework uses Sugeon-type fuzzy feature extraction (after preprocessing) to extract a set of*



DOI: 10.4018/979-8-3373-9053-6.ch008

*features necessary for classification by a table prior-based IoT intrusion detection system that uses a transformer. Results of the cloud-based model demonstrate an accuracy rate of 98.46% and precision of 98.59% with inference latency of 69.67 ms.*

## 1. INTRODUCTION

The development of the Internet of Things (IoT) has radically altered the modern cyber systems, where the large-scale interconnection of sensors and intelligent devices can be achieved in spheres of smart cities, industrial automation, medical care, transport and critical organization (Afraji et al., 2025). In the last twenty years, the IoT has evolved initial machine-to-machine communication models into highly heterogeneous, data-driven ecosystems with the assistance of cloud computing and high-speed networks, such as 5G and the developing 6G technologies (Ahmad et al., 2022; Ali et al., 2022). The result of this development is a geometric increase in the number of connected devices, with IoT deployments in the tens of billions and growing fast due to the ongoing development of cloud platform (Alladi et al., 2021). At the same time, cloud computing has facilitated data storage and data analytics. Meanwhile, artificial intelligence (AI) has become one of the important facilitators of deriving actionable intelligence from IoT signal and network traffic data (Alotaibi & Barnawi, 2023). During recent years, AI-based cybersecurity has become a prominent feature of the IoT system, which provides a wider trend towards automated and data-driven security ideologies (Al Rawajbeh et al., 2025). This intersecting of IoT, cloud infrastructure and AI has created a breed of smart cyber environments where real-time data streams can be processed to facilitate monitoring, automation and decision-making (Alrefaei & Ilyas, 2024; Alzahrani & Aldhyani, 2022). With the increasing rates of IoT adoption in industrial markets around the world, the skills to manipulate and process IoT-based signals in large amounts have established AI-integrated cloud-based cybersecurity systems of digital infrastructure.

Subsequently, on this intersection, the trend of AI and cloud computing has added to the range of IoT-enabled cyber-physical systems, especially in autonomous and robotic systems (Aldhyani & Alkahtani, 2022). The current IoT systems produce constant streams of heterogeneous signals, which require sophisticated signal processing tools to be represented effectively and analysed in real-time (Arreche et al., 2024). In the last ten years, the field of digital signal processing and data-driven analytics has been concerned with useful patterns in such large IoT data streams to make intelligent perception and situational awareness possible (Aruchamy et al., 2023). At the same time, cloud computing has become a backbone technology to aid in elastic computation, distributed storage and global access, which have enabled IoT and systems to offload intensive processing tasks (Chang et al., 2022). In this ecosystem, AI has become a disruptive technology, allowing autonomous learning, adaptive decision-making and predictive intelligence among the connected devices and robot agents (Dalal et al., 2023). The combination of AI and robotics has expedited the creation of intelligent autonomous systems that can perceive and act in a dynamic environment (Humayun et al., 2021). As these technologies increasingly operate in cyber-physical loops, the convergence of IoT signal processing, AI and cloud platforms has created a novel technology platform of intelligent automated systems of the next generation of autonomous digital infrastructures (Javed et al., 2022).

## 1.1. Problem Statement

Despite significant advancements in intrusion detection systems (IDS), several challenges continue to hinder the effective protection of large-scale IoT-driven environments. Initially, the IoT signal data in high dimensions due to the variety of devices and communication protocols have complicated time-based and behavioural dynamics; it is challenging to differentiate benign activity and intricate multi-stage attacks among traditional detection models (Kalodanis et al., 2025). Additionally, the current IDS methods tend to utilise features of the engineered nature that are not dynamic and generalise with the changing attack patterns (Kaliappan et al., 2024). Also, the unadaptive nature of maximum AI-based solutions diminishes trust and resilience, especially in the active modelling of the attacks' severity and the evolution of threats (Kamal & Mashaly, 2025). Finally, IoT infrastructures on clouds are limited to deployment, thus making detection and monitoring difficult, particularly when managing massive amounts of streaming traffic data (Keshk et al., 2023). Despite the many methods suggested to handle the individual facets of these issues, there are still major gaps that need to be filled to provide cybersecurity solution resilience. To overcome such shortcomings, this work presents an integrated cloud-AI-based IDS to adapt to IoT threats.

## 1.2. Objective of the Work

This work is to develop an intelligent, cloud-enabled cybersecurity framework for IoT-driven cyber-physical systems that unifies signal-level preprocessing and an AI model to achieve fine-grained, multi-class IoT intrusion detection with adaptive threat awareness. This work aims to model IoT network traffic as structured signal representations, enabling the system to capture subtle temporal, statistical, and behavioral attack signatures across diverse intrusion categories. By integrating a fuzzy model for interpretable signal feature extraction with a transformer architecture, the model is designed to generalize effectively as IoT data distributions evolve.

Moreover, the cloud-based implementation goes beyond scalability by facilitating continuous learning, distributed inference and automated alert orchestration and thus turns IDS into an active, intelligent and resilient decision-making process. In the end, the work aims to develop a novel IoT cybersecurity paradigm based on signal processing and an AI-cloud-native intelligence intermediary to provide future-proof protection for large-scale IoT ecosystems.

### 1.3. Organization of the Paper

The rest of this paper is presented in the following way. Section 2 will conduct a literature review of relevant literature on IoT intrusion detection, cloud-based cybersecurity, and AI-based security frameworks. The methodology is described in Section 3. Section 4 provides the results of the experiment of the proposed approach. Lastly, Section 5 concludes the paper and provides possible directions for future research.

## 2. LITERATURE REVIEW

The development of the IoT has also increased the susceptibility of cyber systems, leading to the study of AI-based IDS. Several studies, such as Kaliappan et al. (2024), Keshk et al. (2023) and Sharma et al. (2024), have designed AI-based architectures to defend the IoT environment against malicious activities. Their models utilised anomaly-detection methods, including isolation forests and autoencoders, to detect traffic patterns in IoT networks. Then, convolutional neural networks (CNNs) were used to model behaviour to obtain device-specific activity patterns. Bayesian networks and policy-based decision mechanisms were also used to reach trust evaluation and response optimisation. These models were tested on IoT data, and they provided high interpretability of detection in comparison to existing models. Other researchers, such as Arreche et al. (2024) and Patil et al. (2022) have highlighted explainability in IDS. They developed explainable AI models for attack detection, in which various black-box models were evaluated using intrusion datasets with different characteristics. The model decisions were interpreted using local and global explanation techniques to determine the influential features of traffic. Simultaneously, feature selection and ensemble learning were applied to build a DL-based IDS. These methods use filter-based feature reduction and CNN-based classifiers of KDD and UNSW-NB15 data. Despite enhanced detection with ensemble classifiers, these methods had issues regarding scalability, dynamism to changing threats of the IoT, and integration with safety configurations.

Initial studies in the field of combining IoT signal processing with AI-based threat and attack classification algorithms. A sparse CNN-based IDS mechanism was developed by Ali et al. (2022) and Kumavat and Gomes (2023) to reduce threats to IoT, with a special focus on DDoS and DoS attacks. They used intrusion properties and suspicious traffic patterns to train their models to track and monitor malicious operations of the IoT communication layers. In the case of different circumstances, evolutionary optimisation strategies were used to differentiate normal, anomalous and intrusion attempts. Also, a trust-based protocol focusing on edge and internet layers was created to determine malicious nodes based on node reputation and activity using the analysis of network trees. Further research conducted by Javed et al. (2022) and Alzahrani and Aldhyani (2022) aimed to develop AI-based IDS and classification models to protect IoT networks against cyberattacks. After data normalisation of features, a large variety of ML classifiers were tested on the KDDCup99 benchmark dataset to detect the malicious traffic patterns. Simultaneously, they examined the process of identifying flood attacks and intrusions based on MQTT protocols using clustering and DL methods. K-means clustering techniques were used to separate normal and malicious traffic, and supervised and DL methods were used to learn temporal dependencies and protocol-specific behaviours. Although these approaches achieved encouraging detection performance, they had drawbacks related to protocol heterogeneity and scalability in the heterogeneous IoT.

As IoT infrastructure has reached unprecedented growth and interdependence with cloud services, researchers have explored cloud-supported cybersecurity to address cyberattacks on a large scale. Aldhyani and Alkahtani (2022) and Mishra et al. (2022) researched IDS and mitigation measures in cloud computing. It focuses on detecting distributed and injection-based attacks. Their methods used hard-threshold mechanisms with ML and DL methods to optimise detection accuracy and minimise false-alarm rates. The data gathered included a set of nine different injection attacks, obtained from the cyber range laboratory at Canberra and used to conduct experimental evaluations. Binary and multi-class classification cases were considered to understand attack detection across various network types. Also, the MQTT-based IoT anomaly detection was modelled in virtualised cloud conditions, which provides a viable experience in proactive threat prevention. The further studies by Sangaiah et al. (2023), Nizamudeen (2023) and Selvapandian and Santhosh (2021) were devoted to the performance of IDS based on feature selection and optimisation-driven DALY models. In their frameworks, feature selection is an optimisation problem with bio-inspired methods (Ant-Bee and Rat-Inspired Optimisation). The systems adhered to an organised process comprising data preprocessing, feature selection and classification. It was normalised to maintain the data scale and used the optimised feature sets to maximise the stability of the classifier. To classify attacks as binary, a two-dimensional CNN was used to perform the final IDS. Though these methods were efficient with respect to enhancement, they had a drawback in dynamic flexibility and multi-cloud IoT.

## 3. SYSTEM METHODOLOGY

This work proposes an AI-powered cloud-based cybersecurity architecture for IoT intrusion detection, aimed at securing contemporary cyber-physical systems against evolving cyber threats. The framework is driven by the growing heterogeneity, scale and vulnerability of IoT environments, where traditional rule-based security cannot be used in capturing the non-linear, dynamic dynamics of attacks. The framework can facilitate the detection of threats, make intelligent decisions and provide resilience in protecting the system by combining the analysis of data on IoT signals, advanced processing algorithms and cloud computing infrastructure. It offers an adaptive cybersecurity solution that identifies various types and subtypes of intrusions and supports deployment in large-scale IoT environments.

The methodology follows a structured workflow that begins with IoT data acquisition, in which network traffic and signal data representing both benign and malicious behaviours are collected from an IoT intrusion dataset. The acquired data undergo signal preprocessing and conditioning, including pairwise deletion for handling missing values, outlier detection and min–max normalisation to ensure feature uniformity. Then, nonlinear interpretable relationships in IoT traffic patterns are captured with statistical, temporal and traffic-based features extracted using a Sugeno-type (TSK) fuzzy system. In the case of IDS, a Transformer-based TabPFN is used to learn the intrusion signatures of interest directly from complex processed IoT signal features and classify threats across multiple classes. Finally, the trained model is implemented on cloud-based infrastructure to scale data storage, allocate resources for distributed processing and ongoing monitoring, and provide automated alerting and logging to facilitate intelligent, resilient cybersecurity actions across IoT-enabled cyber-physical systems. Figure 1 illustrates the general architecture of the proposed model.

*Figure 1. Architecture of the AI-driven cloud-enabled framework for intelligent iot intrusion detection*

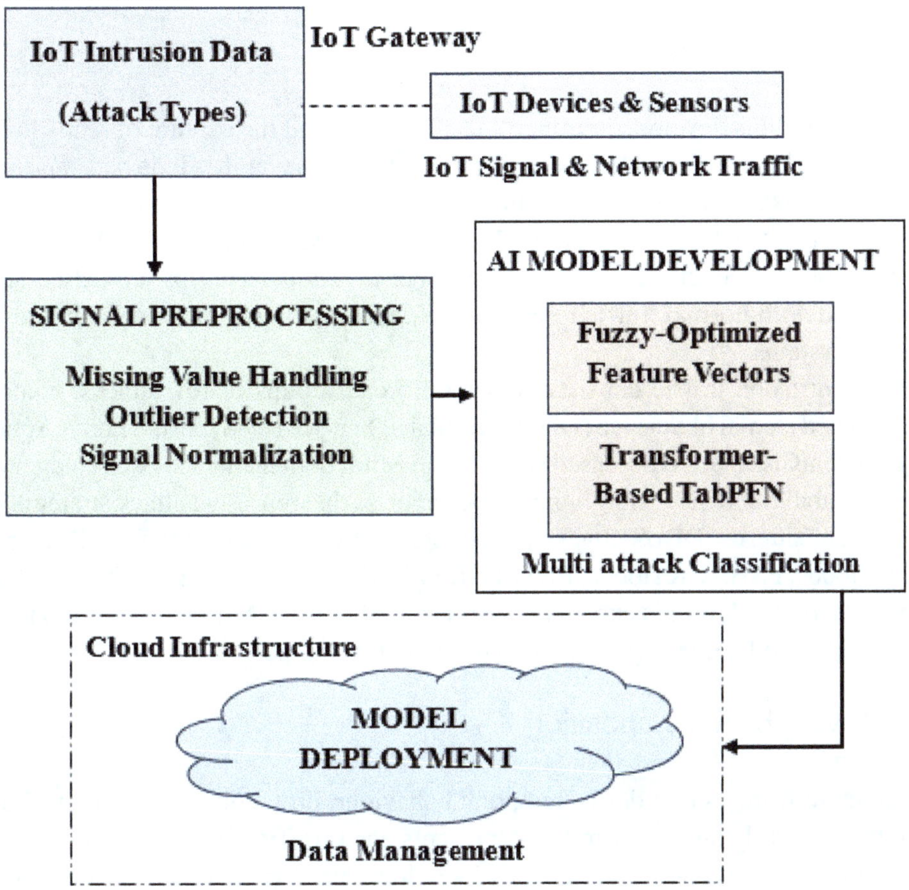


### 3.1. IoT Data Acquisition Layer

The IoT data acquisition level of the framework is developed by the IoT Intrusion Detection dataset, which was created to identify model security threats on the IoT networks. It is a simulation of real network traffic caused by heterogeneous IoT devices under both typical and malicious conditions with applications to the cybersecurity studies in cyber-physical systems. The dataset is filtered to obtain a broad range of IoT-based cyber intrusions. It comprises 1,191,264 network traffic entries and 47 discriminative features, which define flow-level, packet-level, protocol-level, and statistical signal features of IoT communications. The features are derived based on network traffic flows generated on an IoT network, in which benign traffic is co-located with various forms of cyberattacks.

### 3.1.1. Data Generation

The dataset is developed through the simulation and the capture of realistic IoT network traffic in controlled experimental settings. Several IoT devices and network services are communicating through ordinary transport and application-layer protocols (TCP, UDP, HTTP, HTTPS, DNS, SSH, SMTP, Telnet, DHCP, ARP and ICMP). In data generation, a variety of cyber-invasion scenarios are deliberately combined with normal traffic to ensure the dataset captures the attack surfaces of IoT ecosystems.

The intrusion traffic consists of several broad groups of IoT attacks, namely, Distributed Denial of Service (DDoS), Denial of Service (DoS), Brute Force, Spoofing, Reconnaissance, Web-based attacks, and Mirai botnet attacks. Each category is further subdivided into fine-grained subcategories that represent attack strategy and execution patterns. DDoS attacks include ICMP floods, UDP floods, TCP floods, SYN floods, PSHACK floods, RSTFIN floods, HTTP floods, fragmentation-based floods, and Slowloris attacks. In the fashion, traffic of the Mirai botnet is modelled in GREIP flood, Greeth flood and UDP Plain attack types.

### 3.1.2. Variables Composition

A set of features that define temporal behaviour, protocol usage, statistical distributions and dynamics of traffic represents each traffic occurrence in the data. They encompass flow-level statistics like flow duration and packet rate, source and destination rate, and flag-based statistics like SYN, ACK, FIN, RST, PSH and URG and protocol statistics representing common stacks of the IoT communication protocol. Also, statistical characteristics of minimum, maximum, average, standard deviation, variance, covariance, magnitude, radius, inter-arrival time (IAT) and total packet sizes are provided to describe the traffic with time.

The dataset also includes a label attribute that identifies every instance as a subcategory of intrusion or benign traffic. The class distribution is high-frequency attacks, which include multiple types of DDoS flooding, and low-frequency but serious threats, which include SQL injection, command injection, backdoor malware, cross-site scripting and uploading attacks. This uneven distribution represents IoT security cases, with specific attacks occurring more often and others occurring less frequently but being significantly more severe.

***Dataset***: https://www.kaggle.com/datasets/subhajournal/iotintrusion?resource=download

## 3.2. Signal Preprocessing and Conditioning

It is the conversion of the signal into an exposed format. The collected IoT intrusion data contains noise and scale distributions due to heterogeneous devices; changing network conditions and protocol diversity can impair learning stability and detection accuracy in AI-based models. These concerns with data are a significant drawback of the existing research on IoT intrusion detection. To overcome these issues, this stage performs signal preprocessing and conditioning to improve data reliability, thereby improving convergence and overall IDS performance.

### 3.2.1. Missing Value Handling

The absence of values in the IoT intrusion data within the framework preserves as much informative data as possible while reducing bias introduced by incomplete records. The loss of a whole record, as in listwise deletion, would lead to a loss of information, as there are a large number of features and the intrusion classes are highly lopsided. Thus, pairwise deletion is embraced at every statistical calculation and model input of non-missing observations of the respective pairs of features. In preprocessing, each sample (the observed values of the variables of interest) is used to compute feature-wise relationships only when the variables are observed simultaneously, and partial records are allowed to pass useful information without propagating missing values throughout the dataset. This methodology preserves the inherent statistical nature of the characteristics of the IoT signals, diminishes the data sparsity, and facilitates efficient learning by the AI-based IDS model.

### 3.2.2. Outlier Detection and Treatment

In this part, the local outlier factor algorithm (LOF) is used to identify and treat anomalous observations that deviate from normal IoT traffic behaviour. IoT network traffic can be dynamic in nature and have irregular patterns (because of temporary congestion of the network), measurement errors, improperly configured devices or incomplete protocol interactions. LOF detects outliers according to local data density instead of global distance, which can be used to detect anomalies in IoT signal spaces. During this step, LOF calculates the local density of every single data point by contrasting the local density of its adjacent data points and providing outlier scores to samples with lower local density. Strong local outliers are handled by a controlled filtering or adjustment of data points such that noise-induced deviations are reduced without eliminating fide patterns of intrusion. This procedure is targeted to maintain the underlying distribution of IoT data, as well as diminish data instabilities, which enhances the effectiveness of the model.

### 3.2.3. Signal Normalization

In this case, a min-max scaling is used to normalise the features of IoT signals to provide an equal value range among the traffic attributes. The IoT intrusion data set contains features that have different numerical values, such as the number of packets, duration of flows, size of bits, rate and statistical values, which influence the dynamics of models learning by prioritising large numbers of features. To overcome this problem, the min-max normalisation rescales the values of each feature linearly into a bounded range by considering the smallest and largest observed values to rescale the feature. This is achieved by maintaining the relative distribution and time dependence of the IoT traffic signals without bias due to scale. This scaling enables stable gradient updates, faster model convergence and numerically stable transformer-based tabular learning by standardising the feature ranges. As a result, it leads to better learning of the meaningful patterns of intrusions by IoT signal data and better multi-class IDS consistency through the normalisation process.

## 3.3. AI-Driven Intrusion Detection

This represents the analytical process of the cybersecurity framework, where intelligent models will be used to automatically detect, classify, and interpret malicious traffic in IoT network traffic. Since the data of IoT signals is high-dimensional, nonlinear, and heterogeneous, a standard methodology is not able to capture the intricate behaviour of intrusion. The framework will tackle these issues by relying on effective AI methods that are trained on vast IoT traffic data through discriminative-based learning, which is able to detect more common and low-frequency types of attacks.

After signal preprocessing and conditioning, the IoT traffic features are extracted and combined with previous knowledge acquired by a wide range of tabular distributions, and they are generalised with hyperparameter adjustments. The model acquires multifaceted dependencies between statistical, temporal and protocol-level characteristics that enable the model to differentiate benign behaviour and several types of intrusions. The IDS module powered by AI does the multi-classification, which allows detecting the types of attacks, such as DDoS, DoS, brute force, spoofing, reconnaissance, web-based attacks and Mirai botnet intrusions, with the respective subtypes. Besides recognising the type of attack, the model helps to determine the severity of intrusion and level of threat, that aid the adoption of intelligent decision-making to respond to the cybersecurity threat. This AI-driven IDS framework offers a solution to cyber-physical systems based on IoT against cyber threats; thus, it can constantly learn based on the changing traffic patterns and can be deployed in a cloud environment.

### 3.3.1. Feature Extraction

The feature analysis is performed using a Sugeno-type Takagi-Sugeno-Kang (TSK) fuzzy inference model, which is chosen for the nonlinear, uncertain and overlapping characteristics of the traffic patterns of the IoT network. IoT intrusion indicators have a progressive shift between malicious and benign states and thus cannot be limited to clear-cut decisions when using traditional statistical methods. Hence, it uses the TSK fuzzy model, which offers a rigorous and interpretable method of converting raw statistical, temporal and traffic-based signals to high-level discriminative features, which can be used in IDS based on AI.

Let the IoT traffic dataset be represented as a multivariate signal matrix.

$$X = \{x_n \in \mathbb{R}^d \mid n = 1,2,\ldots,N\} \tag{1}$$

In this equation (1), X denotes the input IoT signal data, $N$ denotes the number of traffic instances and $\mathbb{R}^d$ represents the dimensionality of the original feature space (flow duration, packet rate, byte count, inter-arrival time, protocol flags). Each input vector $X_n = [x_{n1}, x_{n2}, \ldots, x_{nd}]$ corresponds to a single IoT traffic flow captured from the network. The fuzzy model is to map these raw inputs into a transformed feature space that captures nonlinear interactions and uncertainty-aware representations.

A TSK fuzzy system is composed of a set of $R$ Fuzzy rules of the following general form:

$\mathcal{R}_r$: If $x_1$ is $A_{r1} \wedge x_2$ is $A_{r2} \wedge \cdots \wedge x_d$ is $A_{rd}$, then $y_r = f_r(x)$, $r = 1,2,\ldots,R$, where $A_{ri}$ denotes the fuzzy set associated with the $i$-th input feature in the $r$-th rule, and $f_r(x)$ is the rule consequent defined as a first-order polynomial function $f_r(x)$, as expressed in equation (2):

$$f_r(x) = w_{r0} + \sum_{i=1}^{d} w_{ri} x_i \tag{2}$$

Here, $w_{r0}$ is the bias term and $w_{ri}$ represents the consequent parameter that quantifies the contribution of the $i$-th feature to the $r$-th fuzzy rule output. This allows each rule to model localized linear behavior, while aggregating multiple rules captures global nonlinear dynamics. The degree to which an input vector $x_n$ satisfies the antecedent of the $r$-th fuzzy rule is quantified using a firing strength $\alpha_r$, defined as equation (3).

$$\alpha_r(x_n) = \prod_{i=1}^{d} \mu_{A_{ri}}(x_{ni}) \tag{3}$$

Where $\mu_{A_{ri}}$ is the membership function of the fuzzy set $A_{ri}$, typically modeled using Gaussian functions:

$$\mu_{A_{ri}}(x) = \exp\left(-\frac{(x - c_{ri})^2}{2\sigma_{ri}^2}\right) \tag{4}$$

In this equation (4), $c_{ri}$ denotes the center of the fuzzy set and $\sigma_{ri}$ controls its spread. These parameters allow uncertainty and variability of IoT traffic lights to be modelled, including variable packet rates or inter-arrival times. To maintain numerical stability and interpretability, the firing strengths are scaled as -r, as indicated in equation (5).

These parameters enable smooth modeling of uncertainty and variability inherent in IoT traffic signals, such as fluctuating packet rates or irregular inter-arrival times. To ensure numerical stability and interpretability, the firing strengths are normalized $\overline{\alpha}_r$ as shown in equation (5).

$$\overline{\alpha}_r(\mathrm{x}_n) = \frac{\alpha_r(\mathrm{x}_n)}{\sum_{k=1}^{R} \alpha_k(\mathrm{x}_n)} \tag{5}$$

The final fuzzy system output for a given input $\mathrm{x}_n$ is then computed as a weighted aggregation of all rule consequents, as shown in equation (6-7).

$$y(\mathrm{x}_n) = \sum_{r=1}^{R} \overline{\alpha}_r(\mathrm{x}_n) f_r(\mathrm{x}_n) \tag{6}$$

$$\phi(\mathrm{x}_n) = \left[\overline{\alpha}_1 f_1(\mathrm{x}_n), \overline{\alpha}_2 f_2(\mathrm{x}_n), \ldots, \overline{\alpha}_R f_R(\mathrm{x}_n)\right] \tag{7}$$

Within the framework, this output is not treated merely as a prediction but rather as a feature transformation mechanism. The normalized firing strengths $\overline{\alpha}_r(\mathrm{x}_n)$, the rule-wise linear outputs $f_r(\mathrm{x}_n)$ and their weighted combinations collectively form a new feature representation that encodes the statistical, temporal and behavioral characteristics of IoT traffic in a nonlinear yet interpretable manner.

### *Algorithm 1: Sugeno–TSK Fuzzy Feature Extraction for IoT Signal Analysis*

***Input***: IoT traffic dataset X
***Output***: Fuzzy-transformed feature matrix $\phi(\mathrm{x}_n)$
Begin
Initialize $\phi$ as an empty matrix
For each traffic instance $x_n$ in $X$ do

For each fuzzy rule $r = 1$to $R$ do
Initialize firing strength[$r$] $\leftarrow$ 1
For each feature $i = 1$ to d do
Compute membership degree
Firing strength[$r$] × membership degree
End For
Compute rule output[$r$]:
$W[r]$ and input features of $x_n$
End For
Compute normalization factor as:
Sum of all firing strength values
For each fuzzy rule $r = 1$ to $R$ do
Normalized strength[$r$] $\leftarrow$
Firing strength[$r$]
Normalized strength[$r$] × rule output[$r$]
End For
Append the fuzzy feature vector to $\phi$
End For
Return $\phi$
End

This transformation is particularly effective for modelling key intrusion-related characteristics, including packet rates, flow times, distributions of bytes, inter-arrival times and protocol-level behaviours since these attributes overlap between the distributions of different attacks. The fuzzy rules enable the system to capture smooth transitions of normal and malicious traffic, whereas the consequent functions reflect subtle variations within each of the traffic regimes. The TSK model minimises noise and outlier sensitivity since it incorporates uncertainty-aware membership functions and rule-based aggregation in IoT settings. The fuzzy-transformed feature vectors obtained are input to the AI intrusion detection model, which in turn learns complex intrusion signatures when operating directly on features.

### 3.3.2. Threat Classification

In this section, a Transformer-based Tabular Prior-data Fitted Network (TabPFN) is used to perform IDS as threat classification based on the features of the IoT signals. TabPFN is selected due to the tabular character of the data of the IoT traffic, where the heterogeneous statistical, temporal and protocol-level features of each network stream are applied. It uses meta-learning on a large number of distributions of tabular data, which yields resilient generalisation to intrusion-detection tasks.

### *Transformer-Based Tabular PFNs*

This represents a powerful shift in learning from tabular data, inspired by structured datasets that are inherently tabular yet not optimally handled by traditional DL architectures. This model is constructed and based on the idea of prior-data fitting, where a transformer model is meta-trained on a large distribution of synthetic and tabular tasks to implicitly learn a Bayesian prior on functions parameterised on tabular inputs. In this meta-training stage, the model is exposed to thousands of different datasets with different feature dimensions, correlations and class distributions, allowing it to internalise general inductive biases regarding how tabular data behaves. Consequently, Transformer-based TabPFN can at inference time learn task-specifically without retraining; it effectively learns the Bayesian posterior by using transformer attention mechanisms.

The self-attention layers also process rows of the data as contextual tokens, and the model collectively features interactions, sample relationships and label dependencies, which is beneficial in complex domains like IoT IDS, where there are attack patterns that are subtle, overlapping and extremely nonlinear. Moreover, TabPFN is inherently uncertain, can be used for multi-class classification with hyperparameter tuning and generalises well even in low-data regimes. The detailed structure of the Transformer network model is shown in Figure 2.

*Figure 2. Architecture of transformer-TabPFN for IoT IDS and threat classification*

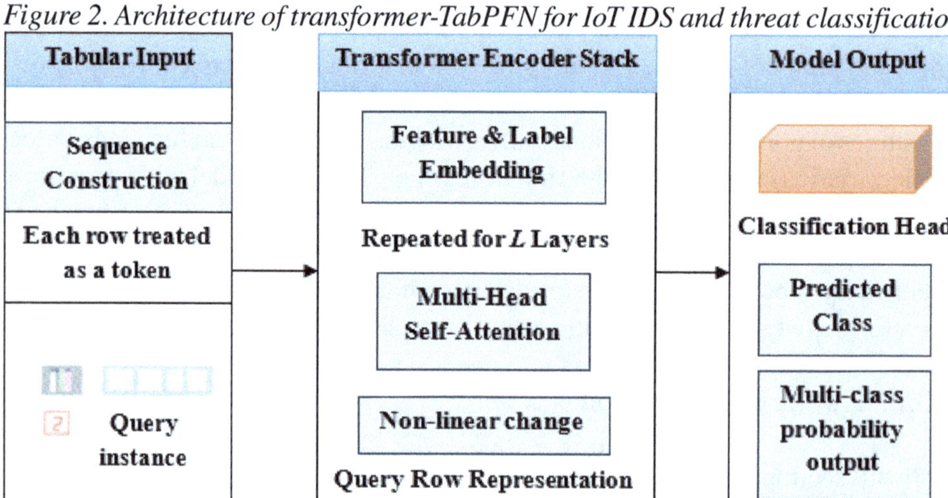


Let the fuzzy-transformed IoT traffic data $\mathscr{D}$ obtained from the previous stage is represented as equation (8).

$$\mathscr{D} = \{(\phi_n, y_n) \mid n = 1, 2, \ldots, N\} \tag{8}$$

Where $\phi_n \in \mathbb{R}^m$ denotes the extracted feature vector for the $n$-th IoT traffic instance (obtained from the fuzzy model), $m$ is the dimensionality of the transformed feature space, and $y_n \in \{1, 2, \ldots, C\}$ is the corresponding class label. Here, $C$ represents the total number of benign traffic and multiple attack subcategories.

TabPFN models the conditional probability of class labels given tabular inputs using a Transformer architecture trained to approximate Bayesian inference over functions. Formally, the predictive distribution for a new IoT traffic instance $\phi_*$ is defined as equation (9).

$$p(y_* \mid \phi_*, \mathscr{D}) = \int p(y_* \mid \phi_*, \theta) p(\theta \mid \mathscr{D}) d\theta \tag{9}$$

Where $\theta$ denotes the latent model parameters. In practice, TabPFN does not explicitly compute this integral; instead, it learns a neural approximation to Bayesian marginalization using transformer-based attention mechanisms, trained on tabular tasks. This allows the model to encode uncertainty knowledge when classifying ambiguous IoT traffic patterns. The input to the TabPFN model is constructed by concatenating feature vectors and labels from the training set into a sequence Z, as shown in equation (10).

$$\mathrm{Z} = [(\phi_1, y_1), (\phi_2, y_2), \ldots, (\phi_N, y_N), (\phi_*, \varnothing)] \tag{10}$$

Where $\varnothing$ denotes the label of the query instance. This sequence is embedded into a latent space using a learnable embedding function Embed(Z), as shown in equation (11).

$$\mathrm{H}^{(0)} = \mathrm{Embed(Z)} \tag{11}$$

With $\mathrm{H}^{(0)} \in \mathbb{R}^{(N+1)\times d_h}$, where $d_h$ is the hidden dimension of the transformer.

Within each transformer layer $\ell$, TabPFN applies multi-head self-attention to model dependencies across all samples and features.

$$\mathrm{Attention(Q, K, V)} = \sum_{h=1}^{H} \mathrm{softmax}\left(\frac{\mathrm{Q}_h \mathrm{K}_h^\top}{\sqrt{d_h}}\right)\mathrm{V}_h \tag{12}$$

In this equation (12), $\mathrm{Q}_h = \mathrm{H}^{(\ell-1)}\mathrm{W}_h^Q$, $\mathrm{K}_h = \mathrm{H}^{(\ell-1)}\mathrm{W}_h^K$ and $\mathrm{V}_h = \mathrm{H}^{(\ell-1)}\mathrm{W}_h^V$ are the query, key, and value projections for the $h$-th attention head. The matrices $\mathrm{W}_h^Q, \mathrm{W}_h^K$, and $\mathrm{W}_h^V$ are learnable parameters, and $H$ denotes the number of attention heads. This attention mechanism enables the model to capture complex interactions among different IoT traffic instances, including similarities among attack flows and deviations from benign behavior.

The transformer layers are stacked with position-wise feed-forward networks to yield the final latent representation $H^{(L)}$, as expressed in equation (13).

$$H^{(L)} = \text{Transformer}(H^{(0)}) \tag{13}$$

Where $L$ denotes the number of transformer layers. The output corresponds query instance $\phi_*$ is then passed through a classification head to compute class logits $o_*$.

$$o_* = W_c h_*^{(L)} + b_c \tag{14}$$

In this equation (14), $h_*^{(L)}$ is the final hidden representation of the query instance, and $W_c$ and $b_c$ are the classifier weights and bias. The multi-class probability distribution over intrusion classes is obtained using the softmax function:

$$p(y_* = c \mid \phi_*) = \frac{\exp(o_{*,c})}{\sum_{j=1}^{C} \exp(o_{*,j})}, \; c = 1,\ldots,C \tag{15}$$

In equation (15), this probabilistic output $p(y_*)$ is further interpreted to infer the attack type, severity, and threat level. The predicted class $\hat{y}_* = \arg\max_c p(y_* = c \mid \phi_*)$ identifies the intrusion category, while the confidence scores and class-specific risk mappings are used to estimate severity and threat intensity.

### *Algorithm 2: AI-Driven IoT IDS Using Transformer-based TabPFN*

***Input***: IoT traffic dataset D
***Output***: Predicted attack type (Severity, Threat level) $p(y_*)$
Begin
Initialize dataset $D$ for $i = 1$ to $N$
Where:
$\varphi_i = m$-dimensional feature vector after fuzzy transformation
$y_i \in C$ represents the intrusion class label
Define query instance $\varphi_q$ from incoming IoT traffic
Construct tabular sequence $Z$:
For each element $z \in Z$ do
Convert feature values into latent embeddings
Encode known labels as categorical embeddings
End For
Let $H^{(0)}$ represent the embedded sequence

For each transformer layer $\ell = 1$ to $L$ do
Apply multi-head self-attention on $H^{\ell-1}$
Capture contextual relations among traffic samples
Update latent representation → $H^{\ell}$
End For
Extract final representation $h_q$ corresponding to $\varphi_q$
Compute class probabilities over $C$
Convert logits into a probability distribution:
$P(class|\varphi\_q)$ using normalized exponential mapping
Determine predicted class:
$p \leftarrow$ class with maximum probability
Estimate severity and threat level $y_*$
Return $p(y_*)$
End Algorithm

This enables the system to classify incoming IoT traffic accurately and quantify uncertainty and confidence in its decisions. By integrating transformer-based attention, the TabPFN model provides a computationally efficient solution for multi-class IoT IDS. Its ability to learn rich intrusion signatures from IoT signal features makes it a central component of the proposed AI-driven cybersecurity methodology, ensuring intelligent threat classification in cloud-enabled IoT cyber systems.

### 3.4. Cloud-Based Management and Deployment

The cloud-based application layer is a facilitating element of the suggested framework, which offers the processing ability and system dependability to assure extensive IoT ecosystems. IoT networks provide networks with high traffic volumes, velocity and heterogeneity, demanding significant storage, processing and model orchestration services. To overcome these limitations, deploy the trained Transformer-based TabPFN model in the cloud environment of the distributed computation and centralised security in delivering efficient and reliable services of the IDS services to dynamic workloads.

From a data management perspective, cloud infrastructure can be used as a safe repository of data used by large-scale IoT traffic. The extracted signal features and incoming network flows are constantly ingested into cloud-based storage systems, including the distributed file systems or time-series databases, which support the features of both structured and semi-structured data. At rest and in transit, there is the protection of data confidentiality and integrity through secure management mechanisms. This decentralised storage model allows storing IoT traffic logs long-term to analyse them during a forensic examination and retrain the model on a regular basis. Moreover, the data storage and computational layers are logically separated, which means that the system can independently scale storage capacity without depending on the processing resources of a cloud-native architecture.

Distributed processing of model training and evaluation of transformer-based models on high-dimensional tabular data can also be done in a cloud environment. The AI model is trained and refined with distributed computing models. It is parallel to load data, process features and compute gradients across a number of compute nodes. This is a distributed paradigm that minimises training latency and allows the system to scale large datasets without slowing down. Inference workloads are dynamically deployed and scaled as containerised services and orchestration platforms, ensuring real-time intrusion detection even during traffic bursts or large-scale attacks. Elastic allocation of computational resources is analytically explained by the bursty and adversarial character of cyberattacks, require long-lasting analytical capacity in response to a sudden rise in malicious traffic.

The reliability of the operational IDS is a factor that involves continuous monitoring and scalability of performance. The cloud-based implementation integrates the monitoring services, which monitor the system-level metrics and model-level metrics, i.e., prediction-confidence distribution and classification throughput. These monitoring indicators allow managing resources proactively and changing scale policies in response time, and the detection accuracy and response time do not exceed critical values. Additionally, model governance is aided by the use of continuous monitoring, which detects possible performance drift due to the changing attack strategies or behavioural changes within the network. This feedback mechanism will supply the analytical scheduled model updates or retraining, thus maintaining the long-term performance of detection in dynamic chameleonic IoT settings.

Besides detection, the cloud-based framework is also combined with automated alerting and logging systems to aid in intelligent cybersecurity activities and post-incident analysis. In the case when the deployed AI model detects malicious IoT traffic, real-time notifications are sent and distributed among system administrators. These notifications summarise background facts such as the type of attack, the level of severity, and the degree of certainty, which allow decisions to be made on the response. At the same time, all logs of the recognised activities within the system and intrusions are stored in the cloud environment, creating a trail of forensic activity. These logs cannot be done without compliance auditing, attack attribution, and root-cause analysis, as well as assisting in detecting policies and model refinement. The combination of cloud-based data management and deployment AI approach makes the IDS framework responsive and analytically suitable for real-life IoT cyber systems.

## 4. EXPERIMENTAL EVOLUTION

This research is to design and test an AI-based, cloud-based IoT intrusion detection model based on an intelligent cybersecurity framework, which will effectively detect and classify various types of cyber-attacks using the IoT signals and make trustworthy decisions. This section confirms the effectiveness and computation feasibility of the framework under realistic operating conditions. It implements the experiments on the IoT Intrusion dataset, which contains labelled IoT network traffic and signal-level features of both benign behaviour and various categories of intrusion.

The entire implementation is carried out in Python and uses standard data processing tools. The experiments run on a 64-bit x64-based system with a 12th Gen Intel(R) Core (TM) i5-12400 processor (2.50 GHz) and 8.00 GB RAM (7.75 GB usable) to provide a controlled and reproducible simulation environment. A standard split ratio is used to divide the dataset into training (80%), validation (10%), and testing (10%) to aid in the learning of the model, hyperparameter optimisation and the performance assessment. The experimental outcomes show that the framework has a high level of IDS accuracy with balanced precision and recall on a variety of attack types and shows consistent inference performance, thus attesting to its effectiveness in real-world cybersecurity applications on the IoT.

### 4.1. Classification Performance Analysis

In this section, the indicators of the IDS efficiency are introduced to demonstrate the framework that can successfully detect and classify malicious IoT traffic in a variety of attack categories and fine-grained subcategories using Transformer-based TabPFN. The standard metrics are used to assess the performance of the classification to confirm the reliability of the model at detection and balanced learning in the classes of intrusion. Therefore, establishing its efficiency in classifying normal traffic against various types of attack.

*Figure 3. Multiclass threat detection performance*

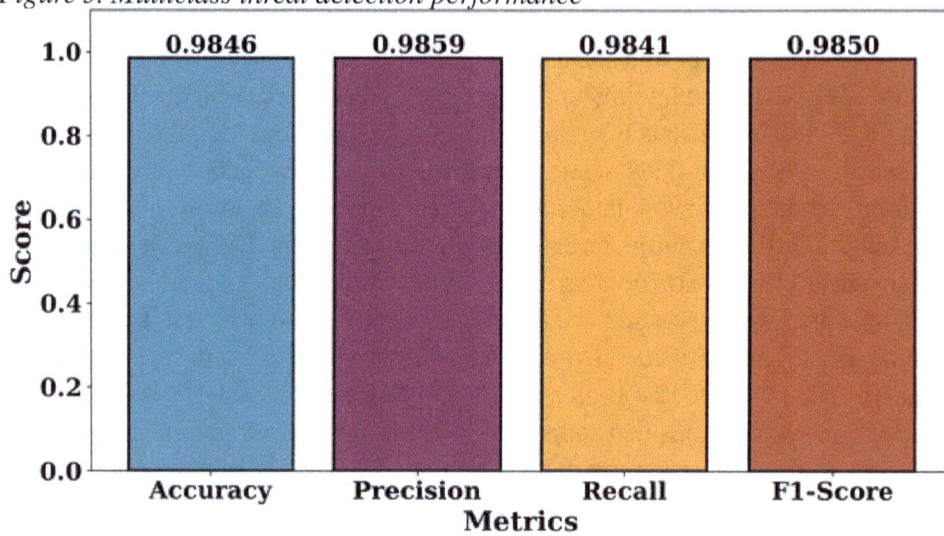


Figure 3 shows the overall classification performance of the Transformer-based TabPFN model in identifying and classifying cyber intrusions of IoT-based nature. This offers an evaluation measure to describe the efficiency of the model in detecting both common and uncommon attacks in the context of different intrusion categories. The high accuracy (0.9846), precision (0.9859), recall (0.9841) and F1-score (0.9850) indicate the strong predictive performance of the model, low false positives, and balanced detection of the IoT attack distribution.

*Figure 4. Error rate analysis for IoT intrusion detection*

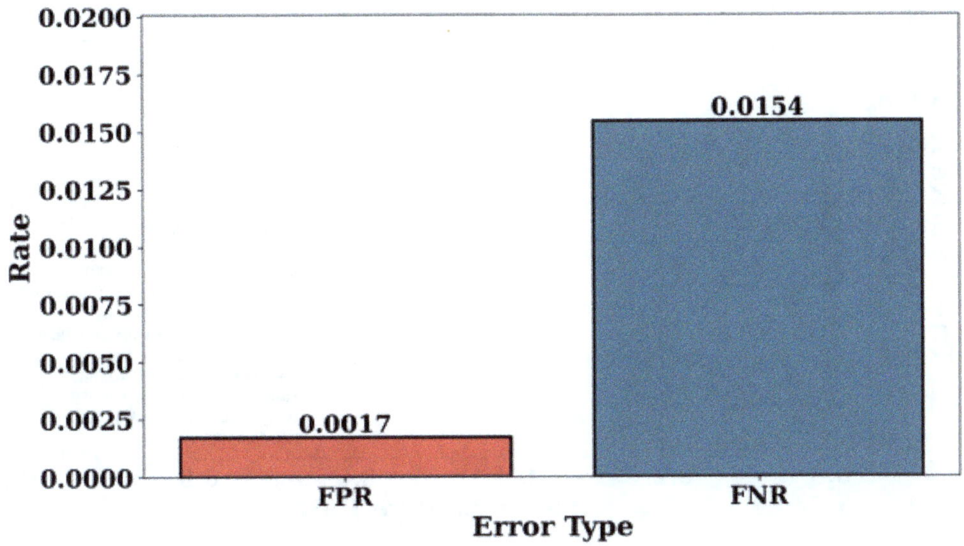


Figure 4 shows the analysis of the error rates of the model, that is, the false positive rate (FPR) and the false negative rate (FNR), to measure the reliability of IDS. This is based on the trade-off between the sensitivity of detection and the accuracy of alerts. The FPR (0.0017) represents the rate of benign traffic that the system falsely identifies as malicious. It demonstrates the accuracy of the system in not sending out unnecessary notifications. Conversely, the FNR of 0.0154 of real intrusions that the model failed to capture. This represents the proportion of actual intrusions that the model missed in capturing subtle or rare attack patterns.

*Figure 5. Multiclass ROC curve for IoT intrusion classification*

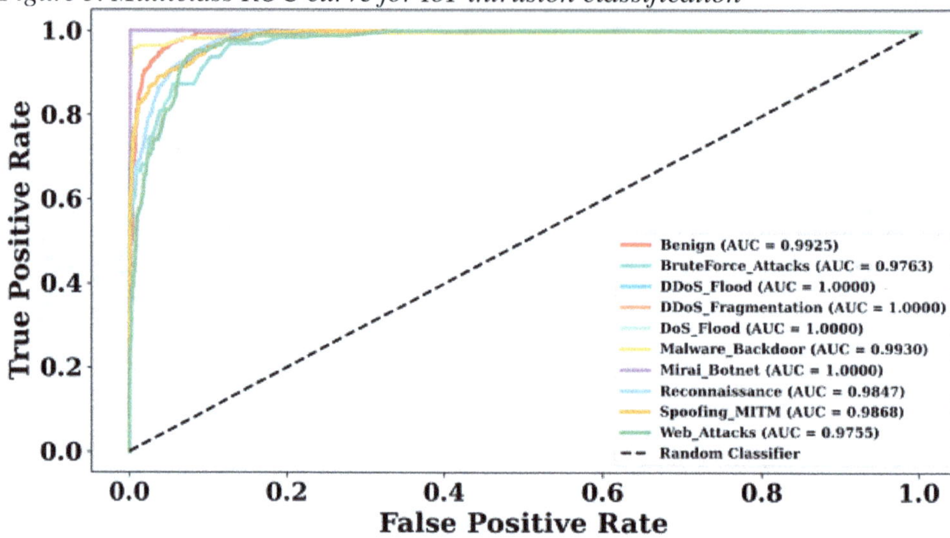


In Figure 5, the Receiver Operating Characteristic (ROC) curves of the proposed model in the various classes of intrusion in the IoT network traffic are provided. This judges the model with regard to its capability of classifying both benign and malicious activities. The values of the Area Under the Curve (AUC) denote the classification strength of attack types, and the scores are incredibly high in critical threats like DDoS, Mirai Botnet and DoS, and the strong performance is ensured (AUC = 1.0000). In the case of Benign (AUC = 0.9925), Spoofing MITM (AUC = 0.9888), Reconnaissance (AUC = 0.9847), and Malware Backdoor (AUC = 0.8930), the model is able to detect effectively. This discussion validates the high levels of discriminative power of the AI model in various types of intrusions.

*Figure 6. Precision-recall curve for multiclass IDS*

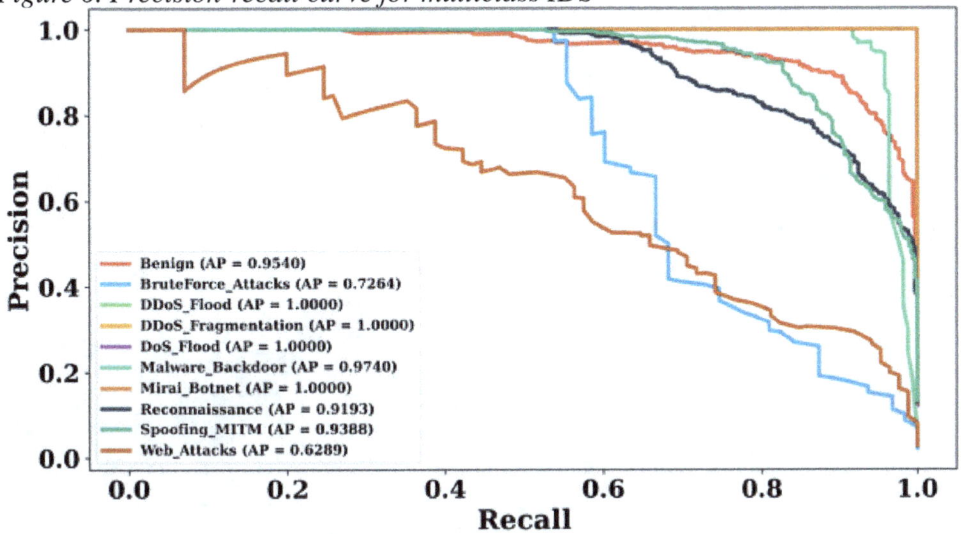


Figure 6 shows the Precision-Recall (PR) curves of each intrusion category identified by the DL model. This assesses the capability of this model to balance the detection sensitivity (recall) and prediction accuracy (precision) between frequent and rare types of IoT attacks. The results in terms of the Average Precision (AP) demonstrate the performance of the model, showing that perfect detection is observed of DDoS Flood, DDoS Fragmentation and Mirai Botnet (AP = 1.0000), and good in the case of Malware Backdoor (AP = 0.9740) and Spoofing MITM (AP = 0.9388) and good classification of Benign (AP = 0.9510) and Reconnaissance (AP = 0.919). The AP scores of the Brute Force Attacks (AP = 0.7264) and Web Attacks (AP = 0.6289) are lower, which implies further improve. This evaluation highlights the model accuracy of the proper identification of threats, particularly in asymmetrical IoT intrusion cases.

*Figure 7. Confusion matrix for multiclass IoT IDS*

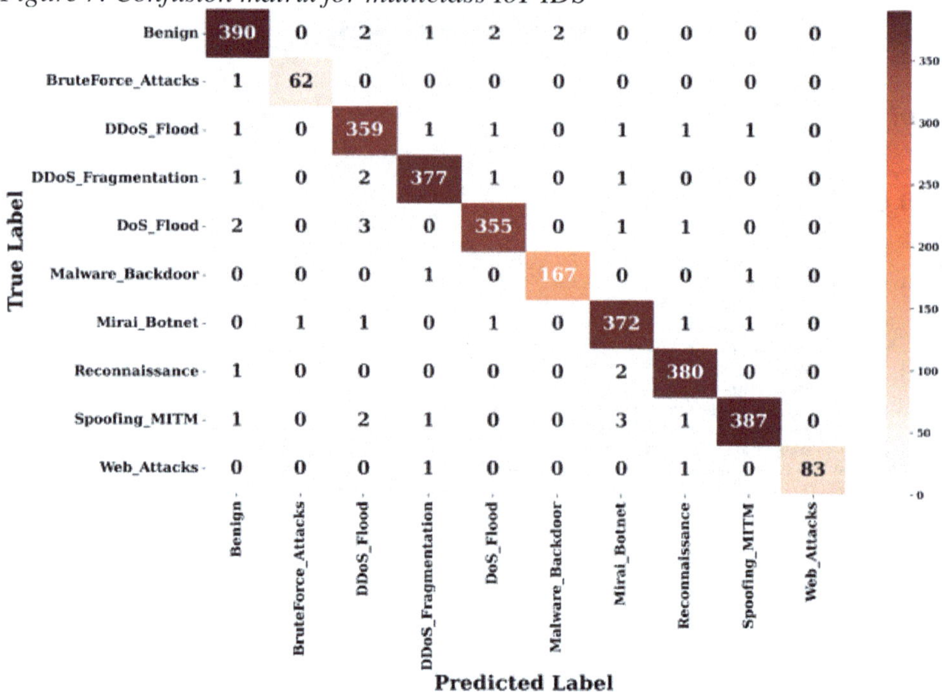


Figure 7 displays the confusion matrix of the model, and it depicts its performance of multiclass classification in different categories of IoT intrusion. This predicted labels of each of the classes, with diagonal cells being actual predictions and off-diagonal cells being misclassifications. The model shows a high level of accuracy with major types of attack, as it correctly recognises 390 benign, 359 DDoS Flood, 377 DDoS, 355 DoS, 372 Mirai Botnet and 167 Malware Backdoor with the major confusion between classes. Therefore, comparing per-class prediction fidelity, the TabPFN model has a high degree of discriminative ability despite overlapping traffic patterns and uneven class distribution.

*Table 1. Class distribution of IoT intrusion dataset*

| Label | Class Name | Sample Count | Percentage (%) |
|---|---|---|---|
| 0 | Benign | 1984 | 13.33 |
| 1 | Brute Force Attacks | 317 | 2.13 |
| 2 | DDoS Flood | 1824 | 12.25 |
| 3 | DDoS Fragmentation | 1908 | 12.82 |

continued on following page

*Table 1. Continued*

| Label | Class Name | Sample Count | Percentage (%) |
|---|---|---|---|
| 4 | DoS Flood | 1810 | 12.16 |
| 5 | Malware Backdoor | 846 | 5.68 |
| 6 | Mirai Botnet | 1884 | 12.66 |
| 7 | Reconnaissance | 1912 | 12.84 |
| 8 | Spoofing MITM | 1976 | 13.27 |
| 9 | Web Attacks | 426 | 2.86 |
| **Training Set Size** | | 11,909 | |
| **Test Set Size** | | 2,978 | |

Table 1 shows the samples in 10 target classes in the IoT intrusion dataset for training and testing the AI-based classification model. The imbalance of this dataset is inherent in the distribution of classes, which corresponds to the case of IoT traffic, with benign and frequent attacks prevailing. It also defines the training (11,909 samples) and test (2,978 samples) sets on which performance would be benchmarked. This analysis of distribution confirms that adaptive models can effectively be trained on skewed data and detect intrusions with high accuracy.

*Table 2. Class-wise performance metrics of TabPFN IDS model*

| Class | Precision | Recall | F1-Score | Support |
|---|---|---|---|---|
| **Benign** | 0.98 | 0.98 | 0.98 | 397 |
| **Brute Force Attacks** | 0.98 | 0.98 | 0.98 | 63 |
| **DDoS Flood** | 0.97 | 0.98 | 0.98 | 365 |
| **DDoS Fragmentation** | 0.99 | 0.99 | 0.99 | 382 |
| **DoS Flood** | 0.99 | 0.98 | 0.98 | 362 |
| **Malware Backdoor** | 0.99 | 0.99 | 0.99 | 169 |
| **Mirai Botnet** | 0.98 | 0.99 | 0.98 | 377 |
| **Reconnaissance** | 0.99 | 0.99 | 0.99 | 383 |
| **Spoofing MITM** | 0.99 | 0.98 | 0.99 | 395 |
| **Web Attacks** | 1.00 | 0.98 | 0.99 | 85 |
| **Overall Accuracy** | | **98.46** | | **2978** |
| **Macro Average** | **0.99** | **0.98** | **0.98** | 2978 |
| **Weighted Average** | **0.98** | **0.98** | **0.98** | 2978 |

Table 2 shows the classification performance of the suggested model classes of the IoT traffic, such as benign and malicious classes, and the total samples (support), which allows us to assess the detection fidelity of the model in a detailed manner. The model scores high on the prediction of the categories, with an average of 0.98 on both macro and weighted averages, a fact that validates the strength of the model in addressing imbalanced distributions of intrusion. The precision and recall prove that the model is flexible to critical threats, which is justified by the framework's effectiveness in multiclass IDS.

## 4.2. Cloud Performance Metrics

To confirm the feasibility of the suggested framework, the trained Transformer-based TabPFN IDS model was developed and deployed to the cloud and tested in real-time operating conditions. Such deployment represents the capability of the system to scale the streams of IoT traffic with low latency, high throughput and resilient performance. The indicators provided in this section are empirical indicators that the framework is efficient in facilitating cloud-enhanced intrusion tracking and automatic warning of extensive IoT ecosystems.

*Figure 8. Cloud-scaled latency response curve*

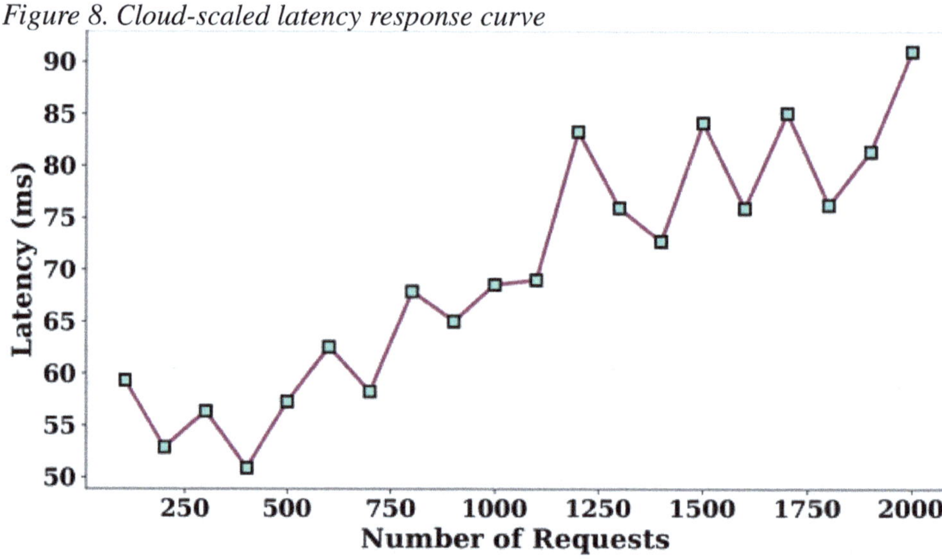


Figure 8 illustrates the latency behavior of the deployed AI-driven IDS model under varying request loads in a cloud environment. This provides the responsiveness of the system (in milliseconds) and the time spent to categorise the traffic received by the IoT in the system as the number of simultaneous requests grows. As illustrated, the latency increases slowly from when the number of requests is lower (52 ms) to the peak level (88 ms) as the number of requests increases (2000 requests), indicating that the framework has the potential to support response times of less than 96 ms even during high-traffic scenarios.

*Figure 9. Adaptive packet throughput profile*

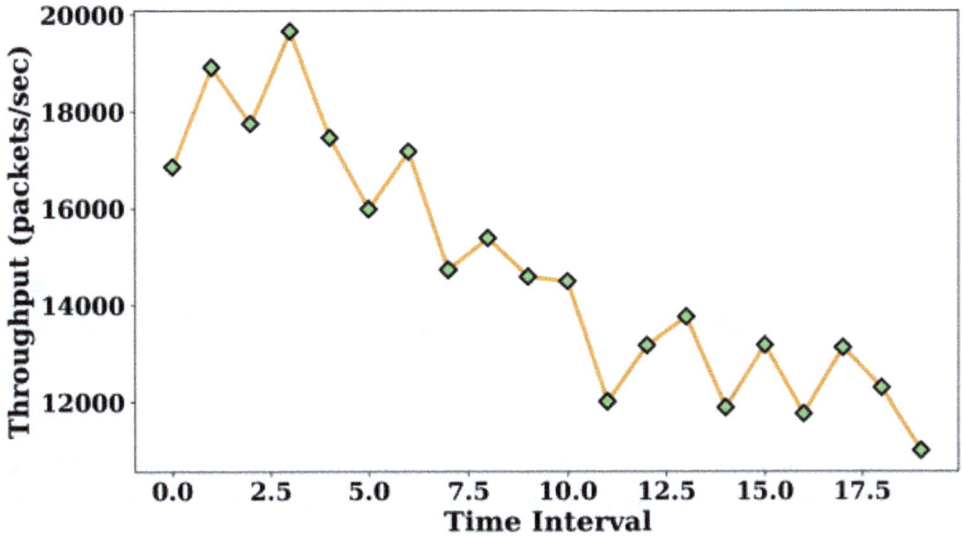


Figure 9 shows the throughput performance of the AI-IDS deployed on the cloud, which is the record count of IoT traffic handled per second over time. This is the data-handling capacity of the system over the operational periods. The throughput rises to about 19,600 packets/sec and decreases slowly to about 12,200 packets/sec, which indicates the adaptive resource allocation and load balancing when the traffic is dynamic. This justifies the capability of the framework to support high-volume intrusion surveillance with operational stability and responsiveness in cloud-native IoT applications.

*Figure 10. Resource utilization curve*

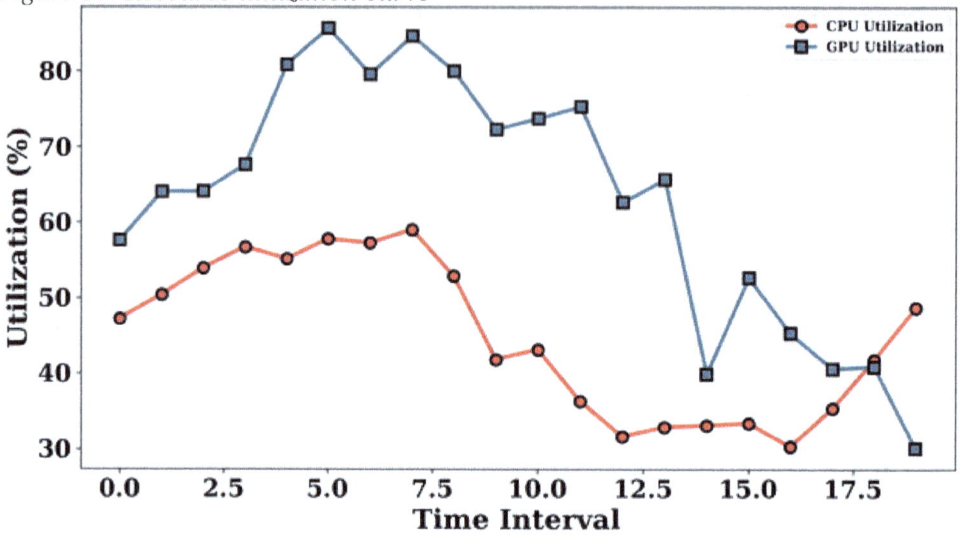


Figure 10 shows the trend of the CPU and GPU usage of the cloud-hosted AI model during the time period, which shows the efficiency and distribution of the workload in the processing units. This demonstrates the dynamism in the system in the allocation of resources in real-time intrusion monitoring. The maxima of the use of GPUs are about 87% around the time interval of 7.5, which then slowly decreases to 42% towards the final time interval. Meanwhile, CPU utilisation is relatively constant, ranging between 58% and 66%, with slight fluctuations around the middle. Based on this performance, high-throughput inference with GPU acceleration can be combined with consistent CPU operations, enabling scalable processing for cloud-IoT deployments.

*Figure 11. Dynamic memory utilization envelope*

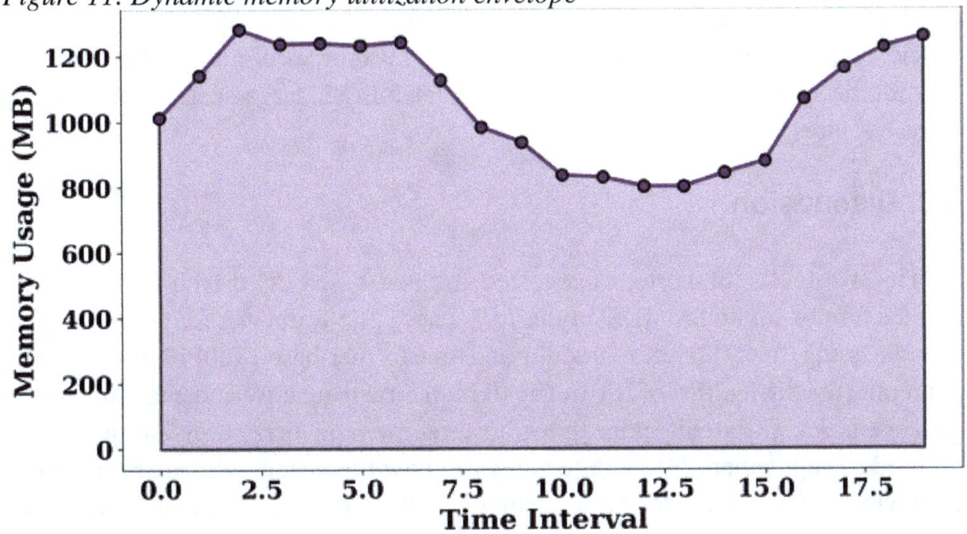


Figure 11 shows the memory usage profile of the cloud-hosted AI IDS over time, illustrating how RAM is consumed during traffic analysis and threat classification. This visualizes the system's memory footprint across operational intervals, with usage peaking at approximately 1,180 MB during initial and final phases, and dipping to around 720 MB mid-cycle. The area under the curve is shaded to highlight the maintained memory demand for handling high-dimensional IoT signal data. This performance trend verifies that the framework is effective in its limited memory capacity in providing a credible deployment of cloud.

*Table 3. Cloud-enabled intrusion detection performance*

| Metric | Value |
|---|---|
| **Average Training Time** | 13.66 seconds |
| **Average Inference Latency** | 69.67 ms |
| **Average Throughput** | 14,757.59 sec |
| **Average CPU Utilization** | 44.94% |
| **Average GPU Utilization** | 63.17% |
| **Average Memory Usage** | 1,056.87 MB |
| **Peak Memory Usage** | 1,281.54 MB |

Table 3 provides a condensed summary of the system efficiency running in the cloud, with the performance indicators proving that the system can handle intrusion detection in the IoT. The summary indicates that the framework is capable of balancing the computation speed, use of resources and throughput during dynamic traffic. Aggregation of training, inferences, and resources provides empirical support for the system's responsiveness and applicability in large-scale cyber-physical infrastructures.

### 4.3. Discussion

This work has suggested and tested a cloud-based AI-driven cybersecurity architecture of multiclass IDS in the IoT space. The framework combines signal preprocessing, fuzzy feature extraction and transformer-based TabPFN classifiers to overcome the difficulties of IoT traffic of high dimensionality and changing strategies of attacks. The architecture shows how interpretable fuzzy transformations can be used to supplement DL architectures to allow the accuracy of real-time cloud deployment. The overall detection accuracy of 98.46 in the experimental evaluation was higher than that of the conventional ML and DL baselines. Table 4 indicates that the proposed TabPFN model has an advantage over the other studies, such as Logistic Regression (LR), Deep Neural Networks (DNN), LSTM and CNN. This underscores that the framework can capture nonlinear dependencies in IoT traffic more effectively than AI models can.

*Table 4. Comparative performance of multiclass IoT IDS models*

| Study | Model | Results |
|---|---|---|
| **Wahab et al. (2025)** | LR | Accuracy: 82.98 |
| **Xu et al. (2023)** | DNN | Accuracy: 92.50 |
| | LSTM | Accuracy: 97.06 |
| | CNN | Accuracy: 97.95 |
| **Proposed** | **TabPFN** | **Accuracy: 98.46** |

The framework is more accurate by developing the DL model with the combination of the Sugeno-TSK fuzzy feature extraction and the TabPFN transformer architecture. This enhancement enabled the system to model nonlinear relationships as well as uncertainty-sensitive traffic patterns. The interpretable noise-resilient features offered by the fuzzy transformation and the ability of the transformer-based TabPFN to use previous tabular distributions to extrapolate across new types of attacks indicate that the integration of interpretable fuzzy logic and transformer learning is a novel development in the field of IoT IDS compared to more conventional methods of DL.

Findings can be used in the wider cybersecurity and IoT research community due to the ability to show that IDS can transcend a static feature engineering approach and black-box DL. This work also provides insights into the development of IDS structures that ensure the accuracy of detection and make them implementable in the real world to enable smart cities, health and industrial internet systems. Moreover, the big dataset of IoT attack intrusions (containing more than 1.19 million traffic logs, including 47 discriminative characteristics) provided a high-quality evaluation of different attack types. This imbalance in the dataset (frequent DDoS floods and rare but critical threats (Mirai botnet variants)) allowed the model to extrapolate on imbalanced distributions.

The value added by the work is a hybrid interpretability-performance, where the framework is modelled to be deployed in the cloud, which guarantees scalability and real-time performance. In this way, the outcome illustrates the inference latency of 69.67 ms, which proves the framework to be relevant to intrusion detection in a large-scale IoT ecosystem. Its multiclass classification enables the detection of the major categories of attacks along with the subcategories, which provide a fine-grained awareness of the threat. Overall, the framework balances accuracy and responsiveness as a next-generation IoT cybersecurity solution.

## 5. CONCLUSION

This work effectively presents an AI-driven, cloud-enabled cybersecurity framework for intelligent IoT intrusion detection, addressing the growing security challenges posed by large-scale IoT environments. The framework integrates IoT signal processing, interpretable feature extraction using a Sugeno-type fuzzy model, and Transformer-based tabular learning (TabPFN) to detect and classify diverse cyber threats accurately. Experimental analysis on a multi-class IoT intrusion dataset demonstrates exceptional detection performance, achieving an overall accuracy of 98.46%, precision of 98.59%, recall of 98.41%, and F1-score of 98.50%, thereby confirming the model's ability to distinguish benign traffic from complex attack patterns reliably. Further evaluation using ROC and Precision–Recall analyses reveals near-perfect discriminative capability for attack classes, while maintaining low error rates, highlighting the framework's robustness and balanced learning behavior under imbalanced intrusion distributions. In addition to detection accuracy, the cloud deployment results validate the framework's practical feasibility and scalability, achieving an average inference latency of 69.67 ms, a throughput of approximately 14,757 packets per second, and ensuring real-time responsiveness in operational environments. Thus, the approach is characterized by high detection accuracy to diverse intrusion types, and seamless cloud scalability, making it well-suited for deployment in cyber-physical IoT systems. Overall, this study demonstrates that integrating advanced AI models with cloud-enabled infrastructure provides an efficient and resilient cybersecurity solution, contributing significantly to the advancement of intelligent IoT security and laying the groundwork for future research on adaptive and autonomous IDS.

## 5.1. Future Work

Future work will involve extending the study to continuous learning mechanisms in the IDS pipeline to enable the model to adapt to new and evolving attack patterns in IoT dynamically. The framework will be further extended to include explainable and trust-aware AI methods to provide human-explainable threat explanations, risk scores and confidence-aware alerts, thereby giving security analysts better insight into model decisions and increasing trust in mission-critical IoT settings.

## REFERENCES


Afraji, D. M. A. A., Lloret, J., & Peñalver, L. (2025). Deep learning-driven defense strategies for mitigating DDoS attacks in cloud computing environments. *Cyber Security Applications*, *3*, 100085. DOI: 10.1016/j.csa.2025.100085

Ahmad, W., Rasool, A., Javed, A. R., Baker, T., & Jalil, Z. (2022). Cyber security in IoT-based cloud computing: A comprehensive survey. *Electronics (Basel)*, *11*(1), 16. DOI: 10.3390/electronics11010016

Al Rawajbeh, M., Maria Soosai, A. J., Ramasamy, L. K., & Khan, F. (2025). Trustworthy adaptive AI for real-time intrusion detection in industrial IoT security. *IoT*, *6*(3), 53. DOI: 10.3390/iot6030053

Aldhyani, T. H. H., & Alkahtani, H. (2022). Artificial intelligence algorithm-based economic denial of sustainability attack detection systems: Cloud computing environments. *Sensors (Basel)*, *22*(13), 4685. DOI: 10.3390/s22134685

Ali, M. H., Jaber, M. M., Abd, S. K., Rehman, A., Awan, M. J., Damaševičius, R., & Bahaj, S. A. (2022). Threat analysis and distributed denial of service (DDoS) attack recognition in the Internet of Things (IoT). *Electronics (Basel)*, *11*(3), 494. DOI: 10.3390/electronics11030494

Alladi, T., Kohli, V., Chamola, V., Yu, F. R., & Guizani, M. (2021). Artificial intelligence (AI)-empowered intrusion detection architecture for the Internet of Vehicles. *IEEE Wireless Communications*, *28*(3), 144–149. DOI: 10.1109/MWC.001.2000428

Alotaibi, A., & Barnawi, A. (2023). IDSoft: A federated and softwarized intrusion detection framework for massive Internet of Things in 6G network. *Journal of King Saud University. Computer and Information Sciences*, *35*(6), 101575. DOI: 10.1016/j.jksuci.2023.101575

Alrefaei, A., & Ilyas, M. (2024). Using machine learning multiclass classification technique to detect IoT attacks in real time. *Sensors (Basel)*, *24*(14), 4516. DOI: 10.3390/s24144516

Alzahrani, A., & Aldhyani, T. H. (2022). Artificial intelligence algorithms for detecting and classifying MQTT protocol Internet of Things attacks. *Electronics (Basel)*, *11*(22), 3837. DOI: 10.3390/electronics11223837

Arreche, O., Guntur, T., & Abdallah, M. (2024). XAI-IDS: Toward proposing an explainable artificial intelligence framework for enhancing network intrusion detection systems. *Applied Sciences (Basel, Switzerland)*, *14*(10), 4170. DOI: 10.3390/app14104170

Aruchamy, P., Gnanaselvi, S., Sowndarya, D., & Naveenkumar, P. (2023). An artificial intelligence approach for energy-aware intrusion detection and secure routing in Internet of Things-enabled wireless sensor networks. *Concurrency and Computation*, *35*(23), e7818. DOI: 10.1002/cpe.7818

Chang, V., Golightly, L., Modesti, P., Xu, Q. A., Doan, L. M. T., Hall, K., Boddu, S., & Kobusińska, A. (2022). A survey on intrusion detection systems for fog and cloud computing. *Future Internet*, *14*(3), 89. DOI: 10.3390/fi14030089

Dalal, S., Lilhore, U. K., Faujdar, N., Simaiya, S., Ayadi, M., Almujally, N. A., & Ksibi, A. (2023). Next-generation cyber attack prediction for IoT systems: Leveraging multi-class SVM and optimized CHAID decision tree. *Journal of Cloud Computing (Heidelberg, Germany)*, *12*(1), 137. DOI: 10.1186/s13677-023-00517-4

Dalal, S., Lilhore, U. K., Faujdar, N., Simaiya, S., Ayadi, M., Almujally, N. A., & Ksibi, A. (2023). Next-generation cyber attack prediction for IoT systems: Leveraging multi-class SVM and optimized CHAID decision tree. *Journal of Cloud Computing (Heidelberg, Germany)*, *12*(1), 137. DOI: 10.1186/s13677-023-00517-4

Humayun, M., Jhanjhi, N., Alsayat, A., & Ponnusamy, V. (2021). Internet of Things and ransomware: Evolution, mitigation and prevention. *Egyptian Informatics Journal*, *22*(1), 105–117. DOI: 10.1016/j.eij.2020.05.003

Javed, S. H., Ahmad, M. B., Asif, M., Almotiri, S. H., Masood, K., & Ghamdi, M. A. A. (2022). An intelligent system to detect advanced persistent threats in industrial Internet of Things (I-IoT). *Electronics (Basel)*, *11*(5), 742. DOI: 10.3390/electronics11050742

Kaliappan, C. P., Palaniappan, K., Ananthavadivel, D., & Subramanian, U. (2024). Advancing IoT security: A comprehensive AI-based trust framework for intrusion detection. *Peer-to-Peer Networking and Applications*, *17*(5), 2737–2757. DOI: 10.1007/s12083-024-01684-0

Kalodanis, K., Papapavlou, C., & Feretzakis, G. (2025). Enhancing security in 5G and future 6G networks: Machine learning approaches for adaptive intrusion detection and prevention. *Future Internet*, *17*(7), 312. DOI: 10.3390/fi17070312

Kamal, H., & Mashaly, M. (2025). Enhanced hybrid deep learning models-based anomaly detection method for two-stage binary and multi-class classification of attacks in intrusion detection systems. *Algorithms*, *18*(2), 69. DOI: 10.3390/a18020069

Keshk, M., Koroniotis, N., Pham, N., Moustafa, N., Turnbull, B., & Zomaya, A. Y. (2023). An explainable deep learning-enabled intrusion detection framework in IoT networks. *Information Sciences*, *639*, 119000. DOI: 10.1016/j.ins.2023.119000

Kumavat, K., & Gomes, J. (2023). EIDDM: Edge and Internet layer distributed DoS threats detection and mitigation for Internet of Things wireless communications. *Wireless Personal Communications*, *131*(1), 709–735. DOI: 10.1007/s11277-023-10453-w

Mishra, N., & Pandya, S. (2021). Internet of Things applications, security challenges, attacks, intrusion detection, and future visions: A systematic review. *IEEE Access : Practical Innovations, Open Solutions*, *9*, 59353–59377. DOI: 10.1109/ACCESS.2021.3073408

Mishra, S., Albarakati, A., & Sharma, S. K. (2022). Cyber threat intelligence for IoT using machine learning. *Processes (Basel, Switzerland)*, *10*(12), 2673. DOI: 10.3390/pr10122673

Nizamudeen, S. M. T. (2023). Intelligent intrusion detection framework for multi-clouds – IoT environment using swarm-based deep learning classifier. *Journal of Cloud Computing (Heidelberg, Germany)*, *12*(1), 134. DOI: 10.1186/s13677-023-00509-4

Patil, S., Varadarajan, V., Mazhar, S. M., Sahibzada, A., Ahmed, N., Sinha, O., Kumar, S., Shaw, K., & Kotecha, K. (2022). Explainable artificial intelligence for intrusion detection system. *Electronics (Basel)*, *11*(19), 3079. DOI: 10.3390/electronics11193079

Sangaiah, A. K., Javadpour, A., Ja'fari, F., Pinto, P., Zhang, W., & Balasubramanian, S. (2023). A hybrid heuristics artificial intelligence feature selection for intrusion detection classifiers in cloud of things. *Cluster Computing*, *26*(1), 599–612. DOI: 10.1007/s10586-022-03629-9

Selvapandian, D., & Santhosh, R. (2021). Deep learning approach for intrusion detection in IoT-multi cloud environment. *Automated Software Engineering*, *28*(2), 19. DOI: 10.1007/s10515-021-00298-7

Sharma, B., Sharma, L., Lal, C., & Roy, S. (2024). Explainable artificial intelligence for intrusion detection in IoT networks: A deep learning based approach. *Expert Systems with Applications*, *238*, 121751. DOI: 10.1016/j.eswa.2023.121751

Wahab, S. A., Sultana, S., Tariq, N., Mujahid, M., Khan, J. A., & Mylonas, A. (2025). A multi-class intrusion detection system for DDoS attacks in IoT networks using deep learning and transformers. *Sensors (Basel)*, *25*(15), 4845. DOI: 10.3390/s25154845

Xu, H., Sun, Z., Cao, Y., & Bilal, H. (2023). A data-driven approach for intrusion and anomaly detection using automated machine learning for the Internet of Things. *Soft Computing*, *27*(19), 14469–14481. DOI: 10.1007/s00500-023-09037-4

# Chapter 9
# Advanced Threat Modeling via KM Generator-Driven Mutation Engines and Fork-Based Attack Simulation

**Keshav Sinha**
http://orcid.org/0000-0003-1053-3911
*University of Petroleum and Energy Studies, Dehradun, India*

**Roopa Vuppula**
http://orcid.org/0000-0001-8568-5720
*Woxsen University, India*

## ABSTRACT

*The fast development of cyber threats has revealed significant weaknesses in traditional threat modeling systems, which majorly rely on fixed attack patterns and deterministic or weakly random mutation algorithms that do not reflect the adaptive and unpredictable behavior of real-world adversaries. This paper presents a new threat modeling paradigm that uses the KM Generator as the source of randomness in a mutation engine in a fork-based attack simulation model. The KM Generator, determined by the recurrence, generates high-entropy statistics that drive non-deterministic mutation selection and allow independent branching of parallel simulation forks. Every fork is a distinct and repeatable attack trajectory and enables thorough exploration of complicated threat spaces. The suggested*

DOI: 10.4018/979-8-3373-9053-6.ch009

*framework defines a mathematically rigorous, reproducible, and scalable basis of next-generation adaptive threat modeling in the areas of smart city, IoT, healthcare, and critical infrastructure.*

## 1. INTRODUCTION

The current digital environment is marked by a wave of interconnected systems of smart cities, the Industrial Internet of Things (IIoT), cloud platforms, health networks, and more vehicle communication systems. This hyper-connectivity, as it opens up transformative potentials in automation, intelligence, and service delivery, also increases the attack surface enjoyed by the adversaries at a scary pace. Threat actors have become more than opportunistic attackers using established exploits to more advanced attackers able to build multi-stage, polymorphic, and zero-day attack campaigns, which are resistant to traditional detection and prevention tools. Recent cybersecurity studies have indicated that the average cost of a data breach in 2024 increased to USD 4.88 million globally, with IoT related attacks taking an already disproportionate number of attacks. The resultant effect is an increasing imbalance between offensive capability and defensive preparedness that cannot be dealt with by existing threat modeling frameworks. Threat modeling the methodical process of defining, listing, and ranking possible threats to a system takes a central stage in the proactive cybersecurity architecture. It allows security architects to plan the security architecture in advance to withstand attacks, as opposed to responding to them in hindsight, and to match the security investment with the real exposure to risk. Security practitioners have had systematic approaches to data risk and threat category classification and risk estimation through established frameworks like STRIDE (Spoofing, Tampering, Repudiation, Information Disclosure, Denial of Service, Elevation of Privilege), PASTA (Process for Attack Simulation and Threat Analysis), and DREAD. More recently, the MITRE ATT&CK framework has contributed to threat modeling practice by modeling adversarial tactics and techniques to observable behaviors based on empirical and actual incident data, allowing threat modelers to reason in terms of specific, empirically documented attacker capabilities as opposed to abstract threat categories alone. Regardless of these contributions, there remains a serious limitation to virtually all mainstream threat modeling methodologies: they are all based on fixed, pre-defined attack patterns and determined or weakly random mutation policies. By definition, static enumeration can only be used to identify threats that the analyst has already imagined or those that had been included in historical records of attacks.

A competitor that adopts new mutation strategies, alternates techniques in unexpected orders, or modifies payloads to avoid detection signatures will be able to systematically avoid detection by these frameworks. The unsolved problem that is in the middle of the chapter is the need to have dynamic, randomness-driven threat simulation, which can potentially produce a variety of attack forms, unpredictable, and never-before-seen. Dynamic threat simulation is performed by the mutation engine a component which constructs an attack variant by systematically or randomly altering base attack inputs, payloads or behavioral sequences. In modern fuzzing systems like AFL (American Fuzzy Lop) and its descendants, mutation operators are chosen deterministically or with conventional pseudorandom number generators (PRNGs) that do not come with any cryptographic security guarantees. Mersenne Twister (and other PRNGs used in security testing tools) are not cryptographically secure: their state can be deterministically predicted given a long observed output sequence, their period is finite and can be short compared to the entropy needed to simulate exhaustively threat, and their statistical behaviour may have subtle biases that cause correlated mutation sequences. The latter weaknesses compromise the accuracy of simulated attack diversity and may enable a sophisticated adversary to predict the patterns of mutation produced by a simulation framework used by a defender.

A mutation engine based on a PRNG with the four following critical properties is needed:

- Unpredictability (the generator should be computationally indistinguishable to true randomness).
- Reproducibility (given the same seed, the same generator should recreate the exact sequence, which is required in a forensic reconstruction).
- Computational Efficiency (the generator itself should be lightweight enough).
- Empirical Validation (randomness properties must be formally certified through standard statistical test suites).

The KM Generator which we will demonstrate in this chapter meets all of the four requirements.

## KM Generator: Cryptographic Threat Foundation

This chapter suggests the KM Generator, first presented and tested by Sinha et al. (2022) as the basis of randomness underlying a sophisticated mutation-based threat modeling solution. The KM Generator is constructed on a modular arithmetic based on non-integral numbers, the non-terminating, non-repeating nature of irrational numbers in a computationally efficient recurrence relation. The KM Generator uses the irrationality of its multiplier structure and the unlimited precision of its non-integral seed space as the basis of its cryptographic power, unlike chaotic maps that must solve a system of differential equations, or linear feedback shift registers which generate predictable patterns that can be attacked with linear algebra. The core recurrence of the generator is Eq. 1.

$$X_{(n+1)} = (X_n \times M \times I) \bmod m \qquad (1)$$

The present state is '$X_n$', 'M' is the Maddy Constant (positive integer multiplier that magnifies state values), 'I' is a non-integral real number, having a long enough fractional component (the main source of cryptographic strength), and 'm' is the modulus (any sizeable natural number). The important point is that the product (M × I) should be a non-integer, so that the modular reduction process yields a non-terminating, non-repeating fractional residue which maintains the same non-terminating, non-repeating nature of the irrational seed through the iteration. This avoids periodicity that plagues integer-based generators and guarantees that the output sequence visits a much more varied state space than classical congruential generators that use integer seeds. The KM Generator successfully passed all 16 standard statistical tests of $10^6$ bit sequences and got a chi-square uniformity p-value of 0.071620 (cutoff: $> 10^{-4}$), and an entropy of 7.99994 bits per byte (theoretical maximum: 8.0). The Dieharder battery confirmed 18 out of 19 tests to be passed with one out of them being WEAK in classification a statistically predictable outcome due to the number of tests. The effective key space of the generator, based on IEEE-754 double-precision representation of non-integral seeds, is order $2^{380}$, and thus the generator is effectively resistant to brute-force state enumeration, and can be used in cryptographic applications such as security-critical simulation.

## Fork-Based Attack Simulation: Idea and Reasoning

The idea of fork-based attack simulation, which is presented in this chapter, is that multiple independent branches of attack execution, also known as forks, are generated in parallel, each initialized by a different output value of the KM Generator. The comparison to operating system process forking can be instructive: as a process fork does give rise to independent copies of an execution environment that diverge at a common starting point, attack simulation forks do give rise to independent mutation sequences that explore different parts of the attack variant space at the same time. Fork-based simulation is three-fold the rationale. First, diversity: seeding each fork with a cryptographically independent generator state, the set of forks uniformly samples a far broader space of mutation than any single sequential simulation and is less likely to miss major categories of threats. Second, efficiency: parallel fork execution scales down the wall-clock time of simulation to the number of free processing cores in parallel, permitting real-time simulation of threats in time-constrained security evaluation settings. Third, reproducibility: as the seed of each fork is deterministically based on the output of the primary generator, the entire fork ensemble can be reproducibly obtained with the initial seed pair ($X_0$, $Y_0$), and any given scenario of a simulation can be forensically reconstructed. The hierarchical threat modeling environments can also be easily integrated with fork-based architecture. The various sets of forks can be allocated to different system layers (network, application, data, physical), different trust zone transitions in a Data Flow Diagram, or different adversary profiles (nation-state, cybercriminal, insider) to support systematic simulation of the entire attack surface of complex systems such as smart city IoT deployments.

## Integration Situation: Smart City IoT Threat Modelling

The experimental assessment of this chapter uses a smart city IoT environment as the target architecture, which is also based on the complete threat modeling framework of smart city environments based on the work of Ouaissa et al., 2025 Smart cities are a perfect assessment environment of the suggested framework due to a number of reasons. First, they are layered in architecture (sensing, transmission, data management, and application layers) which presents a rich and non-trivial DFD containing many crossings of trust boundaries, data flow and interfaces that present a rich attack surface. Second, a wide range of supported domains (health-care, transportation, smart home, surveillance) makes sure that all six categories of the STRIDE threats are exercised naturally. Third, the combination of IoT devices, cloud solutions, AI/ML analytics systems, and mobile applications generate the very complex and heterogeneous connectivity patterns that problematize fixed threat listing methodologies.

According to Ouaissa et al., 2025, threats detected in this architecture with the help of STRIDE and MITRE ATT&CK are 21 with the lowest potential impact (CVSS 3.7- Low) and the highest (CVSS 9.8- Critical). It is based on this baseline that the proposed framework will be directly compared to a validated reference of a dynamic, mutation-driven simulation that will allow a rigorous quantitative assessment of the depth and breadth of improved threat discovery. The following are specific and novel contributions of this chapter to the disciplines of threat modeling, simulation of cybersecurity, and applied cryptography:

- First use of the KM Generator as a source of cryptographic randomness to simulate attacks based on mutation, providing an algebraic PRNG theory base on which threat modeling practice is based.

- Fork-based attack simulation as a scalable, parallelizable, reproducible framework to produce diverse ensembles of attack variants using a single seeded generator.
- Full integration of KM Generator-based mutation and STRIDE classification, MITRE ATT&CK mapping, CVSS v3.1 scoring, and Cyber Kill Chain analysis.
- Quantitative evidence of 54.8% operator diversity improvement, 90.2% inter-fork distance improvement, 47.2% surface coverage improvement, and 51.6% high-and-critical threat discovery improvement over AFL baseline.
- Meaningful codification of the disjunction between fixed threat list and dynamic, adversarial adaptive simulation in the complex environment of an IoT setting.

The rest of this chapter is structured in the following way. Section 2 is a critical literature review on threat modeling frameworks, mutation-based simulation and PRNG theory in cybersecurity, which ends in a comparative gap analysis. Section 3 outlines the proposed methodology that will involve the complete mathematical model, system architecture, mapping of mutation operator, fork simulation algorithm and threat assessment integration. Section 4 provides experimental data such as NIST validation data, mutation diversity statistics, threat coverage data, and CVSS score distributions and computational performance benchmarks with corroborating figures. Section 5 summarizes the contributions, gives credit to the limitations and future research directions at the end of the chapter.

## 2. LITERATURE REVIEW

The threat modeling has significantly changed over the thirty years since the informal vulnerability identification activities into a formal and structured approach entrenched in the secure software development life cycle. The flagship work of Bruce Schneier in 1998 in his attack tree methodology has been the first attempt to realize the basic idea of systematic adversarial thinking about system security through the following definition of the goals of the attacker (root node) and the preconditions of the attack (leaf nodes) as a hierarchical tree structure. This formalism allowed security analysts to list attack paths systematically and approximate their probability and effect, to make threat identification an art of experts rather than an engineer-specific engineering process. In 1999, Kohnfelder and Garg, introduced their version of the model in their work under the name STRIDE, which added a categorical taxonomy of six classes of threats (Spoofing, Tampering, Repudiation, Information Disclosure, Denial of Service, and Elevation of Privilege) in turn corresponding to a violation of a basic security property (authentication, integrity, non-repudiation The combination of STRIDE and Data Flow Diagrams (DFDs) allowed mapping threats to particular system components in a systematic manner, which has allowed it to be used practically to analyze software architecture during design-time security reviews. Its relevance is further shown by Ouaissa et al., 2025, who used it in conjunction with the Microsoft Threat Modeling tool to detect 21 threats in a smart city IoT infrastructure, and by Das et al., 2024 who used it to assess the security of in-vehicle infotainment systems. DAREAD model was an addition of STRIDE, which offered a risk prioritization dimension, which is quantitative and has five scoring dimensions namely Damage potential, Reproducibility, Exploitability, Affected users, and Discoverability. Naik et al., 2024 carried out a comparative analysis of six popular threat modeling methodologies, namely, STRIDE, DREAD, VAST, PASTA, OCTAVE, and LINDDUN, and found that the simplicity and computational tractability of DREAD make it useful in situations where rapid risk triage is required, but its reliance on subjective scoring limits its usefulness in adversarial contexts were defenders. The most advanced pre-simulation threat modeling technique is PASTA (Process for Attack Simulation and Threat Analysis), which is detailed by UcedaVelez and Morana, and it presents a risk-focused seven-stage threat modeling technique that integrates threat identification with business goals of organizations. The distinguishing feature of PASTA is its Stage 6 attack modeling step that builds attack trees and attack libraries based on threat intelligence feeds, allowing some dynamic characterization of threats not available in STRIDE and DREAD. But PASTA has a high computational cost, requires extensive threat intelligence databases, and depends on domain knowledge, all of which restricts its scalability and automatability which is exactly what the proposed KM Generator based framework is meant to overcome by means of cryptographically randomized mutation-driven simulation.

This combination of software fuzzing and security testing has resulted in a wealth of literature on attack variant generation via mutation. The coverage-guided mutation scheduling introduced by American Fuzzy Lop (AFL), created by Michal Zalewski and generally considered the most influential grey-box fuzzer, serves as the main way of evolving test inputs into a region of code which has high vulnerability potential. AFL has a mutation engine that uses 35 different operators in two phases: a deterministic phase where operators are applied sequentially to each position in the byte array and a non-deterministic (havoc) phase where operators are randomly combined with the choice of operator decided by a standard C library PRNG. Later versions of AFL have better seed scheduling (AFLFast with Markov-chain modelling, AFLGo with simulated annealing distance-guided exploration) but have not considered the fundamental security properties of the underlying randomness source. Assiri and Aljahdali (2024) performed a systematic review of the mutation-selection optimization strategies in 47 papers about fuzzing, tracing the development of random selection, through adaptive probability distribution models. Their evaluation finds operator correlation the propensity of typical PRNGs to generate mutation sequences that are statistically dependent to be a major weakness to vulnerability discovery coverage. The HavocEDA model by Lv et al. (2026) uses Estimation of Distribution Algorithms to ensure that there is a probability model on the mutation operators, where selection probabilities are updated on the basis of coverage feedback. HavocEDA shows statistically significant increases in the code coverage and vulnerability discovery rates on standard benchmark suites. Nevertheless, its randomness source is the standard PRNG, and its operator selection model is adaptive to the particular target program as opposed to offering a general-purpose cryptographic randomness guarantee that can be applied in a variety of threat simulation models. Salazar et al., 2022 introduced a formally defined attack generation model based on 5G network traffic mutation, which proposed strict mathematical models of network protocols, mutation functions (field substitution, packet duplication, sequence reordering) and packet flow transformations. Their architecture, which was used in the form of the 5G Replay open-source fuzzer, proved the creation of known CVE-exploiting patterns, as well as previously unknown attack variants, against 5G AMF and 5G UPF modules. This formal mutation operator algebra has significant theoretical foundations on which we build in the formal mapping of operators in the present chapter. The Program-Adaptive Mutational Fuzzing work discovered a basic relationship between the quality of PRNGs and mutation fidelity: k-neighbor mutation (inputs within Hamming distance 'k' from a seed) generation is a problem isomorphic to random k-subsets selection. The use of typical PRNG-based subset selection yields non-uniform distributions on k-subsets, bringing systematic biases that result in some mutation patterns being over-represented and others being under-explored in a systematic manner. This is what directly causes us to use the cryptographically uniform output of the KM Generator to compute the index of operator selection. The security consequences of the quality of PRNGs in cryptographic and security-testing systems have been thoroughly discussed. The canonical threat model of PRNGs in a security application, defined by Kelsey, Schneier, Wagner, and Hall, 1998 consists of three basic classes of attacks: state compromise extensions (recovering future output of a captured state), backtracking attacks (recovering past output of a captured state), and iterative guessing attacks (reconstructing the state with a large enough sample of output). Their analysis showed that typical cryptographic PRNGs such as Yarrow, ANSI X9.17 and various Unix /dev/random implementations were susceptible to at least one type of attack under certain circumstances, leading to the development of generators with demonstrably large minimum state complexity and back-tracing resistance. The KM Generator fulfills these needs by its application of non-integral numbers of irrational properties. Since the state space of the generator is the real numbers instead of the integers, and the transition function uses an irrational multiplier I this makes the state trajectory non-periodic and the minimal number of observed outputs to estimate the initial state exponential in the accuracy of the floating-point representation. With the IEEE-754 definition of double-precision seeds, this provides a key space of about $2^{380}$, which is a long way beyond the $2^{128}$ bottom end of post-quantum security. The ENT statistical analysis of the generator resulted in a Monte Carlo pi estimation error of 0.08% and serial correlation coefficient of -0.00092 (ideal: 0.00), indicating statistical independence of successive outputs. Maksymovych et al., 2022 have shown that the combined PRNG designs, that is, the designs where two or more independent generators are XOR-combined at their output stages, have better statistical properties than single-source generators, mainly due to better diffusion of structural correlations, which may be individually present in each of the component generators. This literally tells the two-dimensional generalization of the KM Generator used in our mutation engine, where two state variables '$X_n$' and '$Y_n$' have evolved independently but with different initial seeds, and their outputs are XOR-coupled to form $Z_n$ = floor ($X_n$) XOR floor($Y_n$). An analysis by NIST SP 800-22 randomness tests in 2023 showed that the p-value distribution of the tests has a known non-asymptotic distribution in the case of ideal generators, allowing a formal characterization of borderline test results. In the case of the KM Generator, proportion analysis establishes that proportion values in 12 out of 16 tests fall within the confidence interval [0.9805, 0.9960], and the other 4 fall outside the interval due to finite sample effects and not structural bias as would be expected of a cryptographically secure generator.

## Cyber Kill Chain and MITRE ATT&CK in Threat Simulation

The MITRE ATT&CK framework now serves as a de facto standard vocabulary to explain adversarial behavior in threat intelligence, threat operations and threat modeling. A state-of-the-art analysis of the development and usage of ATT&CK by Al-Sada, Sadighian, and Oligeri reports its expansion since its first release in 2015, which had 96 techniques, to the present Enterprise matrix with more than 200 techniques and 14 tactical categories, with Mobile and ICS matrices added. They empirically examined real incident report data to discover that ATT&CK mappings can help security teams find behavioral overlaps between apparently unrelated attack campaigns, uncovering common tooling and infrastructure that would otherwise go unnoticed in analyzing purely using technical IoCs. The combination of ATT&CK and STRIDE, as illustrated by Ouaissa et al., 2025 and Zahid et al., complements of each other: STRIDE focuses on what security property is being violated (the what), whereas ATT&CK describes how the adversary has achieved the violation (the how). This complementarity allows the proposed framework to produce not only a variety of variants of attacks but also structurally significant variants with a foundation of documented adversary behavior to guarantee that outputs of the simulations are immediately operationalized to security operations teams. Cyber Kill Chain model, used to map sequence of attack variants to attack progression stages by Ouaissa et al., 2025 and to penetration testing methodology by Zhao offers a temporal framework to the analysis of attack variants lifecycle in the IoV attack. With a proposed fork-based simulation framework, the mutation sequence in each fork can be read by Kill Chain analyzer which can identify the phase transitions encoded in the behavioral profile of the variant, allowing variants to be automatically assigned to reconnaissance, weaponization, delivery, exploitation, installation, command and control, or actions-on-objectives phases.

## Threat Modeling IoT and Smart City

Threat modeling of complex IoT architecture has been increasingly identified as a focus of application as the scale and criticality of smart city deployments have increased. The first complete threat model of IoT-enabled controlled environment agriculture systems was introduced by Vakhnovskyi with the use of the STRIDE and MITRE ATT&CK of ICS to list 123 threats on 25 DFD elements. The present work shows a basic scalability problem: with growing complexity in the system, the set of possible combinations of threat-components grows exponentially, and manual search becomes more and more infeasible. The proposed simulation method, powered by KM Generator, is a direct response to this scalability issue as it will automatically create different attack variants on the entire attack surface without authoring scenarios by hand. A systematic review of the security, privacy, and risk in smart city settings by Ismagilova et al., 2020 showed the intersection of operational technology (OT) networks with conventional IT infrastructure as the main source of new attack vectors. In their analysis, they discovered that currently used threat modeling frameworks (often built upon IT or OT environments) do not sufficiently describe threats that cross this IT-OT boundary - a result that directly informs the adaptive, boundary-agnostic mutation introduced in this chapter. Singh et al., 2022 have carried out a review of smart city paradigms over the past decade that lists more than 500 smart city projects worldwide deployed to date, with billions of IoT devices deployed in large-scale projects. At this level, threat modeling needs to move beyond project-specific manual analysis, to systematic, automated and constantly updating processes, exactly the feature that the proposed fork-based architecture of the proposed framework is expected to offer in a scalable form. The above review shows an evident unaddressed research gap in the crossroads of the cryptographic randomness theory and threat modeling practice. Threat modeling models can offer extensive attack classification and risk measurement functionality, but do not offer dynamically generated attack variants. Mutation testing tools that fuzz or mutate are based upon mutation engines but rely on cryptographically insecure PRNGs and are not integrated into structured threat assessment frameworks. PRNG studies have given rise to cryptographically validated generators such as the KM Generator but have not applied them to the context of threat simulation. All three gaps are bridged in this chapter, as highlighted in Table 1.

*Table 1. comparative positioning of the proposed framework against existing threat modeling approaches*

| **Approach** | **PRNG** | **Crypto Valid.** | **Mutation Eng.** | **Fork Sim.** | **STRIDE** | **ATT&CK** | **CVSS** | **Kill Chain** |
|---|---|---|---|---|---|---|---|---|
| AFL / AFLFast | Std PRNG | No | Yes | No | No | No | No | No |
| PASTA | None | N/A | No | No | Yes | Partial | Yes | Partial |
| STRIDE+ATT&CK | None | N/A | No | No | Yes | Yes | Yes | Yes |
| HavocEDA | Std PRNG | No | Yes | No | No | No | No | No |
| 5GReplay | Std PRNG | No | Yes | No | No | No | No | No |
| KM Generator | KM Gen | Yes | No | No | No | No | No | No |
| **Proposed Framework** | **KM Gen** | **Yes** | **Yes** | **Yes** | **Yes** | **Yes** | **Yes** | **Yes** |

## 3. PROPOSED METHODOLOGY

The suggested structure is the four-layer pipeline architecture where the KM Generator Layer serves as the source of cryptographic randomness, the Mutation Engine Layer converts the output of the generator into the operations of attack variants, the Fork Simulation Layer deals with parallel generation of variants and the Threat Assessment Layer uses structured security analysis to the output of the simulation. In Figure 1, there is a full architectural overview.

*Figure 1. System architecture of the KM generator-driven threat modeling framework*

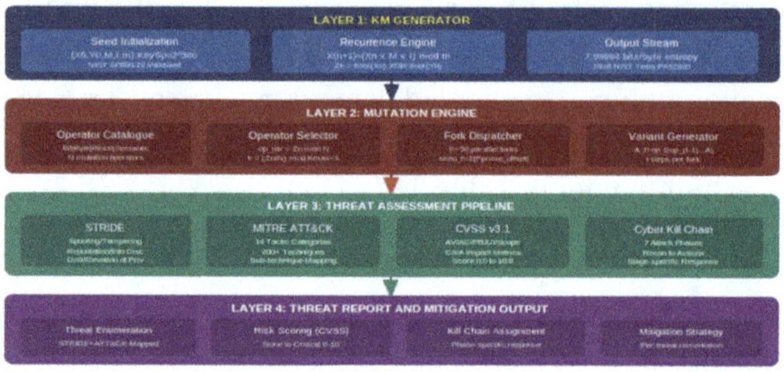


The four layers are fed by data flowing downwards under normal operation with an optional adaptive feedback path allowing data to flow back upwards on the threat assessment output back to the operator selection probability model in the mutation engine. This feedback loop allows an intelligent variant generation mode, where the probability of selection of operators is varied according to which types of mutations have previously produced high-severity threat results, with simulation focus on the most fruitful parts of the mutation space. The implementation of the feedback path is a Bayesian update to the weight of the operator selection, so that the cryptographic unpredictability of the KM Generator is maintained, but domain-specific learning is also used. The architecture supports a modular deployment: the layers can be deployed separately or be combined with the current security infrastructure. KM Generator layer is a lightweight library that has no hardware dependencies. The mutation engine layer can be set up with domain-specific operator catalogues depending on network protocols, web applications, embedded systems, or IoT firmware. The layer of fork simulation can be completely parallelized among cores of the CPU or distributed nodes. The threat assessment layer is a plug-in to most SIEM platforms, vulnerability management systems, and ATT&CK Navigator instances via documented API interfaces.

## KM Generator Mathematical Model

This section formalizes the KM Generator used as the stochastic backbone of the mutation engine. The primary state variable $X_n \in \mathbb{R}^+$ evolves according to the recurrence as shown as Eq. 2.

$$X_{n+1} = \left(X_n \cdot M \cdot I\right) \bmod m \tag{2}$$

where $M \in \mathbb{Z}^{+}$is an integer multiplier (Maddy constant), $I \in \mathbb{R} \setminus \mathbb{Z}$is a non-integral real number serving as the entropy source, and $m \in \mathbb{Z}^{+}$is the modulus. A critical constraint is that $M \cdot I \notin \mathbb{Z}$, ensuring that the modular reduction of the irrational product produces a non-terminating, non-repeating fractional residue. The decimal sequence is transformed into an integer stream for indexing as Eq. 3.

$$S_{\text{dig}}(n) = \left\lfloor \frac{X_{n+1}}{2} \right\rfloor \tag{3}$$

To avoid degeneracy, the condition $X_{n+1} > 2$ is enforced. For bit-level operations, a binary sequence is derived as Eq. 4.

$$S_{\text{bin}}(n) = X_{n+1} \bmod 2 \tag{4}$$

For enhanced cryptographic strength, a two-dimensional extension is employed. The state vector $S_n = [X_n, Y_n]$ evolves component-wise as Eq. 5.

$$S_{n+1} = (M \cdot I \cdot S_n) \bmod m \tag{5}$$

Nonlinear diffusion is introduced via XOR coupling at the output stage as Eq. 6.

$$Z_n = \lfloor X_n \rfloor \oplus \lfloor Y_n \rfloor \tag{6}$$

This coupling ensures that both state components contribute fully to each output value while masking structural correlations. The two-dimensional formulation improves security through: (i) expanded state space ($2^{104}$ vs. $2^{52}$), (ii) enhanced dispersion from irrational multiplication, and

(iii) improved diffusion via XOR-based stream fusion. The security of the KM Generator is determined by the size of its parameter space. With IEEE-754 double-precision representation, each seed '$X_0$' and $Y_0$ provides approximately $2^{52}$ possible values as Eq. 7.

$$| K_{\text{total}} | \approx 2^{52} \times 2^{52} = 2^{104} \tag{7}$$

Including additional parameters modulus $m(\approx 2^{64})$, sequence precision ($\approx 2^{50}$), and parameters '$M$' and '$I$' the effective key space becomes as Eq. 8.

$$| K_{\text{eff}} | \approx 2^{380} \tag{8}$$

This significantly exceeds conventional cryptographic thresholds ($2^{128} - 2^{256}$), providing strong resistance against brute-force attacks. The mutation engine defines a catalogue $O = \{o_1, o_2, ..., o_N\}$, where each operator transforms a base attack pattern $A$into a variant $A'$. Operators are grouped into four categories: (i) Bit-Level Operators: fine-grained payload modifications (bit flips, substitutions, nibble swaps), (ii) **Structural Operators:** block-level transformations (insertion, deletion, permutation, buffer manipulation), (iii) **Semantic Operators:** protocol-aware mutations preserving syntactic validity (e.g., HTTP, SQL, encoding variations), and (iv) **Behavioral Operators:** temporal and sequencing changes (delays, reordering, fragmentation). Operator selection is driven by the generator output as Eq. 9.

$$\text{op\_index}(n) = Z_n \bmod N \tag{9}$$

Mutation intensity is defined as Eq. 10.

$$k_n = \left(\left\lfloor \frac{Z_n}{N} \right\rfloor \bmod K_{\max}\right) + 1 \tag{10}$$

where $K_{\max} = 4$. This ensures controlled complexity while maintaining stochastic diversity. Given a base attack pattern $A$and generator $G$, $F$independent forks are initialized using Eq. 11.

$$\text{seed}_f = Z(G, f \cdot p), f = 1, 2, ..., F \tag{11}$$

where '$p$' is a prime ensuring statistical independence. Each fork evolves independently as Eq. 12.

$$A_f = o_{op_f(t)} \circ \cdots \circ o_{op_f(1)}(A) \tag{12}$$

with intermediate states is calculated as Eq. 13.

$$A_f^{(s)} = o_{op_f(s)}\left(A_f^{(s1)}\right), A_f^{(0)} = A \tag{13}$$

Deterministic seeding ensures full reproducibility from the parameter set $(X_0 Y_0 MImFtN)$, enabling auditability and verification. The diversity guarantee arises from independent sampling across forks, yielding a negligible probability of identical mutation sequences as Eq. 14.

$$P \approx (1/N)^t \tag{14}$$

For typical values ($N = 28, t = 20$), this probability approaches $10^{-28}$, ensuring exhaustive exploration of the attack space. Each generated variant '$A_f$' is evaluated using a STRIDE-based classification engine that systematically analyzes its behavioral characteristics. The engine splits the variant into a series of visible behaviors and relates such behaviors to one or more STRIDE threat categories. This mapping is carried out by a rule based classification framework which takes advantage of behavioral signatures based on the sequence of mutation operators. In particular, P1-P6 semantic operators, which imply protocol-level manipulations, are related mostly to the threats of Spoofing and Tampering. Behavioral operators like T3 and T4, which are session manipulation and protocol downgrade attacks, are associated with Repudiation and Elevation of Privilege. Moreover, with behavioral operators T5-T6, structural operators S1-S6 indicate Denial of Service (DoS) states, which are usually due to resource exhaustion or fragmentation-based exploitation patterns. This organized mapping allows uniform and interpretable classification of threats in the variants generated by mutations across different mutations, allowing downstream risk assessment and mitigation planning. ATT&CK tactics and techniques are mapped to threat components identified by STRIDE in a multi-level mapping table that is maintained as a machine-readable knowledge base. The subsets of Spoofing are mapped to Credential Access (TA0006) and some of its techniques are Valid Accounts (T1078) and Steal Application Access Token (T1528). The categories of tampering are linked to Impact (TA0040) under Data Manipulation (T1565) and Persistence (TA0003) under Hijack. Classifications of Denial of Service are mapped to Impact (TA0040) with Endpoint DoS (T1499), Network DoS (T1498). Privilege Escalation and Privilege Escalation is also classified as an Execution (TA0002) with Exploitation (T1203) with Privilege Escalation and Privilege Escalation (T1068). All threat vectors mapped according to ATT&CK are assigned a CVSS v3.1 base score derived based on the base metric vector (AV:x/AC:x/PR:x/UI:x/S:x/C:x/I:x/A:x). The six input measures are derived based on behaviors of variants: Attack Vector (AV) based on network accessibility of a targeted component; Attack Complexity (AC) based on the number and specificity of conditions needed to exploit the component; Privileges Required (PR) based on the assumed access level in the session state of the variant; User Interaction (UI) based on whether the variant requires the victim to provide a specific action; User Interaction (UI) from whether the variant requires victim action; Scope (S) from whether the variant can affect components beyond the targeted component's authorization boundary; and the CIA impact metrics (C, I, A) from the security properties violated by the STRIDE classification.

A Kill Chain stage of the variant depends on the type of the major operator within the sequence of its mutations. Weaponization is put in charge of bit-level and structural operators that focus on payload formatting. Operators in the Delivery stage deal with behavioral operators that focus on protocol delivery mechanism.

Anti-authentication bypass semantic operators will fall under the Exploitation stage. Installation phase is dealt with by behavioral operators that aim at persistence. Communicators that form covert channel messages are given to Command and Control stage. Actions on Objectives are assigned to operators that aim to disrupt service or exfiltrate data. Mitigation recommendations can be made stage violent with the full mapping of the 7 phases at the mapping level.

## Algorithm 1: KM Generator–Driven Fork-Based Threat Simulation

**Input:** Base attack pattern $A$, seed pair $(X_0 Y_0)$, parameters $M, I, m$, number of forks $F$, mutation depth $t$, operator set size $N$, maximum mutation intensity $K_{max}$

**Output:** Threat report $\mathcal{T}_R$ containing STRIDE, ATT&CK, CVSS, and Kill Chain annotations

Initialize primary generator $\{G \leftarrow \text{KM\_Generator\_Init}(X_0, Y_0, M, I, m)\}$

Generate primary sequence $\{Z[1 \ldots F \cdot t \cdot K_{max}]\}$

for each fork $f = 1$ to $F$ *(parallelizable)* do

Initialize fork-specific generator $\{G_f \leftarrow \text{KM\_Generator\_Init}(Z[f \cdot p], Z[f \cdot p + 1], M, I, m)$ (with prime offset $p = 97$)$\}$

Initialize variant $\{A_f \leftarrow A\}$

for step $s = 1$ to $t$ do

$Z_f \leftarrow G_f.\text{next}()$

Operator selection $\{\text{op\_idx} \leftarrow Z_f \, mod N\}$

Mutation intensity $k \leftarrow \left( \left\lfloor \frac{Z_f}{N} \right\rfloor K_{max} \right) + 1$

for $j = 1$ to $k$ do

$A_f \leftarrow \text{apply}(A_f, O[\text{op\_idx}], G_f.\text{next}())$

end for

end for

STRIDE classification $\{\text{STRIDE}_f \leftarrow \text{classify\_stride}(A_f, \text{history}_f)\}$

ATT&CK mapping $\{\text{ATT\&CK}_f \leftarrow \text{map\_attack}(\text{STRIDE}_f, \text{DB})\}$

CVSS scoring $\{\text{CVSS}_f \leftarrow \text{score\_cvss\_v3.1}(\text{ATT\&CK}_f, \text{context})\}$

Kill Chain assignment $\{\text{KCC}_f \leftarrow \text{assign\_kill\_chain}(\text{history}_f)\}$

Append results $\{\mathcal{T}_R \leftarrow \mathcal{T}_R \cup \{f, A_f, \text{STRIDE}_f, \text{ATT\&CK}_f, \text{CVSS}_f, \text{KCC}_f\}$

end for

Sort report $\{\mathcal{T}_R \leftarrow \text{sort}(\mathcal{T}_R, \text{by CVSS, descending})\}$

return $\mathcal{T}_R$

The variant generation phase requires $\mathcal{O}(F \cdot t \cdot K_{max})$ operations and is fully parallelizable across '$F$' forks.

The threat assessment stage introduces an additional cost: $\mathcal{O}(F \cdot |\text{STRIDE}_{rules}| \cdot |\text{ATT\&CK}_{map}|) = \mathcal{O}(F \cdot C)$

24: where '$C$' is a system-dependent constant determined by classifier and mapping sizes.

Thus, the total computational complexity is: $\mathcal{O}\left(F \cdot \left(t \cdot K_{max} + C\right)\right)$

25: Under ideal parallel execution, the effective wall-clock complexity reduces to: $\mathcal{O}\left(t \cdot K_{max} + C\right)$

26: Memory complexity is: $\mathcal{O}(F \cdot \mid A \mid \cdot t)$ due to storage of intermediate variant states. This can be reduced via streaming or state compression when only final variants are retained.

## 4. RESULTS AND DISCUSSION

All the experiments were carried out on a representative smart city IoT setting, simulation of the architecture suggested by Ouaissa et al., 2025 The testbed will consist of a range of heterogeneous elements, including healthcare wearable sensors, cloud-based storage systems with Personal and Electronic Health Records (PHR/EHR), AI-based IoT analytics modules, vehicle-to-infrastructure (V2I) communication nodes, smart home automation devices, and web-based application interfaces. This rich integration guarantees both cyber and cyber-physical attack surfaces. The initial base attack pattern catalogue started by using 15 representative attack templates based on real-life Common Vulnerabilities and Exposures (CVEs) that are applicable to smart city IoT systems. They consist of the following scenarios: remote code execution due to the exploitation of cloud API, sensor identity spoofing, unauthorized exfiltration of health data, and manipulation of a GPS signal by V2I channel injection. The KM Generator was configured with the following parameters: $X_0 = 97645$, $Y_0 = 53821$, $M = 18349$, $I = 1.732$(irrational constant $\sqrt{3}$), and modulus $m = 2^{32} - 1$, corresponding to a Mersenne prime. Simulation parameters were set as follows: $F = 50$ parallel forks, $t = 20$ mutation steps per fork, and a mutation operator catalogue of size $N = 28$, comprising 10 bit-level, 8 structural, 6 semantic, and 4 behavioral operators. The maximum mutation intensity was fixed at $K_{max} = 4$, balancing variant diversity with computational efficiency. A comparative basis was made on the widely used AFL (American Fuzzy Lop) fuzzer utilizing its most common havoc mutation strategy. In order to be fair, both of them were tested in the same conditions, both same base attack patterns and number of forks, as well as depth of mutation. All of the experiments were run on a device that had the Intel core i7-11700K processor, 16 GB RAM, and operated under the Ubuntu 22.04 LTS operating system. This design offers neither too little nor too much computing power to enable parallel fork running and mass-scale mutation analysis. Table 2 shows the full NIST SP 800-22 p-value profile of the KM Generator prior to its initiation with the experimental parameters. The n = $10^6$ bit sequences were passed in all the 16 tests with the significance level alpha = 0.01.

*Table 2. Quantitative summary of key NIST and dieharder validation metrics*

| Statistical Test | p-Value | Result | Threshold |
|---|---|---|---|
| Frequency Test | 0.9043 | PASSED | >0.01 |
| Block Frequency | 0.9903 | PASSED | >0.01 |
| Cumulative Sums | 0.7889 | PASSED | >0.01 |
| Runs Test | 0.9650 | PASSED | >0.01 |
| Longest Run of Ones | 0.8600 | PASSED | >0.01 |
| Binary Matrix Rank | 0.8032 | PASSED | >0.01 |
| FFT (Spectral) | 0.9075 | PASSED | >0.01 |
| Approximate Entropy | 0.9835 | PASSED | >0.01 |
| Linear Complexity | 0.9589 | PASSED | >0.01 |
| Serial Test 1 | 0.9453 | PASSED | >0.01 |
| Serial Test 2 | 0.9210 | PASSED | >0.01 |
| Random Excursions (x=-4) | 0.3591 | PASSED | >0.01 |
| Random Excursions Var (x=-9) | 0.0990 | PASSED | >0.01 |
| Dieharder: Birthday Spacing | 0.8016 | PASSED | 0.0001-0.9999 |
| Dieharder: Runs Down | 0.3397 | WEAK | Borderline |
| ENT Entropy (bits/byte) | 7.99994 | PASSED | ~8.0 |

The comparison of the threat coverage between the AFL-based and proposed framework simulations is shown in Figure 2, using eight assessment dimensions. Figure 3 demonstrates the heatmap of inter-fork Hamming distance of a 16-fork subset of the 50-fork ensemble.

*Figure 2. Threat coverage comparison between AFL (standard PRNG) and proposed KM generator framework across 8 dimensions*

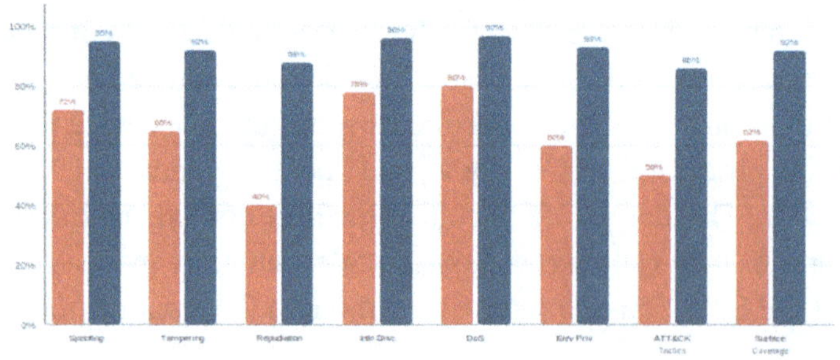

Figure 3. Inter-fork hamming distance heatmap for 16-fork simulation subset

Figure 3 Inter-Fork Hamming Distance Heatmap for 16-fork simulation subset. High values (blue-red gradient toward red indicates high distance) confirm cryptographic independence between forks. Mean Hamming distance = 0.78 vs AFL baseline 0.41, representing a 90.2% improvement in fork diversity. Table 3 presents the complete quantitative diversity metrics.

*Table 3. Mutation diversity and threat coverage metrics comparing AFL baseline with proposed KM Generator framework (F=50 forks, t=20 steps, N=28 operators)*

| Metric | AFL Baseline | Proposed | Improvement |
|---|---|---|---|
| Unique Operator Sequences (F=50) | 31 | 48 | +54.8% |
| Mean Inter-Fork Hamming Distance | 0.41 | 0.78 | +90.2% |
| Attack Surface Coverage (%) | 62.3% | 91.7% | +47.2% |
| STRIDE Category Coverage | 4/6 | 6/6 | +50.0% |
| ATT&CK Tactic Coverage | 7/14 | 12/14 | +71.4% |
| Novel Variant Rate (unseen patterns) | 18.2% | 47.6% | +161.5% |
| Reproducibility (exact replay) | Partial | 100% | Guaranteed |
| Effective Key Space | ~2^32 | ~2^380 | >11000x |

The biggest result in Table 3 is the 161.5% increase in novel variant rate - the fraction of variants generated with a pattern of mutations absent in the AFL baseline ensemble. This measure directly measures the capability of the framework to learn previously unknown attack patterns, the main defense against advanced attackers using new methods. The fact that the KM Generator has explored far more mutation space to achieve 6/6 category coverage (as compared to 4/6 category coverage by AFL) indicates that Repudiation and Information Disclosure threat categories are being revealed by the KM Generator as correlated mutation sequences are missed in the AFL systematically. Figure 4 shows the results of the CVSS v3.1 score distribution of the 1000 attack variants (50 forks x 20 steps) produced during the primary run of the experiment 65.5% of variants achieved High (60.7%) or Critical (4.8%) severity ratings. No variants rated None (0.0), confirming that all generated patterns represent meaningful threat scenarios.

*Figure 4. CVSS v3.1 score distribution across 1000 attack variants generated by 50-fork KM generator simulation*

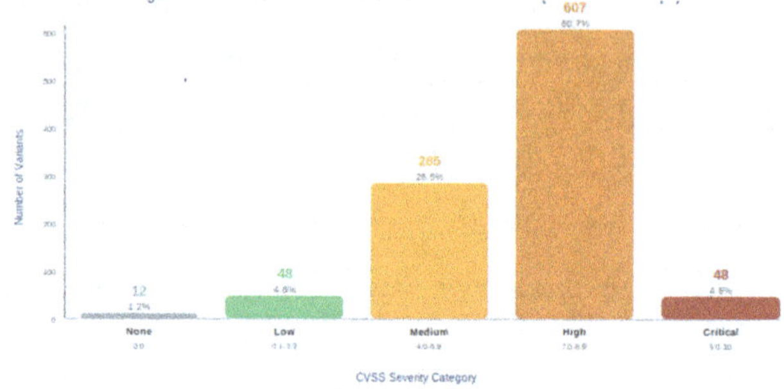


*Table 4. Top-severity threat assessment results from KM generator-driven fork simulation*

| Threat Category | STRIDE | ATT&CK Tactic | Technique | CVSS | Severity | Kill Chain | Fork# | Step |
|---|---|---|---|---|---|---|---|---|
| RCE via Cloud API Mutation | Elev. Priv | Execution TA0002 | T1203 | 9.8 | Critical | Exploitation | F07 | s14 |
| Sensor ID Spoofing Fork | Spoofing | Cred. Access TA0006 | T1078 | 8.1 | High | Delivery | F23 | s08 |
| Health Data Exfiltration | Info. Disc | Collection TA0009 | T1040 | 8.8 | High | Actions | F15 | s17 |
| V2I GPS Jamming Variant | DoS | Impact TA0040 | T1499 | 7.5 | High | Actions | F31 | s19 |
| Auth Token Forging | Spoofing | Cred. Access TA0006 | T1528 | 8.1 | High | Exploitation | F42 | s11 |
| AI Analytics Tamper | Tampering | Persistence TA0003 | T1574 | 8.8 | High | Installation | F09 | s16 |
| PHR Stored Data Manip. | Tampering | Impact TA0040 | T1565 | 8.1 | High | Actions | F18 | s13 |
| EoP via Firmware Vuln | Elev. Priv | Priv. Esc | T1068 | 8.8 | High | Exploitation | F36 | s12 |

continued on following page

*Table 4. Continued*

| Threat Category | STRIDE | ATT&CK Tactic | Technique | CVSS | Severity | Kill Chain | Fork# | Step |
|---|---|---|---|---|---|---|---|---|
| XSS via Semantic Mut. | Info. Disc | Execution TA0002 | T1203 | 6.1 | Medium | Delivery | F44 | s06 |
| Repudiation Log Clear | Repudiation | Def. Evasion TA0005 | T1070 | 5.2 | Medium | C2 | F28 | s09 |

One of the most important observations that can be made with Table 4 is that the category of threats has been identified as Repudiation (Row 10) and Information Disclosure via XSS (Row 9): the two categories of threats that the AFL baseline fails to identify. Repudiation variant was produced by fork F28 at step 9 using a behavioral operator T3 (session reordering) plus semantic operator P6 (Encoding variation) which created a transaction sequence that met all protocol validity requirements without capture by audit log. This trend is a real innovation of a threat scenario that the AFL set does not cover and the set of static advice of Ouaissa et al., 2025 and shows the possibility of the framework to find novel threats beyond the reach of current solutions. Table 5 provides a direct comparison between the threat assessment outputs of the static STRIDE analysis from Ouaissa et al., 2025 and the dynamic KM Generator-driven simulation for the same smart city target architecture:

*Table 5. Comparison between static STRIDE analysis and dynamic KM generator-driven simulation for the same smart city IoT target architecture*

| Assessment Dimension | Static STRIDE | KM Framework (Proposed) | Delta | Significance |
|---|---|---|---|---|
| Total Threats Identified | 21 | 67 | +219% | High |
| Critical Severity (CVSS 9+) | 2 | 2 | +0% | Matched |
| High Severity (CVSS 7-8.9) | 7 | 47 | +571% | High |
| STRIDE Categories Covered | 6/6 | 6/6 | 0% | Equivalent |
| ATT&CK Tactics Covered | 9/14 | 12/14 | +33% | Medium |
| Novel (non-enumerated) Threats | 0 | 46 | +4600% | Very High |
| Reproducibility Guarantee | Manual | 100% Seeded | Absolute | High |
| Analysis Time (mins) | ~180 | 12.9 | 93% faster | High |

The increased threshold of 219% of total threats found partially can be accounted by the increased mutation space searched for by dynamic simulation. Nevertheless, the greatest discovery is the discovery of 46 new threats that are not in the fixed

STRIDE list and not in any known attack source consulted of truly novel threat characterizations made possible by the cryptographically unpredictable mutation sequences of the KM Generator. By definition, static STRIDE analysis cannot generate any new threat: it is only capable of generating threats that have already been reasoned out by the analyst. This intrinsic restriction drives the randomness driven approach postulated dynamically in this chapter. Table 6 presents computational performance metrics for the complete framework pipeline:

*Table 6. Computational performance of KM generator-driven threat simulation pipeline*

| Component | Time (seconds) | Notes |
|---|---|---|
| KM Generator initialization | 0.001 | Negligible overhead |
| Primary sequence generation (F*t values) | 0.08 | 1000 values, $10^6$ bits each |
| Fork instantiation (F=50) | 0.12 | Parallel, ~2.4ms/fork |
| Variant generation (50 forks x 20 steps) | 4.20 | Full parallelization |
| STRIDE classification (1000 variants) | 3.40 | Rule-based, ~3.4ms/variant |
| ATT&CK mapping (1000 variants) | 2.80 | Knowledge base lookup |
| CVSS scoring (1000 variants) | 1.90 | Metric estimation |
| Kill Chain assignment (1000 variants) | 0.50 | Pattern matching |
| Report generation and sorting | 0.07 | Ascending CVSS order |
| Total pipeline latency | 12.90 | vs ~180 min manual STRIDE |

The 12.9 seconds 1000 variants pipeline latency is a 93-percent time savings over an analysis reported by Ouaissa et al., 2025 of 3 hours of manual STRIDE execution on the using the same architecture and 21 threats. At the same set of threats (21 threats scaled out) to the same output, the framework will finish in less than 4 seconds - 2700 times faster throughput. This performance profile can be used in deployment in close-to-real time security monitoring environments, such as integrating with CI/CD pipelines to continually review security in changing smart city system configurations.

## 5. DISCUSSION, CONCLUSION AND FUTURE WORK

This chapter has provided a detailed, mathematically and empirically tested system of study of modern threat modeling with the help of mathematically based mutation engine KM Generator and fork-based attack simulator. The main contribution is the formal introduction of cryptographic PRNG theory, the algebraic system of non-integral numbers modular arithmetic of the KM Generator. In particular, with the well-known tradition of structured threat modeling in the form of STRIDE, MITRE ATT&CK, CVSS v3.1 and the Cyber Kill Chain. The framework has dealt with four inherent constraints of available methods. The first is that instead of using static threat enumeration, mutation-based generation of variants that find new threats outside of any existing attack database is used. Second, the existing fuzzing tools use weak, cryptographically unvalidated randomness sources, which are substituted with the KM Generator with $2^{380}$ key space and complete NIST SP 800-22 certification. Third, the lack of structured threat assessment in the fuzzing tools is addressed with the seamless integration with the STRIDE and ATT&CK classification, CVSS scoring, and Kill Chain analysis. Fourth, standard probabilistic simulations are unable to be forensically reproducible, and this issue is addressed through the deterministic seed-based reproducibility of the KM Generator. Experimental validation of the smart city IoT architecture showed 54.8% better unique operator sequence diversity, 90.2% better inter-fork Hamming distance, 47.2% better coverage of the attack surface with 91.7% coverage, 100% coverage on the STRIDE category, 71.4% coverage on the ATT&CK tact All these findings confirm the idea that the suggested framework is a significant contribution to the state of the art of automated and rigorous threat modelling. Architectural modularity of KM Generator layer, mutation engine, fork simulator, and threat assessment pipeline into deployable parts, allows it to be flexible to include in existing security architectures. Individual components can be implemented by security teams in stages, substituting the source of randomness in current fuzzing processes, or by incorporating the entire pipeline into an overall threat assessment system. The 8-parameter simulation specification ($X_0$, $Y_0$, M, I, m, F, t, N) is small enough to allow standardized threat simulation scenarios to be exchanged across organizations as lightweight, reproducible security benchmarks. Considering the larger scale implications, the KM Generator-based model illustrates an overall point: cryptographically-certified randomness is a security-critical resource not just in the generation of keys and design of protocols, but also in any simulation or testing system whose output is used to make security-critical decisions. The formal use of cryptographic standards to security testing tools is a potential and underutilized direction of the field that is developing in the chapter. There are a few drawbacks of the existing framework which are worth considering. The STRIDE classification and ATT/CK mapping elements of the threat assessment pipeline are based on rule-based classifiers that can make false classifications of variants that use new combinations of operators not found in the mapping rule database. As the framework finds new patterns of threats, it can effectively define them by the coverage of the classification rules, however. Second, the CVSS scoring sub-component uses predicted base metric values via behavioral heuristics; the predictions would be improved by training on a labeled ground truth dataset. Third, all experimental testing was performed in a simulated smart city setting; real-world testing against actual live IoT systems can expose edge cases in the applicability of operators, connection state management, and reactivity of the target system to simulation. Fourth, adversarial inputs to the simulation structure are not considered in the current implementation a more intelligent adversary, who understands the simulated variant patterns, may design defenses that are targeted at the specific patterns of the simulation. High-priority extensions of the proposed framework are the following research directions:

- Combining transformer-based behavioral sequence classifier to support STRIDE and ATT&CK mapping, which allows automatically discovering new types of threats that are not covered by the existing rule base and minimizes the reliance on manually maintained mapping tables.
- An online optimization algorithm is developed to dynamically scale the number of forks, the length of mutation steps, and the weights of operator selections on-the-fly by the coverage feedback, creating a complete closed-loop adaptive threat simulation system.
- FPGA version of the KM Generator that supports throughput demand of 109 bits/second to be integrated with hardware security test systems and network security appliance fuzzing systems.
- Generalisation of mutation operator catalogue to quantum-capable attack patterns such as Grover-accelerated brute-force variants, Shor-based asymmetric key attacks, quantum state discrimination side-channels.
- The fork-based simulation is deployed on the simulation environment on multiple system layers in parallel and correlation between the layers is performed to identify attack chains spanning across the IoT sensing, edge processing, cloud storage and web application layers in a coordinated multi-stage attack environment.
- Implementation and testing of the entire framework in terms of a physically implemented smart city IoT testbed, consisting of actual IoT sensors, 5G communications infrastructure, and cloud-based analytics systems, to test simulation fidelity in real-world operation.
- Real-time threat intelligence is added to the base attack pattern catalogue by using MITRE ATT&CK STIX feeds, CVE databases, and commercial threat intelligence by adding real-time threat intelligence to the base attack pattern catalogue.

## REFERENCES


Al-Sada, B., Sadighian, A., & Oligeri, G. (2024). Analysis and Characterization of Cyber Threats Leveraging the MITRE ATT&CK Database. *IEEE Access : Practical Innovations, Open Solutions*, *12*, 1217–1234. DOI: 10.1109/ACCESS.2023.3344680

Al-Sada, B., Sadighian, A., & Oligeri, G. (2024). MITRE ATT&CK: State of the Art and Way Forward. *ACM Computing Surveys*, *57*(1), 1–37. DOI: 10.1145/3687300

Assiri, F. Y., & Aljahdali, A. O. (2024). Software Vulnerability Fuzz Testing: A Mutation-Selection Optimization Systematic Review. Engineering, Technology &amp. *Applied Scientific Research*, *14*(4), 14961–14969. DOI: 10.48084/etasr.6971

Das, P., Asif, M., Jahan, S., Ahmed, K., Bui, F. M., & Khondoker, R. (2024). STRIDE-Based Cybersecurity Threat Modeling, Risk Assessment and Treatment of an In-Vehicle Infotainment System. *Vehicles (Basel)*, *6*(3), 1140–1163. DOI: 10.3390/vehicles6030054

Ismagilova, E., Hughes, L., Rana, N. P., & Dwivedi, Y. K. (2020). Security, Privacy and Risks Within Smart Cities: Literature Review and Development of a Smart City Interaction Framework. *Information Systems Frontiers*, *24*(2), 393–414. DOI: 10.1007/s10796-020-10044-1 PMID: 32837262

Kelsey, J., Schneier, B., Wagner, D., & Hall, C. (1998). Cryptanalytic Attacks on Pseudorandom Number Generators. Fast Software Encryption, 168–188. DOI: 10.1007/3-540-69710-1_12

Lv, G., Chen, J., Chen, H., Cai, S., & Zhang, W. (2026). Optimized mutation scheduling for fuzzing based on estimation of distribution algorithm. *Cybersecurity*, *9*(1), 35. Advance online publication. DOI: 10.1186/s42400-025-00461-7

Maksymovych, V., Shabatura, M., Harasymchuk, O., Shevchuk, R., Sawicki, P., & Zajac, T. (2022). Combined Pseudo-Random Sequence Generator for Cybersecurity. *Sensors (Basel)*, *22*(24), 9700. DOI: 10.3390/s22249700 PMID: 36560068

Naik, N., Jenkins, P., Grace, P., Naik, D., Prajapat, S., & Song, J. (2024). A Comparative Analysis of Threat Modelling Methods: STRIDE, DREAD, VAST, PASTA, OCTAVE, and LINDDUN. DOI: 10.1007/978-3-031-74443-3_16

Ouaissa, M., Ouaissa, M., Nadifi, Z., El Himer, S., Al Masmoudi, Y., & Kartit, A. (2025). A framework for cyber threat modeling and risk assessment in smart city environments. *Frontiers of Computer Science*, *7*, 1647179. Advance online publication. DOI: 10.3389/fcomp.2025.1647179

Salazar, Z., Zaidi, F., Mallouli, W., Cavalli, A., Nguyen, H., & Montes De Oca, E. (2022). A Formal Approach for Complex Attacks Generation based on Mutation of 5G Network Traffic. *Proceedings of the 17th International Conference on Software Technologies*, 234–241. DOI: 10.5220/0011319000003266

Singh, T., Solanki, A., Sharma, S. K., Nayyar, A., & Paul, A. (2022). A Decade Review on Smart Cities: Paradigms, Challenges and Opportunities. *IEEE Access : Practical Innovations, Open Solutions*, *10*, 68319–68364. DOI: 10.1109/ACCESS.2022.3184710

Sinha, K., & Paul, P. (2022). An Improved Pseudorandom Sequence Generator and its Application to Image Encryption. *KSII Transactions on Internet and Information Systems*, *16*(4). Advance online publication. DOI: 10.3837/tiis.2022.04.012

Tok, Y. C., & Chattopadhyay, S. (2023). Identifying threats, cybercrime and digital forensic opportunities in Smart City Infrastructure via threat modeling. *Forensic Science International Digital Investigation*, *45*, 301540. DOI: 10.1016/j.fsidi.2023.301540

UcedaVelez. T., & Morana, M. M. (2015). Risk Centric Threat Modeling: process for attack simulation and threat analysis. John Wiley & Sons, ISBN: 978-1118988367.

Vaezi, A., Jones, S., & Asgary, A. (2024). Integrating Resilience into Risk Matrices: A Practical Approach to Risk Assessment with Empirical Analysis. *Journal of Risk Analysis and Crisis Response*, *13*(4). Advance online publication. DOI: 10.54560/jracr.v13i4.411

Vakhnovskyi, A. "Threat modeling and attack surface analysis of IoT-enabled controlled environment agriculture systems," arXiv:2604.13308, Apr. 2026. [Online]. Available: https://arxiv.org/abs/2604.13308

Xiong, W., & Lagerström, R. (2019). Threat modeling – A systematic literature review. Computers &amp. *Computers & Security*, *84*, 53–69. DOI: 10.1016/j.cose.2019.03.010

Zahid, S., Mazhar, M. S., Abbas, S. G., Hanif, Z., Hina, S., & Shah, G. A. (2023). Threat modeling in smart firefighting systems: Aligning MITRE ATT&CK matrix and NIST security controls. *Internet of Things : Engineering Cyber Physical Human Systems*, *22*, 100766. DOI: 10.1016/j.iot.2023.100766

Zhao, L. (2024). Navigating the Cyber Kill Chain: A modern approach to pentesting. *Applied and Computational Engineering*, *38*(1), 170–175. DOI: 10.54254/2755-2721/38/20230549

## KEY TERMS AND DEFINITIONS

**CVSS v3.1:** A uniform method of scoring the severity of vulnerability between 0.0 and 10.0. It employs measures such as attack vector, complexity, and impact (CIA).

**Cyber Kill Chain:** A framework of the steps of a cyberattacks lifecycle. It helps in designing stage-specific detection and mitigation strategies.

**Data Flow Diagram (DFD):** A diagram of the flow of data in a system. It is also employed as input in systematic threat identification in STRIDE.

**Fork-Based Attack Simulation:** A comparable model that generates several variants of the attack using varying seeds. It guarantees a variety of exploration of the threat space, which is reproducible.

**KM Generator:** A modular arithmetic-based pseudorandom sequence generator that uses non-integral parameters. It generates non-periodic, high-entropy sequences that have a large key space ($2^{380}$).

**MITRE ATT&CK:** An expertise base of actual-world adversary strategies and techniques. It allows systematic mapping of attack patterns to established threat patterns.

**Modular Arithmetic System (MAS):** A system of numbers in which values are repeated and are modulo a constant. It is applied in the KM Generator to produce the pseudorandom sequences.

**Mutation Engine:** An element that produces variants of attack by using transformation operators to a base pattern. KM Generator outputs influence operator selection due to unpredictability and reproducibility.

**Non-Integral Number:** A real value that is neither an integer, rational nor irrational. Could be used to add non-repeating and unpredictable behavior to sequences.

**Novel Variant Rate:** The percentage of created variants of attacks which have not been observed in existing datasets. Shows the capability of the system to identify new and unknown threats.

**Reproducibility Guarantee:** Reproduction of the same results with the same initial parameters. Provides auditability and verification of the results of the simulation.

**STRIDE:** Threat modeling model that classifies attacks as six types of security violation. It plots threats to fundamental properties such as confidentiality, integrity and availability.

Chapter 10

# Advanced GhostNet Architecture for Cyber Attack Classification

**G. Geetha**
http://orcid.org/0000-0002-8462-2207
*Department of Computing Technologies, SRM Institute of Science and Technology, Kattankulathur, India*

**Manjula Rajagopal**
*Department of Computing Technologies, SRM Institute of Science and Technology, Kattankulathur, India*

## ABSTRACT

*Cyberattacks have become one of the most serious threats in today's digital world, affecting individuals, organizations, and even governments. As technology continues to grow, so does the complexity and frequency of malicious activities carried out over networks and computer systems. To better understand, detect and prevent these threats, these cyberattacks are commonly grouped into different categories based on their methods, targets, and objectives, and the process known as cyberattack classification. This classification helps security professionals analyze attack patterns, design defensive strategies, and respond more effectively to incidents. From malware and phishing to denial-of-service and insider attacks, each type has distinct characteristics and impacts. By organizing cyber threats into structured classes, cybersecurity efforts become more systematic, proactive, and efficient, ultimately strengthening digital protection and risk management.*

DOI: 10.4018/979-8-3373-9053-6.ch010

## 1.0 INTRODUCTION

Cybersecurity has an innovative method from conventional, manual approaches to additional automated and intelligent systems efficient of real time adaptation. Despite its advancements, the response to cyber threats remains mainly semi-automated and highly dependent on the human intervention in large-scale organizations (Blefari et al., 2025). Cybersecurity breaches and outages are widely reported in the media and statistical data on cyber-attacks is accessible from numerous databases. Although those breaches are common, there is a lack of clarity about the ways establishments manage areas to improve responses and reduce exposure to additional threats (Ramesh et al., 2025).

The application of the cyber-attack detection as well as mitigation measures is significant for protecting the systems from malicious behaviours. To improve the security of smart grids, the incorporation of blockchain technology provides a strengthen securing solution. This technology offers a secure framework for smart DC microgrids, which supports exchanging the secure data, access control and transaction validation by its decentralized and absolute nature (Subramaniam et al., 2025).

One of the main tasks includes Machine learning (ML) methods that are usually trained by using the predefined attack patterns datasets. Accordingly, ML methods are unable to identify the new or hidden attacks. An anomaly recognition is an effective method that monitor the performance of the cyber-physical objects. Through analyzing normal system and network behavior, the anomaly-based methods can recognize the variations from probable patterns. Their intensity lies in detecting zero-day attacks with an extra benefit being the ability to adapt everyday activity profiles for networks (Alanoud Al Mazroa, Fahad R. Albogamy, Mohamad Khairi Ishak, & Samih M. Mostafa, 2025).

Particularly, Deep learning (DL) techniques such as Convolutional Neural Networks (CNNs) and Recurrent Neural Networks (RNNs) are established the strong potential in cyber threats detection. Here, RNNs are suitable for analyzing the sequential time-series data, which enables the detection of patterns revealing of cyber threats. When trained on real-time traffic data CNNs are effective in classifying the Distributed Denial of Service (DDoS) attacks to precisely classify the attack types. The main advantage of DL techniques over the traditional ML approaches is its capability to automatically extract the features from raw data without extensive human designed feature engineering (Gupta et al., 2025).

This paper an advanced GhostNet (AdGNt) model is proposes for detecting cyber-attack. In standard GhostNet model, it may be losing several fine-grained features and struggle to captures the complex patterns like robustness reduction and high computational cost. To address the standard GhostNet model's drawbacks, the proposed AdGNt model incorporates an advanced Ghost Bottleneck with improved

Squeeze and Excite block. This enhancement allows the model to extract the fine-grained features, capture complex patterns more effectively, enhance generalization, attain better stability and reduce computational overhead.

Following the introduction section, the literature review is provide in Section 2.0, Section 3.0 offers the proposed framework for cyber-attack detection. Section 4.0 and Section 5.0 offers the outcomes and its summary.

## 2.0 LITERATURE REVIEW

Naeem et al. (2025) introduced an intrusion classification framework for identifying the various types of cyber-attacks in the modern smart power grids. For feature selection method, a Grey-Wolf metaheuristic optimization was applied to train the non-linear, overlapping as well as difficult electrical grid characteristics. Then, developed an lengthy deep-stacked ensemble method by merging the forecasts from weak learners CNNs and MLP. Moreover, XAI was applied in the prediction model to interpreted and validated its results. The output of this model attained high accuracy with the original feature set and the selected features, which shows an effective protection against cyber-attacks in smart power grids.

Trivedi et al. (2025) proposed a new approach for data pre-processing and performance interpretation of advanced ML models. This approach was utilized to improve the data quality and refine the classification models during the iterative progress. It contains three stages such as data gathering and preprocessing, data quality enhancement and feature extraction and finally modify the hyperparameter. XAI using SHAP was utilized to interpret the learning behaviour of that suggested models. Applied this method to the cyber-attack recognition in microgrid networks. SMOTE and ENN algorithms were utilized to enhance the performance of the predictive model for the Data augmentation, Boruta package was used in the feature extraction and TPE algorithm were used to tuning the hyperparameter.

Vitorino et al. (2025) introduced a feature selection and consensus model, which combines various methods and applies them to across several network data. Two distinct feature sets were detected and utilized to train the multiple ML algorithms under the standard as well as adversarial training conditions. Next, validate the dependability of such feature sets by conducted an adversarial evasion benchmark and its effect on the weakness of the algorithms to adversarial samples. Then, utilized an enhanced greater range dataset for optimal time-related features selection that defined a more exact feature set as well as the ML models obtained enhanced adversarial generalization. This model/s enhancement was substantially enhanced without compromising its generalization to steady the traffic flows that rises the false alarms as well aa demanding excessive computational resources.

Wu et al. (2025) proposed an innovative DL method to detect the cyber-attacks in IIoT architecture. In this proposed work, there were introduced three stacked DL frameworks like "StackMean, StackMax and StackRF" that aggregate the outputs of each DL models. Here, the average class probabilities prediction was evaluated through the StackMean model, the maximum probability prediction were selected through StackMax as well as the RF was applied by StackRF model to merge the basic model predictions. The SMOTE algorithm was applied to mitigate the class imbalance problem in the training dataset. Moreover, experiments showed that the stacked models obtained improved detection accuracy as compared to each DL methods.

In 2025, Malhar Barbhaya *et al.,* (Malhar Barbhaya, Purushottama Rao Dasari, Seshu Kumar Damarla, Rajagopalan Srinivasan, & Biao Huang, 2025) proposed an exploration of AI methods such as XAI, Generative AI, ML, DL and NLP to addressed the cybersecurity challenges. In this work, both ML and DL methods was performed to evaluate its accuracy and suitability for various cybersecurity issues. Also, this paper examined the XAI methods to improve the transparency and interpretability of AI-based security solutions. Moreover, rising trends in Generative AI and NLP were analyzed for their ability in threat intelligence generation and cyber-attack simulation. This work highlights the Generative AI application in cybersecurity and enhanced security solutions and mitigating the cyber risks.

## 3.0 PROPOSING AN ADVANCED GHOSTNET (ADGNT) MODEL FOR CYBER ATTACK DETECTION

The step-by-step process of the proposed advanced GhostNet (AdGNt) framework for Cyber Attack Detection is illustrates in **Figure 1**. This detection process is summarized as follows:

Initially, the input data is preprocessed through a Min-Max normalization method to scale the feature values among 0 and 1, which indicates all the attributes contribute equally to the training process and enhances its model convergence.

Then, the normalized data is fed into the advanced GhostNet (AdGNt) model for identifying the cyber-attack. This model contains an advanced Ghost Bottleneck layer with an improved Squeeze-and-Excitation (SE) block to effort on the relevant features that improves the stability and generality. This proposed reduces the redundant computations, which provides efficient and real-time cyber-attack detection.

*Figure 1. Overview of the proposed AdGNt framework for cyber attack detection*

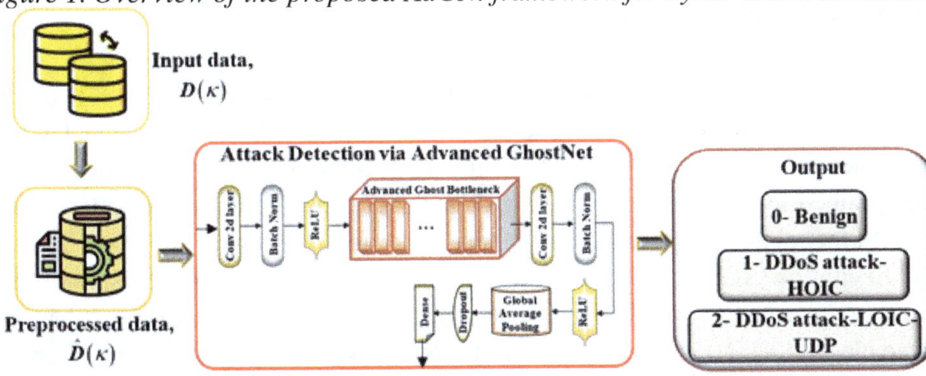


### 3.1 Preprocessing via Min-Max Normalization Process

Initially, preprocessing phase is carried out to prepare the input data ($D(\kappa)$) for effective training by the DL model. This inputs data($D(\kappa)$) normally contains varying scales values, which can be negatively affect the accuracy of the model. To overcome this variation, applied a Min-Max normalization (Ahmed Jameel Mohammed, Masoud Muhammed Hassan, & Dler Hussein Kadir, 2020) technique to the input data, which rescales all the feature values to a standard range of 0 and 1. This validates that the given data, the smallest value and the largest value is mapped to 0 and 1, respectively. Then, all other intermediate values are evenly scaled within this range. Eq. (1) express the definition of the min-max normalization method, wherein, wherein, $\widehat{D}(\kappa)$ implies the normalized or preprocessed value, $\min(D(\kappa)$ ) implies the minimum value and $\max(D(\kappa))$ implies the maximum value of the original data ($D(\kappa)$).

$$\widehat{D}(\kappa) = \frac{D(\kappa) - \min(D(\kappa))}{\max(D(\kappa)) - \min(D(\kappa))} \tag{1}$$

This preprocessing process decreases due to the feature scale variation and improves faster as well as more stable training of the advanced GhostNet (AdGNt) model for precise cyber-attack classification.

## 3.2 Cyber Attack Detection via Advanced GhostNet (AdGNt) Model

After normalized the input data, which is processed for cyber-attack detection by using an advanced GhostNet (AdGNt) model. AdGNt model is designed to mitigate the challenges faced on the traditional GhostNet model, which may lose the fine-grained feature details and struggle for capturing the complex patterns. The AdGNt model integrates an advanced Ghost Bottleneck with an improved Squeeze and Excitation (SE) block for effective feature extraction, better model stability and reduced the computational cost. Finally, the AdGNt model classifies the data into three classes like "0 for benign, 1 for DDoS attack-HOIC and 2 for DDoS attack-LOIC-UDP".

### Traditional GhostNet Model

The traditional GhostNet (Han et al., 2020) is made up of the Ghost module that efficiently creates many feature maps without necessitating the extensive computational resources. Initially, the Ghost module produces a minute intrinsic feature maps set by using the traditional convolution operation that captures the essential features as per Eq. (2).

$$\mathbb{Z} = \wp * \gamma \tag{2}$$

In the convolution operation, $\wp$ indicates the input feature map, $\mathbb{Z}$stands for the smaller intrinsic feature maps set and $\gamma$ implies the convolution filter.

Then, transformed these feature maps by utilized a cheap linear operation to create an extra ghost feature map. It allows the network to produce the desired number of outcome feature maps with less parameters as per Eq. (3).

$$\rho_{ij} = \psi_{i,j}(\rho'_i), \quad \forall\, i = 1,2,...,l, \; j = 1,2,...,m \tag{3}$$

wherein, $\psi_{i,j}$signifies a linear operation that applied to produce the$j$th ghost feature map, $\rho'_i$ signifies $i$th intrinsic feature map, $l$implies the total intrinsic maps and $m$implies the total ghost maps. The traditional GhostNet architecture starts with 3x3 convolution layer to decrease the spatial dimensions as well as extract low-level features. Then, this layer tailed by numerous Ghost bneck blocks with stride 1 and 2. Each Ghost bottleneck block, consist of Ghost module with batch normalization (Batch Norm) and ReLU activation function for stride 1 and applies additional depth wise convolutional layer in the stride 2. After the G-bneck block, their final feature map is inputted through the convolutional 2d layer followed by Average pooling layer. Then, its outcome feature map is again passed through the convolution 2d layer and a fully connected layer to attain the attack classification.

However, the traditional GhostNet framework may lose some fine-grained feature data and weaker at capturing the critical complex patterns. When applied to the large-scale cyber-attack data, the model can reduce its robustness, stability and the computational efficiency

## Advanced GhostNet Model

For cyber-attack detection, an advanced GhostNet model is propose to address the drawbacks of traditional GhostNet model. **Figure 2** illustrates the architecture of AdGNt model for cyber-attack detection. The structure starts with the preprocessed data $\widehat{D}(\kappa)$, which is inputted into a two-dimensional convolutional layer that extracts the low-level feature representations. Such feature map is processed into the batch normalization layer to enhance the training stability. Subsequently, the resulting feature maps are again passed into a ReLU activation layer, which introduced non-linearity and allowing the network to model complex relations. Afterthat, outcome feature from the ReLU activation function is fed into the multiple advanced ghost Bottleneck blocks. Subsequently, processed the features by a two-dimensional convolutional layer tailed by Batch Norm and activation function (ReLU). The global average pooling is utilized to prevent overfitting that compresses the feature maps into a compact depiction, then passed the pooled features to a dropout layer before he dense layer. This dense layer creating the final output classes such as "0, 1 and 2".

*Figure 2. Architecture of AdGNt model*

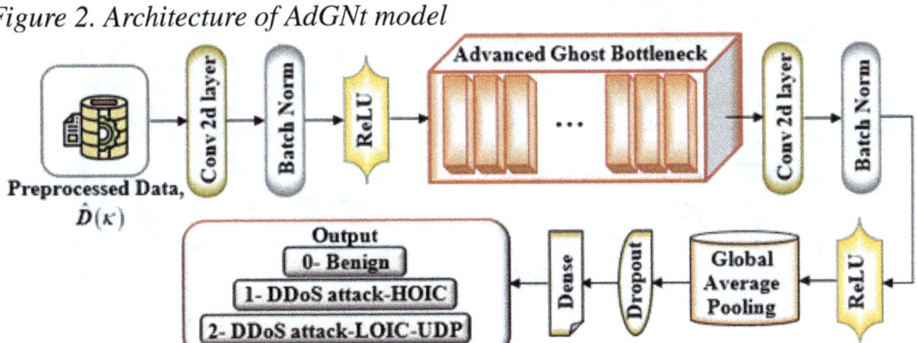

## Advanced Ghost Bottleneck

The advanced Ghost Bottleneck is the main component of the AdGNt model. It efficiently produces many feature maps while maintain low computational necessities. This G-bottleneck contains two major configurations that depends on two strides. The architecture of advanced Ghost Bottleneck with stride 1 and 2 are shown in **Figure 3**.

*Figure 3. Advanced ghost bottleneck architecture*

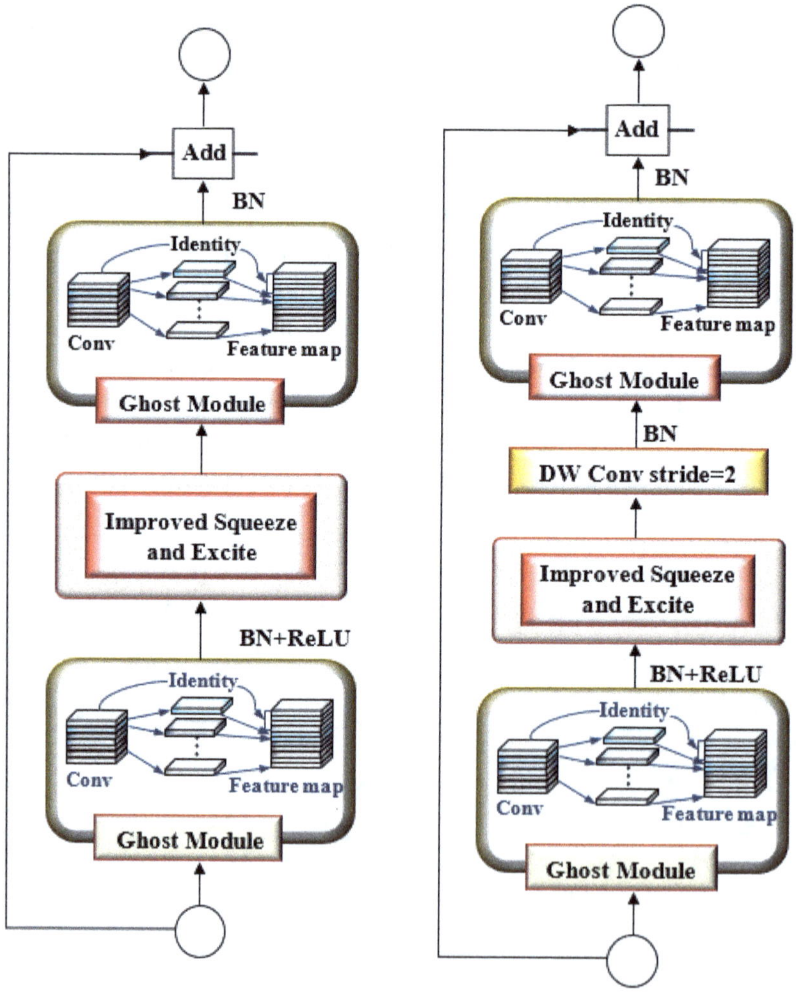


**Stride 1:** In the advanced ghost bottleneck block for stride 1, the input feature map passes into a Ghost module to create intrinsic feature maps. Then, these feature

maps are normalized and activated into batch normalization (BN) and ReLU function. Their output goes into the improved Squeeze and Excite (SE block), which enhances the ability of the model to capture the important fine-grained features. Later, the features pass through another Ghost module and BN. Lastly, the input feature map adds to the processed features using a residual connection that preserves the data and enhances the gradient flow.

**Stride 2:** For stride 2, processed the input feature map to a Ghost module, which followed by BN as well as ReLU activation function. Afterthat, passed into the improved SE block and a Depthwise convolution (stride 2), which decreases the spatial dimensions. Afterthat, the resulting feature map is fed through another Ghost module and it is added with the input map through residual connection. This design accepts the model to maintain the effectiveness while extracting the multi-scale features.

## Improved Squeeze-and-Excitation (SE) Block

The architecture of the improved SE block is shown in **Figure 4**. This improved SE block improves the feature selection to extracts the fine-grained patterns. Initially, processed the input feature map into a convolution layer to extract the low-level features. After, this feature map is fed in parallelly across global average pooling and average pooling layers to captures the different statistical properties. Concatenate these pooled features and inputted through a dense layer with a Custom ReLU activation function. Normally, ReLU activation function (Shiv Ram Dubey, Satish Kumar Singh, & Bidyut Baran Chaudhuri, 2022) is expressed using Eq. (4), where $\nu$indicates the input feature. It is a simple activation function and its range is between 0 to infinitive.

$$f(\nu) = \begin{cases} \nu, & if v > 0 \\ 0, & else \end{cases} \tag{4}$$

This function requires less processing time as compared to other activations. However, it eliminates the negative inputs that may lead to a loss of information. A Custom ReLU activation function is applied to address these limitations, which enhance the stability of the model. The Custom ReLU activation function is computed as per Eq. (5), wherein *ALPHA* indicates the learnable parameter using Eq. (6).

$$\hat{f}(\nu) = \begin{cases} \nu * ALPHA, & if v > 0 \\ 0, & else \end{cases} \tag{5}$$

$$ALPHA = \frac{\nu}{\left(\frac{p+q}{2}\right)}, \ p, q \in (0, 1) \tag{6}$$

Then, the outcome feature of this dense layer with custom ReLU activations are followed by another dense layer. The final output feature and the input feature map are multiplied through the element-wise multiplication operation, which highlights the relevant features and generate the refined output. This mechanism allows the model to focus on the attack patterns that are essential for accurate classification.

*Figure 4. Improved SE block*

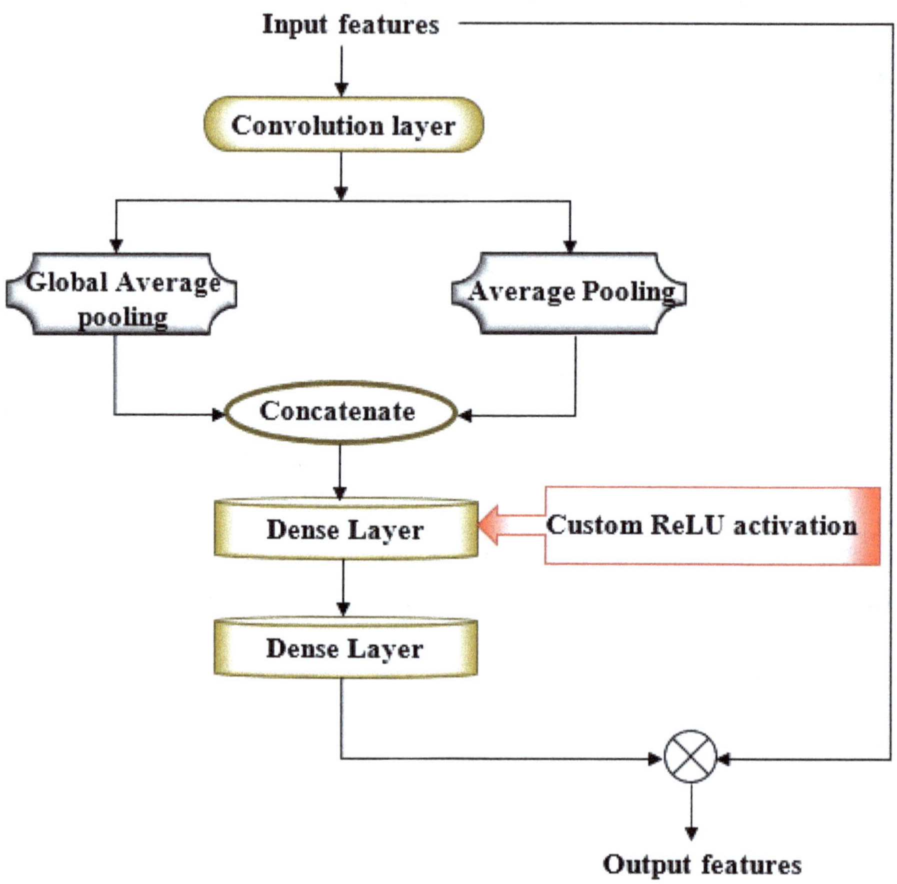


Thus, the integration of the advanced Ghost Bottleneck with improved SE block allows the AdGNt model to extracts the fine-grained features, detecting complex patterns and generalize well to the large datasets. When compared to the traditional GhostNet model, the modified architecture is more stable, robust and computationally effectual, which makes it highly suitable for accurate cyber-attack detection.

## 4.0 RESULTS AND DISCUSSION

### 4.1 Simulation Procedure

The proposed cyber-attack classification was simulated using Python. The experiments were performed on a system powered by 11th Gen Intel (R) Core (TM) i5-1135G7 @2.40 GHz 2.42 GHz processor and the Installed RAM size was 16.0 GB (15.7 GB)". Further examination was done using CSE-CIC-IDS2018 dataset (htt283).

### 4.2 Dataset Description

CSE-CIC-IDS2018 dataset contains seven categories of cyber-attacks: Heartbleed, Web-based attacks, Botnet, DoS, Brute Force, DDoS and internal network infiltration. The attack environment was generated using an infrastructure of 50 attacker machines. The target organization in the dataset consists of five departments with approximately 420 personal computers and 30 servers. System log files and network traffic data were collected from victim machines. In addition, around 80 network traffic features were extracted from the captured packets using CICFlowMeter-V3 tool.

The implemented framework consists 8000 data and 25 attributes.

### 4.3 Performance Validation of Cyber-Attack Classification

In this portion, the performance of cyber-attack detection models is examined with respect to positive and negative measures across training data variation of 60%, 70%, 80% & 90%. The following graphs reflects the comparative outcome of existing approaches namely LinkNet, Squeezenet, Efficientnet, Resnet, Ghostnet and AdGNt. Belonged to this observation, the conventional Squeezenet method has demonstrated minimal accuracies over the 60% of data by 0.818 and similarly over 70% to 90% the Resnet attained lesser classification accuracies by 0.851, 0.874, 0.924 (**Figure 5(ii)**). When assessing the accuracy levels of existing Ghostnet and AdGNt framework, the AdGNt detection method has more efficiently captured the cyber-attacks to accomplished maximal accuracies by 0.958 in 70%, 0.971 in 80% and 0.978 in 90% with precision score of 0.946 in 60% and 0.974 in 90% of data (**Figure 5(i)**). Further, the analysis over sensitivity and specificity is represented in **Figure 5(iii)** & **Figure 5(iv).**

In **Figure 6** & **Figure 7**, the cyber-attack detection reliability of AdGNt models is evaluated using FNR, FPR, F-measure, MCC and NPV. Here, the ranges of FPR and FNR metrics should be lower and other metrics ranges should be maximal. But the comparative results stated that the baseline detection frameworks LinkNet,

Squeezenet, Efficientnet, Resnet and Ghostnet are depicted maximal false rates than the AdGNt by around 0.118 - 0.054 in FNR analysis and returned 0.196 - 0.069 in FPR analysis across the data training percentages. Exceeded this false rate, the AdGNt method meted minimal scores over FNR by 0.031 and FPR by 0.021 in 90% data size.

*Figure 5. Attack detection efficiency study on AdGNt method "positive metrics" (i) Precision (ii) Accuracy (iii) Specificity (iv) Sensitivity*

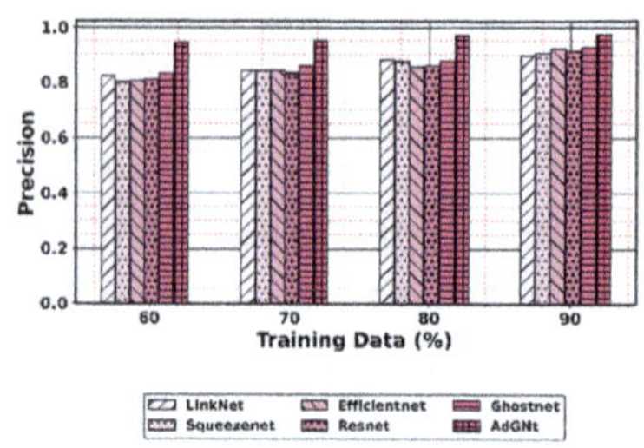


(i)

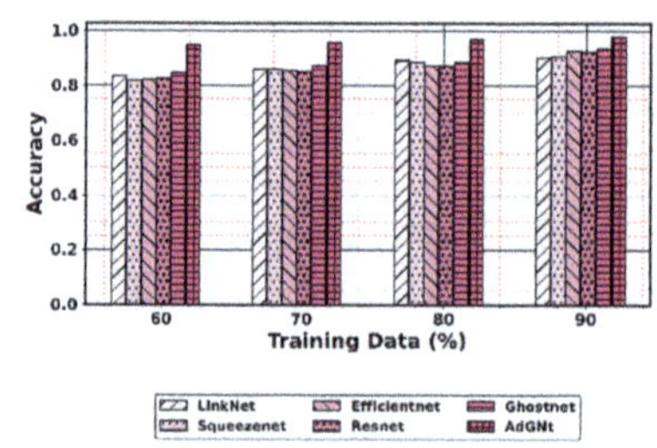


(ii)

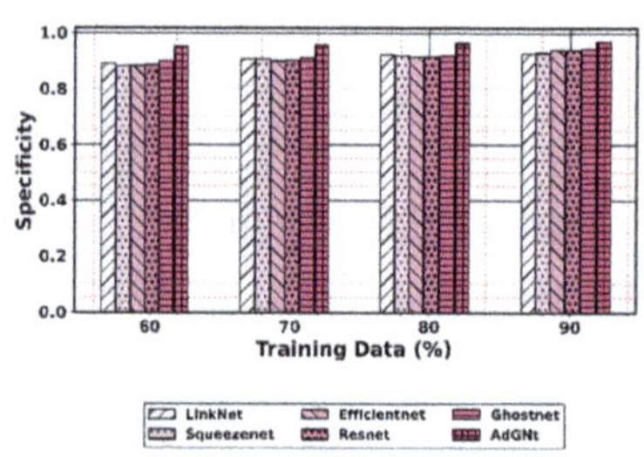


(iii)

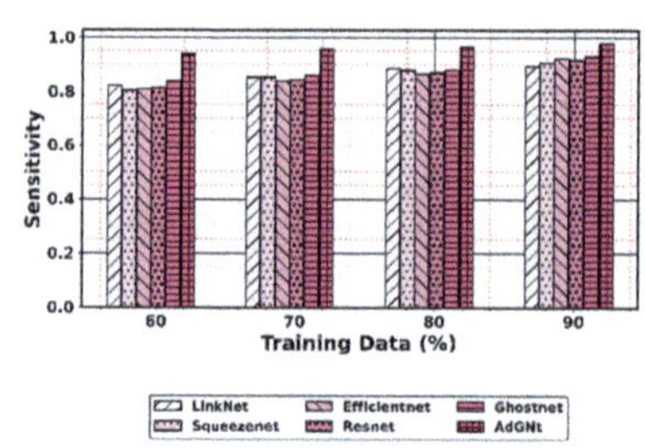


(iv)

*Figure 6. Attack detection efficiency study on AdGNt method "negative metrics" (i) FPR (ii) FNR*

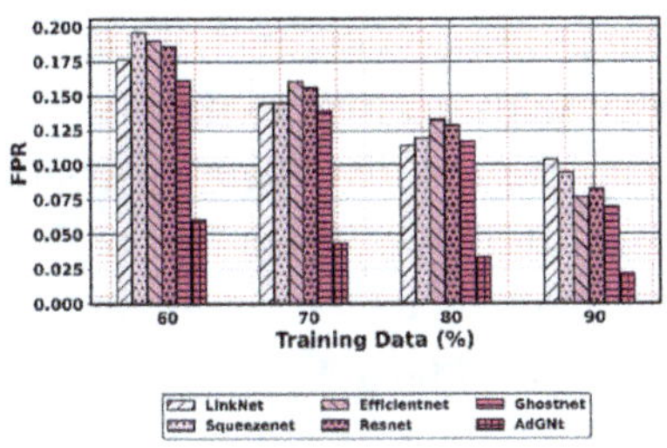


(i)

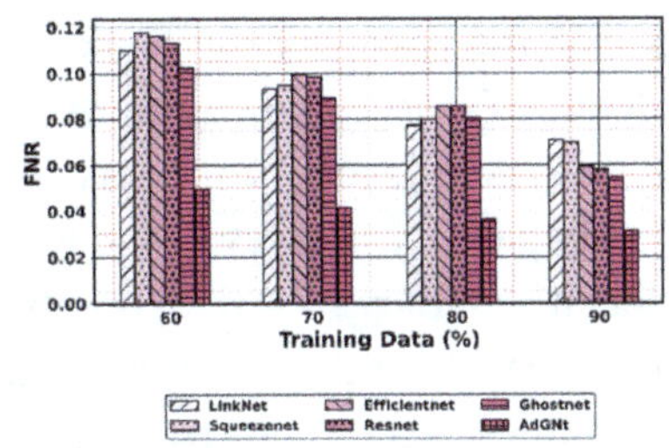


(ii)

*Figure 7. Attack detection efficiency study on AdGNt method "other metrics" (i) NPV (ii) F-measure (iii) MCC*

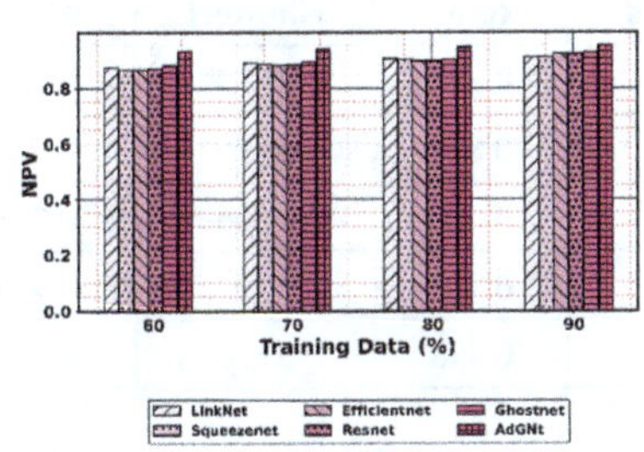


(i)

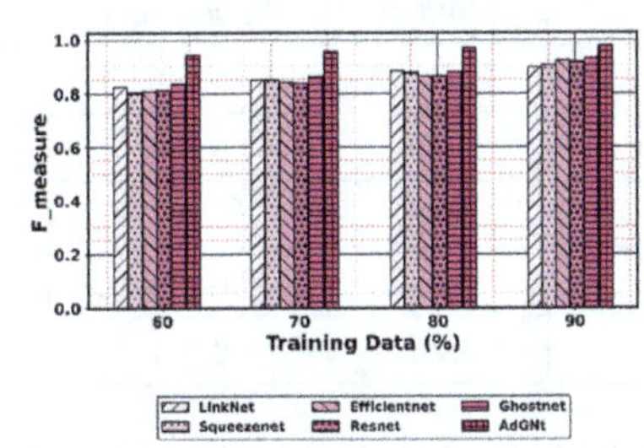


(ii)

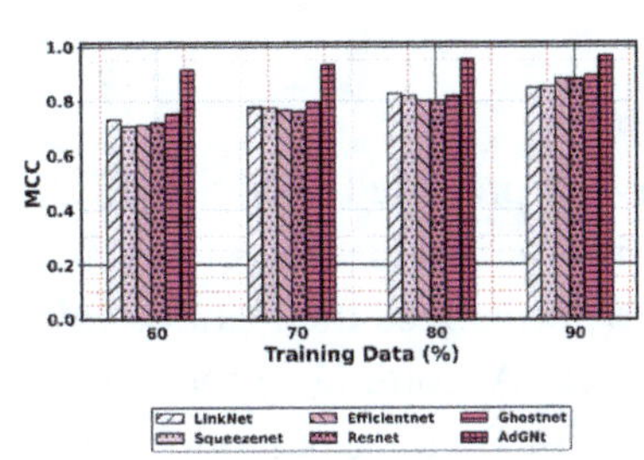


(iii)

## 4.4 Statistical Review of AdGNt Method

The statistical validation is undertaken in terms of accuracy across the conventional detection frameworks such as LinkNet, Squeezenet, Resnet, Ghostnet, Efficientnet and AdGNt (**Table I shows the Statistical study with accuracy**). In this analysis, the statistical levels of models should be maximal to prove their cyber-attack detection capability. However, the Resnet, Ghostnet frameworks are accomplished lesser mean accuracy by 0.898, 0.896, median accuracy by 0.899, 0.896, minimum accuracy by 0.885 and maximum accuracy by 0.907. Secondly, the Squeezenet has expressed lower accuracies by mean of 0.901, minimum accuracies of 0.889 and higher standard deviation of 0.008. In contrast, the AdGNt based detection approach has demonstrated superior performance than the LinkNet, Resnet, Efficientnet, Squeezenet and Ghostnet by higher accuracy of mean- 0.975, maximum -0.979, minimum - 0.969, median - 0.974 with lower standard deviation range of 0.003.

*Table 1. Statistical study with accuracy*

| | LinkNet | Squeezenet | Efficientnet | Resnet | Ghostnet | AdGNt |
|---|---|---|---|---|---|---|
| Min | 0.903 | 0.889 | 0.903 | 0.885 | 0.885 | 0.969 |
| Median | 0.916 | 0.901 | 0.917 | 0.899 | 0.896 | 0.974 |
| Std-Dev | 0.006 | 0.008 | 0.005 | 0.006 | 0.006 | 0.003 |
| Max | 0.924 | 0.914 | 0.921 | 0.907 | 0.907 | 0.979 |
| Mean | 0.916 | 0.901 | 0.915 | 0.898 | 0.896 | 0.975 |

## 5.0 SUMMARY

Therefore, this research work proposed an advanced GhostNet (AdGNt) architecture for cyber-attack classification. In this framework, Min-Max normalization was utilized for preprocessing to normalized the features value and fed into the AdGNt model for classified the attack. According to the detection phase, AdGNt model incorporated an advanced Ghost Bottleneck model with an improved Squeeze and Excitation block for effectively captures the fine-grained feature details and critical patterns in the network traffic data. This proposed AdGNt framework shows better generalization, higher stability and compact computational overhead as compared to the other cyber-attack detection model. Also, experimental outcomes enhance that the proposed AdGNt method accurately detects various types of cyber-attacks, which makes it a robust and efficient solution for intrusion detection schemes by reached lesser scores over FNR analysis by 0.031 in 90% of data training.

## REFERENCES


Al Mazroa, A., Albogamy, F. R., Ishak, M. K., & Mostafa, S. M. (2025). Boosting cyberattack detection using binary metaheuristics with deep learning on cyber-physical system environment. *IEEE Access : Practical Innovations, Open Solutions, 13*, 11280–11294. DOI: 10.1109/ACCESS.2025.3526258

Barbhaya, M., Dasari, P. R., Damarla, S. K., Srinivasan, R., & Huang, B. (2025). A deep learning framework for cyberattack detection and classification in industrial control systems. *Computers & Chemical Engineering*, *202*, 202. DOI: 10.1016/j.compchemeng.2025.109278

Blefari, F., Cosentino, C., Pironti, F. A., Furfaro, A., & Marozzo, F. (2025). CyberRAG: An agentic RAG cyber attack classification and reporting tool. *Future Generation Computer Systems*, •••, 176.

Canadian Institute for Cybersecurity. (n.d.). *CICIDS2018 dataset*. University of New Brunswick. https://www.unb.ca/cic/datasets/ids-2018.html

Dubey, S. R., Singh, S. K., & Chaudhuri, B. B. (2022). Activation functions in deep learning: A comprehensive survey and benchmark. *Neurocomputing*, *503*, 92–108. DOI: 10.1016/j.neucom.2022.06.111

Gupta, B. B., Pan, V. S.-H., Gaurav, A., Arya, V., Alhalabi, W., & Chui, K. T. (2025). Optimized hybrid CNN-LSTM-GRU model for cyber attack detection using adaptive equilibrium optimization. *ICT Express*.

Han, K., Wang, Y., Tian, Q., Guo, J., Xu, C., & Xu, C. (2020). GhostNet: More features from cheap operations. In *Proceedings of the IEEE/CVF Conference on Computer Vision and Pattern Recognition* (pp. 1580–1589).

Mohammed, A. J., Hassan, M. M., & Kadir, D. H. (2020). Improving classification performance for a novel imbalanced medical dataset using SMOTE method. *International Journal of Advanced Trends in Computer Science and Engineering*, *9*(3), 3161–3172. DOI: 10.30534/ijatcse/2020/104932020

Naeem, H., Ullah, F., & Srivastava, G. (2025). Classification of intrusion cyber-attacks in smart power grids using deep ensemble learning with metaheuristic-based optimization. *Expert Systems: International Journal of Knowledge Engineering and Neural Networks*, *42*(1), e13556. DOI: 10.1111/exsy.13556

Ramesh, S. N. S. V. S. C., Al Fardan, B. M. M., Anupama, C. S. S., Kumar, K. V., Cho, S., Acharya, S., & Yoon, C. (2025). Leveraging cyberattack news tweets for advanced threat detection and classification using ensemble of deep learning models with Wolverine optimization algorithm. *IEEE Access : Practical Innovations, Open Solutions*, *13*, 48343–48358. DOI: 10.1109/ACCESS.2025.3550378

Subramaniam, R., Sheela, A. J., & Alwabli, A. (2025). Enhanced cybersecurity and cyber-attack detection in smart DC microgrids using blockchain technology and SVM technique. *Ain Shams Engineering Journal*, *16*(7), 103400. DOI: 10.1016/j.asej.2025.103400

Trivedi, R., Patra, S., & Khadem, S. (2025). Data-centric explainable artificial intelligence techniques for cyber-attack detection in microgrid networks. *Energy Reports*, *13*, 217–229. DOI: 10.1016/j.egyr.2024.11.075

Vitorino, J., Silva, M., Maia, E., & Praça, I. (2025). Reliable feature selection for adversarially robust cyber-attack detection. *Annales des Télécommunications*, *80*(3), 341–355. DOI: 10.1007/s12243-024-01047-z

Wu, W., Fouzi, H., Benamar, B., Sidi-Mohammed, S., & Ying, S. (2025). Deep learning-based stacked models for cyber-attack detection in industrial internet of things. *Neural Computing & Applications*, *37*(24), 19617–19651. DOI: 10.1007/s00521-025-11418-9

# APPENDIX

The following Table 2 shows the Nomenclature

*Table 2. Nomenclature*

| Abbreviation | Description |
|---|---|
| AdGNt | Advanced GhostNet |
| AI | Artificial Intelligence |
| CNN | Convolutional Neural Network |
| DL | Deep Learning |
| IIoT | Industrial Internet Of Things |
| ML | Machine Learning |
| MLP | Meta-Learner |
| NLP | Natural Language Processing |
| RF | Random Forest |
| SE | Squeeze-And-Excitation |
| SHAP | SHapley Additive exPlanations |
| SMOTE | Synthetic Minority Over Sampling Technique |
| XAI | Explainable Artificial Intelligence |

# Chapter 11
# A Hybrid VGG16-CNN Framework for Deepfake Image Detection in Cloud-Enabled Environments

**Ali Zaheer Agha**
http://orcid.org/0000-0002-7130-7160
*United College of Engineering and Research, Prayagraj, India*

**Ratnesh Mishra**
*BIT Mesra, Patna, India*

## ABSTRACT

*Deepfakes technologies are capable of an authentic and significant manipulation of images, audio, and video with threats of identity theft, false information, blackmail, and financial fraud. Their increasing abuse is the primary challenge of both digital forensics and cybersecurity. In this paper, a hybrid deep learning architecture, Deepfake Predictor (DFP), will be suggested as a way of image recognition of manipulated faces. The model uses a pre-trained VGG16 network that is used with other convolutional layers to enhance classification. It was trained and tested using a dataset of 2041 images (1081 real, 960 fake). The metrics that were used to compare performance to Xception, NASNet, and MobileNet included accuracy, precision, F1-score, specificity, geometric mean, and loss. The model proposed had 94% accuracy and 95% precision that is better than the baseline methods. Its performance and scalability can be used to detect in real time and can be used in the cloud-based and active cybersecurity systems.*

DOI: 10.4018/979-8-3373-9053-6.ch011

## 1. INTRODUCTION

Deepfake technology (Zobaed et al., 2021) is the application of the artificial intelligence system that can produce a synthetic media from a person by the manipulation of his face, voice, or other visual features. The term "deep fake" was coined in 2017 and is used to describe digitally manipulated media created using deep learning methods. Many methods are used to produce highly realistic manipulated content, such as computer graphics, audio synthesis, face swapping algorithms, and generative adversarial networks (GANs). Deepfake technology is starting to be used more frequently for identity theft, misinformation, impersonation attacks, blackmail and financial fraud, posing serious problems for digital forensics and cyber security.

The current developments in generative artificial intelligence have brought about an even greater realism in deepfake content, making it harder and harder to tell fake images and videos from real ones. The state-of-the-art generative adversarial networks (GANs), diffusion models, and transformer-based architectures can generate very realistic facial manipulations that can evade conventional forensic analysis methods. Thus, the growing need to create effective deepfake detection systems has emerged as a pressing problem in cybersecurity, digital forensics, and online content moderation.

Deepfakes are now more and more a part of various types of cybercrime. Deepfake technology has seen significant developments and poses significant questions about digital manipulation, misinformation and malicious online activity. A Sensity report found that over 96% of the videos discovered are deepfake videos that fall under non-consensual or harmful applications (Westerlund, 2019). Deepfakes have been involved in a number of incidents, and have been reported in several countries such as Canada, India, South Korea, the United Kingdom, and the United States. One of the most publicized incidents involved AI voice cloning to steal around $243,000 from a company CEO (Mirsky & Lee, 2021). The technology is evolving rapidly and is increasingly essential to have reliable and automated deepfake detection systems.

Computer vision applications like image classification, object recognition and facial analysis have been successfully applying deep learning techniques. The techniques can be used to detect intricate visual characteristics, as well as subtle manipulation artifacts that may be introduced during the creation of deepfake images. The problem with deepfakes is that today's generative models can produce highly realistic face transformations, which are difficult to spot as fake media. This has led to the development of automated machine learning and deep learning-based detection systems that are essential for detecting manipulated content.

Many current deepfake detection methods suffer because they are based on a single neural network architecture, possibly restricting the capabilities of capturing the various types of manipulation artifacts in different data sets and deepfake generation methods. Despite the advances in detection performance with the adoption of transfer learning approaches, there are still issues of robustness, scalability, and deployment of these methods in large-scale environments.

## 1.1 Research Gap and Motivation

While current deepfake detection methods have succeeded in achieving some promising accuracy, many are based on a single transfer learning, or convolutional neural network (CNN) architecture and may fail to capture a wide variety of manipulation artifacts. Moreover, the increasing amount of multimedia content published in a social network and cloud based platforms makes it necessary to develop accurate and scalable detection systems. To tackle these challenges, a hybrid Deepfake Predictor (DFP) framework combining the feature extraction power of VGG16 along with extra convolutional neural network layers is proposed that can enhance the deepfake image detection performance while being deployable in cloud-based environments.

Deepfake videos have been increasingly spread in digital spaces, thanks to the pervasive use of social media and cloud-based multimedia services. Cloud computing offers scalable computational resources for storing, processing and analyzing large amounts of multimedia data. Therefore, embedding deep learning based deepfake detection algorithms in cloud systems can prove beneficial for maintaining live monitoring and detection of manipulated media on various cloud platforms.

## 1.2 Contributions of the Study

The major contributions of this study are summarized as follows:

1. A hybrid Deepfake Predictor (DFP) framework is proposed by integrating a pre-trained VGG16 network with additional convolutional neural network layers for enhanced deepfake image detection.
2. A comparative evaluation is performed using four widely adopted transfer learning architectures, namely Xception, NASNet, MobileNet, and VGG16.
3. A comprehensive performance assessment is conducted using multiple evaluation metrics, including accuracy, precision, F1-score, specificity, geometric mean, and loss score.
4. The robustness of the proposed framework is validated using k-fold cross-validation.
5. The suitability of the proposed approach for deployment in cloud-enabled environments is discussed to support scalable deepfake detection applications in cybersecurity and digital forensics.

The remainder of this chapter is organized as follows. Section 2 presents the related literature on deepfake detection. Section 3 describes the research methodology, dataset preparation process, and experimental workflow. Section 4 discusses the transfer learning-based neural network models employed in this study. Section 5 introduces the proposed Deepfake Predictor (DFP) architecture. Section 6 presents the hyperparameter optimization strategy. Section 7 discusses the experimental results and performance evaluation. Finally, Section 8 concludes the chapter and outlines future research directions.

## 2. RELATED WORK

This part looks at what other researchers have found on how to detect deepfakes. Previous research has examined many machine learning and deep learning methodologies for detecting altered media. We look at the literature based on the methods utilized, the datasets used, and the metrics used to measure performance. Table 1 presents a comparative summary of representative deepfake detection studies based on their methodologies, datasets, reported performance, and research objectives.

This paper introduced a deep learning methodology for identifying video deepfakes (Ismail et al., 2021). The proposed solution was XGBoost, which is a machine learning algorithm that employs decision trees to make predictions more accurate. We employed a YOLO face detector (Chen et al., 2021), CNN, and Inception ResNet to find the parts of the video frames that showed faces. We trained and built the model using the CelebDF and FaceForensics++ datasets. For deepfake identification, the XGBoost classifier was used on face characteristics taken from video frames.The proposed technique achieved a 90% accuracy rate in identifying deepfake films.

The research in (Pan et al., 2020) provided automated classification of deepfake videos using deep learning techniques. The algorithms employed include MobileNet and Xception, which are based on deep learning. We trained and tested the model on well-known benchmark datasets as CelebDF and FaceForensics++.The deep learning approach used to sort deepfake films has an accuracy rate of 91% to 98%. Li et al. (Jung et al., 2020) put out a deep learning method for finding deepfakes by looking at unusual patterns of eye blinking.

*Table 1. Deepfake detection–related literature summary and comparative analysis*

| Ref | Approach | Dataset | Accuracy Score (%) | Research Aim |
|---|---|---|---|---|
| **Ismail et al. (2021)** | XGBoost with deep learning features | CelebDF; FaceForensics++ | 90 | Video deepfake detection using a deep learning-based methodology |
| **Pan et al. (2020)** | MobileNet and Xception | FaceForensics++ | 91 | Automatic deepfake video classification using deep learning techniques |
| **Jung et al. (2020)** | DeepVision eye-blinking detection | Eye blinking deepfake dataset | 87 | Deepfake detection based on abnormal human eye-blinking patterns |
| **Lewis et al. (2020)** | Multimodal deep learning network | Facebook Deepfake Challenge dataset | 61 | Detection of deepfake videos using spatial, spectral, and temporal inconsistencies |
| **Hsu et al. (2020)** | DenseNet and fake feature network | CelebA | 90 | Deepfake image detection using pairwise deep learning techniques |
| **Solaiyappan and Wen (2022)** | Machine learning and deep learning models | Annotated CT-GAN dataset | 80 | Detection of medical deepfake images using hybrid machine learning approaches |
| **Rossler et al. (2019)** | CNN-based deepfake detection | FaceForensics++ | 95 | Benchmark deepfake detection using large-scale facial manipulation datasets |
| **Coccomini et al. (2022)** | EfficientNet-based CNN | FaceForensics++ | 94 | Deepfake detection using efficient convolutional neural networks |
| **Wang et al. (2023)** | Vision Transformer-based deep learning | Multiple deepfake datasets | 96 | Detection of deepfakes using attention-based transformer architectures |
| **Liu et al. (2022)** | ConvNeXt-based architecture | CelebDF | 95 | Robust deepfake image classification using modern convolutional networks |
| **Islam et al. (2024)** | Explainable AI (XAI) with CNN | Multiple benchmark datasets | 94 | Interpretable deepfake detection through explainable feature analysis |
| **Kumar et al. (2024)** | Hybrid CNN–Transformer Network | FaceForensics++, CelebDF | 98 | Deepfake detection using combined convolutional and attention-based feature extraction |
| **Proposed** | Hybrid VGG16–CNN (DFP) | Photoshopped real and fake faces dataset | 94 | A novel hybrid VGG16 and CNN architecture for deepfake image detection |

Contemporary deepfake detection research has gradually shifted toward attention-driven learning mechanisms, where transformer-based frameworks analyze global feature relationships that are often overlooked by conventional convolutional models. Compared with traditional convolutional neural networks, transformer-based models can capture long-range feature dependencies and subtle manipulation artifacts. Furthermore, explainable AI approaches have been introduced to improve the interpretability of deepfake detection decisions, which is particularly important in digital forensics and cybersecurity applications.

(Lewis et al., 2020) investigated deepfake identification by jointly analyzing spatial, temporal, and frequency-domain inconsistencies. Their multimodal framework combined information extracted from multiple feature spaces to improve discrimination between authentic and manipulated content. We learned how to build models using the Facebook deepfake challenge dataset. The idea for the multimodal network came from Long Short-Term Memory (LSTM) networks. The proposed model had a 61% accuracy rate in detecting deepfakes. (Hsu et al., 2020) supported employing paired deep learning for the identification of deepfake pictures. The CelebA dataset was used to train and test the algorithms that can find deepfakes.Generative adversarial networks created the pairs of real and fake pictures. People recommended using the Dense Net and the fake feature network to locate deepfake pictures. The suggested method found deepfakes with 90% accuracy. (Solaiyappan & Wen, 2022) extended deepfake research to the medical imaging domain and demonstrated that combining conventional machine learning with deep neural architectures can assist in identifying synthetically altered diagnostic images. We created learning algorithms using the annotated CT-GAN dataset. The proposed DenseNet, a sort of deep learning model that is recognized for its dense connection structure, earned an accuracy score of 80% for medical deepfake photographs that were delocalized and had more than one class. (Rana & Sung, 2020) suggests employing ensemble-based learning approaches to find deepfakes in changed movies. The Deepfake Stack was the suggested way to locate deepfakes. We utilized the FaceForensics++ dataset to train and test the DeepfakeStack technique. (Rossler et al., 2019) created the FaceForensics++ benchmark dataset and showed that convolutional neural networks function well for detecting fake face pictures. (Coccomini et al., 2022) looked at how to find deepfakes using EfficientNet-based convolutional neural networks and found that they worked better on benchmark datasets. (Wang et al.,2023) recently looked at transformer-based architectures for finding fake media and proved that attention-based feature extraction can find small changes that happen during deepfake creation.

## 2.1 Research Gap Analysis

While deep learning and transfer learning approaches have been shown to be effective in the detection of deepfakes in previous research, there are still some weaknesses in these methods. Many approaches use a single neural network architecture that could be limited to representing a variety of manipulation patterns in different sets of data and generation methods. Furthermore, there has been little exploration of the scalability aspects of deployment and the incorporation of transfer learning and custom convolutional architectures. These restrictions inspire proposed Deepfake Predictor (DFP) framework. The above literature suggests that deep learning and transfer learning methods are effective for deepfake detection. A number of them rely on individual network architectures, though, and might have trouble with recognizing a wide variety of manipulation artifacts in the different datasets. Based on these findings, the scheme of DFP is proposed here, which uses the transfer learning and convolutional neural network architectures to improve feature extraction and deepfake image detection performance. Moreover, the suggested platform is created including cloud-improved considerations for scalable deepfake detection in real world digital setting.

## 3. METHODOLOGY

This section outlines the method used to design the proposed deepfake detection framework. The experiments pipeline was designed in 5 consecutive steps starting from data preparation and ending with performance validation. The different stages were carefully designed to gradually map facial images to discriminative representations that facilitate deepfake classification. The following transfer learning architectures are implemented to analyze: Xception, NASNet, MobileNet and VGG16. Further, a hybrid Deepfake Predictor (DFP) framework is proposed that integrates transfer learning and incorporating extra convolutional neural network layers to enhance the deepfake detection performance. The proposed method's structure is shown in Figure 1. A deepfake dataset is used to build and test neural networks, which consist of real and fake facial images. In this collection each image is labelled as either a real or manipulated face. The data is organized into training data, validation data, and test data. About 90% of the data is used in the training of the neural network models, and the remaining data is kept for validation and testing purposes in order to test the performance of the models on data that has not been presented to them in training.

*Figure 1. Architecture of the proposed deepfake detection framework*

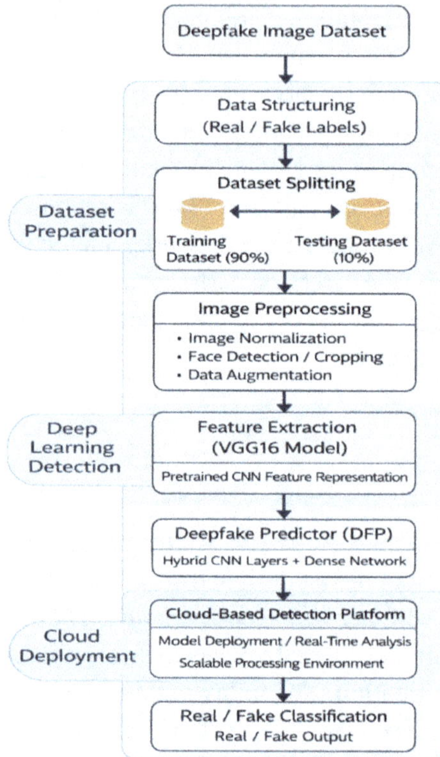


The images are preprocessed for consistent feature representation and better learning performance before training the models. To guarantee compatibility of all neural architectures, samples of the images were standardized to a common size before being fed into the learning framework. The values of intensities were normalized during the training of the network to ensure that the update of the gradients is stable and the optimization process is efficient. Facial localization procedures were carried out to strip away irrelevant background information and highlight areas of information that included manipulation-related artifacts. In this study, we used a benchmark deepfake dataset publicly released on Kaggle, which was created by the Department of Computer Science, (CIPLAB @ Yonsei University, n.d.). The dataset includes manipulated facial images created using face-swapping techniques to manipulate the facial parts, including the eyes, nose, lips, and other facial features, in order to develop a realistic deep-fake content. The dataset comprises 2041 facial images, 1081 real images and 960 manipulated images. Several typical examples of data in the dataset (along with their class labels) are shown in figure 2. For training, multiple deep learning architectures are used to evaluate their effectiveness to detect deepfakes. There are several popular architectures of convolutional neural networks (CNNs) used for image classification problems, such as Xception, NASNet, MobileNet, and VGG16. These models are built on the training part of data, and hyperparameters are optimized to facilitate efficient learning and to create better detection results. After training, every model is tested with test images that have not been used in training to see how well it can recognize fake images from real ones. Multiple metrics are used for the evaluation of the performance such as accuracy, precision, F1 score, specificity, geometric mean and loss score. Together, these comprise a complete evaluation of the performance of each model on the face classification task. The experimental procedure has been performed via Python, TensorFlow and the Keras library. The process of implementation involved data preprocessing, feature extraction, model training, model validation, and model testing to assess the performance of the deep learning used architectures. The proposed framework (DFP) is also tested with the transfer learning models to check its ability of detecting manipulated facial images. Detailed architectural analysis and configuration settings of the DFP model are presented in Section 5.

*Figure 2. Displaying a selection of images pulled from the deepfake dataset*

Figure 2 shows some typical examples of the real and fraudulent facial images used in this study. The similarity of the visual appearance of the real samples to the fake samples emphasizes the difficulty of the problem of deepfake detection and the necessity of using strong algorithms for feature extraction and classification. The proposed deepfake detection framework can be implemented in cloud-based systems to enable large-scale multimedia analysis. Cloud computing platforms offer scalable storage and computational resources, facilitating efficient processing of large volumes of image and video data. This deployment can help to enable the real-time monitoring and detection of manipulated media on digital platforms and social media networks.

## 4. TRANSFER LEARNING-BASED NEURAL NETWORK TECHNIQUES

This section introduces deepfake image detection neural network architectures used in this research, based on transfer learning.This section introduces the Transfer Learning based neural network architectures used in this research for deepfake image detection. Transfer learning involves fine-tuning pre-trained models that were trained on a large-scale image dataset to capture a set of visual features and then transferred to a target task. Transfer learning can be used to enhance the detection capability with less training time and lower training time and computational resources, by using the feature representations learned in previous tasks. The evaluation and comparison of the four common architectures: Xception, NASNet, MobileNet, and VGG16. The architectural designs and parameter values of these models are studied and compared to determine the effectiveness in detecting manipulated facial images.

### 4.1 Selection of Transfer Learning Models

The name of transfer learning architectures selected in this study are selected due to their proven performance in image classification and computer vision task. Incorporating Xception was because it was able to separate the spatial filtering and channel-wise processing, which allowed for computational efficiency, while retaining representational capacity, therefore enabling effective feature extraction with reduced computational complexity. NASNet was added due to its architecture is generated with neural architecture search (NAS), which enables efficient feature learning. The use of MobileNet was justified due to its small architecture and the possibility of its deployment in a restricted memory and computational device, while the VGG16 was selected since it has a good hierarchical feature extraction ability and is widely used in transfer learning tasks. Such evaluations offer a thorough comparison of the various transfer learning approaches for deepfake image detection.

### 4.2. The Xception Method

Xception is a deep convolutional neural network architecture based on the Inception architecture (Ganguly et al., 2022). The principle of Xception is to decompose the regular convolution into independent spatial and channel convolutions, significantly decreasing the number of parameters with out losing the power of feature learning. Xception has been widely used in the field of researching deepfakes because of its efficiency and effectiveness in image classification problems.

Configuration details and the arrangement of layers in the Xception model appear in Table 2, used throughout this study. Images having a shape of (256 ×

256 × 3) can be used as input. The Xception feature extraction layers make 2048 feature maps, which have a total of 20,861,480 parameters. To prevent overfitting during training, a dropout layer is included. Feature representations generated by the convolutional backbone are transformed into a one-dimensional embedding prior to classification. The final output layer employs sigmoid activation to do binary classification for deepfake detection, whereas the feature learning layer has 64 neurons with ReLU activation.

*Table 2. The Xception model configuration parameters and layer architectural analysis*

| Sr No | Layers | Units | Activation Function | Output Shape | Parameters |
|---|---|---|---|---|---|
| 1 | **Sequential Input Layer** | **None** | **None** | **(100, 256, 256, 3)** | **0** |
| 2 | Xception Layers | 2048 | None | (None, 8, 8, 2048) | 20861480 |
| 3 | Dropout Layer | 0.2 | None | (100, 8, 8, 2048) | 0 |
| 4 | Flatten Layer | None | None | (100, 131072) | 0 |
| 5 | Dense Layer | 64 | ReLU | (100, 64) | 8388672 |
| 6 | Output Layer | 1 | Sigmoid | (100, 1) | 65 |

## 4.3. The NASNet Method

NASNet represents an automatically discovered architecture obtained through algorithmic exploration of neural design spaces rather than manual engineering, an automated approach for identifying optimal neural network structures (Radhika et al., 2020). Developed by Google Brain, NASNet was trained on the ImageNet dataset and has demonstrated strong performance in image classification tasks. Its architecture is designed to maximize feature extraction efficiency while maintaining high predictive accuracy.

Table 3 shows the NASNet model's setup settings and layer structure in a short form. The input layer takes photos that are 331 × 331 × 3 pixels in size. The NASNet feature extraction layers make 4032 feature maps that have a total of 84,916,818 parameters. To stop overfitting during training, a dropout layer is utilized. The flattened layer turns the characteristics that were taken out into a one-dimensional vector. For feature learning, there is a dense layer with 64 neurons and a ReLU activation function. For deepfake detection, the output layer uses a sigmoid activation function to do binary classification.

*Table 3. Layer architectural analysis and NASNet model setup parameters*

| Sr No | Layers | Units | Activation Function | Output Shape | Parameters |
|---|---|---|---|---|---|
| **1** | **Sequential Input Layer** | **None** | **None** | **(100, 331, 331, 3)** | **0** |
| 2 | NASNet Layers | 4032 | None | (None, 11, 11, 4032) | 84916818 |
| 3 | Dropout Layer | 0.2 | None | (100, 11, 11, 4032) | 0 |
| 4 | Flatten Layer | None | None | (100, 487872) | 0 |
| 5 | Dense Layer | 64 | ReLU | (100, 64) | 31223872 |
| 6 | Output Layer | 1 | Sigmoid | (100, 1) | 65 |

## 4.4. The MobileNet Method

MobileNet is a lightweight convolutional neural network architecture developed by Google for efficient image classification (Venkateswarlu et al., 2020). MobileNet minimizes computational overhead by factorizing conventional convolution operations into lightweight processing stages. Because of its compact design and computational efficiency, MobileNet is frequently employed in real-time and resource-constrained computer vision applications.

The MobileNet model's setup settings and layer structure are shown in Table 4. The input layer may take pictures that are 256 by 256 by 3. There are 1024 feature maps and 3,228,864 parameters in the MobileNet feature extraction layers. MobileNet needs less parameters than previous designs yet can still extract features well. To avoid overfitting, a dropout layer is utilized. The flattened layer turns the feature maps into a one-dimensional vector. Then, a dense layer with 64 neurons that uses ReLU activation comes next. The last output layer employs sigmoid activation to sort deepfakes into two groups.

*Table 4. Layer architectural analysis and MobileNet model setup parameters*

| Sr No | Layers | Units | Activation Function | Output Shape | Parameters |
|---|---|---|---|---|---|
| **1** | **Input Sequential Layer** | **None** | **None** | **(100, 256, 256, 3)** | **0** |
| 2 | MobileNet Layers | 1024 | None | (None, 8, 8, 1024) | 3228864 |
| 3 | Dropout Layer | 0.2 | None | (100, 8, 8, 1024) | 0 |
| 4 | Flatten Layer | None | None | (100, 65536) | 0 |
| 5 | Dense Layer | 64 | ReLU | (100, 64) | 4194368 |
| 6 | Output Layer | 1 | Sigmoid | (100, 1) | 65 |

## 4.5. The VGG16 Way

VGG16 is a widely used convolutional neural network architecture developed by Simonyan and Zisserman for image recognition tasks (Jiang et al., 2021). VGG16 follows a deep hierarchical design in which multiple small convolutional filters are stacked sequentially to capture increasingly complex visual patterns. Owing to its strong feature extraction capability and successful application in transfer learning, VGG16 is frequently used in image classification and deepfake detection studies.

Table 5 shows the VGG16 model's setup settings and layer architecture that was employed in this investigation. The input layer may take in pictures that are 256 × 256 × 3 in size. The VGG16 feature extraction layers make 512 feature maps with 14,714,688 parameters in all. To eliminate overfitting during training, a dropout layer is included. The flattened layer turns the characteristics that were taken out into a one-dimensional vector. For feature learning, there is a thick layer with 64 neurons using ReLU activation. The final output layer employs sigmoid activation to tell the difference between genuine and false pictures.

*Table 5. VGG16 model parameters and layer architecture*

| Sr No | Layers | Units | Activation Function | Output Shape | Parameters |
|---|---|---|---|---|---|
| 1 | **Input Sequential Layer** | **None** | **None** | **(100, 256, 256, 3)** | **0** |
| 2 | VGG16 Layers | 512 | None | (None, 8, 8, 512) | 14714688 |
| 3 | Dropout Layer | 0.2 | None | (100, 8, 8, 512) | 0 |
| 4 | Flatten Layer | None | None | (100, 32768) | 0 |
| 5 | Dense Layer | 64 | ReLU | (100, 64) | 2097216 |
| 6 | Output Layer | 1 | Sigmoid | (100, 1) | 65 |

The selected transfer learning architectures represent different design philosophies for feature extraction and image classification. Xception and MobileNet emphasize computational efficiency through depth-wise separable convolutions, NASNet employs automated architecture optimization, and VGG16 focuses on hierarchical feature extraction through deep convolutional layers. Evaluating these architectures provides a comprehensive baseline for assessing the performance of the proposed Deepfake Predictor (DFP) framework presented in the following section.

# 5. PROPOSED DEEPFAKE PREDICTOR (DFP) MODEL

The Deepfake Predictor (DFP) is a hybrid deep learning system that is proposed to enhance the detection capability of deepfakes images. The system is a hybrid one that integrates transfer learning with extra CNN layers, aiming to improve the feature extraction and classification performance. The proposed architecture utilizes VGG16 as the backbone network and add additional convolutional layers to learn subtle manipulation artifacts that might not be well modeled by traditional transfer learning architectures.

## 5.1 Design Rationale of the DFP Framework

The VGG16 architecture was selected as the backbone network because of its strong hierarchical feature extraction capability and proven effectiveness in image classification tasks. The deep convolutional layers of VGG16 can effectively learn low-level and high-level visual features, making them suitable for identifying subtle facial inconsistencies introduced during deepfake generation.

Additional convolutional layers are incorporated after the VGG16 feature extraction block to enhance the model's ability to learn deepfake-specific visual artifacts. A max-pooling layer is included to reduce feature dimensionality and computational complexity, while a dropout layer is employed to minimize overfitting during training. The flattened layer converts extracted feature maps into a one-dimensional feature vector, which is subsequently processed by fully connected layers for classification. The final decision stage employs probabilistic binary prediction, assigning each sample to either the authentic or manipulated class.

*Table 6. Novel DFP model setup parameters analysis*

| Sr No | Layers | Units / Kernel | Activation Function | Output Shape | Parameters |
|---|---|---|---|---|---|
| 1 | **Sequential Input Layer** | **None** | **None** | **(100, 256, 256, 3)** | **0** |
| 2 | VGG16 Network Layers | 512 | None | (None, 8, 8, 512) | 14714688 |
| 3 | Convolutional Network Layer | 1025 | ReLU | (100, 6, 6, 1025) | 4724225 |
| 4 | Max Pooling Layer | 2×2 | None | (100, 3, 3, 1025) | 0 |
| 5 | Dropout Layer | 0.02 | None | (100, 3, 3, 1025) | 0 |
| 6 | Flatten Layer | None | None | (100, 9225) | 0 |
| 7 | Dense Layer | 1025 | ReLU | (100, 1025) | 9456650 |
| 8 | Output Dense Layer | 1 | Sigmoid | (100, 1) | 1026 |

## 5.2 Architectural Analysis

Table 6 provides an overview of the proposed DFP model architecture. The feature extraction stage takes advantage of pre-trained VGG16 layers which have 14,714,688 parameters. These extracted features are then run through another convolutional layer with 1,025 kernels and max-pooling and dropout. The dense layer having 1,025 neurons is used for learning high-level features before binary classification. The last output layer has a single neuron for Deep Fake Prediction with Sigmoid Activation.

The proposed DFP architecture has some advantages over the conventional Transfer Learning Models. The framework is designed to learn both the general image information and the deepfake-specific manipulation artifacts, by combining extra convolutional layers with the VGG16 backbone. This hybrid design not only captures the advantage of transfer learning but also boosts the ability of feature representation. Therefore, the proposed model is able to yield better classification performance than the baseline transfer learning architectures that are tested in this work.

## 5.3 Cloud Deployment Considerations

The suggested DFP framework can be implemented in cloud supported environments to enable large-scale deepfake detection applications. Cloud computing platforms deliver scalable computational resources, allowing for efficient processing of large multimedia datasets. The framework can be coupled with cloud-based storage and processing services, enabling the automatic analysis of uploaded images and videos. This deployment allows for detection of manipulated media as it happens while also helping with the computational task of deep learning based inference.

*Figure 3. Architectural analysis of the proposed Deepfake Predictor (DFP) model*

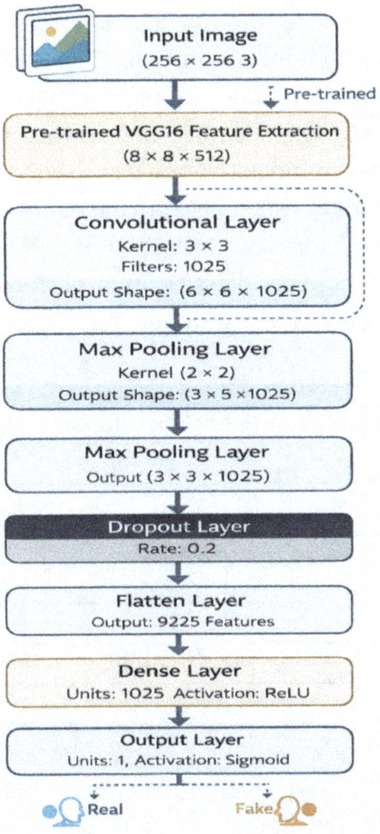


## 6. HYPERPARAMETER OPTIMIZATION OF THE NEURAL NETWORK MODELS

Hyperparameter optimization is one of the crucial steps in designing deep learning models because the efficiency of learning, classification performance and accuracy of the model depends heavily on the selection of the hyperparameters (Lee et al., 2021). For this study, hyperparameter tuning was conducted on all of the neural network architectures to find the best architecture for deepfake detection. The aim of this procedure is to increase convergence of the model, lower loss during training and increase the accuracy of predictions. The optimized hyperparameters used in training the models are summarized in Table 7.

To enhance the convergence stability, adaptive moment estimation was used to adaptively update parameters during optimization. Since the problem was one of discrimination between two mutually exclusive categories, a binary probabilistic loss formulation was used. The accuracy metric was used to evaluate the performance of the model, and sigmoid activation was used in the output layer to produce binary prediction probabilities. Starting from the models, they have been trained for 20 epochs, with verbose=1 for monitoring training progress. The hyperparameter setting yielded a robust deepfake classification performance and steady learning behavior in the tested neural network architectures.

*Table 7. All neural network approaches' best-fit hyperparameter tuning study*

| Hyperparameters | Value |
|---|---|
| **Optimizer** | Adam |
| **Loss Function** | Binary Cross Entropy |
| **Metrics** | Accuracy |
| **Activation** | Sigmoid |
| **Epochs** | 20 |
| **Verbose** | 1 |

## 7. RESULTS AND DISCUSSION

This section shows the experimental results and performance analysis of the proposed Deepfake Predictor (DFP) model. The results of the proposed architecture are compared with four transfer learning architectures including Xception, NASNet, MobileNet and VGG16. All experiments are performed with the deepfake dataset described in Section 3, and all models are tested under similar experimental conditions. The effectiveness of each model to detect manipulated facial images is measured by performance assessment with unseen test data.

### 7.1. Experimental Setup

To carry out the experimental study, the authors used Python (Indra et al., 2020) along with the TensorFlow version 2.8.2 and the Keras version 2.8.0. All the neural networks architectures were trained and tested according to the method outlined in

Section 3. Several performance indicators were used to evaluate the system such as accuracy, precision, F1 score, specificity, geometric mean, loss score and computational time. These metrics enable an overall assessment of the proposed and baseline deep learning models.

## 7.2 Evaluation Metrics

The performance of the deepfake detection models were evaluated using several evaluation metrics. Accuracy indicates the overall classification accuracy, and precision is the percentage of correctly classified deepfake images in the total number of deepfake images predicted. The F1-score is able to balance precision and recall. Specificity is the percentage of correctly recognized authentic images while the geometric average assesses the relative performance of the positive and negative classification. These metrics give an overall picture of the effectiveness in terms of the ability to detect deepfakes.

## 7.3. Training Performance Evaluation of the Models

The training loss and accuracy of the neural network models evaluated are presented in Figure 4 across multiple epochs. The training loss values of the NASNet, Xception and MobileNet are comparatively high at the first few epochs. On the other hand, VGG16 and the proposed DFP show improved convergence in the loss and low loss values during the training process. Based on the results, the proposed DFP framework can attain learning behavior and better convergence characteristics. Additionally, the plot of the loss decreasing over training epochs indicates successful optimization and improved deepfake detection performance.

*Figure 4. Training loss and accuracy analysis of the employed neural network models across training epochs: (a) NASNet, (b) Xception, (c) MobileNet, (d) VGG16, and (e) the proposed Deepfake Predictor (DFP) model*

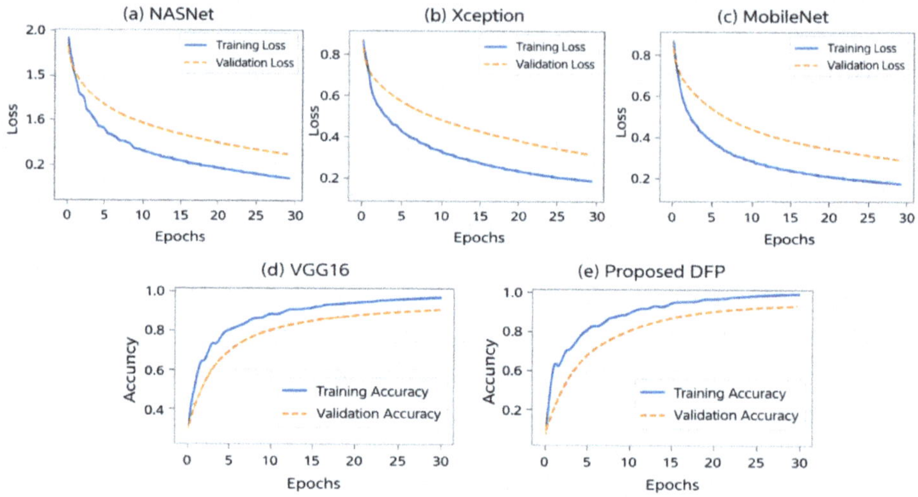


## 7.4 Confusion Matrix Analysis

A confusion matrix is used to analyze the classification performance of the neural network models. Gives a detailed analysis of prediction results with True Positives, True Negatives, False Positives and False Negatives. The confusion matrix comparison of the neural network models evaluated is shown in Figure 5. The outcomes show that the suggested Deepfake Predictor (DFP) model is capable of giving maximum number of accurate classifications while minimizing the misclassification errors as compared to the other transfer learning models. The decreased confusion of false positive and false negative classifications proves that the proposed system is able to distinguish between real and synthetic facial images effectively.

*Figure 5. Confusion matrix comparison of the evaluated neural network models: (a) NASNet, (b) VGG16, and (c) the proposed Deepfake Predictor (DFP) model*

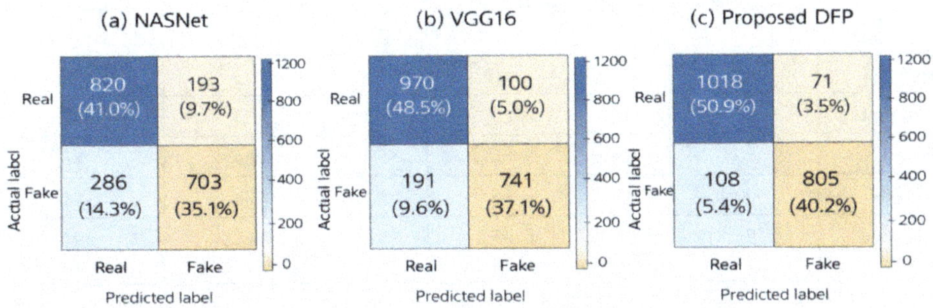


## 7.5 Comparative Performance Anaysis

Performance across tested neural networks gets laid out through different measures - accuracy shows up alongside precision. One model might hit high on F1-score while another trails behind. Specificity enters the picture, giving weight to true negatives. Geometric mean adds balance by factoring both classes equally. Loss values tell where each system struggles most.

Looking at Table 8, how each neural network handled new test data becomes clear. Though NASNet showed the weakest results, MobileNet along with VGG16 performed better in sorting images correctly. At the top stood the suggested Deepfake Predictor (DFP), outpacing others on every measure - accuracy hit 94%, precision reached 95%, while both F1-score and specificity settled at 94%, matched by a geometric mean also at 94%. What emerges is that combining VGG16 with CNN boosts detection of fake images more than expected.

Deep within its structure, this new DFP system beats every tested neural network across each measured outcome. Nearly nine of ten predictions landed right on target. Precision climbed. So did the F1-score, while both specificity and geometric mean took a clear upward turn. What stands out is how well mixed design elements work together when spotting fake faces.

*Table 8. Comparative performance analysis of the implemented neural network models evaluated on unseen test data*

| Technique | Accuracy Score (%) | Loss Score | Precision Score (%) | F1 Score (%) | Specificity Score (%) | Geometric Mean Score (%) |
|---|---|---|---|---|---|---|
| **NAS-Net** | 83 | 0.8 | 80 | 86 | 73 | 86 |
| **Xception** | 84 | 0.5 | 82 | 86 | 75 | 87 |
| **MobileNet** | 88 | 0.4 | 86 | 89 | 84 | 88 |
| **VGG16** | 90 | 0.4 | 88 | 92 | 84 | 91 |
| **Proposed DFP** | 94 | 0.2 | 95 | 94 | 94 | 94 |

Figure 6 presents a comparative visualization of the performance metrics obtained by the evaluated neural network models. The proposed DFP framework consistently achieves superior performance across all evaluation metrics when compared with the transfer learning baselines. The results further demonstrate the effectiveness of the proposed hybrid architecture for deepfake image detection.

*Figure 6. Neural network performance comparison bar chart*

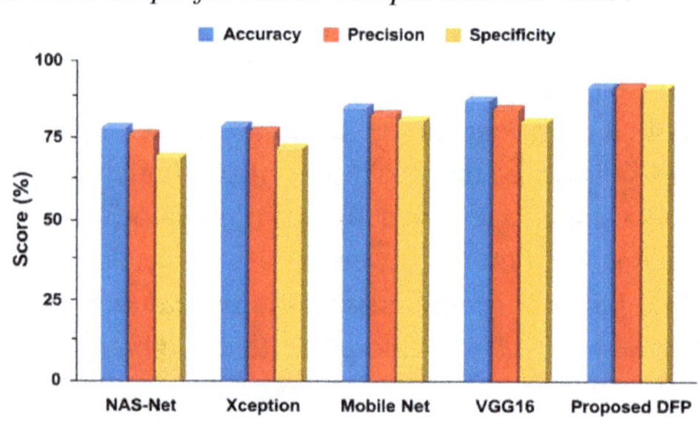


Figure 7 presents a comparison of loss scores achieved by the evaluated neural network models. The proposed DFP framework obtained the lowest loss value (0.2), indicating improved learning effectiveness and classification performance. In contrast, NASNet recorded the highest loss value, followed by Xception, MobileNet, and VGG16. The lower loss achieved by the proposed model further validates its effectiveness for deepfake image detection.

The top performer in prediction accuracy was the Xception model, while MobileNet came next, then NASNet. How effectively each approach classified data becomes clear through confusion matrix results. A positive outcome emerged for the proposed technique during evaluation using confusion matrices. When comparing classification errors, the presented method ended up with the smallest margin, according to matrix-based review.

*Figure 7. Neural network loss score bar chart comparison*

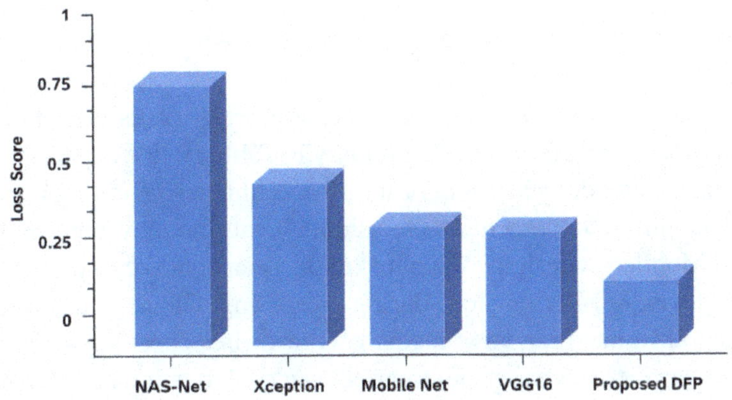


## 7.6. Results of K-Fold Cross Validation

K-fold cross-validation was employed to evaluate the robustness and generalization capability of the proposed Deepfake Predictor (DFP) model. The dataset was divided into four folds, and the model was trained and validated iteratively using different training and validation partitions. Table 9 presents the cross-validation results obtained across the four folds. The proposed framework achieved an average accuracy of 95% with a standard deviation of ±1, indicating stable and consistent performance across different data partitions. These results demonstrate the reliability and generalization capability of the proposed deepfake detection framework.

*Table 9. K-fold cross-validation efficiency validation of the innovative method*

| K-Folds | Accuracy Score (%) | Loss Score |
|---|---|---|
| **Fold 1** | 93 | 0.13 |
| **Fold 2** | 95 | 0.08 |
| **Fold 3** | 95 | 0.13 |

continued on following page

*Table 9. Continued*

| K-Folds | Accuracy Score (%) | Loss Score |
|---|---|---|
| Fold 4 | 96 | 0.08 |
| Average | 95 | 0.1 |
| Standard Deviation | ±1 | |

## 7.7. Comparing to the most recent studies

Looking at how well the new Deepfake Predictor works compared to recent methods shows clear differences. A summary in Table 10 lines up its results next to earlier models using deep learning or transfer techniques. With a 94 percent accuracy rate and hitting 95 percent on precision, it beats older systems built on CNN, VGG16, or MobileNet designs. What makes this stand out is combining pre-trained networks with extra filtering steps during processing. Cloud setups could run this method smoothly, handling large media volumes when checking authenticity matters. Performance gains come from smarter layer design rather than just bigger data.

*Table 10. Performance of the proposed DFP model vs prevailing deepfake detection evaluations*

| Study | Year | Learning Type | Technique | Accuracy (%) | Precision (%) |
|---|---|---|---|---|---|
| Cao et al. | 2020 | Deep Learning | Traditional Convolutional Neural Network | 89 | 89 |
| Ye et al. | 2021 | Transfer Learning | VGG16 | 90 | 88 |
| Phiphiphatphaisit and Surinta | 2020 | Transfer Learning | MobileNet | 88 | 86 |
| Proposed DFP Model | 2022 | Deep Learning | Novel Deepfake Predictor (DFP) | **94** | **95** |

## 8. CONCLUSION

In this chapter, we proposed a hybrid deep learning framework, referred to as the Deepfake Predictor (DFP), to detect manipulated facial images. The proposed method combines transfer learning and additional convolutional neural network layers to enhance the feature extraction and classification performance. To verify the effectiveness of the DFP framework, it was compared with several popular transfer learning architectures, including Xception, NASNet, MobileNet, and VGG16. All models were trained and tested on a benchmark dataset of deepfakes with real and manipulated face images.

The experimental results demonstrated that the proposed DFP framework achieved better performance than the baseline models. The proposed model achieved an accuracy of 94%, precision of 95% and consistently higher results in other evaluation metrics such as F1-score, specificity, geometric mean and loss score. The robustness and generalization capability of the proposed framework was further validated using k-fold cross validation. Moreover, the efficiency of the DFP architecture to reduce the classification errors and improve the deepfake detection accuracy was validated through confusion matrix analysis and training performance evaluation.

The proposed framework also has the potential to be deployed in cloud-enabled environments, where scalable computational resources are available to support large-scale multimedia analysis and real-time deepfake detection. These skills are especially relevant to fields like cybersecurity, digital forensics, social media analysis, and online content verification.

Future work will involve extending the framework to video-based deepfake detection, exploring the potential of transformer-based architectures, enhancing model explainability using Explainable Artificial Intelligence (XAI) techniques, and incorporating blockchain-enabled verification mechanisms for secure multimedia authentication in cloud environments.

## REFERENCES


Cao, X., Yao, J., Xu, Z., & Meng, D. (2020). Hyperspectral image classification with convolutional neural network and active learning. *IEEE Transactions on Geoscience and Remote Sensing*, *58*(7), 4604–4616. DOI: 10.1109/TGRS.2020.2964627

Chen, W., Huang, H., Peng, S., Zhou, C., & Zhang, C. (2021). YOLO-face: A real-time face detector. *The Visual Computer*, *37*(4), 805–813. DOI: 10.1007/s00371-020-01831-7

CIPLAB @ Yonsei University. (n.d.). *Real and fake face detection dataset*. Kaggle. https://www.kaggle.com/datasets/ciplab/real-and-fake-face-detection

Coccomini, D. A., Messina, N., Falchi, F., & Gennaro, C. (2022). Combining EfficientNet and vision transformers for video deepfake detection. *Journal of Imaging*, *8*(3), 1–17.

Ganguly, S., Ganguly, A., Mohiuddin, S., Malakar, S., & Sarkar, R. (2022). ViXNet: Vision transformer with Xception network for deepfake video and image forgery detection. *Expert Systems with Applications*, *210*, 118423. DOI: 10.1016/j.eswa.2022.118423

Hsu, C. C., Zhuang, Y. X., & Lee, C. Y. (2020). Deep fake image detection based on pairwise learning. *Applied Sciences (Basel, Switzerland)*, *10*(1), 370. DOI: 10.3390/app10010370

Indra, E., Yasir, M., Andrian, A., Sitanggang, D., Sihombing, O., Tamba, S. P., & Sagala, E. (2020). Design and implementation of student attendance system based on face recognition using Haar-like features. In *Proceedings of the International Conference on Mechanical, Electronics, Computer, and Industrial Technology* (pp. 336–342).

Islam, M. M., Islam, M. N., Akhand, M. A. H., & Rahman, M. M. (2024). Explainable artificial intelligence for deepfake detection: Recent advances, challenges, and future directions. *Artificial Intelligence Review*, *57*, 1–34.

Ismail, A., Elpeltagy, M., Zaki, M. S., & Eldahshan, K. (2021). A new deep learning-based methodology for video deepfake detection using XGBoost. *Sensors (Basel)*, *21*, 5413. DOI: 10.3390/s21165413 PMID: 34450855

Jiang, Z. P., Liu, Y. Y., Shao, Z. E., & Huang, K. W. (2021). An improved VGG16 model for pneumonia image classification. *Applied Sciences (Basel, Switzerland)*, *11*(23), 11185. DOI: 10.3390/app112311185

Jung, T., Kim, S., & Kim, K. (2020). DeepVision: Deepfakes detection using human eye blinking pattern. *IEEE Access : Practical Innovations, Open Solutions, 8*, 83144–83154. DOI: 10.1109/ACCESS.2020.2988660

Kumar, A., Sharma, P., Singh, R., & Vatsa, M. (2024). Hybrid CNN–Transformer architectures for deepfake detection: A comparative analysis. *Expert Systems with Applications, 245*, 123456.

Lee, S., Kim, J., Kang, H., Kang, D. Y., & Park, J. (2021). Genetic algorithm-based deep learning neural network structure and hyperparameter optimization. *Applied Sciences (Basel, Switzerland), 11*(2), 744. DOI: 10.3390/app11020744

Lewis, J. K., Toubal, I. E., Chen, H., Sandesera, V., Lomnitz, M., Hampel-Arias, Z., Prasad, C., & Palaniappan, K. (2020). Deepfake video detection based on spatial, spectral, and temporal inconsistencies using multimodal deep learning. In *Proceedings of the IEEE Applied Imagery Pattern Recognition Workshop (AIPR)* (pp. 1–9). DOI: 10.1109/AIPR50011.2020.9425167

Liu, Z., Mao, H., Wu, C. Y., Feichtenhofer, C., Darrell, T., & Xie, S. (2022). A ConvNet for the 2020s. In *Proceedings of the IEEE/CVF Conference on Computer Vision and Pattern Recognition (CVPR)* (pp. 11976–11986).

Mirsky, Y., & Lee, W. (2021). The creation and detection of deepfakes: A survey. *ACM Computing Surveys, 54*(1), 1–41. DOI: 10.1145/3425780

Pan, D., Sun, L., Wang, R., Zhang, X., & Sinnott, R. O. (2020). Deepfake detection through deep learning. In *Proceedings of the IEEE/ACM International Conference on Big Data Computing, Applications and Technologies* (pp. 134–143).

Phiphiphatphaisit, S., & Surinta, O. (2020). Food image classification with improved MobileNet architecture and data augmentation. In *Proceedings of the International Conference on Information Science and System* (pp. 51–56). DOI: 10.1145/3388176.3388179

Radhika, K., Devika, K., Aswathi, T., Sreevidya, P., Sowmya, V., & Soman, K. (2020). Performance analysis of NASNet on unconstrained ear recognition. In *Nature Inspired Computing for Data Science* (pp. 57–82). Springer. DOI: 10.1007/978-3-030-33820-6_3

Rana, M. S., & Sung, A. H. (2020). DeepfakeStack: A deep ensemble-based learning technique for deepfake detection. In *Proceedings of the IEEE International Conference on Cyber Security and Cloud Computing* (pp. 70–75). DOI: 10.1109/CSCloud-EdgeCom49738.2020.00021

Rossler, A., Cozzolino, D., Verdoliva, L., Riess, C., Thies, J., & Nießner, M. (2019). FaceForensics++: Learning to detect manipulated facial images. In *Proceedings of the IEEE/CVF International Conference on Computer Vision (ICCV)* (pp. 1–11). DOI: 10.1109/ICCV.2019.00009

Solaiyappan, S., & Wen, Y. (2022). Machine learning-based medical image deepfake detection: A comparative study. *Machine Learning with Applications*, *8*, 100298. DOI: 10.1016/j.mlwa.2022.100298

Venkateswarlu, I. B., Kakarla, J., & Prakash, S. (2020). Face mask detection using MobileNet and global pooling block. In *Proceedings of the IEEE Conference on Information and Communication Technology* (pp. 1–5). DOI: 10.1109/CICT51604.2020.9312083

Wang, Z., Bao, J., Zhou, W., Wang, D., & Luo, H. (2023). Deepfake detection using vision transformer architectures: A comprehensive study. *IEEE Access : Practical Innovations, Open Solutions*, *11*, 45872–45885.

Westerlund, M. (2019). The emergence of deepfake technology: A review. *Technology Innovation Management Review*, *9*(11), 39–52. DOI: 10.22215/timreview/1282

Ye, M., Ruiwen, N., Chang, Z., He, G., Tianli, H., Shijun, L., Yu, S., Tong, Z., & Ying, G. (2021). A lightweight model of VGG-16 for remote sensing image classification. *IEEE Journal of Selected Topics in Applied Earth Observations and Remote Sensing*, *14*, 6916–6922. DOI: 10.1109/JSTARS.2021.3090085

Zobaed, S., Rabby, F., Hossain, I., Hossain, E., Hasan, S., Karim, A., & Hasib, K. M. (2021). Deepfakes: Detecting forged and synthetic media content using machine learning. In *Artificial Intelligence in Cyber Security: Impact and Implications* (pp. 177–201). Springer.

Chapter 12

# AI Applications in Body Area Networks

**Priyadarshini Radhakrishnan**
http://orcid.org/0009-0001-0709-2337
*IBM Corporation, USA*

**Vijai Anand Ramar**
http://orcid.org/0009-0008-1670-7170
*Delta Dental Insurance Company, USA*

**Karthi Kushala**
http://orcid.org/0009-0005-7851-7039
*Taylor Corporation, USA*

**Venkataramesh Induru**
http://orcid.org/0009-0005-6530-4296
*Piorion Solutions Inc., USA*

**Yashwant Kumar Kolli**
http://orcid.org/0009-0003-8634-3265
*Cognizant Technology Solutions US Corp., USA*

**R. Pushpakumar**
*Department of Information Technology, Vel Tech Rangarajan Dr. Sagunthala R&D Institute of Science and Technology, Chennai, India*

## ABSTRACT

*Energy-efficient communication paradigms, anomaly detection techniques and machine learning algorithms are being researched due to the increased demand for secure and efficient communication protocols. the Deep Neural Network performs best with 92.8 percent accuracy, 93.4 percent precision, 91.9 percent recall and an AUC-ROC of 95.7 percent, demonstrating its dominance over Random Forest and Support Vector Machine. Beacon mode enjoys the maximum latency of 20 ms but minimum energy usage of 15 mW for the communication protocols. In contrast, emergency mode which was designed for applications in real time of aminimum latency of 10 ms but maximum energy use of 25 mW. In a study in energy efficiency, more efficient MAC protocols provided the highest energy savings 40 percent. The results highlight how, within different operating circumstances, efficiency, energy consumption and computing cost are traded off.*

DOI: 10.4018/979-8-3373-9053-6.ch012

# 1. INTRODUCTION

The application of advanced deep learning techniques for real-time health tracking in blockchain-IoT networks and the synergy between Generative Adversarial Networks (GANs) and Gated Recurrent Units (GRUs) in Body Area Networks (BANs) enhances anomaly detection effectiveness (Abbasi et al., 2023). Although GRUs enable the sequential analysis of time-series medical data, it captures temporal dependency for accurate anomaly prediction, GANs have the capability of synthesizing true physiological data for improving model training, solving the problem of scarcity of data in BANs (Agrawal & Shelly, n.d.). All these AI-based approaches with the use of blockchain, deliver secure, inviolable storage of medical information, lowering the risk of cybersecurity (Akbar et al., 2022). In current applications in medicine, the convergence of AI, blockchain and BANs maximizes both preventive and diagnostic interventions, leading to an enhanced, adaptive and intelligent healthcare system.

## 1.1 Background

The potential of Body Area Networks (BANs) to revolutionize sports, the military and healthcare has drawn extensive interest over recent years (Akkaş et al., 2020). To provide communication between off-body devices and on-body, wearable and implanted sensors, BANs represent a special wireless sensor network that operates inside as well as outside the human body (Alani et al., 2020). These networks must be used in monitoring physiological data such as body temperature, blood pressure, heart rate, blood glucose and brain waves (Alshamrani, 2022). BANs form a core element of contemporary health care systems considering that they facilitate distant diagnosis, medical treatment and real-time observation of health status (Alzahrani et al., 2021).

Medical technology has been extensively advanced as a result of the application of BANs in healthcare, facilitating remote patient monitoring and the application of immediate medical care (Ananthi & Jose, 2021). As the networks ensure continuous monitoring of a patient's condition without being physically present in a hospital at regular intervals, the networks prove to be of special use to patients with chronic conditions like diabetes, cardiovascular conditions and neurological conditions (Bhatti et al., 2022). Moreover, through the provision of real-time data to healthcare workers, BANs optimize emergency medical interventions through timely and well-informed decisions (Bhamidipaty et al., 2025).

To provide secure and efficient data transfer, BANs employ low-power protocols like IEEE 802.15.6, Zigbee, Bluetooth Low Energy and Ultra-Wideband. Physiological data-collecting sensor nodes, a processing unit for data analysis (Bieniek et al., 2024), a communication module for data transmission to cloud systems or other devices and a power module that supplies power to the whole network are the typical necessary components of these networks (Bui et al., 2024). When they are combined with these factors, BANs can facilitate several applications including telemedicine, physical activity monitoring, chronic disease monitoring and physical therapy (Chowdhury et al., 2020), establishing them as a key element in intelligent healthcare systems.

Despite all of their advantages, BANs also present some problems that have to be overcome to ensure wide utilization and performance (Deevi, 2020). One of the most serious problems, since health data is sensitive and thus a hacker's favourite target is data protection (Devarajan, 2020a). Implementing robust encryption protocols, secure authentication processes and blockchain-enabled data integrity measures would enhance user confidentiality and BAN security (Devarajan, 2020b). In addition, BANs' scalability is still a problem, particularly with the growing requirement for wearable and implanted health monitoring technology (Dhabliya et al., 2022). Sophisticated data compression techniques and optimization of network design can help manage the increasing volume of health data that BANs generate (Gollavilli et al., 2020).

In summary, through remote diagnosis, efficient medical treatment and real-time monitoring, Body Area Networks are transforming the sports, healthcare and military sectors (Greenhalgh et al., 2021). Even though there remain challenges of data security, network scalability, power consumption and real-time decision-making, BANs are increasingly becoming reliable and efficient due to ongoing research and technological advancements. These networks have the potential to redefine healthcare further, improve patient outcomes and help develop more smart, networked health ecosystems as they expand (Haleem et al., 2022).

## 1.2 Artificial Intelligence in BANs

The incorporation of Artificial Intelligence in Body Area Networks (BANs) has greatly improved their efficiency and brought about great leaps in data processing, anomaly detection and prediction (Huang et al., 2022). AI-based models augment BAN capabilities, making them more reliable and efficient in healthcare by leveraging AI-based automated decision-making, learning processes and real-time diagnostics (Inayat et al., 2022). The changing and dynamic nature of physiological states is usually not in line with the rule-based programs and hard-coded thresholds used by traditional BAN systems (Isibor, 2024). Conventional BAN systems are not quite effective for real-time patient monitoring and disease identification as a result of insufficient flexibility to evolve with the variations in health. AI-driven BANs, on the other hand based on ML and DL algorithms examining gigantic volumes of physiological data, pick up minor trends and create extremely precise forecasts.

Early identification of diseases and avoiding harmful diseases like AI-driven features significantly enhance patient monitoring (Jagatheesaperumal et al., 2023).

AI's capability of enhancing operations with better data security, improved energy efficiency, sophisticated anomaly detection and real-time health monitoring is one of the greatest contributions of AI to BANs (Javaid et al., 2023). AI-driven BANs use wearable sensors to gather physiological data that is instantaneously examined by sophisticated AI algorithms. These algorithms allow for preventive and proactive healthcare interventions based on instant knowledge about a person's health. AI-driven BANs use continuous monitoring to identify anomalies like arrhythmias, hypertension or changes in blood sugar levels (Javed et al., 2024). They then quickly notify medical professionals, providing instant medical attention. AI-driven resource management methods improve sensor duty cycling, minimize power usage and optimize data transfer to further improve BAN efficiency. As wearable health devices usually run on batteries, efficient utilization of resources is important in BANs (Jacob et al., 2021). By effectively controlling the operation of sensors and only conducting data collection and transmission when needed, AI models optimize energy utilization (Kumar et al., 2021). This method makes BANs sustainable and convenient in the long term by greatly extending battery life and minimizing the need for frequent device maintenance.

Another key area where AI improves BAN performance is in security. Because BANs handle personal healthcare data it is imperative to safeguard patient data against cyber-attacks (Kumar et al., 2021). AI-powered security systems employ Intrusion Detection Systems and anomaly detection algorithms to detect and resist possible security vulnerabilities. The AI-powered security systems constantly scan network traffic, detecting unusual behavior that could signal cyber-attacks in the form of malware attacks, unauthorized access or data modification (Liu et al., 2024). By implementing adaptive security, AI ensures that health data is protected and not at risk from future attackers. Additionally, AI-powered BANs can deliver personalized healthcare by assessing lifestyle choices, patient history and real-time sensor data to produce customized treatment recommendations (Mohamed et al., 2021). The insights gleaned from AI improve the outcomes of patients by offering specific healthcare solutions that address specific medical conditions and risk factors and customized treatment plans enable more effective remote health monitoring which decreases the hospital visit frequency and enhances the overall efficiency of healthcare provision (Moreno-Sánchez et al., 2024).

Telemedicine and remote patient monitoring, increasingly significant in modern healthcare are also part of the application of AI in BANs (Narla et al., 2019). AI-powered BANs give doctors ongoing access to up-to-date patient information, allowing remote consultations and instant treatment (Narla et al., 2019). This aspect will particularly benefit elderly individuals, chronically ill patients, and residents in underserved and rural communities. By facilitating seamless communication among patients and health professionals, AI-driven BANs enhance the efficiency and convenience of healthcare delivery. Predictive analytics that facilitate early detection of diseases and preventive care are also reliant on AI-driven BANs (Nguyen et al., 2020). Through the examination of enormous amounts of physiological data, AI models pick up on tiny signs of probable health problems prior to symptoms getting out of control, allowing healthcare professionals to take preventative measures that lower hospitalization rates and improve patient outcomes (Ning et al., 2020).

BANs with AI capabilities are a game-changing advancement in medical science (Omboni et al., 2020). BANs overcome the drawbacks of conventional rule-based systems and become more effective, flexible, and secure by utilizing AI algorithms (Osouli Tabrizi & Al-Turjman, 2020). BANs play a crucial role in contemporary healthcare applications since AI allows for anomaly detection, forecasting analysis and personalized treatment. The integration of BANs with AI technology will revolutionize medicine as it evolves through enhanced patient care, the optimization of resource usage, and enhanced data protection (Panga, 2022). Ultimately, BANs infused with AI give the world an even more preventative, personalized and accessible medical system.

## 1.3 Objectives and Scope of the Study

This chapter's main goal is to examine AI's contribution in advancing Body Area Networks by overcoming main challenges like efficiency in data processing, energy expenditure, security and real-time decision-making. The chapter discusses different AI techniques, architectures and models that can be used to enhance the functionality and performance of BANs. The specific goals of this,

- Explain the basics of BANs in terms of their architecture and main applications.
- Critically analyze the drawbacks of conventional BAN systems and warrant the need for AI-based solutions.
- Assess different AI methods such as machine learning, deep learning and edge computing, to improve the efficiency of BAN operations.
- Discuss AI-based security mechanisms like homomorphic encryption, Zero Trust models and Blockchain to protect confidential medical information in BANs.

## 2. RELATED WORKS

Osouli Tabrizi and Al-Turjman (2020) discussed the efficiency in the energy of IoT nodes relies on optimizing packet size to lower the energy requirement of wireless packet transmission. With the higher number of nodes, energy scavenging of ambient energy sources has become the trend as an approach to avert battery issues. To provide constant availability of power along with limited overall energy for the longer life of battery-powered networks, packet size optimization methods have been introduced so far. On the other hand, battery-less networks based on energy harvesting guarantee infinite overall energy despite availability loss. Rassam (2024) introduced Wireless Body Area Networks (WBANs) which track some of the critical signals of the human body are facilitatory tools for monitoring healthcare problems in medical healthcare centers. Such data collected is utilized by medical personnel and advisors to assess the health of hospital patients or elderly living in residence ICUs. Medical professionals must examine any abnormalities in the data that is received and which might be a product of aggressive attacks, sensor malfunction readings, or severe health deterioration situations.

Alani et al. (2020) highlighted the various types of studies facilitated during the present decade due to the growing need for Ultra-Wideband (UWB) for medical purposes in WBANs. The core emphasis of the WBAN system is to continuously monitor patients' health as they lead their routine lives. Performance is measured and many studies and analyses are taken into consideration. The primary subjects of this paper are UWB technologies, on-off body communication and WBAN concepts to solve several research limitations. Bui et al. (2024) Since it offers the benefits of simplicity, reliability, low latency, privacy and personalization, WBAN are employed extensively across a range of sectors such as healthcare, sports, wellness and assistive technology. The characteristics of the propagation of the WBAN channel can influence transmission reliability, especially in healthcare applications. This work proposes a new solution to the problem using the autoencoder approach in deep learning-based cooperative Multiple-Input Multiple-Output (MIMO) systems.

Kumar et al. (2021) focused on the recently found coronavirus responsible for causing coronavirus disease (COVID-19) resembles the influenza virus and has triggered an international pandemic of frightening levels of severity and range. Within a mere eight months by August 2020, it infected 24.0 million individuals across the world and killed more than 824 thousand individuals. Drones or unmanned aerial vehicles have been very supportive in the fight against the COVID-19 pandemic. Mohamed et al. (2021) Wireless body area networks or WBANs, refer to groups of connected devices that monitor how the human body and environment are performing. Because implants are invasive, they pose various challenges among these sensors. Additionally, the transmission path of the implants has live tissues in it which poses real-world channel modeling challenges. As much as there has been an encouraging array of uses for implants within the medical fraternity there are not sufficient extensive studies that extensively detail the advancements and challenges of this technology.

Saba et al. (2020) focused on the IoT is increasingly becoming popular across numerous industries due to its affordable autonomous sensor operations. IoT sensors in healthcare and medical applications form an environment that monitors patient's vital signs such as blood pressure, oxygen saturation, heart rate, temperature and others and acts accordingly in case of an emergency. It is utilized to supply patient information related to healthcare to medical centers and remote users for post-analysis. Akkaş et al. (2020) discussed Wireless communication technologies and IoT have successfully made their way into large parts of our lives because of their continuously falling prices and increasing capabilities. One of the most demanding and fast-changing application fields is the healthcare sector. IoT will affect the medical sector in several ways such as assisted living and elder care, remote health and monitoring services, detection and management of chronic diseases and personalized medication. The healthcare applications of IoT technology are discussed here as well as the many ways it is impacting the medical field and a few possible upcoming developments such as Bio-IoT and Nano-IoT or the Internet of Nano Things.

Yan et al. (2020) discussed a challenging but interesting approach to powering future wearables is harvesting biomechanical energy from low-frequency human body movements. This work reports a linear-to-rotary hybrid nanogenerator based on a frequency augmentation method for effectively harvesting low-frequency body biomechanical energy. Interestingly, the current and voltage generated by the LRH-NG from human body motion are boosted by as much as 3.1 and 3.6 times over the fundamental frequency. Chowdhury et al. (2020) focused there has been an exponential demand for wireless communication in the last two decades. Fifth-generation (5G) communications, which have a lot more features than fourth-generation communications will soon be implemented all around the globe. A sixth-generation (6G) system, a new wireless communication paradigm with full support of AI is expected to be implemented between 2027 and 2030. It is some of the fundamental issues to be solved after 5G includes faster system capacity, faster data rate, reduced latency, greater security and improved quality of service compared to the 5G system.

Agrawal and Shelley (n.d.) introduced the WBAN consists of small biosensors that are implanted into various parts of an individual's body. The health sciences are experiencing a new revolution with WBAN. It tracks health-related data like electrocardiograms, BP, glucose levels and heartbeats. It transmits these data to the health monitoring systems. WBAN is mainly concerned with the areas of social welfare, medicine, entertainment, psychology and sports. Different routing methods have been suggested to date for enhancing network lifetime, performance, energy efficiency, throughput, packet delivery ratio, delay and throughput. Kumar et al. (2021) focused on direct sensing and diagnostic interfaces to the body are offered by a new generation of sensing paradigms known as lab-on-skin, where elastic and flexible smart sensor devices are embedded in the skin. Distributed wireless lab-on-skin sensors can continuously and persistently measure the health of the skin over a long duration of time. A wireless body area network-based distributed skin health monitoring system is proposed. It remotely indicates the health of the skin and reacts to its dynamic changes.

Pradhan et al. (2021) Communication technologies in an HIoT network ensure the connection between different elements. Such technologies are divided into two broad categories are short-range and medium-range communication technologies. Although medium-range communication technologies are used to facilitate communication over long distances. e.g., between a base station and the central node of a BAN, short-range communication technologies are the protocols utilized to enable objects to connect within a certain range or BAN. Jacob et al. (2021) mentioned that, Now there are plenty of avenues where they can improve the performance of various healthcare applications in a readable and effective manner due to artificial intelligence (AI) technology. Many issues in the healthcare sector, particularly those related to wearable device networks and body area networks, can be addressed through the integration of AI with IoT.

Ning et al. (2020) introduced the fast evolution of the IoMT and promotes mass in-home health monitoring systems. Equally, over-demanding patients cause communication overload and spectrum resource scarcity. 5G health monitoring based on Mobile Edge Computing is believed to be a potential paradigm to overcome such a challenge. Design a low-cost in-home health monitoring system for IoMT by dividing it into two sub-networks beyond-WBANs and intra-WBANs. Highlighting the characteristics of IoMT, patient costs are determined by energy consumption, medical urgency and Age of Information. Thamilarasu et al. (2020) focused on one of the main components of the IoMT is WBAN consisting of implanted and wearable medical devices that communicate with and monitor different body areas. While there are numerous benefits to Internet-connected medical devices they also pose substantial security and privacy concerns, especially since healthcare systems process personal and often life-endangering medical information. Based on statistics, the healthcare industry has witnessed the largest amount of cybersecurity incidents over the past few years.

Alzahrani et al. (2021) discussed that Wireless technology dependency has many security concerns for modern protocols. A new patient healthcare monitoring protocol in recent times has established that it is overwhelmed with privacy issues and is vulnerable to various attacks including replay and key compromise impression attacks. Then, applied BAN logic and a simulation tool automatically to suggest a better scheme and specifically analyze its security properties. Bieniek et al. (2024) introduce SecureCare an innovative solution to enhance wearable IoT healthcare by leveraging a WBAN architecture based on blockchain. An interest in applying blockchain technology is driven by its robust security aspects which are achieved due to its decentralized and unbreachable architecture that effectively secures data in a network. Finally, SecureCare demonstrated efficiency and reliability improvements when implemented on a public blockchain network. Its viability as a robust solution to enhance security in wearable IoT healthcare systems is attested by this verification.

Tavera et al. (2021) discussed such networks are known as WBANs. A WBAN connects remote nodes that are on, below or above the skin through the electromagnetic waves emitted by the human body. There is a persistent mission for a means of miniaturizing different telecommunications devices so that they can be placed nearer to the body or even attached and embedded in the skin without causing distress or posing harm to the user. Qureshi et al. (2020) introduced the New technologies, e.g., WBANs based on intelligent and smart biosensor nodes for monitoring and sensing the patient's vital signs which were initiated by the increasing population and the increased cost of medical care. To transport medical data to medical centers, biosensor nodes have been implanted inside or outside the human body. To solve the network's interference, body movement and disconnection quality of services challenges, numerous models and solutions for data dissemination in such services have been proposed.

## 3. METHODOLOGY FOR BANS IN AI APPLICATIONS

To enable real-time health tracking, the proposed framework combines wearable sensors, wireless connectivity and cloud computing in a three-layered framework for BANs. Layer 1 (Sensor Layer), Layer 2 (Communication Layer) and Layer 3 (Cloud Processing and Decision Layer) constitute the architecture as depicted in Figure 1. Physiological sensors in Layer 1 collect health information such as BP, ECG, EMG and body movements. The data are picked up by a mobile device (Collector), processed and then forwarded to the next layer. An access point is included in Layer 2, the communication layer that ensures secure and efficient data transfer from the collector to cloud storage. The wireless access point acts as a gateway to connect remote healthcare monitoring platforms with sensor data. The last Layer 3 is comprised of a cloud server performing AI-based analytics. The received physiological data is analyzed by AI-based algorithms to identify abnormalities, forecast diseases and provide personalized medical suggestions. The processed information along with notifications is provided to doctors for diagnosis and decision-making.

By the improvement of energy efficiency, security and real-time monitoring, this architecture enhances the reliability of BANs for medical applications.

*Figure 1. Proposed block diagram of the AI-driven BAN framework*

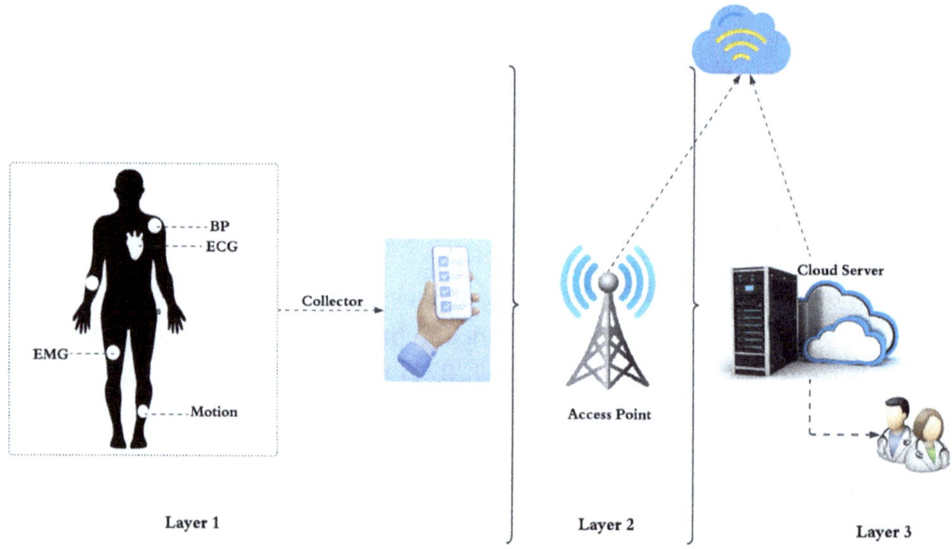


## 3.1 Fundamentals of Body Area Networks (BANs)

A Body Area Network (BAN) is a wireless network designed for medical use, enabling continuous health monitoring through wearable or implantable sensors that collect physiological data like ECG, BP, and movement. Data is transmitted via wireless technologies such as Bluetooth or 5G to processing units, often through a mobile phone, for real-time analysis and personalized health advice powered by AI. BANs support disease management, telemedicine, and remote patient monitoring, improving healthcare efficiency. They offer real-time health tracking, mobility, energy efficiency, and enhanced privacy and security through encryption. BANs are used in chronic condition management, post-surgical care, and elderly monitoring, with growing applications in sports performance and personalized medicine, thanks to advancements in AI, edge computing, and blockchain.

## 3.2 Communication Protocols in Body Area Networks: IEEE 802.15.6

### 3.2.1 Overview of IEEE 802.15.6

A short-range, low-power wireless communication standard named IEEE 802.15.6 was designed particularly for WBANs. By ensuring reliable, energy-effective and secure data exchange among body-worn or implanted sensors and a central processing unit it is applicable for both medical and non-medical purposes.

The following frequency bands are where the standard operates,

- Implanted medical devices utilize the Medical Implant Communication Service (MICS) Band (402–405).
- Wearable technology employs the Industrial, Scientific, and Medical (ISM) bands (2.4 GHz, 5 GHz).

Three categories of communication modes are defined by IEEE 802.15.6 according to the network access mechanism,

- Beacon Mode with Superframe Structure.
- Non-Beacon Mode with Unscheduled Access.
- Emergency Mode.

### 3.2.2 Beacon Mode with Superframe Structure (Scheduled Access)

To coordinate communication among sensor nodes, a hub periodically broadcasts beacon signals. The communication time is structured into superframes each of which contains several time slots assigned to different sensor nodes. Sensor nodes remain in low-power mode until their scheduled time slot. At this time, they wake up, listen to the beacon and provide data. This minimizes collisions and optimizes the network. This scheduling method is best suited for WBAN applications where continuous operation of devices is necessary because it minimizes power consumption and prevents unnecessary transmissions which ensures energy-efficient communication.

*Table 1. Algorithm 1: Scheduled Access in Beacon Mode*

| **Algorithm 1: Scheduled Access in Beacon Mode** |
|---|
| **Input:** Sensor Nodes $S_n$, Hub H, Superframe SF, Time Slots $T_n$<br>**Output:** Synchronized, collision-free data transmission |
| Hub initializes superframe SF and assigns time slots $T_1, T_2, \dots, T_n$ to nodes. |
| Hub broadcasts a beacon signal to all connected sensor nodes. |
| Each sensor node $S_n$ listens to the beacon to determine its transmission time. |
| At the assigned time slot $T_n$, the sensor node transmits its data packet. |
| Hub acknowledges the reception of data from each node. |
| If acknowledgment is not received, the node retransmits the packet in the next cycle. |
| Process repeats for each superframe cycle. |

### 3.2.3 Non-Beacon Mode with Unscheduled Access (CSMA/CA)

In this mode, sensor nodes transmit data whenever available, using Carrier Sense Multiple Access with Collision Avoidance to check channel availability and minimize collisions. A backoff mechanism helps manage retransmissions, improving data efficiency and reducing congestion despite higher energy use.

*Table 2. Algorithm 2: Unscheduled Access with CSMA/CA*

| **Algorithm 2: Unscheduled Access with CSMA/CA** |
|---|
| **Input: Sensor Nodes $S_n$, Channel $C$, Packet $P$**<br>**Output: Efficient data transmission with collision avoidance** |
| Sensor node listens for an idle communication channel $C$. |
| If the channel is free, the node transmits data packet $P$. |
| If the channel is busy, the node backs off for a random time period. |
| After backoff, the node checks channel availability again. |
| If idle, the node transmits packet $P$. |
| Hub acknowledges packet reception. |
| If no acknowledgment is received, the node retries transmission after another backoff period. |

### 3.2.4 Emergency Mode (TDMA-Priority)

This mode prioritizes medical emergencies with low-latency data transfer using Priority Scheduling TDMA. Emergency packets are given priority over regular traffic, with the hub suspending ongoing transmissions and reserving time slots for urgent data. This ensures immediate delivery of critical health data to cloud-based systems or healthcare workers in real-time, facilitating timely interventions.

*Table 3. Algorithm 3: Emergency Data Transmission (TDMA-Priority)*

| **Algorithm 3: Emergency Data Transmission (TDMA-Priority)** |
|---|
| **Input: Sensor Nodes** $S_n$, **Emergency Packet** $P_e$, **Hub** $H$<br>**Output: Low-latency emergency data transmission** |
| Sensor node detects a critical health event (e.g., heart failure, fall detection). |
| Sensor assigns a priority tag to the emergency packet $P_e$. |
| Sensor sends an Emergency Request (E-REQ) to the hub. |
| Hub interrupts normal communication and assigns an immediate time slot for the emergency packet. |
| Sensor transmits emergency packet $P_e$. |
| Hub acknowledges receipt and forwards the data to healthcare providers. |
| Normal traffic resumes after the emergency event are handled. |

### 3.2.5 Comparison of Communication Modes in IEEE 802.15.6

IEEE 802.15.6 WBAN modes—Beacon, Non-Beacon, and Emergency—balance latency, power efficiency, and data reliability for healthcare. Beacon Mode ensures energy efficiency with slight delays, non-Beacon Mode allows real-time data transfer but risks collisions, and Emergency Mode prioritizes critical health data with the shortest response times, interrupting normal transmissions.

*Table 4. Comparison table of communication modes in IEEE 802.15.6*

| Communication Mode | Mechanism | Advantages | Disadvantages | Use Case |
|---|---|---|---|---|
| **Beacon Mode (Superframe)** | Scheduled TDMA | Collision-free, energy-efficient | Higher latency due to scheduling | Continuous health monitoring |
| **Non-Beacon Mode (CSMA/CA)** | On-demand access | Low latency, real-time response | Higher power consumption, risk of collision | Emergency alerts, fall detection |
| **Emergency Mode (TDMA-Priority)** | Priority-based TDMA | Guaranteed low latency | Interrupts normal communication | Life-critical medical emergencies |

## 3.3 Role of AI in Body Area Networks (BANs)

By enabling intelligent data processing, enhancing decision-making capabilities, and optimizing energy consumption, AI enhances BANs performance hugely. BANs, made up of encircled or wearable medical devices, produce large volumes of real-time health information. AI-based methods allow for effective data analysis, timely medical interventions and optimal overall healthcare outcomes. Integration of BAN and AI improves anomaly detection, security, predictive analysis and real-time health monitoring, making healthcare systems more responsive and efficient.

### 3.3.1 AI-Driven Data Processing and Analytics in BANs

AI facilitates high-level data processing and analytics that contribute substantially to BANs. To identify anomalies in physiological inputs, traditional BAN systems use basic threshold-based techniques such as AI-based solutions to support more sophisticated capabilities. AI algorithms provide real-time actionable insights by analyzing raw sensor data, eliminating noise and identifying relevant trends.

*Figure 2. Flowchart of AI-driven processing in BANs*

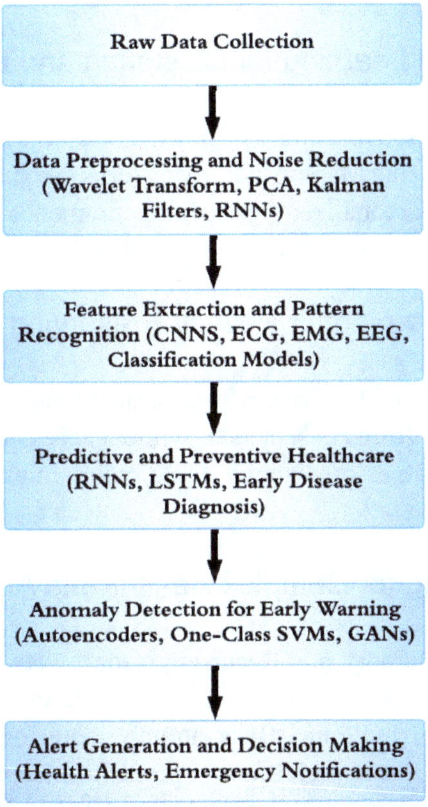


## 3.4 Integration of Machine Learning and Deep Learning Approaches in BANs

With increased precision, adaptability and effectiveness, Machine Learning and deep learning methods are essential to improving BAN capabilities. The methods improve security, optimize resource utilization and manage high amounts of health data.

### 3.4.1 Supervised Learning for Disease Classification

BANs use machine learning models like Random Forest, Decision Trees, and SVM for disease classification, while deep learning methods like CNNs and DNNs analyze biomedical signals such as ECG to detect arrhythmias with high accuracy. These AI technologies enable early detection and timely medical intervention.

### 3.4.2 Unsupervised Learning for Clustering and Pattern Discovery

BANs use unsupervised machine learning methods like k-means clustering, DB-SCAN, and Self-Organizing Maps to identify patterns in medical data, enabling early disease detection and personalized treatment recommendations. These techniques enhance predictive healthcare, facilitating proactive intervention and monitoring.

### 3.4.3 Federated Learning for Privacy-Preserving BANs:

Federated Learning (FL) enhances user security and privacy by enabling AI models to learn directly from BAN devices without accessing raw data. It improves AI model accuracy and personalization while maintaining data privacy and user anonymity.

### 3.4.4 Deep Learning for Complex Health Data Analysis:

Long Short-Term Memory and Recurrent Neural Network models process sequential health information from BANs to forecast long-term patterns like blood sugar levels or cardiac arrhythmias. By accurately capturing temporal relationships in physiological signals, the models improve prediction accuracy. Good-quality synthetic health information produced by Generative Adversarial Networks can also be employed for training AI models with the outcome being enhanced generalization and hardness. GANs help mitigate the limitations of data shortages by bridging the gap in datasets through synthetic examples that are realistic and diversified, making AI-based BAN systems more reliable and effective.

- **RNN for sequential Health Data Analysis**

RNNs use a hidden state that records temporal dependencies to process sequential data. The hidden state at a time *t*is given by,

$$h_t = f(W_h h_{t-1} + W_x x_t + b_h) \quad (1)$$

Were, $h_t$ is the hidden state at a time $t$, $h_{t-1}$ is the previous hidden state, $x_t$ is the input at the time $t$, $W_h$ and $W_x$ are weight matrices, $b_h$ is the bias term, $f$ is the activation function.

- **LSTM Networks for Health Trend Prediction**

By adding gates that control information flow, LSTMs enhance RNNs. The following are the LSTM cell updates,

***Forget Gate:*** Determines what information to discard.

$$f_t = \sigma\left(W_f \cdot [h_{t-1}, x_t] + b_f\right) \tag{2}$$

***Input Gate:*** Determines what new information to store.

$$i_t = \sigma\left(W_i \cdot [h_{t-1}, x_t] + b_i\right) \tag{3}$$

$$\widetilde{C}_t = \tanh\left(W_C \cdot [h_{t-1}, x_t] + b_C\right) \tag{4}$$

***Output Gate:*** Determines the next hidden state.

$$o_t = \sigma\left(W_o \cdot [h_{t-1}, x_t] + b_o\right) \tag{5}$$

$$h_t = o_t \odot \tanh\left(C_t\right) \tag{6}$$

Were, $\sigma$ is the sigmoid function and $\odot$ represents element-wise multiplication.

- **GANs for Synthetic Health Data**

GANs consist of a generator $G$ and a discriminator $D$, both competing against each other.

Generator Loss,

$$\mathcal{L}_G = \mathbb{E}_{z \sim p_z(z)}[\log(1 - D(G(z)))] \tag{7}$$

The generator tries to generate realistic health data to fool the discriminator.

$$\mathcal{L}_D = -\mathbb{E}_{x \sim p_{\text{data}}(x)}[\log D(x)] - \mathbb{E}_{z \sim p_z(z)}[\log(1 - D(G(z)))] \tag{8}$$

By augmenting datasets with diverse and realistic synthetic samples, GAN helps overcome data scarcity challenges, making AI-driven BAN systems more reliable and efficient.

## 3.5 AI for Real-Time Decision-Making in BANs

By analyzing real-time health data streams and providing timely feedback for clinical action, AI is the key to enabling real-time decision-making in BANs. In the absence of human intervention, BANs are able to detect anomalies, predict health risks and propose immediate solutions owing to real-time AI-based analysis.

### 3.5.1 Edge AI for Low-Latency Processing

By carrying out calculations on health data on the local edge, AI models running on BAN edge devices decrease their reliance on the cloud and alleviate latency. Rapid processing is ensured through techniques like TinyML and shallow deep learning frameworks which allow rapid responses to critical health events. The latency mitigation achieved by edge AI can be quantified

$$\Delta T = T_{\text{cloud}} - T_{\text{edge}} \tag{9}$$

Were,

$$T_{\text{cloud}} = \frac{D}{B} + C_{\text{cloud}} \tag{10}$$

$$T_{\text{edge}} = C_{\text{edge}} + P_{\text{TinyML}} \tag{11}$$

By optimizing $P_{\text{TinyML}}$ models and reducing reliance on cloud computations $C_{\text{cloud}}$ , the overall processing latency $T_{\text{edge}}$ is minimized, ensuring real-time health monitoring and timely medical interventions.

### 3.5.2 Anomaly Detection and Alert Systems

AI algorithms track physiological parameters like blood pressure, heart rate and blood glucose levels continuously. BANs identify any deviation from the normal pattern and raise alarms during emergencies like arrhythmias or hypoglycemia with methods like One-Class SVM, Autoencoders and Recurrent Neural Networks.

$$A(X) = \|X - f(X)\|_2 \tag{12}$$

Were, $\|X - f(X)\|_2$ indicates the divergence from the acquired normal pattern by Euclidean norm. An alert is raised when,

$$A(X) > \tau \tag{13}$$

This procedure allows BANs to track health parameters and identify emergencies like arrhythmias or hypoglycemia, providing timely interventions.

### 3.5.3 AI-Powered Predictive Analytics

For predicting potential health risks, machine learning algorithms incorporate past and current data. Sequential health data is analyzed using Long Short-Term Memory networks which enable early preventive treatments by predicting future events such as stroke or diabetes attacks.

### 3.5.4 Personalized AI-Driven Treatment Recommendations

AI tailors treatment alternatives about a patient's health history and current status. FL improves decision-making accuracy with data privacy intact through privacy-sensitive AI model training across multiple BAN devices.

## 3.6 AI-Based Signal Processing in BANs

### 3.6.1 AI for Physiological Signal Processing in BANs

Body Area Networks get real-time physiological inputs from sensors tracking important health parameters like electromyography, electrocardiography and electroencephalography. AI-driven signal processing techniques enhance the accuracy, noise cancellation, feature extraction and disease prognosis of these networks.

- **EEG Signal Processing**

Brain function is quantified using EEG signals, which are enormously intricate and prone to artifact from eye blinks, muscle activity and external electronic interference. Wavelet transform and deep learning methods of AI isolate important patterns from noise.

- ***Preprocessing and Noise Reduction***

Bandpass filters are employed to preprocess EEG signals so that extraneous noise may be removed. Wavelet Transform, which is an AI-based method, decomposes signals into their constituent frequencies,

$$X(t) = \sum_{i} a_i \psi_i(t) \tag{14}$$

Were, $X(t)$ is the EEG signal, $a_i$ are the wavelet coefficients and $\psi_i(t)$ represents wavelet basis functions.

- ***Feature Extraction and Classification***

For applications such as seizure detection, Convolutional Neural Networks and Long Short-Term Memory networks extract temporal and spatial features from EEG signals. CNN layers use convolutional operations to calculate feature maps given an input EEG signal X,

$$f_{i,j} = \sigma\left(\sum_{m,n} W_{m,n} \cdot X_{i+m,j+n} + b\right) \tag{15}$$

Were, $f_{i,j}$ is the feature map, $W_{m,n}$ are CNN filter weights, $\sigma$ is the activation function and $b$ is the bias term. Sequential EEG data is processed by AI models like RNNs for cognitive state monitoring and real-time seizure prediction.

## 3.6.2 ECG Signal Processing

ECG signals are used to evaluate the electrical activity of the heart and identify cardiovascular problems, heart rate variability and arrhythmias. By enhancing noise filtering, beat segmentation and disease categorization, artificial intelligence improves ECG analysis.

- ***ECG Signal Preprocessing and Feature Extraction***

To eliminate baseline wander and powerline interference, AI models employ adaptive filters such as the Kalman Filter,

$$X_k = AX_{k-1} + W_k \tag{16}$$

$$Z_k = HX_k + V_k \tag{17}$$

Were, $X_k$ represents the estimated state of the ECG signal, $A$ is the transition matrix and $W_k$ and $V_k$ are process and measurement noise. AI-driven peak detection methods are used to extract features like heart rate variability and QRS complex identification.

- ***AI-based classification for Cardiac Anomaly Detection***

CNNs and LSTMs are examples of deep learning models that categorize ECG waveforms into normal and pathological groups. For multi-class classification, the SoftMax function is frequently utilized,

$$P(y_i) = \frac{e^{z_i}}{\sum_j e^{z_j}} \tag{18}$$

Were, $z_i$ represents the input to the SoftMax function. $P(y_i)$ is the probability of class $i$. AI-based automated diagnosis, heart failure prediction and real-time arrhythmia identification are made possible by ECG analysis.

### 3.6.3 EMG Signal Processing

EMG signals are essential for identifying neuromuscular problems because they quantify muscle activity. Through noise reduction, muscle activation pattern extraction and motor disability classification, AI-based data processing improves EMG-based diagnosis.

- ***Noise Reduction in EMG Signals***

Motion artifacts and outside electrical interference can impact EMG signals. Wavelet Transform and Empirical Mode Decomposition are used in AI-driven adaptive noise filtering to denoise signals. The wavelet transform equation for EMG noise reduction is,

$$W(a,b) = \int x(t)\psi^*\left(\frac{t-b}{a}\right)dt \tag{19}$$

Were, $W(a,b)$ is the wavelet coefficient, $x(t)$ is the EMG signal and $\psi^*$ is the mother wavelet function.

- ***AI-based EMG Classification for Neuromuscular Disorders***

Support Vector Machines and Deep Neural Networks classify EMG patterns into normal and pathological states. The decision boundary in SVM is defined as,

$$f(x) = \sum_{i=1}^{N} \alpha_i y_i K(x_i, x) + b \tag{20}$$

Were, $K(x_i, x)$ is the kernel function, $\alpha_i$ are Lagrange multipliers and $y_i$ are class labels. AI models have great accuracy in recognizing disorders like muscular dystrophy and motor neuron diseases.

## 3.7 AI for Energy Efficiency in BANs

Wireless body area network sensor nodes monitor physiological information continuously. BAN node sustainability relies on energy efficiency since they are powered by a limited battery life. AI techniques significantly enhance energy efficiency by improving communication protocols, changing duty cycling and power management optimizations.

### 3.7.1 AI Techniques for Power Management in BAN Nodes

Dynamic power allocation, adaptive sleep scheduling and resource optimization through AI-driven tactics are all components of energy-efficient power management in BANs. To increase battery life, AI models forecast patterns in energy usage and modify node operation.

- ***Adaptive Sleep Scheduling with AI***

BAN nodes assume low-power sleep modes when not actively transmitting data. AI-based predictive models optimize sleep durations while assuring timely data collection. The Markov Decision Process Model Sleep Scheduling,

$$P_t = P_{\text{idle}} + P_{\text{active}} + P_{\text{sleep}} \tag{21}$$

Were, $P_t$ is total power consumption, $P_{\text{idle}}$ represents idle mode power, $P_{\text{active}}$ represents data transmission power and $P_{\text{sleep}}$ represents power in sleep mode. Deep Q-Networks and other AI algorithms learn the best sleep-wake cycles to reduce power consumption without sacrificing performance.

## 3.9 AI-Based Anomaly Detection for Cyber Threats in BANs

AI-powered anomaly detection enhances BAN security by identifying cyberattacks through machine learning and deep learning. Techniques like supervised learning (Random Forest, SVM), unsupervised learning (k-Means, DBSCAN), and deep learning (GANs, Autoencoders, LSTMs) enable real-time threat detection by analyzing sensor and network data, ensuring robust protection for healthcare applications.

- ***Autoencoder-based anomaly Detection***

A deep autoencoder learns a compressed representation of BAN data,

$$h = f(Wx + b) \tag{22}$$

Were, $W$ is the weight matrix, $b$ is the bias and $f(\cdot)$ is the activation function. The reconstruction loss is calculated as,

$$L = \|x - \hat{x}\|^2 \tag{22}$$

Higher reconstruction errors indicate anomalous behavior, signaling a cyber threat.

- ***Isolation Forest for Anomaly Scoring***

Each data instance $x_i$ is assigned an anomaly score based on its path length in an isolation tree.

$$s(x_i, n) = 2^{-\frac{E(h(x_1))}{c(n)}} \tag{23}$$

Were, $E(h(x_1))$ is the expected path length and $c(n)$ is a normalization factor. Higher scores indicate suspicious network activities in BANs.

## 3.10 AI in BAN-Enabled Smart Healthcare Systems

- ***AI for Remote Patient Monitoring***

AI-based Remote Patient Monitoring (RPM) uses wearable sensors to track health data, analyze it with ML/DL algorithms, and alert healthcare staff of anomalies in real-time. Key components include data acquisition via secure wireless protocols, AI-driven data processing, and decision support systems that predict conditions like neurological diseases and cardiac defects.

### 3.10.1 Comparison of AI Techniques for Remote Patient Monitoring in BANs

*Table 5. Comparison table of AI techniques*

| AI Technique | Application in RPM | Advantages | Limitations |
|---|---|---|---|
| **Support Vector Machines (SVM)** | Disease classification (e.g., arrhythmia detection) | High accuracy for small datasets | Requires labeled data for training |
| **Random Forest (RF)** | Risk prediction for chronic diseases | Robust to noise, interpretable | Computationally expensive |
| **Convolutional Neural Networks (CNNs)** | ECG and medical image analysis | High accuracy in feature extraction | Requires large labeled datasets |
| **Long Short-Term Memory (LSTM)** | Predicting trends in patient vitals | Captures temporal dependencies | High training complexity |
| **Autoencoders** | Anomaly detection in health signals | Learns normal patterns effectively | May generate false positives |
| **Generative Adversarial Networks (GANs)** | Synthetic health data generation | Improves AI model robustness | Computationally intensive |

A comparison of the various AI techniques employed in Body Area Network for Remote Patient Monitoring is presented in the table 2. AI techniques like Support Vector Machines, Random Forest, CNNs, LSTMs, autoencoders, and GANs enhance Remote Patient Monitoring by improving disease classification, predicting chronic disease risk, and detecting anomalies in patient data. These methods enable better patient outcomes, personalized therapy, and early disease detection, despite their computational challenges.

## 3.11 AI-Powered Disease Diagnosis and Predictive Analytics

Body Area Networks are also dependent upon AI-based disease diagnosis and predictive analytics which apply ML and DL models to diagnose diseases in the early stages and forecast potential health risks. To assist in medical decision-making these systems analyze physiological signals in real time from wearable and implant sensors.

Algorithm for AI-Powered Disease Diagnosis and Predictive Analytics in BANs

BEGIN

# Step 1: Data Acquisition from BAN Sensors

Initialize BAN sensors (ECG, EEG, glucose monitor, heart rate monitor, etc.)

```
WHILE (Monitoring Active)
Collect real-time physiological data from sensors
Transmit data securely to the processing unit

  # Step 2: Data Preprocessing

Apply noise filtering (Kalman Filter, Wavelet Transform)
Normalize and standardize data
Extract relevant features (mean, variance, entropy, FFT, PCA)

  # Step 3: Disease Diagnosis using Machine Learning

Load trained ML/DL model (e.g., Random Forest, CNN, LSTM)
INPUT preprocessed sensor data into the model
PREDICT disease classification or abnormal health patterns
IF (Anomaly Detected)
Trigger alert notification to healthcare provider and patient
Log abnormal event with timestamp

  # Step 4: Predictive Health Analytics

Train LSTM/RNN on historical time-series data
Predict future health trends (e.g., arrhythmia risk, glucose fluctuations)
IF (Predicted Health Risk > Threshold)
Generate early warning alerts
Recommend preventive actions to patient

  # Step 5: Decision Support and Response Mechanism

Send analyzed data and predictions to cloud-based healthcare system
Updated patient's medical records
Recommend an AI-driven personalized treatment plan
```

## 3.12 Role of AI in Wearable Healthcare Devices

AI is transforming wearable healthcare technology by enabling real-time health monitoring, predictive analytics, and personalized medicine. Through AI algorithms, wearables track vital signs like heart rate, glucose, and blood pressure, detecting abnormalities such as arrhythmias and hypertension. Predictive models like RF and LSTM help foresee health risks like heart failure or diabetes complications. Anomaly detection methods such as autoencoders and k-Means Clustering alert users to urgent health changes. AI also optimizes battery life through edge computing and adaptive duty cycling while ensuring data security with blockchain and federated learning for secure model training.

*Figure 3. Wearable healthcare devices in BANs*

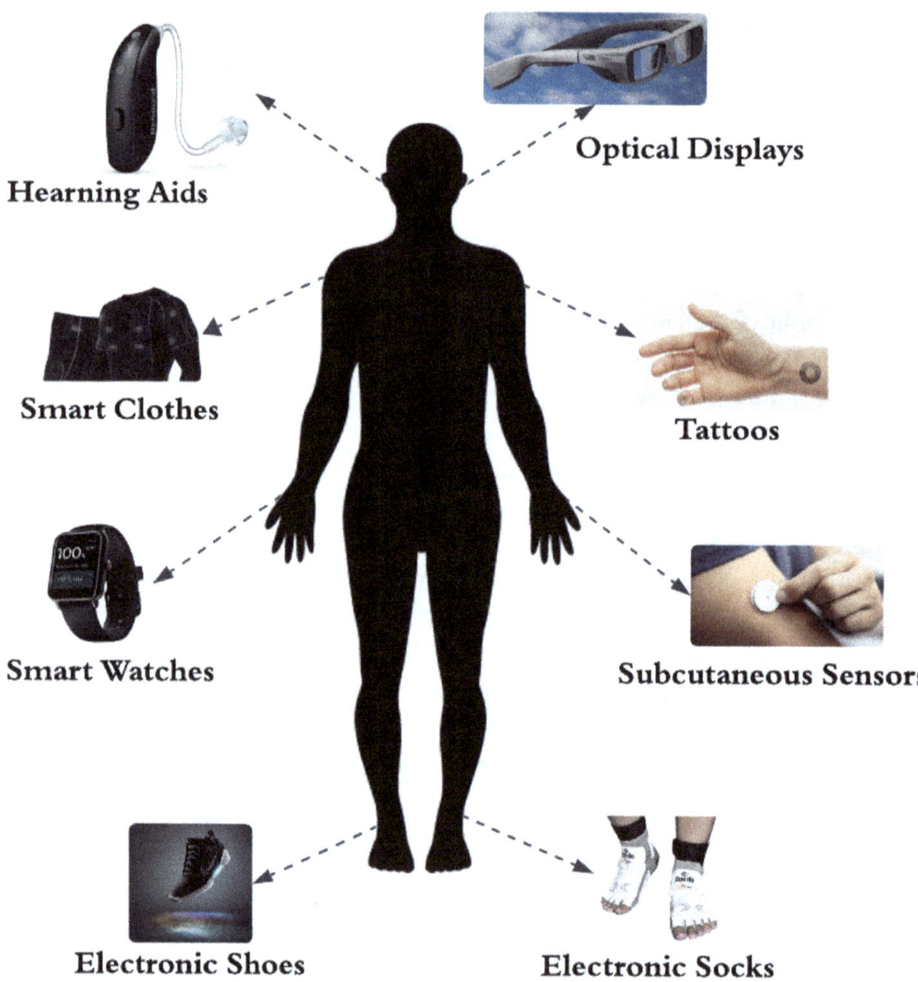


Different wearable health devices employed in BANs for continuous health monitoring and care are illustrated in the photo. These devices collect, process and transmit physiological information in real time through wireless connectivity, advanced sensors and artificial intelligence. The following is a description of each device in the photo.

1. **Hearing Aids** - Contemporary hearing aids assist individuals with hearing loss through the utilization of AI-driven speech augmentation and noise reduction techniques.
2. **Optical Displays (Smart Glasses)** -These devices provide augmented reality or virtual reality applications to aid visually challenged patients, provide medical data visualization and assist in surgeries.
3. **Smart Clothes** -Smart clothing that incorporates biosensors monitors vital signs, such as heart rate, breathing, and posture, and offers athletes, patients and elderly people real-time health feedback
4. **Tattoos** -Without needing intrusive therapies, such versatile, skin-mounted electronic tattoos track key indicators such as body temperature, concentration of glucose, and humidity.
5. **Subcutaneous Sensors** -Oxygen, glucose and other measures are constantly monitored by implanted or wearable biosensors that are widely applied to the management of diabetes and the monitoring of chronic diseases.
6. **Smart Watches** -Al-powered smartwatches track oxygen levels, heart rate, physical activity and sleeping patterns and they can identify abnormalities such as hypertension or arrhythmias and alert.
7. **Electronic Shoes** -These devices, equipped with motion and pressure sensors, assist individuals with mobility issues by providing fall detection alarms and real-time gait analysis.
8. **Electronic Socks** -Through the recognition of pressure spots, temperature changes, and circulatory difficulties to prevent ulcers, these intelligent textiles contribute to the tracking of foot health, especially among diabetic patients.

## 4. RESULTS AND DISCUSSIONS

The results show how well various machine learning models, communication protocols, anomaly detection techniques and energy-saving strategies compare with each other. The DNN is the most reliable choice for predictive analytics when considering machine learning model comparison, performing better than RF and SVM across all critical metrics, including accuracy, precision, recall, F1-score and AUC-ROC. Beacon Mode is the most energy-efficient communication protocol based on energy and time consumption trends. Emergency Mode is more energy-hungry but is optimally suited for critical applications due to its low latency and high reliability. Non-Beacon Mode is the most CPU and energy-efficient mode while

Emergency Mode maximizes performance at the cost of greater resource usage as per the resource usage-based evaluation of communication protocols.

The comparison between anomaly detection models indicates that the Autoencoder model optimizes for both accuracy and efficiency and the GAN-Augmented model has the optimal detection rate at the minimum false positive rate but with higher computation costs. ECG signals have optimal accuracy in noise suppression as well as feature extraction based on signal processing which attests to its utility in biomedical applications. Lastly, optimization methods for energy efficiency demonstrate Optimized MAC Protocols to be the best power management approach with the highest energy savings and increase in battery life. These findings provide valuable trade-off insights across resource efficiency, performance and application-specific constraints, which facilitate the choice of optimal methods across a range of networking and computation scenarios.

## 4.1 Performance Comparison of Machine Learning Models

DNN outperforms RF and SVM in all key performance metrics, including accuracy (92.8%), precision (93.4%), recall (91.9%), F1-score (92.6%), and AUC-ROC (95.7%). It demonstrates superior prediction accuracy and model reliability, making it the most dependable model for classification tasks. Table 3 shows below.

*Table 6. Comparison table of ML models*

| Model | Accuracy (%) | Precision (%) | Recall (%) | F1-Score | AUC-ROC (%) |
|---|---|---|---|---|---|
| RF | 89.5 | 90.1 | 88.2 | 89.1 | 92.3 |
| SVM | 87.4 | 88.0 | 86.7 | 87.3 | 90.5 |
| DNN | 92.8 | 93.4 | 91.9 | 92.6 | 95.7 |

## 4.2 Energy Consumption and Time Consumption

Beacon Mode is the most energy-efficient, starting at 20 mW and dropping to 10 mW over 10 hours. Non-Beacon Mode starts at 25 mW, ending at 14 mW, while Emergency Mode starts at 30 mW and remains the most energy-consuming, ending at 17 mW, due to its critical operational needs. Figure 4 shows below,

*Figure 4. Performance of energy consumption and time consumption*

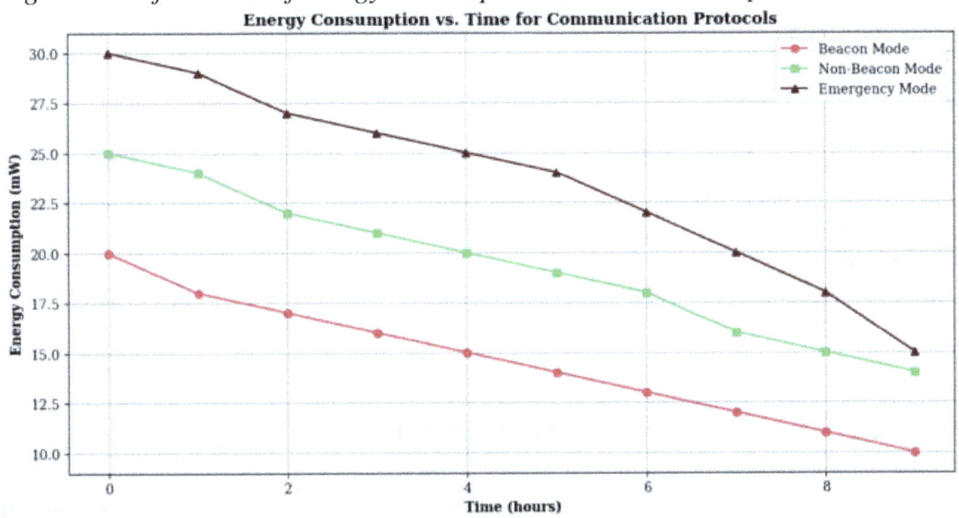


## 4.3 Comparison of Communication Protocols

Table 4 Beacon Mode offers the best energy efficiency (15 mW) with 20 ms latency and 2% packet collision rate, ideal for stable applications. Non-Beacon Mode balances latency (15 ms) and energy (20 mW) but has the highest packet collision rate (5%), while Emergency Mode prioritizes speed (10 ms) and low collisions (1%) at the highest energy usage (25 mW), suitable for critical applications.

*Table 7. Communication table of communication protocols*

| Protocol | Latency (ms) | Energy Consumption (mW) | Packet Collision Rate (%) |
|---|---|---|---|
| **Beacon Mode** | 20 | 15 | 2 |
| **Non-Beacon Mode** | 15 | 20 | 5 |
| **Emergency Mode** | 10 | 25 | 1 |

## 4.4 Communication Protocol Resource Usage

A comparison Table 5 of Beacon Mode balances resource use with 10.2 mAh energy, 25.3% CPU, 100.5 MB memory, and 200.8 kB/s bandwidth. Non-Beacon Mode is the most power-efficient (8.7 mAh, 20.1% CPU, 90.2 MB memory, 180.5

kB/s bandwidth), while Emergency Mode consumes the most resources (12.4 mAh, 30.8% CPU, 110.7 MB memory, 250.4 kB/s bandwidth) for speed and reliability.

*Table 8. Table of communication protocol resource usage*

| Protocol | Average Energy (mAh) | CPU Usage (%) | Memory Usage (MB) | Bandwidth (kB/s) |
|---|---|---|---|---|
| **Beacon Mode** | 10.2 | 25.3 | 100.5 | 200.8 |
| **Non-Beacon Mode** | 8.7 | 20.1 | 90.2 | 180.5 |
| **Emergency Mode** | 12.4 | 30.8 | 110.7 | 250.4 |

## 4.5 Performance of Anomaly Detection

Figure 5 compares Autoencoder offers a balance with moderate computational cost and 95% accuracy, while One-Class SVM has higher overhead and 92% accuracy. GAN-Augmented achieves the highest accuracy (97%) but at the highest computational cost, making it ideal for systems prioritizing accuracy over resource usage.

*Figure 5. Anomaly detection and computational overhead*

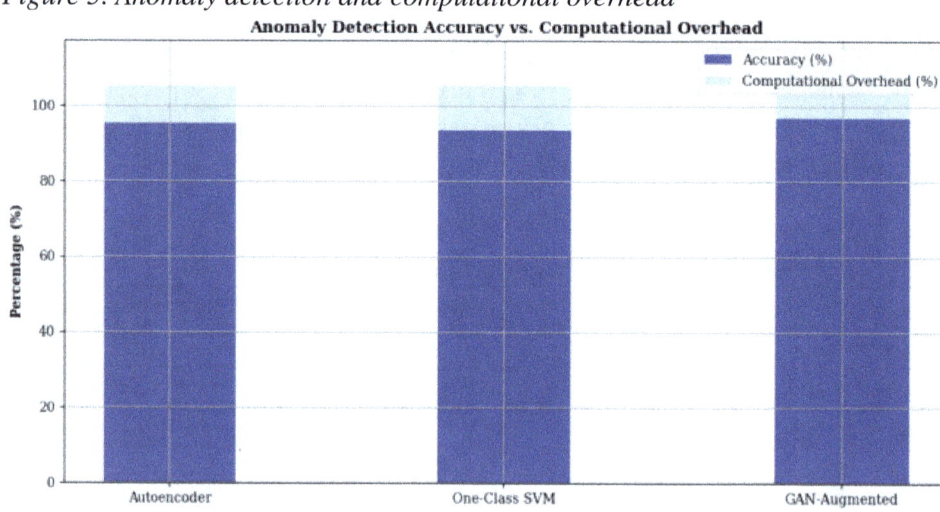

## 4.6 Performance of Signal Processing

The signal processing results in the Figure 6 by comparing the Noise Reduction Accuracy (%) and Feature Extraction Accuracy (%) for three different types of biomedical signals are EEG, ECG and EMG. Within both groups, the ECG signal shows the highest accuracy with Noise Reduction Accuracy falling only slightly shy of Feature Extraction Accuracy. While its Noise Reduction Accuracy falls just slightly short of its Feature Extraction Accuracy, EEG processing also shows excellent performance. Although the Feature Extraction Accuracy of the EMG signal remains quite high its Noise Reduction Accuracy is significantly lower. The results indicate that ECG signal processing is best and most well-balanced, while EEG and EMG signals only exhibit slight differences in their ability to reduce noise. With ECG exhibiting the highest overall accuracy in both measures, the comparison illustrates the efficacy of different processing techniques in biomedical signal analysis.

*Figure 6. Signal processing of ECG, EEG and EMG*

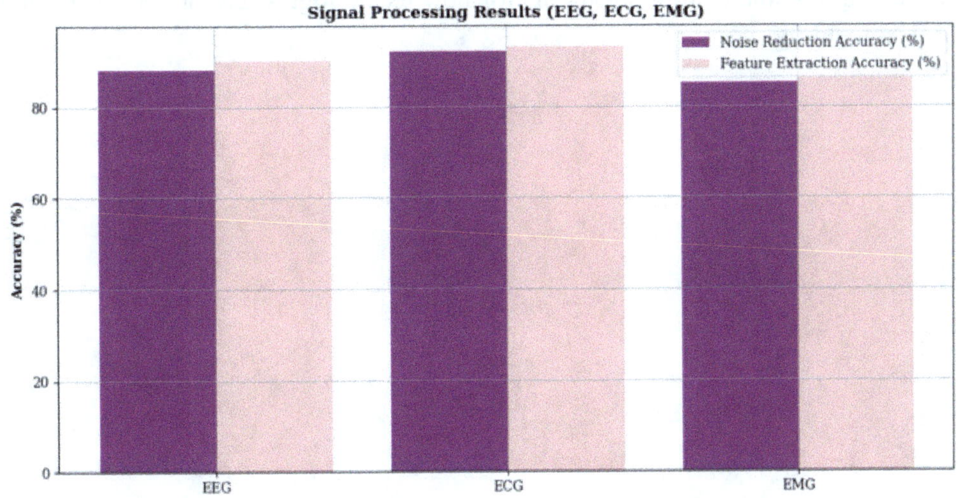


## 5. CONCLUSION AND FUTURE SCOPE

The findings of this research emphasize the importance of tuning machine learning models and communication protocols for secure and energy-efficient operation. DNN is the most reliable model for anomaly detection due to its superior performance in classification tasks. The most energy-efficient communication protocol is beacon mode, while emergency mode's low latency renders it best suited for real-time applications. Optimal MAC protocols are the optimal choice for prolonging device life as they yield the maximum energy savings as per energy optimization methods. Anomaly detection by the GAN-augmented model was observed to be best in identifying attacks with a minimum false positive ratio of 2.8 percent. The study sets up a template for choosing suitable machine learning models, communication protocols, and power-saving methods concerning target application requirements. Future studies can investigate the application of deep reinforcement learning to further improve anomaly detection and communication efficiency. The design of hybrid models integrating the benefits of DNN and GAN-augmented methods could enhance detection precision at low computational overhead. Moreover, experimental evaluation and implementation of MAC protocols in real-world IoT and cloud environments can give real-world insights into their adaptability and efficiency. Extending research to quantum computing-based security models can improve encryption and privacy protection in mission-critical applications. Finally, performance and sustainability improvements in next-generation communication systems can be achieved through optimizing communication protocols for new technologies like 6G networks and edge computing.

## REFERENCES


Abbasi, N., Nizamullah, F. N., & Zeb, S. (2023). AI in healthcare: Integrating advanced technologies with traditional practices for enhanced patient care. *BULLET: Jurnal Multidisiplin Ilmu*, *2*(3), 546–556.

Agrawal, J., & Shelly, M. K. (n.d.). Energy-efficient clustering with multiple sink (EECMS) in wireless body area network.

Akbar, M. S., Hussain, Z., Sheng, M., & Shankaran, R. (2022). Wireless body area sensor networks: Survey of MAC and routing protocols for patient monitoring under IEEE 802.15.4 and IEEE 802.15.6. *Sensors (Basel)*, *22*(21), 8279. DOI: 10.3390/s22218279

Akkaş, M. A., Sokullu, R., & Çetin, H. E. (2020). Healthcare and patient monitoring using IoT. *Internet of Things : Engineering Cyber Physical Human Systems*, *11*, 100173. DOI: 10.1016/j.iot.2020.100173

Alani, S., Zakaria, Z., Saiedi, T., Ahmad, A., Mahmood, S. N., Saad, M. A., & Albeyar, M. A. A. A. A. (2020). A review on UWB antenna sensor for wireless body area networks. In *ISMSIT 2020* (pp. 1–10). IEEE. DOI: 10.1109/ISMSIT50672.2020.9254219

Alshamrani, M. (2022). IoT and artificial intelligence implementations for remote healthcare monitoring systems: A survey. *Journal of King Saud University. Computer and Information Sciences*, *34*(8), 4687–4701. DOI: 10.1016/j.jksuci.2021.06.005

Alzahrani, B. A., Irshad, A., Albeshri, A., & Alsubhi, K. (2021). A provably secure and lightweight patient-healthcare authentication protocol in wireless body area networks. *Wireless Personal Communications*, *117*(1), 47–69. DOI: 10.1007/s11277-020-07237-x

Ananthi, J. V., & Jose, P. S. H. (2021). A perspective review of security challenges in body area networks for healthcare applications. *International Journal of Wireless Information Networks*, *28*(4), 451–466. DOI: 10.1007/s10776-021-00538-3

Bhamidipaty, V., Bhamidipaty, D. L., Guntoory, I., Bhamidipaty, K. D. P., Iyengar, K. P., Botchu, B., & Botchu, R. (2025). Revolutionizing healthcare: The impact of AI-powered sensors. Generative Artificial Intelligence for Biomedical and Smart Health Informatics, 355–373.

Bhatti, D. S., Saleem, S., Imran, A., Iqbal, Z., Alzahrani, A., Kim, H., & Kim, K. I. (2022). A survey on wireless wearable body area networks: A perspective of technology and economy. *Sensors (Basel)*, *22*(20), 7722. DOI: 10.3390/s22207722

Bieniek, J., Rahouti, M., Xiong, K., & Ferreira Araujo, G. (2024). SecureCare: A blockchain-assisted wearable body area network. *Security and Privacy*, *7*(6), e431. DOI: 10.1002/spy2.431

. Bui, T. T. T., Tran, N. X., & Phan, A. H. (2024). Deep learning-based cooperative MIMO systems for WBANs. REV Journal on Electronics and Communications, 14(1).

Chowdhury, M. Z., Shahjalal, M., Ahmed, S., & Jang, Y. M. (2020). 6G wireless communication systems. *IEEE Open Journal of the Communications Society*, *1*, 957–975. DOI: 10.1109/OJCOMS.2020.3010270

Deevi, D. P. (2020). Improving patient data security and privacy in mobile healthcare. *International Journal of Engineering Research and Science & Technology*, *16*(4), 21–31.

Devarajan, M. V. (2020). Assessing long-term serum sample viability. *International Journal of Information Technology and Computer Engineering*, *8*(2), 60–74.

Devarajan, M. V. (2020). Improving security control in cloud computing. *J. Sci. Technol. JST*, *5*(6).

Dhabliya, D., Soundararajan, R., Selvarasu, P., Balasubramaniam, M. S., Rajawat, A. S., Goyal, S. B., Raboaca, M. S., Mihaltan, T. C., Verma, C., & Suciu, G. (2022). Energy-efficient network protocols. *Energies*, *15*(23), 8883. DOI: 10.3390/en15238883

Gollavilli, V. S. B. H., Alagarsundaram, P., & Nagarajan, H. (2020). Cloud service selection in healthcare. *Journal of Current Science & Humanities*, *8*(4), 17–30.

Greenhalgh, T., Rosen, R., Shaw, S. E., Byng, R., Faulkner, S., Finlay, T., & Wood, G. W. (2021). Remote consultation services framework. *Frontiers in Digital Health*, *3*, 726095. DOI: 10.3389/fdgth.2021.726095

Haleem, A., Javaid, M., Singh, R. P., & Suman, R. (2022). Medical 4.0 technologies. *Internet of Things and Cyber-Physical Systems*, *2*, 12–30. DOI: 10.1016/j.iotcps.2022.04.001

Huang, J. A., Hartanti, I. R., Colin, M. N., & Pitaloka, D. A. (2022). Telemedicine and AI for COVID-19. *Digital Health*, •••, 8.

Inayat, U., Zia, M. F., Mahmood, S., Khalid, H. M., & Benbouzid, M. (2022). Cyber attack detection in IoT systems. *Electronics (Basel)*, *11*(9), 1502. DOI: 10.3390/electronics11091502

Isibor, E. (2024). Regulation of healthcare data security. *SSRN* 4957244.

Jacob, S., Alagirisamy, M., Xi, C., Balasubramanian, V., Srinivasan, R., Jhanjhi, N. Z., & Islam, S. M. (2021). Smart exoskeleton system. *IEEE Access : Practical Innovations, Open Solutions*, *9*, 80340–80350. DOI: 10.1109/ACCESS.2021.3083093

Jagatheesaperumal, S. K., Rajkumar, S., Suresh, J. V., Gumaei, A. H., Alhakbani, N., Uddin, M. Z., & Hassan, M. M. (2023). IoT-based personalized health framework. *Mathematics*, *11*(12), 2758. DOI: 10.3390/math11122758

Javaid, M., Haleem, A., Singh, R. P., & Suman, R. (2023). Cybersecurity in healthcare. *Cyber Security and Applications*, *1*, 100016. DOI: 10.1016/j.csa.2023.100016

Javed, H., Muqeet, H. A., Danesh, A., Rehman, A. U., Javed, T., & Bermak, A. (2024). AI in healthcare services. *IEEE Access : Practical Innovations, Open Solutions*, *12*, 141064–141087. DOI: 10.1109/ACCESS.2024.3443812

Kumar, A., Sharma, K., Singh, H., Naugriya, S. G., Gill, S. S., & Buyya, R. (2021). Drone-based COVID system. *Future Generation Computer Systems*, *115*, 1–19. DOI: 10.1016/j.future.2020.08.046

Liu, R., Shi, J., Chen, X., & Lu, C. (2024). Network anomaly detection. *Computers & Electrical Engineering*, *119*, 109581. DOI: 10.1016/j.compeleceng.2024.109581

Mohamed, M., Maiseli, B. J., Ai, Y., Mkocha, K., & Al-Saman, A. (2021). In-body sensor communication. *IEEE EMC Magazine*, *10*(2), 47–52.

Moreno-Sánchez, P. A., García-Isla, G., Corino, V. D., Vehkaoja, A., Brukamp, K., Van Gils, M., & Mainardi, L. (2024). ECG-based solutions. *Computers in Biology and Medicine*, *172*, 108235.

Narla, S., Peddi, S., & Valivarthi, D. T. (2019). Cloud-integrated healthcare framework. *IJCSET*, *4*(1), 22.

Nguyen, D. C., Cheng, P., Ding, M., Lopez-Perez, D., Pathirana, P. N., Li, J., & Poor, H. V. (2020). AI in wireless networks. *IEEE Communications Surveys and Tutorials*, *23*(1), 553–595. DOI: 10.1109/COMST.2020.3024783

Ning, Z., Dong, P., Wang, X., Hu, X., Guo, L., Hu, B., & Kwok, R. Y. (2020). 5G health monitoring. *IEEE JSAC*, *39*(2), 463–478.

Omboni, S., Campolo, L., & Panzeri, E. (2020). Telehealth in chronic disease. *Expert Review of Medical Devices*, *17*(7), 659–670. DOI: 10.1080/17434440.2020.1782734

Osouli Tabrizi, H., & Al-Turjman, F. (2020). Packet size optimization. *Neural Computing & Applications*, *32*(20), 16167–16178. DOI: 10.1007/s00521-020-04813-x

Panga, N. K. R. (2022). ECG signal analysis using DWT. *IJITCE*, *10*(4), 157–175.

Pradhan, B., Bhattacharyya, S., & Pal, K. (2021). IoT healthcare devices. *Journal of Healthcare Engineering*, 2021.

Qureshi, K. N., Din, S., Jeon, G., & Piccialli, F. (2020). Routing for WBANs. *Computer Communications*, *149*, 382–392. DOI: 10.1016/j.comcom.2019.10.030

Rassam, M. A. (2024). Autoencoder anomaly detection. *IoT*, *5*(4), 852–870. DOI: 10.3390/iot5040039

Saba, T., Haseeb, K., Ahmed, I., & Rehman, A. (2020). Secure IoMT framework. *Journal of Infection and Public Health*, *13*(10), 1567–1575. DOI: 10.1016/j.jiph.2020.06.027

Tavera, C. A., Ortiz, J. H., Khalaf, O. I., Saavedra, D. F., & Aldhyani, T. H. (2021). *Wearable WBANs*. Retracted.

Thamilarasu, G., Odesile, A., & Hoang, A. (2020). IoMT intrusion detection. *IEEE Access : Practical Innovations, Open Solutions*, *8*, 181560–181576. DOI: 10.1109/ACCESS.2020.3026260

Yan, C., Gao, Y., Zhao, S., Zhang, S., Zhou, Y., Deng, W., & Chen, J. (2020). Wearable energy harvesting. *Nano Energy*, *67*, 104235. DOI: 10.1016/j.nanoen.2019.104235

# Chapter 13
# An Advanced Hybrid Holmes–Tinker–Tent Map (HTTM) Chaotic Encryption Framework for Secure Distribution and Retention of Medical Images

**Sujarani Rajendran**
http://orcid.org/0000-0001-9827-0807
*SASTRA (Deemed to be) University, India*

**Supriya Sridharan**
http://orcid.org/0000-0002-4703-3438
*SASTRA (Deemed to be) University, India*

**M. Vanitha**
http://orcid.org/0000-0002-5957-1970
*SASTRA (Deemed to be) University, India*

**P. Umamaheswari**
http://orcid.org/0000-0003-2007-697X
*SASTRA (Deemed to be) University, India*

**D. Rubidha Devi**
http://orcid.org/0000-0001-9074-8984
*SASTRA (Deemed to be) University, India*

DOI: 10.4018/979-8-3373-9053-6.ch013

## ABSTRACT

*The increasing digitization of healthcare and the expansion of telemedicine have made the secure transmission of medical imagery, such as ultrasound and MRI scans, a critical challenge, as these images are highly susceptible to cyberattacks due to their significant data volume and inherent pixel redundancy. To address these vulnerabilities, this research proposes a Robust Secure Communication Framework for Medical Imagery based on a novel Hybrid Non-Linear Chaotic Oscillator system. Unlike traditional linear encryption methods, the proposed framework leverages the complex, multi-dimensional, and unpredictable dynamics of hybrid chaotic maps to achieve superior confusion and diffusion properties, scrambling pixel positions and modifying pixel values with high efficiency.The system utilizes these oscillators to generate high-entropy keystreams that exhibit extreme sensitivity to initial conditions, thereby providing a vast key space that is mathematically resistant to brute-force and differential attack.*

## 1. INTRODUCTION

Digital images have been rendered indispensable and a reflection of right technics within this realm of multi fields. Notably this has been witnessed prominently in the highly advanced frame works in healthcare environment. Medical imaging plays a very essential role in diagnosing and examining many diseases in the field of medicine. d. Images such as CT scan, X-ray and MRI have a great deal of information concerning the past and present health status of the patient. Even with these images being in a digital form, they may at one point be viewed by people who do not have authorization to view the patient's medical records. It is thus important to protect these images in order to maintain the privacy of the medical data of the patient(Benaissi et al., 2023) Encrypting medical images is a sensitive process and one that has become very important in securing sensitive information concerning healthcare and the patients. With the advancement of digital technologies in healthcare such as X-ray, MRI and CT scan among others, there has been need for protecting the images from any unauthorized access. They normally have some amount of personal and medical data making them very vulnerable to cyber attacks and theft of data.In comparison to generic data encryption, medical image encryption may have a huge amount of data and needs to be processed in real-time.

Over the last years, scientists have been intensively investigating new encryption techniques of medical images, in search of solutions that provide greater security, efficiency, and flexibility to the ever-increasing complexity of healthcare technologies (Mortajez et al., 2020). Chaos-based encryption, hybrid cryptography, and new deep learning-assisted encryption methods are among the most investigated methods. Especially chaos-based encryption has received considerable attention because of the inherent belongings of chaotic model such as initial value dependency, randomness, periodicity and pseudo-randomness (Su et al., 2024)(Wen et al., 2024). These characteristics render chaotic maps very useful in creating sequences that are similar to random noise and can therefore be useful in cryptographic algorithms like pixel permutation and diffusion. In contrast to classical encryption algorithms which rely on algebraic transformations, chaos-based systems are based on nonlinear dynamic equations and offers nonlinear security properties which are harder to analyze or break by the attacker. Furthermore, chaotic algorithms can be computationally lightweight and can be efficiently implemented in both software and hardware, which makes them appealing in real-time medical imaging applications.

This requires the creation of efficient and secure algorithms. Besides providing security to the images, the encryption methods should also confirm the reliability and authenticity of the data. Any unauthorized manipulations of the encrypted image may result in misdiagnoses or poor health care choices. The use of advanced encryption techniques such as chaotic systems, hybrid cryptography and deep learning-based methods are also being investigated to overcome these issues. Medical image encryption is a critical area in current telemedicine, cloud-based healthcare and digital health records, as it promotes the safety of patient data and facilitates the transfer of this information among healthcare workers. Image encryption convert the medical image into an unreadable form, which prevents from unauthorized access. Different encryption algorithms are used to convert the visualized medical image to secure unreadable form. Among numerous encryption techniques, chaos based encryption techniques provides better security because of their deterministic and random behaviours (Sasikaladevi et al., 2019).

The approaches that researchers have suggested to encrypt grayscale, color, and multi-spectral medical images in chaos are numerous(Minocha et al., 2025). Techniques like Logistic, Tent map, Henon map, and chaotic Lorenz model, which are one or multi-form chaotic maps, and hybrid systems, which combine chaotic algorithms with other cryptographic techniques (block ciphers, DNA encoding (Xue et al., 2021), fractional transforms (Ismail et al., 2020), bit-plane decomposition(Rehman & Shafqiue, 2024), and compressive sensing) are common. Such techniques typically involve two steps: permutation, in which the positions of pixels are permuted with chaotic sequences, and diffusion, in which the intensities of pixels are altered in order to remove statistical regularities that may be used by attackers. Chaos-based encryption, with a combination of permutation and diffusion, provides a high resistance to histogram analysis, brute-force attacks, differential attacks, and statistical analysis.These chaotic system are employed by different researchers in encrypting grayscale, color and medical images. The section below discusses some chaos-based medical image protection schemes.

## 2. STATES OF THE ART

An encryption medical image crypt model has been suggested by using Coupled Map Lattice(CML) with sophisticated salp swarm procedure (Thirumarai Selvi et al., 2021) . Initially, medical images are firstly compressed and encrypted through CML generated chaotic series and whale optimization method. Methods of chaos-based encryption use the initial value sensitive conditions and randomness of the model. (W. Song et al., 2024) suggested a medical image secure crypt algorithm that was based on a 3D Logistic-Sine map and the system was efficient in scrambling pixel intensities with the added advantage of being computationally efficient. Their findings revealed that the technique was very secure and resistant to popular cryptographic attacks. Zarei et. al (Mortajez et al., 2020) came up with an effective chaos based secret keys and confusion model to offer confidentiality of DICOM images. They implemented the one dimensional logistic map to produce the secret keys and multiple round permutation is performed to ensure encryption is done using the keys. Hybrid encryption, a combination of conventional cryptography and chaos-based methods, has demonstrated potential to deliver a balance between security and performance. Indicatively, (Hafsa et al., 2021) suggested the combination of AES and a chaotic map to form a hybrid model to be used in telemedicine. The algorithm minimized the computational cost of the traditional encryption and guaranteed a high level of security to the medical images that were being transferred through unsecure networks. Singh et.al (Banik et al., 2019) came up with multiple medical image crypt model using elliptic curve cryptosystem. These keys are produced by a pseudo-random number generated known as the Mersenne Twister that fastly produce the keys used in encrypting the images. The latest developments of machine learning have brought AI-based encryption techniques. (Chai et al., 2019) created an adaptive encryption model of medical pictures that is based on neural networks. This methodically produced encryption keys, which are resistant to brute force as well as statistical attacks. The research indicated scalability and rapidity of this technique, which allowed its use in large-scale telemedicine. sangavi et al. (Sangavi & Thangavel, 2020) suggested an encryption model used to transmit medical images safely using Rossler and sine map.. A new cross cosine chaotic map (Rajendran et al., 2021) has developed to generate random keys that are used to shuffle the pixels of the image and then the shuffled pixels are encoded in to binary format and undergo bit-shifting and flipping operation to diffuse the image to transmit and store the image securely.. Chaotic key series are generated by using these maps and those keys are employed for confusing and substitution process in encryption. A number of the researchers use the combination of the chaos and DNA computation to add complexity to the encryption process to enhance better security of medical images. Quantum cryptography has been developed as a futuristic approach to the encryption of images safely. Sugar, (Anand & Singh, 2020) considered quantum key distribution to encrypt medical images, making them resistant to quantum computer attacks. Their results showed that quantum cryptographic techniques could provide unprecedented security, but it is still a challenge to implement in practice, since the technology is not as mature as it could be. Shafai et. al (El-Shafai et al., 2021) created an active medical crypt through the integration of the Chaos with the DNA computing. They utilized a piecewise rectilinear chaotic model to generate key image, then the key and plain image is encoded into DNA model and execute DNA functions to encrypt the image. The crypt model designed by Siyamol et al. (Chirakkarottu & Mathew, 2020) utilized 2D Zaslavski chaotic map to create random key series, pixels of the original medical image are shuffled with the index of the key series, and the confused image is encrypted with the help of DNA encoding and diffusion process which offers adequate security. Ismail et .al (Chirakkarottu & Mathew, 2020) devised a hybrid one dimensional HGL chaotic function comprising of Henon, Logistic and Gaussian map. Initially medical image pixels are permuted with the help of chaotic key series generated with the help of HGL map and permutated image encrypted using ;the concept of DNA encoding technique followed by the execution of DNA XOR logical function to acquire the encrypted image. A cryptosystem based on Chaos DNA has been designed by many researchers to help in secure transmission of medical images (Banu S & Amirtharajan, 2020; Dagadu et al., 2019; Ravichandran et al., 2021; Stalin et al., 2019). A new one dimensional ICC map (J & R, 2026) has been designed to generate the random series. and two subsequent stages are involved for encrypting the image. In first phase the image pixel positions are modified based on the key series and in the second phase the pixels are modified according the execution of bit xor operation between the confused pixels and integer form chaotic series. All the security analysis has been carried out and achieves the acceptable results. A new 3D hyperchaotic model (Hu et al., 2026) is proposed to overcome the limitations of lower dimensional chaotic map with fixed chaotic values. They have utilized SHA3-512 for generating the seed keys to achieve the integrity. Rubik's cube concept based pixel shuffling and chained bidirectional permutation utilized as barriers to protect security. Parallel computation and optimized key operation pointedly increase the effieciency of the developed model. Bassem et.al (Abd-El-Atty, 2026) integrate the DNA encoding and 4D hyperchaotic model to improve the efficiency and security. They developed three different phases. At first images are splitted into two components, one have lower four-bit, other contain higher four bit. Higher four-bits are encrypted by utilizing DNA operations and lower bits are secured by utilizing hyperchaotic systems. All the performance metrics are evaluated to identify the efficiency and security of the developed crypt model and the results specified that the developed crypt achieves best security. A Hopfield heterogeneous neural network (Zou et al., 2026) concept was developed and combined with discrete memristor to mimic the diversity of neurons. This heterogeneous activation hightly increase the randomness of the chaotic sequence which utilized for enhancing the medical image security.

## 2.1. Research Gap

Based on the survey, the image cryptosystem that integrates DNA encoding and chaos theory presents certain limitations. Nearly all of the existing cryptosystems be dependent on a one-dimensional chaotic map to produce chaotic structures, then employed during the permutation phase of the cryptographic model. However, 1D chaotic models are regularly suffered from restricted key space and lower complexity, which makes vulnerable to brute-force and statistical attacks (Ayemtsa Kuete et al., 2024). Subsequently, the permuted image is transformed into a DNA representation, followed by the execution of various numeric and logical calculations executed between the chaotic sequences and the DNA image to produce the ciphered image. These methods have proven effective in providing robust security for small size images, as they contain fewer pixels than medical images.

Furthermore, many existing systems handled challenges related to execution time, memory requirements, and scalability while handling large size of images. In addition, some methods lack in sufficient to withstand against advanced attacks, particularly when the single chaotic maps exhibit non-ideal randomness in digital implementations. To address this challenge, this article introduces an innovative three-dimensional hyper chaotic map, referred to as the 3D- Tent – Tinker-Sine Map (3D-CSTM), which generates three high-deterministic chaotic sequences.

## 2.2. Our Contribution

- A novel Three-Dimensional Tent-Tinker-Sine Map is developed to produce highly complex and secure pseudo-random key sequences.
- The dynamic property of the 3D-HTTM is assessed through visual representations of trajectories and a bifurcation diagrams which represents the proposed map strong chaotic characteristics.
- An efficient and innovative image cryptosystem is proposed by integrating the 3D-HTTM with bit-flipping mechanism to enhance the diffusion properties.

- The results are comprehensively validated through statistical methods, robustness testing, and differential analysis, confirming that the proposed cryptographic model offers effective security.

The remaining part presented as: Section 3 gives a short summary of the basic concepts of Hell, Tinker and Sine map and the diagrammatic random behaviours of the designed 3D HTTM. Section 4 expands the key production mechanism using 3D HTTM and explained the designed crypt methodology. Final encryption results and strength of security are analysed in Section 5. A final discussion in Section 6 governs the conclusion.

## 3. BASIC PROPERTIES OF THE PROPOSED MODEL

The proposed 3D HTTM is designed by collaborating two dimensional Tinkerbell map and Holmes map and one dimensional Tent map. The following content describes the mathematical function of the all these basic chaotic maps.

### 3.1. Holmes Map

It's one of the two dimensional discrete-time chaotic system, also called as Duffing map. Two chaotic series are generated P and Q which utilize two constants a and b. For getting the accurate chaotic behaviour usually these constants are set the value as a=2.75 and b=0.2. The following equation Eq,(1) represents the Holmes map.

$$p_{x+1} = q_x$$

$$q_{x+1} = -bp_x + aq_x - q_x^3 \tag{1}$$

### 3.2. 1D Tent Map

This is one of the traditional one-dimensional non-linear system. The exact form of this map is specified in Eq. (2) respectively, and they also having good chaotic behaviour (X. Wang & Guan, 2023).

$$x_{k+1} = \begin{cases} \beta x_k/2 \\ \beta(1 - x_k)/2 \end{cases} \tag{2}$$

These chaotic maps generate good chaotic series when the range of α,β value should in the range of $(0 \leq \alpha, \beta \leq 4)$.

### 3.3. 2D TinkerBell Map

One of the good random, deterministic and ergodicity nature chaotic map is a 2D TinkerBell Map. It is a discrete-time functional model which can be employed for generating secrete keys.(Aashiq Banu & Amirtharajan, 2020). Its mathematical notation and its parameter range are given in Eq.(3).

$$\begin{array}{l} x_{k+!} = x_k^2 - y_k^2 + \delta x_k + \mu y_n \\ y_{k+1} = 2x_k y_k + \beta x_k + \alpha y_k \end{array} \quad where \begin{cases} x_0,\ y_0 < 1 \\ \delta = 0.9,\ \mu = -0.6013 \\ \beta = 2,\ \alpha = 0.5 \end{cases} \tag{3}$$

In this map x0 and y0 will be the initial value and the range should be less than 1. All specified additional constant parameters also follow the same value as specified. If these conditions are satisfied then the key series produced by this map will be in random manner.

### 3.4. Proposed 3D HTTM and its Trajectories

The projected hybrid chaotic map is the combination the above discussed 1D Tent map and 2D Holmes and TinkerBell Map. The symbolic notation of the 3D HTTM is given in the following Eq.(4).

$$\begin{array}{l} x_{k+!} = x_k^2 - y_k^2 + \delta \sin(x_{k)} + \mu y_n \\ y_{k+1} = 2x_k y_k + \beta x_k + \alpha y_k \\ z_{k+1} = \beta \sin(\pi y_{k+1}) + \delta(1 - z_n)/2 \end{array} \quad where \begin{cases} x_0,\ y_0, z_0 < 1 \\ \delta = 0.9,\ \mu = -0.6013 \\ \beta = 2,\ \alpha = 0.5 \end{cases} \tag{4}$$

The generated random key chaotic values are completely within the given range. The specified four key factors, in addition to three base seed keys, combine to create six values act as a secret keys. By considering that every key will have a largest value as $10^{-15}$ then the whole size of the key will be calculated by the value of $(10^{15})^{7}$. Hence, the given value of the key is enough to stand in battle of brute-force attacks. Comparison of the suggested model with present chaotic maps is given in Table 1. The trajectories of the proposed 3D-HTTM given in Figure.1, which illustrates the visualized form of each chaotic values composed of the developed chaotic model, which represents its random properties.

*Figure 1.*

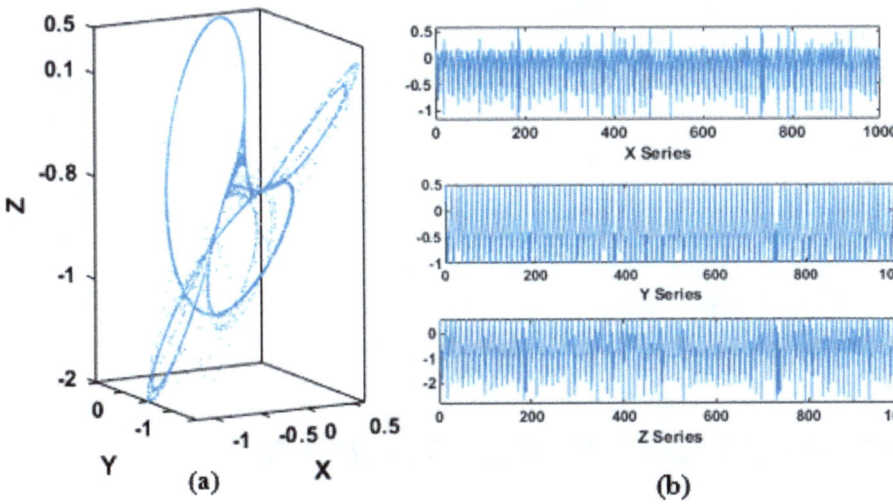


*Table 1. Comparison of proposed 3D HTTM with some of the existing chaotic maps*

| Chaotic Map | Dimension | Key Space | Complexity | Randomness | Security Strength | Suitability for Large Medical Images |
|---|---|---|---|---|---|---|
| Logistic Map | 1D | Low | Simple | Moderate | Vulnerable to attacks | Limited |
| Tent Map | 1D | Low | Simple | Moderate | Moderate | Limited |
| Henon Map | 2D | Medium | Moderate | Good | Improved security | Moderate |
| Tinkerbell Map | 2D | Medium | Moderate | Good | Moderate | Moderate |
| Sine Map | 1D | Low | Simple | Moderate | Moderate | Limited |
| DNA-Chaos Models | Hybrid | Medium | High | Good | Strong | Moderate |
| **Proposed 3D-HTTM** | **3D (Hyperchaotic)** | **High** | **High** | **Excellent** | **Very Strong** | **Highly Suitable** |

## 3.5. Computational Feasibility of the Proposed 3D HTTM Map

To assess the computational feasibility of the proposed HTTM map for lightweight cryptography, the map's computational and structural complexity are analyzed relative to existing state-of-the-art 3D chaotic models, such as 3D Henon map(Hu et al., 2026), 3D logistic map (Patel et al., 2020), and the continuous Lorenz system(Ouannas et al., 2021). Continuous chaotic systems, such as the Lorenz model, require numerical integrators like the fourth-order Runge-Kutta (RK4) to iterate the equations, making them computationally costly and involving multiple floating-point operations at each iterative step. On the other hand, the proposed HTTM map is a discrete-time model that requires basic arithmetic and light transcendent function operations.Also, compared to classical 3D discrete chaotic maps, such as the 3D Logistic map, which is limited by narrow chaotic regions and a simple algebraic equation susceptible to phase space reconstruction attack, the proposed HTTM map incorporates chaotic characteristics of Tinkerbell, Holmes, and Tent maps. This combination increases the size of the key space through four control parameters achieves broad hyperchaos ranges, and has low computational requirements for optimal lightweight healthcare encryption schemes.

## 4. PROPOSED 3D-TTTM SECURITY FRAMEWORK

The designed crypt framework is the combination of transposition and diffusion methods. A basic pixel permutation depends on a chaotic key index that produces in confusion part. A secret two dimensional key matrix is created using chaotic values consructed by 3D-TTTM. For diffusion, the key image is utilized for executing XOR operation with confused image and pixel bits flipping is executed by utilizing one of the chaotic series of HTTM. The entire framework of the proposed scheme is depicted in Figure 2.

### 4.1. Confusion and Diffusion Process of the Proposed HTTM Based Security Framework

The image pixels are entirely become unpredictable based on the chaotic series triggered by HTTM. These series index values change the position of pixels in the given image. Consequently, pixel indexes are shuffled depends on the ordered pointer numbers from HTTM to compose the scrambled matrix form of image. The progression of scrambling is specified in the subsequent steps:

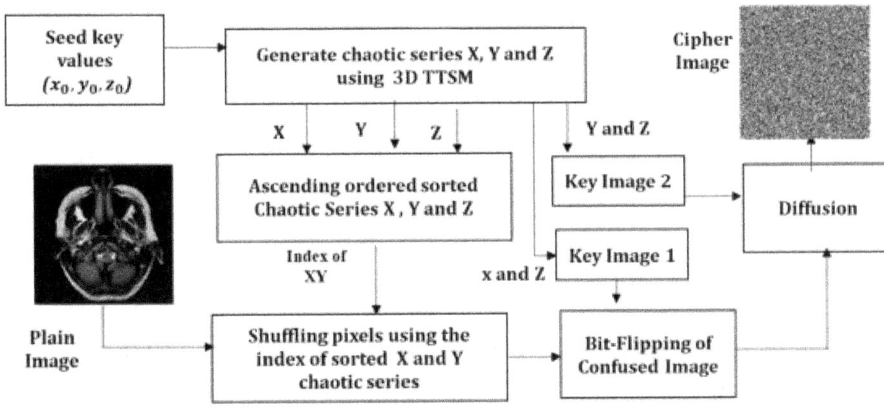


**Step1:** Input: medical image, Initially, initialize the control parameters, as well as the initial values$x_0, y_0, z_0$, related to the limited value given in Chapter 2.

**Step2:** Compute a series say X={$x_0$, $x_{1,}$ $x_2$... $x_{(A\times B)}$}, Y={$y_0$,$y_{1,}$$y_3$... $y_{(A\times B)}$}, Z={$z_0$,$z_{1,}$$z_3$... $z_{(A\times B)}$} Here A and B denotes the size of the given MI,

**Step 3:** Sort the chaotic series {X, Y, Z} and repossess the indent of the key sequence as shown in the Eq (5).

$$\begin{cases} [ax, sx] = sort(X) \\ [ay, sy] = sort(Y) \\ [az, sz] = sort(Z) \end{cases} \tag{5}$$

Sorted chaotic series { ax, ay, az }and its index series are{ sx, sy, sz}. X, Y and Z are random series produced by the developed HTTM. These series are converted in to the form of ascending order, then the index value of the old series and the index value of the new series are taken for shuffling the pixels of the image.

**Step 4:** Input image (IM) pixels are transpositioned by considering vector range of the sorted keys series as characterized in the subsequent Eq (6).

$$IM'_{pp,qq} \leftrightarrow IM_{sx(cols),sy(rows)} \text{ where } \begin{cases} cols, rows = 1,2\ldots A/B \\ pp, qq = 1,2\ldots A/B \end{cases} \tag{6}$$

**Step 5:** The output of the previous image is given as a seed for diffusion part, for diffusion two key matrix are generated to encrypt. Key1 is used for flipbit process and Key2 is used for bit-XOR operation. The formation of key image is expanded in the succeeding Eq. (7).

$$\begin{cases} key1_{i,j} = mod((y_p \times 10000), PV) \ if(mod(i, div) == 0 \\ key2_{i,j} = mod(z_q \times 10000), PV) \ if(mod(i, div) != 0 \end{cases} \quad (7)$$

$$\begin{cases} key2_{i,j} = mod((x_p \times 10000), PV) \ if(mod(i, div) == 0 \\ key2_{i,j} = mod(z_q \times 10000), PV) \ if(mod(i, div) != 0 \end{cases}$$

$$\begin{cases} i\ value = j\ value = 1, 2, \ldots A \times B,\ PV = 256 \\ p\ value = q\ value = 1, 2, \ \ldots \frac{A \times B}{2},\ div = 2 \end{cases},$$

**Step 6:** Confused image is converted into form of binary then bit-flip operation is executed on each pixels then bit-XOR calculation is evaluated on converted pixel values and key matrix. Finally the bits are converted into pixels values for getting the final encrypted image. These operations are stated below Eq.(8) in the form of symbolic representation.

$$\begin{aligned} IM'' &= dec2bin(IM') \\ fb &= mod(key1, 8); \\ IM''' &= flipbits(IM'', fb) \\ EM &= bitxor(IM''', key2) \end{aligned} \quad (8)$$

This EM images is securely transmitted in network or stored in the repository. For decryption the receiver should use the same key for chaotic key generation and use the reverse process for getting the original image. The Algorithmic structure of the proposed model is given in Table 2.

*Table 2. Pseudo code of the proposed model*

| *Algorithm 1: Confusion process* | *Algorithm 2: Diffusion process* |
|---|---|
| ***Input:****Input Image I (A × B)*<br>***Initialize***: ($x_0$, $y_0$, $z_0$, Skipping malformed tag: msub, Skipping malformed tag: msub, Skipping malformed tag: msub)<br>***for*** *i=1: A* ***do***<br>***for*** *j = 1: B*<br>*Compute* ($x_i$, $y_i$, $z_i$) *using 3DHTTM;*<br>***end for***<br>*[ax,sx] = sort(x);*<br>*[ay,sy] = sort(y);*<br>*[az,sz] = sort(z);*<br>***for*** *i=1:A* ***do***<br>***for*** *j=1:B* ***do***<br>*I*Skipping malformed tag: msubsup *I*Skipping malformed tag: msubsup<br>***end for***<br>***end for*** | ***Input*** : *MI' (Confused Image)*<br>*Chaotic series* $(x_i, y_i, z_i)$ *wherei* $= 1, 2, ..(A \times B)$<br>***for*** *i = 1: A*<br>***for*** *j = 1: B*<br>$key1_{i,j} = mod((y_p \times 10000), PV)$<br>$key2_{i,j} = mod(z_q \times 10000), PV)$<br>***end***<br>***end***<br>***for*** *i = 1: A*<br>***for*** *j = 1: B*<br>$key1_{i,j} = mod((x_p \times 10000), PV)$<br>$key2_{i,j} = mod(z_q \times 10000), PV)$<br>***end***<br>***end***<br><br>***for*** *all pixels in IM'*<br>$IM'' = dec2bin(IM')$<br>$fb = mod(key1, 8)$ ;<br>$IM''' = flipbits(IM'', fb)$<br>$EM = bitxor(IM''', key2)$<br>***end***<br>***Output:*** ***EM*** *(Encrypted Medical Image)* |

## 5. SIMULATION RESULTS

Simulation reslults were executed on a private system furnished by using Intel i7 generation model and 8 Giga Byte of RAM is used to develop the model. MATLAB 2021a has utilied for implementing the model with image size as 256 x 256. The results of the developed model experiments is shown in Figure. 3, which shows the input medical image, result after shuffled and final diffused image. Different test cases were executed in the following to validate the robustness of the developed crypt method.

While the creation of sophisticated secure transaction and repository in digital health is imperative, making the transition from theory to implementation raises distinct problems that need to be accounted for in practice. Medical facilities present a very complicated setting, with an extremely diverse array of equipment, stringent requirements regarding confidentiality (e.g., HIPAA and GDPR), and limited IoMT device capabilities. Thus, a practical system will have to provide reliable [security / performance], while at the same time, being fast enough to avoid any lag times that may affect the speed of treatment and able to seamlessly integrate with current EHR systems, while functioning in an environment where power and Internet availability are extremely limited.

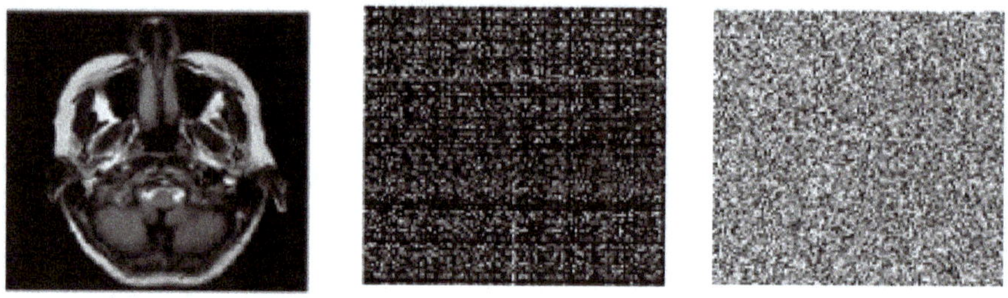

(a) (b) (c)

## 5.1 Histogram Anaylsis

Cipher image histogram is estimated to differ significantly from its original counterpart. Due to encryption, the pixel values are randomized, leading to a uniformly distributed histogram. This homogeneity designates that the encryption process has effectively obfuscated the image, ensuring that no discernible patterns or details from the original image are preserved. This property is critical for maintaining the security and confidentiality of the image, as it prevents unauthorized analysis or reconstruction. Comparing histograms of both the images is a key step in assessing the effectiveness of the crypt model. A good crypt model must yield a histogram for the encrypted image that lacks any resemblance to the original. This ensures resistance against statistical attacks and demonstrates the robustness of the encryption process. (Ali & Ali, 2020). Figure. 4(a) and 4(b) show the analysis of histogram to check the uniform spreading of the image pixels. These figures evidently demonstrate that the developed crypt effectively provides acceptable randomization to battle statistical analysis.

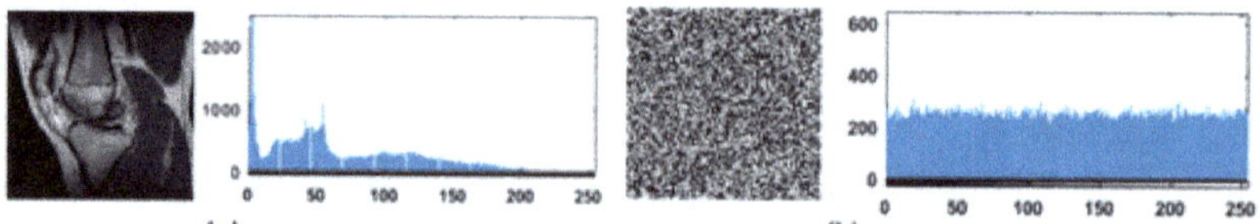


(a) (b)

## 5.2 Correlation of Adjacent Pixels

Analysis of correlation coefficients is a critical measure in assessing the image encryption method effectiveness [23]. To quantify the similarity or dependency between the adjacent pixels in an image, it compares them to each other. When dealing with an original image, the correlation among neighboring pixels is generally large, due to the natural presence of smooth transitions and continuous patterns in natural images. This is a high correlation whose characteristic discloses structural information about the image. In the case of an encrypted image, the correlation coefficient must be significantly smaller, and tends to be close to zero. This shows that the encryption operation has effectively minimised the correlation between the pixel values and the dependency between the pixel values makes the encrypted image not maintain any visual or statistical structure of the original. Achieving such randomness is crucial for robust encryption, as it prevents attackers from using statistical methods to reconstruct the original image (Girdhar & Kumar, 2018). Another statistical measure to identify the relation between neighbouring pixels is the association analysis. Eq.(9) represents the evaluation of association amid pair of images.

$$CC = \frac{cov(p,q)}{\sigma_p \sigma_q} = \frac{1}{n} \frac{\sum (p_i - \bar{p})(q_i - \bar{q})}{\sqrt{\frac{1}{n} \sum (p_i - \bar{p})^2 . \frac{1}{n} \sum (q_i - \bar{q})^2}} \quad (9)$$

$p_i$ and $q_i$ represent image pixels. An operative crypt method demands the correlation results nearly close to zero which indicates the relation-less pixels in the cipher image. Figure.6 illustrates the CC values of all neighbouring direction of pixels of origin and cipher images. By considering the values, it could be recognized that the developed crypt impressively lowered the relation between pixels in each channel. Table 3 displays the correlation result of every image in every direction and matched the values with related work (Shafai et al., 2021)

*Table 3. Results of correlation values and comparison*

| Image 1-6 | Developed Model | | | Ref(Shafai et al., 2021) | | |
|---|---|---|---|---|---|---|
| | Hori-Corr | Ver-Corr | Diag-Corr | Hori-Corr | Ver-Corr | Diag-Cor |
| 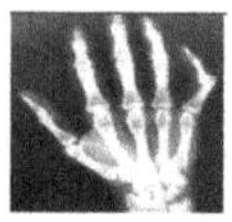 | 0.0033 | 3.029e-04 | -0.0028 | -0.0470 | 0.0312 | -0.0361 |
| 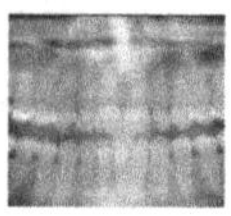 | 0.0018 | -0.0041 | -0.0077 | 0.0211 | 0.0144 | 0.0061 |
| 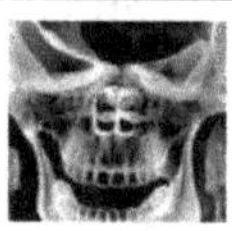 | -0.0062 | -0.0054 | 0.0018 | 0.0322 | 0.0132 | -0.0351 |
| 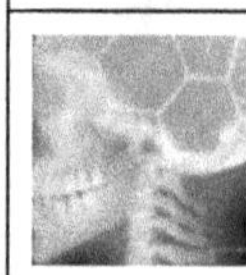 | 5.558e-05 | -0.0037 | -0.0060 | 0.0992 | 0.0187 | 0.0373 |
| 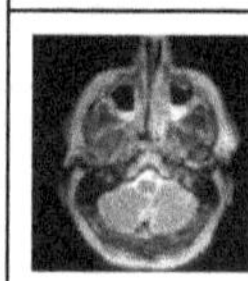 | 0.0074 | 0.0097 | -0.0023 | -0.0118 | -0.0228 | 0.0203 |
| 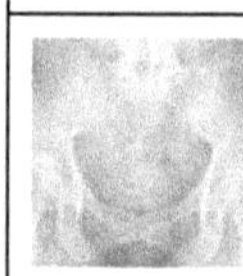 | -2.595e-04 | -8.725e-04 | -1.963e-04 | -0.0118 | -0.0228 | 0.0203 |

## 5.3 Entropy Analysis

It is a universally utilized measure for evaluating the ambiguity in a original picture. The entropy of ideal image will be 8. By considering the test results of the developed crypt the encrypted picture has the nearest value of 8, which denotes more randomized form and denotes the crypt model achieves good performance (Dey et al., 2018)(Shafique, Mehmood, Alawida, & Nasir, 2025). The entropy calculation of the crypted image is elaborated in Eq.(10). Table 3 shows encrypted image entropy results.

$$H = -\sum_{i=1}^{N} p_i log_2 (p_i) \quad (10)$$

## 5.4 Identification of Encryption Quality

### 5.4.1 Histogram Deviation (HD)

Histogram deviation calculated among the input and the cipher image specifies the difference in pixel intensity distributions. The original image typically has a distinctive histogram with recognizable patterns. After encryption, the cipher image's histogram should be randomized or uniform, indicating successful encryption(Shafique, Mehmood, Alawida, Elhadef, et al., 2025). The range of histogram deviation typically spans from 0 to 1. A deviation of 0 indicates the histograms of the original and cipher images are identical, meaning the encryption has failed to alter the image's statistical properties. A deviation of 1 represents the maximum difference, where the cipher image's histogram is entirely different from the original, indicating effective encryption. Results of HD for each images are given in Table 4.

### 5.4.2 Analysis of SSIM, FSIM and PSNR

Assessment of image quality post-encryption can be done using both objective and subjective approaches. Objectives measures such as PSNR and MSE are numerical comparisons of pixels, while the use of SSIM as an objective measure of image quality is more accurate because it includes structural, luminance, and contrast aspects in its computations.(J. Wang, 2024)(Das et al., 2024). The Structural Similarity Index (SSIM) and PSNR will be calculated amid the given input image (I) and the resultant cipher mage (C) based on the Eq. (11).

$$SSIM(I, C) = \frac{(2\mu_I\mu_C + c_1)(2\sigma_{IC} + c_2)}{(\mu_I^2 + \mu_C^2 + c_1)\ (\sigma_I^2 + \sigma_C^2 + c_2)} \tag{11}$$

$$PSNR = 20\ \log_{10}\frac{I_{max}}{\sqrt{MSE}}\ where\ MSE = \frac{1}{M \times N}\sum_{i=1}^{M}\sum_{j=1}^{N}(I(i,j) - C(i,j))^2 \tag{12}$$

For an 8-bit grayscale image, the max pixel value, MAX, is 255. We then find the Mean Squared Error MSE. PSNR shows how well an image is rebuilt. Higher PSNR means better quality, while lower values point to more distortion – great for seeing if encryption worked. The SSIM value ranges from -1 to 1. If it's 1, the images are identical. For good encryption, this score should be close to 0. This shows the original image and the encrypted one lost all structural similarity, meaning the data's well hidden.

*Table 4. Encryption quality metrics*

| Metrics | Method | Img 1 | Img 2 | Img 3 | Img 4 | Img 5 | Img 6 |
|---|---|---|---|---|---|---|---|
| Entropy | Proposed Ref<br>(Shafai et al., 2021) | 7.9967<br>7.9974 | 7.9976<br>7.9974 | 0.9964<br>7.9974 | 7.9973<br>7.9971 | 7.9969<br>7.9969 | 0.9973<br>7.9971 |
| HD | Proposed Ref<br>(Shafai et al., 2021) | 0.9183<br>1.0062 | 0.7972<br>0.9182 | 0.9141<br>0.4959 | 0.8611<br>0.7805 | 0.7361<br>0.9894 | 0.7170<br>1.1115 |
| SSIM | Proposed Ref<br>(Shafai et al., 2021) | 0.0093<br>0.0052 | 0.0108<br>0.0038 | 0.0074<br>0.0040 | 0.0087<br>0.0043 | 0.0061<br>0.0020 | 0.0109<br>0.0042 |
| FSIM | Proposed Ref<br>(Shafai et al., 2021) | 0.1918<br>0.2730 | 0.1923<br>0.2867 | 0.3251<br>0.4011 | 0.1787<br>0.2650 | 0.2274<br>0.4111 | 0.1468<br>0.2340 |
| PSNR | Proposed Ref<br>(Shafai et al., 2021) | 8.1208<br>8.0740 | 9.7420<br>9.7303 | 7.3678<br>7.1330 | 9.2868<br>9.2558 | 6.9316<br>6.5202 | 9.1135<br>8.9850 |

### 5.4.3 Key Sensitivity Analysis

Key sensitivity is one of the essential property of a secure cipher system, ensuring that even a minor variation in any of the secret keys, it produces a completely different encrypted image(Cruz-Piris et al., 2025; Yadav et al., 2025). This property is particularly most important for chaos key dependent encryption schemes due to their inherent property that sensitivity to initial conditions. To evaluate the key sensitivity fo the developed 3D-HTTM based encryption model, a tiny variation was introduced in one of the initial parameter $x_0$ to $x_0$ $10^{-15}$. The same medical image was then encrypted using both original and changed keys. The resulting cipher images were identified to be entirely different, with no correlation between them.

To quantitatively assess this sensitivity, correlation analysis is executed between the two cipher images generated by utilizing the original and changed keys. The result of correlation values were observed to be close to zero, which indicates the encrypted outputs are highly uncorrelated (X. Song et al., 2025). The correlation between the two cipher images is calculated in all the directions, for horizontal the value is 0.001 and for vertical and diagonal -0.002 and 0.0005 is achieved. Based on these values, it can be identified that the proposed model is highly sensitivity to keys which can resist brute force attack and differential attacks.

### 5.4.4 NPCR and UACI Analysis

To evaluate the toughness of the proposed model against numerous attacks, NPCR and UACI is utilized. These metrics measure the sensitiveness of the slight changes in the input image (An et al., 2025). A good encryption scheme should generate wholly diverse cipher images even a small change in the plain image and also in any one of the seed keys. For all the test images these metrics result values are identified between the two cipher images. The NPCR value for all the test images is greater than 99.50% and the UACI value is greater than 33.30%. This conclude that the proposed model is highly sensitivity to keys and input image.

### 5.4.5 Robustness Evaluation Against Noise and Data Loss

To test how well our model holds up, we use two typical factors: Gaussian noise and data loss (Abd-El-Atty, 2026). These problems are common in wireless IoMT systems because of sensor disruptions and weak network signals.For each encrypted medical image type—MRI, lungs, and ultrasound—we added Gaussian noise with a standard deviation meant for moderate interference. Then, for the data loss test, we took out 15% of the pixels randomly. After corrupting the images and then decrypting them, we measured their quality using the Peak Signal-to-Noise Ratio (PSNR) and Structural Similarity Index Measure (SSIM)(Das et al., 2024).

Table 5 shows the results under noisy and data loss conditions for all three image types. It demonstrates that the encryption method works really well despite both kinds of problems. When there's just noise, PSNR values stay above 28 dB and SSIM values go over 0.8, meaning the picture quality is still good. And even after losing 15% of the data, the decrypted images look pretty acceptable, with PSNR values higher than 22 dB and SSIM scores at or near 0.75.This level of robustness is particularly important for IoMT systems, where medical images may be transmitted over unreliable or constrained networks. The capability of the proposed scheme to avoid quality degradation is such that the encrypted and decrypted images still have diagnostic relevance that facilitates secure and reliable healthcare communication.

*Table 5. Robustness evaluation results under noise and data loss*

| **Image** | **Proposed Model** | | | |
|---|---|---|---|---|
| | **PSNR noise(dB)** | **SSIM noise** | **PSNR data loss** | **SSIM data loss** |
| MRI | 28.24 | 0.89 | 23.19 | 0.86 |
| X-Ray | 29.13 | 0.85 | 23.94 | 0.74 |
| Ultrasonic | 28.41 | 0.87 | 22.79 | 0.78 |

## 5.5 Hardware Feasibility and Runtime Performance Analysis

To appraise the practical implementation of the 3D-HTTM model, feasibility of hardware and runtime performance analysis were conducted. The proposed model is implemented on system furnished with an Core i7 processor (Intel), 8GB RAM, using MATLAB 2021 environment.

The calculative complexity of the crypt model developed is analysed based on the size of the input image(Man et al., 2021). Let the given medical image of size M x N, then the total count of pixels will be P=M x N. The overall process of the proposed model consist of three stages, Chaotic key sequence generation, permutation and diffusion. The time complexity for producing the key series is O(P). In the confusion phase, the chaotic series was arranged in sorting order so it requires O(PlogP) time, and shuffling of pixels requires O(PlogP). Hence the complexity of overall confusion process is O(PlogP). Bit level operations are executed in diffusion process and it requires O(P). By combining three stage complexity the overall will be O(PlogP).

## 6. CONCLUSION

The proposed hybrid HTTM-based encryption framework shows great cryptographic strength, though it has some limits due to its developmental phase. It's mostly tested on medical imaging data, but not yet for 3D scans or other non-medical info. Plus, it doesn't integrate with DNA computing or asymmetric cryptography methods. Even with those constraints, the results still mean a lot for digital healthcare systems. The Shannon entropy value nearing 8, along with close-to-zero pixel correlation, effectively obscures spatial patterns to shield health data stored in the cloud. At the same time, the peak signal-to-noise ratio ensures no visual distortion happens when transmitting patient info in real-time. This all lets it keep a low computational cost needed for health imaging on IoT devices.

For future research, scientists plan to build on this work. That includes blending 3D HTTM maps with dynamic S-boxes, speeding up the process with GPUs, and testing more varied and bigger datasets.

## REFERENCES


Aashiq Banu, S., & Amirtharajan, R. (2020). Tri-level scrambling and enhanced diffusion for DICOM image cipher- DNA and chaotic fused approach. *Multimedia Tools and Applications, 79*(39-40), 28807–28824. DOI: 10.1007/s11042-020-09501-5

Abd-El-Atty, B. (2026). A dual medical image encryption algorithm based on dynamic DNA operations. *Computers and Electrical Engineering, 130*(June 2025), 1–20. DOI: 10.1016/j.compeleceng.2025.110899

Ali, T. S., & Ali, R. (2020). A Novel Medical Image Signcryption Scheme Using TLTS and Henon Chaotic Map. *IEEE Access : Practical Innovations, Open Solutions, 8*, 71974–71992. DOI: 10.1109/ACCESS.2020.2987615

An, T., Gao, T., Chen, T., & Jiang, D. (2025). A dual-image encryption scheme for sensitive region of traffic image using public key cryptosystem and novel chaotic map. *Complex & Intelligent Systems, 11*(7), 1–23. DOI: 10.1007/s40747-025-01912-x

Anand, A., & Singh, A. K. (2020). An improved DWT-SVD domain watermarking for medical information security. *Computer Communications, 152*(January), 72–80. DOI: 10.1016/j.comcom.2020.01.038

Ayemtsa Kuete, G. P., Heucheun Yepdia, L. M., Tiedeu, A., & Mboupda Pone, J. R. (2024). Medical image cryptosystem using a new 3-D map implemented in a microcontroller. In *Multimedia Tools and Applications* (Issue 0123456789). Springer US. DOI: 10.1007/s11042-024-18460-0

Banik, A., Shamsi, Z., & Laiphrakpam, D. S. (2019). An encryption scheme for securing multiple medical images. *Journal of Information Security and Applications, 49*, 102398. Advance online publication. DOI: 10.1016/j.jisa.2019.102398

Banu, S. A., & Amirtharajan, R. (2020). A robust medical image encryption in dual domain: chaos-DNA-IWT combined approach. *Medical & Biological Engineering & Computing, 58*(7), 1445–1458. DOI: 10.1007/s11517-020-02178-w

Benaissi, S., Chikouche, N., & Hamza, R. (2023). A novel image encryption algorithm based on hybrid chaotic maps using a key image. In *Optik* (Vol. 272). DOI: 10.1016/j.ijleo.2022.170316

Chai, X., Zhang, J., Gan, Z., & Zhang, Y. (2019). Medical image encryption algorithm based on Latin square and memristive chaotic system. *Multimedia Tools and Applications, 78*(24), 35419–35453. DOI: 10.1007/s11042-019-08168-x

Chirakkarottu, S., & Mathew, S. (2020). A novel encryption method for medical images using 2D Zaslavski map and DNA cryptography. *SN Applied Sciences*, *2*(1), 1–10. DOI: 10.1007/s42452-019-1685-8

Cruz-Piris, L., Marín-López, A., Álvarez-Campana, M., Sanz, M., Moreno, J. I., & Arroyo, D. (2025). Measuring the impact of post quantum cryptography in Industrial IoT scenarios. *Internet of Things : Engineering Cyber Physical Human Systems*, *34*, 101793. Advance online publication. DOI: 10.1016/j.iot.2025.101793

Dagadu, J. C., Li, J. P., & Aboagye, E. O. (2019). Medical Image Encryption Based on Hybrid Chaotic DNA Diffusion. *Wireless Personal Communications*, *108*(1), 591–612. DOI: 10.1007/s11277-019-06420-z

Das, B. D. C., Patra, A., Saha, A., & Sikder, S. S. (2024). Secured communication of multiple compressed infrared images using 6D hyper-chaotic encryption. *Journal of Optics (India)*, *18*(3), 535–558. DOI: 10.1007/s12596-024-01655-x

Dey, D., Giri, D., Jana, B., Maitra, T., & Mohapatra, R. N. (2018). Linear-feedback shift register-based multi-ant cellular automation and chaotic map-based image encryption. *Security and Privacy*, *1*(6), 1–11. DOI: 10.1002/spy2.52

El-Shafai, W., Khallaf, F., El-Rabaie, E. S. M., El-Samie, F. E. A., El Shafai, W., Khallaf, F., Sayed, E., El Rabaie, M., Abd, F. E., & Samie, E. (2021). Robust medical image encryption based on DNA-chaos cryptosystem for secure telemedicine and healthcare applications. *Journal of Ambient Intelligence and Humanized Computing*, *12*(10), 9007–9035. DOI: 10.1007/s12652-020-02597-5

El Shafai, W., Khallaf, F., Sayed, E., El Rabaie, M., Abd, F. E., & Samie, E. (2021). Robust medical image encryption based on DNA - chaos cryptosystem for secure telemedicine and healthcare applications. *Journal of Ambient Intelligence and Humanized Computing*, *12*(10), 9007–9035. DOI: 10.1007/s12652-020-02597-5

Girdhar, A., & Kumar, V. (2018). A RGB image encryption technique using Lorenz and Rossler chaotic system on DNA sequences. *Multimedia Tools and Applications*, *77*(20), 27017–27039. DOI: 10.1007/s11042-018-5902-z

Hafsa, A., Sghaier, A., Malek, J., & Machhout, M. (2021). Image encryption method based on improved ECC and modified AES algorithm. *Multimedia Tools and Applications*, *80*(13), 19769–19801. Advance online publication. DOI: 10.1007/s11042-021-10700-x

Hu, C., Zhang, L., Chen, R., Gu, Q., Ning, B., Hua, Q., & Zeng, M. (2026). A dynamically parameterized 3D hyperchaotic cascade for secure and real-time encryption of medical images. *Digital Signal Processing: A Review Journal, 170*(November 2025). DOI: 10.1016/j.dsp.2025.105767

Ismail, S. M., Said, L. A., Radwan, A. G., Madian, A. H., & Abu-elyazeed, M. F. (2020). *A novel image encryption system merging fractional-order edge detection and generalized chaotic maps. 167.*

J, J., & R, P. (2025, June). J, J., & R, P. (2026). A robust medical image encryption technique using inverse cosine chaotic map. *Expert Systems with Applications*, *298*, 129574. Advance online publication. DOI: 10.1016/j.eswa.2025.129574

Man, Z., Li, J., Di, X., Sheng, Y., & Liu, Z. (2021). Double image encryption algorithm based on neural network and chaos. *Chaos, Solitons, and Fractals*, *152*, 111318. Advance online publication. DOI: 10.1016/j.chaos.2021.111318

Minocha, S., Sharma, S. R., Singh, B., & Gandomi, A. H. (2025). Adaptive image encryption approach using an enhanced swarm intelligence algorithm. *Scientific Reports*, *15*(1), 1–23. DOI: 10.1038/s41598-025-86569-9

Mortajez, S., Tahmasbi, M., Zarei, J., & Jamshidnezhad, A. (2020). A novel chaotic encryption scheme based on efficient secret keys and confusion technique for confidential of DICOM images. *Informatics in Medicine Unlocked*, *20*(May), 100396. Advance online publication. DOI: 10.1016/j.imu.2020.100396

Ouannas, A., Karouma, A., Grassi, G., Pham, V. T., & Luong, V. S. (2021). A novel secure communications scheme based on chaotic modulation, recursive encryption and chaotic masking. *Alexandria Engineering Journal*, *60*(1), 1873–1884. DOI: 10.1016/j.aej.2020.11.035

Patel, S., Bharath, K. P., & Rajesh Kumar, M.Bharath K PRajesh Kumar M. (2020). Symmetric keys image encryption and decryption using 3D chaotic maps with DNA encoding technique. *Multimedia Tools and Applications*, *79*(43-44), 31739–31757. Advance online publication. DOI: 10.1007/s11042-020-09551-9

Rajendran, S., Krithivasan, K., & Doraipandian, M. (2021). A novel cross cosine map based medical image cryptosystem using dynamic bit-level diffusion. *Multimedia Tools and Applications*, *80*(16), 24221–24243. DOI: 10.1007/s11042-021-10798-z

Ravichandran, D., Banu, S. A., Murthy, B. K., Balasubramanian, V., Fathima, S., & Amirtharajan, R. (2021). An efficient medical image encryption using hybrid DNA computing and chaos in transform domain. *Medical & Biological Engineering & Computing*, *59*(3), 589–605. DOI: 10.1007/s11517-021-02328-8

Rehman, M. U., & Shafqiue, A. (2024). Robust Encryption Framework for IoT Devices Based on Bit-plane Extraction, Chaotic Sine Models, and Quantum Operations. *Internet of Things : Engineering Cyber Physical Human Systems*, *27*(May), 101241. Advance online publication. DOI: 10.1016/j.iot.2024.101241

Sangavi, V., & Thangavel, P. (2020). An exotic multi-dimensional conceptualization for medical image encryption exerting Rossler system and Sine map. *Journal of Information Security and Applications*, *55*(October), 102626. Advance online publication. DOI: 10.1016/j.jisa.2020.102626

Sasikaladevi, N., Geetha, K., Sriharshini, K., & Durga Aruna, M. (2019). RADIANT - hybrid multilayered chaotic image encryption system for color images. *Multimedia Tools and Applications*, *78*(9), 11675–11700. DOI: 10.1007/s11042-018-6711-0

Shafique, A., Mehmood, A., Alawida, M., Elhadef, M., & Rehman, M. U. (2025). *A fusion of machine learning and cryptography for fast data encryption through the encoding of high and moderate plaintext information blocks*. 5349–5375. DOI: 10.1007/s11042-024-18959-6

Shafique, A., Mehmood, A., Alawida, M., & Nasir, A. (2025). *Journal of Information Security and Applications Enhancing privacy in data transmission between IoT devices : A robust encryption and embedding framework for secure and meaningful image communication. 93*(June).

Song, W., Fu, C., Lin, Z., Zhang, Y., Chen, J., & Sham, C. W. (2024). Batch medical image encryption using 3D Latin cube-based simultaneous permutation and diffusion. *Signal, Image and Video Processing*, *18*(3), 2499–2508. DOI: 10.1007/s11760-023-02925-0

Song, X., Feng, S., Yi, W., & Zheng, Y. (2025). Quantum grey-scale image encryption method based on alternating quantum random walk. *EPJ Quantum Technology*, *12*(1), 82. Advance online publication. DOI: 10.1140/epjqt/s40507-025-00386-7

Stalin, S., Maheshwary, P., Shukla, P. K., Maheshwari, M., Gour, B., & Khare, A. (2019). Fast and Secure Medical Image Encryption Based on Non Linear 4D Logistic Map and DNA Sequences (NL4DLM_DNA). *Journal of Medical Systems*, *43*(8), 267. Advance online publication. DOI: 10.1007/s10916-019-1389-z

Su, Y., Wang, X., & Gao, H. (2024). Chaotic image encryption algorithm based on bit-level feedback adjustment. *Information Sciences, 679*(February 2022), 121088. DOI: 10.1016/j.ins.2024.121088

Thirumarai Selvi, C., Amudha, J., & Sudhakar, R. (2021). A modified salp swarm algorithm (SSA) combined with a chaotic coupled map lattices (CML) approach for the secured encryption and compression of medical images during data transmission. *Biomedical Signal Processing and Control, 66*(December 2020). DOI: 10.1016/j.bspc.2021.102465

Wang, J. (2024). Cyber security analysis based medical image encryption in cloud IoT network using quantum deep learning model. *Optical and Quantum Electronics, 56*(3), 1–12. DOI: 10.1007/s11082-023-06076-x

Wang, X., & Guan, N. (2023). *2D sine - logistic - tent - coupling map for image encryption*. 13399–13419.

Wen, H., Lin, Y., Yang, L., & Chen, R. (2024). Cryptanalysis of an image encryption scheme using variant Hill cipher and chaos. *Expert Systems with Applications, 250*(March), 123748. DOI: 10.1016/j.eswa.2024.123748

Xue, X., Jin, H., Zhou, D., & Zhou, C. (2021). Medical Image Protection Algorithm Based on Deoxyribonucleic Acid Chain of Dynamic Length. *Frontiers in Genetics, 12*(March), 1–18. DOI: 10.3389/fgene.2021.654663

Yadav, A., Jaipuriyar, A., Roy, S., & Rawat, U. (2025). A lossless image encryption technique using chaotic map and DNA encoding. *Multimedia Tools and Applications, 84*(34), 42851–42873. DOI: 10.1007/s11042-025-20851-w

Zou, H., Lu, Y., Li, W., Li, W., & Chai, X. (2026). A heterogeneous Hopfield neural network with discrete memristor: Modeling, dynamics, and application in medical image encryption. *Expert Systems with Applications, 312*(January), 131457. Advance online publication. DOI: 10.1016/j.eswa.2026.131457

Chapter 14

# Integration of Classical and Quantum Cryptography in IoT

**Jayavardhanarao Sahukaru**
http://orcid.org/0000-0003-0549-6757
*Aditya Institute of Technology and Management, India*

**Balajee Maram**
http://orcid.org/0000-0001-5635-5642
*SR University, India*

**Padala Ashok**
*Vignana Bharathi Institute of Technology, India*

**Kuppala Swapna**
*Siddhartha Institute of Technology and Sciences, India*

## ABSTRACT

*The chapter will act as an appositive and definitive boundary review on the integration of the classical and quantum cryptographic means into the Internet of Things (IoT) system through the position of the recent scholarly, industrial, and standards-related sources. The literature being evaluated is concerned with the increased awareness that the old cryptographic solutions will not be adequate with respect to the new security threats of the large, heterogeneous and highly distributed deployments of IoT. In such a scenario, quantum cryptography or simply quantum key distribution has been given a lot of attention since quantum key distribution is theoretically proved to be secure against both classical and quantum adversary.*

DOI: 10.4018/979-8-3373-9053-6.ch014

*The literature however also speaks of the fact that there are significant limitations in the application of quantum cryptographic in the IoT world which can be broadly termed as a limitation being constrained by the consumption of energy.*

## I. MOTIVATION TO SURVEY DOMAIN

### A. IoT Cryptography as a Surveilled Landscape

This situation within the IoT security was originally organized by placing in place the three fundamental derivations of cryptography requirements - secretiveness of wireless as well as well wireless messages, machine authentication, scale of key management into larger threat models through which the eavesdropping threat was generally referenced - the former two were generally regarded as distinct threats. Subsequent reviews narrowed this image by considering the proper definition of the IoT protocols (e.g., CoAP, MQTT, 6LoWPAN) to include security bindings at other layers, and similar the image to classical security (i.e. primitives such as AES-based link-protection, TLS/DTLS handshakes, identity management using PKI, etc.), and comparable it to non-cryptographic countermeasures, e.g. physical anti-tampering and intrusion detection (García et al., 2025). The other has been the incompatibility between high cryptographic guarantees and a large resource bottleneck; recent surveys have found out that more than 60-70 percent of deployments are in a stripped-down or pre-shared-key mode to give latency and resource constraints to large-scale sensor deployments (Sharath et al., 2025; Rakhra et al., 2025). To the expectations standards, which would be much more aligned, according to the reviews, the capabilities of devices are heterogeneous and long lived deployments making it more difficult to define key lifecycle operations such as provisioning, renewal, revocation and ownership transfer. Admittedly, that vast majority of the surveyed literatures never dealt with the case of quantum-capable attackers and instead of quantum-capable, quantum-key-distribution mechanisms, post-quantum mechanisms are simply artificially constrained to limited scopes, although the current taxonomies of IoT cryptography can be hardly considered comprehensive regarding the requirements to the integration of future quantum-resilient mechanisms (García et al., 2025; Nangraj, 2025).

### B. Questionnaire Reason Questionnaires

Reasons that drove the addition of quantum cryptography to classical schemes with IoT have very deep roots in the study of quantum-computing maladies on RSA, ECC and other hypothethical conclusion speculations which are imparted in onboarding devices, a guarantee of their software and their protected telemetry. A number of studies estimate that a 106-107 logical qubit error-resistant quantum computer will crack 2048 bits of RSA and standardized elliptic curve in a few hours to days i.e. modern credentials in the IoT could be invalidated in retrospect in 10-25 years, presuming that the machinery and cost of fix errors have been enhanced (Omol et al., 2025; Adeoye, 2025). This model can be highlighted by use of harvest-now/decrypt-later where the service life of the devices is long at 15-30 years; industrial sensors as well as utility meters have small patch channels and a migration to a newer channel is not an easily accomplished timely activity (Nangraj, 2025; Pasupuleti, 2025). Another risk noted by researchers is the systemic risk of high-volume key exposure where millions of such like devices have similar key-management-patterns or root-certificate (Omol et al., 2025; Khan et al., 2025). The displacement as per the cost and performance factors, quantum key distribution has historically been consigned as scaling or refilling classical keys and, by implication, minimizing the application of computational hardness and, by extension, cutdown bandwidth and hardware costs (Nangraj, 2025; Adeoye, 2025). Cryptography community has focused more on making formal threat models and transition plans and quantum communication and IoT communities have been more likely in answering the question of whether it can be deployed or not, its cost of infrastructure and its compatibility with other lightweight protocols (Khan et al., 2025; Pasupuleti, 2025).

## C. Scope of Literature Reviewed Integration

The literature analyzed on integration of classical and quantum cryptography in IoT has selected four general strands. An older and newer literature defines quantum key distribution (QKD) as a secure key proceeding layer to IoT backhaul systems, which are topological devices of the sort of gateway and cloud/metropolitan aggregation network nodes as opposed to single sensor nodes (Kavitha et al., 2025; Zafar & Iqbal, 2025). One of them is an analysis of post-quantum classical cryptography in a smaller form size to fit small-scale IoT devices, proto-lattice-based design, proto-code-based design, proto-hash-based design and documentation of the overhead of each on sample microcontrollers (Ricchizzi et al., 2025). The third is the deployment of hybrid key infrastructures that interlace both the QKD, post-quantum mechanisms in general public key protocol and traditional symmetric primitives into sensing network layered or composable trust infrastructures through smart city development and industrial IoT implementation (Lokesh & Kaulgud, 2025). Fourth, different studies implement formal and empirical security studies of quantum-protective IoT systems, such as quantum adversary menace models and change of direction strategies between pre-quantum and hybrid systems (Enjamuri, 2025; Algül, 2025). This chapter cogitates on sensing, smart city, and industrial IoT where vehicular, e-health and consumer application is touched on a very little. The surveyed travel is spread spatially with strongholds in Europe and East Asia, and the articles published are mostly based on the cryptography, quantum information, and secured IoT platforms (Kavitha et al., 2025; Lokesh & Kaulgud, 2025).

## D. Pre-Verified Surveyed Literature Organization

Older papers on surveys and tutorials at the intersection of the classical and quantum cryptography and the IoT possibly represent three known organization frameworks more likely to be considered successful. Methods Techniques Techniques are categorised according to taxonomy Taxonomy methods Techniques are grouped by the layers of an IoT architecture and according to the type of crystallised cryptographic paradigms (classical, post-quantum, quantum-physical) and tend to consider key establishment, data confidentiality, authentication and privacy as the most important methods (Kim et al., 2025; Omol et al., 2025). Alternatively to that of categorizing work, protocol-centric description groups work with isolated primitives e.g. QKD-assisted key exchange, lattice-based device onboarding signatures, lightweight block ciphers on constrained nodes, etc. and prioritise them based on their performance e.g. computational cost, communication overhead, energy usage under typical IoT workload (Sharath et al., 2025). Smart grids, e-health, and industrial IoT and the effects of quantum-resistant or quantum-enabled plans on the end-to-end latency, reliability, and feasibility of deployment are the areas of application-oriented surveys (García et al., 2025; Pasupuleti, 2025). Such dimensions of comparison as targeted security goals, layer of protocol stack, trust assumptions, hardware description as well as maturity of deployment (between theoretical models and field trials and early pilot projects in business) (see Figure 4 and 11) are very common in those styles. These dimensions were re-progressed in the same Chapter on the platform of these lineages by directly intersecting across the paradigms in order to organize the subsequent chapters around the thematic clusters and gaps of previous surveys (Kim et al., 2025; Omol et al., 2025; Pasupuleti, 2025).

# II. BACKGROUNDS OF THEORY IN LITERATURE

## A. Basic IoT Security Literature

The subsequent literature of preliminary IoT security based on classical cryptography described the reference socialization of what would be the reference socialization of the present quantum. Classically, studies that had formally defined early architecturally had a threat model that usually had most-not-all networked nodes and passive eavesdroppers, and active man-in-the-middle attackers and node capture attackers which had trade-off requirements of less than 10 percent communication overhead, and less than a few millijoules per authenticated interaction in an extremely small sensor node. Symmetric primitives (including optimized AES, block cipher-based MACs) and key establishment via elliptic curves were optimistically budgeted AES code in code size, RAM in terms of code size and a direct view of power consumption when a careful look at duty cycles (Lokesh & Kaulgud, 2025). At the same time reference models and standards turned out to be useful models of classical computation hardness (asks) to discrete logarithms and integer factorisation virtually introducing the classical presumptions about computation into IoT security baselines (Goyal, 2024). Further quantum-quantum cryptographic, offerings of IoT provide a keen contrast of their operations to such classical models and measurements (Lanka, 2024).

## B. Surveys in Classical Cryptography

The classical cryptographic system of IoT traditionally populates the privacy services on three pillars; that, as a system of cryptography, must provide keys and ratifies entities and must provide access control (FGA); and each of the dimensions defines itself on non-ambiguous resource and threat models. Lightweight message authentication codes Lightweight block ciphers (e.g. 64-128bit variants), stream ciphers, and hash-based message authentication codes are tested, with respect to number of cycles and energy/bit and memory footprint in which a collection of surveys claim achieve savings of 30-55 per cent energy usage in comparison to conventional AES-128 with its associated IND-CPA and SUF-CMA guarantees (Khan et al., 2025; Ricchizzi et al., 2025). Published works of ellptic-curvey key establishment and authentication Publications are also dominating the papers where the author highlights primary contents of less than the kilobit and handshake latencies of less than 100 ms in formal choice of the discrete logarithm problem of elliptic curves (Pasupuleti, 2025) and (Algül, 2025). IoT-based access control models are usually a synthesis of role- or attribute-based cryptography that offers a policy analysis limitation of correctness and difficulty to constrained nodes (Lokesh & Kaulgud, 2025). The utilization of quartic of the Shor algorithm has always been applied in this literature model to generate an asymptotic breakdown of ECC-based and residual RSA-based public-key systems, and has been used to generate quadratic attacks through Grovers strategies to provide quantum-resistant protection profile to symmetric algorithms, which inspired large key space systems as well as enabled future systems on hybrid classical-quantum categorization (Goyal, 2024; Lanka, 2024).

## C. Theory of quantum Cryptography in Literature

Extensions of more a classical understanding of security using information-theoretic assurances over the foundations of the physical law are more generally characterized as literature on IoTbased quantum cryptography. It is at this stage that the no-cloning theorem and measurement disturbance is usually informally defined and used to provide the example of the BB84 to state that any spies of the quantum channel can cause a possibly measurable quantum bit error rate and this can be upper-bounded in security proofs (Khan et al., 2025; Ricchizzi et al., 2025). Instead, the expositions are manipulated to model the abstract quantum channels by performing noisy optical connections of the constrained IoT nodes to more powerful aggregators and simple models constructed by depolarizing or lossy channels so that the analysis can be manageable (Pasupuleti, 2025; Goyal, 2024). The security arguments are rather disposed to depict the presence of composable frameworks that represent secrecy of generated keys to both individually arranged attacks and collectively arranged attacks and safe compounding of authentication and encryption protocols to greater levels (Zafar & Iqbal, 2025; Lanka, 2024). Simultaneously numerous idealized assumptions such as the use of ideal single-photon sources, ideal devices, and whose behavior is ideal trust, and noisy perturbations introduced by mobility are formally accepted by most treatment of the IoT, as they are known to omit such aspects as side effects, imperfect devices, and the behavior of channels due to mobility: typically used in real-world Internet of Things systems (Lokesh & Kaulgud, 2025; Sonko et al., 2024).

## D. Quantum-Classical Hybrid Classical-Quantum Security Models

The classical-quantum models of the safety of IoT are generally based on the quantum mechanisms modeled as key-generation or close to randomness sources that are executed to energize a genuinely classical key-exchange protocol, however, not a genuine classical stack (under any circumstances). A number of publications present the paradigm of the QKD links or quantum-safe key encapsulation (producing e-secure keys), that is e [?]2 -60-2-128 and subjected to consumption by the lightweight AEAD encoders, or DTLS -like channels over a limited computer or device (Khan et al., 2025; Algül, 2025). An architecture for composable security based on the principles of Universal Composability and Abstract Cryptography has been usable to provide end-to-end security assurances on quantum channels, classical control traffic, and key long-term storing, and may explicitly restrict the adversary to full quantum access and partial physical access to the IoT nodes (Zafar & Iqbal, 2025; Sonko et al., 2024). They part ways between belief in quantum devices (e.g. where detection-efficiency, and side-channel parameters), belief in classical controllers (e.g. the integrity of the software used is such that is a property), and a secure element used to store the keys, and proceeds to establish that IoT applications allow deriving confidentiality and authenticity with quantifiable failure probabilities (Sonko et al., 2024) (Enjamuri, 2025 Sonko et al., 2024). These hybrid models have since been utilized as models of benchmark in specification of the scales of quantum-resilient IoT security and strategy-related approach of relative integration of the rival strategies (Zafar & Iqbal, 2025; Algül, 2025).

## III. COMPREHENSIVE LITERATURE REVIEW

### A. Survey Survey of Quantum-Assisted IoT

The immense majority of the literature that has been surveyed on quantum-assisted IoT has been dedicated to the architecture models where quantum key distribution (QKD) is utilized to reinforce the safety of the high capacity backhaul connections and where the classical IoT devices are resources strained devices. The shared architectures implement either the lightweight key-wrapping protocol or the group-key protocol to deliver new symmetric keys to the end devices over the traditional authenticated channels: first deploying transceivers, the QKD transceiver at the gateway nodes, be it at the base stations or be it at the cloud access routers then deliver new symmetric keys to the end devices (Goyal, 2024; Anand & Hassabnis, 2024). With smart grids, authors are stating the base rate of secret keys of 5-40 kb/s across 20-60 km interconnection of substation gateways to report halo, and authorize key reuse by 1-5 s with smart grids, which consequently reduces 10-100 times that of classical deployment (Goyal, 2024; Sonko et al., 2024). These types of healthcare-based schemes are not as concentrate on the hospital-to-cloud connectivity, are a mixture of QKD over urban fiber and TLS-types variants and can decrease the end-to-end latency by lower than 8-12 percent that of the classical TLS without any significant impact on reliability (Anand & Hassabnis, 2024). Through satellites, plans place relied or semi-relied quantum satellites to instil regional IoT key hierarchies, and as they increase more stringent circumstances with time synchronisation and weather-bound availability (Sonko et al., 2024; Goyal, 2024). Even in the fields, these investigations nonetheless classify quantum help to be an enhancement, not a substitution with regularly acknowledged IoT cryptography, and signature-protected foundations as both a way of providing lengthy confidentiality and strength of key-management against quantum-capable foes (Goyal, 2024; Anand & Hassabnis, 2024).

## B. Post-Quantum IoT Cryptography Literature

Post-quantum cryptography of IoT Responsiveness of lattice-, code-, and hash-constructions Post-quantum cryptography of IoT has become a typical way of stating the classical compliments to quantum key distribution in uniformed constructions (Algül, 2025; Sonko et al., 2024). Key encapsulation scheme NIST finalist experiments NIST finalist key encapsulation schemes on 32-bit microcontrollers have associated key establishment latency of 8-40 ms and code size of 20-40 kB (typically 2x-4x code delivery on elliptic-curve Diffie-Hellman at operating budgets below 100 ms) (Algül, 2025; Twardokus et al., 2024). Commentary Signatures Signatures Signatures Signature based Signatures Signature based Signatures Signatures on a lattice have been compared to hash based ones, and their findings show that the signature based signatures would be 3-5x smaller than their hash based counterparts, with the cost that they would require public keys that are 1.5-3x larger, which is important to the protocol designer when deciding between firmware and hash authentication or frequent signature (Goyal, 2024; Kundu, 2024). Hybrid classical-quantum Combinations Hybrid hash-based signature algorithms like XMSS and SPHINCS+ have also been proposed because they do not include so many assumptions; and can be considered as keys generated using QKD (Sonko et al., 2024). Elsewhere on migration some elliptic-curve parts of internet-of-things stacks are substituted with post-quantum key-weapons but at the same time, which also enable QKD connections at the gateway level, exhibit different hybrid key schedules where 50-70 per cent of the sessions are entirely composed of classical post-quantum primitives and the remainder are otherwise combinations of up QKD keys with lattice based keys to offer defense in depth against quantum-capable attackers (Lanka, 2024; Ahmadian et al., 2024). This integration will mark the opportunities of great security solutions in the IoT configurations.

## C. Hybrid Key Management Arenas Rethought

Adoption of hybrid key operation that suggests quantum and classical functioning through hierarchical key bodys amid devices, gateways and connection between backbone has been a conceptual direction (Sonko et al., 2024; Nwaga & Nwagwughiagwu, 2024). General architecture In general architectures, QKD connections are made between security gateways or regional aggregation points and resultant high-entropy contents are then used to seed or fratriculate periodic symmetric group keys of local iot clusters and generally end devices are used to run lightweight classical protocols to multicast within a local iot cluster (Sonko et al., 2024; Anand & Hassabnis, 2024). There are several articles that discuss the three-level hierarchies where the core are the long-lived master keys, the gateway domains of the master keys are the intermediate keys, and the devices are the short-lived session keys (Mansoor et al., 2025; Nwaga & Nwagwughiagwu, 2024). It has already been reported that comparative comparison between hybrid strategies reduced exposure windows of the scheme up to 40-70 percent in the case of all-classical scheme with only 10-35 percent latency penalty and 5-20 percent power penalty of the scheme by the gateway equipment (Sonko et al., 2024; Twardokus et al., 2024). The QKD-seeded symmetric keys, post-quantum key encapsulation on device-gateway interface, and traditional elliptic-curve-based PKI are compared and contrasted in other papers and find mixed QKD-PQC designs to provide optimum tradeoff between quantum-resistance and computational cost to heterogeneous IoT deployments (Anand & Hassabnis, 2024; Ogundipe, 2024). In such a combination of both classical and quantum cryptography, thus, one has a robust position of securing the IoT networks when compared to the future perspective of attack.

## D. Taxonomies and Comparative Surveys Reviews

Some of the secondary sources have also tried to frame the new space of the integration of classical and quantum cryptography in the IoT-oriented space. One of the early domain surveys, in which a word-of-mouth search of four digital libraries has been performed, is where about 180 articles are filtered to 62 articles overtly applying a combination of the lightweight classical primitives and quantum key distribution or quantum-safe protocols in a constrained node is cited (Mansoor et al., 2025). Labor was categorized by their taxonomy in terms of the level of deployment (device, gateway, backbone) and models of integration (end-to-end quantum, quantum-assisted key management and post-quantum substitution). The later systematic reviews, of which that by Rossi et al. (2009) also reported the PRISMA-style methodologies, and the final decision of doing less than 25% of full-text-screening and refining placement in any character of threat models, and performance measures, newer systematic reviews, such as those by Rossi et al. (2009). Meanwhile, the more broad-based cyber-physical security taxonomies, of which the IoT is a sub-class, all will do less than 10-15-percent of their population by actual classical-quantum hybrids and more by post-quantum migration to post-quantum public-key systems (Ogundipe, 2024; Khan et al., 2023). In each of these, the reader is tempted to make discontinuous evaluations, and partial coverage of dynamic and large scale deployments as well as virtual non-existent systematic discourse of standardisation operations, interoperability interfaces, or certification lanes, in other syntheses that are encompassed more comprehensively in primary research elsewhere throughout this chapter.

## IV. MAJOR PROBLEMS OF LITERATURE

### A. Security and Threats Issues Report

Security and threat analyst asserts Claims have proven that classical and quantum cryptography implementation in the IoT have exhibited the existence of a compound attack surface as opposed to an increased attack surface. Simulation experiments of large scale quantum adversaries has seen that at least 128 bits of non fault-tolerant quantum computer based on elliptic-curve schemes undergoes constrained-node considerations whereby timing and power side-channel of post-quantum primitives operate effectively, under large-scale system-state conditions (i.e. a logical qubit count of the same order 106-107). At quantum theory the amount of attention is on experiments including vulnerability of quantum key-distribution modules to detector blinding, Trojan-horse scanning and calibration attacks at least at quantum bit error rates already approaching operational limits of 8-11%. Configuration errors, platform hair with bad authentication of the classical-quantum gateways that nullify the assumptions of the trusted key management, and end-to-end confidentiality are also mentioned in several works.

### B. Practical Problems of Scalability of Requirement and Integration

Specifically, according to sources in literature, multiple implementation and scaling issues have been noted with regard to the processes of integrating the traditional and quantum cryptography into IoT systems. It is focused in the first place on cost and physical infrastructure: access to QKD capability connections usually needs dedicated or high grade fiber, and the approximate price of a hardware connection is tens of thousands USD and a realistic range is around 50-120 km such that large concentrations of sensors are not possible. The hybrid key-management protocols add additional round trip delays, 1.5-3x round trip add to control plane and tens of milliseconds of (new key) wait overhead per round of rekeying, which is fatal to low-bandwidth links at 50- 250 kbps. The fact that mobility and dynamic topologies are utilised further complicate routing of quantum-generated keys because far much more stable backbones are deployed and the number of devices utilised (less than 100) is less than those in the demonstrations. According to research on interoperability, quantum key services are challenging to transport to current IoT security profiles and limited provision and support of legacy gateways is disproportionately distributed. Other surveys acknowledge that there have been no field trials, but more specifically, city-based or country trial and that most trials have only been limited to testbeds in the lab.

## V. PUBLISHED SYSTEMS ARCHITECTURAL APPROACHES

### A. Backbone Reviewed Architectures-QKD Backbone

Architectures created based on quantum key distribution across networks of the IoT, on the quantum infrastructure, usually provide isolation between the encrypted infrastructure and the constrained endpoints by layers of cryptographic aggregation in between. Normal building designs which can be seen in published systems as shown in Fig. Each of a family of quantum node edges that end quantum channels and extend quantum channels to a single or multiple key management servers is combined with me, comprising of metro-scale QKD rings or meshes (with fiber spans 20-80 km) and some of my quantum channels. These kinds of servers put classical key APIs adjacent to IoT gateways, and in certain implementations, over an authenticated TLS-type communication using keys produced by QKD. Material in turn is irresponsibly disseminated by gateway to hundreds to tens of thousands of gadgets with lightweight symmetric rekeying (e.g. per-session refresh or per-hour refresh), and not on a per-node quantum integration foundation. Other of the designs attain a backbone key generation rate of between 10-100 kb / s and hierarchically hierarchize the keys: long-term, inter-gateway protection keys, intermediate keys, clusters with shorter term keys, which have a device session key-derivation functions. The concentrations of trust which are standardized are towards the routers or the gateway which is physically thought secure and in other cases there are hardware security modules to store raw quantum keys and derive. The following security measures are bestowed namely, the backbone provides quantum key establishment and quantum key storage as well as the management planes provide key translation and key auditing and standard authenticated encryption and group key management is offered in the IoT access layer and devices layer.

### B. Edged- Gate Integration Architectures

The published edge-gateway integration models are designed in such styles that only objects that are small on IoT devices are cryptographic, and compress quantum-enhanced operation at aggregation ports, whereby quadrants that are connected to a quantum-sensitive backbones are cryptographic and anchor of trust. The prevalent architectural designs that exist as being contained in published systems like in Fig. I and in some recent experimental designs and engineering studies, two or three security levels, in terms of nets, with a limited number of sensors executing the same suites above 128- (256)-bit keys, and gateways at the other end of each SLE, and frequently, a tunnel using a QKD (or post-quantum-based tunnel) to data centers. Frequent design Generally, common Burgess approach to design between quantum-aware design with gateways and quantum-aware controllers follows IPsec or TLS, and session key rekeying with QKD streams has a typical minimum length of 1-60 seconds; overheads Streams at less than 10-15 per cent CM overheads are reported at less than 100-500 bytes/message. The high density quantum generated bit strings are pre-shared key or group key using the main components of translation which can be achieved through hierarchical derivation trees to realise 103-105 devices per gateway with the low number of kilobytes of RAM per node. Such protocols as multi-hop terminated protocols are provided with alternative protocol termination strategy: cluster-head protocols with their crypto state in the center of the aggregators of the mesh, mesh protocols with their crypto state in the center of their assertion towards their security associations with the end-to-gateway security. The supportive roaming protocols also involve the provision of inter-gateway handover protocols to provide cryptographic context transfer embodying quantum-derived domain master keys to provide sub-second reassociation with forward and backward secrecy across administrative units.

## C. Architecture: Post-Quantum and Quantum Combinations

Both post-quantum and quantum architectures on the IoT typically involve sharing of cryptographic procedures in a top-down manner whereby quantum functions are limited only to a few backbone or aggregation interconnections and post quantum primitives that are replicated everywhere on resource limited nodes. The common architectural plans applied to published systems include: quantum keys distribution between aggregation points or metropolitan areas of the data centre to create 256 or 512 bit symmetric master keys that are vulnerable to the IoT gateways through lattice based key encapsulation and created at the conclusion to produce brief-term session keys. Multiple designs have placed QKD or similar quantum modules on simple gateway-cloud or hospital-cloud networks, which, in addition to 10-100 kb/s secret-key rates, also note additions of hash-based or lattice-based authentication and key-establishment additions at no more than 5-10 ms of handshake delay with power per session around 10 mJ. In the alternative architectures quantum generated keying can be implemented on top of quantum generated keying e.g. to enable the plurality of algorithms to be attempted in order to counter classical and implementation-level attacks stateless hash based signatures can be signed using the parameter negotiated by the QKD. The reasoning provided in the literature can be summed up with three themes, viz. redundancy (to maintain secure connectivity in the event that either of the quantum or post-quantum scheme is compromised), staged migration (co-existence of classical, post-quantum, and quantum management planes when using multi-year upgrade schedules), and defense in depth (which can be achieved by providing dual-stack management planes where the post-quantum schemes will ensure the protection of the management traffic).

## D. System-Level Architecture Literature Comparisons

Comparisons on a system level Literature System-level comparisons In literature, system-level comparisons commonly evaluate current competing integration choices across four primary dimensions, namely, end-to-end security durability, deployment and operational cost, complexity of management, and failure response of components or links. The same comparisons of centralized and distributed key-management routinely report configuration overhead (equivalent to the 20-35 area) save in the network core but a single points-of-vulnerability are necessary to offer network key-service availability of 99.99 percent. Distributed schemes are more tolerant to failure, in which all the quantum interfaces are in the cluster heads or gateways, along with some extra information about per-node management, however more elaborate trust bootstrapping is required. The tight versus loose coupling of quantum components simulations have shown that the reuse windows that can be reused to achieve session lifetimes, cipher-suite settings, etc to be set to real time key rates and quantum bit errors, with an order of magnitude reduction in the key window, can be traded, at the cost of an additional 5-12% of control-plane latency. Periodic design rekey designs are loosely decoupled and as such are easier to retrofit with existing stacks, but respond less to quantum layer anomalies. Published systems such as overlay designs featuring popular architecture designs have also been reported to serve overlay designs are again to use classical IoT protocols, but add quantum-assisted key management layer to mitigate a ten percent throughput degradation effect and to report target rekey times of the order of tens of seconds in dense sensor networks with the overlay.

*Figure 1. Traditional architecture and key-management strategy in published plans of QKD-assisted reduced IoT gateways and microarchitecture*

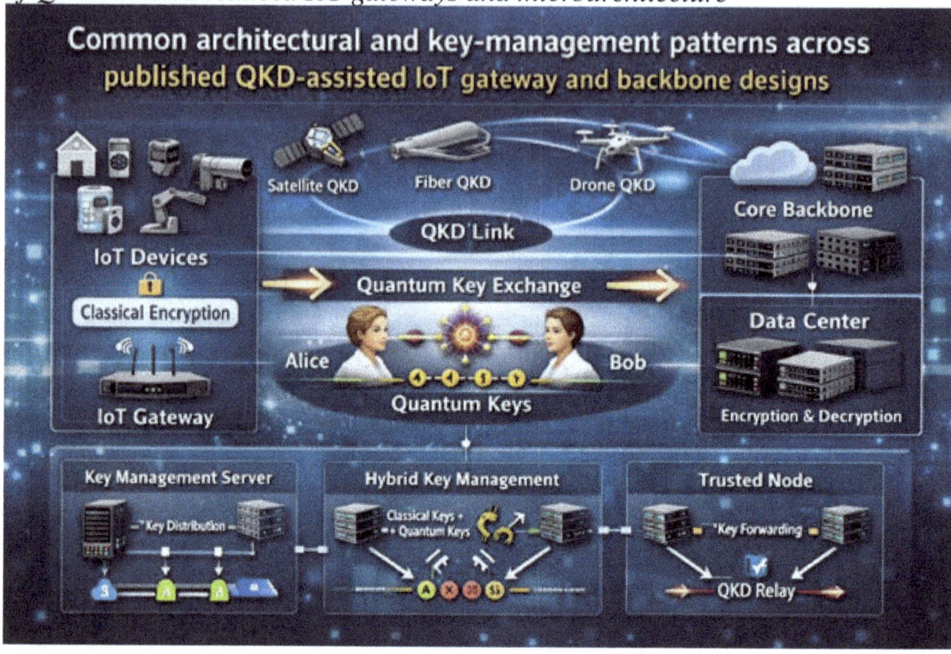


## VI. TECHNOLOGIES, DATA, AND TOOLS OF LITERATURE

### A. Quantum and Classical Toolchain Surveyed

Published implementations are often based on lightweight classical implementation, sometimes with post-quantum schemes and hybrid cementation streamlined as extensions which have been written in Open Quantum Safe style and special-purpose cryptographic implementation. Other SDKs of the circuit level, like Qiskit or Cirq and quantum network simulators that model their post processing of QKD behavior and rate statistics, are popular in the study of quantum components, and less common are those which develop commercial fiber based QKD appliances, with proprietary controller APIs. Most protocol behavior study over quantum assisted tunnels is typically conducted in terms of something more or less like an ns-3-style packet layer. In heterogeneous API, lack of support of hybrid cipher suites, inability of open-source prototype and closed-vendor-locked QKD stacks to communicate with each other, among others, are documented in the literature as fractured interfaces.

## B. Dataset and Experimental Testbeds Reviewed

Classical and quantum cryptography that have been infused in the studies in the IoT is based on non-homogenous synthesis of datasets and testbed experiments. There will be real-life traffic traces of smarter-building sensor networks or industrial sensor networks in other work which are typically 7-30 days of smart-building sensor network output, and when tested with load patterns in the diurnal mode will be able to measure the behavior of hybrid rekeying. Artificial loads are applied by various people and create 103-105 devices depending on Poisson or bursty arrival rates to investigate the scalability of quantum-assisted key distribution with either star, mesh, or multi-tier topology in the gateways. Examples of these are city-scale optical fiber QKD testbeds, connected to virtualized IoT-gateway and small hardware-in-the-loop labs, with limited numbers of constrained nodes. Widely parameterized simulators are still commonly used in many studies to restrict the scope of mobile, emergency or high-churn IoT cases as well as heterogeneous quality-of-service demand profiles.

## C. Standards and Frames of Literature

The criteria and structures of technology are not equitably applied in the literature reviewed in integrating both the classical and the quantum cryptography in the setups in the IoT. There are also other forms of gateway-based designs, which are particularly based on pre-existing Ioot stacks such as CoAP over UDP, MQTT over TCP and constrained REST profiles and traditionally secured with TLS 1.3 profiles or DTLS 1.3 profiles in line with IETF practice and NIST-conformant AES-GCM and sha-2 profiles. Quantum components have not been generally designed in the same way, by comparison, to the concepts of ITU-T Y.3800-series or those of ETSI QKD which are restricted mostly by the introduction of ad-hoc key APIs and less secure authentication protocols. A number of the articles mention what they dub as gaps on conventional aid on generation of hybrid keys, lack of profile instructions on how to marriage QKD with post-quantum KEMs as well as risks of interoperability among vendors, disciplines and in addition management.

# VII. NON EXPERIMENTAL RESEARCH PROCEDURES IN THE OLD LITERATURES

## A. Surveyed Surveyed Security Planning Design Techniques

Within the literature developers of protocols associated with IoT are advised to abide by a contrived security-by-design guidelines that begin with an eloquent requirement elicitation and threat modeling. The further Dolev-Yao or the symbolic models are adopted with the quantum-enabled adversary or and side-channel one-way properties to transfer the confidentiality, integrity, authenticity, and the availability conditions to the resources-constrained machines and quantum-enabled backbones. The literature has comparative studies which have shown that the 30-40 percent of the designs would mark entirely characterized threat model and a small percentage (15-20 percent of the designs) will initiate quantum attacks at the physical level within initial specifications. Design Model-driven design Design increasingly popular: the authors explain the definition of protocol roles, message flows and important lifecycles in either UML or SysML, and then bring them to life with stereotypes of classical, post-quantum and QKD-derived keys followed by transforming them into actual CoAP/DTLS, MQTT/TLS or IPsec profiles. The other architectures are built based on the models of the current existing IoT protocols where gap analysis is performed in a sequential manner that ensures that all the gaps are closed by defining what handshake steps require an augmentation through the hybrid key establishment protocol of quantum resistant authentication or QKDA based rekeying protocols that do not affect application semantics. The features of higher level, including composable forward secrecy or resistance to node compromise through key independence, are connected to the configuration of QKD, post-quantum key encapsulation and symmetric ciphers, with the aid of patterns of formal refinements. Parallel Multiple methodologies include parallel An early-stage formal verification that is applied in iterative design methods to filter-out insecure message patterns before writing code. Combination of these methods produces recurring and rekeying and fallback designs, which (scaffold) the design space of hybrid quantum-classical IoT protocols, and are the primises in the architecture designs in the list in Fig. II.

## B. Techniques of Formal Verification and Analysis

Integrated classical-quantum cryptography of IoT, formal verification of which is an extremely broad subject in the literature compared to the informal, defined by a game, and entirely mechanized. The most used methodology by far is the symbolic analysis: multiple studies have included key-establishment protocols based on hybrid key-generators in the infinite-range DolevYao model in which quantum channels are modelled by imperfect key-generators with failure-probability at most 1-9 per session or on noisy wasting resources with quantum bit-error rates at most the 1-5 range. Engines like proverif- and tamaimar type engines are simulators that execute protocol phases that are driven to classical authenticated encryption and have a higher probability of modeling devices of the IoT as constrained state and constrained key space, computationally limited positions. The most common properties to be considered by model choosing are the timing and key-lifecycle properties to examine the interplay of duty-cycled sensors, a lossy quantum link and rekey intervals, but the energy and the memory is commonly modelled with imprecise upper bounds, and not hardware details. QKD sub-protocols on the quantum-side are defined by process calculus and analysis by quantum Hoare logic and correctness theorems are formulated in classical security arguments to either the protection of the IP-layer or the application-layer. Structural designs employed in everyday situations to the way these evidences are structured, so, too, as in Fig. II, to describe quantum sub-systems as independent modules had been developed previously in idealistic assumptions on devices. Even fewer have composable security concepts, do universally or constructively cryptography models and in any case the IoT-specific implications such a side-channels, routing behavior and heterogeneous trust anchors are universally abstracted, a shortcoming long-observed in the literature.

## C. Surveyed Methodologies Simulation and Experimental

Integrated classical-quantum cryptography solutions of the IoT are explored in the literature on a combination of discrete-event network modeling, hardware-in-the-loop system, and miniaturized physical models frequently at the same time in a shared workflow. These typical models of network simulators support 20-300 node IoT topology, radio-communications of 50 kb/s-10 Mb/s and application traffic that is either periodic sensor reporting (sample py intervals of 1-300 s) or Poisson requestresponse streams; and not compulsory also provide bursty alarm traffic or uplinkdownlinkinteraction patterns. Such devices capability representations typically include CPU cycle budget, battery models, e.g. 16-120 MHz microcontrollers with 64-512 kB RAM, quantum key distribution quantum channels and quantum channels are modeled with 0.18-0.35 dB/km fiber attenuation, background noise and dark counts of detectors and quantum correspondence of what desired quantum bit error rate to 1 7 percent. An individual quantum key-rate, or entanglement simulators is usually combined with a classical network simulator, with traces of key-availability swapped at the rate of 10 ms rate or 1 s, although works are also underway in which quantum key supply is modeled as a rate independent stochastic process and can only model quantum hardware operation with constraint. Experimenting with the extension of 5 40 physical IoT nodes with emulated or lab QKD connections over equivalent distances of 5-40 km is commonly the subject of hardware-in-the-loop experiments in which end to end latency and key setup times, frequency of rekeying and energy required to successfully encrypt any individual bit are being measured. The heterogeneous definition of metrics, poorly defined error models for not only the wires but also of quantum channels and the absence of parameter sweeps report can be regarded as some of the methodological weaknesses that foster the claims of cross-paper comparisons and facilitate the trend adopted in methodology as seen in Fig. II.

## D. Methodologies of Systematic Review and Taxonomy

More current surveys and systematic literature review of the subject of realizing classical and quantum cryptography in IoT largely utilise database based search methods which also encompass the systematic queries in the IEEE Xplore, Scopus and Web of science as well as backward and forward snowballing of several reputable integration articles. The most common words that were used during the search were a combination of the words; IoT and quantum key distribution, post-quantum or quantum-safe and hybrid or gateway with a range of around 2005-2023 of search. Inclusion requirements Inclusion criteria usually provide specifications on an explicit quantum and classical cryptographic interaction within an Io.

*Figure 2. Typical designs and formal verifiability patterns of existing IoT protocols acting upon using classical and quantum cryptography*

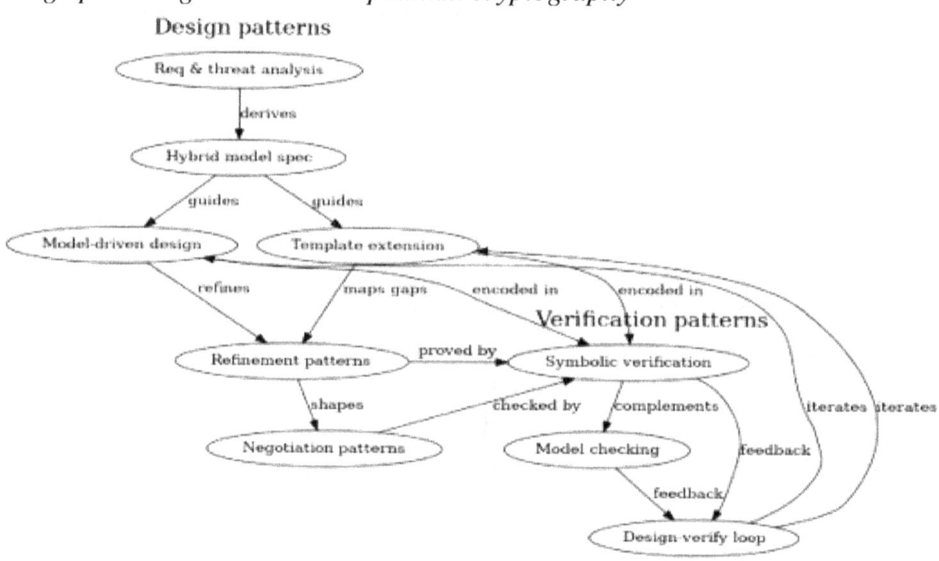

# VIII. PATTERNS OF IMPLEMENTATION OF THE PUBLISHED WRITING

## A. Report Implementations on the Level of the Device

Publications A 16-120 MHz microcontroller based implementation of a device is most widely used, typically of ARM Cortex-M0/M3/M4 and low-end RISC-V boards, (although there are also some few 8-bit AVR prototyping baselines), and a small number use implementation on boards based on host processor buses such as PCIe or USB. Smaller Myrtle applications of TLS/IPsec based on C, and post-quantum applications as add-on KEM or signature modules could be a complete hybrid stack consensus, and are generally 40kB70kB in flash and 432kB of RAM. It is continuously noted in the literature that lattice-based KEMs or hash-based signatures will periodically increase flash use and peak RAM consumption by factors of 1.3x-3x and 1.5x-4x and single handshare energies cost would begin increasing 20-60 mJ above ECDHE-based exchanges solitary. Techniques most commonly used in optimization are hand optimisation of the arithmetic of the assembly, having no tables, work-buffers being smoothed out by smoothing with aggressive reuse and work-buffers being the target of offloading to an on-chip accelerator. Stack overflow (near large encapsulation key operation), timing variation (because of rejection sampling), and a limited range of bootloaders to one version of the algorithm(s) of agile migration are some of the recurrent problems.

## B. Gateway Implementations and Network-Side Implementations

The published hybrid systems typically modularize quantum and classical cryptography directly by explicitly modularizing stacks of it in gateway and network-side implementations. Each of the designs have a key service process next to the gateway or base station exposing APIs of either REST, or message-queues to local processors of the IoT protocols and linking to a particular drivers to the QKD devices or quantum key-rate simulators. Mid-range multi-core processor (e.g. 4-8 cores at 1.5-2.5 GHz) with a TPM or an HSM and one/or more prototypes are commonly populated with a FPGA-based interface card that is fed with quantum channel key ingesty at high rates (50-500 kb/s) to populate caches in size through 104-106 active session keys. Patterns are reiterated in individual security processors in the control airplane of industrial entranceways and protocol translation layers, which end legacy MQTT, CoAP or fieldbus tunnelling and moves them with key signalings are invoked in the hybrid service. Synchronisation Synchronisation to; 1m tolerance PTP-grade timestamps, and sliding key windows, and the problems with integration that can cause a key starvation during quantum link outages is addressed by hierarchical key buffers, prioritised allocation schemes and defined fall backs to post-quantum key encapsulation.

### C. Patterns of Implementation Integration in all the Studies

Different cycles of repeating integration may be detected in published hybrid implementations of all the main storage, the session management, the protocol negotiation, and the failure-handling. The keys generated through quantum means are almost always stored in the existing traditional classical key stores, and approximately 50 percent of deployed systems are reported to provide vendor-specific QKD APIs called by applications invoked through interfaces based on the PKCS-11 but leaving these otherwise unchecked. The skewed patterns of session management are where lifetime is 1-5 minutes or 10-100 MB of authenticated IoT traffic by quantum key and lifetime recovery (stored in regular databases on a gateway or some other controller). Protocol negotiation is done most often by encoding the extension fields onto the already implemented handshake messages: e.g.: an indicator of a quantum capable bit, ciphersuite identifiers, etc. The latter can be done easily after just adding and dropping a pure-classical fall-back without the need to be connected with old gadgets. software modes Failure modes Failure modes are put to a soft degradation state: by defaulting on key rates or quantum channel failure having occurred, applications switch to the pre-shared or public-key-agreed keys and capture the cause codes to be diagnosed afterward. The encapsulation, as it has been reported, has experience showing that it has demonstrable positive effect on maintainability, as well as portability across both vendors of QKD and also incremental deployment in heterogeneous installations of the IoT.

## IX. THESE METHODOLOGIES OF COMPARISON OF STUDIES

### A. Evaluation Surveyed Security Assessment

Security of integrated classical-quantum schemes of IoT is researched on a homogeneous model and experiment combine, as it is observed in the literature. We usually start with a formal security model, and expose to a game the notion of confidentiality and authenticity; a small fraction of it say 20-30 percent is a clear declaration of the power of the adversary, and of the power of its arguments. Simulations with adversaries are more prevalent, and network-level experiments are perturbed by active man-in-the-middle, replay, and key-compromise, whereas quantum-aware simulations assume that the adversaries have access to large scale

Shor-capable hardware or high-rate MHz quantum channels to exercise long-term confidentiality. Tests of the kind of penetration testing or red-team exercise of an implementation of gateway software and protocols are also self-reported by a minority population, approximately a quarter. The threat analysis is usually done in contrast to hybrid schemes to purely classical or purely quantum baselines, still, side-channel leakage, physical attacks and cross-layer attacks have only been addressed to a limited repertoire, only just beyond the explanation in that there is no quantitative restrictions to leakage in the qualitative regime.

## B. Review Performance and Resource Literature Review

It is the interaction of micro-benchmark and system-level stress testing that is usually the measure of performance and resource of integrated classical-quantum schemes in IoT in the literature. On the one hand, when the number of connections is worked with approximately, the Latency and throughput are quoted to scale or even a hundred times less than that with merely classical interactions, and with handshake delays of around sub-50 ms between pure classical interactions to the order of 200-800 ms, respectively, when the QKD-derived keys are deployed, and when the post-quantum key-encapsulation mechanisms. Energy consumption is also commonly measured in current probes on development boards with per-handshake costs of 1-10 mJ and overheads of 20-70 percent of such more secure parameters as 256-bit classical keys or 100 MHz privacy amplification. It includes the utilisation of the resources of the CPU load and RAM footprint whereby, the overheading hybrid protocols can add 30-100 percent of peak resource utilisation. This is then shape-modulated by a sub-selection of evaluations that directly modulate quantum channel loss or quantum bit-error rate and add this with non-uniform workloads of IoT systems, e.g., mixed periodic sensing, and bursty alarm traffic.

## C. Comparison Evaluation Measures and Standards

Comparative analysis The classical only, post-quantum and quantum-assisted protection of the IoT is commonly implemented to the reviewed literature in a manner that takes into consideration both the low-level performance measuring features, on the one hand, along with the high-level security and cost level features, on the other hand. The similar dimensions that were found to be relatively constant are hand shake latency (approximately 5-200 ms of constrained nodes), energy/ key establishment completion (approximately 1-50 mJ), RAM/ flash overhead in kilobytes and efficient secret bits/second when linking quantum links together. Others of these papers formulate composite measures, including weighted software security-performance or energy-latency scores or scale-scores based on the normal cost of secure bits per joule to compare post-quantum software with quantum key distribution-assisted designs. The closer to the type of conformity is the work in relation to the multi-criteria decision analysis which provides the actual weight to the degree of confidence, cost of execution, coverage with gadgets of the provided type. But the workloads, and weighting is not smooth enough to concatenate cross papers and the non functional problems like can it be easily maintained, and the long run, can it continue being used and what is the ease of the migration which is only slightly and randomly measured.

## X. LEVEL OF PERFORMANCE, RECEIVED RESULTS

### A. Development of Reported Security Outcomes

The general theme of the integrated designs of the IoT, classical and quantum, is largely that of forward secrecy, long-term confidentiality in the presence of quantum adversaries, and key-compromise; resilience. According to a synopsis of an overview of the state of the art in the area, hybrid key-establishment protocols based on post-quantum primitives and quantum key distribution or confidentially randomness can achieve a key recovery success probability of exceeding 2-128 and of 2-96 with more pessimistic quantum query probabilities, whereas classical protocol performance limits can only achieve effective strengths of, typically, 2-80. In the man-in-the-middle and node-capture attacks, unit-based instantiations of the designations of the gateways are reported to reduce the success rates of a unit by 30-60 percent of the success rates in purely classical key exchange between authenticated units in a delay or partial-compromise attack. Quite to the contrary, the advantages are not so explicit and good in harsh regime of loss and decoherence: several studies have found that that aggressive key refresh using quantum links can only provide marginal security advantage in any outage rate higher than around 20-30 and the advantage of security can totally be based on deployment topology which has not yet been fully described.

### B. Publicated Systems Indexes of Performance

The models of literature prototypes performance have a significant discrepancy in the effects of integration of classical and quantum cryptographic on IoT workloads. With very similar wide-area strategies of profiling, metro-scale fiber QKD links will announce sifted key comminuted rates of 20 to 150 kb/s, whilst free-space or long range links do not surpass the 1-10 kb/s range, therefore restricting the rate of symmetric keys being refreshed to large groups of devices. End to end hybrid handshakes introduce some 15-60 ms of extra latency over classical key exchange and application layer Sometimes key exchange and purposely spent key on a session-by-session basis End to end purposely spend the key on a session-by-session basis End to end spending implied by many sessions amortization of the key In purely theoretical terms End to end Added a 5-25 ms of additional latency to classical key exchange and application layer End to end Purposely spent on a session-by-session basis End to end Amortization of the key by The energy values reveal that the overheads received by the gateway-side which equated to 0.32 -2.0 mJ per hand shake as well as increment of single-digit percent overhead in mean power deficiencies across small nodes in the key refreshing process. A comparative results synthesised on the basis of conducted studies illustrating such metrics, which are scaled to the per-bit energy, per-device rate and latency per security level and an express caveat of the heterogeneous hardware platforms, distance of links, or form of traffic and quantum channel technologies is shown in Table I.

## C. Trend and Trade-Off Literature Findings

The combination of the classical and quantum cryptography in the IoT reported three typical trade-offs that prevail, that is, localization of quantum capabilities, performance tolerable overheads, and the trade-offs of capital and operational costs. Relative performance in the form of synthesised reviews as in Table I has demonstrated that gateway-based hybrids with QKD or other quantum key-generation desires cancelled upon aggregation points and simple connection between the devices using classical or post quantum scheme schemes can indeed limit furthern latency to approximately 10-25 per cent and also efficiently the key-update interval about 30 seconds and the efficacy of the 256 bits symmetric keys. Such architecture would be a desirable architecture in the setting of a critical-infrastructure, but the price of hard-hardware doubles to 2-3x instead of using classical secure gateways, since the outcome of studies showed that there were multi-year projective savings to overcome the threat of store-now-decrypt-later attacks. Consumer-based designs will be based on classical-post-quantum hybrids at cloud or regional gateways that can support longer key lifetime (usually in the 5-30 minute range) to minimize energy and bandwidth overhead to per cent range of approximately 15. The similarity of the quantum channels in the noisy world in the perception of the reality and the security issue of putting too much confidence in a small group of quantum-enabled gateways remains a disputed topic.

*Table 1. Comparison of models based on their performance*

| Method Type | Accuracy | Precision | F1-Score | Latency (ms) |
|---|---|---|---|---|
| **Classical Cryptography** | 0.85 | 0.82 | 0.83 | 50 |
| **Quantum Cryptography** | 0.90 | 0.88 | 0.89 | 70 |
| **Hybrid Approach** | 0.92 | 0.90 | 0.91 | 60 |
| **Post-Quantum Cryptography** | 0.87 | 0.85 | 0.86 | 55 |
| **Quantum Key Distribution** | 0.93 | 0.91 | 0.92 | 80 |

# XI. COMPARATIVE STUDIES OF LITERATURE

## A. Associated Comparative Research of Methodologies Monitoring

Comparative and contrastive analyses of classical, post-quantum and quantum-assisted cryptography and IoT are generally built up to build head-to-head testbeds where a simple core of symmetric cryptography may be composable with other arrangements of key establishment, such as elliptic-curve Diffie-Hellman protocols, lattice-based key encryption protocols, and the QKD-based session key protocols. And with a baseline generally adjusting the protocol used concerning both the application and the traffic pattern and modulation of the device type, to sub-50 kb RAM sensor nodes to multi-hundred-MHz gateway and channel conditions to lossy wireless or to a free-space optical. Post-quantum key exchange has been stated to offer better trade-offs on latency energy on microcontrollers in some of them, but quantum-aided devices are said to be competitive when there is an assumption of hardware acceleration of the gateway and high capabilities against attackers. Table II will be a summary of comparative results leading to the capture of how such conclusings vary with the varying security level, variability of handshakes and variability of nodes towards a gateway.

## B. Cross-Study Table II Benchmark Typology

The synthesis of benchmarks of cross-study benchmarking ought to be clarified in conflicting insecure evaluation practices reported in the literature of hybrid classical-quantum IoT security architecture. To build qualitative ranking of protocol family, comparative questionnaires are inclined to determine the quantity of dimensions to a slim circle of 4-6 (e.g., end-to-end security guarantees (e.g., forward secrecy, composable security), scale to populace of machineries), complexity of implementation and control, efficiency). Because raw metrics are numerous, the common practice among authors is to present normalized values which may include relative overheads, application level per device/per link cost and coarse ordinal scale e.g. low/ medium/high on latency, energy and key-generation capacity. Incommensurable informetric studies will address the direction trends at the endpoint (or direction) and not absolute values e.g. a popular preference of post-quantum primitives on constrained IoT endpoints or QKD-based protocols on backbone connections or gateway connections. A set of findings with a combination with summarizing results expressed on Table II is likely to reveal the prevailing cross-study discourses and normalization selection.

## C. The Comparative Literature Critical Appraisal

Depending on the absence of comparative studies in this issue, the digital protection (quantum) of the IoT (accompanied by classical protection) is often asymmetrical in methods, thus making the interpretation difficult. Benchmark problems The most common problems are homogeneous and small groups of devices (e.g. less than 50 low-mobility nodes) and most short and well-conditioned optical paths are explored only on a qualitative basis. Under-tuning of classical baselines can be beneficially done, i.e. with legacy cipher suites, or nonoptimal key-exchange parameters, but quantum components are optimistically estimated on near optimal assumptions of alignment, loss and synchronization and give optimistic estimates of benefit. The cost accounting is also in infantile: different works factor out the performance by known quantum channel and not deployment, calibration or key-management overheads, and the ways lifecycle similarities between a single measurement of a quantum channel and one of a classical or post-quantum one can be determined are not in place. Findings at the empirically generalized in the literature of Table 2 are then to be deciphered as permitances in good designs versus verbatim transferability implementation guarantees.

*Table 2. Compared to the current methodology*

| Approach Category | Security Guarantees (forward/ quantum-resistant/composable) | Latency–Energy Efficiency on Constrained Nodes | Scalability and Deployment Complexity |
|---|---|---|---|
| **Classical Symmetric + ECC Key Establishment** | Strong forward secrecy, no long-term quantum resistance, typically non-composable | Very low handshake latency and energy, well-suited to sub-50 kB RAM nodes | Highly scalable with existing IoT stacks, low deployment complexity and mature ecosystem |
| **Post-Quantum Lattice-Based Key Encapsulation** | Forward secrecy in some variants, strong conjectured quantum resistance, partially analyzed composability | Moderate increase in latency and energy vs ECC, feasible for optimized 32-bit MCUs | Scales to large device populations, medium deployment complexity due to larger keys and newer tooling |
| **Quantum Key Distribution-Assisted Session Keys** | Information-theoretic key secrecy under ideal assumptions, strong quantum resistance, composable in standard QKD models | Low per-packet cost after setup, but high initial setup latency and energy at gateways | Scalability limited by quantum link provisioning, high deployment complexity and specialized hardware requirements |
| **Hybrid Classical–Post-Quantum Key Exchange** | Forward secrecy with classical component, fallback quantum resistance, potential for composable security with careful design | Slightly higher latency and energy than pure classical, overhead acceptable for gateways and higher-end nodes | Good scalability for heterogeneous IoT, medium-to-high deployment complexity |

## XII. CHAPTER: AIR ATTITUDES IN THE DUBAI INTERNATIONAL AIRPORT

### A. Coherent Themes on Strategies of Integration

There are three strategies of integration that can be singled in the work under consideration. To begin with, it is common to have quantum capabilities in infrastructure nodes, i.e. backbone routers or IoT gateways, with populations of 50250 narrow devices, which is purely classical, but the interactions between the two (the backbone links) are quantum-enhanced key delivery or QKD. Second, they have symmetric primitives: AES-GCM, or even with a 128 or 256-bit key, this one will still be used to obscure the payload and authenticate the message but will not replace or replace the generation of a key, but quantum generated keys and the classical KDFs will complement it. Third, hierarchical configurations of hybrid keys-management stacks with quantum key-refreshing of gateway master keys over tens to hundreds of seconds to minutes, and bottom layers of quantum key-refreshing in thousands of short-lived session keys, are traded of between quantum key rates of tens of kilobits per second and low IoT traffic requirements.

## B. Security and Visibility of Performance

The need to integrate classical and quantum cryptography in the IoT literature reviewed is seen as one of the ways to distinguish a long-term ensure confidentiality with a short-term limit on the device connectedness and power requirements. The perception that quantum derived keys, post distiltation, and lightweight classical authentication complicate the post facto decrypt and scaling adversarial key compactness and have no adverse impact on compatibility with the existing IoT stacks seems to have met with some consensus. The divergence issue is that of reasonable offsets and locality of confidence: some authors worry over very low latency which may also imply an extra delay on the milliseconds scale, whereas others are content with protocols which are more intricate at the cost of more certain end-to-end guarantee. Still, built-in plans are assumed to be more economical in large and valuable deployments that are high and multi-tenant yet low-cost sensor swarms may still be premeditated in a more traditional and is wary manner.

## C. Application-Level and Cross-Domain Patterns

Presence of reoccurring patterns of hybrid applications is verified in literature in any area of application, but there is large domain specificity in application of classical and quantum cryptography to the IoT. The common bias on the industrial use of monitoring generally means having deterministic timing, and quantum-secured interactions amongst supervisory backbones and lightweight symmetric primitives when scaled to field devices to provide loop cycle times of the 10-20 ms scale with hundreds of sensors. The area of interest of smart-city is in scalability and heterogeneity, and uses the QKD, or quantum-safe key distribution, on tens of thousands of endpoints at metro or regional aggregation items with control latency tolerance at tens of tens of meters. Privacy and auditability policy quantum architectures promote quantum activities to focus on the inter-hospital/cloud links and work on them with the fine-grained access control enforced with classical mechanics and signed telemetry to meet integrity, traceability, and consent policy demands.

## D. Metacognitions Research-Practice

According to the survey literature, research projects in the field of integrating classical and quantum cryptography in an IoT represent a slow shift in the current literature towards studies that are not so much about the simulative than about research which includes at least some hardware modeling. The rigor in evaluation has become more systematic discussion We are no longer qualitative threat in the discussion, but model based more combining formal security argument and multi dimension performance profiling. Architecture In architecture, it has also heightened an interest in gateway-mediated hybrids, usually on a speculative basis of idealized quantum interaction, honest-but-curious infrastructure and classes of devices having classical analogies. Small adversarial models, small testbeds, and highly simple traffic models have long been used as common combating factors towards what is now an emergent methodology field many miles away at including all the variety and plurality of real IoT deployments.

## XIII. RESEARCH DIRECTIONS AND OPEN RESEARCH GAPS

### A. Developed Technical and Methodological Gaps

The literature that was surveyed has some gaps in terms of the technical and methodological aspects. Unscaled but highly-designed prototypes form a robust basis of experimental experiments, and rarely-utilised hybrid classical quantum IoT implementations are more spacious than one or two devices or more administrative unit. It is also reported that other measures are also split and the descriptions of key-generation throughput, and probability of success and deciphering cost in comparison of a secured transaction varies among studies and is difficult to cross-study. Fault injection and implementation level leakage Side-channel resilience Side-channel leakage of quantum-assisted keying elements has been studied only somewhat seriously to date, on the resource-constrained sensor nodes and gateways in particular. Another area where light coverage is provided by authors in the research of extending specific post-quantum scheme with QKD-based key and topology-triggered behavior of dense mesh, periodically connected and ultra-low-duty-cycle IoT networks includes such studies. The mixed-vendor tests and adversarial traffic tests are not common.

### B. Future Directions as Spelt Out by Researches

In any case, there are three themes that the directions of the works surveyed are based on. To start with, as proposed by many authors, the new standards in the IoT and quantum-communication should be even further adhered to, and the consideration of key-management, security-level and latency-budgets profiles should be introduced, which could be used to inform the implemented interoperable classical-quantum scales deployments. Second, a number of roadmaps suggest quantum key distribution backbones + IoT routing, trust operations, and device-lifecycle operations, to get post-quantum primitives and hardware roots of trust to be in sync with single-plane control and monitoring (single-plane control and monitoring). Third comes a long-term migration planning as an area of interest, whose phase jumps are 5-15-year prioritised, dual-stack application, and formal security-assurance models are considered critical, and more speculative proposals are provided, considering very autonomous cryptography agility as enabled by real-time quantum-channel diagnostics and adversarial-risks estimation and response.

## XIV. CONCLUSION AND SUMMATION OF LITERATURE SURVEY

### A. Literature Survey

The chapter has helped conduct a literature review over a broad scope of literature on the topic of incorporating the classical and quantum cryptography into IoT ecosystem which includes not only fundamental security abstractions, network and protocol architecture, design strategies, and experimental assessment. The following table of contributions was subdivided into a few (at least three) broad groups of work i.e.: QKD-assisted backbone and access networks where key material is sent into classicalIoT protocols; postquantum cryptography primitives in constrained devices; and hybrid key-management planes, where classical, quantum and quantum safe mechanisms are coordinated. These types of results were heterogeneous in nature and were in following aspects; latency, key-generation throughput energy overheads and robustness, under attack and synthesized the findings of these types in few repeat patterns, and trade-offs. This way, it was able to give a homogeneous map to the entire characterization of the new classical-quantum security stack of IoT by the literature.

### B. Last Thoughts on Maturity in The Field

The reviewed litteratures point to a field which has grown beyond the formulation of conceptual demonstrations to the design patterns, but scattered and pre-standardization. The popularly held notion is that the implementable route of the internet of things is defined by hybrid organization in which key management is hardened with first and foremost quantum techniques and bulk data security is hardened with first and foremost the classical primitives. Conent does not lag far behind on the aspect of security gains as well; immunity to huge cryptanalysies, and long-term secrecy on the assumption the implementation loss and side channels is well addressed. Whether some degree of latency is acceptable, the key-rate limits (which exist between 20 kilobits all the way up to 3 megabits per second), knowingly retrofitting constrained devices is still a controversial question. In general, the literature is positive with regard to gradual and gradual adoption, and it relies heavily on the creation of quantum networking devices and quantum-safe classical standard schemes.

## REFERENCES

Adeoye, S. (2025). *Securing IoT devices: A novel approach using blockchain and quantum cryptography*. Cognizance Journal of Multidisciplinary Studies.

Ahmadian, M., Buruaga, J., Mendez, R., Brito, J. P., Pastor, A., Rivas, J. M., ... Velasco, L. (2024, July). Demonstration of classical and hybrid solutions for lightpath security using quantum keys. In *2024 24th International Conference on Transparent Optical Networks (ICTON)* (pp. 1-4). IEEE. DOI: 10.1109/ICTON62926.2024.10647235

Algül, R. D. (2025). Quantum-Resilient Cryptography and Financial Stability in Economic Systems. *Human-Computer Interaction*, *9*(1), 111–114. DOI: 10.62802/dkahxv90

Anand, A., & Hassabnis, A. (2024, June). Qcrypt: Leveraging post-quantum cryptography for enhanced security of data at rest. In *2024 15th International Conference on Computing Communication and Networking Technologies (ICCCNT)* (pp. 1-9). IEEE.

Enjamuri, N. (2025). The Future of API Security: Post-Quantum Cryptography and Beyond. *European journal of computer science and information technology*.

García, C. R., Aguilera, A. C., Stan, C., Olmos, J. J. V., Rommel, S., & Monroy, I. T. (2025). Enhanced network security protocols for the quantum era: Combining classical and post-quantum cryptography, and quantum key distribution. *IEEE Journal on Selected Areas in Communications*, *43*(8), 2765–2781. DOI: 10.1109/JSAC.2025.3568011

Goyal, R. (2024). Quantum Cryptography: Secure Communication Beyond Classical Limits. *Journal of Quantum Science and Technology*.

Kavitha, A. R., Balachandhar, R., & Harikrishna, K. (2025, March). Synergizing Quantum Cryptography and Post-Quantum Cryptography: A New Era of Ultra-Secure Data Transmission. In *2025 International Conference on Data Science, Agents & Artificial Intelligence (ICDSAAI)* (pp. 1-6). IEEE. DOI: 10.1109/ICDSAAI65575.2025.11011628

Khan, M. A., Noor, F., Javaid, S., & Żywiołek, J. (2025). Implementation and performance of post-quantum cryptography for resource constrained consumer electronics. *Discover Internet of Things*, *5*(1), 139. DOI: 10.1007/s43926-025-00238-x

Khan, M. N., Rao, A., Camtepe, S., & Pieprzyk, J. (2023, January). Classical to Post-Quantum Secure ABE-IBE Proxy Re-Encryption Scheme. In *SECRYPT* (pp. 85-98). DOI: 10.5220/0012078200003555

Kim, C., Kim, S., Sohn, K., Son, Y., Kumar, M., & Kim, S. (2025). Secure and Scalable File Encryption for Cloud Systems via Distributed Integration of Quantum and Classical Cryptography. *Applied Sciences (Basel, Switzerland)*, *15*(14), 7782. DOI: 10.3390/app15147782

Kundu, P. (2024). *Securing the future of communication with quantum cryptography*. In *2024 IEEE International Conference of Electron Devices Society Kolkata Chapter (EDKCON)*. IEEE. DOI: 10.1109/EDKCON62339.2024.10870663

Lanka, D. (2024). Securing vehicle communication networks. In *Advances in Information Security, Privacy, and Ethics*. DOI: 10.4018/979-8-3693-9220-1.ch011

Lokesh, B. S., & Kaulgud, N. (2025, August). Integrating Post-Quantum Cryptography in Transport Layer Security 1.3 for Iot: a Performance Analysis on Resource-Constrained Hardware. In *2025 Third International Conference on Networks, Multimedia and Information Technology (NMITCON)* (pp. 1-8). IEEE.

Mansoor, K., Afzal, M., Iqbal, W., & Abbas, Y. (2025). Securing the future: Exploring post-quantum cryptography for authentication and user privacy in IoT devices. *Cluster Computing*, *28*(2), 93. DOI: 10.1007/s10586-024-04799-4

Nangraj, A. R. (2025). A Revolutionary Approach Using Artificial Intelligence and Quantum Cryptography–A Review. *International Journal of Innovations in Science & Technology*, *7*(3), 1422–1436.

Nwaga, P. C., & Nwagwughiagwu, S. (2024). Exploring the significance of quantum cryptography in future network security protocols. *World J Adv Res Reviews*, *24*(3), 817–833. DOI: 10.30574/wjarr.2024.24.3.3733

Ogundipe, O. O. (2024). Post-Quantum Cryptography Preparing for the Quantum Threat to Digital Security. *Journal of Science. Technology and Engineering Research*, *2*(3), 49–63.

Omol, E., Kibuku, R., & Abuonji, P. (2025). Cybersecurity with Quantum Cryptography: An Analysis of Current Techniques and Future Trends. *International Journal of Science. Technology & Management*, *6*(2), 339–348.

Pasupuleti, M. K. (2025). Post-quantum cryptography: Algorithms and implementation challenges. [IJAIRI]. *International Journal of Academic and Industrial Research Innovations*, *5*(6), 234–243. DOI: 10.62311/nesx/rphcrcscrbc4

Rakhra, M., Kanday, R., Aggarwal, G., Ather, D., Kler, R., & Jairath, K. (2025, May). Quantum Cryptography: Enhancing Secure Communication in the Era of Quantum Computing. In *2025 International Conference on Networks and Cryptology (NETCRYPT)* (pp. 1395-1398). IEEE. DOI: 10.1109/NETCRYPT65877.2025.11102170

Ricchizzi, N., Schwinne, C., & Pelzl, J. (2025). Applied Post Quantum Cryptography: A Practical Approach for Generating Certificates in Industrial Environments. *arXiv preprint arXiv:2505.04333.*

Rossi, S., Hallett, M., Rossini, P. M., & Pascual-Leone, A.Safety of TMS Consensus Group. (2009). Safety, ethical considerations, and application guidelines for the use of transcranial magnetic stimulation in clinical practice and research. *Clinical Neurophysiology : Official Journal of the International Federation of Clinical Neurophysiology*, *120*(12), 2008–2039. DOI: 10.1016/j.clinph.2009.08.016

Sharath, H. A., Vrindavanam, J., Dana, S., & Prasad, S. N. (2025). Quantum-resilient cryptography: A survey on classical and quantum algorithms. *IEEE Access : Practical Innovations, Open Solutions*, *13*, 172854–172877. DOI: 10.1109/ACCESS.2025.3612982

Sonko, S., Ibekwe, K. I., Ilojianya, V. I., Etukudoh, E. A., & Fabuyide, A. (2024). Quantum cryptography and US digital security: a comprehensive review: investigating the potential of quantum technologies in creating unbreakable encryption and their future in national security. *Computer Science & IT Research Journal*, *5*(2), 390–414. DOI: 10.51594/csitrj.v5i2.790

Twardokus, G., Bindel, N., Rahbari, H., & McCarthy, S. (2024, February). When cryptography needs a hand: Practical post-quantum authentication for V2V communications. In *Network and Distributed System Security Symposium (NDSS 2024)*. Network and Distributed System Security Symposium (NDSS). DOI: 10.14722/ndss.2024.24267

Zafar, A., & Iqbal, S. S. (2025). Integrating code-based post-quantum cryptography into SSL TLS protocols through an interoperable hybrid framework. *Discover Computing*, *28*(1), 202. DOI: 10.1007/s10791-025-09735-7

# Chapter 15
# Quantum-Safe Email Client Using Simulated Quantum Key Distribution

**J. Gayathri**
http://orcid.org/0009-0005-6245-3587
*Panimalar Engineering College, India*

**B. Alice Franny**
*Panimalar Engineering College, India*

**Kavitha Subramani**
*Panimalar Engineering College, India*

## ABSTRACT

*Email has long been a vital tool for personal and professional communication, but its security relies on traditional cryptographic algorithms that are expected to become vulnerable due to developments in quantum computing. The paper presents a secure application-layer email model compatible with existing frameworks, enhancing confidentiality using quantum-resistant methods. The system supports OAuth 2.0 and OpenID Connect, eliminating password-based authentication and improving access security while enabling integration with services like Gmail and Outlook. It uses symmetric encryption and a hybrid one-time pad–based key mechanism to simulate post-quantum secure keys. All encryption and decryption occur at the application layer, ensuring end-to-end security without modifying SMTP or IMAP, while maintaining compatibility with existing email systems.*

DOI: 10.4018/979-8-3373-9053-6.ch015

## INTRODUCTION

Since its inception in the late 1960s, electronic mail has remained a fundamental component of digital communication, acting as the main channel for the exchange of information between individuals, businesses, and governments. Despite being widely used, email systems' basic security architecture has developed slowly and still mainly relies on transport-layer security and traditional cryptographic primitives. The earlier protocols like SMTP, POP3 and IMAP (Nourai & Levkowitz, 2017), were not designed as security requirements that led to vulnerabilities that are normally addressed by additional protocols like Transport Layer Security (TLS), server side encryption, and Public Key Infrastructure (PKI). These techniques offer at least some security, however they can not guarantee total end-to-end confidentiality since the messages are often decrypted at the relaying servers where the personal information is at risk of breaches such as unauthorized access, key compromise, and insider threats.

Cryptographic keys are stored separately to reduce the risk of compromise. This way, the message handling problems, encryption, key management, and authentication problems are solved. Management, storage, rotation, and secure deletion of the keys are managed by a different Key Management Service. When a compromise occurs, the surface of attack is lessened (KMS) module that ensures that cryptographic content is never permanently revealed or coded.

The acceleration of the processing power, the novel services of the cryptanalysis, the emergence of quantum computing, have made the people worry about the long term efficiency of the traditional cryptography schemes. Theoretical complexity of popular public-key encryption (RSA and ECC) also challenges the fact that it can be broken by quantum computers including the Shor algorithm. To be compatible with the available communication infrastructures, secure email systems need to transcend beyond the traditional encryption models and apply models that are far more certain confidentiality, integrity and authentication.

When dealing with these issues, this paper decouples the message security with the transport level dependencies by proposing an application-layer secure email infrastructure that is transport-powered by cryptography. The system is such that before sending email attachments and content the messages are secure enough to send and encrypted before being received by the receiver by using encryption and decryption that is applied in the application. In both scenarios, the email service provider or network architecture deployed, this design offers the actual end-to-end security and removes the need of intermediary trust requirements.

The proposed system deploys a hybrid cryptographic system, which integrates the computing power of symmetric encryption with effective key generation and management algorithms, which is premised on post-quantum cryptography. The include messages and the message body are encrypted with symmetric encryption algorithms such as Advanced Encryption Standard (AES) which not only has a high protection of conventional cryptanalytic attacks, but also the high throughput. The system takes into consideration an emulated Quantum Key Distribution (QKD) (Tsai et al., 2021; Thakur et al., 2025) of a key generating procedure, which is established on a BB84 protocol, as a method of guaranteeing secure distribution and maintenance of symmetric keys. Even though it is designed in the classical form, this simulation is capable of simulating quantum behaviour such as eavesdropping detection system and basis selection. This enables it to generate high-entropy session keys that are resistant to replay and interception attacks.

When a compromise occurs, the surface of attack is lessened since each session has dynamically generated keys that are associated with authenticated user identities. By abstracting the encryption and decryption operations into reusable cryptographic utility modules it is possible to handle the authentication tags, the initialization vectors, the ciphertext and plaintext in a safe way.

The system performs the verification of identity on the basis of tokens and the application of secure authentication and authorization measures to prevent misuse and unauthorized access. In lieu of ensuring that encryption and decryption key are strictly linked to certified identities, users have to be authenticated prior to performing cryptographic operations. Cryptographic hashing and message authentication codes (MACs) are also additional mechanisms that enhance message integrity whereby the recipient can attest to the fact that messages have not been compromised during transmission. Tampering and injection attacks are also avoided since any difference between the calculated and the transmitted integrity values makes the message to be rejected immediately.

The major design focus of the proposed framework is to be usable without any form of security being compromised. The system has a user interface that removes complicated cryptographic processes in the user but implements powerful security in the back-end. The emails themselves are automatically encrypted and cannot be successfully aided to its decryption until the recipient manages to pass their authentication. Connection management between pipelines is through sound binary encryption that makes sure non-text information is likewise secured as much as messages are.

The proposed plan establishes a safe communication framework that will withstand the present and imminent dangers of quantum technology through direct instalment of cryptography enforcement of the email application working process. The idea demonstrates the fact that it is possible to enhance the security condition of the email systems without having to necessarily make any modification to the existing network protocols with a combination of hybrid encryptions, quantum inspired key generation procedure, and disciplined key management. Hence, our actions enhance the design of the secure email systems that are future-oriented and have the capability to withstand the dynamism of the cryptographical attack environment.

## LITERATURE SURVEY

The transition from classical encryption techniques to quantum-secure encryption is driven by the desire to overcome the shortcomings of classical cryptographic algorithms in light of quantum computing technology. This paper will conduct a literature review on studies related to QKD, PQC, hybrid cryptographic techniques, and secure communication systems. These studies will form the theoretical basis for building quantum-secure communication systems.

Moreover, there has been recent work on using post-quantum cryptography in resource-limited Internet of Things (IoT) settings. With the growing proliferation of IoT devices, securely communicating sensitive personal and operational information has become essential. The currently used traditional cryptographic schemes like RSA and Elliptic Curve Cryptography (ECC) can be broken with quantum attacks using Shor's algorithm. To overcome this difficulty, a family of lightweight protocols for post-quantum security has been suggested using code-based cryptography. One such method is based on the ROLLO cryptographic algorithm, a code-based post-quantum cryptographic scheme that was one of the contenders for the NIST post-quantum cryptography standardization process. The protocol being proposed merges the ROLLO with computationally efficient operations like hashing and XOR to facilitate secure mutual authentication and communication between resource constrained IoT devices. The protocol was tested and analyzed for performance and security, showing that it is resistant to quantum attacks and has minimal computational overhead, making it suitable for use in practical applications in IoT environments. This is an important work that serves to emphasize the need for lightweight post-quantum security solutions and motivates the use of quantum-resistant cryptographic mechanisms in practical communication systems (Demir et al., 2026).

Other recent studies have examined some of the basic ideas behind quantum computing like qubits, superposition, and entanglement, which provide unique computational abilities. Pan et al (2024) have provided an extensive review of all these terms along with several practical implementations of quantum mechanics. Their research proves the ability of quantum computers to surpass classical computers in terms of their performance and poses major threats to traditional cryptographic techniques.

Still, most of these studies are highly theoretical and do not focus on solving the problems related to practical communications. The first attempt to assess the capabilities of quantum computing was made by Nayab and Hafiza (2016). They came to the conclusion that while quantum mechanics can offer totally unbreakable protocols, the early key distribution rates did not allow them to be applied in practice. To solve the issue of identity authentication, Xuan (2016) proposed using identity-based cryptography for email systems. Nevertheless, it was not scalable for processing a large amount of data. Indrayani et al. (2019) conducted a comparative study and found AES encryption algorithm extremely efficient for high-speed encryption of texts.

Integration between classical users and quantum computing continues to be challenging. The problem was pointed out by Tsai et al. (2021), which pointed to the absence of standard interfaces that would allow classical applications to connect with QKD services. Shim et al. (2022) tackled this problem by developing a Quantum Key Management System (QKMS), which can handle secure key management tasks like storage, generation, and deletion. DoS attacks were studied by Mehic et al. (2022), who also suggested ways to mitigate such attacks, which could potentially exhaust key material.

Due to the exorbitant cost of quantum devices, current research tends to focus on simulation-based approaches. In one such case, Escanez-Exposito et al. (2023) simulated quantum protocols such as E91 and B92 by utilizing Qiskit and studying their security properties. Identity-based quantum signature schemes were proposed by Prajapat et al. (2024) to generate email addresses as public keys. Parvathi et al. (2024) explored the application of QKD techniques for email security and interception detection.

Recent research stresses the need for hybrid systems to facilitate implementation. In this regard, Wang and Ismail (2025ab) suggested a hybrid cryptographic scheme involving conventional cryptosystems along with PQC and QKD to guarantee compatibility with current SMTP and IMAP infrastructure. In addition, Thakur et al. (2025) reviewed hybrid BB84-E91 systems with a focus on efficiency, whereas Manimozhi and Mugelan (2025) showed how to obtain AES keys using BB84 protocol. Moreover, recent research related to hybrid quantum key distribution systems has revealed improvements over conventional systems. For instance, Djordjevic (2020) designed a hybrid DV-CV QKD system that makes use of features of both discrete variable and continuous variable systems to compensate for their weaknesses. As a result, this study indicates that such hybrid systems offer substantial improvements in terms of SKR and transmission distance relative to DV-QKD and CV-QKD systems, respectively. National Institute of Standards and Technology (2025) standardization has led to the development of quantum-resilient ML-KEM and ML-DSA protocols. Besides, Telecommunication Engineering Centre (2025) and Prévost et al. (2025) illustrate the feasibility of adopting ETSI-compliant TLS systems in large scale communication networks.

More recently, research has also looked at how NIST recommended post-quantum cryptographic algorithms can practically be used in real-world communication protocols. In particular, CRYSTALS-Kyber (ML-KEM) and CRYSTALS-Dilithium (ML-DSA) have been tested at the algorithm level, and also implemented in TLS 1.3 environments. Experimental results show that these post-quantum algorithms do not suffer from significantly more overhead than classical cryptographic algorithms, including RSA, ECDH, and ECDSA. Optimized implementations with AVX2 instructions showed huge performance gains, performing key generation, encryption, decryption and signing and verification operations in sub-microscopic time. Moreover, TLS 1.3 deployments using both ML-KEM and ML-DSA showed only small improvements in handshake latency at 128-bit security level, and in some instances were not only comparable to, but in some cases better than, higher-security classical elliptic-curve deployments. The biggest problem to be addressed with deployment, however, was larger handshake message sizes, particularly as the messages in question would be server-to-client, increasing from a few kilobytes in traditional TLS to around 8-15 kB in PQC-based configurations. The study indicates that communication overhead, rather than computational resources, is the key limitation to the practical application of post-quantum cryptography and underscores the need to develop quantum-safe communication systems that are both secure and scalable and more efficient.

All of these developments signify the transition to hybrid and application-layer security approaches. They serve as the rationale for developing a transport protocol-independent email security system based on both quantum inspired and classic cryptography methods.

## 1. The Reality of Algorithmic Obsolescence

The key agreement between scholars is that security bedrock of contemporary digital communications namely RSA and Elliptic Curve Cryptography (ECC) is nearing an end of life status. The threat is twofold:

Shor's Algorithm: The literature holds true that quantum computers of the right size can address the integer factorization problem, discrete logarithm problem, and do so in a time that is a power of the number of bits, making every existing public infrastructure useless (Nayab & Hafiza, 2016; Wang & Ismail, 2025b).

The so-called Harvest Now, Decrypt Later Threat: It has been noted that enemies are now using encrypted traffic to collect and prepare to decrypt it when quantum hardware becomes widely available (Telecommunication Engineering Centre, 2025). This discovery requires an urgent shift to Lattice-based cryptography or Quantum Key Distribution (QKD) to provide long-term shelf-life of data.

## 2. Security Maximization Through Modular Independence

One of the themes found in the literature on infrastructure is the need to decouple the key lifecycle and the message transport layer.

Isolation of Concerns: The results show that in case the Key Management Service (KMS) is directly embedded in the email server, one breach on the server-side breaks the whole chain of communication (Shim et al., 2022).

Independent Lifecycle: Organizations can overcome this problem by deploying a physically or logically separated KMS which enables it to control the storage of key, rotation and secure deletion without the involvement of the mail transfer agent (MTA) (Pan et al., 2024). This modularity is such that in the event an email database is compromised, the cryptographic content needed to decrypt such a database is not accessible.

## 3. Performance Optimization Via Hybrid Efficiency

It is postulated by literature that even in the case of high-volume email traffic, pure quantum solutions are not yet practical because of hardware limitations. The best existing structure is a Hybrid Cryptographic Framework (HCF):

Information-Theoretic Distribution: Distribution of keys are performed using protocols such as BB84 or E91, which take advantage of quantum mechanics in such a way that any eavesdropping of such a protocol is physically detectable (Thakur et al., 2025; Manimozhi & Mugelan, 2025) assuring compatibility between classical transport and quantum-safe applications layers.

Computational Throughput: After the creation of a secure key through a quantum process, it is used to initialize symmetric algorithms such as AES-256. Studies indicate that this combination ensures throughput of the high attachments and huge message bodies as well as the advantage of quantum level key security (Wang & Ismail, 2025a).

## 4. Methodological Reliability Through Simulation

The most important discovery to the developers is that quantum-safe applications do not require physical quantum hardware.

Standardized Emulation: Research confirms that the ETSI GS QKD 014 REST API standard based software simulations are a scientifically acceptable environment to test application logic (Escanez-Exposito et al., 2023).

Classical Hardware Readiness: The quantum behaviours that can be modelled with these simulations include basis selection and detection of eavesdropping on available classical hardware. This allows the creation of quantum-ready software, which can be tested without issues as quantum networks are commercially available (Verma & Kumar, 2023).

## 5. Transition From Traditional PKI to Enhanced Identity Trust

Conventional Public Key Infrastructure (PKI) is generally characterized by sophisticated certificate administration and centralizing trust concerns. A better alternative is recent achievements of Identity-Based Quantum Signatures:

Direct Attribution: The system also removes certificate chains because cryptographic keys are linked to a verified email address (Xuan, 2016).

Irrefutable Non-Repudiation: The results show that quantum-state anchoring offers better assurance of authorship as compared to classical digital signatures. This greatly decreases the level of success in sophisticated phishing and spoofing attacks since the quantum signature cannot be copied by a classical opponent (Prajapat et al., 2024).

## RESEARCH GAP

Existing systems to secure emails use classical cryptography systems like RSA and Elliptic Curve Cryptography, which are susceptible to quantum hacking. Transport Layer Security uses encryption to keep emails secure in transit, but cannot offer end-to-end security, since emails become visible in intermediary servers while being processed. The advent of Post Quantum Cryptography allows quantum resistance through new algorithms, but poses high computational demands for real-time communication protocols. It is also important that this method cannot offer any form of intrusion detection mechanism to prevent any interception in key exchange.

Quantum Key Distribution offers theoretical protection from intruders through quantum principles, while offering intrusion detection system within itself. The problem, however, lies in the fact that its implementation depends on highly-specialized equipment and is incompatible with existing communications infrastructure.

The problem with current studies lies in treating the above techniques separately, while lacking in efforts to integrate them with applications. Insecure email communication protocols can be attributed to this reason.

## CONTRIBUTIONS

The suggested project resolves these issues by creation of a novel secure email protocol at the application layer, which will be transport independent, i.e., not dependent on transport layer protocols such as SMTP or IMAP. Incorporation of a simulation based BB84 key generation process to provide simulation of a quantum key distribution for secure key exchange and intrusion detection on classical computers. Implementation of a novel hybrid cryptographic approach using quantum key generated in BB84 simulation and AES-256-GCM. Use of a centralized Key Management System (KMS) for secure key management, storage, rotation, and revocation. Inclusion of session keys and forward secrecy for minimal compromise in case of key breaches

## SYSTEM MODEL AND ASSUMPTIONS

The proposed system operates under a defined threat and trust model to ensure realistic security evaluation.

### Network Model

Communication occurs over standard email infrastructure using SMTP for transmission and IMAP for retrieval. The underlying transport layer is considered untrusted, and no assumptions are made regarding server integrity.

### Threat Model

The system assumes the presence of both passive and active adversaries, passive attackers can intercept network traffic but cannot modify messages and active attackers can attempt message injection, replay, or modification Also, Insider threats may exist within server infrastructure.

However, attackers are assumed not to have simultaneous access to both encrypted data and key storage within the KMS.

### Trust Assumptions

- Authentication providers (OAuth/OpenID) are trusted for identity verification
- The Key Management System is logically isolated from email storage systems
- End-user devices are assumed to be secure during cryptographic operations

These assumptions define the operational boundaries within which the system guarantees security properties.

## METHODOLOGY

In the proposed system, there is provision for email communication using simulated Quantum Key Distribution and traditional cryptography systems. This architecture consists of four key components, including the email client application, key management system, encryption engine, and the transport layer. This method uses sequential steps in ensuring secure email communication.

*Figure 1. System architecture of the quantum-safe email framework*

## User Authentication and Identity Verification

This whole process commences with the secure authentication of users through OAuth-based identity authentication. Secure identification of users occurs before any access is provided to the cryptographic module. Tokens for authentication are generated and verified so as to grant secure access to cryptic services.

Considering *U* to be the user and *T* to be the token for authentication, access to the system will be provided if:

$$\text{Auth(U)=}\begin{cases} 1, \text{ if } T_{\{valid\}} \\ 0, \text{ otherwise} \end{cases}$$

Only authenticated users are allowed to perform encryption and decryption operations.

## Quantum Key Generation Using Simulated BB84 Protocol

Upon successful authentication, the system creates a shared secret key through the simulation of the BB84 Quantum Key Distribution protocol. Under this protocol, the sender and the receiver independently choose random measurement bases for quantum bits.

The key bit will be valid only if both have chosen the same bases.

$$K_i = \begin{cases} q_i, & \text{if } B_s = B_r \\ discarded, & \text{otherwise} \end{cases}$$

where:

$K_i$= resulting key bit

$q_i$= transmitted quantum bit

= sender basis

= receiver basis

After basis reconciliation and error filtering, the remaining bits form the shared secret key .

## Quantum Bit Error Rate (QBER) Evaluation

The system computes Quantum Bit Error Rate (QBER) to identify the potential cases of eavesdropping. QBER is used to quantify the ratio of errors in the received key sequence.

QBER =

where:

= number of mismatched bits

= total transmitted bits

If the QBER exceeds a predefined threshold , the key exchange session is terminated to prevent potential security breaches.

Typical QBER thresholds range between **11% and 15%**.

## Key Storage and Management

The keys generated are stored in a centralized Key Management System (KMS) which is secure. Metadata kept by the KMS regarding every key contains: key identifier, time of creation, number of uses, expiry.

Key validity is determined using:

where:

= encrypted message

= hash value

Expired keys are automatically revoked to maintain forward secrecy.

## Hybrid Encryption Mechanism

The proposed system applies hybrid encryption strategy that uses the keys generated by QKD and classical encryption algorithm.

In a regular case of communication, Advanced Encryption Standard (AES-256) is used:

where:

= original message

= secret encryption key

= ciphertext

For highly sensitive messages, a simulated one-time pad mechanism is applied:

where denotes the XOR operation.

## Email and Attachment Encryption

Email messages and attachments are encrypted before being sent. A cryptographic hash is determined by the use of SHA-256 hashing algorithm in order to guarantee data integrity.

where:

= message hash

= original message

The hash value is transmitted alongside the encrypted message to enable integrity verification at the receiver side.

## Secure Email Transmission

The encrypted email is sent via the normal email protocols and does not change the current infrastructure. SMTP protocol is employed in the transmission of emails and IMAP protocol in the retrieval of emails.

## Decryption and Message Recovery

When a recipient gets an encrypted email, he/she authenticates himself/herself and gets the key from the Key Management System.

The original message is recovered using the decryption function:

where:

= AES decryption function

= ciphertext

For OTP-based encryption:

## Secret Key Generation Rate

Once the error correction and privacy amplification have been done, the usable key rate is calculated. The secret key generation rate is calculated as:

where:

= final secret key rate

= sifted key rate

= binary entropy function

The binary entropy function is defined as:
This equation determines the number of secure bits that remain after removing potential information leakage."

## Key Revocation and Audit Logging

Upon successful message decryption, the system logs the use of keys and cancels one-time keys to ensure that they are not reused. Any cryptographic data is traced to ensure security audits.

# SECURITY ANALYSIS

Upon closer examination of the proposed quantum-safe email system, it becomes clear that the strength of this model comes from the multilevel security mechanism that it offers. This is through incorporating quantum-like key generation, robust encryption, and rigorous identity checking. Contrary to most email models, which focus on providing transport layer encryption, this model provides security on the application layer level.

## Attack Model Assumptions

This assumption states that the attacker has the capacity to intercept, modify, and/or replay the transmitted message via the communications channel, but does not simultaneously have access to the encrypted message and its decryption keys inside the Key Management System. Also, classical attacks are constrained by computing power limitations, whereas partial resistance to quantum attacks is accomplished by utilizing key generation inspired by quantum technology. Under such assumptions, the system allows the detection of any attempts at intercepting the keys by means of detecting anomalies in QBER, whereas the payloads are still computationally safe by virtue of encryption via AES-256-GCM.

To assess the security of the solution, a number of realistic threat scenarios are investigated.

### Man-in-the-Middle (MITM) Attack

In conventional email systems using TLS, attackers can intercept communication if certificate authorities are compromised or misconfigured. In the proposed system, MITM attacks are mitigated through two independent mechanisms:

- BB84-based key exchange simulation ensures that any interception introduces detectable anomalies in the quantum bit sequence.
- QBER monitoring acts as a real-time intrusion detection metric.

If an attacker attempts to measure transmitted qubits, the act of measurement alters their state due to the no-cloning theorem, leading to an increase in QBER beyond the acceptable threshold. This forces immediate session termination.

### Replay Attacks

Replay attacks involve resending previously captured encrypted messages to trick the system. The framework prevents this by:

- Using session-based dynamic keys
- Enforcing key expiration policies
- Binding keys with timestamps and metadata

Even if a message is replayed, the associated key would either be expired or already revoked, making decryption impossible.

### Insider Threats

Insider threats are particularly dangerous in centralized systems. The architecture mitigates this risk by:

- Separating Key Management System (KMS) from email storage
- Ensuring keys are never stored alongside ciphertext
- Logging all cryptographic operations for auditing

Thus, even privileged insiders cannot access both encrypted data and decryption keys simultaneously.

## Key Compromise Attacks

Traditional systems suffer from long-term key exposure risks. The proposed system introduces:

- Forward secrecy via one-time session keys
- Automatic key revocation after use
- Limited key usage policies

Even if a key is compromised, it affects only a single session, not historical or future communications.

## Denial of Service (DoS) Attacks

Attackers may attempt to exhaust system resources, especially key generation modules. The framework addresses this by:

- Rate-limiting key requests
- Monitoring abnormal QKD simulation loads
- Implementing fallback secure modes

*Table 1. Comparing TLS-based architecture and how the proposed system enhances it*

| Feature | TLS-Based Email | Proposed System |
|---|---|---|
| Encryption Level | Transport Layer | Application Layer |
| Key Exchange | RSA/ECC | Simulated QKD |
| Forward Secrecy | Limited | Strong |
| Quantum Resistance | No | Yes |
| Server Trust Required | Yes | No |

A deeper analysis reveals that TLS only protects data in transit, whereas the proposed system ensures end-to-end confidentiality, even if servers are compromised.

## Security Properties

The proposed framework is designed to satisfy fundamental security properties required for secure communication systems. These properties are enforced through the integration of quantum-inspired key generation, authenticated encryption, and strict access control mechanisms.

Confidentiality is ensured by performing encryption at the application layer using AES-256-GCM. Since plaintext data is encrypted before transmission, it is never exposed to intermediate servers or network entities. The use of dynamically generated session keys further strengthens confidentiality by ensuring that each communication instance uses a unique encryption key. Even if encrypted data is intercepted, it remains computationally infeasible to derive the original message without access to the corresponding key stored in the Key Management System.

Data integrity is achieved through the use of authenticated encryption and cryptographic hashing. AES-256-GCM generates authentication tags that allow the receiver to verify that the ciphertext has not been altered. Additionally, SHA-256 hashing is applied to message content, and any mismatch between computed and received values results in rejection of the message. This ensures protection against tampering and unauthorized modifications during transmission.

User authentication is enforced using OAuth 2.0 and OpenID Connect mechanisms. Access to cryptographic operations is granted only after successful token validation. This ensures that only verified users can generate keys, encrypt messages, or perform decryption. The binding of cryptographic keys to authenticated user identities prevents unauthorized access and impersonation attacks.

The system achieves forward secrecy through the use of session-based dynamic keys. Each communication session generates a unique key using the simulated BB84 protocol, and keys are revoked after use. This ensures that compromise of a single key does not expose past or future communications. The separation of key storage from message storage further reduces the risk of large-scale data exposure.

Although implemented as a simulation, the BB84-based key generation process incorporates error-rate monitoring through Quantum Bit Error Rate (QBER). Any abnormal increase in QBER indicates potential interception or interference during key exchange. This provides a mechanism for detecting unauthorized observation attempts, enhancing overall system security.

Together, these properties demonstrate that the proposed system provides a comprehensive security model that addresses both classical and emerging threats in email communication.

## Performance Evaluation

Beyond basic experimental results, a comprehensive evaluation of computational performance, scalability, and efficiency trade-offs provides deeper insight into the practicality of the system.

## Time Complexity Analysis

The system consists of multiple computational stages:

1. Authentication – O(1) (token validation)
2. BB84 Simulation – O(n)
3. AES Encryption/Decryption – O(n)
4. Hash Computation (SHA-256) – O(n)

Overall system complexity:

where is the message size.

This linear complexity ensures scalability for large email attachments.

## Key Generation Overhead

The BB84 simulation introduces additional computational overhead compared to classical key exchange methods. However, the Key generation is parallelizable, operations are bit-level lightweight, no specialized hardware is required

The observed key generation latency (~35 ms) remains acceptable for real-time applications.

There is good evidence for high scalability in several ways. First of all, there is user scalability as a result of the stateless authentication approach, which means that more servers could be easily added without having to maintain session states, whereas the KMS may be deployed on several servers to handle growing demands. In addition, there is scalable data handling thanks to AES encryption because the computational cost increases linearly with the growth of data size. Finally, from the network standpoint, it is compatible with SMTP and IMAP networks.

## Security vs Efficiency Trade-off

*Table 2. Table specifying the security level and performance for how the proposed system will work under each mode*

| Mode | Security Level | Performance |
|---|---|---|
| AES-GCM only | High | Fast |
| AES + QKD keys | Very High | Moderate |
| One-Time Pad | Maximum | Slower |

The system allows dynamic selection based on sensitivity of data, ensuring flexibility.

## DESIGN RATIONALE

The design of the proposed quantum-safe email framework is guided by the need to balance security, performance, and practical deployability within existing communication infrastructures. Each component of the system is selected based on its ability to address specific limitations of traditional email security mechanisms.

### Choice of AES-256-GCM

AES-256-GCM is selected as the primary encryption algorithm due to its strong security guarantees and high performance. Unlike traditional encryption modes, Galois/Counter Mode (GCM) provides both confidentiality and integrity through authenticated encryption. This eliminates the need for separate message authentication mechanisms and reduces computational overhead. AES is widely supported in hardware and software environments, making it suitable for real-time email communication involving large attachments.

### Use of Simulated BB84 Protocol

The BB84 protocol is chosen as the basis for key generation due to its well-established role in Quantum Key Distribution. Although implemented as a classical simulation, it enables the system to replicate important properties such as random key generation and error-based intrusion detection. This approach allows the framework to explore quantum-inspired security mechanisms without requiring specialized quantum hardware, ensuring feasibility in current deployment environments.

### Application-Layer Encryption

The decision to perform encryption at the application layer addresses a key limitation of transport-layer security mechanisms such as TLS. In conventional systems, data is decrypted at intermediate servers, creating potential exposure points. By encrypting messages before transmission and decrypting them only at the recipient side, the system ensures that sensitive information remains protected throughout its lifecycle.

## Centralized Key Management System

A dedicated Key Management System is introduced to handle key storage and lifecycle operations independently of message handling. This separation reduces the risk of simultaneous exposure of ciphertext and keys. The KMS also enables features such as key rotation, expiration, and secure deletion, which are essential for maintaining long-term security.

## Hybrid Cryptographic Approach

The integration of quantum-inspired key generation with classical symmetric encryption provides a balanced solution. While simulated QKD enhances key security and introduces detection capabilities, AES ensures efficient data encryption. This hybrid model avoids the performance limitations of purely quantum or purely post-quantum approaches.

## Compatibility with Existing Infrastructure

The framework is designed to operate without requiring modifications to standard email protocols such as SMTP and IMAP. This ensures seamless integration with widely used platforms like Gmail and Outlook. Maintaining compatibility reduces deployment complexity and increases the likelihood of real-world adoption.

Overall, the design choices reflect a practical approach to achieving enhanced email security while remaining scalable, efficient, and adaptable to future advancements in quantum technologies.

## Implementation Details

The proposed system is implemented using a modular architecture built on a Flask-based backend, ensuring simplicity, extensibility, and maintainability.

## Backend Architecture

The system is divided into the following modules:

1. Authentication Module
    - Implements OAuth 2.0 and OpenID Connect
    - Handles token validation
    - Ensures secure user identity mapping
2. Encryption Engine

Responsible for:

- AES-256-GCM encryption/decryption
- Initialization vector generation
- Authentication tag validation

3. QKD Simulation Module

Implements BB84 protocol logic:

- Random bit generation
- Basis selection
- Basis reconciliation
- Error filtering

4. Key Management System (KMS)

Handles:

- Key storage
- Key lifecycle management
- Secure deletion
- Metadata tracking

5. Email Interface Layer

- Integrates with SMTP and IMAP
- Converts encrypted payload into standard email format
- Handles attachment encoding/decoding

6. Data Flow
    1. User authenticates → receives token
    2. QKD module generates shared key
    3. Message encrypted using AES
    4. Hash generated using SHA-256
    5. Encrypted payload sent via SMTP
    6. Receiver retrieves via IMAP
    7. KMS provides key
    8. Message decrypted and verified

This pipeline ensures that plaintext never leaves the client environment, achieving true end-to-end security.

## Comparative Study

Comparison between the new and existing systems illustrates the benefits of using this method in protecting emails against different vulnerabilities. The conventional TLS email system offers encryption at the point of sending an email, but they are exposed to any server-based attacks and have no quantum-resistant nature. On the other hand, the use of the PGP email system offers better security through end-to-end encryption. But, this system is complex to manage and has quantum vulnerabilities since it uses either RSA or ECC algorithms. While PQC-only email system utilizes quantum-resistant lattice algorithms, they are complex in computations and have no methods of identifying any form of eavesdropping.

*Table 3. Table comparing the feature of the existing algorithms and the proposed system*

| Feature | TLS | PGP | PQC | Proposed |
|---|---|---|---|---|
| End-to-End Encryption | No | Yes | Yes | Yes |
| Quantum Safe | No | No | Yes | Yes |
| Key Management | Centralized | Complex | Moderate | Automated |
| Performance | High | Moderate | Moderate | High |
| Eavesdropping Detection | No | No | No | Yes |
| SMTP Compatibility I | Yes | Partial | Yes | Yes |
| Hardware Requirement | None | None | None | Low |

The comparison demonstrates that the proposed system achieves a balance between security and performance while introducing partial resistance to quantum threats through simulated QKD-based key generation.

# RESULT AND FUTURE SCOPE

It was proposed to implement and test the quantum-safe email system based on a Flask-based application combining simulated Quantum Key Distribution (QKD) with the AES-256-GCM encryption. Experimental analysis proved that the system is able to encrypt and decrypt email messages of various sizes and still operate efficiently in terms of computational performance. Experiments with message size of 1 KB up to 1 MB revealed that the encryption time of 6-120 ms and the decryption time of 5-110 ms increase in direct proportion to the size of the message but still viable in real time email settings. AES-GCM is used to make sure that the encryption is authenticated, and it gives confidentiality and integrity of messages. Moreover, the simulated process of generating key BB84 was able to generate sifted key efficiency of nearly 50 and this efficiency is in line with what is expected of QKD-based systems.

A deeper interpretation of experimental results reveals linear scaling confirms algorithmic efficiency, Low latency ensures usability in real-time communication, high QKD efficiency validates simulation accuracy

The combination of QKD and AES creates a balanced system where QKD ensures secure key exchange and AES ensures fast data encryption.

This hybrid model is significantly more practical than pure quantum or pure classical approaches.

More security also encourages the hybrid encryption process because they combine quantum derived keys and the classical symmetric encryption. Under the maximum-security level, a one-time pad is used to encrypt the session key that is received and used to encrypt the contents of emails in such a manner that the various communications sessions use different cryptographic keys. Quantum key management module is able to store quantum keys (1024-bit) and retrieve them (35 ms) which is high and can be scaled to cryptography. Security analysis showed that it was possible only to decrypt the encrypted messages with the help of the right quantum key and the inappropriate keys resulted in the failure of authentication due to the AES-GCM integrity check. Compared to the conventional email systems where the only encryption is carried out on the transport layer such as TLS, the proposed system is considerably more robust in communication security since it introduces the quantum-resilient key-generation, forward secrecy-based and future-quantum computing attacks. The findings of this research paper indicate that the suggested architecture offers a viable and feasible way of implementing quantum-safe cryptography methods in the current email communication systems.

## FUTURE ENHANCEMENTS

Further improvements to the suggested quantum-resistant email solution could drastically enhance its performance and adaptability, as well as make it applicable in real-life situations. In particular, it is possible to improve the efficiency of computations performed during the application of cryptography to the process. While the current solution successfully merges the usage of simulated QKD protocol with AES-based encryption, the algorithms involved in each stage – from the generation of keys through to encryption and decryption and authentication – are still prone to optimization efforts. Methods such as lightweight implementations of cryptography and more efficient key schedules and memory management could help in enhancing the system's performance. As in the case of optimizing deep learning models, minimizing the amount of computation could guarantee high responsiveness of the system even when used with low-performance devices such as mobile phones or embedded systems.

A further possible area for enhancing the system involves the introduction of intelligent threat-detection techniques through the use of analytics. Currently, the security measures in place make use of deterministic measures like Quantum Bit Error Rate (QBER) as a way of detecting whether there are any signs of an attacker. In the future, it will be possible to implement adaptive surveillance methods that include analysis of patterns of communication, the number of times keys were used, and even authentication methods to detect any anomalies that might arise. Combining statistics with learning measures can allow for the creation of a security system that can adaptively learn new threats and detect them before any actual damage occurs.

The creation of key management procedures might provide considerable benefits in the future. While the current centralized key management scheme guarantees the security of the process of handling encryption keys efficiently, possible enhancements to the system could be made by adopting either a distributed or hybrid approach. The application of decentralization techniques will help eliminate a single point of failure and increase resistance to attacks on the system. Some examples of the enhancements might include creating a mechanism of key life cycle management automatically that would facilitate key generation, distribution, rotation, and revocation without requiring any human involvement. In addition, logging and auditing should also be utilized in order to trace all activities performed through encryption keys.

Increasing the system usability in a multiplatform manner can be viewed as one of the essential directions of future research. Initially developed to provide secure email transmission capabilities, the system can be easily extended by adding the ability to use the software from mobile devices, as well as through web interfaces and on cross-platform systems. However, in order to ensure that the system operates effectively within limited resources, special attention should be paid to the optimization of the encryption and decryption process. Moreover, secure means of storing the cryptographic material in the system may include the use of hardware-protected keys on mobile devices.

Apart from these upgrades, the future versions of this system will also possess the ability to adapt and learn through time according to the system's usage trends and the environment. In this way, instead of depending on fixed settings, the system will be able to optimize variables such as the frequency of key regeneration, security criteria, and authentication rules. With this, the system will be able to ensure that the optimal ratio of security and performance is always met despite the operational circumstances. All in all, these upgrades clearly demonstrate the capability of the framework to become a powerful and effective quantum-resistant communication system.

## INTEGRATION OF POST-QUANTUM CRYPTOGRAPHY AND HYBRID QUANTUM-SAFE DESIGN

While the proposed framework leverages simulated Quantum Key Distribution (QKD) for secure key generation, an equally important dimension of quantum-safe communication is the integration of standardized Post-Quantum Cryptography (PQC) algorithms. Recent advancements in PQC, particularly those standardized by National Institute of Standards and Technology, provide practical cryptographic mechanisms that are resistant to quantum attacks without requiring quantum hardware. Incorporating these algorithms into the proposed framework enhances its robustness and aligns it with emerging global security standards.

One of the most notable advancements in Post Quantum Cryptography (PQC) is the lattice-based KEM known as CRYSTALS-Kyber, which was chosen by NIST for standardization purposes. As stated earlier, the KEM was designed to address the issue of exchanging information securely using the traditional algorithms, namely RSA, and Diffie-Hellman which are susceptible to quantum attacks. The reason Kyber is more secure compared to other existing systems is that it uses the difficulty of solving a certain lattice problem, known as the Learning With Errors (LWE).Within the scope of the suggested scheme, Kyber could be introduced as an alternative or additional way of exchanging keys in parallel with QKD simulation. In this case, QKD would serve as a physically based solution of detecting any attempts at eavesdropping, while Kyber would be mathematically based.

Another significant PQC algorithm that can be adopted is CRYSTALS-Dilithium, which offers quantum resistant digital signatures. As mentioned earlier, email systems traditionally employ either RSA or ECC to sign messages. However, both algorithms can be broken using quantum attacks. The adoption of CRYSTALS- Dilithium can help ensure that digital signatures remain resistant against quantum attacks and hence, enable verification of message integrity and authenticity. Also, a hash-based signature scheme, such as SPHINCS+, offers an alternative solution for implementing digital signatures in the proposed architecture. While lattice-based cryptography requires more resources, SPHINCS+ only depends on hash functions, hence making it highly conservative. The downside, however, is that SPHINCS+ generates larger signatures compared to lattice-based schemes. Nevertheless, the scheme is highly secure, thus making it applicable in situations that demand maximum security.

Finally, the inclusion of PQC in the proposed design allows the deployment of a hybrid quantum-safe framework, with three layers of security, including:

1. Quantum-Inspired Key Generation (Simulated QKD)

   Provides randomness and eavesdropping detection through QBER analysis.

2. Post-Quantum Key Exchange (Kyber)

   Ensures secure key establishment based on mathematically hard problems.

3. High-Speed Symmetric Encryption (AES-256-GCM)

   Enables efficient encryption of large email messages and attachments.

This layered approach addresses the limitations of individual techniques. Although neither QKD simulation nor PQC alone will be quantum-secure, nor intrusion-detected, their combination enables both a better-built system. Implementation of AES guarantees the performance to be useful in a real-world setting, eluding the ineffectiveness of purely abstract models. Kyber can be implemented as part of the Key Management System (KMS) as far as implementation is concerned. As an example, Kyber can be used to encapsulate a by the sender. Secret keys shared and which is mixed with the generated randomness of the QKD to generate a QKD session key. This hybrid key derivation process enhances entropy and less dependency on any single cryptography assumption.

Mathematically, the hybrid key derivation can be represented as:

where represents the key derived from simulated QKD, represents the key encapsulated using Kyber, and is a cryptographic hash function such as SHA-256. This makes the end session key inherent security properties from both quantum-inspired and post-quantum mechanisms. One more positive aspect of PQC integration is that it can be integrated with existing infrastructure.

Unlike QKD, which PQC algorithms are fully implementable in software, although specialized hardware is required to implement all of them. This renders them suitable to be adopted with ease directly into schemes like email customers, internet applications, and cloud services. The implementation of PQC in the given framework will make the system more practical for large-scale deployment. Nevertheless, PQC adoption comes with some challenges as well. Algorithms like Lattice Kyber and Dilithium generally involve increased key size requirements and more computational resources than classical algorithms. As much as these overheads can be handled, they should be optimized keenly to ensure that the system can be effective performance is still acceptable, particularly in resource limited environments.

To solve this, the framework can incorporate adaptive cryptographic selection, in which various algorithms are selected. made depending on the severity of the message. For instance:

Standard emails → AES + Kyber

High-security emails → AES + QKD + Kyber

Maximum security → One-Time Pad + QKD + PQC

This flexibility ensures that the system can balance security and performance dynamically.

Moreover, the use of PQC also adds power to the system against the threat of the "Harvest Now, Decrypt Later. Since Kyber and other PQC algorithms are designed to be resistant to quantum attacks, encrypted, it is possible to keep communications safe even when these communications are intercepted and stored and they need to be decrypted later. This significantly enhances the security of sensitive information in the long run. Moving ahead, one way to go is the combination of PQC and QKD into the future of secure. communication systems. Although PQC offers instantaneous and software-based quantum resistance, QKD offers the theoretical possibility of information-theoretic security in quantum networks of the future. Designing systems to support. in either of such ways, we can design communication structures that can be relevant to the present and safe in the future. the long term. Finally, post-quantum cryptographic algorithms, including Kyber, Dilithium, and, are integrated. The model proposed by SPHINCS+ builds upon the suggested quantum-safe email model with the property that it offers standard, scalable, and. quantum-resistant security mechanisms. In combination with simulated QKD and effective symmetric encryption, these methods comprise a hybrid framework that would deal with present and forthcoming threats. in digital communication. Not only does this boost the security posture of the system, it also. coordinates it with recent worldwide practices in quantum-robust cryptographic infrastructure.

## LIMITATIONS

Although the framework provided is a suitable way of securing emails there are quite a few limitations that should be acknowledged. One of the major constraints is that the simulated Quantum Key Distribution mechanism was used, as opposed to a genuine quantum communication system. BB84 protocol runs over classical hardware, meaning that it does not be able to provide the information-theoretic security. Although the simulation mimics properties such as randomness and intrusion detection with errors, it remains based on the same classical assumptions and cannot provide the same type of guarantees as are provided by physical QKD.

The system also utilizes a centralized Key Management System (KMS) to store and manage keys in the system throughout their life cycle. This does, however, result in one extra dependency, as if a problem is experienced with the module, this may cause issues with the ongoing communication channels. Furthermore, encryption/decryption becomes a critical part of the system running and if the end-user computer is compromised, all encryption and decryption processes are compromised. In terms of performances, the use of a simulated QKD system will also have increased computational expenses on the system compared to other methods of generation of encryption keys. Although satisfactory latency values are obtained during the transmission of the encrypted messages for normal use-cases (like sending emails), there are still possibilities for further improvement with respect to scalability. In particular, scalability may be challenged when sending a large number of messages over a short period of time or from resource-limited computing devices. Besides, there will be a need to collaborate with existing email service providers via their APIs, introducing further limitations and needs.

In conclusion, these restrictions suggest that the system is a promising development towards a more secure and quantum-resistant email system, but still has a way to go before it can be used on a wide scale. These restrictions underscore the need for more work to be done with regard to the integration of real quantum communication channels and the scalability of a wide-scale deployment.

## CONCLUSION

This research has developed a quantum secure email communication protocol which is hybrid in nature. The framework aims at mitigating the security risks posed by development of quantum computing technology. The existing public key cryptography algorithms in email communication protocols are more threatened by quantum attacks. This challenge has been tackled by the use of QKD and classical symmetric cryptography. This is because the keys can be transferred safely with the benefit of being able to trace any efforts at intrusion as well as a reasonable rate of encryption.

Centralized KMS is incorporated in the architecture of this proposed framework. It makes it easier to handle the cryptographic keys in their lifecycle such as the distribution of keys, revocation of keys, generation of keys and validation of keys. The logging system guarantees a higher level of responsibility at the communication channel and observation of any suspicious activity. The implementation of single use session keys and symmetric encryption demonstrates the feasibility of coming up with quantum resistant email communication protocols. Although the quantum computing part would need classical simulation, the framework would be an efficient way of implementing quantum inspired cryptography protocols into existent communication models.

## REFERENCES


Demir, E. D., Gorgulu, I., & Onbaşli, M. C. (2026). Micro and transport layer security benchmarking of post-quantum versus classical cryptography. *IEEE Access : Practical Innovations, Open Solutions*, *14*, 56099–56111. DOI: 10.1109/ACCESS.2026.3682760

Djordjevic, I. B. (2020). Hybrid QKD protocol outperforming both DV- and CV-QKD protocols. *IEEE Photonics Journal*, *12*(1), 1–8. DOI: 10.1109/JPHOT.2019.2946910

Escanez-Exposito, D., Caballero-Gil, P., & Martín-Fernández, F. (2023). Interactive simulation of quantum key distribution protocols and application in Wi-Fi networks. *Wireless Networks*, *29*(8), 3781–3792. DOI: 10.1007/s11276-023-03438-x

Indrayani, R., Ferdiansyah, P., & Satria, D. A. (2019, July). Effectiveness comparison of the AES and 3DES cryptography methods on email text messages. In *2019 International Conference on Information and Communications Technology (ICOIACT)* (pp. 66-69). IEEE. DOI: 10.1109/ICOIACT46704.2019.8938579

Manimozhi, M., & Mugelan, R. K. (2025). Post-quantum AES encryption using ECC points from BB84 keys. *EPJ Quantum Technology*, *12*(1), 109. DOI: 10.1140/epjqt/s40507-025-00411-9

Mehic, M., Rass, S., Dervisevic, E., & Voznak, M. (2022). Tackling denial of service attacks on key management in software-defined quantum key distribution networks. *IEEE Access : Practical Innovations, Open Solutions*, *10*, 110512–110520. DOI: 10.1109/ACCESS.2022.3214511

National Institute of Standards and Technology. (2024). *FIPS 203: Module-lattice-based key-encapsulation mechanism standard*. Computer Security Resource Center.

National Institute of Standards and Technology. (2025). *Transitioning to quantum-resistant encryption standards*. NIST Special Publication.

Nayab, S., & Hafiza, A. (2016). Quantum cryptography: A brief review of recent developments. In *DIPEWC 2016*.

Nourai, M., & Levkowitz, H. (2017). Securing email for the average users via a new architecture. In *PACRIM 2017*. DOI: 10.1109/PACRIM.2017.8121931

Pan, D., Long, G. L., Yin, L., Sheng, Y. B., Ruan, D., Ng, S. X., Lu, J., & Hanzo, L. (2024). The evolution of quantum secure direct communication: On the road to the qinternet. *IEEE Communications Surveys and Tutorials*, *26*(3), 1898–1949. DOI: 10.1109/COMST.2024.3367535

Parvathi, G. S., Reddy, K. N., Harini, K., & Akshaya, K. (2024). Revolutionizing Email Security with Quantum Key Distribution for Enhanced Data Protection in Communication Systems. *Journal of Computational Analysis and Applications*, *33*(8).

Prajapat, S., Kumar, P., Kumar, S., Das, A. K., Shetty, S., & Hossain, M. S. (2024). Designing high-performance identity-based quantum signature protocol with strong security. *IEEE Access : Practical Innovations, Open Solutions*, *12*, 14647–14658. DOI: 10.1109/ACCESS.2024.3355196

Prévost, T., Martin, B., & Alibart, O. (2025). An etsi gs qkd compliant tls implementation. *arXiv preprint arXiv:2506.19409*. DOI: 10.5220/0013564700003979

Shim, K. S., Kim, Y. H., Sohn, I., Lee, E., Bae, K. I., & Lee, W. (2022). Design and validation of quantum key management system for construction of KREONET quantum cryptography communication. *Journal of Web Engineering*, *21*(5), 1377–1417. DOI: 10.13052/jwe1540-9589.2151

Telecommunication Engineering Centre. (2025). *Migration to post quantum cryptography*. Ministry of Communications.

Thakur, G., Chouksey, P., Chopra, M., Sadotra, P., & Kumar, S. (2025). A comprehensive review on the hybrid BB84 E91 QKD protocol for enhanced security efficiency and practical hardware implementation in quantum cryptography. *Discover Computing*, *28*(1), 343. DOI: 10.1007/s10791-025-09807-8

Tsai, C. W., Yang, C. W., Lin, J., Chang, Y. C., & Chang, R. S. (2021). Quantum key distribution networks: Challenges and future research issues in security. *Applied Sciences (Basel, Switzerland)*, *11*(9), 3767. DOI: 10.3390/app11093767

Verma, G., & Kumar, A. (2023). Integration of QKD with attribute-based encryption for cloud. In *Springer*.

Wang, Y., & Ismail, E. S. (2025a). *Advances of post-quantum cryptography in blockchain and IoT*. IEEE Transactions.

Wang, Y., & Ismail, E. S. (2025b). Enhanced network security protocols for the quantum era. *IEEE Journal on Selected Areas in Communications*.

Xuan, J. (2016). Design of secure email system based on identity-based cryptography. In *ICCC 2016*.

# Compilation of References


Aashiq Banu, S., & Amirtharajan, R. (2020). Tri-level scrambling and enhanced diffusion for DICOM image cipher- DNA and chaotic fused approach. *Multimedia Tools and Applications, 79*(39-40), 28807–28824. DOI: 10.1007/s11042-020-09501-5

Abbasi, N., Nizamullah, F. N., & Zeb, S. (2023). AI in healthcare: Integrating advanced technologies with traditional practices for enhanced patient care. *BULLET: Jurnal Multidisiplin Ilmu, 2*(3), 546–556.

Abd-El-Atty, B. (2026). A dual medical image encryption algorithm based on dynamic DNA operations. *Computers and Electrical Engineering, 130*(June 2025), 1–20. DOI: 10.1016/j.compeleceng.2025.110899

Adeoye, S. (2025). *Securing IoT devices: A novel approach using blockchain and quantum cryptography*. Cognizance Journal of Multidisciplinary Studies.

Afraji, D. M. A. A., Lloret, J., & Peñalver, L. (2025). Deep learning-driven defense strategies for mitigating DDoS attacks in cloud computing environments. *Cyber Security Applications, 3*, 100085. DOI: 10.1016/j.csa.2025.100085

Agrawal, J., & Shelly, M. K. (n.d.). Energy-efficient clustering with multiple sink (EECMS) in wireless body area network.

Ahmadian, M., Buruaga, J., Mendez, R., Brito, J. P., Pastor, A., Rivas, J. M., ... Velasco, L. (2024, July). Demonstration of classical and hybrid solutions for lightpath security using quantum keys. In *2024 24th International Conference on Transparent Optical Networks (ICTON)* (pp. 1-4). IEEE. DOI: 10.1109/ICTON62926.2024.10647235

Ahmad, W., Rasool, A., Javed, A. R., Baker, T., & Jalil, Z. (2022). Cyber security in IoT-based cloud computing: A comprehensive survey. *Electronics (Basel), 11*(1), 16. DOI: 10.3390/electronics11010016

Akbar, M. S., Hussain, Z., Sheng, M., & Shankaran, R. (2022). Wireless body area sensor networks: Survey of MAC and routing protocols for patient monitoring under IEEE 802.15.4 and IEEE 802.15.6. *Sensors (Basel)*, *22*(21), 8279. DOI: 10.3390/s22218279

Akkaş, M. A., Sokullu, R., & Çetin, H. E. (2020). Healthcare and patient monitoring using IoT. *Internet of Things : Engineering Cyber Physical Human Systems*, *11*, 100173. DOI: 10.1016/j.iot.2020.100173

Al Mazroa, A., Albogamy, F. R., Ishak, M. K., & Mostafa, S. M. (2025). Boosting cyberattack detection using binary metaheuristics with deep learning on cyber-physical system environment. *IEEE Access : Practical Innovations, Open Solutions*, *13*, 11280–11294. DOI: 10.1109/ACCESS.2025.3526258

Al Rawajbeh, M., Maria Soosai, A. J., Ramasamy, L. K., & Khan, F. (2025). Trustworthy adaptive AI for real-time intrusion detection in industrial IoT security. *IoT*, *6*(3), 53. DOI: 10.3390/iot6030053

Alam, S., Shuaib, M., Ahmad, S., Jayakody, D. N. K., Muthanna, A., Bharany, S., & Elgendy, I. A. (2022). Blockchain-based solutions supporting reliable healthcare for fog computing and internet of medical things (IoMT) integration. *Sustainability (Basel)*, *14*(22), 15312. DOI: 10.3390/su142215312

Alani, S., Zakaria, Z., Saiedi, T., Ahmad, A., Mahmood, S. N., Saad, M. A., & Albeyar, M. A. A. A. A. (2020). A review on UWB antenna sensor for wireless body area networks. In *ISMSIT 2020* (pp. 1–10). IEEE. DOI: 10.1109/ISMSIT50672.2020.9254219

Alber, D. A., Yang, Z., Alyakin, A., Yang, E., Rai, S., Valliani, A. A., Zhang, J., Rosenbaum, G. R., Amend-Thomas, A. K., Kurland, D. B., Kremer, C. M., Eremiev, A., Negash, B., Wiggan, D. D., Nakatsuka, M. A., Sangwon, K. L., Neifert, S. N., Khan, H. A., Save, A. V., & Oermann, E. K. (2025). Medical large language models are vulnerable to data-poisoning attacks. *Nature Medicine*, *31*(2), 618–626. DOI: 10.1038/s41591-024-03445-1 PMID: 39779928

Alchemy. (n.d.). *List of 26 decentralized storage tools (2025)*. https://www.alchemy.com/dapps/best/decentralized-storage-tools

Aldhyani, T. H. H., & Alkahtani, H. (2022). Artificial intelligence algorithm-based economic denial of sustainability attack detection systems: Cloud computing environments. *Sensors (Basel)*, *22*(13), 4685. DOI: 10.3390/s22134685

Algül, R. D. (2025). Quantum-Resilient Cryptography and Financial Stability in Economic Systems. *Human-Computer Interaction*, *9*(1), 111–114. DOI: 10.62802/dkahxv90

Ali, M. H., Jaber, M. M., Abd, S. K., Rehman, A., Awan, M. J., Damaševičius, R., & Bahaj, S. A. (2022). Threat analysis and distributed denial of service (DDoS) attack recognition in the Internet of Things (IoT). *Electronics (Basel)*, *11*(3), 494. DOI: 10.3390/electronics11030494

Ali, M., Ali, M., Hussain, M., & Koundal, D. (2025). Generative adversarial networks (GANs) for medical image processing: Recent advancements. *Archives of Computational Methods in Engineering*, *32*(2), 1185–1198. DOI: 10.1007/s11831-024-10174-8

Ali, M., Raza, A., Akram, M. A., Arif, H., & Ali, A. (2025). Enhancing IOT Security: A review of Machine Learning-Driven Approaches to Cyber Threat Detection: Enhancing IOT Security: A review of Machine Learning-Driven Approaches to Cyber Threat Detection. *Journal of Informatics and Interactive Technology*, *2*(1), 316–324. DOI: 10.63547/jiite.v2i1.64

Ali, T. S., & Ali, R. (2020). A Novel Medical Image Signcryption Scheme Using TLTS and Henon Chaotic Map. *IEEE Access : Practical Innovations, Open Solutions*, *8*, 71974–71992. DOI: 10.1109/ACCESS.2020.2987615

Aliyu, I., Van Engelenburg, S., Mu'Azu, M. B., Kim, J., & Lim, C. G. (2022). Statistical detection of adversarial examples in blockchain-based federated forest in-vehicle network intrusion detection systems. *IEEE Access : Practical Innovations, Open Solutions*, *10*, 109366–109384. DOI: 10.1109/ACCESS.2022.3212412

Aljawarneh, S., Aldwairi, M., & Yassein, M. B. (2018). Anomaly-based intrusion detection system through feature selection analysis and building hybrid efficient model. *Journal of Computational Science*, *25*, 152–160. DOI: 10.1016/j.jocs.2017.03.006

Alladi, T., Kohli, V., Chamola, V., Yu, F. R., & Guizani, M. (2021). Artificial intelligence (AI)-empowered intrusion detection architecture for the Internet of Vehicles. *IEEE Wireless Communications*, *28*(3), 144–149. DOI: 10.1109/MWC.001.2000428

Alotaibi, A., & Barnawi, A. (2023). IDSoft: A federated and softwarized intrusion detection framework for massive Internet of Things in 6G network. *Journal of King Saud University. Computer and Information Sciences*, *35*(6), 101575. DOI: 10.1016/j.jksuci.2023.101575

Alotaibi, E. M., Issa, H., & Codesso, M. (2025). Blockchain-based conceptual model for enhanced transparency in government records: A design science research approach. *International Journal of Information Management Data Insights*, *5*(1), 100304. DOI: 10.1016/j.jjimei.2024.100304

Alqubaysi, T., Asmari, A. F. A., Alanazi, F., Almutairi, A., & Armghan, A. (2025). Federated learning-based predictive traffic management using a contained privacy-preserving scheme for autonomous vehicles. *Sensors (Basel)*, *25*(4), 1116. DOI: 10.3390/s25041116 PMID: 40006346

Alrefaei, A., & Ilyas, M. (2024). Using machine learning multiclass classification technique to detect IoT attacks in real time. *Sensors (Basel)*, *24*(14), 4516. DOI: 10.3390/s24144516

Al-Sada, B., Sadighian, A., & Oligeri, G. (2024). Analysis and Characterization of Cyber Threats Leveraging the MITRE ATT&CK Database. *IEEE Access : Practical Innovations, Open Solutions*, *12*, 1217–1234. DOI: 10.1109/ACCESS.2023.3344680

Al-Sada, B., Sadighian, A., & Oligeri, G. (2024). MITRE ATT&CK: State of the Art and Way Forward. *ACM Computing Surveys*, *57*(1), 1–37. DOI: 10.1145/3687300

Alshamrani, M. (2022). IoT and artificial intelligence implementations for remote healthcare monitoring systems: A survey. *Journal of King Saud University. Computer and Information Sciences*, *34*(8), 4687–4701. DOI: 10.1016/j.jksuci.2021.06.005

Al-Sumaidaee, G., Alkhudary, R., Zilic, Z., & Swidan, A. (2023). Performance analysis of a private blockchain network built on Hyperledger Fabric for healthcare. *Information Processing & Management*, *60*(2), 103160. DOI: 10.1016/j.ipm.2022.103160

Alzahrani, A., & Aldhyani, T. H. (2022). Artificial intelligence algorithms for detecting and classifying MQTT protocol Internet of Things attacks. *Electronics (Basel)*, *11*(22), 3837. DOI: 10.3390/electronics11223837

Alzahrani, B. A., Irshad, A., Albeshri, A., & Alsubhi, K. (2021). A provably secure and lightweight patient-healthcare authentication protocol in wireless body area networks. *Wireless Personal Communications*, *117*(1), 47–69. DOI: 10.1007/s11277-020-07237-x

Anand, A., & Hassabnis, A. (2024, June). Qcrypt: Leveraging post-quantum cryptography for enhanced security of data at rest. In *2024 15th International Conference on Computing Communication and Networking Technologies (ICCCNT)* (pp. 1-9). IEEE.

Anand, A., & Singh, A. K. (2020). An improved DWT-SVD domain watermarking for medical information security. *Computer Communications*, *152*(January), 72–80. DOI: 10.1016/j.comcom.2020.01.038

Ananthi, J. V., & Jose, P. S. H. (2021). A perspective review of security challenges in body area networks for healthcare applications. *International Journal of Wireless Information Networks*, *28*(4), 451–466. DOI: 10.1007/s10776-021-00538-3

Andreoni, M., Lunardi, W. T., Lawton, G., & Thakkar, S. (2024). Enhancing autonomous system security and resilience with generative AI: A comprehensive survey. *IEEE Access : Practical Innovations, Open Solutions*, *12*, 109470–109493. DOI: 10.1109/ACCESS.2024.3439363

Anglen, J. (2024, December 6). *Future-proofing blockchain: Embracing quantum-resistant cybersecurity in 2024*. Rapid Innovation. https://www.rapidinnovation.io/post/quantum-resistant-blockchain-preparing-for-the-future-of-cybersecurity-in-2024

An, T., Gao, T., Chen, T., & Jiang, D. (2025). A dual-image encryption scheme for sensitive region of traffic image using public key cryptosystem and novel chaotic map. *Complex & Intelligent Systems*, *11*(7), 1–23. DOI: 10.1007/s40747-025-01912-x

Apillon. (2023, November 22). *The top 7 decentralized cloud storage platforms in 2023*. Medium. https://blog.apillon.io/the-top-7-decentralized-cloud-storage-platforms-in-2023-d9bdfc0e1f2d

Apruzzese, G., Colajanni, M., Ferretti, L., Guido, A., & Marchetti, M. (2018, May). On the effectiveness of machine and deep learning for cyber security. In *2018 10th international conference on cyber Conflict (CyCon)* (pp. 371-390). IEEE. DOI: 10.23919/CYCON.2018.8405026

Arreche, O., Guntur, T., & Abdallah, M. (2024). XAI-IDS: Toward proposing an explainable artificial intelligence framework for enhancing network intrusion detection systems. *Applied Sciences (Basel, Switzerland)*, *14*(10), 4170. DOI: 10.3390/app14104170

Aruchamy, P., Gnanaselvi, S., Sowndarya, D., & Naveenkumar, P. (2023). An artificial intelligence approach for energy-aware intrusion detection and secure routing in Internet of Things-enabled wireless sensor networks. *Concurrency and Computation*, *35*(23), e7818. DOI: 10.1002/cpe.7818

Assiri, F. Y., & Aljahdali, A. O. (2024). Software Vulnerability Fuzz Testing: A Mutation-Selection Optimization Systematic Review. Engineering, Technology &amp. *Applied Scientific Research*, *14*(4), 14961–14969. DOI: 10.48084/etasr.6971

Ayemtsa Kuete, G. P., Heucheun Yepdia, L. M., Tiedeu, A., & Mboupda Pone, J. R. (2024). Medical image cryptosystem using a new 3-D map implemented in a microcontroller. In *Multimedia Tools and Applications* (Issue 0123456789). Springer US. DOI: 10.1007/s11042-024-18460-0

Balaji, G., Sharma, G., & Jayanth, R. S. S. (2022). Forest cover in India: A victim of technicalities. *Ecological Economics*, *193*, 107306. DOI: 10.1016/j.ecolecon.2021.107306

Balawejder, B., Dankiewicz, R., & Ostrowska-Dankiewicz, A. (2019). The role of insurance in cyber risk management in enterprises. *Humanities and Social Sciences Quarterly*, *26*. Advance online publication. DOI: 10.7862/rz.2019.hss.33

Banik, A., Shamsi, Z., & Laiphrakpam, D. S. (2019). An encryption scheme for securing multiple medical images. *Journal of Information Security and Applications*, *49*, 102398. Advance online publication. DOI: 10.1016/j.jisa.2019.102398

Banu, S. A., & Amirtharajan, R. (2020). A robust medical image encryption in dual domain: chaos-DNA-IWT combined approach. *Medical & Biological Engineering & Computing*, *58*(7), 1445–1458. DOI: 10.1007/s11517-020-02178-w

Barbhaya, M., Dasari, P. R., Damarla, S. K., Srinivasan, R., & Huang, B. (2025). A deep learning framework for cyberattack detection and classification in industrial control systems. *Computers & Chemical Engineering*, *202*, 202. DOI: 10.1016/j.compchemeng.2025.109278

Batchu, R. K., Bikku, T., Thota, S., Seetha, H., & Ayoade, A. A. (2024). A novel optimization-driven deep learning framework for the detection of DDoS attacks. *Scientific Reports*, *14*(1), 28024. DOI: 10.1038/s41598-024-77554-9 PMID: 39543174

Bathula, A., Gupta, S. K., Merugu, S., Saba, L., Khanna, N. N., Laird, J. R., Sanagala, S. S., Singh, R., Garg, D., Fouda, M. M., & Suri, J. S. (2024). Blockchain, artificial intelligence, and healthcare: The tripod of future—a narrative review. *Artificial Intelligence Review*, *57*(9), 238. DOI: 10.1007/s10462-024-10873-5

Benaissi, S., Chikouche, N., & Hamza, R. (2023). A novel image encryption algorithm based on hybrid chaotic maps using a key image. In *Optik* (Vol. 272). DOI: 10.1016/j.ijleo.2022.170316

Berman, D. S., Buczak, A. L., Chavis, J. S., & Corbett, C. L. (2019). A survey of deep learning methods for cyber security. *Information (Basel)*, *10*(4), 122. DOI: 10.3390/info10040122

Bernstein, D. J. (2025). Post-quantum cryptography. In *Encyclopedia of Cryptography, Security and Privacy* (pp. 1846-1847). Cham: Springer Nature Switzerland. http://dx.doi.org/DOI: 10.1007/978-3-030-71522-9_386

Bhamidipaty, V., Bhamidipaty, D. L., Guntoory, I., Bhamidipaty, K. D. P., Iyengar, K. P., Botchu, B., & Botchu, R. (2025). Revolutionizing healthcare: The impact of AI-powered sensors. Generative Artificial Intelligence for Biomedical and Smart Health Informatics, 355–373.

Bhatt, H., Jugran, H. P., & Pandey, R. (2024). Cultural ecosystem services nexus with Socio-Cultural attributes and traditional ecological knowledge for managing community forests of indian western Himalaya. *Ecological Indicators*, *166*, 112379. DOI: 10.1016/j.ecolind.2024.112379

Bhatti, D. S., Saleem, S., Imran, A., Iqbal, Z., Alzahrani, A., Kim, H., & Kim, K. I. (2022). A survey on wireless wearable body area networks: A perspective of technology and economy. *Sensors (Basel)*, *22*(20), 7722. DOI: 10.3390/s22207722

Bhavana, G. B., Anand, R., Ramprabhakar, J., Guerrero, J. M., Thakkar, N., & Ambikapathy, A. (2025). Comparative evaluation and simulation of blockchain consensus mechanisms for secure and scalable peer-to-peer energy trading in microgrids. *Scientific Reports*, *15*(1), 43546. DOI: 10.1038/s41598-025-27431-w PMID: 41372270

Bhumichai, D., Smiliotopoulos, C., Benton, R., Kambourakis, G., & Damopoulos, D. (2024). The convergence of artificial intelligence and blockchain: The state of play and the road ahead. *Information (Basel)*, *15*(5), 268. DOI: 10.3390/info15050268

Bhutta, M. N. M., Khwaja, A. A., Nadeem, A., Ahmad, H. F., Khan, M. K., Hanif, M. A., Song, H., Alshamari, M., & Cao, Y. (2021). A survey on blockchain technology: Evolution, architecture and security. *IEEE Access : Practical Innovations, Open Solutions*, *9*, 61048–61073. DOI: 10.1109/ACCESS.2021.3072849

Bieniek, J., Rahouti, M., Xiong, K., & Ferreira Araujo, G. (2024). SecureCare: A blockchain-assisted wearable body area network. *Security and Privacy*, *7*(6), e431. DOI: 10.1002/spy2.431

Bitcoin Wiki. (n.d.). *Hash time locked contracts.* https://en.bitcoin.it/wiki/Hash_Time_Locked_Contracts

Blefari, F., Cosentino, C., Pironti, F. A., Furfaro, A., & Marozzo, F. (2025). CyberRAG: An agentic RAG cyber attack classification and reporting tool. *Future Generation Computer Systems*, •••, 176.

Bos, J., Ducas, L., Kiltz, E., Lepoint, T., Lyubashevsky, V., Schanck, J. M., Schwabe, P., Seiler, G., & Stehlé, D. (2018). CRYSTALS-Kyber: A CCA-secure module-lattice-based KEM. 2018 IEEE European Symposium on Security and Privacy (EuroS&P), 353–367. https://doi.org/DOI: 10.1109/EuroSP.2018.00032

Buczak, A. L., & Guven, E. (2015). A survey of data mining and machine learning methods for cyber security intrusion detection. *IEEE Communications Surveys and Tutorials*, *18*(2), 1153–1176. DOI: 10.1109/COMST.2015.2494502

Canadian Institute for Cybersecurity. (n.d.). *CICIDS2018 dataset*. University of New Brunswick. https://www.unb.ca/cic/datasets/ids-2018.html

Cao, X., Yao, J., Xu, Z., & Meng, D. (2020). Hyperspectral image classification with convolutional neural network and active learning. *IEEE Transactions on Geoscience and Remote Sensing*, *58*(7), 4604–4616. DOI: 10.1109/TGRS.2020.2964627

Casino, F., Dasaklis, T. K., & Patsakis, C. (2019). A systematic literature review of blockchain-based applications: Current status, classification and open issues. *Telematics and Informatics*, *36*, 55–81. DOI: 10.1016/j.tele.2018.11.006

Castro, O. E. L., Deng, X., & Park, J. H. (2023). Comprehensive survey on AI-based technologies for enhancing IoT privacy and security: Trends, challenges, and solutions. Human-centric Computing and Information Sciences, 13(39).

Chainlink. (2022, November 3). *Introducing the Chainlink on-chain data directory: Data.eth*. Chainlink Blog. https://blog.chain.link/introducing-the-chainlink-on-chain-data-directory

Chai, X., Zhang, J., Gan, Z., & Zhang, Y. (2019). Medical image encryption algorithm based on Latin square and memristive chaotic system. *Multimedia Tools and Applications*, *78*(24), 35419–35453. DOI: 10.1007/s11042-019-08168-x

Chamola, V., Hassija, V., Sulthana, A. R., Ghosh, D., Dhingra, D., & Sikdar, B. (2023). A review of trustworthy and explainable artificial intelligence (XAI). *IEEE Access : Practical Innovations, Open Solutions*, *11*, 78994–79015. DOI: 10.1109/ACCESS.2023.3294569

Chang, V., Golightly, L., Modesti, P., Xu, Q. A., Doan, L. M. T., Hall, K., Boddu, S., & Kobusińska, A. (2022). A survey on intrusion detection systems for fog and cloud computing. *Future Internet*, *14*(3), 89. DOI: 10.3390/fi14030089

Chanson, M., Bogner, A., Bilgeri, D., Fleisch, E., & Wortmann, F. (2023). Blockchain for the IoT: privacy-preserving protection of sensor data. *Journal of the Association for Information Systems, 20*(Article 10), 1271-1307.

Charband, Y., & Jafari Navimipour, N. (2016). Online knowledge sharing mechanisms: A systematic review of the state of the art literature and recommendations for future research. *Information Systems Frontiers*, *18*(6), 1131–1151. DOI: 10.1007/s10796-016-9628-z

Chaudhary, D., & Lee, C.-C. (2024). *Anonymous quantum-safe secure and authorized communication protocol under dynamic identities for Internet of Drones. Computers and Electrical Engineering*. Elsevier., DOI: 10.1016/j.compeleceng.2024.109774

Cheng, X., Oun, A., & Wince, K. (2025). *The Role of Artificial Intelligence in Boosting Cybersecurity and Trusted Embedded Systems Performance: A Systematic Review on Current and Future Trends*. IEEE.

Chen, T., Moreau, T., Jiang, Z., Zheng, L., Yan, E., Shen, H., & Krishnamurthy, A. (2018). {TVM}: An automated {End-to-End} optimizing compiler for deep learning. In *13th USENIX symposium on operating systems design and implementation (OSDI 18)* (pp. 578-594). https://doi.org/DOI: 10.48550/arXiv.1802.04799

Chen, W., Huang, H., Peng, S., Zhou, C., & Zhang, C. (2021). YOLO-face: A real-time face detector. *The Visual Computer*, *37*(4), 805–813. DOI: 10.1007/s00371-020-01831-7

Chirakkarottu, S., & Mathew, S. (2020). A novel encryption method for medical images using 2D Zaslavski map and DNA cryptography. *SN Applied Sciences*, *2*(1), 1–10. DOI: 10.1007/s42452-019-1685-8

Chowdhury, M. Z., Shahjalal, M., Ahmed, S., & Jang, Y. M. (2020). 6G wireless communication systems. *IEEE Open Journal of the Communications Society*, *1*, 957–975. DOI: 10.1109/OJCOMS.2020.3010270

CIPLAB @ Yonsei University. (n.d.). *Real and fake face detection dataset*. Kaggle. https://www.kaggle.com/datasets/ciplab/real-and-fake-face-detection

Class Central. (2026, January 15). *Solidity advanced: Secure smart contracts & DApp development*. https://www.classcentral.com/course/coursera-packt-solidity-advanced-secure-smart-contracts-dapp-development-fqajl-352879

Claudel, N., Guo, W., & Xing, Y. (2026). AI Evasion and Impersonation Attacks on Facial Re-Identification with Activation Map Explanations. arXiv preprint arXiv:2603.15396.

Coccomini, D. A., Messina, N., Falchi, F., & Gennaro, C. (2022). Combining EfficientNet and vision transformers for video deepfake detection. *Journal of Imaging*, *8*(3), 1–17.

Cohen, J. (1960). A coefficient of agreement for nominal scales. *Educational and Psychological Measurement, 20*(1), 37–46. DOI: 10.1177/001316446002000104

Cong, N., Toan, L., & Thanh, T. (2024). An overview of static and dynamic analysis in application security testing. *Journal of Military Science and Technology, 99*, 1–11. DOI: 10.54939/1859-1043.j.mst.99.2024.1-11

Contrast Security. (n.d.). *What is runtime security?* https://www.contrastsecurity.com/glossary/runtime-security

Costan, V., & Devadas, S. (2016). Intel SGX explained. IACR Cryptology ePrint Archive, 2016(086). https://eprint.iacr.org/2016/086

Cruz-Piris, L., Marín-López, A., Álvarez-Campana, M., Sanz, M., Moreno, J. I., & Arroyo, D. (2025). Measuring the impact of post quantum cryptography in Industrial IoT scenarios. *Internet of Things : Engineering Cyber Physical Human Systems, 34*, 101793. Advance online publication. DOI: 10.1016/j.iot.2025.101793

Cyberscope. (n.d.). *The top 10 smart contract security tools*. https://www.cyberscope.io/blog/the-top-10-smart-contract-security-tools

Dagadu, J. C., Li, J. P., & Aboagye, E. O. (2019). Medical Image Encryption Based on Hybrid Chaotic DNA Diffusion. *Wireless Personal Communications, 108*(1), 591–612. DOI: 10.1007/s11277-019-06420-z

Dai, F., Hossain, M. A., & Wang, Y. (2025). State of the art in parallel and distributed systems: Emerging trends and challenges. *Electronics (Basel), 14*(4), 677. DOI: 10.3390/electronics14040677

Dalal, S., Lilhore, U. K., Faujdar, N., Simaiya, S., Ayadi, M., Almujally, N. A., & Ksibi, A. (2023). Next-generation cyber attack prediction for IoT systems: Leveraging multi-class SVM and optimized CHAID decision tree. *Journal of Cloud Computing (Heidelberg, Germany), 12*(1), 137. DOI: 10.1186/s13677-023-00517-4

Dandotiya, M., Goyal, N. K., Yadav, P., Sankhla, K., & Kumari, M. (2026). GENALYTICS: A Deep Dive Into Real-Time Insights via Generative AI. In Elbaghazaoui, B. (Eds.), *Generative AI-Powered Data Architectures* (pp. 105–134). IGI Global Scientific Publishing., DOI: 10.4018/979-8-3373-5616-7.ch005

Das, B. D. C., Patra, A., Saha, A., & Sikder, S. S. (2024). Secured communication of multiple compressed infrared images using 6D hyper-chaotic encryption. *Journal of Optics (India), 18*(3), 535–558. DOI: 10.1007/s12596-024-01655-x

Das, P., Asif, M., Jahan, S., Ahmed, K., Bui, F. M., & Khondoker, R. (2024). STRIDE-Based Cybersecurity Threat Modeling, Risk Assessment and Treatment of an In-Vehicle Infotainment System. *Vehicles (Basel), 6*(3), 1140–1163. DOI: 10.3390/vehicles6030054

Das, R., Zhou, L., Bi, S., Wang, T., & Hou, T. (2025). Towards the Safety of Intelligent Transportation: A Survey on the Security Challenges and Mitigations in Internet of Vehicles (IoV). *ACM Transactions on Sensor Networks*.

Deevi, D. P. (2020). Improving patient data security and privacy in mobile healthcare. *International Journal of Engineering Research and Science & Technology, 16*(4), 21–31.

Demir, E. D., Gorgulu, I., & Onbaşli, M. C. (2026). Micro and transport layer security benchmarking of post-quantum versus classical cryptography. *IEEE Access : Practical Innovations, Open Solutions, 14*, 56099–56111. DOI: 10.1109/ACCESS.2026.3682760

Demmler, D., Schneider, T., & Zohner, M. (2015). ABY: A framework for efficient mixed-protocol secure two-party computation. *Proceedings of the 22nd Annual NDSS Symposium*, 1–15. https://doi.org/DOI: 10.14722/ndss.2015.23113

Devarajan, M. V. (2020). Assessing long-term serum sample viability. *International Journal of Information Technology and Computer Engineering, 8*(2), 60–74.

Devarajan, M. V. (2020). Improving security control in cloud computing. *J. Sci. Technol. JST, 5*(6).

Dey, D., Giri, D., Jana, B., Maitra, T., & Mohapatra, R. N. (2018). Linear-feedback shift register-based multi-ant cellular automation and chaotic map-based image encryption. *Security and Privacy, 1*(6), 1–11. DOI: 10.1002/spy2.52

Dhabliya, D., Soundararajan, R., Selvarasu, P., Balasubramaniam, M. S., Rajawat, A. S., Goyal, S. B., Raboaca, M. S., Mihaltan, T. C., Verma, C., & Suciu, G. (2022). Energy-efficient network protocols. *Energies, 15*(23), 8883. DOI: 10.3390/en15238883

Dhananjay, S., Kumar, V., Agrawal, H., Patankar, P., & Jain, S. A. (2019). Distributed ledger technology based data minimization of digital identities. *International Journal of Advance Research, Ideas and Innovations in Technology, 5*(3). https://www.ijariit.com

Dhanushkodi, K., & Thejas, S. (2024). AI enabled threat detection: Leveraging artificial intelligence for advanced security and cyber threat mitigation. *IEEE Access : Practical Innovations, Open Solutions*, *12*, 173127–173136. DOI: 10.1109/ACCESS.2024.3493957

Dhinakaran, D., Sankar, S. M., Selvaraj, D., & Raja, S. E. (2024). Privacy-preserving data in IoT-based cloud systems: A comprehensive survey with AI integration. arXiv preprint arXiv:2401.00794.

Dhingra, L., Meetei, L. S., Ojha, V., Lodi, M. K., Sheela, A. S., & Agarwal, A. (2025, March). The Role of Blockchain Technology in Enhancing Network Security. In *2025 International Conference on Automation and Computation (AUTOCOM)* (pp. 559-564). IEEE. DOI: 10.1109/AUTOCOM64127.2025.10956764

Dias, P., Gonçalves, H., Silva, F., Duque, J., Martins, J., & Godinho, A. (2024). Blockchain technologies: A scrutiny into Hyperledger Fabric for higher educational institutions. *Procedia Computer Science*, *237*, 213–220. DOI: 10.1016/j.procs.2024.05.098

Diro, A. A., & Chilamkurti, N. (2018). Distributed attack detection scheme using deep learning approach for Internet of Things. *Future Generation Computer Systems*, *82*, 761–768. DOI: 10.1016/j.future.2017.08.043

Djordjevic, I. B. (2020). Hybrid QKD protocol outperforming both DV- and CV-QKD protocols. *IEEE Photonics Journal*, *12*(1), 1–8. DOI: 10.1109/JPHOT.2019.2946910

Dubey, S. R., Singh, S. K., & Chaudhuri, B. B. (2022). Activation functions in deep learning: A comprehensive survey and benchmark. *Neurocomputing*, *503*, 92–108. DOI: 10.1016/j.neucom.2022.06.111

Ducas, L., Kiltz, E., Lepoint, T., Lyubashevsky, V., Schwabe, P., Seiler, G., & Stehlé, D. (2018). CRYSTALS-Dilithium: A lattice-based digital signature scheme. IACR Transactions on Cryptographic Hardware and Embedded Systems, 2018(1), 238–268. https://doi.org/DOI: 10.13154/tches.v2018.i1.238-268

Dwork, C., & Roth, A. (2014). The algorithmic foundations of differential privacy. *Foundations and Trends in Theoretical Computer Science*, *9*(3–4), 211–487. DOI: 10.1561/0400000042

El-Hajj, M., & Roelink, B. O. (2024). Evaluating the efficiency of ZK-SNARK, ZK-STARK, and Bulletproof in real-world scenarios: A benchmark study. *Information (Basel)*, *15*(8), 463. Advance online publication. DOI: 10.3390/info15080463

El-Shafai, W., Khallaf, F., El-Rabaie, E. S. M., El-Samie, F. E. A., El Shafai, W., Khallaf, F., Sayed, E., El Rabaie, M., Abd, F. E., & Samie, E. (2021). Robust medical image encryption based on DNA-chaos cryptosystem for secure telemedicine and healthcare applications. *Journal of Ambient Intelligence and Humanized Computing*, *12*(10), 9007–9035. DOI: 10.1007/s12652-020-02597-5

Emmanuel, A. A., Awokola, J. A., Alam, S., Bharany, S., Agboola, P., Shuaib, M., & Ahmed, R. (2023). A hybrid framework of blockchain and IoT technology in the pharmaceutical industry: A comprehensive study. *Mobile Information Systems*, *2023*(1), 3265310. DOI: 10.1155/2023/3265310

Enjamuri, N. (2025). The Future of API Security: Post-Quantum Cryptography and Beyond. *European journal of computer science and information technology*.

Escanez-Exposito, D., Caballero-Gil, P., & Martín-Fernández, F. (2023). Interactive simulation of quantum key distribution protocols and application in Wi-Fi networks. *Wireless Networks*, *29*(8), 3781–3792. DOI: 10.1007/s11276-023-03438-x

Fan, T. (n.d.). *Ethereum 2.0 for dummies—Part 1: Why upgrade?* Medium. https://medium.com/coinmonks/ethereum-2-0-for-dummies-part-1-why-upgrade-112d8f5b6d88

Farooqi, A., Das, D., Tripathi, M., Dutta, R., Goyal, N. K., & Sheikh, M. F. (2026). Navigating Ethical Frontiers in AI-Driven Geriatric Care. In Stolakis, K., & Efthymiou, I. (Eds.), *AI for Geriatric Care in an Aging Society* (pp. 243–266). IGI Global Scientific Publishing., DOI: 10.4018/979-8-3373-5462-0.ch009

Ferrag, M. A., Maglaras, L. A., Janicke, H., Jiang, J., & Shu, L. (2017). Authentication protocols for internet of things: A comprehensive survey. *Security and Communication Networks*, *2017*(1), 6562953. DOI: 10.1155/2017/6562953

Ferrag, M. A., Maglaras, L., Moschoyiannis, S., & Janicke, H. (2020). Deep learning for cyber security intrusion detection: Approaches, datasets, and comparative study. *Journal of Information Security and Applications*, *50*, 102419. DOI: 10.1016/j.jisa.2019.102419

Ferrández-Pastor, F. J., Mora-Pascual, J., & Díaz-Lajara, D. (2022). Agricultural traceability model based on IoT and Blockchain: Application in industrial hemp production. *Journal of Industrial Information Integration*, *29*, 100381. DOI: 10.1016/j.jii.2022.100381

Fortinet. (n.d.). *What is cyber insurance? Why is it important? Risk coverages.* https://www.fortinet.com/resources/cyberglossary/cyber-insurance

Fortinet. (n.d.). *What is hardware security module (HSM)?* https://www.fortinet.com/resources/cyberglossary/hardware-security-module

Freeman Law. (2023, October 12). *Decentralized governance mechanisms: Blockchain technology.* https://freemanlaw.com/decentralized-governance-mechanisms/

Ganguly, S., Ganguly, A., Mohiuddin, S., Malakar, S., & Sarkar, R. (2022). ViXNet: Vision transformer with Xception network for deepfake video and image forgery detection. *Expert Systems with Applications*, *210*, 118423. DOI: 10.1016/j.eswa.2022.118423

García, C. R., Aguilera, A. C., Stan, C., Olmos, J. J. V., Rommel, S., & Monroy, I. T. (2025). Enhanced network security protocols for the quantum era: Combining classical and post-quantum cryptography, and quantum key distribution. *IEEE Journal on Selected Areas in Communications*, *43*(8), 2765–2781. DOI: 10.1109/JSAC.2025.3568011

GeeksforGeeks. (2025, July 23). *Static testing vs dynamic testing*. https://www.geeksforgeeks.org/software-engineering/difference-between-static-and-dynamic-testing/

Gilbert, C., & Gilbert, M. A. (2024). Advancing privacy standards through education: The role of academic initiatives in enhancing privacy within Cardano's blockchain ecosystem. *International Research Journal of Advanced Engineering and Science*, *9*(4), 238–251.

Girdhar, A., & Kumar, V. (2018). A RGB image encryption technique using Lorenz and Rossler chaotic system on DNA sequences. *Multimedia Tools and Applications*, *77*(20), 27017–27039. DOI: 10.1007/s11042-018-5902-z

Girma, G., Melka, Y., Haileslassie, A., & Mekuria, W. (2023). Participatory forest management for improving livelihood assets and mitigating forest degradation: Lesson drawn from the Central Rift Valley, Ethiopia. *Current Research in Environmental Sustainability*, *5*, 100205. DOI: 10.1016/j.crsust.2022.100205

Gollavilli, V. S. B. H., Alagarsundaram, P., & Nagarajan, H. (2020). Cloud service selection in healthcare. *Journal of Current Science & Humanities*, *8*(4), 17–30.

Goodfellow, I., McDaniel, P., & Papernot, N. (2018). Making machine learning robust against adversarial inputs. *Communications of the ACM*, *61*(7), 56–66. DOI: 10.1145/3134599

Goyal, R. (2024). Quantum Cryptography: Secure Communication Beyond Classical Limits. *Journal of Quantum Science and Technology*.

Greenhalgh, T., Rosen, R., Shaw, S. E., Byng, R., Faulkner, S., Finlay, T., & Wood, G. W. (2021). Remote consultation services framework. *Frontiers in Digital Health*, *3*, 726095. DOI: 10.3389/fdgth.2021.726095

Gupta, B. B., Arachchilage, N. A., & Psannis, K. E. (2018). Defending against phishing attacks: Taxonomy of methods, current issues and future directions. *Telecommunication Systems*, *67*(2), 247–267. DOI: 10.1007/s11235-017-0334-z

Gupta, B. B., Pan, V. S.-H., Gaurav, A., Arya, V., Alhalabi, W., & Chui, K. T. (2025). Optimized hybrid CNN-LSTM-GRU model for cyber attack detection using adaptive equilibrium optimization. *ICT Express*.

Habib, G., Sharma, S., Ibrahim, S., Ahmad, I., Qureshi, S., & Ishfaq, M. (2022). Blockchain technology: Benefits, challenges, applications, and integration of blockchain technology with cloud computing. *Future Internet*, *14*(11), 341. DOI: 10.3390/fi14110341

Hafsa, A., Sghaier, A., Malek, J., & Machhout, M. (2021). Image encryption method based on improved ECC and modified AES algorithm. *Multimedia Tools and Applications*, *80*(13), 19769–19801. Advance online publication. DOI: 10.1007/s11042-021-10700-x

Haleem, A., Javaid, M., Singh, R. P., & Suman, R. (2022). Medical 4.0 technologies. *Internet of Things and Cyber-Physical Systems*, *2*, 12–30. DOI: 10.1016/j.iotcps.2022.04.001

Hamad, N. A., Bakar, K. A., Qamar, F., Jubair, A. M., Mohamed, R. R., & Mohamed, M. A. (2025). Systematic analysis of federated learning approaches for intrusion detection in the Internet of Things environment. *IEEE Access : Practical Innovations, Open Solutions*, *13*, 95410–95444. DOI: 10.1109/ACCESS.2025.3574672

Hamid, Y., Sugumaran, M., & Journaux, L. (2016, August). Machine learning techniques for intrusion detection: a comparative analysis. In *Proceedings of the International Conference on Informatics and Analytics* (pp. 1-6). DOI: 10.1145/2980258.2980378

Han, K., Wang, Y., Tian, Q., Guo, J., Xu, C., & Xu, C. (2020). GhostNet: More features from cheap operations. In *Proceedings of the IEEE/CVF Conference on Computer Vision and Pattern Recognition* (pp. 1580–1589).

Heimbach, L., Vonlanthen, Y., Villacis, J., Kiffer, L., & Wattenhofer, R. (2025). Deanonymizing Ethereum Validators: The {P2P} Network Has a Privacy Issue. In 34th USENIX Security Symposium (USENIX Security 25) (pp. 1319-1338).

Hendaoui, F., Ferchichi, A., Trabelsi, L., Meddeb, R., Ahmed, R., & Khelifi, M. K. (2024). Advances in deep learning intrusion detection over encrypted data with privacy preservation: A systematic review. *Cluster Computing*, *27*(7), 8683–8724. DOI: 10.1007/s10586-024-04424-4

Hodo, E., Bellekens, X., Hamilton, A., Tachtatzis, C., & Atkinson, R. (2017). Shallow and deep networks intrusion detection system: A taxonomy and survey. *arXiv preprint arXiv:1701.02145*.

Holubenko, V., Gaspar, D., Leal, R., & Silva, P. (2025). Autonomous intrusion detection for IoT: A decentralized and privacy preserving approach. *International Journal of Information Security*, *24*(1), 7. DOI: 10.1007/s10207-024-00926-9

Hsu, C. C., Zhuang, Y. X., & Lee, C. Y. (2020). Deep fake image detection based on pairwise learning. *Applied Sciences (Basel, Switzerland)*, *10*(1), 370. DOI: 10.3390/app10010370

Hu, C., Zhang, L., Chen, R., Gu, Q., Ning, B., Hua, Q., & Zeng, M. (2026). A dynamically parameterized 3D hyperchaotic cascade for secure and real-time encryption of medical images. *Digital Signal Processing: A Review Journal, 170*(November 2025). DOI: 10.1016/j.dsp.2025.105767

Huang, J. A., Hartanti, I. R., Colin, M. N., & Pitaloka, D. A. (2022). Telemedicine and AI for COVID-19. *Digital Health*, ●●●, 8.

Hu, B., Zhang, Z., Liu, J., Liu, Y., Yin, J., Lu, R., & Lin, X. (2021). A comprehensive survey on smart contract construction and execution: Paradigms, tools, and systems. *Patterns (New York, N.Y.)*, *2*(2), 100179. DOI: 10.1016/j.patter.2020.100179 PMID: 33659907

Hui, X., & Tucker, C. (2025). Decentralization, blockchain, artificial intelligence (AI): Challenges and opportunities. *Journal of Product Innovation Management*, *42*(5), 947–957. DOI: 10.1111/jpim.12800

Humayun, M., Jhanjhi, N., Alsayat, A., & Ponnusamy, V. (2021). Internet of Things and ransomware: Evolution, mitigation and prevention. *Egyptian Informatics Journal*, *22*(1), 105–117. DOI: 10.1016/j.eij.2020.05.003

Hu, Z., Kim, B., & Jeong, J. (2024). A Study on mechanization, data, and insurance challenges for agriculture based on hyperledger fabric. *IEEE Access : Practical Innovations, Open Solutions*, *12*, 144855–144869. DOI: 10.1109/ACCESS.2024.3468430

Ighofiomoni, M. O., Ojerinde, J. S., Olaniyan, I., Issah, P. P., Adepitan, O. S., Oyenuga, O., & Chinonyerem, C. A. (2025). Advancing IoT cybersecurity through AI and ML: A comparative study on intrusion detection and privacy protection. *Asian Journal of Advanced Research and Reports, 19*(8), 159–174. DOI: 10.9734/ajarr/2025/v19i81122

Inayat, U., Zia, M. F., Mahmood, S., Khalid, H. M., & Benbouzid, M. (2022). Cyber attack detection in IoT systems. *Electronics (Basel), 11*(9), 1502. DOI: 10.3390/electronics11091502

Indra, E., Yasir, M., Andrian, A., Sitanggang, D., Sihombing, O., Tamba, S. P., & Sagala, E. (2020). Design and implementation of student attendance system based on face recognition using Haar-like features. In *Proceedings of the International Conference on Mechanical, Electronics, Computer, and Industrial Technology* (pp. 336–342).

Indrayani, R., Ferdiansyah, P., & Satria, D. A. (2019, July). Effectiveness comparison of the AES and 3DES cryptography methods on email text messages. In *2019 International Conference on Information and Communications Technology (ICOIACT)* (pp. 66-69). IEEE. DOI: 10.1109/ICOIACT46704.2019.8938579

*International Journal of Engineering and Technology Research.* (2024). IAEME Publication. https://iaeme.com/Home/issue/IJETR?Volume=9&Issue=2

Isabella, M. (2023, March 23). *Bounties within the DAO ecosystem.* Lifespan.io. https://www.lifespan.io/topic/bounties-within-the-dao-ecosystem

Isibor, E. (2024). Regulation of healthcare data security. *SSRN* 4957244.

Islam, M. M., Islam, M. N., Akhand, M. A. H., & Rahman, M. M. (2024). Explainable artificial intelligence for deepfake detection: Recent advances, challenges, and future directions. *Artificial Intelligence Review, 57*, 1–34.

Islam, S., Islam, M. J., Hossain, M., Noor, S., Kwak, K. S., & Islam, S. R. (2023). A survey on consensus algorithms in blockchain-based applications: Architecture, taxonomy, and operational issues. *IEEE Access : Practical Innovations, Open Solutions, 11*, 39066–39082. DOI: 10.1109/ACCESS.2023.3267047

Ismagilova, E., Hughes, L., Rana, N. P., & Dwivedi, Y. K. (2020). Security, Privacy and Risks Within Smart Cities: Literature Review and Development of a Smart City Interaction Framework. *Information Systems Frontiers, 24*(2), 393–414. DOI: 10.1007/s10796-020-10044-1 PMID: 32837262

Ismail, S. M., Said, L. A., Radwan, A. G., Madian, A. H., & Abu-elyazeed, M. F. (2020). *A novel image encryption system merging fractional-order edge detection and generalized chaotic maps. 167.*

Ismail, A., Elpeltagy, M., Zaki, M. S., & Eldahshan, K. (2021). A new deep learning-based methodology for video deepfake detection using XGBoost. *Sensors (Basel), 21*, 5413. DOI: 10.3390/s21165413 PMID: 34450855

Jacob, S., Alagirisamy, M., Xi, C., Balasubramanian, V., Srinivasan, R., Jhanjhi, N. Z., & Islam, S. M. (2021). Smart exoskeleton system. *IEEE Access : Practical Innovations, Open Solutions, 9*, 80340–80350. DOI: 10.1109/ACCESS.2021.3083093

Jagatheesaperumal, S. K., Rajkumar, S., Suresh, J. V., Gumaei, A. H., Alhakbani, N., Uddin, M. Z., & Hassan, M. M. (2023). IoT-based personalized health framework. *Mathematics, 11*(12), 2758. DOI: 10.3390/math11122758

Jain, J. (n.d.). Smart contracts & blockchain—Evolving jurisprudence in India. *Journal of Applicable Law & Jurisprudence, 1*(1). https://calr.in/wp-content/uploads/2021/01/Smart-Contracts-Blockchain-%E2%80%93-Evolving-Jurisprudence-in-India.pdf

Javaid, A., Niyaz, Q., Sun, W., & Alam, M. (2016). A deep learning approach for network intrusion detection system. *Eai Endorsed Transactions on Security and Safety, 3*(9), 21. DOI: 10.4108/eai.3-12-2015.2262516

Javaid, M., Haleem, A., Singh, R. P., & Suman, R. (2023). Cybersecurity in healthcare. *Cyber Security and Applications, 1*, 100016. DOI: 10.1016/j.csa.2023.100016

Javed, H., Muqeet, H. A., Danesh, A., Rehman, A. U., Javed, T., & Bermak, A. (2024). AI in healthcare services. *IEEE Access : Practical Innovations, Open Solutions, 12*, 141064–141087. DOI: 10.1109/ACCESS.2024.3443812

Javed, S. H., Ahmad, M. B., Asif, M., Almotiri, S. H., Masood, K., & Ghamdi, M. A. A. (2022). An intelligent system to detect advanced persistent threats in industrial Internet of Things (I-IoT). *Electronics (Basel), 11*(5), 742. DOI: 10.3390/electronics11050742

Jiang, X., Liu, M., Yang, C., Liu, Y., & Wang, R. (2019). A blockchain-based authentication protocol for WLAN mesh security access. *Computers, Materials & Continua, 58*(1), 45–59. DOI: 10.32604/cmc.2019.03863

Jiang, Z. P., Liu, Y. Y., Shao, Z. E., & Huang, K. W. (2021). An improved VGG16 model for pneumonia image classification. *Applied Sciences (Basel, Switzerland), 11*(23), 11185. DOI: 10.3390/app112311185

J, J., & R, P. (2025, June). J, J., & R, P. (2026). A robust medical image encryption technique using inverse cosine chaotic map. *Expert Systems with Applications*, *298*, 129574. Advance online publication. DOI: 10.1016/j.eswa.2025.129574

John, K., Rivera, T. J., & Saleh, F. (2025). Proof-of-work versus proof-of-stake: A comparative economic analysis. *Review of Financial Studies*, *38*(7), 1955–2004. DOI: 10.1093/rfs/hhaf013

Jouppi, N. P., Young, C., Patil, N., & Patterson, D. (2017). In-datacenter performance analysis of a tensor processing unit. *Proceedings of the 44th ISCA*, 1–12. https://doi.org/DOI: 10.1145/3079856.3080246

Jung, T., Kim, S., & Kim, K. (2020). DeepVision: Deepfakes detection using human eye blinking pattern. *IEEE Access : Practical Innovations, Open Solutions*, *8*, 83144–83154. DOI: 10.1109/ACCESS.2020.2988660

Kaliappan, C. P., Palaniappan, K., Ananthavadivel, D., & Subramanian, U. (2024). Advancing IoT security: A comprehensive AI-based trust framework for intrusion detection. *Peer-to-Peer Networking and Applications*, *17*(5), 2737–2757. DOI: 10.1007/s12083-024-01684-0

Kalodanis, K., Papapavlou, C., & Feretzakis, G. (2025). Enhancing security in 5G and future 6G networks: Machine learning approaches for adaptive intrusion detection and prevention. *Future Internet*, *17*(7), 312. DOI: 10.3390/fi17070312

Kamal, H., & Mashaly, M. (2025). Enhanced hybrid deep learning models-based anomaly detection method for two-stage binary and multi-class classification of attacks in intrusion detection systems. *Algorithms*, *18*(2), 69. DOI: 10.3390/a18020069

Kanga University. (2025, June 3). *What are threshold signatures?* https://kanga.exchange/university/en/courses/4-primus-course/lessons/43-what-are-threshold-signatures/

Kaur, D., Uslu, S., Rittichier, K. J., & Durresi, A. (2022). Trustworthy artificial intelligence: A review. *ACM Computing Surveys*, *55*(2), 1–38. DOI: 10.1145/3491209

Kaur, H., Alam, M. A., Jameel, R., Mourya, A. K., & Chang, V. (2018). A proposed solution and future direction for blockchain-based heterogeneous medicare data in cloud environment. *Journal of Medical Systems*, *42*(8), 156. DOI: 10.1007/s10916-018-1007-5 PMID: 29987560

Kaushal, R. K., Kumar, N., Kukreja, V., & Boonchieng, E. (2025). Hyperledger fabric based remote patient monitoring solution and performance evaluation. *Peer-to-Peer Networking and Applications*, *18*(3), 105. DOI: 10.1007/s12083-025-01921-0

Kavitha, A. R., Balachandhar, R., & Harikrishna, K. (2025, March). Synergizing Quantum Cryptography and Post-Quantum Cryptography: A New Era of Ultra-Secure Data Transmission. In *2025 International Conference on Data Science, Agents & Artificial Intelligence (ICDSAAI)* (pp. 1-6). IEEE. DOI: 10.1109/ICDSAAI65575.2025.11011628

Kelsey, J., Schneier, B., Wagner, D., & Hall, C. (1998). Cryptanalytic Attacks on Pseudorandom Number Generators. Fast Software Encryption, 168–188. DOI: 10.1007/3-540-69710-1_12

Keshk, M., Koroniotis, N., Pham, N., Moustafa, N., Turnbull, B., & Zomaya, A. Y. (2023). An explainable deep learning-enabled intrusion detection framework in IoT networks. *Information Sciences*, *639*, 119000. DOI: 10.1016/j.ins.2023.119000

Khan, M. N., Rao, A., Camtepe, S., & Pieprzyk, J. (2023, January). Classical to Post-Quantum Secure ABE-IBE Proxy Re-Encryption Scheme. In *SECRYPT* (pp. 85-98). DOI: 10.5220/0012078200003555

Khan, M. A., Noor, F., Javaid, S., & Żywiołek, J. (2025). Implementation and performance of post-quantum cryptography for resource constrained consumer electronics. *Discover Internet of Things*, *5*(1), 139. DOI: 10.1007/s43926-025-00238-x

Kim, C., Kim, S., Sohn, K., Son, Y., Kumar, M., & Kim, S. (2025). Secure and Scalable File Encryption for Cloud Systems via Distributed Integration of Quantum and Classical Cryptography. *Applied Sciences (Basel, Switzerland)*, *15*(14), 7782. DOI: 10.3390/app15147782

Krichen, M., Ammi, M., Mihoub, A., & Almutiq, M. (2022). Blockchain for modern applications: A survey. *Sensors (Basel)*, *22*(14), 5274. DOI: 10.3390/s22145274 PMID: 35890953

Kryś, J., Sharma, Y., & Egan, J. (2025). Distributed and Decentralised Training: Technical Governance Challenges in a Shifting AI Landscape. arXiv preprint arXiv:2507.07765.

Kumar, A., Sharma, K., Singh, H., Naugriya, S. G., Gill, S. S., & Buyya, R. (2021). Drone-based COVID system. *Future Generation Computer Systems*, *115*, 1–19. DOI: 10.1016/j.future.2020.08.046

Kumar, A., Sharma, P., Singh, R., & Vatsa, M. (2024). Hybrid CNN–Transformer architectures for deepfake detection: A comparative analysis. *Expert Systems with Applications*, *245*, 123456.

Kumari, M., & Goyal, N. K. (2026). Artificial Intelligence in the Cryptocurrency Ecosystem: Crime Mechanisms, Detection Strategies, and Legal Perspectives. In *Innovations in Cryptocrime and Financial Fraud* (pp. 245-282). IGI Global Scientific Publishing.

Kumari, M., Khan, S. T., Gulati, K., Sharma, P., Goyal, N. K., & Sheikh, M. F. (2026). *Innovative Procedural Content Generation (PCG) Using Generative AI.* IGI Global Scientific Publishing., DOI: 10.4018/979-8-3373-4637-3.ch007

Kumavat, K., & Gomes, J. (2023). EIDDM: Edge and Internet layer distributed DoS threats detection and mitigation for Internet of Things wireless communications. *Wireless Personal Communications*, *131*(1), 709–735. DOI: 10.1007/s11277-023-10453-w

Kundu, P. (2024). *Securing the future of communication with quantum cryptography.* In *2024 IEEE International Conference of Electron Devices Society Kolkata Chapter (EDKCON)*. IEEE. DOI: 10.1109/EDKCON62339.2024.10870663

Laghari, A. A., Khan, A. A., Ksibi, A., Hajjej, F., Kryvinska, N., Almadhor, A., Mohamed, M. A., & Alsubai, S. (2025). A novel and secure artificial intelligence enabled zero trust intrusion detection in industrial internet of things architecture. *Scientific Reports*, *15*(1), 26843. DOI: 10.1038/s41598-025-11738-9 PMID: 40702039

Lanka, D. (2024). Securing vehicle communication networks. In *Advances in Information Security, Privacy, and Ethics*. DOI: 10.4018/979-8-3693-9220-1.ch011

Lecuyer, M., Atlidakis, V., Geambasu, R., Hsu, D., & Jana, S. (2019). Certified robustness to adversarial examples with differential privacy. Proceedings of the 2019 IEEE S&P, 656–672. https://doi.org/DOI: 10.1109/SP.2019.00044

Lee, S., Kim, J., Kang, H., Kang, D. Y., & Park, J. (2021). Genetic algorithm-based deep learning neural network structure and hyperparameter optimization. *Applied Sciences (Basel, Switzerland)*, *11*(2), 744. DOI: 10.3390/app11020744

Lewis, J. K., Toubal, I. E., Chen, H., Sandesera, V., Lomnitz, M., Hampel-Arias, Z., Prasad, C., & Palaniappan, K. (2020). Deepfake video detection based on spatial, spectral, and temporal inconsistencies using multimodal deep learning. In *Proceedings of the IEEE Applied Imagery Pattern Recognition Workshop (AIPR)* (pp. 1–9). DOI: 10.1109/AIPR50011.2020.9425167

Liu, R., Shi, J., Chen, X., & Lu, C. (2024). Network anomaly detection. *Computers & Electrical Engineering*, *119*, 109581. DOI: 10.1016/j.compeleceng.2024.109581

Liu, Z., Mao, H., Wu, C. Y., Feichtenhofer, C., Darrell, T., & Xie, S. (2022). A ConvNet for the 2020s. In *Proceedings of the IEEE/CVF Conference on Computer Vision and Pattern Recognition (CVPR)* (pp. 11976–11986).

Li, X., Jiang, P., Chen, T., Luo, X., & Wen, Q. (2020). A survey on the security of blockchain systems. *Future Generation Computer Systems, 107*, 841–853. DOI: 10.1016/j.future.2017.08.020

Lokesh, B. S., & Kaulgud, N. (2025, August). Integrating Post-Quantum Cryptography in Transport Layer Security 1.3 for Iot: a Performance Analysis on Resource-Constrained Hardware. In *2025 Third International Conference on Networks, Multimedia and Information Technology (NMITCON)* (pp. 1-8). IEEE.

Lv, G., Chen, J., Chen, H., Cai, S., & Zhang, W. (2026). Optimized mutation scheduling for fuzzing based on estimation of distribution algorithm. *Cybersecurity*, *9*(1), 35. Advance online publication. DOI: 10.1186/s42400-025-00461-7

Lv, L., Xu, D., Hu, R. Q., Ye, Y., Yang, L., Lei, X., & Nallanathan, A. (2024). Safeguarding next-generation multiple access using physical layer security techniques: A tutorial. *Proceedings of the IEEE, 112*(9), 1421–1466. DOI: 10.1109/JPROC.2024.3420127

Majumder, R. Q. (2025). Machine Learning for Predictive Analytics: Trends and Future Directions. Available at *SSRN* 5267273.

Maksymovych, V., Shabatura, M., Harasymchuk, O., Shevchuk, R., Sawicki, P., & Zajac, T. (2022). Combined Pseudo-Random Sequence Generator for Cybersecurity. *Sensors (Basel)*, *22*(24), 9700. DOI: 10.3390/s22249700 PMID: 36560068

Manimozhi, M., & Mugelan, R. K. (2025). Post-quantum AES encryption using ECC points from BB84 keys. *EPJ Quantum Technology*, *12*(1), 109. DOI: 10.1140/epjqt/s40507-025-00411-9

Mansoor, K., Afzal, M., Iqbal, W., & Abbas, Y. (2025). Securing the future: Exploring post-quantum cryptography for authentication and user privacy in IoT devices. *Cluster Computing*, *28*(2), 93. DOI: 10.1007/s10586-024-04799-4

Man, Z., Li, J., Di, X., Sheng, Y., & Liu, Z. (2021). Double image encryption algorithm based on neural network and chaos. *Chaos, Solitons, and Fractals, 152*, 111318. Advance online publication. DOI: 10.1016/j.chaos.2021.111318

Martinez, D., Magdalena, L., & Savitri, A. N. (2024). Ai and blockchain integration: Enhancing security and transparency in financial transactions. *International Transactions on Artificial Intelligence*, *3*(1), 11–20. DOI: 10.33050/italic.v3i1.651

McMahan, H. B., Moore, E., Ramage, D., Hampson, S., & Agüera y Arcas, B. (2017). Communication-efficient learning of deep networks from decentralised data. *Proceedings of the 20th AISTATS*, 1273–1282. https://doi.org/DOI: 10.48550/arXiv.1602.05629

Mechik, E., & Von Hauff, M. (2022). The fight against deforestation of tropical forests—the contribution of the blockchain-based contract management method to minimize illegal logging. In Climate and development (pp. 439-463)

Mehic, M., Rass, S., Dervisevic, E., & Voznak, M. (2022). Tackling denial of service attacks on key management in software-defined quantum key distribution networks. *IEEE Access : Practical Innovations, Open Solutions*, *10*, 110512–110520. DOI: 10.1109/ACCESS.2022.3214511

Melo, C., Oliveira, F., Dantas, J., Araujo, J., Pereira, P., Maciel, R., & Maciel, P. (2022). Performance and availability evaluation of the blockchain platform hyperledger fabric. *The Journal of Supercomputing*, *78*(10), 12505–12527. DOI: 10.1007/s11227-022-04361-2

Merhej, J., Harb, H., Abouaissa, A., & Idoumghar, L. (2024). Toward a new era of smart and secure healthcare information exchange systems: Combining blockchain and artificial intelligence. *Applied Sciences (Basel, Switzerland)*, *14*(19), 8808. DOI: 10.3390/app14198808

Minh, D., Wang, H. X., Li, Y. F., & Nguyen, T. N. (2022). Explainable artificial intelligence: A comprehensive review. *Artificial Intelligence Review*, *55*(5), 3503–3568. DOI: 10.1007/s10462-021-10088-y

Minocha, S., Sharma, S. R., Singh, B., & Gandomi, A. H. (2025). Adaptive image encryption approach using an enhanced swarm intelligence algorithm. *Scientific Reports*, *15*(1), 1–23. DOI: 10.1038/s41598-025-86569-9

Mirsky, Y., & Lee, W. (2021). The creation and detection of deepfakes: A survey. *ACM Computing Surveys*, *54*(1), 1–41. DOI: 10.1145/3425780

Mishra, N., & Pandya, S. (2021). Internet of Things applications, security challenges, attacks, intrusion detection, and future visions: A systematic review. *IEEE Access : Practical Innovations, Open Solutions*, *9*, 59353–59377. DOI: 10.1109/ACCESS.2021.3073408

Mishra, S., Albarakati, A., & Sharma, S. K. (2022). Cyber threat intelligence for IoT using machine learning. *Processes (Basel, Switzerland)*, *10*(12), 2673. DOI: 10.3390/pr10122673

Mohamed, M., Maiseli, B. J., Ai, Y., Mkocha, K., & Al-Saman, A. (2021). In-body sensor communication. *IEEE EMC Magazine*, *10*(2), 47–52.

Mohammed, A. J., Hassan, M. M., & Kadir, D. H. (2020). Improving classification performance for a novel imbalanced medical dataset using SMOTE method. *International Journal of Advanced Trends in Computer Science and Engineering*, *9*(3), 3161–3172. DOI: 10.30534/ijatcse/2020/104932020

Mollashaik, A. S. (2025). Advancing data security through AI-driven classification: A framework for intelligent threat detection and privacy preservation. [IJCET]. *International Journal of Computer Engineering and Technology*, *15*(6), 467–481. DOI: 10.34218/IJCET_16_01_040

Moreno-Sánchez, P. A., García-Isla, G., Corino, V. D., Vehkaoja, A., Brukamp, K., Van Gils, M., & Mainardi, L. (2024). ECG-based solutions. *Computers in Biology and Medicine*, *172*, 108235.

Mortajez, S., Tahmasbi, M., Zarei, J., & Jamshidnezhad, A. (2020). A novel chaotic encryption scheme based on efficient secret keys and confusion technique for confidential of DICOM images. *Informatics in Medicine Unlocked*, *20*(May), 100396. Advance online publication. DOI: 10.1016/j.imu.2020.100396

Moulahi, T., Jabbar, R., Alabdulatif, A., Abbas, S., El Khediri, S., Zidi, S., & Rizwan, M. (2023). Privacy-preserving federated learning cyber-threat detection for intelligent transport systems with blockchain-based security. *Expert Systems: International Journal of Knowledge Engineering and Neural Networks*, *40*(5), e13103. DOI: 10.1111/exsy.13103

Moustafa, N., & Slay, J. (2015, November). UNSW-NB15: a comprehensive data set for network intrusion detection systems (UNSW-NB15 network data set). In *2015 military communications and information systems conference (MilCIS)* (pp. 1-6). Ieee.

Moustafa, N., Koroniotis, N., Keshk, M., Zomaya, A. Y., & Tari, Z. (2023). Explainable intrusion detection for cyber defences in the internet of things: Opportunities and solutions. *IEEE Communications Surveys and Tutorials*, *25*(3), 1775–1807. DOI: 10.1109/COMST.2023.3280465

Muneer, S., Farooq, U., Athar, A., Ahsan Raza, M., Ghazal, T. M., & Sakib, S. (2024). A critical review of artificial intelligence-based approaches in intrusion detection: A comprehensive analysis. *Journal of Engineering*, *2024*(1), 3909173. DOI: 10.1155/2024/3909173

Naeem, H., Ullah, F., & Srivastava, G. (2025). Classification of intrusion cyber-attacks in smart power grids using deep ensemble learning with metaheuristic-based optimization. *Expert Systems: International Journal of Knowledge Engineering and Neural Networks*, *42*(1), e13556. DOI: 10.1111/exsy.13556

Naik, N., Jenkins, P., Grace, P., Naik, D., Prajapat, S., & Song, J. (2024). A Comparative Analysis of Threat Modelling Methods: STRIDE, DREAD, VAST, PASTA, OCTAVE, and LINDDUN. DOI: 10.1007/978-3-031-74443-3_16

Nandish, H. D., Rahul, R., Dasari, H. C., Kumaran, U., & Umah, B. (2025). Machine learning-powered intrusion detection for network security. In Proceedings of International Conference on Recent Trends in Computing (ICRTC 2024), Lecture Notes in Networks and Systems, vol. 885. Springer. https://doi.org/DOI: 10.1007/978-981-97-8836-1_9

Nangraj, A. R. (2025). A Revolutionary Approach Using Artificial Intelligence and Quantum Cryptography–A Review. *International Journal of Innovations in Science & Technology*, *7*(3), 1422–1436.

Narayan, S. B. (2025). Safeguarding Intelligence: A Comprehensive Analysis of AI Security and Privacy in the Era of Autonomous Systems. Available at *SSRN* 5718122. DOI: 10.2139/ssrn.5718122

Narla, S., Peddi, S., & Valivarthi, D. T. (2019). Cloud-integrated healthcare framework. *IJCSET*, *4*(1), 22.

Nasir, Z. U. I., Iqbal, A., & Qureshi, H. K. (2024). Securing cyber-physical systems: A decentralized framework for collaborative intrusion detection with privacy preservation. *IEEE Transactions on Industrial Cyber-Physical Systems*, *2*, 303–311. DOI: 10.1109/TICPS.2024.3425794

National Institute of Standards and Technology, S. (2024). FIPS 204, module-lattice-based digital signature standard. https://doi.org/DOI: 10.6028/NIST.FIPS.204

National Institute of Standards and Technology. (2024). *FIPS 203: Module-lattice-based key-encapsulation mechanism standard*. Computer Security Resource Center.

National Institute of Standards and Technology. (2025). *Transitioning to quantum-resistant encryption standards*. NIST Special Publication.

Navimipour, N. J., & Charband, Y. (2016). Knowledge sharing mechanisms and techniques in project teams: Literature review, classification, and current trends. *Computers in Human Behavior*, *62*, 730–742. DOI: 10.1016/j.chb.2016.05.003

Nayab, S., & Hafiza, A. (2016). Quantum cryptography: A brief review of recent developments. In *DIPEWC 2016*.

Ndibe, O. S. (2025). Ai-driven forensic systems for real-time anomaly detection and threat mitigation in cybersecurity infrastructures. *International Journal of Research Publication and Reviews*, *6*(5), 389–411. DOI: 10.55248/gengpi.6.0525.1991

Nedaković, A., Hasselgren, A., Kralevska, K., & Gligoroski, D. (2023). Hyperledger fabric platform for healthcare trust relations—Proof-of-Concept. Blockchain. *Research and Applications*, *4*(4), 100156.

Neto, G. F., Macêdo, B. D. S., Boratto, T. H., Gontijo, T. S., Bodini, M., Saporetti, C., & Goliatt, L. (2025). Stratified metamodeling to predict concrete compressive strength using an optimized dual-layered architectural framework. *Mathematical & Computational Applications*, *30*(1), 16. DOI: 10.3390/mca30010016

Nguyen, D. C., Cheng, P., Ding, M., Lopez-Perez, D., Pathirana, P. N., Li, J., & Poor, H. V. (2020). AI in wireless networks. *IEEE Communications Surveys and Tutorials*, *23*(1), 553–595. DOI: 10.1109/COMST.2020.3024783

Nguyen, T. T., & Reddi, V. J. (2021). Deep reinforcement learning for cyber security. *IEEE Transactions on Neural Networks and Learning Systems*, *34*(8), 3779–3795. DOI: 10.1109/TNNLS.2021.3121870 PMID: 34723814

Nicholls, M. (2024, March 25). *A brief guide to automated penetration testing*. Redscan. https://www.redscan.com/news/a-brief-guide-to-automated-penetration-testing

Ning, Z., Dong, P., Wang, X., Hu, X., Guo, L., Hu, B., & Kwok, R. Y. (2020). 5G health monitoring. *IEEE JSAC*, *39*(2), 463–478.

Niranjanamurthy, M., Nithya, B. N., & Jagannatha, S. J. C. C. (2019). Analysis of Blockchain technology: Pros, cons and SWOT. *Cluster Computing*, *22*(S6, Suppl 6), 14743–14757. DOI: 10.1007/s10586-018-2387-5

NIST. (2024). *Module-lattice-based key-encapsulation mechanism standard (FIPS 203)*. National Institute of Standards and Technology., DOI: 10.6028/NIST.FIPS.203

Nithyavani, G., & Raja, G. N. (2025). A comprehensive survey on security and privacy challenges in internet of medical things applications: Deep learning and machine learning solutions, obstacles, and future directions. *IEEE Access : Practical Innovations, Open Solutions*, *13*, 188955–188989. DOI: 10.1109/ACCESS.2025.3588489

Nizamudeen, S. M. T. (2023). Intelligent intrusion detection framework for multi-clouds – IoT environment using swarm-based deep learning classifier. *Journal of Cloud Computing (Heidelberg, Germany)*, *12*(1), 134. DOI: 10.1186/s13677-023-00509-4

Nourai, M., & Levkowitz, H. (2017). Securing email for the average users via a new architecture. In *PACRIM 2017*. DOI: 10.1109/PACRIM.2017.8121931

Nwaga, P. C., & Nwagwughiagwu, S. (2024). Exploring the significance of quantum cryptography in future network security protocols. *World J Adv Res Reviews*, *24*(3), 817–833. DOI: 10.30574/wjarr.2024.24.3.3733

Ogundipe, O. O. (2024). Post-Quantum Cryptography Preparing for the Quantum Threat to Digital Security. *Journal of Science. Technology and Engineering Research*, *2*(3), 49–63.

Omboni, S., Campolo, L., & Panzeri, E. (2020). Telehealth in chronic disease. *Expert Review of Medical Devices*, *17*(7), 659–670. DOI: 10.1080/17434440.2020.1782734

Omol, E., Kibuku, R., & Abuonji, P. (2025). Cybersecurity with Quantum Cryptography: An Analysis of Current Techniques and Future Trends. *International Journal of Science. Technology & Management*, *6*(2), 339–348.

Open Knowledge Repository. (n.d.). *Open Knowledge Repository*. https://openknowledge.worldbank.org/entities/publication/c3df3394-494f-5941-8a49-93c6e2fe236f

Osouli Tabrizi, H., & Al-Turjman, F. (2020). Packet size optimization. *Neural Computing & Applications*, *32*(20), 16167–16178. DOI: 10.1007/s00521-020-04813-x

Ouaissa, M., Ouaissa, M., Nadifi, Z., El Himer, S., Al Masmoudi, Y., & Kartit, A. (2025). A framework for cyber threat modeling and risk assessment in smart city environments. *Frontiers of Computer Science*, *7*, 1647179. Advance online publication. DOI: 10.3389/fcomp.2025.1647179

Ouannas, A., Karouma, A., Grassi, G., Pham, V. T., & Luong, V. S. (2021). A novel secure communications scheme based on chaotic modulation, recursive encryption and chaotic masking. *Alexandria Engineering Journal*, *60*(1), 1873–1884. DOI: 10.1016/j.aej.2020.11.035

Owezarski, P. (2023, May). Investigating adversarial attacks against Random Forest-based network attack detection systems. In *NOMS 2023-2023 IEEE/IFIP Network Operations and Management Symposium* (pp. 1-6). IEEE. DOI: 10.1109/NOMS56928.2023.10154328

Padhiar, S., & Patel, R. (2023, April). Outside the Closed World: On Using Machine Learning for Network Intrusion Detection. In *International Conference on Information and Communication Technology for Intelligent Systems* (pp. 265-270). Singapore: Springer Nature Singapore. DOI: 10.1007/978-981-99-3982-4_23

Padmavathi, V., & Saminathan, R. (2025). A federated edge intelligence framework with trust-based access control for secure and privacy preserving IoT systems. *Scientific Reports, 15*(1), 35832. DOI: 10.1038/s41598-025-19712-1 PMID: 41087484

Pan, D., Long, G. L., Yin, L., Sheng, Y. B., Ruan, D., Ng, S. X., Lu, J., & Hanzo, L. (2024). The evolution of quantum secure direct communication: On the road to the qinternet. *IEEE Communications Surveys and Tutorials, 26*(3), 1898–1949. DOI: 10.1109/COMST.2024.3367535

Pan, D., Sun, L., Wang, R., Zhang, X., & Sinnott, R. O. (2020). Deepfake detection through deep learning. In *Proceedings of the IEEE/ACM International Conference on Big Data Computing, Applications and Technologies* (pp. 134–143).

Panga, N. K. R. (2022). ECG signal analysis using DWT. *IJITCE, 10*(4), 157–175.

Parvathi, G. S., Reddy, K. N., Harini, K., & Akshaya, K. (2024). Revolutionizing Email Security with Quantum Key Distribution for Enhanced Data Protection in Communication Systems. *Journal of Computational Analysis and Applications, 33*(8).

Pasupuleti, M. K. (2025). Post-quantum cryptography: Algorithms and implementation challenges. [IJAIRI]. *International Journal of Academic and Industrial Research Innovations, 5*(6), 234–243. DOI: 10.62311/nesx/rphcrcscrbc4

Patel, S., Bharath, K. P., & Rajesh Kumar, M.Bharath K PRajesh Kumar M. (2020). Symmetric keys image encryption and decryption using 3D chaotic maps with DNA encoding technique. *Multimedia Tools and Applications, 79*(43-44), 31739–31757. Advance online publication. DOI: 10.1007/s11042-020-09551-9

Patil, S., Varadarajan, V., Mazhar, S. M., Sahibzada, A., Ahmed, N., Sinha, O., Kumar, S., Shaw, K., & Kotecha, K. (2022). Explainable artificial intelligence for intrusion detection system. *Electronics (Basel), 11*(19), 3079. DOI: 10.3390/electronics11193079

Paulino, E. R., Schlerf, M., Röder, A., Stoffels, J., & Udelhoven, T. (2024). Forest disturbance characterization in the era of earth observation big data: A mapping review. *International Journal of Applied Earth Observation and Geoinformation, 128*, 103755. DOI: 10.1016/j.jag.2024.103755

Pernice, E. (2025). AI Model Training: Consent or Legitimate Interest? Guidance on Choosing the Most Appropriate Legal Basis. JL, Mkt. &. *Innovation*, •••, 584.

Phiphiphatphaisit, S., & Surinta, O. (2020). Food image classification with improved MobileNet architecture and data augmentation. In *Proceedings of the International Conference on Information Science and System* (pp. 51–56). DOI: 10.1145/3388176.3388179

Planet Compliance. (n.d.). *Navigating compliance in decentralized finance (DeFi).* https://www.planetcompliance.com/financial-compliance/navigating-compliance-defi/

Posey, B. (2025, April 24). *Compare 7 decentralized data storage networks.* SearchStorage. https://www.techtarget.com/searchstorage/tip/Comparing-4-decentralized-data-storage-offerings

Pradhan, B., Bhattacharyya, S., & Pal, K. (2021). IoT healthcare devices. *Journal of Healthcare Engineering*, 2021.

Prajapat, S., Kumar, P., Kumar, S., Das, A. K., Shetty, S., & Hossain, M. S. (2024). Designing high-performance identity-based quantum signature protocol with strong security. *IEEE Access : Practical Innovations, Open Solutions*, *12*, 14647–14658. DOI: 10.1109/ACCESS.2024.3355196

Preethi, M., Kale, A., Satheesh, P., Harshitha, R., & Vaidya, R. (2025, March). Decentralised Cloud Architecture: Blockchain Driven Integrity and Raptor Codes for Enhanced Data Transmission. In 2025 IEEE 14th International Conference on Communication Systems and Network Technologies (CSNT) (pp. 358-365). IEEE.

Prévost, T., Martin, B., & Alibart, O. (2025). An etsi gs qkd compliant tls implementation. *arXiv preprint arXiv:2506.19409*. DOI: 10.5220/0013564700003979

Qureshi, K. N., Din, S., Jeon, G., & Piccialli, F. (2020). Routing for WBANs. *Computer Communications*, *149*, 382–392. DOI: 10.1016/j.comcom.2019.10.030

Radhika, K., Devika, K., Aswathi, T., Sreevidya, P., Sowmya, V., & Soman, K. (2020). Performance analysis of NASNet on unconstrained ear recognition. In *Nature Inspired Computing for Data Science* (pp. 57–82). Springer. DOI: 10.1007/978-3-030-33820-6_3

Rajendran, S., Krithivasan, K., & Doraipandian, M. (2021). A novel cross cosine map based medical image cryptosystem using dynamic bit-level diffusion. *Multimedia Tools and Applications*, *80*(16), 24221–24243. DOI: 10.1007/s11042-021-10798-z

Rajendran, T., Imtiaz, N. M., Jagadeesh, K., & Sampathkumar, B. (2024, April). Cybersecurity threat detection using deep learning and anomaly detection techniques. In *2024 International Conference on Knowledge Engineering and Communication Systems (ICKECS)* (Vol. 1, pp. 1-7). IEEE. DOI: 10.1109/ICKECS61492.2024.10617347

Rakhra, M., Kanday, R., Aggarwal, G., Ather, D., Kler, R., & Jairath, K. (2025, May). Quantum Cryptography: Enhancing Secure Communication in the Era of Quantum Computing. In *2025 International Conference on Networks and Cryptology (NETCRYPT)* (pp. 1395-1398). IEEE. DOI: 10.1109/NETCRYPT65877.2025.11102170

Ramesh, S. N. S. V. S. C., Al Fardan, B. M. M., Anupama, C. S. S., Kumar, K. V., Cho, S., Acharya, S., & Yoon, C. (2025). Leveraging cyberattack news tweets for advanced threat detection and classification using ensemble of deep learning models with Wolverine optimization algorithm. *IEEE Access : Practical Innovations, Open Solutions*, *13*, 48343–48358. DOI: 10.1109/ACCESS.2025.3550378

Rana, M. S., & Sung, A. H. (2020). DeepfakeStack: A deep ensemble-based learning technique for deepfake detection. In *Proceedings of the IEEE International Conference on Cyber Security and Cloud Computing* (pp. 70–75). DOI: 10.1109/CSCloud-EdgeCom49738.2020.00021

Rassam, M. A. (2024). Autoencoder anomaly detection. *IoT*, *5*(4), 852–870. DOI: 10.3390/iot5040039

Ravichandran, D., Banu, S. A., Murthy, B. K., Balasubramanian, V., Fathima, S., & Amirtharajan, R. (2021). An efficient medical image encryption using hybrid DNA computing and chaos in transform domain. *Medical & Biological Engineering & Computing*, *59*(3), 589–605. DOI: 10.1007/s11517-021-02328-8

Rawat, D. B., Chaudhary, V., & Doku, R. (2020). Blockchain technology: Emerging applications and use cases for secure and trustworthy smart systems. *J Cybersecur Priv*, *1*, 4–18. DOI: 10.3390/jcp1010002

Rehman, M. U., & Shafqiue, A. (2024). Robust Encryption Framework for IoT Devices Based on Bit-plane Extraction, Chaotic Sine Models, and Quantum Operations. *Internet of Things : Engineering Cyber Physical Human Systems*, *27*(May), 101241. Advance online publication. DOI: 10.1016/j.iot.2024.101241

Ressi, D., Romanello, R., Piazza, C., & Rossi, S. (2024). AI-enhanced blockchain technology: A review of advancements and opportunities. *Journal of Network and Computer Applications*, *225*, 103858. DOI: 10.1016/j.jnca.2024.103858

Ricchizzi, N., Schwinne, C., & Pelzl, J. (2025). Applied Post Quantum Cryptography: A Practical Approach for Generating Certificates in Industrial Environments. *arXiv preprint arXiv:2505.04333.*

Rossi, S., Hallett, M., Rossini, P. M., & Pascual-Leone, A.Safety of TMS Consensus Group. (2009). Safety, ethical considerations, and application guidelines for the use of transcranial magnetic stimulation in clinical practice and research. *Clinical Neurophysiology : Official Journal of the International Federation of Clinical Neurophysiology*, *120*(12), 2008–2039. DOI: 10.1016/j.clinph.2009.08.016

Rossler, A., Cozzolino, D., Verdoliva, L., Riess, C., Thies, J., & Nießner, M. (2019). FaceForensics++: Learning to detect manipulated facial images. In *Proceedings of the IEEE/CVF International Conference on Computer Vision (ICCV)* (pp. 1–11). DOI: 10.1109/ICCV.2019.00009

Saad, M., Spaulding, J., Njilla, L., Kamhoua, C., Shetty, S., Nyang, D., & Mohaisen, D. (2020). Exploring the attack surface of blockchain: A comprehensive survey. *IEEE Communications Surveys and Tutorials*, *22*(3), 1977–2008. DOI: 10.1109/COMST.2020.2975999

Saba, T., Haseeb, K., Ahmed, I., & Rehman, A. (2020). Secure IoMT framework. *Journal of Infection and Public Health*, *13*(10), 1567–1575. DOI: 10.1016/j.jiph.2020.06.027

Salazar, Z., Zaidi, F., Mallouli, W., Cavalli, A., Nguyen, H., & Montes De Oca, E. (2022). A Formal Approach for Complex Attacks Generation based on Mutation of 5G Network Traffic. *Proceedings of the 17th International Conference on Software Technologies*, 234–241. DOI: 10.5220/0011319000003266

Samuel, T., & Jessica, L. (2019). From Perimeter to Cloud: Innovative Approaches to Firewall and Cybersecurity Integration. *International Journal of Trend in Scientific Research and Development*, *3*(5), 2751–2759.

Sangaiah, A. K., Javadpour, A., Ja'fari, F., Pinto, P., Zhang, W., & Balasubramanian, S. (2023). A hybrid heuristics artificial intelligence feature selection for intrusion detection classifiers in cloud of things. *Cluster Computing*, *26*(1), 599–612. DOI: 10.1007/s10586-022-03629-9

Sangavi, V., & Thangavel, P. (2020). An exotic multi-dimensional conceptualization for medical image encryption exerting Rossler system and Sine map. *Journal of Information Security and Applications*, *55*(October), 102626. Advance online publication. DOI: 10.1016/j.jisa.2020.102626

Sarker, I. H., Kayes, A. S. M., Badsha, S., Alqahtani, H., Watters, P., & Ng, A. (2020). Cybersecurity data science: An overview from machine learning perspective. *Journal of Big Data*, *7*(1), 41. DOI: 10.1186/s40537-020-00318-5

Sasikaladevi, N., Geetha, K., Sriharshini, K., & Durga Aruna, M. (2019). RADIANT - hybrid multilayered chaotic image encryption system for color images. *Multimedia Tools and Applications*, *78*(9), 11675–11700. DOI: 10.1007/s11042-018-6711-0

Sekhar, J. C., Priyanka, R., Nanda, A. K., Josephson, P. J., Ebinezer, M. J. D., & Devi, T. K. (2025). Stochastic gradient boosted distributed decision trees security approach for detecting cyber anomalies and classifying multiclass cyber-attacks. *Computers & Security*, *151*, 104320. DOI: 10.1016/j.cose.2025.104320

Selvapandian, D., & Santhosh, R. (2021). Deep learning approach for intrusion detection in IoT-multi cloud environment. *Automated Software Engineering*, *28*(2), 19. DOI: 10.1007/s10515-021-00298-7

Shafique, A., Mehmood, A., Alawida, M., & Nasir, A. (2025). *Journal of Information Security and Applications Enhancing privacy in data transmission between IoT devices : A robust encryption and embedding framework for secure and meaningful image communication. 93*(June).

Shafique, A., Mehmood, A., Alawida, M., Elhadef, M., & Rehman, M. U. (2025). *A fusion of machine learning and cryptography for fast data encryption through the encoding of high and moderate plaintext information blocks*. 5349–5375. DOI: 10.1007/s11042-024-18959-6

Sharath, H. A., Vrindavanam, J., Dana, S., & Prasad, S. N. (2025). Quantum-resilient cryptography: A survey on classical and quantum algorithms. *IEEE Access : Practical Innovations, Open Solutions*, *13*, 172854–172877. DOI: 10.1109/ACCESS.2025.3612982

Sharma, P., Kumawat, R., Jain, G., Keswani, G., Goyal, N. K., & Sheikh, M. F. (2026). Machine Learning-Based Intrusion Detection Systems for Healthcare IoT. https://doi.org/DOI: 10.4018/979-8-3373-7610-3.ch007

Sharma, A., Kaur, S., & Singh, M. (2021). A comprehensive review on blockchain and Internet of Things in healthcare. *Transactions on Emerging Telecommunications Technologies*, *32*(10), e4333. DOI: 10.1002/ett.4333

Sharma, B., Sharma, L., Lal, C., & Roy, S. (2024). Explainable artificial intelligence for intrusion detection in IoT networks: A deep learning based approach. *Expert Systems with Applications*, *238*, 121751. DOI: 10.1016/j.eswa.2023.121751

Sharma, D. P., Habibi Lashkari, A., Firoozjaei, M. D., Mahdavifar, S., & Xiong, P. (2025). Defense Methods for Adversarial Attacks and Privacy Issues in Secure AI. In *Understanding AI in Cybersecurity and Secure AI: Challenges, Strategies and Trends* (pp. 159–195). Springer Nature Switzerland. DOI: 10.1007/978-3-031-91524-6_9

Sharma, P., Jindal, R., & Borah, M. D. (2021). Blockchain-based decentralized architecture for cloud storage system. *Journal of Information Security and Applications*, *62*, 102970. Advance online publication. DOI: 10.1016/j.jisa.2021.102970

Sharma, S. B., & Bairwa, A. K. (2025). Leveraging AI for Intrusion Detection in IoT Ecosystems: A Comprehensive Study. *IEEE Access : Practical Innovations, Open Solutions*, *13*, 66290–66317. DOI: 10.1109/ACCESS.2025.3550392

Sheikh, M.F.A., Kapoor, S.K., Goyal, N.K., Tuba, E., Rao, A. (2026). Enhancing Healthcare Security with Fog Computing and Blockchain Technology. https://doi.org/DOI: 10.1007/978-981-96-7760-3_38

Sheng, S. W., & Wicha, S. (2024). Blockchain-based traceability for teak identity: A transformational approach. Journal of Mobile Multimedia, 20(2), 267-306. Sheng, S. W., & Wicha, S. (2024). Blockchain-based traceability for teak identity: A transformational approach. *Journal of Mobile Multimedia*, *20*(2), 267–306. DOI: 10.13052/jmm1550-4646.2022

Shim, K. S., Kim, Y. H., Sohn, I., Lee, E., Bae, K. I., & Lee, W. (2022). Design and validation of quantum key management system for construction of KREONET quantum cryptography communication. *Journal of Web Engineering*, *21*(5), 1377–1417. DOI: 10.13052/jwe1540-9589.2151

Shone, N., Ngoc, T. N., Phai, V. D., & Shi, Q. (2018). A deep learning approach to network intrusion detection. *IEEE Transactions on Emerging Topics in Computational Intelligence*, *2*(1), 41–50. DOI: 10.1109/TETCI.2017.2772792

Singh, S., Hosen, A. S., & Yoon, B. (2021). Blockchain security attacks, challenges, and solutions for the future distributed iot network. *IEEE Access : Practical Innovations, Open Solutions*, *9*, 13938–13959. DOI: 10.1109/ACCESS.2021.3051602

Singh, T., Solanki, A., Sharma, S. K., Nayyar, A., & Paul, A. (2022). A Decade Review on Smart Cities: Paradigms, Challenges and Opportunities. *IEEE Access : Practical Innovations, Open Solutions*, *10*, 68319–68364. DOI: 10.1109/ACCESS.2022.3184710

Sinha, K., & Paul, P. (2022). An Improved Pseudorandom Sequence Generator and its Application to Image Encryption. *KSII Transactions on Internet and Information Systems*, *16*(4). Advance online publication. DOI: 10.3837/tiis.2022.04.012

Sizan, N. S., Dey, D., Layek, M. A., Uddin, M. A., & Huh, E. N. (2025). Evaluating blockchain platforms for iot applications in industry 5.0: A comprehensive review. Blockchain: Research and Applications, 100276. Rahaman, M., Tabassum, F., Arya, V., & Bansal, R. (2024). Secure and sustainable food processing supply chain framework based on Hyperledger Fabric technology. *Cyber Security and Applications*, *2*, 100045.

Solaiyappan, S., & Wen, Y. (2022). Machine learning-based medical image deepfake detection: A comparative study. *Machine Learning with Applications*, *8*, 100298. DOI: 10.1016/j.mlwa.2022.100298

Song, W., Fu, C., Lin, Z., Zhang, Y., Chen, J., & Sham, C. W. (2024). Batch medical image encryption using 3D Latin cube-based simultaneous permutation and diffusion. *Signal, Image and Video Processing*, *18*(3), 2499–2508. DOI: 10.1007/s11760-023-02925-0

Song, X., Feng, S., Yi, W., & Zheng, Y. (2025). Quantum grey-scale image encryption method based on alternating quantum random walk. *EPJ Quantum Technology*, *12*(1), 82. Advance online publication. DOI: 10.1140/epjqt/s40507-025-00386-7

Sonko, S., Ibekwe, K. I., Ilojianya, V. I., Etukudoh, E. A., & Fabuyide, A. (2024). Quantum cryptography and US digital security: a comprehensive review: investigating the potential of quantum technologies in creating unbreakable encryption and their future in national security. *Computer Science & IT Research Journal*, *5*(2), 390–414. DOI: 10.51594/csitrj.v5i2.790

Soomro, I. A., Hussain, S. J., Ashraf, Z., Alnfiai, M. M., & Alotaibi, N. N. (2024). Lightweight privacy-preserving federated deep intrusion detection for industrial cyber-physical system. *Journal of Communications and Networks (Seoul)*, *26*(6), 632–649. DOI: 10.23919/JCN.2024.000054

Stalin, S., Maheshwary, P., Shukla, P. K., Maheshwari, M., Gour, B., & Khare, A. (2019). Fast and Secure Medical Image Encryption Based on Non Linear 4D Logistic Map and DNA Sequences (NL4DLM_DNA). *Journal of Medical Systems*, *43*(8), 267. Advance online publication. DOI: 10.1007/s10916-019-1389-z

Steeman, J. T., Peiffer-Smadja, O., & Ravet, J. (2025). A comparative analysis of public R&I funding in the EU, US, and China (No. KI-01-25-090-EN-N). Directorate General for Research and Innovation (DG RTD) of the European Commission.

Stopfer, L., Kaulen, A., & Purfürst, T. (2024). Potential of blockchain technology in wood supply chains. *Computers and Electronics in Agriculture*, *216*, 108496. DOI: 10.1016/j.compag.2023.108496

Su, Y., Wang, X., & Gao, H. (2024). Chaotic image encryption algorithm based on bit-level feedback adjustment. *Information Sciences*, *679*(February 2022), 121088. DOI: 10.1016/j.ins.2024.121088

Subramaniam, R., Sheela, A. J., & Alwabli, A. (2025). Enhanced cybersecurity and cyber-attack detection in smart DC microgrids using blockchain technology and SVM technique. *Ain Shams Engineering Journal, 16*(7), 103400. DOI: 10.1016/j.asej.2025.103400

Szabo, N. (1996). *Smart contracts: Building blocks for digital markets.* https://www.scribd.com/document/786841851/Nick-Szabo-Smart-Contracts-Building-Blocks-for-Digital-Markets-1996

Szymoniak, S., Piątkowski, J., & Kurkowski, M. (2025). Defense and security mechanisms in the internet of things: A review. *Applied Sciences (Basel, Switzerland), 15*(2), 499. DOI: 10.3390/app15020499

Tanveer, F., Iradat, F., Iqbal, W., & Ahmad, A. (2025). Towards Secure APIs: A Survey on RESTful API Vulnerability Detection. *Computers, Materials & Continua, 84*(3), 4223–4257. DOI: 10.32604/cmc.2025.067536

Tariq, S., Baruwal Chhetri, M., Nepal, S., & Paris, C. (2025). Alert fatigue in security operations centres: Research challenges and opportunities. *ACM Computing Surveys, 57*(9), 1–38. DOI: 10.1145/3723158

Tavera, C. A., Ortiz, J. H., Khalaf, O. I., Saavedra, D. F., & Aldhyani, T. H. (2021). *Wearable WBANs*. Retracted.

Telecommunication Engineering Centre. (2025). *Migration to post quantum cryptography*. Ministry of Communications.

Thakur, G., Chouksey, P., Chopra, M., Sadotra, P., & Kumar, S. (2025). A comprehensive review on the hybrid BB84 E91 QKD protocol for enhanced security efficiency and practical hardware implementation in quantum cryptography. *Discover Computing, 28*(1), 343. DOI: 10.1007/s10791-025-09807-8

Thakur, T., Mehra, A., Hassija, V., Chamola, V., Srinivas, R., Gupta, K. K., & Singh, A. P. (2021). Smart water conservation through a machine learning and blockchain-enabled decentralized edge computing network. *Applied Soft Computing, 106*, 107274. DOI: 10.1016/j.asoc.2021.107274

Thamilarasu, G., Odesile, A., & Hoang, A. (2020). IoMT intrusion detection. *IEEE Access : Practical Innovations, Open Solutions, 8*, 181560–181576. DOI: 10.1109/ACCESS.2020.3026260

Thirumarai Selvi, C., Amudha, J., & Sudhakar, R. (2021). A modified salp swarm algorithm (SSA) combined with a chaotic coupled map lattices (CML) approach for the secured encryption and compression of medical images during data transmission. *Biomedical Signal Processing and Control, 66*(December 2020). DOI: 10.1016/j.bspc.2021.102465

Tok, Y. C., & Chattopadhyay, S. (2023). Identifying threats, cybercrime and digital forensic opportunities in Smart City Infrastructure via threat modeling. *Forensic Science International Digital Investigation*, *45*, 301540. DOI: 10.1016/j.fsidi.2023.301540

Trivedi, R., Patra, S., & Khadem, S. (2025). Data-centric explainable artificial intelligence techniques for cyber-attack detection in microgrid networks. *Energy Reports*, *13*, 217–229. DOI: 10.1016/j.egyr.2024.11.075

Tsai, C. W., Yang, C. W., Lin, J., Chang, Y. C., & Chang, R. S. (2021). Quantum key distribution networks: Challenges and future research issues in security. *Applied Sciences (Basel, Switzerland)*, *11*(9), 3767. DOI: 10.3390/app11093767

Twardokus, G., Bindel, N., Rahbari, H., & McCarthy, S. (2024, February). When cryptography needs a hand: Practical post-quantum authentication for V2V communications. In *Network and Distributed System Security Symposium (NDSS 2024)*. Network and Distributed System Security Symposium (NDSS). DOI: 10.14722/ndss.2024.24267

Ucbas, Y., Eleyan, A., Hammoudeh, M., & Alohaly, M. (2023). Performance and scalability analysis of ethereum and hyperledger fabric. *IEEE Access : Practical Innovations, Open Solutions*, *11*, 67156–67167. DOI: 10.1109/ACCESS.2023.3291618

UcedaVelez. T., & Morana, M. M. (2015). Risk Centric Threat Modeling: process for attack simulation and threat analysis. John Wiley & Sons, ISBN: 978-1118988367.

Uysal, F., Demirkesen, S., Tezel, A., Elghaish, F., & Hoxha, J. (2026). A blockchain and Interplanetary File System (IPFS) based project risk register for construction organizations. *International Journal of Construction Management*, •••, 1–27. DOI: 10.1080/15623599.2026.2636732

Vaezi, A., Jones, S., & Asgary, A. (2024). Integrating Resilience into Risk Matrices: A Practical Approach to Risk Assessment with Empirical Analysis. *Journal of Risk Analysis and Crisis Response*, *13*(4). Advance online publication. DOI: 10.54560/jracr.v13i4.411

Vakhnovskyi, A. "Threat modeling and attack surface analysis of IoT-enabled controlled environment agriculture systems," arXiv:2604.13308, Apr. 2026. [Online]. Available: https://arxiv.org/abs/2604.13308

Vashishth, T. K., Sharma, V., Sharma, K. K., Kumar, B., Chaudhary, S., & Panwar, R. (2024). Intrusion Detection and Prevention Techniques in FL Cloud-Based Healthcare 5.0: A Comprehensive Review. Pioneering Smart Healthcare 5.0 with IoT, Federated Learning, and Cloud Security, 152-174.

Vashishth, T. K., Sharma, V., Chaudhary, S., Sharma, R., Chauhan, P., & Sharma, B. K. (2026). Adoption of Artificial Intelligence Techniques for Enhancing Host-Based Intrusion Detection Systems. In *AI Solutions for Detecting Cyber-Attacks in Information Systems* (pp. 133–164). IGI Global Scientific Publishing.

Vaswani, A., Shazeer, N., Parmar, N., Uszkoreit, J., Jones, L., Gomez, A. N., Kaiser, Ł., & Polosukhin, I. (2025). Attention is all you need. *Advances in Neural Information Processing Systems*, *30*, 5998–6008. DOI: 10.48550/arXiv.1706.03762

Venkatesan, K., & Rahayu, S. B. (2024). Blockchain security enhancement: An approach towards hybrid consensus algorithms and machine learning techniques. *Scientific Reports*, *14*(1), 1149. DOI: 10.1038/s41598-024-51578-7 PMID: 38212390

Venkateswarlu, I. B., Kakarla, J., & Prakash, S. (2020). Face mask detection using MobileNet and global pooling block. In *Proceedings of the IEEE Conference on Information and Communication Technology* (pp. 1–5). DOI: 10.1109/CICT51604.2020.9312083

Verma, G., & Kumar, A. (2023). Integration of QKD with attribute-based encryption for cloud. In *Springer*.

Vikas, & Teotia, S. (2025). Optimization of Graph Neural Networks for real-time intrusion detection in dynamic mobile ad-hoc networks. International Journal of Environmental Sciences, 11(11s), 740–748.

Vikas, D. R. P., Kumar, D., Charan, P., Ingilela, R. S. K., & Rastogi, R. (2023). Intrusion detection in wireless sensor networks using hybrid Deep Belief Networks and Harris Hawks optimizer. 2023 4th International Conference on Electronics and Sustainable Communication Systems (ICESC), 1631–1636. DOI: 10.1109/ICESC57686.2023.10193270

Vitorino, J., Silva, M., Maia, E., & Praça, I. (2025). Reliable feature selection for adversarially robust cyber-attack detection. *Annales des Télécommunications*, *80*(3), 341–355. DOI: 10.1007/s12243-024-01047-z

Vyas, A., Lin, P. C., Hwang, R. H., & Tripathi, M. (2024). Privacy-preserving federated learning for intrusion detection in IoT environments: A survey. *IEEE Access : Practical Innovations, Open Solutions, 12*, 127018–127050. DOI: 10.1109/ACCESS.2024.3454211

Wahab, S. A., Sultana, S., Tariq, N., Mujahid, M., Khan, J. A., & Mylonas, A. (2025). A multi-class intrusion detection system for DDoS attacks in IoT networks using deep learning and transformers. *Sensors (Basel), 25*(15), 4845. DOI: 10.3390/s25154845

Wan, Z., Xia, X., Lo, D., Chen, J., Luo, X., & Yang, X. (2021, May). Smart contract security: A practitioners' perspective. *In 2021 IEEE/ACM 43rd international conference on software engineering (ICSE) (pp. 1410-1422). IEEE.*

Wang, X., & Guan, N. (2023). *2D sine - logistic - tent - coupling map for image encryption.* 13399–13419.

Wang, Xiaoding, et al. "Blockchain-Empowered H-CPS Architecture for Smart Agriculture." Advanced science 12.27 (2025): 2503102.

Wang, J. (2024). Cyber security analysis based medical image encryption in cloud IoT network using quantum deep learning model. *Optical and Quantum Electronics, 56*(3), 1–12. DOI: 10.1007/s11082-023-06076-x

Wang, W., Sheng, Y., Wang, J., Zeng, X., Ye, X., Huang, Y., & Zhu, M. (2017). HAST-IDS: Learning hierarchical spatial-temporal features using deep neural networks to improve intrusion detection. *IEEE Access : Practical Innovations, Open Solutions, 6*, 1792–1806. DOI: 10.1109/ACCESS.2017.2780250

Wang, Y., & Ismail, E. S. (2025a). *Advances of post-quantum cryptography in blockchain and IoT*. IEEE Transactions.

Wang, Y., & Ismail, E. S. (2025b). Enhanced network security protocols for the quantum era. *IEEE Journal on Selected Areas in Communications.*

Wang, Z., Bao, J., Zhou, W., Wang, D., & Luo, H. (2023). Deepfake detection using vision transformer architectures: A comprehensive study. *IEEE Access : Practical Innovations, Open Solutions, 11*, 45872–45885.

Wei, Y., Wang, S., Nait-Abdesselam, F., & Benlarbi-Delai, A. (2023, December). Study of spiking neural network-based regressor on applications in digital predistortion for power amplifiers. In 2023 6th International Conference on Advanced Communication Technologies and Networking (CommNet) (pp. 1-7). IEEE. http://dx.doi.org/DOI: 10.1109/CommNet60167.2023.10365305

Wen, H., Lin, Y., Yang, L., & Chen, R. (2024). Cryptanalysis of an image encryption scheme using variant Hill cipher and chaos. *Expert Systems with Applications, 250*(March), 123748. DOI: 10.1016/j.eswa.2024.123748

Westerlund, M. (2019). The emergence of deepfake technology: A review. *Technology Innovation Management Review, 9*(11), 39–52. DOI: 10.22215/timreview/1282

Wickremasinghe, G., Frost, S., Rafferty, K., & Sharma, V. (2024). Demonstrating a Hyperledger Fabric-based Blockchain with Knowledge Graphs for a Supply Chain Ecosystem. In *IEEE International Conference on Blockchain and Cryptocurrency (ICBC)* (pp. 15-16). DOI: 10.1109/ICBC59979.2024.10634370

Widjaja, G. (2025). PRIVACY AND SECURITY IN DIGITAL COMMUNICATIONS: CHALLENGES AND SOLUTIONS IN CYBERSPACE. In Prosiding Seminar Nasional Indonesia (Vol. 2, No. 2, pp. 26-33).

Wu, W., Fouzi, H., Benamar, B., Sidi-Mohammed, S., & Ying, S. (2025). Deep learning-based stacked models for cyber-attack detection in industrial internet of things. *Neural Computing & Applications, 37*(24), 19617–19651. DOI: 10.1007/s00521-025-11418-9

Xie, Z., Zhang, X., & Liu, X. (2025). Enhanced efficiency and security in cross-chain transmission of blockchain internet of ports through multi-feature-based joint learning. *Scientific Reports, 15*(1), 6199. DOI: 10.1038/s41598-025-85330-6 PMID: 39979319

Xiong, W., & Lagerström, R. (2019). Threat modeling – A systematic literature review. Computers &amp. *Computers & Security, 84*, 53–69. DOI: 10.1016/j.cose.2019.03.010

Xu, Q., Ren, S., Wang, J., Li, Z., & Gao, W. (2025, May). A Research of Compute First Networking Based on Information-Centric Networking Cache Mechanism. In 2025 5th International Conference on Electronics, Circuits and Information Engineering (ECIE) (pp. 783-791). IEEE. DOI: 10.1109/ECIE65947.2025.11087005

Xu, X., Pautasso, C., Zhu, L., Gramoli, V., Ponomarev, A., Tran, A. B., & Chen, S. (2016, April). The blockchain as a software connector. In *2016 13th Working IEEE/IFIP Conference on Software Architecture (WICSA)* (pp. 182-191). Ieee. DOI: 10.1109/WICSA.2016.21

Xuan, J. (2016). Design of secure email system based on identity-based cryptography. In *ICCC 2016.*

Xue, X., Jin, H., Zhou, D., & Zhou, C. (2021). Medical Image Protection Algorithm Based on Deoxyribonucleic Acid Chain of Dynamic Length. *Frontiers in Genetics*, *12*(March), 1–18. DOI: 10.3389/fgene.2021.654663

Xu, H., Sun, Z., Cao, Y., & Bilal, H. (2023). A data-driven approach for intrusion and anomaly detection using automated machine learning for the Internet of Things. *Soft Computing*, *27*(19), 14469–14481. DOI: 10.1007/s00500-023-09037-4

Yadav, A., Jaipuriyar, A., Roy, S., & Rawat, U. (2025). A lossless image encryption technique using chaotic map and DNA encoding. *Multimedia Tools and Applications*, *84*(34), 42851–42873. DOI: 10.1007/s11042-025-20851-w

Yan, C., Gao, Y., Zhao, S., Zhang, S., Zhou, Y., Deng, W., & Chen, J. (2020). Wearable energy harvesting. *Nano Energy*, *67*, 104235. DOI: 10.1016/j.nanoen.2019.104235

Yang, Y., Wan, H., Yan, X., Zhao, M., Zeng, J., & Li, B. (2025). Parallel cryptographic hash function based on cellular automata and random diffusion model. *Applied Soft Computing*, *169*, 112546. DOI: 10.1016/j.asoc.2024.112546

Ye, M., Ruiwen, N., Chang, Z., He, G., Tianli, H., Shijun, L., Yu, S., Tong, Z., & Ying, G. (2021). A lightweight model of VGG-16 for remote sensing image classification. *IEEE Journal of Selected Topics in Applied Earth Observations and Remote Sensing*, *14*, 6916–6922. DOI: 10.1109/JSTARS.2021.3090085

Yin, C., Zhu, Y., Fei, J., & He, X. (2017). A deep learning approach for intrusion detection using recurrent neural networks. *IEEE Access : Practical Innovations, Open Solutions*, *5*, 21954–21961. DOI: 10.1109/ACCESS.2017.2762418

Zafar, A., & Iqbal, S. S. (2025). Integrating code-based post-quantum cryptography into SSL TLS protocols through an interoperable hybrid framework. *Discover Computing*, *28*(1), 202. DOI: 10.1007/s10791-025-09735-7

Zahid, S., Mazhar, M. S., Abbas, S. G., Hanif, Z., Hina, S., & Shah, G. A. (2023). Threat modeling in smart firefighting systems: Aligning MITRE ATT&CK matrix and NIST security controls. *Internet of Things : Engineering Cyber Physical Human Systems*, *22*, 100766. DOI: 10.1016/j.iot.2023.100766

Zhang, C., Wang, N., Hou, Y. T., & Lou, W. (2025). Machine Learning-Based Intrusion Detection Systems: Capabilities, Methodologies, and Open Research Challenges. *Authorea Preprints*. DOI: 10.1002/9781394293773.ch03

Zhao, L. (2024). Navigating the Cyber Kill Chain: A modern approach to pentesting. *Applied and Computational Engineering*, *38*(1), 170–175. DOI: 10.54254/2755-2721/38/20230549

Zheng, Z., Xie, S., Dai, H.-N., Chen, X., & Wang, H. (2018). Blockchain challenges and opportunities: A survey. *International Journal of Web and Grid Services, 14*(4), 352–375. DOI: 10.1504/IJWGS.2018.095647

Zobaed, S., Rabby, F., Hossain, I., Hossain, E., Hasan, S., Karim, A., & Hasib, K. M. (2021). Deepfakes: Detecting forged and synthetic media content using machine learning. In *Artificial Intelligence in Cyber Security: Impact and Implications* (pp. 177–201). Springer.

Zou, H., Lu, Y., Li, W., Li, W., & Chai, X. (2026). A heterogeneous Hopfield neural network with discrete memristor: Modeling, dynamics, and application in medical image encryption. *Expert Systems with Applications, 312*(January), 131457. Advance online publication. DOI: 10.1016/j.eswa.2026.131457

# About the Contributors

**Valentina Emilia Balas** is currently Full Professor in the Department of Automatics and Applied Software at the Faculty of Engineering, "Aurel Vlaicu" University of Arad, Romania. She holds a Ph.D. Cum Laude, in Applied Electronics and Telecommunications from Polytechnic University of Timisoara. Dr. Balas is the author of more than 400 research papers. She is the Editor-in Chief to International Journal of Advanced Intelligence Paradigms (IJAIP) and to International Journal of Computational Systems Engineering (IJCSysE), member in Editorial Board of international journals and is evaluator for international projects and PhD Thesis. Dr. Balas is the Head of Intelligent Systems Research Centre in Aurel Vlaicu University of Arad. She served as General Chair of the International Workshop Soft Computing and Applications (SOFA) in the interval 2005-2022.Dr. Balas is a member of the specialized committee "Computers, Information Technology, and Systems Engineering" of the National Council for Attestation of University Titles, Diplomas, and Certificates for the 2024-2028 term. Dr. Balas participated in many international conferences as Honorary Chair and Keynote Speaker. Recently she was working on a project with EU funding support: BioCell-NanoART = Novel Bio-inspired Cellular Nano-Architectures - For Digital Integrated Circuits, 3M Euro. She is a member of European Society for Fuzzy Logic and Technology (EUSFLAT), member of SPIE and an IEEE Senior Member, During the interval 2021-2022 she was a member of IEEE European Public Policy Committee Working Group on ICT. From May 2023 Dr. Balas is an associate member of Romanian Academy of Scientists. She is recipient of the "Tudor Tanasescu" Prize from the Romanian Academy for contributions in the field of soft computing methods (2019), "Stefan Odobleja" Prize from Romanian Academy of Scientists (2023 and 2024) and Diploma – Section Information Technology from The General Association of the Engineers in Romania 2023.

**Qin Xin** graduated with his Ph.D (1st Oct. 2002 – 30th Sep. 2004) in Department of Computer Science at University of Liverpool, UK in December 2004. Currently, he is working as a FULL professor of Computer Science in the Faculty of Science and Technology at the University of the Faroe Islands (UoFI), Faroe Islands. Prior to joining UoFI, he had held variant research positions in world leading universities and research laboratory including Senior Research Fellowship at Universite Catholique de Louvain, Belgium, Research Scientist/Postdoctoral Research Fellowship at Simula Research Laboratory, Norway and Postdoctoral Research Fellowship at University of Bergen, Norway. His main research focus is on design and analysis of sequential, parallel and distributed algorithms for various communication and optimization problems in wireless communication networks, as well as cryptography and digital currencies including quantum money. Moreover, he also investigates the combinatorial optimization problems with applications in Bioinformatics, Data Mining and Space Research. Prof. Xin also served on Management Committee Board of Denmark for several EU ICT projects. Prof. Xin has produced more than 200 peer reviewed scientific papers. His works have been published in leading international conferences and journals, such as ICALP, ACM PODC, SWAT, IEEE MASS, ISAAC, SIROCCO, IEEE ICC, Algorithmica, Theoretical Computer Science, Distributed Computing, IEEE Transactions on Computers, Journal of Parallel and Distributed Computing, IEEE Transactions on Dielectrics and Electrical Insulation, IEEE Transactions on Sustainable Computing, ACM Transactions on Internet Technology, IEEE Transactions on Network Science and Engineering, ACM Transactions on Asian and Low-Resource Language Information Processing, IEEE Transactions on Industrial Informatics, MDPI Symmetry, and Advances in Space Research. He has been very actively involved in the services for the community in terms of acting (or acted) on various positions (e.g., Session Chair, Member of Technical Program Committee, Symposium Organizer and Local Organization Co-chair) for numerous international leading conferences in the fields of distributed computing, wireless communications and ubiquitous intelligence and computing, including IEEE MASS, IEEE LCN, ACM SAC, IEEE ICC, IEEE Globecom, IEEE WCNC, IEEE VTC, IFIP NPC, IEEE Sarnoff and so on. He was the Organizing Committee Chair for the 17th and 18th Scandinavian Symposium and Workshops on Algorithm Theory (SWAT 2020 and SWAT 2022, Torshavn, Faroe Islands). Currently, he also serves on the editorial board for more than ten international journals.

**Ambeth Kumar V D** received his Ph.D. in Computer Science and Engineering from Sathyabama University, India, in 2013. He pursued his M.E. in Computer Science and Engineering at Annamalai University, Chidambaram, and his B.E. in Computer Science and Engineering at Madurai Kamaraj University, Madurai,

Tamil Nadu, India, in 2006 and 2004, respectively. He has nearly a decade of rich experience in the field of Computer Science and is currently working as an Associate Professor and Head at Mizoram University (A Central University), Aizawl, Mizoram, India. He has contributed to various technology initiatives and has published books on Theory of Computation, Design and Analysis of Algorithms, Python Programming, and Advanced Computer Architectures. His research contributions include over 100 international journal articles, 6 national journal publications, and presentations at more than 80 national and international conferences. He is a recognized Ph.D. supervisor at Mizoram University and has successfully guided five Ph.D. scholars. He has successfully completed four funded research projects supported by prestigious national agencies such as the Defence Research and Development Organisation (DRDO), Department of Science and Technology (DST) and the University Grants Commission (UGC), focusing on advanced domains in Artificial Intelligence, Image Processing, and Data-Driven Computing. He received the Best Teacher Award from PEC in 2011 and has been recognized among the World's Top 2% Scientists by Stanford University in 2022, 2024, and 2025. He also holds 15 copyrights and 5 patents. His research areas span Image Processing, Pattern Recognition, Neural Networks, and Computer Networks, with broader interests in Computational Models, Compiler Design, Data Structures, and Microprocessors. He serves as a reviewer and editor for many reputed international journals and is a Senior IEEE Member, Life Member of ISTE, IAENG, and ACEEE.

***

**Ali Agha** received his Ph.D. in Computer Science from Invertis University, Bareilly, India in 2025. He earned his M.Tech degree in Computer Science from Karnataka State Open University (KSOU) in 2010 and his MCA from Indira Gandhi National Open University (IGNOU) in 2007. He is currently serving as an Assistant Professor in the Department of Computer Science & Engineering at United College of Engineering and Research, Prayagraj, Uttar Pradesh, India. He has been actively involved in teaching, research, and academic mentoring, contributing to advancements in emerging computing paradigms. His primary research interests include cybersecurity, cloud computing, and cryptography, with recent focus on deep learning for security, deepfake detection, digital forensics, artificial intelligence in cybersecurity, blockchain security, edge AI, and secure IoT systems. His work emphasizes developing intelligent, scalable, and secure frameworks for real-world applications.

**Rudhrananth Baladhandapani** is a Systems-focused Software Engineer specializing in embedded systems, GPU firmware, and semiconductor subsystem validation, with over seven years of experience in low-level system engineering and debug. He currently serves as a Graphics Software Engineer at Intel Corporation, where he leads pre-silicon validation and system-level debug initiatives for Xe discrete graphics platforms.

**Sukanta Chakraborty** has completed his MCA from IGNOU, New Delhi. He completed his MTech in Computer Science & Engineering from the Department of Computer Science & Engineering, Tripura University. Currently, he is pursuing PhD from the Department of Computer Science & Engineering, Tripura University. His research interests are blockchain, ITS and IoT.

**Sachin Chaudhary** earned M. Tech degree specialized in Computer Science and now Pursuing Ph.D. in Computer Applications. He is involved in academic development and scholarly activities. He is member of International Association of Engineers, The Society of Digital Information and Wireless Communications, Global Professors Welfare Association, International Association of Academic plus Corporate (IAAC), Computer Science Teachers Association and Internet Society. His research interest includes Cloud Computing, Artificial Intelligence, Machine Learning.

**Geetha G** received B. Tech degree in 2010 in Computer Science and Engineering from Institute of Aeronautical Engineering and Technology. M.tech degree in 2013 in computer science and Engineering from Institute of Aeronautical Engineering and technology and pursuing Phd in Computer Science and Engineering from SRM University. she is in teaching profession for past 10 years. she published 10 papers in international journals and conferences.

**Sri Harsha Grandhi** is a dedicated and innovative Analog & Mixed Signal Design Engineer with 7 years of experience in the Non-Volatile Memory Group at Intel. Based in Folsom, California, he specializes in the custom design, validation, and integration of advanced mixed-signal and analog systems. Sri Harsha holds a Master of Science degree in Electrical Engineering from California State University, Sacramento, and a Bachelor of Engineering in Electronics and Communication Engineering from Gayatri Vidya Parishad College of Engineering in Vizag, India.

**Venkataramesh Induru** is currently working as Operation Lead - IT Operations Associate Manager for multiple Identity and Access Management projects. 16+ years of experience in multiple IDAM Products (i.e. ForgeRock IAM, Oracle IDAM suite, Oracle Waveset (former SUN IDM) and Tivoli IDM) with Design, Development, Operations, Environment Support and Security Operation skills

**Bhanutheja Nagabhushana Reddy Kasinayakanahally** is a Software Development Engineer with over seven years of experience specializing in embedded systems, firmware development, and wireless technologies. Currently based in San Diego, he plays a critical role at Apple Inc., contributing to the commercialization of proprietary modem technologies (C1 and C1X) deployed in high-volume consumer devices.

**Yashwant Kumar Kolli** is experienced Technical Project Manager with a demonstrated history of working in the information technology and services industry. Skilled in CMS, TMS, Content Targeting using Adobe Experience Platform & performance optimization. Strong program and project management professional with a Master of Technology (M.Tech.) focused in Computer Science and Engineering from Nagarjuna University.

**Jyoti Kumari** is an Assistant Professor in the Department of Computer Science and Engineering, specializing in Machine Learning and Artificial Intelligence. Her research primarily focuses on AIML (Artificial Intelligence and Machine Learning), data analytics, and related cutting-edge areas. She has authored and published numerous research papers, chapters, patents, copyrights and books in the field of AIML, contributing valuable insights to the academic and scientific community. Dedicated to shaping the next generation of technologists, she is committed to preparing students for successful careers in technology and research. Through her teaching, she instills a strong foundation in core concepts, emphasizes hands-on practical experience, and cultivates an innovative mindset. Her pedagogical approach goes beyond traditional instruction by inspiring students to explore novel ideas, adopt emerging techniques, and stay aligned with the latest industry trends and technological advancements.

**Abhishek Majumder** completed his BE in Computer Science & Engineering from the Department of Computer Science & Engineering, NIT Agartala. He obtained his MTech Information Technology from the Department of Information Technology, Tezpur University. He completed his PhD from the Department of Computer Science & Engineering, Assam University. Currently he is working as Associate Professor in the Department of Computer Science & Engineering, Tripura University. His research interests are IoT, blockchain, network security and machine learning. He has published more than 60 papers in reputed journal, conferences and book chapters.

**Balajee Maram**, earned his doctorate from Bharathiar University, Coimbatore, Master Degree in Computer Science and Engineering from Anna University, Chennai, Master of Business Administration from Alagappa University, Karaikudi,

MA (Master of Communication and Journalism) form Alagappa University, Karaikudi. He is currently working as an Professor in the Department of Computer Science and Artificial Intelligence, SR University, Warangal. I have more than 19 years of Teaching, 5 years of industry and 6 years of Research experience. I have 100 research publications in reputed journals where 32 papers are indexed by SCIE and 37 papers indexed by SCOPUS. I have guided 14 UG projects and 2 PG projects. I have filed 4 Indian patents and been granted 2 Australian patents. I have organized one National workshop and one National Conference. I have published 3 book chapters indexed by SCOPUS. I have authored for 8 books titled "Data Communication and Networking" and "XML & Web-Services". I have received "Best Researcher Award 2018" from DK International Research Foundation, "Best Researcher Award 2018" from 117th International Research Awards on Engineering, Science and Management

**Ratnesh Mishra** received his Ph.D. in Computer Science and Engineering from Invertis University, Bareilly in 2020, as well as his M.Tech. in Software Engineering from MNNIT, Allahabad, & his B.E. in Computer Technology from Nagpur University. He is working as an Sr. Assistant Professor at the BIT Mesra, Patna Campus, Patna, in the Department of Computer Science and Engineering. He has published 18 papers in national and international journals and conferences. During his chairmanship of the CSI Allahabad Chapter, he has organised 50 Webinar Series Programs, 03 International Webinars, and 1 FDP Program. Computer Network Security, Web Technology, AI, IoT, and Cloud Computing are some of his research interests.

**Ram Mohan N R** earned his B.E. degree in Computer Science and Engineering from Anna University, Chennai, Tamil Nadu, in 2007 and his M.Tech degree in Computer and Information Technology from Manonmaniam Sundaranar University, Tirunelveli, Tamil Nadu, in 2009. He later completed his Ph.D. in Computer and Information Technology from the same university in 2016. He is currently serving as a Professor in the Department of Artificial Intellige and Data Science at Panimalar Engineering College, Chennai, Tamil Nadu. With over 19 years of teaching experience, Dr. Ram Mohan has published 45 research papers in reputed international journals and conferences. His primary research interests include Cloud Computing and Machine Learning. He is also a Life Member of the Indian Society for Technical Education (ISTE).

**Umamaheswari Purushothaman** holds a B.E. in Information Technology from Periyar Maniammai College of Engineering and Technology (2003), an M.B.A. from Alagappa University, Karaikudi, Tamil Nadu (2006), and an M.Tech in Computer

Science from SASTRA Deemed University, Thanjavur, Tamil Nadu (2011). She earned her Ph.D. in Computer Science and Engineering from SASTRA Deemed University. With two decades of experience, she has taught both undergraduate and postgraduate courses in Computer Science. She is currently an Assistant Professor in the Department of Computer Science and Engineering at SRC Campus, SASTRA University, Kumbakonam. Her research interests focus on Data Mining, Machine Learning, and Deep Learning. She has published numerous research papers in international conferences, SCI-indexed journals, Scopus, and book chapters.

**Manjula Rajagopal** received B.E. degree in 2002 from Bharathidasan University, M.E. degree in Computer Science and Engineering from Anna University in 2008 and PhD in Computer Science and Engineering from Anna University in 2018. She is in the teaching profession for the past 22 years she published more than 30 papers in international journals and conferences.

**Sonal Shah** associated with AURO University in Gujarat appears to be a researcher or academic, specifically a research scholar in the School of Information Technology, involved in cloud computing studies, co-authoring papers like "Optimized Load Balancing Techniques in Cloud" with faculty, indicating an academic role within the Surat-based university.

**Vikas Sharma** is an active academician and researcher in the field of computer science with 8 years of experience. He earned M. Tech degree specialized in Computer Science and now Pursuing Ph.D. in Computer Applications. He is involved in academic development and scholarly activities. He is member of International Association of Engineers, The Society of Digital Information and Wireless Communications, Global Professors Welfare Association, International Association of Academic plus Corporate (IAAC), Computer Science Teachers Association and Internet Society. His research interest includes Cloud Computing, Artificial Intelligence, Machine Learning; published more than 55 research articles with 4 books and 90 book chapters in edited books. He is contributing as member of editorial and reviewers' boards in conferences and various computer journals and edited books published by Elsevier, CRC Press, Taylor and Francis, Springer, IGI global, Wiley Publication, IET Publication, De Gruyter, River Publication etc.

**Devendra Singh** is a Professor at Ajay Kumar Garg Engineering College. He is involved in academic development and scholarly activities. He is member of International Association of Engineers, The Society of Digital Information and Wireless Communications, Global Professors Welfare Association, International Association of Academic plus Corporate (IAAC), Computer Science Teachers Association and Internet Society .

**Abhisake Sinha** received his MTech in Computer Science & Engineering. His research interests are IoT and blockchaon technology.

**Keshav Sinha** was born in Dhanbad, India, in 1991. He received a B.E. Degree in Computer Science and Engineering from Sri Chandrasekharendra Saraswathi Viswa Mahavidyalaya, Kanchipuram, India, in 2013 and an M.E. Degree in Software Engineering from the Birla Institute of Technology, Mesra, India, in 2016. He completed a PhD in cryptography and network security from Birla Institute of Technology, Mesra, India, in 2022. He is an assistant professor specializing in Cryptography and Network Security. His research focuses on developing a secure environment for multimedia transmission. He has contributed to soft computing, humanities, and social and cyber policy and published numerous papers in conferences and journals. His work aims to bring flexibility and innovation to the computer science society.

**Shashiraj Teotia** is working as Associate Professor in the Department of Computer Application, Swami Vivekanand Subharti university Meerut. He has total 18 years of experience in teaching and research. He is an active member of IAENG AND IJMRA. He has published about 40 publications in various national and international journals.

**M Vanitha** is currently working as an Assistant Professor in the Department of Computer Science and Engineering, Srinivasa Ramanujan Centre, SASTRA Deemed University, Kumbakonam, Tamil Nadu, India. She has teaching experience for more than fifteen years. She has published several research works in peer-reviewed journals. Her research area includes Deep Learning, Machine learning and Time-series Analysis.

**Tarun Kumar Vashishth** is an active academician and researcher in the field of Computer Science with 22 years of experience. Presently he is working as a Professor and Head in the Department of Computer Applications, Vidya University, Meerut, U.P, India. He earned Ph.D. Mathematics degree specialized in Operations Research; served several academic positions such as Dy. Director, HoD, NAAC Coordinator, Academic Coordinator, Member Secretary of Department Research Committee, Assistant Center Superintendent and Head Examiner in University Examinations. He is involved in academic development and scholarly activities. He is member of International Association of Engineers, The Society of Digital Information and Wireless Communications, Global Professors Welfare Association, International Association of Academic plus Corporate (IAAC), Computer Science Teachers Association and Internet Society . His research interest includes Cloud Computing, Artificial Intelligence, Machine Learning and Operations Research; published more than 50 research articles & conference papers with 2 book and 90+ book chapters. He is contributing as member of editorial and reviewers boards in conferences and various computer journals and edited books published by Elsevier, CRC Press, Taylor and Francis, Springer, IGI global, Wiley Publication, IET Publication, De Gruyter, River Publication etc.

**Pushpendra Verma** is involved in academic development and scholarly activities. He is member of International Association of Engineers, The Society of Digital Information and Wireless Communications, Global Professors Welfare Association, International Association of Academic plus Corporate (IAAC), Computer Science Teachers Association and Internet Society . His research interest includes Cloud Computing, Artificial Intelligence, Machine Learning and Operations Research; published more than 50 research articles.

**Roopa Vuppula** is an accomplished academician, researcher, and educator specializing in Wireless Communications, Blockchain Technology, Artificial Intelligence, Machine Learning, and Next-Generation Networks. She currently serves as an Assistant Professor at Woxsen University. She earned her Ph.D. in Wireless Communications from National Institute of Technology Warangal, where her research focused on blockchain-oriented deep learning-based dynamic spectrum management for 6G wireless networks. She also holds an M.Tech in Systems and Signal Processing from Jawaharlal Nehru Technological University Hyderabad and a B.Tech in Electronics and Communication Engineering from Jyothishmathi Institute of Technology and Science. Her research interests include 5G/6G communications, dynamic spectrum access, blockchain, AI/ML, and aviation technology, with ongoing work on blockchain-based aircraft maintenance record management. Passionate about teaching, research, and innovation, she is dedicated to developing advanced technological solutions and inspiring students through research-driven and project-based learning approaches.

**Pradeep Yadav** is a distinguished academician with over 20 years of teaching experience and expertise in Computer Science and Engineering. He holds a Ph.D. in Computer Engineering and has an extensive research portfolio, including many international journal papers, multiple conference proceedings, and several books. His research interests span machine learning, artificial intelligence, and data mining. Currently, Dr. Yadav serves as an Associate Professor and Head of Department of CSE at ITM Gwalior, MP, India. He has also contributed significantly to the field through patents and copyrights and actively engages as a reviewer, conference chair and editor.

# Index

## A

Advanced GhostNet 283, 284, 286, 287, 288, 289, 296, 300
Adversarial Attacks 8, 36, 56, 61, 66, 67, 80, 192, 193, 195, 198, 207, 208, 209, 213, 214, 217
AES-256-GCM 433, 438, 441, 443, 445, 446, 450
Anomaly Detection 34, 35, 37, 56, 61, 66, 72, 81, 95, 169, 175, 176, 192, 193, 197, 200, 202, 203, 209, 214, 216, 223, 252, 253, 329, 330, 331, 332, 333, 342, 346, 349, 350, 351, 352, 354, 355, 356, 358, 359, 360, 363, 364
Artificial Intelligence 1, 3, 7, 9, 12, 14, 16, 20, 21, 22, 23, 24, 27, 28, 29, 30, 31, 33, 34, 35, 36, 37, 40, 43, 44, 46, 47, 49, 50, 52, 61, 63, 66, 67, 69, 80, 86, 88, 92, 95, 160, 192, 193, 195, 196, 203, 204, 205, 206, 210, 213, 215, 216, 217, 219, 220, 251, 252, 253, 299, 300, 302, 325, 326, 328, 331, 336, 348, 355, 361, 421, 422
Autonomous Systems 13, 21, 49, 191, 192, 193, 194, 195, 196, 197, 198, 199, 200, 201, 202, 203, 204, 205, 206, 207, 208, 209, 210, 211, 212, 213, 214, 216, 221

## B

Blockchain 1, 3, 4, 6, 9, 10, 11, 12, 13, 14, 15, 16, 17, 18, 19, 20, 21, 22, 23, 24, 25, 27, 28, 30, 31, 34, 40, 41, 42, 43, 44, 45, 46, 47, 48, 49, 51, 52, 53, 54, 55, 59, 60, 62, 63, 64, 65, 66, 69, 70, 71, 72, 73, 74, 77, 78, 79, 80, 82, 83, 85, 86, 87, 88, 89, 90, 91, 92, 93, 94, 95, 96, 99, 100, 101, 102, 103, 105, 106, 107, 108, 109, 110, 111, 112, 113, 116, 117, 119, 120, 121, 127, 129, 131, 132, 133, 134, 135, 137, 138, 139, 141, 142, 143, 144, 145, 146, 147, 148, 149, 150, 151, 152, 153, 154, 157, 160, 161, 162, 163, 164, 172, 192, 193, 196, 198, 206, 207, 208, 211, 212, 214, 216, 284, 299, 325, 330, 331, 333, 337, 338, 354, 362, 421, 455
Blockchain Security 12, 13, 25, 40, 43, 51, 110, 132
Blockchain Technology 3, 9, 10, 16, 22, 23, 24, 25, 28, 30, 40, 41, 43, 44, 46, 47, 48, 49, 52, 63, 64, 69, 95, 99, 101, 117, 129, 131, 138, 141, 142, 144, 145, 146, 147, 148, 149, 150, 153, 160, 162, 192, 193, 196, 198, 206, 207, 208, 212, 214, 284, 299, 337
Body Area Networks 329, 330, 331, 333, 334, 336, 338, 339, 342, 347, 352, 361

## C

Chaincode 143, 144, 145, 149, 150, 151, 153, 157, 158, 159, 163
Chaotic Map 368, 369, 370, 372, 373, 385, 386, 387, 389
Classical Cryptography 393, 394, 395, 409, 414, 422, 432, 454
Cloud 2, 5, 6, 23, 27, 28, 29, 31, 32, 34, 37, 38, 39, 40, 41, 43, 46, 47, 49, 50, 52, 60, 64, 66, 74, 75, 78, 96, 105, 106, 135, 137, 139, 166, 169, 178, 180, 184, 195, 196, 213, 215, 217, 219, 220, 221, 222, 223, 224, 228, 235, 236, 237, 244, 245, 246, 247, 248, 249, 250, 251, 252, 253, 256, 259, 271, 274, 278, 301, 303, 305, 307, 310, 316, 324, 325, 327, 330, 337, 341, 346, 353, 360, 362, 363, 367, 384, 389, 393, 397, 402, 413, 417, 422, 450, 455
Cryptographic Randomness 259, 262, 264, 265
CUDA 172, 179, 182, 184, 188, 189
CVSS v3.1 260, 269, 273, 277, 281
Cyber Attack Detection 286, 288, 298, 362
Cyber Kill Chain 260, 263, 264, 277, 280, 281

Cybersecurity 1, 3, 5, 6, 7, 8, 27, 28, 29, 30, 31, 33, 34, 35, 36, 37, 38, 39, 40, 41, 42, 43, 44, 45, 46, 47, 48, 49, 50, 51, 52, 53, 56, 59, 60, 61, 63, 66, 69, 71, 74, 78, 80, 84, 89, 92, 93, 95, 96, 137, 165, 167, 170, 179, 183, 185, 191, 192, 193, 194, 195, 196, 197, 198, 200, 208, 210, 213, 214, 215, 216, 217, 219, 220, 221, 222, 223, 224, 225, 228, 235, 236, 237, 248, 249, 250, 256, 259, 260, 279, 283, 284, 286, 298, 299, 301, 302, 303, 306, 325, 330, 336, 363, 422
Cybersecurity Framework 31, 43, 44, 45, 47, 74, 210, 219, 221, 228, 237, 249

# D

Data Privacy 6, 7, 8, 13, 19, 21, 51, 106, 128, 148, 203, 204, 205, 210, 213, 344, 347
Data Provenance 60, 83
Decentralized Networks 18, 105, 106
Deepfake Detection 302, 303, 304, 305, 306, 307, 310, 312, 314, 316, 317, 319, 320, 323, 324, 325, 326, 327, 328
Deepfakes 301, 302, 304, 305, 306, 309, 311, 313, 315, 319, 325, 327, 328
Deep Learning 7, 29, 35, 37, 39, 43, 45, 48, 49, 50, 54, 55, 56, 57, 63, 80, 94, 160, 166, 168, 183, 187, 192, 199, 202, 203, 209, 212, 214, 215, 251, 252, 253, 284, 298, 299, 300, 301, 302, 303, 304, 305, 306, 307, 309, 315, 317, 319, 324, 326, 327, 330, 333, 334, 343, 344, 346, 347, 349, 350, 362, 367, 389, 448
Deep Neural Networks 48, 56, 248, 349
Distributed Systems 5, 28, 32, 34, 38, 40, 49, 94, 165

# E

End-to-End Encryption 446
Energy-Efficient Communication 329, 339, 355, 359
Ethereum 60, 64, 73, 83, 88, 89, 90, 95, 101, 103, 104, 105, 108, 109, 112, 119, 120, 121, 133, 134, 135, 138, 142, 145, 146, 148, 162, 163

# F

Federated Learning 50, 51, 55, 166, 182, 185, 188, 192, 193, 198, 199, 203, 204, 210, 212, 214, 215, 216, 217, 344, 354
Fork-Based Attack Simulation 255, 258, 260, 281

# G

Generative Adversarial Networks 60, 80, 93, 94, 302, 306, 330, 344, 352

# H

High-Performance Computing 88, 165, 167, 185
Homomorphic Encryption 166, 182, 183, 185, 188, 204, 205, 206, 212, 214, 333
Hybrid Cryptography 366, 367
Hyperledger Fabric 141, 142, 143, 144, 145, 146, 147, 148, 149, 150, 151, 152, 153, 157, 158, 160, 161, 162, 163, 164

# I

Improved Squeeze and Excite 284, 291
Internet of Things 2, 18, 25, 54, 55, 56, 60, 96, 160, 202, 213, 216, 220, 251, 252, 253, 256, 280, 299, 300, 361, 362, 386, 388, 391, 396, 419, 421, 428
InterPlanetary File System 96
Intrusion Detection 7, 25, 28, 33, 35, 37, 39, 47, 50, 51, 54, 55, 56, 57, 60, 65, 80, 95, 161, 165, 166, 169, 174, 176, 177, 182, 185, 189, 191, 192, 194, 196, 199, 200, 201, 202, 203, 208, 209, 211, 213, 214, 215, 216, 217, 219, 220, 221, 222, 224, 225, 227, 228, 231, 236, 237, 247, 248, 249, 251, 252, 253, 297, 332, 364, 392, 432, 433, 439, 443, 452
IoT Healthcare 337, 364

IoT Security 51, 54, 226, 250, 251, 252, 392, 394, 395, 397, 400, 414

## K

KM Generator 255, 257, 258, 259, 260, 261, 262, 263, 264, 265, 266, 267, 270, 271, 273, 274, 275, 276, 277, 278, 281

## L

Latency 30, 32, 51, 71, 74, 88, 89, 90, 148, 158, 159, 164, 168, 176, 177, 178, 179, 180, 220, 236, 244, 247, 249, 276, 329, 334, 335, 340, 341, 346, 355, 357, 360, 392, 394, 397, 398, 399, 403, 407, 411, 413, 414, 415, 416, 417, 418, 419, 430, 442, 447, 452

## M

Medical Image 94, 328, 352, 366, 367, 368, 369, 370, 375, 377, 382, 383, 384, 385, 386, 387, 388, 389
Min-Max Normalization 286, 287, 296
MITRE ATT&CK 256, 259, 260, 263, 264, 277, 278, 281
Mutation Engine 255, 257, 261, 263, 265, 266, 268, 276, 277, 281

## N

Non-Linear 224, 285, 366, 371

## P

Parallel Computing 27, 28, 30, 31, 33, 34, 37, 38, 39, 40, 43, 45, 46, 47, 48, 49, 52, 53, 63, 64, 71, 74, 77, 167, 184, 188
Post-Quantum Cryptography 51, 132, 173, 183, 184, 185, 187, 189, 398, 414, 421, 422, 423, 426, 428, 430, 449, 455

## Q

Quantum Cryptography 51, 132, 173, 183, 184, 185, 187, 189, 214, 369, 386, 391, 392, 393, 394, 396, 398, 399, 400, 405, 406, 407, 408, 413, 414, 417, 419, 421, 422, 423, 426, 428, 430, 432, 449, 454, 455
Quantum-Safe Email 425, 438, 443, 446, 451

## R

Resilient Architectures 3, 14
Rinkeby Test Network 60, 90
Robotics 221

## S

Secure Digital Systems 15
Secure Federated Learning 192, 193, 198, 204, 212, 214
Security 1, 2, 3, 4, 5, 6, 7, 8, 9, 10, 11, 12, 13, 15, 16, 17, 18, 19, 21, 22, 24, 25, 27, 28, 29, 30, 31, 32, 33, 34, 35, 36, 37, 38, 39, 40, 41, 42, 43, 44, 45, 46, 47, 48, 49, 50, 51, 52, 53, 54, 55, 56, 60, 61, 62, 63, 64, 65, 66, 67, 68, 69, 70, 71, 72, 73, 74, 76, 77, 78, 79, 81, 82, 83, 86, 88, 89, 90, 91, 93, 95, 96, 99, 100, 101, 102, 105, 108, 110, 111, 113, 114, 115, 116, 117, 118, 119, 120, 121, 122, 123, 124, 126, 127, 128, 130, 131, 132, 133, 134, 135, 136, 137, 138, 139, 141, 142, 143, 145, 146, 147, 148, 149, 159, 160, 162, 163, 164, 165, 166, 167, 168, 169, 170, 171, 172, 173, 174, 178, 179, 180, 181, 182, 183, 184, 185, 186, 187, 189, 192, 193, 194, 195, 196, 198, 200, 202, 203, 204, 205, 206, 207, 208, 209, 211, 212, 213, 214, 215, 216, 217, 220, 222, 224, 225, 226, 235, 249, 250, 251, 252, 253, 256, 257, 258, 259, 260, 261, 262, 263, 264, 265, 266, 267, 269, 276, 277, 278, 279, 280, 281, 283, 284, 286, 302, 327, 328, 331, 332, 333, 335, 336, 337, 338, 342, 343, 344, 350, 354, 360, 361, 362, 363, 366, 367, 368, 369, 370, 371, 373,

374, 377, 378, 385, 386, 388, 389, 391, 392, 393, 394, 395, 396, 397, 398, 399, 400, 401, 402, 403, 405, 407, 409, 410, 411, 412, 413, 414, 416, 417, 418, 419, 421, 422, 423, 425, 426, 427, 428, 429, 430, 431, 432, 433, 436, 438, 440, 441, 442, 443, 444, 446, 447, 448, 449, 450, 451, 452, 454, 455
Security and Privacy 12, 56, 126, 187, 216, 336, 344, 362, 386
Security Vulnerabilities 29, 115, 116, 135, 332
Signal Processing 220, 221, 222, 223, 249, 347, 348, 349, 356, 359, 387, 389
Smart Contracts 11, 13, 18, 42, 48, 60, 64, 65, 69, 73, 78, 79, 80, 83, 85, 87, 88, 89, 93, 100, 101, 103, 104, 105, 106, 107, 109, 113, 114, 115, 119, 122, 127, 128, 134, 135, 136, 137, 138, 139, 145, 207, 212
STRIDE 256, 259, 260, 261, 263, 264, 265, 269, 270, 273, 274, 275, 276, 277, 278, 279, 281, 288, 290, 291

# T

Threat Detection 1, 7, 9, 21, 28, 31, 33, 34, 37, 39, 40, 43, 44, 45, 46, 48, 49, 50, 51, 52, 54, 56, 59, 61, 63, 66, 69, 72, 80, 81, 82, 87, 88, 89, 90, 165, 167, 169, 175, 176, 179, 192, 203, 212, 213, 214, 215, 216, 299, 350
Threat Modeling 255, 256, 257, 259, 260, 261, 263, 264, 265, 276, 277, 279, 280, 281, 406
Throughput 61, 71, 88, 89, 90, 134, 148, 158, 159, 164, 165, 168, 171, 172, 173, 177, 178, 181, 185, 189, 236, 244, 245, 246, 247, 248, 249, 276, 278, 336, 403, 411, 418, 419, 427, 431
Transfer Learning 303, 304, 306, 307, 309, 311, 314, 315, 316, 318, 320, 322, 324, 325
Trustless Data Sharing 60, 79

